THE ECONOMICS OF GLOBAL TURBULENCE

THE ECONOMICS OF GLOBAL TURBULENCE

The Advanced Capitalist Economies from
Long Boom to Long Downturn, 1945—2005

ROBERT BRENNER

VERSO

London • New York

This edition published by Verso 2006
'Economics of Global Turbulence' © New Left Review 1998
Preface and Afterword © Robert Brenner 2006
All rights reserved

The moral rights of the author have been asserted

1 3 5 7 9 10 8 6 4 2

Verso
UK: 6 Meard Street, London W1F 0EG
USA: 180 Varick Street, New York, NY 10014–4606
www.versobooks.com

Verso is the imprint of New Left Books

ISBN 10: 1-85984–730–7
ISBN 13: 978-1-85984–730–5

British Library Cataloguing in Publication Data
A catalogue record for this book is available from the British Library

Library of Congress Cataloging-in-Publication Data
A catalog record for this book is available from the Library of Congress

Typeset in Palatino Linotype by Andrea Stimpson
Printed and bound in Great Britain by William Clowes Ltd, Beccles, Suffolk

To Alfred and Elizabeth Brenner

CONTENTS

LIST OF FIGURES AND TABLES

Figures

Tables

LEGEND TO TABLES

GDP	gross domestic product
GK	gross capital stock
K/L	capital/labour ratio
LPy	labour productivity
Mfgr	manufacturing
NK	net capital stock
NKPRI	net capital stock prices
Non-mfgr	non-manufacturing
NY	net output
NY/NK	output-capital ratio
NY/NK real	real output-capital ratio (capital productivity)
NPR	net profit rate
NPSH	net profit share
NW	nominal wage
PPRI	product price
PW	product wage
RW	real wage
TFP	total factor productivity (output per unit of input of labour and capital)
ULC	unit labour costs

ACKNOWLEDGEMENTS

I owe an enormous debt to Perry Anderson, who has offered unstinting intellectual and moral support to this project since its inception, providing comprehensive critiques of my text and suggestions for improvement, as well as to Mark Glick, Andrew Glyn, and Bob Pollin, who have generously put at my disposal masses of their hard-won data, explained to me how to use it, commented upon multiple drafts, and spent countless hours discussing with me issues of economic theory and data, vastly improving the final product. I also wish to express my profound gratitude to the late David Gordon, John Ashworth, Gopal Balakrishnan, Michael Bernstein, Sam Bowles, Alex Callinicos, Jim Cronin, Gérard Duménil, Sam Farber, Bob Fitch, Mike Goldfield, Loren Goldner, Michael Howard, Dominique Lévy, Lars Mjoset, Jonathon Moses, John Roemer, Rune Skarstein, Dick Walker and Erik Wright, all of whom provided careful readings of my text and offered very helpful criticisms. I want to thank as well Robin Blackburn for his patience, comradeship, support and substantive critiques in seeing the text through to its original publication in *New Left Review*, Steve Kern and Julian Stallabrass for their extensive help in improving its style and clarity, and Dave Huth for crunching out unending series of numbers and teaching me how to do it. I owe a special debt to Susan Watkins, who, late in the day, read through the whole text and provided invaluable advice on form and content, paving the way for its completion. John Rodgers has offered me a huge amount of ongoing help and collaboration in the tedious, but indispensable, tasks of data gathering and calculation, required to put together profit rates for various countries and multiple sectors. I am very grateful for his generosity. The team at Verso, headed by Tom Penn and including Pat Harper, Sophie Skarbek-Borowska, and Andrea Stimpson, brought a complex manuscript through the process of production with a high degree of professionalism, and I want to express to them my gratitude. Sebastian Budgen edited the text, from start to finish, and did much to improve its style and presentation, and for this I am deeply grateful to him. Tom Mertes has offered me massive assistance in countless ways over a seemingly endless period—gathering data, helping with style, critiquing content, suggesting ideas, and much more. His help and support was truly indispensable in enabling me to bring the work to conclusion, and I cannot adequately thank him. My greatest debt is, once more, to Teri Edgar, not only for help of every sort with this book since its inception, but for being there and offering her love through the long process by which it came to see the light of day.

ACKNOWLEDGMENTS

PUBLISHER'S NOTE

'The Economics of Global Turbulence' was first published as a Special Report on the World Economy in *New Left Review* 229, May–June 1998; it is reproduced here with small amendments for style or for clarification. The tables and graphs have been updated where possible to take account of revised data. The Preface and the Afterword are new texts as are the two Appendices.

Preface

DYNAMICS OF TURBULENCE

The evolution of the advanced capitalist economies since World War II naturally divides itself into two roughly equal parts, each about a quarter-century in length: a period of prosperity from the later 1940s to 1973 and an era of slowed growth and increasing economic turbulence from 1973 onwards, marked by deeper recessions and the return of devastating financial crises absent since the Great Depression. The objective of *The Economics of Global Turbulence* is to offer a unified interpretation of this trajectory: the historic postwar boom, the transition from boom to downturn that took place between the mid 1960s and the mid 1970s, and the long slowdown that followed. It is, above all, the long downturn—the extraordinarily extended phase of reduced economic dynamism and *declining* economic performance, persisting through the end of the old millennium and into the new—that this work seeks to explain.

Theory and History

The difficulty of providing a systematic account of the evolution of postwar development is self-evident. At its core, the problem is to provide a consistent framework that can cope at once with major shifts over time in the system as a whole—a series of phases, differing one from another in their patterns of growth—and with regional variation—the main poles of accumulation, diverging from one another in their political economies. What is needed is to integrate theory and comparative history, an imposing task. The job is made all the harder by the paucity of already existing accounts, an insufficiency exacerbated by the default of orthodox economics. The latter barely recognizes the problem and is, in any case, ill-suited for confronting it due to its lack of a theory of capital accumulation. The major existing alternative, which initially had orthodox and heterodox versions, finds the source of the shift from long boom to long downturn in the increased power of and pressure from labour exerted against capital, itself the result in part of the long extension of the postwar economic upturn.[1] But, with the benefit of hindsight, this thesis would seem to have been definitively undermined by the failure of the decisive weakening of labour vis-à-vis capital during the 1970s and 1980s to bring about the restoration of system-wide economic vitality. In any case, in what follows, I offer an extended criticism of it, in order to lay the basis for presenting my own interpretation.

---

1 See, especially, P. Armstrong et al., *Capitalism Since 1945*, London 1991, a fundamental work on the period.

My way into the problem of providing a theoretical-cum-comparative historical account of the postwar economy is through an analysis of the path of profitability. The realized rate of profit is the direct measure of firms' ability to derive surpluses from their plant, equipment, and software. It is also the best available predictor of the rate of return that firms can expect on their new investment. As a result, the rate of profit is the fundamental determinant of the rate at which the economy's constituent firms will accumulate capital and expand employment, therefore of its output, productivity and wage growth, and, in turn, of the increase of its aggregate demand, both investment and consumer. From this point of departure, an initial account immediately follows. What made possible the inauguration and long perpetuation of the postwar boom in the US, Europe, and Japan was the achievement, over the period between the late 1930s and late 1940s, of elevated rates of profit and their maintenance during the following two decades. What brought the postwar boom to an end was the sharp fall in profitability for the advanced capitalist economies taken individually and together between 1965 and 1973, focused on the manufacturing sector but extending to the private economy as a whole, beginning in the US but soon encompassing Western Europe and Japan. The reason that, as of 2000, there had been no clear revival of the global economy is that there had been no decisive recovery of the profit rate system-wide, or in the US, Western Europe, or Japan considered separately. The challenge posed by these results is, of course, to account for the pattern of profitability itself—both for the system as a whole and for its various regional and national components—and to show how that pattern illuminates the actual history of postwar economic development—again at the levels both of the global economy and of its constituent parts. To respond to that challenge is, simply stated, the project of this book.

My interpretation proceeds, in schematic terms, at three interrelated levels. At the bottom level, so to speak, I offer a mechanism that can account for a tendency for the rate of profit to fall. This takes as its starting point the anarchy and the competitiveness of capitalist production. These require individual capitals to cut costs in order to survive by introducing fixed capital embodying ever more efficient technology, but to do so not only without reference to the reproductive requirements of other capitals, but by threatening their profits and indeed their very existence. The outcome in aggregate is, on the one hand, to bring about the unprecedented development of the productive forces. But it is, on the other hand, to prevent firms with higher-cost methods of production frozen in their already-existing plant, equipment, and software from realizing their fixed capital investments. This manifests itself in over-capacity and, in turn, reduced profitability.

In order to bring to bear the abstract account of a tendency for the profit rate to fall on the concrete trajectory of postwar economic evolution, I forge an intermediate conceptual link between them. Also built upon the dynamics of fixed capital, this conceptualization provides a rationale for expecting capitalist expansion to take the form of uneven development, as a consequence of the interaction between, on the one hand, an early-developing bloc of capital that initially is technologically and socio-economically more advanced, as well as politically dominant, and, on the other hand, later-developing blocs of capital that are at first technologically and socio-economically backward, as well as politically subordinate, yet able to exploit the potential advantages of coming late and of cultivating new, hitherto less developed regions. The point of departure is the proposition that investment tends to occur in waves, or blocs, of interrelated placements of fixed capital, their constituent elements embodying technologies of roughly the same vintage. The outcome is a hypothetical pattern of development as follows: the early-developing bloc of capital tends, for an extended period, to dominate its own markets, discouraging challengers; the newly emerging blocs of capital, repelled by the earlier bloc from its markets, end up profiting by means of developing new regions and exploiting new labour forces to an important degree in separation from the earlier developer; and, finally, the capitals of the later-developing blocs increasingly challenge those of the earlier-developing bloc by combining lower-cost inputs and equal or more advanced technology, making for an intensification of inter-capitalist competition that undermines the ability of large masses of fixed capital investments to realize themselves, leading to the onset of over-capacity and declining rates of profit.

The ultimate point of this conceptual framework is, of course, to make possible the construction of a convincing narrative of international economic evolution since World War II. What I argue is that, during the first postwar quarter-century, the economic history of the advanced capitalist countries traced a pattern of uneven development leading eventually to falling rates of profit across their economies that resulted from the inability to valorize great blocs of fixed capital, along the lines just sketched. The reproduction of high rates of profit and economic prosperity was long made possible by a powerful symbiosis, underwritten by the US state, between an earlier-developing bloc of capital in the US—characterized by technological leadership, more advanced socio-economic evolution, and the hegemonic position internationally of its state and capitalist class—and later-developing blocs of capital in Western Europe and Japan—marked by technological followership, retarded socio-economic evolution, and the hegemonized position of the associated states and capitalist classes—which developed at first largely in separation from the earlier-developing one. The later-developing blocs secured their dynamism in the last instance by means of a mercantilist orientation toward manufacturing exports made possible by their statism and organized capitalisms; the earlier-developing bloc achieved its vibrancy by means of a free market, globalizing orientation toward foreign direct investment and financial internationalization, made possible by the international predominance of its state, not to say its militarism cum imperialism.

But the extension and deepening of this very syndrome ultimately proved self-undermining. Between 1965 and 1973, producers from the earlier- and later-developing blocs ultimately entered into intensified international competition which, by bringing about stepped-up downward pressure on prices, made it impossible for large swathes of already existing fixed capitals to valorize themselves. The ensuing over-capacity made for sharply falling profitability system-wide, focused on the international manufacturing sector but also engulfing the private economies of the US, Western Europe and Japan, individually and in aggregate. The outcome was, in a breathtakingly short space of time, to propel the world economy from long boom to long downturn.

Nevertheless, if adducing the foregoing mechanisms explains the onset of the long downturn, it also poses an enormous further question: why did the long downturn persist for so very long? This question is made all the more pressing in light of the fact that, over the next quarter-century and beyond, firms, assisted by governments, throughout the advanced capitalist world engaged in an ever more self-conscious, systematic, and all-encompassing effort to restore their profit rates by means both of the obsessive reduction of costs, above all direct and indirect labour costs, and the transformation of their ways of doing business. They detonated an ever more vicious assault on the organizations of the working class, so as to force down the growth and, in some cases, the level of compensation and social services. They sought to neoliberalize the global economy by deregulating commodity and labour markets, privatizing state enterprises, and freeing up the formerly repressed financial sector, while seeking to force open markets for commodities, foreign direct investment, financial services, and short-term capital throughout the less developed countries. They shifted capital out of high-cost, low- profit manufacturing lines, especially into financial services, and turned increasingly to speculation. They stepped up foreign direct investment for the purpose of relocating manufacturing in selected regions of what had been the Third World in order to combine low-cost but increasingly skilled and well-educated labour with the best possible techniques, while meanwhile seeking to profit throughout much of the global South by means of the rapid inflow and outflow of hot money to and from newly freed-up markets in financial assets. In fact, all of these interrelated measures of cost reduction, neoliberalization, and globalization—unleashed with ever-increasing intensity from the start of the 1970s by the advanced capitalist economies—constituted little more or less than an ever more frenzied attempt to cope with the pervasive and persistent problem of reduced profitability. But the overriding fact remains that far from restoring economic dynamism, these measures failed to prevent the performance of the advanced capitalist economies from *worsening* as time went on. As a consequence, as of 2000, the long downturn remained very far from overcome.

In the last part of this text, as well as the Afterword, I seek to elucidate these processes and explain the unexpected persistence of the long downturn by focusing on, and attempting to account for, what I believe to be the fundamental source of the problem—the failure of private sector profitability to recover in the advanced capitalist economies, resulting, in the first instance, from the paradoxical long-term persistence of chronic over-capacity in international manufacturing. This I attempt to accomplish by elaborating and extending the framework I advanced to account for the long boom and the onset of the long downturn, focused upon the inter-related dynamics of fixed capital and uneven development. This has two aspects, a demand side and a supply side. On the one hand, in response to falling profit rates, firms were obliged to slow the growth of investment and employment, while seeking to reduce the growth and level of their costs, particularly labour costs, in the multifarious ways indicated above. The outcome, in the face of the persistent failure of profitability to recover, was a chronic and worsening problem of investment, consumer, government, and therefore aggregate demand. On the other hand, contrary to expectations, the great firms of the advanced capitalist world sought only tardily and with the greatest reluctance to respond to their profitability problems by withdrawing their capital stock from oversubscribed lines of production. Instead, they defended their positions in the world market as long as possible by improving their competitiveness by expanding investment as much as they were able, even in the face of reduced rates of return. At the same time, one after another region of East Asia—from the Northeast Asian Newly Industrializing Countries (NICs), to the

Southeast Asian Little Tigers, to the Chinese behemoth— extended ever further the processes of uneven development that had set off the long downturn by succeeding in exploiting the potential advantages of coming late in much the same manner as had their Western European and Japanese predecessors. Proceeding up the technological ladder with unprecedented speed, especially by means of ever-deepening regional integration made possible by accelerating foreign direct investment as well as by trade, they rained down ever greater torrents of increasingly sophisticated manufacturing products on already over-supplied world markets, increasing still further the stress on world manufacturing profit rates.

Nevertheless, the intensification of over-capacity in world manufacturing markets (which resulted from both the unexpected persistence of incumbents from the advanced capitalist world and the unprecedented ingress of entrants from the developing world, especially East Asia) in the face of a deepening problem of insufficient aggregate demand (which resulted from universal cost-cutting and the slowdown of investment and job creation consequent upon the decline of profitability) did not lead, as might otherwise have been expected, to a large-scale shakeout of high-cost, low-profit means of production by making for serious recession or depression. This was because the governments of the advanced capitalist world, led to an ever-increasing extent by the US, made sure that titanic volumes of credit were made available, through ever more varied channels, direct and indirect, both public and private, to firms and households to soak up the surplus of supply over demand, especially in the wake of the serious cyclical downturns that periodically threatened stability. Rather than system-shaking crisis, we therefore witnessed the continuation, stretching over three decades, of persistently reduced rates of profit that made for ever-decreasing economic vitality on a global scale, along with ever more destructive asset price bubbles and financial implosions, and increasingly severe cyclical downturns. The upshot was the predicament facing the world economy as it entered the new millennium: namely, the still further continuation of the long downturn against a background of over-supplied lines of production, decelerating aggregate demand, and a mountain of over-priced paper assets, all made possible by the accumulation of private and public debt at unprecedented speed and at historic levels.[2] (See p. 7, Figure 0.3; p. 8, Figure 0.4; p. 304, Figure 15.6.)

The Long Downturn: An Enduring Problem

With the exception of the Afterword, the text published here was completed at the height of both the New Economy boom and the East Asian financial crisis of 1997–98. It interpreted the accompanying global turbulence as a tell-tale sign that the international economy had still failed to transcend the long downturn. It insisted that, beneath the glossy surface of the 'Fabulous Decade', the foundations on which the global system was developing remained rickety. It concluded that 'Redundant production would for still another time undermine the gains from trade, and competition would end up trumping complementarity,' with the consequence that accelerating supply of world exports in the face of shrinking markets 'would

---

2   These arguments have provoked considerable discussion and debate. See especially the two special issues devoted to them of *Historical Materialism*, no. 4, Summer 1999, and no. 5, Winter 2000, as well as forums in *Challenge. The Magazine of Economic Affairs*, vol. xlii, May–June 1999 and *Monthly Review*, vol. li, June 1999.

undercut [profits] and thereby the recovery, in this way cutting short a system-wide secular upturn and risking a serious new turn downward of the world economy'. Economic developments since that time have, I believe, largely vindicated its basic approach. The long downturn has continued, extending itself into the opening years of the twenty-first century. It has done so largely as a consequence of the paradox-ical persistence of chronic over-capacity in the international manufacturing sector, which has been mainly responsible for the persistence of reduced profit rates in man-ufacturing and, in turn, the overall private economies of the advanced capitalist economies. Secularly reduced profit rates have themselves been largely responsible for the secularly reduced GDP, investment, productivity, and wage growth that have prevailed since the 1970s. It is in the context of the perpetuation of the long down-turn—and the ongoing problem of manufacturing over-capacity and reduced manufacturing and private sector profitability—that one should, I would argue, interpret the frenetic boom and stock-market bubble of the second half of the 1990s, the equity price crash and deep recession of 2000–1, and the so far weak and precar-ious cyclical recovery that has ensued.[3]

Nevertheless, the standard intellectual response to the problem of the long down-turn has not been to provide alternative accounts, but rather, explicitly or implicitly, to deny its very existence. Business and government publicists have contended that, since the start of the 1980s, the deregulation of industry has led to accelerated inno-vation; the freeing up of financial markets has brought cheaper and more efficient allocation of capital; the destruction of unions has made for more flexible labour markets; the reduction of taxation has created increasing incentives at the margin both to invest and to labour; and the weakening of state intervention has unfettered entrepreneurship. As a consequence, far from continuing to sputter, the economy has assumed ever-increasing vitality, culminating in the marvel of the New Economy boom of the later 1990s. More sober economists and economic historians have sought to deny not the reality of reduced dynamism and slowed growth, but rather the need to offer any special explanation for it. From their point of view, the long period of weakened economic performance manifests a kind of return to equilibrium—to standard, and indeed quite respectable, growth—after what they view as the unique experience of the postwar boom. What really needs to be explained, they contend, is the economy's unprecedented dynamism during the first postwar quarter-century, attributable in their eyes to the unusual build-up of pent-up technological capacity during the crisis-bound inter-war period. This, they insist, was exhausted during the long postwar upturn, bringing about a recur-rence of normality after 1973.[4] In fact, neither of these views remotely corresponds to the economy's actual trajectory during the past three decades.

The contention, so dear to the hearts of business advocates and neoliberal politi-cians, as well as some neoclassical economists, that the turn to ever-freer markets and ever-deeper austerity must bring, and has brought, ever-greater economic vigour is in defiance of the evidence. The fact is that, for the advanced capitalist economies (the US, the EU, and Japan) taken singly or together, economic perform-

---

3   See Afterword.
4   N. Crafts and G. Toniolo, 'Postwar Growth: An Overview', in Crafts and Toniolo, eds., *Economic Growth in Europe Since 1945*, Cambridge 1996.

ance has worsened, business cycle by business cycle, since the end of the postwar boom in terms of all of the main macroeconomic indicators: the growth of GDP, capital stock, labour productivity, and real compensation. Economic performance was less good during the 1990s than the 1980s, which lagged the 1970s, which was, of course, far worse than the economic performance of the 1950s and 1960s.[5] This even as neoliberal economic policy, highlighted by balanced budgets and the pre-eminence of central banks, came to govern the economy in ever-purer form.

As to the US, site of a supposed stock-market-driven high-tech miracle that enabled it to break beyond the secular stagnation that continued to weigh down its less agile counterparts in Europe and Japan, economic performance during the first half of the 1990s was worse than in any other five-year period during the whole postwar era. The unquestionable economic acceleration of the second half of the 1990s did raise the figures for the decade as a whole above those of the 1980s, but was itself obliged to depend in large part on the enormous fillip to both consumption and investment provided by the wealth effect of the historic and ill-fated stock-market bubble of those years. That wealth effect was responsible for no less than one-quarter of total GDP increase between 1995 and 2000, which, without it, would have averaged a mediocre 3 per cent rather than 4 per cent. Even with it, the US economy did no better in the 1990s than in the much-maligned 1970s. Indeed, in the *five* supposedly miraculous years between 1995 and 2000, US economic performance, in terms of the main macroeconomic indicators, was not better than in the *twenty-five* years between 1948 and 1973, when state intervention and regulation, trade union power, the repression of finance, and taxation of corporations were all at their greatest, ostensibly fettering economic performance.[6]

Nor, despite the near-universal impression to the contrary, was the US's performance in this period clearly superior to that of its main overseas rivals in terms of the ultimate criterion, the growth of productivity. It must be stressed that, over the course of the long downturn, the overall economic performance of Germany and Western Europe more generally, as well as Japan, deteriorated in relative terms even more profoundly than that of the US. Yet the fact remains that, between 1993 and 2003, the European Union as a whole (including Spain, Greece, and Portugal) achieved a slightly higher rate of growth of GDP per hour than did the US, at 1.8 per cent versus 1.6 per cent.[7] By the end of this period, moreover, it had pretty much closed the enormous historic productivity gap between itself and the US, its aggregate level of GDP per hour in 2003 being just 5 per cent below that of the US. By this latter date, levels of GDP per hour in Germany, France, and Italy had all climbed slightly above that of the US (between 1 per cent and 3 per cent), while those of the Netherlands, Belgium, Luxemburg, and Norway had risen substantially higher (between 6 and 31 per cent).[8]

Nor can lagging economic performance in the US and throughout the advanced capitalist economies since 1973 be explained away as an optical illusion resulting from

5   See below, 'Declining Economic Dynamism, 1960–2005', p. 240, Table 13.1.

6   R. Brenner, *The Boom and the Bubble*, London 2002, p. 47, Table 1.10 and p. 221, Table 9.1.

7   K. Daly, 'Euroland's Secret Success Story', Goldman Sachs Global Economics Paper, no. 102, 16 January 2004, pp. 1–3, 8, 10.

8   OECD, *Science and Technology Scoreboard 2003—Towards a Knowledge-based Economy*, Table D.2, 'Income and productivity levels in the OECD, 1950–2002' (online). Cf. B. van Ark, 'Does the European Union Need to Revive Productivity Growth', Groningen Growth and Development Centre Research Memorandum GD-75, April 2005, p. 9, Table 2. The rate of US manufacturing productivity growth between 1995 and 2000,

the misleading vantage point of the ostensibly aberrant immediate postwar decades. The postwar golden age in the US was, in historical terms, unquestionably impressive, but it was not in a league of its own, as is evident when compared to the previous long upturn, between 1890 and 1913. The growth of labour productivity, of per capita income, and of real wages was higher in the boom after World War II than that before World War I, although not by all that much. On the other hand, the growth of GDP and of investment proceeded as rapidly or more so in the latter epoch than the former. The long boom from 1950 through 1973 thus surpassed the long expansion from 1890 through 1913, but it remains reasonable to group them together.

By contrast, the long downturn after 1973 can be clearly and properly identified as such, because its economic performance was so weak, compared not only to that of the post-World War II boom but also to the pre-World War I long boom. It fell palpably short of both of these long expansions with respect to virtually all of the main macroeconomic indicators. The long downturn is precisely that ... and, lasting through the end of the millennium, far too extended to be passed off as just another down phase of the latest Kondratieff cycle (leaving aside the vexed question of their existence).[9]

Did the onset of slowed growth reflect the using up of technological potential, which had reached unprecedented heights as a consequence of the long drought of investment during the Great Depression and which endowed the economy of the first postwar decades with exceptional dynamism? This appears to be the reigning orthodoxy among macroeconomists, but it is impossible to justify in terms of the actual trends of productivity.[10] There was, in the first place, no exhaustion whatsoever of technological potential in the manufacturing sector. After maintaining roughly the same 3 per cent level from 1938 through 1973 and then falling off briefly in the 1970s, manufacturing productivity actually accelerated from 1980 onwards, achieving during the 1990s the highest rate of growth for any ten-year period during the postwar epoch. In any case, were the trajectory of productivity expressive of the using up of a technological backlog, one would expect it to have followed a path of gradual, more or less continuous, decline. As it was, productivity growth for the private economy as a whole remained high, and remarkably steady, over the long period between 1938 and 1973. It then declined suddenly and deeply between 1973 and 1980 and did not come close to recovering between 1980 and 2000. If technological capacity was being drawn on so as to make possible the long boom, why did productivity growth outside manufacturing fail to fall for decades? Why did it suddenly collapse? And why did it stagnate for so very long? Given the timing and the discontinuity, the productivity growth fall-off seems better understood as a consequence rather than cause of the economic slowdown — specifically as the result of the slowed growth of the capital

---

at 4.7 per cent, was without question outstanding, but it was not clearly better than that of its leading rivals, including France at 5.2 per cent, a recession-plagued Japan at 4.2 per cent, and west Germany at 4.9 per cent (through 1998, when data for west Germany ceases to be available).

9   For the comparison of macroeconomic performance during the long downturn and the pre-World War I and post-World War II expansion, see R. Brenner, 'The Capitalist Economy, 1945–2000', in D. Coates, ed., *Varieties of Capitalism, Varieties of Approaches*, Basingstoke 2005, p. 215 and Table 11.1.

10   W. J. Baumol, 'Productivity Growth, Convergence, and Welfare: What the Long-Run Data Show', *American Economic Review*, vol. lxxvi, December 1986, especially pp. 1081-2; P. Krugman, *Peddling Prosperity*, New York 1994, pp. 59–63.

Table 1. Long Booms and Long Downturn: 1890–1913 and 1950–73 versus 1973–96.

(Average per cent change)

	1890–1913	1950–1973	1973–1996
GDP	4.0	4.0	2.9
GDP/hour	2.2	2.6	1.2
GDP/capita	2.1	2.5	1.8
Real wage (mfgr)	1.6	2.2	0
Gross capital stock	5.4	3.2	–
Gross capital stock/hour	3.4	1.7	–

Sources: A. Maddison, *Dynamic Forces in the World Economy*, 1991, pp. 71, 140, 142; A. Maddison, *The World Economy: Historical Statistics*, 2003, pp. 84–86, Table 2b, and pp. 87–89, Table 2c; Bureau of Economic Analysis, National Income and Product Accounts, Table 7.1; (BEA website); A. Rees, *Real Wages in Manufacturing, 1890–1914*, 1969, p. 120; Bureau of Labor Statistics, Hourly Earnings of Production and Non-Supervisory Workers (BLS website); Bureau of Labor Statistics, Consumer Price Index-U (1982–1984) (BLS website) (wages are for manufacturing instead of whole economy, as wages outside of manufacturing are unavailable for earlier period)

stock consequent on reduced profitability, as well as the reduced increase of the capital-labour ratio resulting from the profound stagnation of wages.[11]

Perhaps most telling of all, decreasing dynamism was accompanied by radically increased instability. Especially from around 1980, the financial sector internationally was increasingly liberated by deregulation from its postwar shackles. The result was a stunning return of the financial crises that had been largely repressed and practically nonexistent during the first postwar quarter-century and beyond. The world economy was once again gripped by an ever-lengthening series of debt-based financial-bubble-cum-speculative-booms, issuing inevitably in devastating crashes. Not accidentally, these reached something of a culmination during the 1990s, when capital market liberalization was extended from the core to the developing world, and a succession of financial expansions and financial meltdowns crippled not only the Turkish, Russian, Brazilian, and Argentinian economies, but also, by the end of the decade, the East Asian NICs, Japan, and the US itself.[12]

The ultimate testimony to the economy's continuing debility can be read off trends in the standard of living, as well as income distribution. The income shares of both the top 1 per cent and top 5 per cent of US households had ascended to their twentieth-century peaks in 1928, at 19.6 per cent and 34.7 per cent respectively. But they had then fallen during the next 45 years, to reach their lowest points of the

11   US Department of Commerce, *Historical Statistics of the United States*, Washington, DC 1970, Series D 685, p. 162.

12   Bank of International Settlements, *71st Annual Report, 1 April 2000–31 March 2001*, Basel, 11 June 2001, pp. 123–4. 'When financial systems were heavily regulated and central banks focused on controlling the money or credit aggregates [before the 1980s], the scope for damaging financial cycles was constrained … [S]uch regulated environments … were less prone to the large cyclical swings seen in today's more liberalized environment.' Cf. E. Prasad et al., *Effects of Financial Globalization on Developing Countries*, IMF, Washington, DC March 2003.

century in 1973, the last year of the postwar boom, at 7.7 per cent and 20.6 per cent respectively. Yet from this nadir they both rose without cease throughout the long downturn to approach, though not quite to reach, their 1928 high points in 1998, at 14.6 per cent and 29.4 per cent respectively. This trend toward the polarization of income found its counterparts in the trajectory of the poverty rate and family income. Between 1959 and 1973, the poverty rate fell from 22.4 per cent to 11.1 per cent. But from 1973 to 1995, it rose to 13.8 per cent and by 2000 was still slightly above its level in 1973, at 11.3 per cent. Whereas median family income more than doubled in the postwar boom between 1947 and 1973, between 1973 and 1995 it increased by less than 12 per cent, despite the enormous increase in women's labour force participation (although it did leap up by 16 per cent between 1995 and 2000). Throughout the long downturn, gains for the wealthy and corporate owners have been secured overwhelmingly at the expense of working people and the poor, especially because they have been accompanied by such slowed growth. The economy has functioned decreasingly well, but for the wealthy ever more satisfactorily.[13]

Between 1973 and 2000, the average annual growth of real wages (excluding benefits) for private sector production and non-supervisory workers (who compose roughly 80 per cent of the labour force) was a flat zero (0.5 per cent for the long 1990s business cycle). But this repression of real wage growth was clearly indispensable for capital, in view of the parallel slowdown of productivity growth, the ultimate indicator of economic dynamism, or lack thereof. Between 1973 and 2000, labour productivity (GDP/hour) increased at an average annual rate of just 1.2 per cent (1.7 per cent for the 1990s). This was less than half that from 1948 to 1969, at 2.65 per cent, and barely half the average annual rate of productivity increase for the ninety-year period between 1890 and 1980 of 2.3 per cent. Over the course of the 1990s, the average rate of profit for the private economy still remained 15 per cent below its level of the postwar boom. But it would have languished at a far lower level had real wages been allowed to rise at anything remotely approaching the average annual rate of 1.6 per cent they had attained in the last decade of the postwar boom (1964–73).[14] What vitality the economy still maintained derived from—had been conditioned upon—depriving production and non-supervisory workers of any real wage increase for a quarter of a century.

The truth is that even today, nearly five years into the new, post-New Economy business cycle that began in February 2001, the standard macroeconomic indicators provide no clear sign that the long downturn has been overcome. Between 2000 and 2005, average annual GDP growth for the EU and Japan was lower than for any other five-year period since 1950, while that for the US barely equalled its rate between 1990 and 1995, hitherto the worst five-year interval of the postwar era. Indeed taking into account all of the standard macroeconomic indicators, the advanced capitalist economies   performed   less   well   than   in   any   other   postwar

13   T. Piketty and E. Saez, 'Income Inequality in the United States, 1913–1998', *Quarterly Journal of Economics*, vol. cxvii, February 2003, pp. 8–10, Table II; L. Mishel et al., eds., *The State of Working America 2002/2003*, Ithaca 2003, Table 5.1, p. 312.

14   Historical Data for the 'B' Tables of the Employment Situation Release, in Employment, Earnings, and Hours from the Current Employment Statistics Survey, US Bureau of Labor Statistics website, adjusted with CPI-U-1982-4 (1964–77) and CPI-U-RS (1978–2000); A. Maddison, *Dynamic Forces in Economic Development*, Oxford 1991, p. 71; 'Industry Analytical Ratios for the Total Economy', 2 June 2005 (folder provided on request by the BLS).

quinquennium (see p. 240, Table 13.1). This was despite the fact that, during this period, the US government unleashed the greatest macroeconomic stimulus in its history. Meanwhile, financial imbalances and asset price bubbles exceeded even their record-breaking predecessors of the later 1990s and loomed like dark clouds over the global economy. The long downturn remains to be transcended ... and continues to require explanation.

Introduction

THE PUZZLE OF THE LONG DOWNTURN

At the end of the 1960s, in the wake of the longest stretch of uninterrupted economic expansion in US history, Nobel prize economists Robert Solow and Paul Samuelson pronounced exultant obituaries on destructive capitalist economic instability. 'The old notion of a ... "business cycle" is not very interesting any more', said Solow. 'Today's graduate students have never heard of Schumpeter's apparatus of Kondratieffs, Juglars, and Kitchins, and they would find it quaint if they had.' After fifty years of study, joked Samuelson, the National Bureau of Economic Research had 'worked itself out of one of its jobs, the business cycle.'[1] With the neoclassical-Keynesian synthesis now in the hands of every enlightened government, recessions, according to top Kennedy–Johnson advisor Arthur Okun, were 'now ... preventable, like airplane crashes', and business fluctuations as a threat to the smooth operation of the modern economy were 'obsolete'.[2]

Economic policy-makers had become so confident in their ability to effectively control the capitalist economy that, just past the peak of the boom, the OECD could predict without qualification that the future would be indistinguishable from the recent golden past. As it concluded in its early 1970s study on the prospects of the advanced capitalist world, 'The output of goods and services in the OECD area as a whole has nearly doubled in the past decade and a half. There is little evidence of any general slowing-down in the rate of growth, so that there is a strong presumption that the gross domestic product of the OECD area may again double in the next decade and a half ... Nor is it likely that the sources of the high rates of growth expected in the 1970s will quickly disappear; on the contrary ... Governments, therefore, need to frame their policies on the assumption that the forces making for rapid economic growth are likely to continue and that potential GDP for the OECD area might quadruple between now and the end of the century.'[3] The miracle of the market, superintended by the state, could now virtually guarantee perpetual growth.

---

1   *Economic History Review*, 2nd series, vol. xxiii, August 1970, p. 410; V. Zarnowitz, ed., *The Business Cycle Today*, New York 1972, p. 167. Samuelson made this remark at a conference marking the Bureau's fiftieth anniversary.

2   Arthur Okun, *The Political Economy of Prosperity*, Washington, DC 1970, p. 33. Okun was one of the main architects of the 'New Economics' of the 1960s and a chairman of the Council of Economic Advisors under Lyndon Johnson. His book was completed in November 1969. With the nation, at that point, as he put it, 'in its one-hundred-and-fifth month of unparalleled, unprecedented, and uninterrupted economic expansion', Okun had no hesitation in referring to 'The Obsolescence of the Business Cycle Pattern' (p. 32).

3   OECD, *The Growth of Output 1960–80. Retrospect, Prospect and Problems for Policy*, Paris 1974, p. 166.

The Long Downturn

The triumphalism of Samuelson, Solow, Okun, and the OECD could hardly have been more ill-timed. At the very moment that they were making their remarks, the world economy was entering into a long and increasingly serious downturn, which, even now, a quarter-century later, shows only a few signs of abating. Reports of a cure for periodic capitalist economic crisis, indeed secular stagnation, were premature. Today, as the world economy enjoys its recovery from the fourth major recession since the end of the 1960s, the average rate of unemployment in the leading capitalist economies—leaving out the US—is at least as high as the average during the Great Depression decade of the 1930s.[4] As international equities prices soar daily to new records, moreover, most of the economy of East Asia (excluding Japan)—the site during 1996 of as much investment as took place that year in the US, and source of perhaps 20 per cent of the world's exports—languishes in depression. Japan itself teeters on the brink, threatening to pull the rest of the world down with it.

In the US, it is true, the unemployment rate has fallen to 4.3 per cent and inflation is back down to the levels of the mid 1960s. The rate of profit on capital stock, depressed for more than two decades, has, moreover, been creeping back up toward the high levels of the postwar boom, and 1997 was indeed a banner year. The fact remains that the marked improvement in the condition of US capital has been achieved to a very large degree at the direct expense of its main economic rivals and especially its working class, and has occurred against a background of fundamentally dismal economic performance right through 1996. The recovery of manufacturing vitality, perhaps the central achievement of the US economic revival, was made possible only on the basis of the most massive, decade-long devaluation of the dollar against the yen and the mark. It could not, moreover, prevent the growth of productivity for the economy as a whole—perhaps the best available indicator of an economy's dynamism—from falling to its lowest levels in US history, for the near-quarter-century between 1973 and 1996. During that period, the growth of GDP per hour worked has averaged 1.3 per cent. This is *barely two-thirds* the historic average for the previous century, and the average for the 1990s (through 1996) has been no higher. In this context, the defence of profitability throughout the period, and its partial recovery in the 1990s, has been predicated upon a repression of wages without precedent during the last century, and perhaps since the Civil War. Between 1973—when they reached their peak—and 1990, real hourly wages (leaving aside benefits) for production and non-supervisory workers in the private business economy *fell* by 12 per cent, declining at an average annual rate of 0.7 per cent, and they failed to rise *at all* during the decade of the 1990s, up to 1997. Real hourly wages (excluding benefits) for production and non-supervisory workers in the manufacturing sector had pretty much the same trajectory, declining at an average annual rate of 0.8 per cent, or a total of 14 per cent, between their 1977 peak and 1990, and also failing to rise at all during the 1990s. In the year 1997, real wages in the private business economy and in manufacturing were, respectively, at the

---

4   In 1996, unemployment in the eleven countries of the European Union averaged 11.3 per cent, for the twenty-eight OECD countries including the US 7.3 per cent, in the US, 5.0 per cent. OECD, *Economic Outlook*, no. 62, December 1997, p. a24, Table 21. The average annual rate of unemployment for the sixteen leading capitalist economies for the years 1930–38 (inclusive) was 10.3 per cent. A. Maddison, *Dynamic Forces in Capitalist Development*, Oxford 1991, pp. 170–1, Table 6.2.

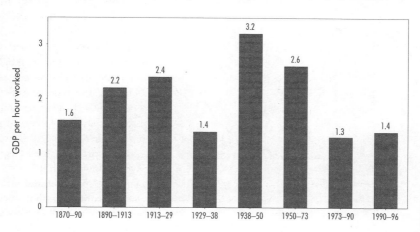

Figure 0.1. The growth of labour productivity in the US, 1870–1996.

Sources: A. Madison, *Dynamic Forces in Capitalist Development*, 1991, p. 71, Table 3.13; BLS Industry Analytical Ratios and Basic Data for the Total Economy. See also Appendix II.

same levels that they had been in 1967 and 1972! In total contrast, between 1890 and 1973, the average annual growth of real hourly wages in manufacturing was 2 per cent, and there was no decade during that entire period, including that of the 1930s, in which it was less than 1.2 per cent.[5]

Even US Deputy Treasury Secretary Lawrence Summers, a leading apostle of the US economic model, has been obliged to acknowledge 'the ironies of the current economic boom'. As he noted in a recent speech before a large crowd of Silicon Valley executives, 'a child born today in New York is less likely to live to the age of five than a child born in Shanghai'.[6] Summers might have added that the cyclical upturn of the 1990s has done little or nothing to improve the lot of the poor. In 1996 the poverty rate was 13.7 per cent (36.5 million people), clearly higher than in 1989, and at the end of 1997, the extent of hunger and homelessness was actually rising. Perhaps most telling in light of current celebrations of a supposed American economic miracle, the current cyclical upturn of the 1990s has, in terms of the main macroeconomic indicators of growth—output, investment, productivity, and real compensation— been even less dynamic than its relatively weak predecessors of the 1980s and the 1970s (not to mention those of the 1950s and 1960s). As the *Financial*

5   A. Rees, *Real Wages in Manufacturing, 1890–1914*, Princeton 1961, p. 120. Henceforth, all wage data is for compensation – that is, included wages and salaries plus benefits – and is for all employees, not just production and non-supervisory workers, unless otherwise stated. Moreover, the terms 'wages' and 'compensation' are used interchangeably to mean compensation, unless otherwise stated.

6   'Treasury Official Warns Against Complacency, Cites Great Depression', *Los Angeles Times*, 29 April 1998; F. Fiore and R. Brownstein, 'All But the Poor Got Richer in '96', *Los Angeles Times*, 30 September 1997; N. Timmins, 'Poverty on the Increase in US', *Financial Times*, 11 December 1997.

Figure 0.2. The growth of real wages in US manufacturing, 1890–2004.

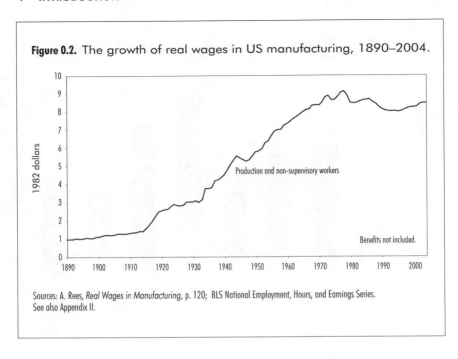

Sources: A. Rees, *Real Wages in Manufacturing*, p. 120; BLS National Employment, Hours, and Earnings Series.
See also Appendix II.

Times editorialized at the start of 1997, 'Conventional wisdom is that the US economy has been motoring along in the 1990s, while Europe and Japan have been left behind in its dust. Not so. US performance has been mediocre at best, while the difference between it and the other two has been largely cyclical.'[7]

The brute fact that has thus made a mockery of the pretensions to prescience and control of mainstream economists and capitalist governments alike has been the reality of *long-term* and *system-wide* economic downturn, the seriousness of which can be demonstrated merely by comparing the macroeconomic profiles of the leading advanced capitalist economies in two successive phases, from 1950 through 1970 and from 1970/1973 through to the present. The sharp deterioration in the economic performance of the advanced capitalist economies over the last quarter-century, compared to that of the first quarter-century of the postwar epoch, is self-evident. Throughout these economies, average rates of growth of output, capital stock (investment), labour productivity, and real wages for the years 1973 to the present have been one-third to one-half of those for the years 1950–73, while the average unemployment rate has been more than double. (See p. 5, Table 0.1.)

The reduction in the average rate of profit on capital stock, particularly in manufacturing, over the past quarter-century is particularly striking because the rate of profit is not only the basic indicator but also the central determinant of

7   'The Leader and the Laggards', *Financial Times*, 9 January 1997. For example, between 1990 and 1996, whereas in the 'booming' US real hourly compensation (including benefits) in manufacturing rose by a total of 3 per cent, in recession-bound Germany and Japan, they rose, respectively, by totals of 15 and 17 per cent. See also below "Declining Economic Dynamism, p. 269, Table 17.

Table 0.1. Comparing the postwar boom and the long downturn.

(Average annual rates of change, except for net profit and unemployment rates, which are averages.)

Manufacturing

	Net Profit Rate		Output		Net Capital Stock		Gross Capital Stock		Labour Productivity		Real Wage	
	1950–70	1970–93	1950–73	1973–93	1950–73	1973–93	1950–73	1973–93	1950–73	1973–93	1950–73	1973–93
US	24.4	14.5	4.3	1.9	3.8	2.3	–	–	3.0	2.4	2.6	0.5
Germany	23.1	10.9	5.1	0.9	5.7	0.9	6.4	1.7	4.8	1.7	5.7	2.4
Japan	40.4	20.4	14.1	5.0	14.5	5.0	14.7	5.0	10.2	5.1	6.1	2.7
G-7	26.2	15.7	5.5	2.1	–	–	4.8	3.7	3.9	3.1	–	–

G-7 net profit rate extends to 1990; German net capital stock covers 1955–1993; Japanese net profit rates and net capital stock cover in manufacturing 1955–1991.

Private Business

	Net Profit Rate		Net Output		Capital Stock		Gross Capital Stock		Labour Productivity		Real Wage		Unemployment Rate	
	1950–70	1970–93	1950–73	1973–93	1950–73	1973–93	1950–73	1973–93	1950–73	1973–93	1950–73	1973–93	1950–73	1973–93
US	12.9	9.9	4.2	2.6	3.8	3.0	–	–	2.7	1.1	2.7	0.2	4.2	6.7
Germany	23.2	13.8	4.5	2.2	6.0	2.6	5.1	3.0	4.6	2.2	5.7	1.9	2.3	5.7
Japan	21.6	17.2	9.1	4.1	–	–	9.4	7.1	5.6	3.1	6.3	2.7	1.6	2.1
G7	17.6	13.3	4.5	2.2	–	–	4.5	4.3	3.6	1.3	–	–	3.1	6.2

G-7 net profit rate extends to 1990; German net capital stock covers 1955–1993.

Sources: OECD, *National Accounts, 1960–1997*, volume II, Detailed Tables; OECD, *Flows and Stocks of Fixed Capital*, various issues; P. Armstrong, A. Glyn, and J. Harrison, *Capitalism Since 1945*, Oxford 1991, data appendix, and their 'Accumulation, Profits, State Spending: Data for Advanced Capitalist Countries 1952–83', Oxford Institute of Economics and Statistics, July 1986 (updated by A. Glyn). (Henceforth, AGH).

the system's health.[8] The average rate of profit expresses the economy's capacity to generate a surplus from its capital stock and therefore constitutes a good first approximation of its potential to accumulate capital (invest), and thereby increase productivity and grow.[9] The average rate of profit also expresses the degree to which the system is vulnerable to economic shocks: if the dispersion of profit rates is held constant, the (changing) average rate of profit will determine the proportion of firms on the edge of survival and thereby the potential for serious recession or depression. Finally, because investors are unable to predict or control the market, they must, as a rule, rely on the *realized* rate of profit to estimate the expected rate of profit and, on that basis, to decide how to allocate their funds.[10] The rate of profit will thus determine the relative attractiveness of sinking one's funds in capital stock, which implies productive commitment and furnishes returns only over the long run, compared with shorter-term placements in employing labour only, in the purchase and sale of goods, in speculation, or in personal consumption.[11]

Between 1970 and 1990, the manufacturing rate of profit for the G-7 economies taken together was, on average, about 40 per cent lower than between 1950 and 1970. In 1990, it remained about 27 per cent below its level in 1973 and about 45 per cent below its peak in 1965.[12] These changes were tell-tale signs, as well as key determinants, of the marked deterioration of the whole economy in the period after the early 1970s. As I shall try to demonstrate, the major decline in the profit rate throughout the advanced capitalist world has been the basic cause of the parallel, major decline in the rate of growth of investment, and with it the growth of output, especially in manufacturing, over the same period. The sharp decline in the

8   The profit rate, r, is defined, standardly, as the ratio of profits, P, to the capital stock, K, ($r = P/K$). The output-capital ratio (Y/K) is the ratio of nominal output, or value added, Y, to the capital stock. The profit share (P/Y) is the ratio of profits to output, or value added. (In this text, all of the foregoing variables are always presented in net terms, that is, with depreciation taken out, unless otherwise indicated). Thus, by de-composing, the profit rate equals the profit share times the output-capital ratio: $r = P/Y \times Y/K$. Changes in profitability can be effected only through changes in the profit share or the output-capital ratio (or through the impact of changes in capacity utilization on these components). All profit rates given are pre-corporate profits tax (but post-indirect business tax), unless otherwise specified. Profit rates (and other basic data) are standardly given for the 'private business economy' (or the 'private economy'), which refers to the whole non-farm economy minus the government sector and also minus government enterprises. Sometimes profit rates (and other basic data) are given for the 'business economy', which refers to the whole non-farm economy, minus the government sector but including government enterprises. Capital stock equals plant and equipment and in this text is always non-residential, unless otherwise stated. For a full exposition, see Appendix 1 on 'Profit Rates and Productivity Growth: Definitions and Sources'.

9   Those who wish to invest can of course also draw on existing sources of credit, so it is necessary to take into account the interest rate, as well as the realized profit rate, in explaining how much investment takes place.

10   Preventing the theory from more directly grasping reality is the fact that investors know, or at least think they know, aspects of the future bearing on the profit rate, with the result that the expected rate of profit on the basis of which they make their decisions reflects the realized rate of profit, but with certain modifications.

11   For systematic discussions of the significance of the rate of profit, see the major work by G. Duménil and D. Lévy, *The Economics of the Profit Rate. Competition, Crises and Historical Tendencies of Capitalism*, Aldershot 1993, as well as Andrew Glyn's important recent article, 'Does Aggregate Profitability Still Matter?', *Cambridge Journal of Economics*, vol. xxi, September 1997.

12   The G-7 economies are the US, Germany, Japan, the UK, France, Italy, and Canada. The calculations of the aggregate profit rate, the aggregate profit share, and the aggregate capital stock for the G-7 economies are from P. Armstrong, A. Glyn, and J. Harrison, *Capitalism Since 1945*, London 1984; second edition, Oxford 1991, data appendix.

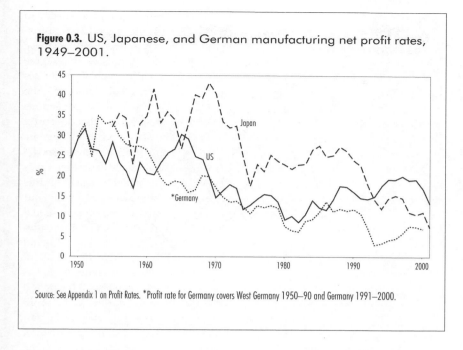

Figure 0.3. US, Japanese, and German manufacturing net profit rates, 1949–2001.

Source: See Appendix 1 on Profit Rates. *Profit rate for Germany covers West Germany 1950–90 and Germany 1991–2000.

rate of growth of investment—along with that of output itself—is, I shall argue, the primary source of the decline in the rate of growth of productivity, as well as a major determinant of the increase of unemployment. The declines in the rate of growth of employment and productivity are at the root of the sharp slowdown in the growth of real wages.

To explain the origins and evolution of the long downturn through an analysis of the causes and effects of changes in profitability is thus the objective of this study. In Chapter One, my point of departure is the family of *supply-side* theories which constitute the consensus interpretation. These theories, simply put, attribute the downturn and failure of recovery to increased pressure on profits from workers. Because pressure from labour grew, direct and indirect wage growth outran productivity growth, setting off the downturn; then, because pressure from labour failed to decline sufficiently, direct and indirect wage growth failed to adjust downward enough to match the decline in productivity growth, thereby perpetuating the downturn. After noting variations on this basic interpretation, I specify several fundamental conceptual problems with it, and point to a number of basic empirical trends that impugn its ability to explain the long downturn. Then, using the general standpoint from which I criticized the supply-side interpretation, I offer an alternative approach which takes as its point of departure the *unplanned, uncoordinated, and competitive* nature of capitalist production, and in particular individual investors' unconcern for and inability to take account of the effects of their own profit-seeking on the profitability of other producers and of the economy as a whole.

In this view, the fall in *aggregate* profitability that was responsible for the long downturn was the result of not so much an autonomous vertical squeeze by labour

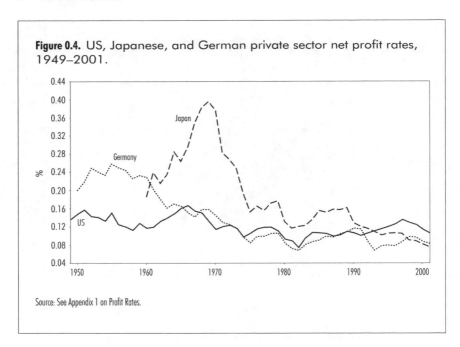

Figure 0.4. US, Japanese, and German private sector net profit rates, 1949–2001.

Source: See Appendix 1 on Profit Rates.

on capital, as the over-capacity and over-production that resulted from intensified, horizontal intercapitalist competition. The heightening of intercapitalist competition was itself brought about by the introduction of lower-cost, lower-price goods into the world market, especially in manufacturing, at the expense of already existing higher-cost, higher-price producers, their profitability and their productive capacity. The long downturn, from this standpoint, has persisted largely because the advanced capitalist economies have proved unable to accomplish profitably sufficient reductions and reallocations of productive power so as to overcome over-capacity and over-production in manufacturing lines, and thereby to restore profitability, especially given the growing presence of East Asia in world markets. With profitability failing to recover, investment growth and in turn output growth has fallen over the long term, bringing about secularly reduced productivity growth and wage growth, and rising unemployment.

In the remainder of this text, focusing for practical reasons on the US, German, and Japanese cases, I try to show that the foregoing approach can comprehend the economic evolution of the advanced capitalist world, providing a better account of the data than the supply-side theories.[13] In Parts Two, Three, and Four, therefore, I offer interpretations, respectively, of the long boom (1950–65), the fall in prof-

---

13   Concentrating on these three economies does introduce distortions. Still, in 1950, taken together, they accounted for 60 per cent of the output (in terms of purchasing-power parities) of the seventeen leading capitalist economies and by 1994 that figure had risen to 66 per cent. A. Maddison, *Monitoring the World Economy 1820–1992*, Paris 1995, Table C-16a. Each of these economies stood, moreover, at the hub of great regional blocs, which they effectively dynamized and dominated. In addition, the interaction among these three economies was, as I shall argue, one of the keys to the evolution of the advanced capitalist world throughout the postwar period.

itability and the turn from boom to crisis (1965–73), and the long downturn (1973–present), in terms of the systematically *uneven development* of the advanced capitalist economies in the postwar years—manifested, through most though not all of the epoch, in slow growth in the earlier-developing leader economy of the US in relationship to accelerated expansion in the later-developing follower economies of Japan and Germany, and in turn East Asia. I attempt to demonstrate that the way in which this pattern of uneven development worked itself out supports my more general interpretation of the long downturn in terms of intensified competition leading to over-capacity and over-production and a secular fall in profitability, especially in manufacturing.

PART ONE
The Trajectory of the Profit Rate

Chapter 1

SUPPLY-SIDE EXPLANATIONS: A CRITIQUE

To begin at a very general level, the capitalist mode of production distinguishes itself from all previous forms by its tendency to relentless and systematic development of the productive forces. This tendency derives from a system of social-property relations in which economic units—unlike those in previous historical epochs—must depend on the market for everything they need and are unable to secure income by means of systems of surplus extraction by extra-economic coercion, such as serfdom, slavery, or the tax-office state. The result is twofold. First, individual units, to maintain and improve their condition, adopt the strategy of maximizing their rates of profit by means of increasing specialization, accumulating surpluses, adopting the lowest-cost technique, and moving from line to line in response to changes in demand with respect to supply for goods and services. Second, the economy as a whole constitutes a field of natural selection by means of competition on the market which weeds out those units that fail to produce at a sufficient rate of profit.

The combination of individual price-cost maximizing and systemic natural selection through competition could have been expected to make for an extremely productive system, and, over the long historical run, it surely has. The accumulation of capital brings about the growth of the size of the labour force. It also brings about the growth of the productiveness of the labour force, meaning that the labour force is able to produce the consumption goods it needs and the tools it needs to produce those goods in less and less time, with the result that capitalists have to pay relatively less and less for the reproduction of their labour power, on the assumption (for purposes of exposition) that real wages remain constant. The outcome should be a dual tendency, doubly favourable to capital. If they have no trouble selling what they produce, capitalists should net both a rising mass of profits, proportional to the growth of the labour force, and a rising rate of profit, resulting from the increased productivity of the labour force.

The Persistence of Malthusianism

The inherent dynamism of the capitalist economy over the long run, its tendency to improve the productive forces, would seem to rule out that well-known form of crisis, which was built into virtually all pre-capitalist agricultural economies—the Malthusian/Ricardian type of crisis, brought about by the secular tendency to the declining growth of labour productivity, especially in agriculture, under the pressure of population growth. But, if that is the case, we confront a basic question: if a tendency to declining productivity growth is *not* at the root of capitalist crises, what is?

Historically and currently, the most common response to this question has been simply to deny its premise and to find the source of economic crisis under capitalism precisely in the economy's declining capacity to develop the productive forces. Malthus and Ricardo, of course, saw an inevitable tendency to stagnation or crisis as resulting from an apparently inexorable tendency to falling labour productivity in agriculture. As poorer and poorer soil was brought into cultivation in response to population growth, profits were bound to be squeezed between rising rents and subsistence wages that had to increase as food became more costly to produce. In its original guise, this classical position has been rendered obsolete by the application of science-based technologies to agriculture; but, in more up-to-date forms, it has retained much of its original allure.

Even today, most accounts of the onset and persistence of the current long downturn in the world economy take as their point of departure the successive oil crises of the early and late 1970s, and especially the so-called 'productivity crisis'. This is true of explanations emanating not only from the Right but from the Left as well. According to several major left-wing schools, the fall in profitability responsible for the long downturn originated in a secular decline in productivity growth which was itself the consequence either of the declining effectiveness of the so-called Fordist system of organizing the labour process, or of rising worker resistance and slacking on the shop floor, or of a combination of the two. These 'social Malthusian' accounts actually dovetail rather closely, in practice—though not, of course, in their underlying rationale—with orthodox Marxist theory, which sees the economy's tendency to increase productivity by relying to an ever greater extent on indirect relative to direct labour as leading inexorably to a fall in the rate of profit. Paradoxically, this theory, too, has a Malthusian character, because it also posits a decline in profitability as resulting from declining productivity. According to the orthodox Marxist thesis, in order to compete, capitalists must cut costs by increasing mechanization, manifested in a rising organic composition of capital (capital-labour ratio). But, in so doing, they cannot avoid bringing about a fall in the aggregate rate of profit because the rise in the organic composition of capital issues in an increase in the output-labour ratio that is insufficient to counteract the parallel fall in the output-capital ratio that it also brings about. The rate of profit falls, from this perspective, because, with the real wage assumed constant, investment in mechanization cannot but result in an increase in labour productivity (real output-labour ratio) that is more than cancelled out by a decrease in capital productivity (real output-capital ratio). Were this theory correct, what would logically be entailed is the impeccably Malthusian proposition that the rate of profit can be expected to fall because, as a direct result of capital accumulation, overall productivity—productivity *taking into account both labour and capital inputs*—can be expected to decline.[1]

---

1   As Marx liked to put it, the rise in the organic composition of capital brings about a fall in the rate of profit in the very process of bringing about an increase in *labour* productivity, the ratio of output to labour (by bringing about, as he failed to emphasize, an even greater decrease in the ratio output to capital). 'The rate of profit falls, although the rate of surplus-value remains the same or rises, because the proportion of variable capital to constant capital decreases with the development of the productive power of labour. The rate of profit thus falls, not because labour becomes less productive, but because it becomes more productive.' *Theories of Surplus Value*, Vol. II, Moscow 1971, p. 439. Marx was, of course, fiercely

The Wage-Squeeze Thesis

Of course, as any economist will aver, no decline in productivity growth, however severe, is sufficient in itself to cause problems for the macroeconomy. Falling productivity growth can result in a squeeze on profitability only if there is a failure of real wage growth to adjust downward in tandem. The fact is, however, that today an extraordinarily wide range of economists believe that a slowdown in productivity growth to which (direct and indirect) wage growth failed to adjust is *precisely what happened* over the last two decades or so in the advanced capitalist economies, and that exactly this development is at the root of our economic troubles.

The consensus of today's economists thus explains the long downturn in terms of the failure of wage growth to fall in line with declining productivity growth by combining the theses of Malthusianism ('the productivity crisis' and 'the oil crisis') and of downward 'wage inflexibility' (resulting from a politicized labour market). That it does so is hardly surprising, for mainstream economics has implicit faith in the market as a self-sufficient, self-regulating mechanism for the economy. It can therefore conceive of major problems for the economy as arising only 'exogenously' to the market: either as a consequence of political interference which prevents the market mechanism from bringing about the necessary economic adjustment or as a consequence of a failure of technological progress, the origins of which are separate from the economy's own functioning.

To the extent, then, that the problem of the long downturn in the world economy has been systematically posed, it has called forth a paradoxical near-consensus. Marxists and radicals have joined liberals and conservatives in explaining the long downturn as a 'supply-side' crisis, resulting from a squeeze on profits, reflecting pressure on capital from labour that is 'too strong'. In so doing, they have characterized

---

anti-Malthusian. The Malthusian character of his theory of the fall of the rate of profit is therefore highly incongruous, though logically unavoidable, given that it has the decline in profitability result from a decline in productivity, taking into account both capital and labour inputs. It also flies in the face of commonsense. For, if, as Marx himself seemed to take for granted (see *Capital*, Vol. III, New York 1967, pp. 264–65) capitalists are assumed, in response to competition, to adopt technical changes that raise their own rate of profit by reducing their total cost (labour plus capital, or direct and indirect labour) per commodity, it seems intuitively obvious that the ultimate result of their innovation, when it is generally adopted in their line, can only be to reduce the exchange value of the goods produced in their line and thus, directly or indirectly, to reduce the exchange value of the wage, and thus to *raise* the average rate of profit, given again the (Marxian) assumption that the real wage remains constant. It certainly cannot be to reduce the rate of profit. Formal proofs of this result can be found in N. Okishio, 'Technical Change and the Rate of Profit', *Kobe University Economic Review*, vol. vii, 1961, as well as in J. Roemer, 'Technical Change and the "Tendency of the Rate of Profit to Fall"', *Journal of Economic Theory*, vol. ii, March 1978, and 'The Effects of Technological Change and the Real Wage on Marx's Falling Rate of Profit', *Australian Economic Papers*, June 1978. For the orthodox Marxist thesis to hold, therefore, requires the assumption—again paradoxical in terms of Marx's own premises—that capitalists adopt new techniques that *decrease their own rate of profit*—and, again, end up reducing overall productivity. This implication of Marx's falling profit rate thesis is recognized and embraced by A. Shaikh, who advances the argument that the rate of profit falls because individual firms are obliged to maximize their profit *margin* (that is, their rate of return on circulating capital) in order to effectively compete in terms of prices and so are indeed obliged to adopt techniques which raise their organic composition of capital and thereby increase their total cost per commodity, even though this brings down their profit rate on total capital—both circulating and fixed. 'Political Economy and Capitalism: Notes on Dobb's Theory of Crisis', *Cambridge Journal of Economics*, vol. ii, 1978; 'Marxian Competition Versus Perfect Competition: Further Comments on the So-Called Choice of Technique', *Cambridge Journal of Economics*, vol. iv, 1980; 'Organic Composition of Capital', in *The New Palgrave. A Dictionary of Economics*, ed. J. Eatwell et al., London 1987, Vol. iii, pp. 755–7.

the current crisis in terms just the opposite of those that have often been used to characterize the long downturn of the interwar period, a crisis widely viewed as a 'demand-side' or 'under-consumption' crisis, resulting from an overly high profit rate, reflecting pressure from labour that was 'too weak'.

A series of variations on the supply-side theme have been argued by a large number of analysts across a broad political spectrum. The standard, or classical, version of the theory—what could be called the Full Employment Profit Squeeze theory—finds its origins over a century ago, and is still advocated today.[2] This boils down to the proposition that, in the medium run, capital accumulation leads to crisis because it proceeds without sufficient regard for the material conditions necessary for its continuation: the supply of labour (and raw materials) thus fails to keep up with the demand that results from ongoing investment, leading to rising labour (and primary commodity) costs, which begin to interfere with satisfactory profit-making.[3]

1. The 'Contradictions of Keynesianism'

Nevertheless, the majority of contemporary versions of the supply-side approach distinguish themselves from the classical statement by arguing that the enhanced power of labour purportedly behind the secular squeeze on profits has been the result not merely of tight labour markets, but also the operation of certain historically specific institutional arrangements and government policies first put into effect in the period following World War II. Indeed, in its most fully developed form, the thesis is that the long downturn finds its roots in what might be loosely called the contradictions of Keynesianism. The operation of those very institutional arrangements and government policies that ostensibly made possible the postwar boom by solving the problem of effective demand are thus claimed to be responsible for the supply-side problems that have brought about the long downturn.[4]

The Key to the Boom

In the supply-side, 'contradictions of Keynesianism' view, the foundations of the long boom are thus to be found in the continuous growth of demand, which

---

2   K. Marx, 'The Law of the Accumulation of Capital', *Capital*, Vol. 1, ch. 25, sec. 1, But see below, p. 24, footnote 14.

3   For variations on this basic position, see A. Glyn and B. Sutcliffe, *British Capitalism, Workers, and the Profits Squeeze*, London 1972, and 'The Critical Condition of British Capital', *New Left Review* 66, March–April 1971; Armstrong et al., *Capitalism Since 1945*; R. Boddy and J. Crotty, 'Class Conflict and Macro-Policy: The Political Business Cycle', *Review of Radical Political Economics*, vol. ii, 1975; 'Class Conflict, Keynesian Policies and the Business Cycle', *Monthly Review*, vol. xxvi, October 1974; Makoto Itoh, *The World Economic Crisis and Japanese Capitalism*, London 1990.

4   Leading advocates of this viewpoint from the Left include representatives of the US Social Structure of Accumulation (SSA) School (notably Samuel Bowles, the late David Gordon, and Tom Weisskopf) and representatives of the French Regulation School (notably Michel Aglietta, Robert Boyer, and Alain Lipietz). The advocates of the Full Employment Profit Squeeze thesis joined representatives of the SSA and the French Regulation Schools in presenting a fully elaborated version of the theory in the collective work *The Golden Age* (ed. Stephen Marglin and Juliet Schor, Oxford 1990). See especially the essay by A. Glyn, A. Lipietz, A. Hughes, and A. Singh, 'The Rise and Fall of the Golden Age'. Standard-bearers of pretty much the same position from the liberal centre include Jeffrey Sachs. See, in particular, Sachs's interesting early formulation in 'Wages, Profits, and Macroeconomic Adjustment', *Brookings Papers on Economic Activity*, no. 2, 1979. Among the major economists of the Right associated with the position is Assar Lindbeck of Sweden.

made possible both the transcendence of the under-consumption supposedly behind the interwar crisis and the emergence of a high level of business confidence in the postwar epoch.[5] The key to the growth of demand was, according to the theory, the rise of labour after 1945 to a recognized place in the political economy of the advanced capitalist countries. The rise of labour found its expression in the establishment of, often government-sanctioned, arrangements between capital and labour to ensure that the growth of wages would keep up with the growth of productivity and prices—the so-called 'capital-labour accord'. The emergence of the welfare state—notably, the growth of unemployment insurance which tended to operate in counter-cyclical fashion—was also deemed critical, although not so much for increasing demand, since it was financed largely out of workers' taxes, as for stabilizing it. Governments' adoption of Keynesian fiscal and monetary policies also stabilized demand, smoothing out the business cycle and maintaining high employment.[6]

Nevertheless, according to the supply-side, 'contradictions of Keynesianism' thesis, success in securing economic growth proved to be self-undermining in the long run because the operation of those very arrangements which, by hypothesis, brought about that expansion of demand which underpinned the postwar boom had the long-term effect of skewing the balance of market and socio-political power in favour of labour and broadly speaking the citizenry, and against capital.

Problems on the Supply Side

In the classical statement of this position, Michal Kalecki found the contradictions of Keynesianism to lie—somewhat paradoxically in light of later appropriations of his theme—primarily outside the boundaries of the economy per se. In line with the 'Keynesian' theory that he had originated—independently from Keynes—Kalecki argued that there was no economic limit to the degree to which Keynesian policies of demand management could extend a boom. There were, however, in his view, very definite *political* limits to the degree to which it could do so. The growing power of labour on the shop floor and in the economy more generally (which would result from demand-subsidized full employment) and the encroachment of the state on the private sector (which would result from increased government spending) would eventually undermine that business confidence which the implementation of Keynesian policies had originally secured. Increasingly alarmed businessmen would press government to cut back on spending and would feel obliged to reduce investment, despite the still high rate of profit. Their politically motivated economic

---

5   For the under-consumptionist interpretation of the interwar crisis as a corollary of the supply-side interpretation of the long downturn, see S. Bowles, D. Gordon, and T. Weisskopf, *After the Wasteland. A Democratic Economics for the Year 2000*, Armonk 1990, pp. 29–30; M. Aglietta, *The Theory of Capitalist Regulation. The US Experience*, London 1979, pp. 94, 285–6; R. Boyer, 'Technical Change and the "Theory of 'Regulation'"', in G. Dosi et al., ed., *Technical Change and Economic Theory*, London 1988, pp. 82–3. For a critique, see R. Brenner and M. Glick, 'The Regulation Approach: Theory and History', *NLR* 188, July–August 1991, pp. 76–86.

6   Left-wing advocates of the 'contradictions of Keynesianism' approach tend to play down the significance of government fiscal policy in providing the demand that made for postwar stability and growth, emphasizing instead the expansion of the welfare state, especially unemployment insurance, and new institutions regulating labour-capital relations, which ostensibly kept wages up with prices and productivity. But I use the term Keynesianism more generally to refer to all of these aspects.

response would thus bring about a downturn even though the economic conditions for it were not present.[7]

Subsequent advocates of the 'contradictions of Keynesianism' argument have followed the broad outline laid out by Kalecki but with two important differences. First, they have gone beyond Kalecki in their account of those institutional mechanisms which, according to the theory, provided the foundations of the postwar boom and, in so doing, increased the market and socio-political power of labour. Second, *contra* Kalecki, they have argued that the enhancement of the power of labour and the citizenry *directly* undermined the accumulation process by bringing about a squeeze on profits. From the perspective of today's 'contradictions of Keynesianism' theorists, the operation of the capital-labour accord, the growth of the welfare state, and the commitment on the part of governments to Keynesian policies were, by the later 1960s, both maintaining the growth of demand so as to further bring down unemployment and making for enhanced confidence on the part of workers that the weapon of increased unemployment would not be invoked in the future. Meanwhile, the increased availability and level of unemployment insurance was reducing not only the risk, but also the cost, of job loss. At the same time, contractually sanctioned arrangements between capital and labour that provided for keeping wages up with both productivity and the cost of living were making it increasingly difficult for employers to compensate for rising labour costs by raising prices. Finally, the cost of the welfare state was weighing increasingly heavily on the national income.

As the boom reached its peak and labour demand outran labour supply, workers exploited their enhanced leverage to launch a powerful wave of labour militancy across the advanced capitalist economies. The outcome was an 'explosion of wages'.[8] At the same time, according to some accounts, workers withheld their energy and care on the shop floor, setting off a long-term decline in the growth of productivity.[9] The result was the onset of a secular wages-productivity squeeze on profits, made worse by the failure of the welfare state to shrink sufficiently.

Nor, according to the supply-side theory, did reduced profitability lead to adjustment via the reduction of working-class pressure. Over the course of the 1970s, 1980s and beyond, in response to reduced profitability, employers unleashed an offensive, aiming to curb the growth of wage and other costs, while reducing investment and bringing about the growth of unemployment. Meanwhile, governments throughout the advanced capitalist economies sought to get costs under control in both the private and public sectors by introducing tight credit policies, as well as major cuts in welfare-state spending. The resulting reduction in the subsidy of demand further forced up unemployment. Even so, according to the supply-side theory, there was no successful process of adjustment. Despite reduced growth and hugely increased joblessness, workers were able to maintain and make use of the institutionally based power that

7   M. Kalecki, 'Political Aspects of Full Employment' (1943), in *Selected Essays on the Dynamics of the Capitalist Economy, 1933–70*, Cambridge 1971.

8   For early arguments concerning the wage explosion, see W.D. Nordhaus, 'The Worldwide Wage Explosion', *Brookings Papers on Economic Activity*, 1972; P. Wiles, 'Cost Inflation and the State of Economic Theory', *Economic Journal*, vol. lxxxiii, June 1973.

9   See, for instance, Bowles et al., *After the Wasteland*, pp. 53–4, 69–72, 83, 100–4, 111–14; R. Boyer, 'Technical Change and the Theory of Regulation', p. 86; Armstrong et al., *Capitalism Since 1945*, p. 179.

was the legacy of the postwar boom to prevent the restoration of labour market 'flexibility' and sufficient reductions in social-welfare costs. They thereby prevented the recovery of profitability. According to the theory, the continuing power of workers also precluded the use of Keynesian measures to restore growth and employment. For, by hypothesis—given the continuing untoward influence, direct and indirect, of organized workers over the labour market—increased government subsidy of demand to reduce unemployment would lead once more either to runaway inflation or a renewed squeeze by wages on profits.[10]

2. Conceptual Difficulties with the Supply-Side Thesis

There is, of course, no reason to deny that, *all else held constant*, ongoing capital accumulation tends to increase the demand for labour relative to supply and thus to increase wages, probably the rate of growth of wages, and, more generally, the bargaining position of workers. It follows that, to the extent that policies and institutions subsidize demand and thereby bring about increased levels of capital accumulation, *all else being equal*, the resulting reduction of unemployment will further enhance workers' capacity to squeeze profits, all the more so if the availability and level of government unemployment insurance, as well as institutionalized arrangements with employers, reduce the risk and cost of job loss. The question is, however, whether it is legitimate to hold that all else is equal. This question has two aspects which need to be carefully distinguished. There is first an issue concerning *origins or onset*: can an extended process of capital accumulation leading to full employment be expected to bring down profitability? But, second and more decisive, there is an issue concerning *endurance and non-adjustment*: even supposing that full employment does lead to wage growth outrunning productivity growth, can the resulting fall in profitability be expected to persist, and thereby bring about a *temporally extended* economic downturn?

From Full Employment to Squeeze on Profits?

Full Employment as Profit-Enhancing: The Kaleckian Objection. While the growth of demand leading to full employment will tend to strengthen labour's bargaining position, it will, as it does so, tend to bring about counterbalancing effects that enhance profitability. As Michal Kalecki, the originator of the 'contradictions of Keynesianism' thesis, pointed out, increased employment tends not only to bring about upward pressure on wages, but also to lead to higher sales and capacity utilization, thereby lowering unit costs and raising profitability. As an economy approaches full employment, it may very well experience a heightening of profitability, even as wage growth accelerates.[11]

10   For critical introductions to the mainstream explanations of the downturn's continuance, see R. Z. Lawrence and C. L. Schultz, 'Overview', and P. R. Krugman, 'Slow Growth in Europe: Conceptual Issues', in Lawrence and Schultz, eds, *Barriers to European Growth*, Washington, DC 1987. For Left versions, see S. Bowles, D. Gordon, and T. Weisskopf, 'Business Ascendancy and Economic Impasse: A Structural Retrospective on Conservative Economics, 1979–87', *Journal of Economic Perspectives*, vol. iii, Winter 1989; A. Glyn, 'The Costs of Stability: The Advanced Capitalist Countries in the 1980s', *NLR* 195, September–October 1992.

11   M. Kalecki, 'Political Aspects of Full Employment', p. 138. 'The attitude [of business in opposing the maintenance of full employment through government spending financed by loans] is not easy to explain. Clearly higher output and employment benefits not only workers, but businessmen as well, because their profits rise.'

The Substitution of Capital for Labour Leading to Relatively Reduced Labour Demand and to Increased Productivity Growth. While the acceleration of real wage growth—resulting from increased demand for labour with respect to supply—tends to directly squeeze profits by outrunning productivity growth, it tends simultaneously to encourage the substitution of capital for labour, thus speeding up technical innovation.[12] Technical innovation induced by rising wages tends to reduce the pressure of labour demand with respect to labour supply in two ways. First, it tends to be labour saving. Second, it tends to increase overall productivity (the ratio of output to total input, including both labour and capital inputs), thereby reducing the amount of labour required, and therefore the amount of labour demanded, for any given level of output.

To look at the other side of the same coin, technical change tends not only to increase the relative availability of labour, it also tends to increase efficiency, reducing total (capital plus labour) costs for any given output. The fact, then, that real wages grow, or even accelerate, clearly does not automatically mean that profitability falls. Why shouldn't the growth of productivity, driven both by wage growth leading to the substitution of capital for labour and by the pressures of inter-firm competition, be rapid enough to keep the rate of return from falling?

The Growth of the Supply of Labour: Immigration and the Export of Capital. When the demand for labour rises, the resulting increase in wages tends to provoke an increase in labour supply by way of the action of the labour and capital markets themselves. Workers from abroad find it more attractive to immigrate, and—unless they are restrained by political means—their entry will reduce the tightness of the labour market. Simultaneously, the profitability of combining means of production with lower-waged labour elsewhere increases; as a result, either more capital is exported or capitalists in other places accelerate their investment. The effective size of the labour pool thus tends to expand relative to supply, and wage pressure is reduced. I am making the assumption here that there will in fact be available other, cheaper labour that can be combined with means of production embodying something like the current level of technology without a loss of efficiency (that is, at lower unit cost). But this assumption appears warranted in light of what seems to be a double reality.

First, in the course of any historically extended wave of capital accumulation, as a consequence of the growth of demand for labour and of competition for labour between more efficient and less efficient producers, labour forces inevitably secure increases in wages far greater than can be understood as compensation for their increased skill—the increased productiveness of the workers themselves, aside from the machinery they operate. More generally, labour forces in regions with long histories of economic development tend to receive wages which are substantially higher than can be explained simply by reference to their relative level of productiveness. Second, over similarly extended time periods, technical change tends to reduce the skill required to produce any given array of products, with the result that the labour force that can make those products without loss of efficiency is continually enlarged, and the wage required to pay it correspondingly

---

12   For this line of criticism of the consensus view, see R. J. Gordon, 'Productivity, Wages, and Prices Inside and Outside of Manufacturing in the US, Japan, and Europe', *European Economic Review*, vol. xxxi, 1987.

reduced.[13] The outcome is that, as their wages rise over the course of a boom, workers in the most advanced, longest developing regions tend to price themselves out of the market in consequence of the relative rise of what might be called their wages-skill ratio.

In sum, it cannot be assumed that a trend to full employment will in any straightforward way put a squeeze on profits. The very processes of extensive capital accumulation and institutionally founded enhancements of the power of labour which the supply-side theorists understand to bring down the profit rate tend, in so doing, to call forth counteracting tendencies that make for the increase of profitability and thereby tend to prevent an actual profit squeeze from taking place. Still, it would be absurd to deny that full employment leading to an enhancement of labour's leverage can ever precipitate a fall in the profit rate, and I shall have occasion to refer to several historical instances of this phenomenon. But, even if the Full Employment Profit Squeeze thesis can sometimes explain a significant fall in profitability, it is hard to see how it could account for a long-term reduction in the profit rate of the sort that has produced the long downturn.

Can the Power of Labour Prevent Adjustment?

From Tight Labour Market to Economic Crisis? The point is that where tight labour markets do make for declining profitability, firms will inevitably respond to their reduced rates of return by reducing investment. As a result, sooner rather than later, the labour market will loosen sufficiently to allow for a reduction of pressure on wages and thus for the restoration of profitability and the renewal of capital accumulation. Under capitalism, the taking of profits and wages does not occur merely as an outcome of the immediate interaction between capital and labour, although that surely is an important aspect of the distributional process. Rather, production, employment, and distribution are themselves dependent upon prior, autonomous decisions to invest, and these are entirely under the control of capital. Employers will find no motivation to invest at any given place and time unless they can secure a satisfactory rate of return. Employers must, in other words, demand a satisfactory rate of profit *as the condition for investing*, because a satisfactory rate of return is the fundamental condition for competitiveness and thus the continuing viability of the firm. In shifting distribution back in their own favour, employers are not confined to confronting their workers directly, but can respond to profit-reducing increases in labour costs by decreasing the rate of capital accumulation, thereby bringing about, in aggregate, a reduction in the growth of demand with respect to the supply of labour which produces a rise in unemployment sufficient to moderate labour's demands. The implication is that capital accumulation leading to the outrunning of labour supply by labour demand can be expected to squeeze profits only in *the short run* and therefore seems incapable of precipitating a secular, system-wide long downturn. The Full Employment Profit Squeeze theory can

---

13   See K. Akamatsu, 'A Theory of Unbalanced Growth in the World Economy' (1938), *Weltwirschaftliches Archiv*, vol. lxxxvi, 1961, as well as the literature on the product cycle, starting from R. Vernon, 'International Investment and International Trade in the Product Cycle', *The Quarterly Journal of Economics*, vol. lxxx, May 1966. See also M. Shinohara, *Industrial Growth, Trade, and Dynamic Patterns in the Japanese Economy*, Tokyo 1982.

account for some instances of reduction in profitability, but it cannot explain a long downturn.[14]

The 'Inflexible' Labour Market and the Power of Labour. The more elaborated versions of the 'contradictions of Keynesianism' approach—those centred more explicitly on the welfare state and postwar institutions regulating capital-labour relations—were formulated precisely to remedy the foregoing weaknesses of the straightforward Full Employment Profit Squeeze theory in accounting for a long-term, system-wide economic downturn. Supply-side theorists have thus taken it as their task to argue that the rise of unemployment which normally results from the reduction of investment set off by reduced profitability cannot in fact be expected to function as a disciplinary device sufficient to restore the conditions for capital accumulation. Their central contention is that, over the course of the postwar epoch, rising unemployment became insufficient to oblige labour to moderate its wage claims because workers succeeded in institutionalizing sufficient power at various levels—the shop floor, the industry or union and the state—to prevent the proper functioning of the labour market. Governments, say the supply-side theorists, were so committed to the maintenance of full employment and/or the provision of high unemployment benefits that the threat of being fired lost its teeth. Unions, they contend, have found ways to control their labour markets even in the face of high unemployment, protecting their own 'insiders' at the expense of 'outsiders'.[15] As a result, they conclude, 'disequilibrium' or profit-squeezing wages have been able to persist alongside high levels of unemployment for an extended period of time. Put another way, the economy does not return to full employment because, were it to do so, wage growth would again outrun productivity growth and squeeze profits.[16]

There is nothing logically wrong with the idea that the power of labour, exercised either on the basis of its own institutions and norms or through the state, can skew the operation of the labour market in favour of workers—for *given* firms, industries, regions, or even national economies, for *given* periods of time. The fact remains that this conclusion, even where it holds empirically, is of limited relevance. The operation of the labour market does, of course, have an irreducible political aspect; wages are, in significant respects, determined 'politically' by class conflict, as well as the operation of social norms and values, along with state intervention. But it is one thing to assert that strategic socio-political action always plays

14   Marx certainly did not see his rising-employment profit-squeeze dynamic as directly applicable to— or likely to lead to crisis in—the real world. He presented it, quite explicitly, in abstraction from what he believed to be the system's inexorable (counter-) tendencies both to productivity increase (through the growth of the organic composition of capital leading to technical change) and the expansion of the available labour force (through the growth of the surplus army of unemployed). He saw it, moreover, as strictly limited by capitalists' ability to predicate investment on a satisfactory rate of return. See *Capital*, Vol. I, ch. 25, sections 2–5, as well as 1. 'Nothing is more absurd, then, than to explain the fall in the rate of profit in terms of a rise in wage rates, even though this too may be an exceptional case.' *Capital*, Vol. III, ch. 14, section 5.

15   A sharp statement of the argument can be found in A. Lindbeck, 'What is Wrong with the West European Economies?', *The World Economy*, vol. viii, June 1985. See also A. Lindbeck and D. J. Snower, 'Wage Setting, Unemployment, and Inside-Outside Relations', *American Economic Review*, vol. lxxvi, May 1986; J.B. Donges, 'Chronic Unemployment in Western Europe Forever?' *The World Economy*, vol. viii, December 1985; Bowles, Gordon, Weisskopf, 'Business Ascendancy and Economic Impasse'.

16   See also below, pp. 160ff.

a part in determining the wage, quite another to argue that such action can so squeeze profits as to cause a *long-term, system-wide downturn*. Labour cannot, as a rule, bring about a temporally extended, systemic downturn because, as a rule, what might be called the potential sphere of investment for capital in any line of production generally extends beyond the labour market that is affected by unions and/or political parties or is regulated by norms, values, and institutions supported by the state. So firms can generally circumvent and thereby undermine the institutionalized strength of workers at any given point by investing where workers lack the capacity to resist. Indeed, they must do so, or they will find themselves outflanked and competitively defeated by other capitalists who will.

This basic dynamic may be slowed but not fundamentally transformed by state institutions. If government intervention is making for a significant squeeze by labour on profits either indirectly (as a consequence, for example, of maintaining high levels of unemployment insurance or implementing Keynesian policies for full employment) or directly (as a result, for example, of taxing capital and allocating increased public services to labour) the outcome will be the same as if labour were acting alone. In the first instance, capitalists will find their competitive position undercut; in the longer run, they will either redirect their investments to points of higher profitability or find themselves unable to compete because other capitalists have done so.

Because all elements of society depend on private investment for economic growth, for employment, and for tax revenue to finance state expenditures, governments are obliged to make the profitability of 'their' capitalists a priority, at least given that capitalist property relations are unchallenged. One of the more paradoxical consequences of this reality is that, especially since World War II, trade unions and social-democratic parties have generally accepted the principle of the primacy of profits and sought to enforce it on their followers. In direct proportion to the degree they have been well-organized, powerful, and representative of the working class as a whole, trade unions and social-democratic parties have thus consciously and systematically sought to keep wage growth from threatening profitability in the interest of the capital accumulation and growth that they deem to be the precondition for working-class material gains. To the extent that an increase in workers' material demands had been responsible for the decline in profitability over the past couple of decades, official trade unions and social-democratic parties would certainly have used their power precisely to reverse that development.[17]

The general principle may be stated as follows: victories by labour in economic conflicts tend to be relatively localized; reductions in profitability resulting from the successful exertion of workers' power tend therefore to be correspondingly localized; nevertheless, there is a generalized, system-wide pressure on employers to make the average rate of profit on pain of extinction. To the extent therefore that workers' gains reduce their employers' rate of profit below the average, they undercut capital accumulation, creating the conditions, in the medium run, for their own eradication.

---

17   'Wage restraint was an essential feature of the Golden Age model [in the countries ruled by social-democratic parties] and, if anything, it became more central to the efforts of these countries to deal with the new difficulties of the seventies and eighties.' E. Huber and J. Stephens, 'Internationalization and the Social Democratic Model: Crisis and Future Prospects', *Comparative Political Studies*, vol. xxxi, 1998.

Workers' action may certainly reduce profitability in given locales in the short run, but it cannot, generally speaking, make for an extended downturn because it cannot, as a rule, bring about a spatially generalized (system-wide) and temporally extended decline in profitability. Nevertheless, what needs to be explained in the current case is precisely a squeeze on profits and a corresponding downturn in the advanced capitalist economies from which no economy has been immune, which has enveloped all economies at the roughly the same time and same pace, and which has been temporally very extended.

3. Basic Evidence Against the Supply-Side Argument

Because the supply-side theorists explain the long downturn in terms of the operation of institutions and impact of policies, they are obliged to explain it in historically and nationally specific terms. They must therefore interpret the onset and subsequent outcomes of the squeezes on profitability that afflicted each of the advanced capitalist economies essentially on a case-by-case basis, in terms of the specific historical evolution of institutions and policies in those economies that ostensibly led to the enhancement of labour's economic and political leverage. But how can such interpretations be successfully accomplished, in view of the obvious facts that the downturn has been *universal, simultaneous* and *long-term*?

The Universality of the Long Downturn. It is a reality worth conjuring with that none of the advanced capitalist economies was able to escape the long downturn. Neither the weakest economies with the strongest labour movements, like Great Britain, nor the strongest economies with the weakest labour movements, like Japan, remained immune. Is it plausible that what explains the downturn is that workers *everywhere* accumulated sufficient power to squeeze profits?

The Simultaneity of the Onset and Various Phases. The advanced capitalist economies experienced the onset of the long downturn at the same moment—between 1965 and 1973. These economies have, moreover, experienced the successive stages of the long downturn more or less in lock step, sustaining simultaneous recessions in 1970–1, 1974–75, 1979–82 and from 1990–91. It is one thing to argue that economic and institutional developments among the advanced capitalist countries were rather similar in the postwar epoch—although if one considers the Japanese case, or compares the US with most European cases, even that may seem less than obvious. But it is quite another to contend that the paths of institutional development and policy formation, the experience of capital accumulation and technological change, and the evolution of capital-labour relations—and politics more generally—could have been so similar in the major capitalist economies as to have brought about, at the same moment, virtually identical shifts in the labour market situation and the balance of class forces so as to determine essentially the same *evolution of profitability* in those economies. In view of the very high degree to which labour's power has been differentially determined by conditions within and circumscribed by national boundaries, it is difficult to understand how the exertion of power by labour could explain the internationally coordinated evolution of the long downturn.

The Length of the Downturn. Finally, the fact that the downturn has gone on for so very long would seem to be fatal for the supply-side approach. It is not hard to believe that particular unions, workers movements, or social-democratic governments could have brought down the profit rate in given places for given periods. But, if one takes into account both the alternatives available to employers (specifically their ability to reallocate investment away from points where profits have been squeezed) and labour's long-term interests (specifically its dependence upon and concern for—in the absence of any alternative—the continuation of capital accumulation), it is almost impossible to believe that the assertion of workers' power has been both so effective and so unyielding as to have caused the downturn to continue throughout the advanced capitalist world for close to a quarter-century.

4. From Criticism to an Alternative

My alternative approach to the long downturn takes as its point of departure the results of the foregoing critique. The attempts of the supply-side theorists to understand crises essentially in terms of maldistribution—under-consumption in the case of the interwar crisis, a profit squeeze in the case of the current downturn—has led them to focus too exclusively upon the 'vertical' (market and socio-political) power relations between capitalists and workers. As a result, they have tended to underplay not only the productive benefits, but also the economic contradictions, that arise from the 'horizontal' competition among firms that constitutes the capitalist system's economic mainspring. My point of departure is thus simultaneously that capitalism tends to develop the productive forces to an unprecedented degree, and that it tends to do so in a destructive, because *unplanned and competitive*, manner.

Relatedly, the emphasis of the supply-side theorists on institutions, policy and power has led them to frame their analyses too heavily on a country-by-country basis, in terms of national states and national economies—to view the international economy as a sort of spill-over of national ones and to see systemic economic problems as stemming from an agglomeration of local ones. In contrast, I shall take the international economy—*the capital accumulation and profitability of the system as a whole*—as a theoretical vantage point from which to analyze both its booms and its crises, and those of its national components.

Finally, while the supply-side theorists specify processes that *could* lead to rising costs and a squeeze on profits in *given locales* over the *short run*, they have failed to take sufficiently into account the *compensatory* economic, political, and social mechanisms that are set off, more or less automatically, precisely as a consequence of any squeeze by labour or the citizenry on profits—mechanisms by which rising costs, through their negative effect on profitability and on the inducement to invest, create pressures both to bring about cost reductions in the 'affected' regions and to redirect investment beyond them.

To put this final point more positively, an adequate theory of crisis must explain not only why what individuals and collectivities do in pursuit of their interests leads to an aggregate pattern of production and distribution in which profitability is undermined, thereby reducing the capacity and incentive to invest. It must also explain why that same pattern leads producers to take remedial action that fails to bring about an adjustment and ends up exacerbating the difficulties of the initial situation. If we are to understand not only the historical regularity of secular capitalist development, but also the historical regularity of secular capitalist downturn, we therefore need a theory of a malign invisible hand to go along with Adam Smith's benign one—a theory which can encompass a self-generating *series of steps* resulting from individual (and collective) profit maximizing which leads not towards adjustment, but rather away from it.

In line with this prescription, I shall present an account of the long downturn which finds the source of the profitability decline, schematically speaking, in the tendency of producers to develop the productive forces and increase economic productiveness by means of the installation of increasingly cheap and effective methods of production, without regard for existing investments and their require-ments for realization, with the result that aggregate profitability is squeezed by reduced prices in the face of downwardly inflexible costs. I shall explain the perpetuation of the crisis by demonstrating that the profit-maximizing steps cap-itals find it rational to take in response to the reduction in their profitability not only fail to resolve the problem that brought down profitability in the first place, but have the effect, in aggregate, of making necessary and rational additional responses which further undercut aggregate profitability. In the face of their reduced profitability, numbers of firms thus find that it makes most sense to persist in their line rather than leave it and search for a better alternative; meanwhile, numbers of other still lower-cost producers find it individually profitable to enter into those same lines despite the lines' reduced profitability. As a consequence of the resulting consolidation of over-capacity and over-production and of reduced profitability (or the even further fall thereof), investment and output growth will decline and wage growth will be cut back, leading, in turn, to both a decline of productivity growth and a decline in the growth of effective demand (both investment and consumption), which put still further downward pressure on prof-itability. This sequence, as shall be seen, can be reversed and profitability restored only when sufficient high-cost, low-profit means of production can be forced from lines affected by over-capacity/over-production and reduced profitability, and successfully reallocated to sufficiently high-profit lines.

Chapter 2

AN ALTERNATIVE APPROACH TO THE LONG DOWNTURN

I start from the premise that, under capitalist social-property relations, the generalization of the individual norm of profitability maximization combined with the pressure of competition on a system-wide scale tends to bring about the growth of the productive forces and overall productivity, with the result that, on the assumption that the real wage remains constant, both the rate and the mass of profit *rise*, assuming there are no problems of realization.[1] But, given capitalism's unplanned, competitive nature, realization problems cannot be assumed away. The same cost-cutting by firms which creates the potential for aggregate profitability to rise creates the potential for aggregate profitability to fall, leading to macroeconomic difficulties.

1. Cost-Cutting Technology Leading to Over-Production

In a world where firms can predict what their competitors will do and perfectly adjust, cost-cutting technical change poses no problem. Cost-cutting firms will add output so as exactly to fill the space of demand left unoccupied by the decreased output resulting from the using up of means of production by higher-cost producers. The outcome, initially, is a higher rate of profit in the line because the cost-cutter needs fewer inputs to produce, so enjoys a higher rate of profit on, its output than was hitherto garnered on the exactly equivalent output by the firm reducing its output. The output of the cost-cutting firm has thus been produced at a lower cost than the same output had been hitherto produced by the other (higher-cost) firms in the line; since aggregate output and by assumption aggregate demand remain the same and aggregate cost has been reduced, the average rate of profit in the line rises. From this point, the higher-cost firms will either emulate the cost-cutter or will cede space to it by reducing their means of production in the line precisely to the extent that the cost-cutter increases its capacity. The price for the line's output will thus fall to reflect the reduced cost required to produce it and purchasers outside the line will share the gain, as capitalists pay less than before for inputs and/or workers are able to purchase more goods than previously with their money wage. The outcome, so long as workers do not secure all of the gains from the reduced price in the form of increased real wages, will be an increase in the rate of profit for the economy as a whole.

Nevertheless, in the real world of economic competition, individual capitalist producers can neither control nor predict the market for their goods; investments

---

1   I wish to thank Mark Glick and Michael Howard for their invaluable help with formulations in this chapter.

yield profits only after the fact, once they have proved themselves in a potentially destructive competitive war. Under these conditions, the only path to survival and security involves risk-taking by investing in new, more technically advanced means of production and combining these with the lowest possible wage. In this way, the lowest possible cost and price is achieved, thus maximizing either one's rate of profit or one's share of the market, and the goal is to maintain the resulting advantage for the longest period possible. Yet, when one firm secures the lowest cost of production and puts its goods on the market at a correspondingly reduced price so as to increase its market share, its doing so poses a serious problem for the other firms which are producing with older, higher-cost techniques.

Rather than merely replacing, at the established price, the output hitherto but no longer produced by a higher-cost firm which has used up some of its means of production—as in the aforementioned case of perfect foresight and perfect adjustment—real-world cost-cutting firms, by virtue of their reduced costs, will reduce the price of their output and expand their output and market share *at the expense* of the higher-cost competitors, while still maintaining for themselves the established rate of profit.[2] Given the reduced price, some firms, the least cost-effective, will be obliged to scrap means of production because they can no longer make a profit on it; the others will have to at least endure reduced profitability because of their excessively high costs. Because the cost-cutters' rate of profit remains the same as before and because the higher-cost firms' rates of profit are reduced, the outcome is an aggregate reduction of the rate of profit in the line. Under these conditions, the line can be said to be characterized by over-capacity or over-production because—or in the sense that—there is insufficient demand to allow the higher-cost firms to maintain their former rates of profit; they have been obliged to cease using some of their means of production and can make use of the rest only by lowering their price and thus their profitability. There is over-capacity and over-production, *with respect to the hitherto existing profit rate.*

While few would deny that the foregoing process is indeed normal to the capitalist economy, most would deny its problematic character. It is true, they would say, that the cost-cutters' expansion of lower-priced output leads to increased competition and (what is the same thing) over-capacity/over-production in the line, manifested in exit for some of the higher-cost means of production and temporarily reduced profitability for the rest. But it is also true, they would argue, that this situation is 'out of equilibrium' and thus only transitional, for some firms are not, at this point, doing as well as they could do and can thus be expected, more or less immediately, to take action. Those firms which have experienced reduced profitability can be expected either to leave the line, or to adopt the new technique of the innovating cost-cutter—or in some other way to match its costs. If they do not do so, the innovating firm will take the whole market. The outcome should thus be, sooner rather than later, the restoration of the previously established rate of profit in the line, though now on the basis of the cost-cutter's lowered price and cost. Ultimately, this should lead to an increase in the rate of profit for the economy as a whole (including the line initially subject to reduced profitability), just as in

---

2   I assume here that the cost-cutting firms compete among themselves, as well as with the higher-cost firms, to drive down the rate of profit to its already-established level.

the case of perfect foresight/perfect adjustment, assuming again that workers cannot garner all of the gains that accrue to the economy as a whole from the now lowered price of the line's products. Joseph Schumpeter, 'the Marx of the bourgeoisie', saw this process as the genius of capitalism. What he termed 'creative destruction'—the beating out of less productive by more productive means of production—is, after all, what makes capitalism ever more productive.

2. The Failure to Adjust

Schumpeter may, however, have underestimated the potentially destructive side of his creative destruction. *If they possess fixed capital,* firms which sustain reduced profitability as a result of the introduction of lower-cost and lower-priced goods by cost-cutters in their line *cannot* be assumed to respond by more or less immediately leaving the line; this is because it is rational for them to remain in the line so long as the new, lowered price allows them at least to make the average rate of return on their circulating capital—that is, the additional investment in labour power, raw materials, and semi-finished goods that is required to put their fixed capital into motion. The reason for this is that their fixed capital is 'sunk', that is, already paid for—or requiring interest payments that must continue whether or not the capital is in use. They can thus regard it as, in practical terms, costless and its further use as free. It therefore makes sense for higher-cost firms to seek to hold onto their share of the market by lowering their price, unless and until the price of the cost-cutting firm's goods falls so low as to prevent them from securing the average rate of return even on their circulating capital.[3] This calculus has two major consequences.

First, firms can, by virtue of their earlier placement of capital, deter the introduction of lower-cost, lower-priced goods by competitors with the potential to cut costs. This is because a cost-cutting firm that is incapable of imposing a price which is not only below that currently prevailing in the line but sufficiently low to force some incumbents to leave the line—because the rate of profit on their circulating capital has been driven below the average—will be incapable of increasing its market share without reducing its own rate of profit. Should such a firm reduce the price and attempt to maintain its old rate of profit, *all* of the incumbents would find it rational to match the price so as to maintain at least the average rate of profit on their circulating capital—even if that was reduced on their total capital. The result would be to prevent the cost-cutter from increasing market share at that price and to force it to reduce the price further, and thus its rate of profit below the established rate, in order to gain market share. Even firms capable of producing at lower cost and price in a line cannot therefore profitably expand their market share unless they are capable of making a sufficient place for their output by forcing sufficient productive capacity from the line. Put another way, they can take increased market

3   The mechanism here presented making for maladjustment is discussed in the late nineteenth-century literature on 'ruinous competition', which often sought to justify cartels and trusts. That literature also focused on the barrier to exit placed by fixed capital as sunk capital, and specifically on the continuation of over-capacity and over-production with respect to the profit rate on total capital that results from incumbents' willingness to continue producing so long as they secure normal profitability on their circulating capital See, for example, A.T. Hadley, *Economics*, New York 1901, pp. 292–5. For a useful introduction to this literature, see H. Hovenkamp, 'The Antitrust Movement and the Rise of Industrial Organization', *Texas Law Review*, vol. lxviii, November 1989, esp. pp. 122–43. I wish to thank Mark Glick for calling my attention to this body of writing.

share without experiencing a reduction in their own profitability only to the extent that they can force others to yield market share by scrapping.

This said, a further point should be emphasized. While, by virtue of their possession of fixed capital, high-cost firms possess a powerful deterrent to cost-cutters intent on expanding their market share (specifically, of cost-cutters with the ability to reduce cost and price below that prevailing in the line but insufficiently to drive out some incumbents), this does not at all ensure that such cost- and price-cutting will not take place. The cost- and price-cutter may have a strategic reason to accept the lower rate of profit or, alternatively, may miscalculate. In either case, the consequence of its action is not only over-capacity/over-production but reduced profitability in the line for all, including the cost- and price-cutter itself.

Second, cost-cutting, price-reducing firms that are capable of replacing some incumbents—by reducing their price sufficiently to make it impossible for the latter to make the average rate of profit even on their circulating capital and thereby forcing them to scrap fixed capital—will be able both to continue to secure the established rate of profit and increase their market share on the basis of their lower price. Yet, they will, in so doing, bring about a reduction in the average rate of profit in the line because their new low price will have a (doubly) undermining effect on the profitability of the other firms in the line, forcing them to cede market share and accept lowered prices for their (higher-cost) goods.[4] Firms which can no longer make the average rate of profit even on their circulating capital will be forced to cede market share. Initially, in the short run, they may be able to get away with only reducing capacity utilization, because the firm with the lower cost as yet has insufficient productive capacity to take as much market share away from them as its lowered price would warrant. To the degree that their capacity is reduced, however, these higher-cost firms will suffer the reduced profitability that results from the fact that output (sales) is reduced but capital costs are not. Eventually, as the cost-cutting firm expands its capacity, they will be forced to scrap and leave the line. Those firms that can still make the average rate of profit on their circulating capital will find that it makes sense to remain in the line, but will nonetheless endure reduced profitability on their total capital since their costs remain the same, but the price at which they must sell is now reduced.

With respect to the higher-cost firms who remain, then, the 'normal' process of adjustment—whereby higher-cost firms leave the line and are replaced by lower-cost producers—simply does not occur, because of those firms' possession of fixed capital. The line's output now has the lower price imposed by the cost-cutting entrant. Its population consists of the cost-cutting firm making the old rate of profit on the basis of its reduced production costs plus the firms that have failed to cut costs having to take a reduced profit rate. Technically speaking, as a result of the lower-cost firm's appropriation of market share, through the imposition of its lower

---

4   The idea that problems could arise due to cost-cutters' introduction of price-reducing technical changes that prevent incumbents from fully realizing their investments on fixed capital goes back at least as far as Marx. An interesting and helpful exposition of this notion and its implications can be found in J. Weeks, *Capital and Exploitation*, Princeton 1981, pp. 186, 211–17. See also the texts on economic crisis by S. Clarke, notably *Keynesianism, Monetarism, and the Crisis of the State*, Aldershot 1988. I am indebted to Loren Goldner for many stimulating discussions of this issue, as well the opportunity to read his essay 'The American Working Class and the Current World Crisis' (unpublished manuscript).

price, over-investment leading to over-capacity and over-production has arisen in the line, again *with respect to the previously and still prevailing rate of profit*. Some higher-cost firms have been obliged to scrap fixed capital because they have lost market share; for the same reason, those higher-cost incumbents who remain have been able to hold onto their place (meet some of the demand) only by selling their goods at less than the old rate of return. The outcome is that, rather than leading to a higher rate of profit, the entry of a lower-cost, lower-price producer brings about a lower rate of profit in the line. The line is nonetheless 'in equilibrium' and no further transition can be expected to take place for the time being since all of its incumbents are presumably making the best profit rate they can. The line's reduced profit rate is typically registered both in a declining output-capital ratio and a declining profit share, because, in arithmetical terms, it is simply the result of the higher-cost firms' inability to raise their prices sufficiently over their (given) capital and wage costs due to the competitive price pressure of the cost-cutting entrant.

A final, major issue needs to be clarified before the relevance of the foregoing mechanisms for the problem of explaining economic crises and extended slow-downs can begin to be examined. This issue is the impact on profitability *in the economy as a whole* of the reduced price that determined the fall of profitability in the line affected by over-capacity and over-production. We know that, to the extent that the reduced price in the line leads, as above, to a reduction of profitability in that line, that same reduced price will provide an equivalent increase in income to others in the economy who purchase those goods as their inputs. The question is, who actually secures these gains—other capitalists in the form of a higher rate of profit resulting from lower production costs or workers in the form of a higher real wage? This question cannot be answered a priori, but it may be possible nonetheless to advance our argument by taking into account the limiting case.

In the event that other capitalists outside the lowered profit line secured *all* and workers secured *none* of the gains from the lowered price that brought about the reduction of profits in the lowered-profit line, capitalists' increase in profitability outside the lowered-profit line would balance out the decrease in profitability in the lowered-profit line and aggregate profitability for the economy as a whole would stay the same. But this scenario seems an unlikely one, because conditions do not ordinarily exist that could enable capitalists to prevent workers from securing any gains from the reduced price in the form of higher real wages. On the assumption that the line's output is 'typical'—that is, it is consumed in the same proportion as consumption takes place in the economy as a whole, in accord with the established distribution of the consumption of consumer goods and of capital goods—the gains from the reduction in price will roughly accord with the estab-lished distribution of income between labour and capital, i.e. the profit share. In any case, if labour is able to get *any* of the gains from the decrease in prices, then the aforementioned processes—by which a decline in profitability in a given line results from the failure of higher-cost, lower- profit producers in possession of fixed capital who suffer reduced profitability to leave the line—will indeed result in a fall in profitability for the economy as a whole. This is because the fall in profitability (the loss of profits) that results from the fall in price in the line will fail to be fully compensated by the rise in profitability (the gain in profits) outside that line: all of the losses sustained within the line stemming from the reduced price are sustained by capital; but not all of the gains accrued outside the line from the same reduced price are accrued by capital. To what *extent* there is a fall in profitability for the economy as a whole depends, of course, on the details of the given case.

3. Fixed Capital, Uneven Development, and Downturn

The question that imposes itself is whether the sort of processes just envisioned— whereby unplanned-for, unforeseen innovation, and cost-cutting more generally, leads to over-capacity and over-production—are likely to occur on a large enough scale and over a long enough period to seriously damage the economy. Certain aspects of the investment process under capitalism as it has evolved historically do, I would argue, make such an outcome more than a possibility.

The Vulnerability of Fixed Capital

There has been an historical tendency for production to be improved through investment in ever greater masses of fixed capital. Successful technical advance— most notably via economies of scale—has tended to require initial investments that can be realized only over many years, as for example in steel mills, or car factories, or chemical plants. Today this tendency has been much intensified as a consequence of the enormous expenditures on research and development upon which large-scale fixed capital investments are usually predicated. As a result, in many lines, great masses of capital tend to be vulnerable to new productions with more advanced techniques operating at lower costs.

The degree to which an economy's fixed capital is vulnerable to cost-cutting competition is increased because investment tends to take place in waves and be embodied in large, technically interrelated, developmental blocs.[5] This occurs because each investment tends to depend on others to provide the demand to its output and the inputs for its production process. Think of the interrelated rise of railroads and shipbuilding, coal mining, iron and steel production, and machine-tool production in the British economy of the middle third of the nineteenth century, or the interrelated expansion of automobile, steel, iron, coal, and petroleum production, along with highway construction, in the US economy in the years following World War II.

The vulnerability of fixed capital, as it is embodied in waves of investment or developmental blocs, tends to be exacerbated by its inertia. Fixed capital thus tends to perpetuate itself at the same technological level as a consequence of the 'technical interrelatedness' that characterizes the structure of production both internal to and among the producing units.[6]

As a result of technical interrelatedness internal to the unit, existing plants tend to find it difficult to adopt specific inventions without significantly altering or

5   This notion is suggested in E. Dahmen, 'Technology, Innovation, and International Industrial Transformation', in L.H. Dupriez, ed., *Economic Progress*, Louvain 1955, where it is explicitly introduced in connection with what Dahmen calls *'the struggle between the old and new'* (emphasis added) and the potential of the latter to cause aggregate economic disruption.

6   For the following two paragraphs, see M. Frankel, 'Obsolescence and Technological Change in a Maturing Economy', *American Economic Review*, vol. xlv, June 1955, the analysis of which is extended in C. P. Kindleberger, 'Obsolescence and Technical Change', *Bulletin of the Oxford University Institute of Economics and Statistics*, vol. xxiii, 1961.

entirely transforming their layout. Yet, it often makes no sense to accept the costs of making the required alteration or transformation, because the remainder of the productive unit—aside from the specific part to be improved by bringing in the invention—is perfectly efficient and would be costly to change. Existing units of production therefore find it irrational to bring in technical advances that newly constructed units would find it rational to install, with the result that there is a tendency for such units to replace worn-out parts with roughly identical new ones and so conserve fixed capital in its old form rather than to transform it in accord with the improvement of technology. The same sort of problem that arises within individual units may arise within sets of interconnected units. It may thus be difficult to innovate in one part without changing some or all of the others. For example, the laying down of small-gauge railroad tracks in Britain in the first part of the nineteenth century made it difficult to adopt the newer more powerful locomotives that later became available because a transformed and enlarged system of tracks would have been difficult to adopt without undertaking the large capital investment required to transform the existing mineheads, ports, and iron and steel facilities which had been designed to fit the old railroad system. The task was made all the more difficult by the coordination problems which arose because the railroads and the associated facilities had different owners. The problem of interrelatedness among units within a productive system may thus be added to the problem of interrelatedness of equipment within units tending to further increase the inertial character of a developmental bloc and thereby increase its vulnerability to new, lower-cost production based on new techniques.

The New Prey on the Old

If one thus views investment as taking place in the course of capitalist development in waves, in which large masses of fixed capital are embodied in interrelated and partly self-conserving blocs, one can envision the dangers which arise with the advent of new blocs of interrelated productions at higher levels of productivity, or simply lower costs. Large masses of capital can quickly become vulnerable, as firms of the older bloc are obliged to face reduced prices for their higher-cost output and to confront the necessity of premature scrapping and lowered rates of profit on their fixed capital. Nevertheless, such large-scale processes of technical change and cost-cutting more generally leading to reduced profitability need not—and do not generally—take place in a continuous, unilineal way. Certain forces tend to delay and counter this tendency, even if they do not permanently forestall it.

First, all else being equal, existing firms tend to repel new entrants from the markets they occupy. They do so because they tend, at least for a time, to be more cost-effective than potential competitors. They do so as well because, by virtue of the aforementioned deterrent power they derive from their existing placements of fixed capital, they have the capacity to delay the entry of even lower-cost competitors for longer than their pure cost effectiveness would seem to warrant.[7]

---

7   As Schumpeter was at pains to emphasize, moreover, in the modern epoch, corporations routinely ensure the returns on their investments in capital stock embodying technological advances by securing, by all sorts of politico-institutional means, the (temporary) protection of their market from competitors. *Capitalism, Socialism, and Democracy*, New York 1950, ch. 8.

Second, a corollary of the above point, investors often can make the best profits if they can develop new geographical regions. As a result of the implicit shield to competition offered by their location, producers in new regions can typically avoid having immediately to confront the established dominant firms of the old bloc, thereby gaining space and time to perfect their production and improve their competitiveness. In addition, production can be cheaper in later-developing economies because producers have the potential to emulate the advanced techniques of their rivals from the old bloc while availing themselves of less expensive labour and paying lower rents than in developed areas where living standards have increased in accord with the growth of labour productivity—and faster than increases in the productiveness of the labour force per se. The evolution of technique itself, marked by de-skilling and standardization, tends to magnify this advantage by facilitating the combination of ever more advanced technology and ever less skilled labour. Producers in later-developing economies sometimes have the further advantage of trade protection and, beyond that, advanced institutional forms making for greater competitiveness—through merging bank and industrial capital, facilitating coordination among producers that provide one another's markets, regulating capital-labour relations, and driving state intervention.

Schematically speaking, the operation of these mechanisms may be seen to bring about a specific ideal-typical pattern of economic evolution. Initially, the older bloc will tend to operate to a significant degree in separation from the competition of newer blocs. In part, this is because, by virtue of their existing fixed capital, its firms are able to deter entry due to either their straightforward superiority in terms of costs of production or to their ability to price their products, if necessary, in terms of their circulating capital costs alone. In part, it is because the newly placed capitals of the new bloc are able to secure their best profits by exploiting, with lower productive costs, new labour forces and new markets in new regions in relative freedom from the competition of the established producers. The trend to declining profitability that derives from the difficulties of producers of the older bloc in realizing fixed capital investments in the face of competition from lower-cost producers of the newer bloc tends therefore to be delayed for a time, staved off temporarily by the resistance to entry of the established producers, and also compensated by the higher than average profitability of investments in newer areas.

Nevertheless, in the longer run, capitalists serving new regions on the basis of lower-cost production will tend to improve and expand their productive capacity to a point where they not only open new markets with new labour forces, but can profitably enter into already occupied markets. Over time, these producers find it ever easier to penetrate markets hitherto dominated by the firms of the older bloc, especially because they can do so by increasing the output of plants already serving their new markets rather than by incurring the risk of setting up new plants for the specific purpose of invading the old markets. Markets thus tend to be unified and new blocs of capital come into direct competition with the old.

From Over-Capacity to Long Downturn

Initially, elements of the older bloc will thus face lower prices, be stuck with higher-costs, and suffer reduced profit rates. Some capitals will be forced to scrap, but others, rather than switching lines in pursuit of the highest rate of return on their total capital, will find that they can secure the best return by maintaining their market share by means of lowering their price, since they can still achieve at least the average rate of profit on their new investments in circulating capital on the basis of the new lowered price. Since, ideal-typically, the representatives of the new bloc have expanded their share by setting the new, lower price at a level at which they themselves still make only the average rate of profit, the result is to consolidate the situation of generally reduced aggregate rate of profit in the affected lines at a kind of new equilibrium (all of the producers are presumably maximizing their profit rates to the extent possible). The economy enters the downturn, then, because the measures that individual economic actors are obliged to take to counteract their own reduced profitability serve to reproduce the problem of reduced profitability at the aggregate level. Nevertheless, the processes tending to prolong the downturn are not by any means exhausted with the higher-cost producers' recourse to their sunk capital.

From Proprietary Assets to Counter-Offensive. In terms of their additional investments in circulating capital, the higher-cost firms of the older bloc are still making at least the same rate of profit as before, presumably at least the 'average rate'. They have, moreover, though long years of operation in their lines, accumulated otherwise unattainable information about markets, favourable relationships with suppliers and purchasers, and above all technical know-how which together constitute perhaps their greatest assets. Because this proprietary intangible fixed capital, no less than their tangible fixed capital, can be realized only in their established lines of production and would be lost were they to switch lines, they might very well possess a better opportunity for investing profitably and producing competitively where they are already ensconced than anywhere else. Having just been victimized by unforeseen cost-cutting, they will have every reason to defend their markets and counterattack by speeding up the process of innovation through investment in additional fixed capital. The adoption of such a strategy on the part of the firms originally caught with high costs will tend to provoke the original cost-reducing innovators to accelerate technical change themselves, further worsening the already existing over-capacity and over-production.

From Declining Demand Growth to Difficulty Reallocating. While the possession of tangible and proprietary intangible fixed assets biases firms to stay where they are even in the face of reduced profitability, the slowed growth of demand that is the unavoidable expression of the reduced growth of investment, of employment, and of wages that inevitably results from falling profit rates makes it more difficult to reallocate to new lines. In periods of high profitability and rapid growth of GDP, the economy brings about the reallocation of capital into new lines of production almost automatically. The generalized rise of incomes, both wages and profits, which is an expression of the cheapening of goods that follows from the growth of productivity which can be expected to result from the rapid growth of investment, frees up purchasing power so as to raise demand for goods which were hitherto 'too costly'. Opportunities to profit by producing such goods thus increases, and firms have little difficulty recognizing them. But, in periods in which over-capacity and over-production have brought down profitability, the demand for hitherto too-costly goods obviously must slow down because discretionary incomes must grow at a decelerated pace in response to the slower productivity growth that follows from decreased investment. It becomes harder to find alter-native lines in which old levels of profitability can be maintained for the simple reason that such lines are emerging and expanding less rapidly.

To complicate matters, the growth of demand from the particular lines plagued by over-capacity and over-production falls disproportionately, bringing about a shift in the overall pattern of demand. Firms find it more difficult to discern where sufficient profits can actually be made. To reallocate successfully, firms will thus face, to a greater extent than previously, the difficult prospect of creating demand by creating new supply, that is, by making new products that meet previously unrecognized needs. Yet, because investable surpluses have also been growing more slowly as a consequence of reduced profitability, they are likely to find the required stepped-up expenditures on research and development particularly dif-ficult to accomplish and the risks thereby entailed especially daunting.

Entry of Still Lower-Cost Producers. Just as the mere over-supply of a line of pro-duction cannot be counted on to force enough exit to restore its profitability, that same over-supply is insufficient to deter further entry that could bring down its profit rate further. On the contrary. The initial fall in profitability that results from processes of uneven development bringing about over-capacity and over-production can be expected to intensify the worldwide drive for even lower production costs for the same products through the combination of even cheaper labour with even higher levels of technique in still later-developing regions. To the extent this drive succeeds—typically by means of the emulation by later developers of the produc-tion methods of the earlier developers—it only intensifies the initial problem.

From Increased Credit to Increased Inertia. The fact that credit is usually available even to firms with relatively high costs and relatively low profit rates tends to greatly complicate the adjustment process. No mere reduction of profitability on total capital, or even inability to profit on circulating capital, can be expected to lead firms to view as necessary and inevitable the eventual reallocation of their capital else-where or the closing down of their business. Firms will tend to respond to such reverses, as far as possible, by taking out loans so as to be able to increase invest-ment in the hope of improving competitiveness, or just to hold on in the hope that the market will improve. Such assumption of debt obviously allows individual firms that have been set back by aggregate over-capacity and over-production greater longevity in their lines. But, precisely by facilitating the survival of low-profit firms, firms that might in its absence have gone out of business, the growth of borrowing tends to exacerbate over-capacity and over-production, and to slow the restoration of profitability, increasing instability and vulnerability to economic disruption.

'The Productivity-Wage Profit Squeeze'. The very fall in profitability that results from over-capacity and over-production will tend, finally, to further slow the process of adjustment by *itself* generating further downward pressure on the profit rate, because, as a consequence of the reduced growth of investment that it induces, it will tend to bring about not only, as already noted, reduced growth of effective demand, but also the reduced growth of productivity. Reduced growth of invest-ment tends to reduce the growth of productivity of labour (output per labour input) because it generally means reducing the growth of plant and equipment per person. But, it also tends to reduce the growth of productivity taking into account both capital and labour inputs ('total factor productivity'), because a placement of capital

can be expected, in itself, to bring improvement—'endogenously', in the jargon, by bringing about economies of scale, learning by doing, and the like ... as well as because the reduced growth of output and demand that generally accompany slowed investment can be expected to increase risk, lower expectations, and put a dampener on product and process innovation. Longer term 'crises of productivity' are thus more likely to be understandable as a consequence than as a cause of secular problems of profitability. In turn, because a slowdown in productivity growth means that a smaller surplus will be generated at any given rate of wage growth than previously, it obviously complicates the process of adjustment to over-capacity and over-production by making the restoration of profitability that much more difficult to accomplish.

4. The Postwar Economy from Boom to Stagnation

In the remainder of this text, I will try to demonstrate that the mechanisms presented above lay behind the processes by which the postwar economy moved from long boom to long downturn. These processes, I shall argue, worked themselves out during the postwar period by way of a specific, historical pattern of uneven development and international competition. In this process of uneven international evolution, what had been the earlier-developing and dominant blocs of the international economy, notably the US (and also the UK), suffered from the disadvantages of having held technological leadership, having evolved further in socio-economic terms, and having held hegemonic status in the world economy. Meanwhile, certain of the later-developing blocs of the international economy, focused on Japan and Germany—and, later, parts of East Asia—benefited by exploiting the potential advantages of being followers technologically, less developed socio-economically, and internationally hegemonized. It was the combination of and interaction between the older- and later-developing blocs that largely determined both the character of the long boom and the nature of the long downturn to which it gave rise.

Through the initial era of postwar development—the period of the boom proper, lasting until the mid 1960s—the older US and the newly emerging European and Japanese blocs experienced paths of growth that were not only highly uneven, but also, to a surprising degree, *separate*, especially in one crucial respect. Trade grew rapidly, but it began everywhere from very low levels. In particular, even as late as the early 1960s, the US economy remained to an extraordinary degree self-contained, as US domestic producers confined themselves largely to the home market and were able, for the most part, by virtue of their high levels of productivity, as well as the protection provided by distance, to defend that market against their overseas rivals—while providing rapidly increasing foreign direct investment to the rest of the world. Meanwhile, the Japanese and the German economies were themselves securing high levels of growth through achieving high rates of investment and productivity growth, particularly in manufacturing, especially by achieving extremely elevated rates of export growth. The German and Japanese economies were, it must be stressed, able to turn their impressive growth trajectories into spectacular ones only by virtue of their ability to capture, mostly from US (and UK) producers, *increasing shares* of an international market that was growing at least half again as fast as rapidly advancing world production. In this sense, the followers could develop as successfully as they did only by virtue of their international economic relationship with the leader, specifically its markets. Still, although US-based producers lost significant export share—and suffered some import penetration—during this period, such losses initially had a limited effect on overall US economic performance as a consequence of US producers' restricted dependence upon world trade and their continued domination of their own home market.[8] In any case, the huge gains from trade for the system as a whole far overshadowed the restrictions on growth endured by the economic leaders due to their declining competitiveness.

But uneven development did not long remain only favourable in its effects. From the early 1960s, especially as a consequence of the dramatic reduction of trade barriers at the end of the 1950s, the growth of trade accelerated spectacularly and unexpectedly. US manufacturing producers suddenly found their markets, both abroad and at home, under radically increased pressure from the lower-cost, lower-price exports of the later-developing blocs, especially Japan. As a consequence of the resulting downward pressure on prices, they were unable to realize their existing investments at their previously established rates of profit, suffering falling output-capital ratios, as well as reduced profit shares, and thus declining profitability. The upshot of what was effectively a process of over-investment leading to over-capacity and over-production in manufacturing on an international scale—especially given the enormous fraction of the total for the advanced capitalist economies represented by US production—was a major fall in the aggregate profitability of the advanced capitalist economies, located primarily in manufacturing, in the years between 1965 and 1973.

Falling aggregate profitability brought extended economic difficulty, the long downturn, because it failed to lead to adjustment—and it was soon experienced throughout the advanced capitalist world. Many US manufacturing firms which sustained reduced profitability on their total capital investments nonetheless continued to hold onto much of their market share, while presumably securing at least the established rate of profit on their circulating capital. Meanwhile, between 1969 and 1973, as part and parcel of the same processes of intensifying competition that brought down profitability in the US, the explosion of Japanese and German current account surpluses and US current account deficits—catalyzed by the rise of record US federal deficits—precipitated the collapse of the Bretton Woods system and with it a major devaluation of the dollar, leading to a dramatic restructuring of relative costs internationally in favour of US producers. The mark and the yen sustained major increases in value against the dollar, and, as a result, some of the burden of profitability decline was shifted away from the US economy and the international crisis was extended to both Germany and Japan.

Nevertheless, this was only the beginning of what turned out to be a very extended downturn. There was no easy exit from the crisis, because the processes of adjustment that were required to bring it to an end failed to go into effect to a sufficient degree. Rather than leave their lines, US manufacturing corporations, aided by the even further devaluation of the dollar, sought to improve their

8   The same processes of appropriation of market share by German and Japanese competitors from the US could thus have a major positive effect on the former economies, while only having a minor negative effect on the US economy, the latter being so much larger.

profitability and competitiveness by launching a powerful wave of investment during the 1970s and radically reducing the growth of wage costs, direct and indirect. Faced with cheaper US goods on the world market, and given the generally slower growth of international demand, manufacturers in Japan and Germany faced an intensification of the same sort of stepped-up price pressure that their US counterparts had experienced in the immediately preceding period and the same downward pressure on their profits. But, rather than reallocate resources, they, too, accepted reduced rates of return and sought, as far as possible, to continue producing as before, helped out in this by the steady supply of loans from highly accommodating financial institutions. There was, in other words, no smooth movement out of lines of reduced profitability stemming from over-capacity and over-production as firms politely ceded position. On the contrary, producers sought to maintain themselves by doing what they had always done, only in less costly ways. They thereby intensified their competitive warfare, exacerbating over-capacity and over-production, with highly destructive consequences.

The process of uneven development out of which the crisis had initially emerged did not, moreover, come to an end, but continued apace, highlighted by the dramatic entry into international manufacturing of newly established producers based in East Asia. These later-developing manufacturers used Japanese-style institutions to combine increasingly advanced techniques with low wages to make possible a stunning, Japanese-style invasion into world export markets. The result was to exacerbate the problem of over-capacity and over-production in manufacturing, helping to prevent the recovery of profitability and to perpetuate the downturn through the 1980s and into the 1990s. Secularly reduced aggregate profitability brought much increased instability, but failed to lead to depression because the massive growth of both public and private debt, made possible largely by the enormous expansion of government borrowing, prevented the series of major recessions that shook the international economy in 1974–75, 1979–82 and 1990–91 from spiralling out of control. But the very same processes that allowed the international economy to avoid depression prolonged the downturn because they prevented that shakeout of high-cost, low-profit firms, especially in manufacturing, that was requisite to the recovery of aggregate profitability.

From the end of the 1970s, the epoch-making turn from Keynesian debt-creation to monetarist credit restriction and intensified austerity did accelerate the destruction of redundant capital, especially in manufacturing, but it simultaneously made more difficult the necessary allocation of investment funds into new lines. Meanwhile, from the mid 1980s, on the basis of another round of massive dollar devaluation against the yen and the mark, there began a major new shift in the locus of the most competitive manufacturing production—in favour of the US and against Germany and Japan. In the US, while growth remained slow, profitability did begin to rise, dramatically so towards the mid 1990s. This was in part because wage growth was so effectively held down and the dollar so heavily devalued against the currencies of Germany and Japan. But it was also in part because the US manufacturing sector achieved a certain rationalization and revitalization, largely through shedding redundant, ineffective capital and intensifying labour.

Even so, especially because the advanced capitalist economies sustained the ever greater curtailment of the growth of domestic demand—as wage and employment growth was further reduced and restrictive macroeconomic policies became ever tighter and more universally applied, but investment growth failed to recover— there was no transcendence of the underlying problem of reduced system-wide manufacturing profitability. Instead, over-capacity and over-production were perpetuated and exacerbated throughout the advanced capitalist world, as almost all of the leading economies oriented themselves to an ever greater extent toward growth through manufacturing exports in the face of ever more slowly growing domestic markets. The question that therefore imposed itself as the world economy approached the end of the century was whether a new, US-based investment boom could finally precipitate an international recovery through a profound deepening of the world division of labour, or whether the worldwide explosion of exports would bring even more redundant production and deeper stagnation.

PART TWO
The Long Upturn

Chapter 3

THE PATTERN OF THE POSTWAR BOOM

During the first quarter-century of the postwar epoch, the advanced capitalist world experienced record rates of growth. Nevertheless, its extraordinary dynamism was very unevenly distributed. While the earlier-developing US economic bloc tended to repel new investment, the new economic blocs with which the Japanese and German economies were associated tended to attract it. The postwar growth of the US economy was not therefore especially impressive, either in comparison to that of its major competitors, or with respect to its own record in earlier periods. Between 1950 and 1973, the average annual growth of GDP, capital stock, and the capital-labour ratio, as well as the percentage of investment in output, were thus markedly lower than they had been between 1890 and 1913—although labour productivity growth was a bit higher. In sharp contrast, the postwar rates of growth enjoyed by many European economies, particularly Germany, were far greater than they had ever been, while Japan's productive performance over the same years was without equal by any other economy over a comparable period of time in world history. It was the US economic bloc's *relatively* slow path of development, at first largely in separation from, then in increasingly intense interaction with, the dynamic developmental trajectories of these later-developing blocs that was largely responsible for the overall pattern of postwar economic development, first during the boom, then during the downturn.

Table 3.1. Comparing the pre-World War I to the post-World War II booms.
(Average annual per cent change, except for Investment/GDP ratio.)

	GDP		GDP/hour		Capital Stock		Gross Stock/hour		Gross Capital Investment/ GDP	
	1890/ 1913	1950/ 73	90/13	50/73	90/13	50/73	90/13	50/73	90/13	50/73
US	3.9	3.6	2.2	2.5	5.4	3.2	3.4	1.7	15.8	13.2
Germany	3.2	5.9	1.9	4.9	3.1	6.6	1.5	5.5	–	17.2
Japan	2.7	9.3	1.7	8.0	3.0	9.1	1.9	7.3	11.1	23.7

Source: A. Maddison, *Dynamic Forces in Capitalist Development*, Oxford 1991, pp. 41, 50, 71, 140, 142, 210, 274.

At the point at which the European and Japanese economies completed their postwar recoveries, roughly around 1950, the US economy had already been experiencing rapid growth for more than a decade, thereby increasing its already substantial lead over all other national economies. Nevertheless, as a consequence of the very developments by which it consolidated its dominant position, the US economy found it difficult to maintain its momentum. Its initially advanced technology as embodied in already existing fixed capital, its more evolved socio-economic structure as expressed in its high degree of industrialization and correspondingly reduced agricultural sector, and its internationally hegemonic position as manifested in the dominant global position of its financiers, multi-national corporations, and, of course, its state, all constituted significant barriers to its continued dynamism. In contrast, its leading rivals, in Germany and Japan, were able to realize the potential advantages of technologically following the leader, of socio-economic backwardness and of a 'hegemonized' position.[1]

Catch-Up and the Weight of Fixed Capital

In the course of a decade-long spurt of capital accumulation from the end of the 1930s, US producers profited from interwar and wartime waves of innovation to install the most advanced plant and equipment in the world. But the existence of this great mass of fixed capital turned out to be a mixed blessing. At the start of the period, the US capital stock was the material instantiation of American firms' overwhelming international technological leadership. But, as time went on, its possessors, by virtue of their sunk capital, were able to discourage further entry into the US market, even by producers with lower costs, and thereby to slow the process of technological change and the growth of productivity within the US.

US producers' leading emerging rivals in Germany and Japan faced almost precisely the opposite conditions. As a result of US technical achievements, German and Japanese producers had the possibility of catch-up—drawing upon a huge backlog of hitherto unused, advanced techniques, which they could embody in new fixed-capital investments at relatively low cost. At least for a time, moreover, they could exploit this advantage to an increasing degree, because technological change tended to make possible, through simplification (de-skilling), the combination of an ever broader range of advanced equipment with labour of relatively low skill, to which the German and Japanese economies had access at a lower price than the US. German and Japanese producers were not, moreover, deterred from putting into place new, more productive plant and equipment, as were their US counterparts, by the existence of great masses of recently placed fixed capital.

The fact remains, however, that catch-up alone can explain little, for it must itself be explained, being anything but an automatic process. Leaders, especially through

---

1   The classic account of the 'penalty of taking the lead' is found in T. Veblen, *Imperial Germany*, New York 1915, but much more fully developed ideas concerning the advantages of coming late—as well as about the innovative institutional forms that make possible the realization of these advantages—in relationship to the broader processes of uneven development, both within and between economies, are to be found in the discussions among Russian Marxists, between the 1890s and 1930s, notably Lenin, Trotsky, Tugan-Baranowsky, and Parvus. In *Economic Backwardness in Historical Perspective*, Cambridge, Mass., 1962, chs 1 and 2, A. Gerschenkron famously develops some of the notions originally limned out by his Russian forbears, especially Trotsky, but without bothering to refer to these sources.

their unmatched capacity for technological innovation, often increase their lead over laggards, rather than watch it disappear. This was the situation with the US economy itself for three-quarters of a century before 1950. Followers, moreover, often lack the social structure and/or the requisite institutional framework and/or the labour force skills to exploit the potential for rapid productivity gains at low cost provided by the technological achievements of the leader.[2] The catch-up process was unquestionably central for the German and Japanese economies in the quarter-century after 1950, but this was only because these economies' capacities for rapid capital accumulation and large-scale technological change had recently been so enhanced in each case by the domestic socio-economic and politico-institutional transformations of the immediate post-World War II period, because the hitherto existing barriers to the international free flow of goods and of capital were so dramatically lowered over the course of the 1950s and 1960s, and because, in particular, the US, functioning as hegemon, was willing to accept its rivals' and trading partners' statism and organized capitalism—and not least their protectionism and undervalued currencies—in order to further their postwar dynamism and, in this way, the expansion of markets for US exports and broadfields for US foreign direct investment.

As it was, catch-up, for these economies, was only a part of the story. In the process of carrying through vast expansions of their capital stock, the manufacturing economies of both Germany and Japan secured unparalleled opportunities not only for emulation, but also for innovation through learning by doing. By investing a great deal at a rapid pace, they not only quickly grasped new technologies, but also transformed them. As they became wealthier, moreover, these economies could, at both the private and the public levels, afford greater expenditures on both research and development, and training and education. In catching up, they could therefore often forge ahead of the US leader, as they in fact did over the course of the 1950s and 1960s in one key industry after another—textiles, steel, automobiles, machine tools, consumer electronics.

The Orientation of the Labour Movement

The US labour movement had remade and revitalized itself in the historic struggles for industrial unionism of the 1930s. It had, however, been profoundly weakened by wartime bureaucratization and postwar political repression. Still, the very manner in which the US economy had arrived at world economic dominance endowed labour with unexpected leverage. Long-term processes of industrialization had largely eliminated the reserves of labour that were once found in agriculture and small business; any major wave of capital accumulation would therefore quickly induce tight labour markets. Moreover, at least through the mid 1950s, US industry was essentially immune from the sort of intense overseas competition that could oblige unions to think twice before advancing demands on employers. US labour thus remained more than strong and militant enough to push up wages rapidly, especially when cyclical upturns pushed down unemployment, as at the time of the Korean War.

In contrast to their counterparts in the US, manufacturers in Germany and Japan were able to found their postwar expansion on the basis of labour forces that

2 For further discussion of the role of catch-up in postwar development, see below, pp. 272–80.

received extremely low wages relative to their skill. In both societies, a large part of the working population remained in agriculture or in small industrial and retail shops, much of it being disguisedly unemployed. Their industrial reserve armies, supplemented in the German case by large-scale immigration from the East, could thus exert strong downward pressure on wages over an extended period, at least through the later 1950s. The large agricultural and small business sectors of both economies also opened up an easy path to major productivity gains for the economy as a whole, as labour could be transferred at low cost from low-productivity operations into high-productivity manufacturing.

The gains to capital from this transfer process were protected, moreover, through the decisive defeat of postwar labour revolts and the emergence in their wake of newly burgeoning conservative trade union organizations which gave top priority to the needs of capital accumulation. During the 1930s, in both Germany and Japan, fascist and authoritarian regimes had destroyed domestic labour organizations. But militant worker rebellions broke out in both countries in the wake of military defeat, initially encouraged by the pro-union policies of the occupying forces. With the advent of the Cold War, however, US Occupation authorities did an about-face: they joined conservative governments and hard-line employers to systematically repress (as in Japan) or contain (as in Germany) these uprisings. It is true that after World War II, with the consolidation of formally democratic regimes in both countries, the German and Japanese labour movements achieved for the first time a relatively secure and recognized place in the political economy. This gave them considerable leverage in maintaining working class living standards. But the fact remains that, especially in view of the strength that the working classes in both Germany and Japan had managed to briefly accrue on the morrow of World War II, the postwar boom in both countries was predicated more on the defeat of labour than on its recognition, more on the explicit subordination of labour than the consolidation of any putative 'capital-labour accord'. In particular, the extended waves of capital accumulation that founded the long upturn during the decade of the 1950s were conditioned on the achievement of extraordinarily high rates of profit, which were themselves premised upon the suppression of labour and its consequent acceptance of low and (relative to productivity growth) slowly increasing wages. It was thus the long postwar expansion itself which made possible labour's substantial material gains and its ulterior (partial) socio-political integration through the emergent trade union bureaucracies—not vice versa.

The defeat and subordination of labour cannot, of course, be understood merely as a reflection of these economies' later development, but was the result, in both Germany and Japan, of large-scale class struggle, relentlessly pursued by the employers into the early and middle 1950s. Nevertheless, once sufficiently controlled so as to find radical institutional change off the agenda, German and Japanese workers tended to see little choice but to hitch their fate to that of 'their own' firms. In view of the latecomer status of firms in both places and their consequent need to establish themselves against their well-entrenched counterparts in the US, this meant identifying themselves with those firms' struggle for international competitiveness. They were able to accomplish the latter with more effectiveness (from the standpoint of capital) than could their counterparts in the US (and UK) especially by means of the establishment and operation of firm- and plant-level institutions, which allowed for the more precise adjustment of workers' demands to the requirements of profitability—enterprise unions in Japan, works councils in Germany.

Free Trade and State Intervention

Rapid economic growth in the US during the decade from the late 1930s to the late 1940s raised barriers to further improvement by leaving in its wake masses of fixed capital capable of deterring further entry and investment, by using up factor supplies, especially surplus labour, and by facilitating labour resistance. But it did so, in addition, by giving rise to a constellation of leading social forces which were either incapable of intervening politically to reverse what had become the relatively unfavourable conditions for capital accumulation at home, or positively committed to improving conditions for economic expansion abroad, even at the expense of domestic manufacturing. US producers had risen to their position of dominance by exploiting their uniquely large domestic market. But, especially in the wake of the investment boom of the 1940s, their leading representatives, the great manufacturing corporations and international bankers, understood that many of the best opportunities for profit would henceforth lie abroad, as the other advanced capitalist economies rebuilt and expanded, soon under a protectionist umbrella. What these forces needed from the US government was support for a policy of free flow of goods and investment funds that would allow the multinationals and international bankers to make direct investments and loans abroad and allow imports to flow back into the country. Their ability to secure this support was enhanced by the fact that, at least through the first postwar decade, US-based exporters tended to need free trade to enable their prospective customers abroad to sell sufficiently in the US to earn the currency that they needed to buy US goods.

The US government was strongly committed to the industrial reconstruction of its leading potential rivals as a central aspect of its struggle against communism. It was thus even more willing than it might otherwise have been to serve the needs of its greatest capitalists by subscribing to an internationalist economic perspective, despite the fact that this approach would, in the medium run, put those of its manufacturers who were mainly domestically based at a distinct disadvantage with respect to their leading overseas competitors. In fact, the international economic arrangements constituted at Bretton Woods, as actually implemented in practice, turned out to instantiate an informal bargain: on the one hand, the US, with its dollar key currency, was enabled to run large balance of payments deficits to finance its overseas military bases and its foreign aid, as well as the foreign direct investments of its corporations; on the other hand, those countries which were at once its allies and economic rivals were allowed to control in various ways access to their domestic markets for commodities and capital. On the condition that its allies/rivals would not seek to cash in too many of their dollars for gold, the US government opened up the US market to their exports, while accepting without complaint their protectionism and their restrictions on the outward and inward mobility of capital, even forbearing to push too hard or too fast for the re-establishment of currency convertibility. It thereby helped to create the conditions for the secular decline of competitiveness of US domestic manufacturing. But free trade and the over-valued dollar not only encouraged the export offensives of US manufacturers' leading overseas rivals, but also facilitated the overseas investment drives of America's greatest multinational corporations, allowing them to purchase the factors of production on the cheap and to send part of the output that they produced in their overseas affiliates back to the US as imports, often in the form of intermediate goods to be worked up into final goods by their home plants.

The constellations of leading social forces that emerged to shape the postwar German and Japanese economies were the converse of those found in the US. The advantages possessed by German and Japanese manufacturers by virtue of their later development thus went beyond those that were bound to be exhausted over time—cheap labour recruited from the countryside, access to the latest techniques by borrowing from the US, and the benefits of a particular position in the product cycle. Their advantages came to include more permanent politico-institutional arrangements which had a longer-term impact, making for the maintenance of favourable conditions for capital accumulation. Because German, and especially Japanese, manufacturing firms were able to embed themselves within advanced institutional forms for organizing intra-manufacturing, finance-manufacturing, and capital-labour relations that had no counterpart in the US, as well as to secure state support for industry of a kind unavailable in the US, these firms were able to achieve a level and quality of investment and a capacity to control costs inexplicable in purely market terms. These political and economico-institutional arrangements allowed manufacturers access to cheaper capital, increased socialization of risk, greater protection (even if partial and temporary) from international competition, longer time horizons for returns on investment, more favourable opportunities to invest in human capital, and greater investments in socially necessary, but individually unprofitable, endeavours, particularly infrastructure, education, and research and development.

Precisely how and why these arrangements originated when they did in Germany and Japan is a historical question, made more complex by the fact that they emerged and underwent major transformation over a long term, going back to the second half of the nineteenth century. Still, follower economies such as Japan and Germany have, as a rule, provided more favourable ground for the constitution of such arrangements than economic leaders. Because of their initial relative weakness with respect to their counterparts in the leading economies, their manufacturers, financiers, and governments have required such arrangements as a condition for successfully competing through trade.[3] Industry and banking have thus tended to ally or 'merge', and to receive the support of the state in creating, through economic and political means, the capacity to contest the producers of the dominant economy for shares of the world market. In contrast, the leading manufacturers and financiers and the governments of the leading economy—typified by nineteenth-century Britain, as well as the postwar US—have found it in their interest to eschew such institutional forms and types of intervention. This is in part because they have needed them less. But it is also because, as a consequence of their superior competitiveness, they have been able

---

3   The argument, it must be emphasized, is *not* the functionalist one that the institutional requirements of late development caused them to be put into place by late developers, for the fact that institutions are needed for successful development cannot explain why they came into existence. It is, rather, that because late development tended to have certain institutional requisites, in those places where late development took place successfully, such institutions were usually to be found and played a central role.

to orient themselves, much more than have their counterparts in the follower economies, to searching for the best opportunities for profit-making on a world scale, either through direct overseas investment or international lending, and because the institutional and policy requisites for such activities are so very different from, and obviously quite often opposed to, those needed for the development of domestic manufacturing.

Like such producers in other later-developing economies, German and Japanese manufacturers tended to subject themselves to the discipline of the banks and the state, because they were more dependent upon them for access to desperately needed investment funds and protection against overseas competition. By the same token, banks in Germany and Japan, like those of other later-developing economies, tended, in view of their own competitive weakness as international lenders, as well as the competitive weakness of their counterparts in manufacturing, to find their profits to be more dependent than those of their counterparts in earlier-developing economies on securing the competitive-productive success of domestic industry in international markets. They therefore tended to involve themselves more deeply with, and could therefore give much greater material assistance to, domestic manufacturers, not only through providing cheaper finance, but also through offering vital economic information and by helping to secure various forms of economic coordination—cartels, vertical and/or horizontal integration, and the like.

Finally, relative to their US counterpart, the German and Japanese governments found themselves subject to the coordinated, insistent pressure of combined manufacturing and financial interests to provide policies oriented to the growth of domestic production rather than investment and lending overseas. At the same time, their own general interest in supporting successful capital accumulation as the basic condition for realizing their own needs for state fiscal solidity, high employment, and social stability, led them, more unambiguously, to provide improved and protected conditions for capital investment at home, especially to buttress export-oriented manufacturing. These governments not only attempted to provide manufacturing exporters with under-valued currencies, as well as subsidies and various degrees of protection from foreign imports. They sought to secure, in addition, 'low pressure' macroeconomic environments, imposing balanced budgets and relatively tight credit to achieve low inflation in the interest of overseas sales.

By contrast, as overseas competition intensified, the separation in the US (and the UK) of purely domestically based producers from the highly influential banks and the multinationals put them at a profound disadvantage in their attempts to secure from the state favourable exchange rate, tariff, and industrial policies. Postwar US governments therefore found themselves far freer to pursue the generally quite compatible requirements of ensuring the stability and security of the international capitalist system, and providing for the interests of their own multinationals and banks. The main form of aid provided by the US government to domestic manufacturing was by way of the subsidy of demand through the construction of a large new state sector, heavily oriented to the military, often at the expense of other, more productive forms of public spending. This subsidy to demand increasingly involved Keynesian budget deficits and no doubt increased economic stability by raising business confidence. But it proved relatively inflationary and, especially in light of its enormous military component, may well have done as much harm as good to US manufacturing competitiveness. Whereas a focus on the US market had historically expressed the unparalleled strength of US domestically based manufacturing, its growing, and increasingly embattled, confinement to that market in the quarter-century after World War II manifested its growing weakness.

Economic Internationalization and Export-Oriented Mercantilism

The interdependent evolution of the internationalizing leading economy of the US and of the export-oriented follower economies of Germany and Japan turned out to instantiate a highly dynamic, but ultimately highly unstable, symbiosis. While the Japanese and the German economies may have founded their economic dynamism on their ability to develop the home market, they were able to achieve such impressive growth trajectories only by maximizing the growth of exports, and here their ability to appropriate markets formerly held by US (and UK) producers turned out to be decisive. In both economies, a mutual feedback between investment-driven and export-driven growth processes was at the heart of development. Success in containing costs, via relatively low wage growth (despite high rates of capital accumulation) and relatively high productivity growth (made possible by high rates of capital accumulation), thus provided the indispensable condition for the pursuit of export-oriented trajectories of growth. In turn, these trajectories made for otherwise unattainable levels of productivity advance. They did so, in the first place, by facilitating economies of scale made possible through the exploitation of the world market—the largest there is—in individual product lines. They did so, secondly, by making possible the maintenance of manufacturing sectors of a size which would have been insupportable by the home market alone: inflated manufacturing sectors thus brought stepped-up rates of overall productivity increase, since manufacturing lines offered better opportunities for productivity gain than most others.[4]

The fact remains that the very opportunity to undertake dynamic export-oriented growth depended not only on the emergence, during the postwar epoch, of a fast-growing world economy that was demanding, as its income grew, ever greater quantities of the very goods which German and Japanese producers were (or were becoming) especially well-fitted to provide—machinery, metals, chemicals, vehicles, and the like—but even more on the huge, dependable, and easily penetrable markets of the US and (to some extent) the UK. Both the German and Japanese economies prospered to no small degree by virtue of their ability to dynamize rapidly progressing regional economic blocs in Europe and East Asia by supplying them with increasingly high-powered capital goods.[5] Still, it was the ability of German and Japanese manufacturers to wrest *ever greater shares* of the world market from US (and UK) producers that ultimately made possible their postwar 'miracles'. Again, however, this capacity to seize market share could only come into play because of the willingness of the US government to tolerate not only the broad opening of the US economy to overseas penetration, but even a certain decline in US manufacturing competitiveness in the interests of US military and political hegemony, international economic stability, and the rapid expansion overseas of US multinational corporations and banks.

4   See N. Kaldor, 'Conflicts in National Economic Objectives', *Economic Journal*, vol. lxxxi, March 1971.

5   For 'Germany as the pivot of advance' in Western Europe, see A. Milward, *The European Rescue of the Nation-State*, Berkeley 1992, pp. 134–73.

It was the extraordinary advantages, not least institutional and policy advantages, enjoyed by Germany and especially Japan on the *supply side*—not new arrangements for keeping domestic demand up with production, as in the 'contradictions of Keynesianism' story—which were thus responsible for their unusually rapid growth. In sharp contrast, the new institutional arrangements and policies that helped to raise and maintain demand in the US economy proved powerless to overcome its supply-side disabilities and reverse what turned out to be its not very impressive pattern of growth. In fact, in combination with its free-trade, free-investment approach to the international economy, the US government's Keynesian subsidies to demand played a not insignificant part in further spurring the exports and thus capital accumulation of US manufacturers' leading competitors, at first largely alongside, but ultimately in confrontation with that of the US. Indeed, the failure of US and UK producers to prevent German and especially Japanese manufacturers from appropriating—and being able to *count on* appropriating—ever greater shares of the world market from the US and the UK should be understood as the indispensable condition *on the demand side* for the German and Japanese manufacturing economies to pursue such extraordinarily rapid paths of capital accumulation.

It should be clear at the outset that rapid growth in this mode was hardly unproblematic, even for the Germans and Japanese. The growth of their domestic demand was held back so as to keep costs down and thereby buttress the growth of exports. But the resulting tendency of the German and Japanese economies to sustain large external surpluses via the outrunning of imports by exports brought pressures for either prices or the currency to rise. The hot-housed growth of exports tended, then, to be self-undermining, and, over the long run, economic development in both Germany and Japan instantiated an uphill struggle to improve productivity faster than the currency (and thus relative costs) appreciated, a struggle negotiated only with great difficulty by each.

In the longer run, the contradictions were even more profound. The obverse side of German and Japanese manufacturing export success was the tendential decline of US manufacturing competitiveness, the tendential rise of US external deficits, and the tendential decline of the US currency. Implied was the declining capacity of the US market to absorb its allies' and rivals' goods and thus to serve as the 'motor of last resort' of their economies. The very processes by which the German and Japanese economies achieved rapid growth during the postwar boom tended to destroy the foundations of their success. During the 1950s and much of the 1960s, for Germany and Japan, and even the US, such problems were largely in the future. But they would not be put off indefinitely.

Chapter 4

THE US ECONOMY: THE COSTS OF LEADERSHIP

At the end of the 1930s, the US economy took off, following a decade of depression that had prepared the boom by destroying huge amounts of redundant, obsolescent capital, while creating mass unemployment. Under the stimulus of European rearmament and US war preparations, and then the war effort itself, US producers were suddenly able to combine low wages (resulting from years of high unemployment and maintained by wartime government controls) with a large backlog of unused advanced technology (some of it carried over from the technologically dynamic 1920s, some of it developed but unused during the depression years, and some of it spun off by the feverishly developing war industries) to achieve some of the highest rates of profit registered in the US during the twentieth century. Between 1940 and 1945, the rate of profit for the private economy was, on average, about 50 per cent above its level in 1929 and 60–70 per cent higher than the average for the years 1900–29.[1]

The wartime rise of profitability was literally epoch-making, because it provided the fundamental basis for a powerful and extended boom, which lasted throughout the war and which was hardly interrupted by what turned out to be the surprisingly smooth and rapid transition to a peacetime economy. Driving the boom was the extremely rapid growth of investment in response to the high rate of profit: between the years 1938 and 1950, gross investment in both the private economy and the manufacturing sector grew at an average annual rate of around 11 per cent. Even before the war, the US economy was the most technically advanced in the world. As the only major economy to avoid serious wartime destruction, it was able to widen its lead substantially, as the decade-long investment boom brought about generally solid productivity growth, and truly impressive productivity growth in the immediate postwar era. Between 1938 and 1950, output per hour increased at the average annual rate of 2.7 per cent both in the private business economy and manufacturing—and 3.8 per cent and 5.5 per cent for these sectors, respectively, in the four years between 1946 and 1950—making it possible for the US economy to rapidly extend its domination of world trade.[2] During the years 1945–49 inclusive, merchandise exports averaged $12.5 billion, two-and-a-half times the level of

---

1 G. Duménil, M. Glick and D. Lévy, 'The Rise of the Rate of Profit During World War II', *Review of Economics and Statistics*, vol. lxv, May 1993; G. Duménil and D. Lévy, 'The US Economy Since the Civil War: Sources and Construction of Series', *CEPREMAP*, 31 December 1991, p. 28. Compare G. Duménil, M. Glick and J. Rangel, 'The Rate of Profit in the United States', *Cambridge Journal of Economic*, vol. xi, 1987, pp. 351–4.

2 US Department of Commerce, *Historical Statistics of the United States. Colonial Times to 1970*, Washington, DC 1970, p. 162.

1929 and triple the level of 1940, and the excess of merchandise exports over imports totalled $25 billion. By 1950, the US share of advanced-country manufacturing exports had climbed to 27.1 per cent, from 21.3 per cent in 1929 and 20.5 per cent in 1937.[3] Newly dynamic export growth thus helped to compensate for the fall-off in military spending so as to sustain demand and help drive the economy. Overall, between 1938 and 1950, the growth of real GNP averaged 6.5 per cent per annum, at least 50 per cent above the US historic average for periods of boom.[4]

1. Towards Stagnation in the 1950s

From the end of the Korean War, if not earlier, there was a palpable loss of dynamism. In the wake of the extended process of advanced industrialization that the US had experienced by the end of the 1920s and of its impressive wartime and immediate postwar boom, the US economy began to grow much more slowly. Indeed, at the end of the 1950s, the economy appeared to many to be in trouble, especially in view of the marked weakening of its performance during the second half of the decade, after the Korean War had ceased to impart its powerful artificial stimulus. Between 1955 and 1961, GDP grew at an average annual rate of only 2.5 per cent, far below the average annual rates of 5.8 per cent between 1938 and 1955 and 4.8 per cent between 1950 and 1955. The fall-off was even greater in the manufacturing sector, where output grew at an average annual rate of only 1.4 per cent between 1955 and 1961, compared to 5.1 per cent between 1950 and 1955. Over the course of the 1950s, unemployment remained ominously higher after the completion of each successive cyclical downturn than it had during the previous one. During the second half of the decade, the average rate of unemployment increased by more than one-third, compared to the first half (5.5 per cent for 1956–61, 4.0 per cent for 1950–55) and as late as 1963 remained at 5.7 per cent.[5] As a student of the economy of the 1950s put it at the time, 'Looking at the decade as a whole, most persons would judge the growth rate of output as rather sluggish. If the latter part of the decade is made the reference point, the rate would be judged unsatisfactory, particularly when compared with the 1920s or the long-run performance of the economy prior to the great depression of the 1930s.'[6]

The economy's decelerating growth from the end of the 1940s to the start of the 1960s led some observers initially to interpret the pattern of postwar economic development in terms of 'capitalist stagnation', arising from the predominance of 'monopoly capital'. From this perspective, the relatively slow rate of growth and relatively high levels of unemployment could be attributed to the control of the economy by giant monopolistic corporations, and this for two reasons. First, monopolistic firms tend to limit their output, the best way to maximize profits in the face of given demand curves for their products. Second, monopolistic firms tend to restrict the growth of their capital investments, because a reduced rate of

---

3 US Department of Commerce, *Historical Statistics*, p. 884; H. G. Vatter, *The US Economy in the 1950s*, New York 1961, p. 43; A. Maizels, *Industrial Growth and World Trade*, Cambridge 1963, p. 220. Henceforth, the term 'exports' refers to real exports of goods and services, unless otherwise specified.

4 H. Van Der Wee, *Prosperity and Upheaval. The World Economy 1945–80*, Berkeley 1986 (first edition 1983), p. 30.

5 Vatter, *The US Economy in the 1950s*, p. 120.

6 Ibid., p. 8. Compare B. G. Hickman, *Growth and Stability of the Postwar Economy*, Washington, DC 1960.

investment is the best way to allow for the full realization of their already existing fixed capital.[7]

The notions of 'monopoly capital' and 'capitalist stagnation' soon revealed themselves, however, to be reifications of quite *temporary* and specific aspects of the economy of the US in the 1950s. They could carry conviction on the morrow of World War II because of the overwhelming preponderance of US industry within the world market, the oligopolistic control exerted by handfuls of US companies over major industries within the US market, and the corresponding debilitation of the US's main potential competitors. But they could not continue to command adherence in the face of the dramatic and (to many) unexpected developments of the succeeding period. The long and dynamic postwar expansion of the *world* economy from the late 1940s through the early 1970s and the profound intensification of international competition, brought about most notably by German and Japanese 'monopolies' at the expense of US 'monopolies', put paid to the idea that capitalism per se had entered a stage of structural stagnation as a result of the monopoly control over the market exerted by its giant firms. Still, these same developments did confirm and bring to the fore the very real *relative* stagnation of the US economy in comparison with Europe and Japan, as well as when compared to its own historical record of growth.

The US private economy *was* slow-growing, in relative terms, especially during the 1950s, but also over the whole period after 1950. The prevalent pattern of investment and growth did, moreover, look much like that foreseen by the theory attributing stagnation to monopoly capital. But the roots of the problem were, for the most part, to be found elsewhere.[8] Simply stated, the economy of the territorial US developed unimpressively because its manufacturing sector offered relatively limited opportunities for profitable investment, compared to those available in manufacturing outside the US. There was thus an increasing divergence between the requirements for individual firms to make a profit, especially in manufacturing, and the requirements for aggregate economic growth within the US.

First of all, the large, relatively recent fixed-capital investments of the corporations that dominated the US market discouraged these corporations' further investment, because such investments required time to be fully realized. These investments constituted, as we have seen, powerful deterrents to investment by others, even some with lower costs. This was because corporations could, as has

---

7   The basic statement of this view is P. Baran and P. Sweezy, *Monopoly Capital*, New York 1964. The publication date should be noted. Baran and Sweezy's view that the emergence of monopoly is the key to the specificity of the operation of the contemporary economy was founded upon the work of Kalecki and Steindl, as well as the monopolistic-oligopolistic price theory of Robinson and Chamberlain. See especially Steindl's *Maturity and Stagnation*, New York 1950. Baran and Sweezy's position was associated with a broader intellectual current associated with the idea that the postwar economy was tending to structural stagnation. Leading representatives of this current included a number of mainstream Keynesians identified with 'stagnationist' theses since the 1930s who continued to apply them to the economy of the 1950s, most notably Alvin Hansen. See A. H. Hansen, *Full Recovery or Stagnation?*, New York 1938, as well as *Economic Issues of the 1960s*, Cambridge, Mass. 1960, pp. 50–1.

8   This is not to deny that, within the US economy for a brief period following the war, especially during the years when overseas competitors had yet to make their presence felt, small numbers of great corporations within major industries—auto, steel, and so forth—could effectively collude to fix prices.

been stressed, if necessary reduce their rate of return in response to cost-cutting competitors up to the point at which they could still make the average rate of return on their circulating capital alone.[9] Many potential entrants, even cost-cutters, could therefore expect a lower rate of profit than could incumbents—assuming the potential entrants did not in fact enter.[10] Put another way, the rate of profit that could be derived by new investors from new capital placements, especially in manufacturing, appeared higher than it actually was. In this restricted sense one can legitimately refer to the existence of 'oligopolistic competition' as a fetter on investment in this period.

For the US economy, the main consequence of its possession of so much recently placed fixed capital was to discourage the growth of investment. In turn, the reduced growth of investment may well have contributed to the declining growth of manufacturing productivity which, in combination with the rapid growth of wages, issued in a problem of rising costs in manufacturing, both absolute and relative. During the mid to late 1950s, US manufacturers faced a squeeze on profits from wages, but this was not all. For the first time in the twentieth century, firms producing in the US found themselves saddled with *relatively* high costs of production and *relatively* low profitability in an increasing number of manufacturing lines, as later-emerging producers based in Europe and Japan combined relatively high levels of technology with relatively low wages. This trend not only reduced the incentive to invest at home, but also gave multinational corporations and international lenders a stronger incentive to invest abroad. The pursuit by individual US capitals of their own self-interest in securing the highest rate of profit thus led, in aggregate, to a tendency to stagnation in the US domestic economy, especially in manufacturing.

Following a large jump in investment in both manufacturing and the private business economy as a whole in 1950–51, investment in new plant and equipment grew exceedingly slowly. In manufacturing, investment was essentially flat for the four years 1951 through 1955, and its average level for the years 1956 through 1960 was only 8.2 per cent higher than that of the previous five years. Manufacturing investment was below the level it attained in 1956 and 1957 (when investment totals were almost identical) in every subsequent year until 1964. In the private business economy, investment in plant and equipment grew at an average annual rate of 2.3 per cent for the four years 1951–55 and peaked in 1957 at a level about 23 per cent above that of 1951. But, at the height of the last (very weak) cyclical upturn of the decade (early 1958 to mid 1960), investment was more than 10 per cent below what it had been at the height of the previous upturn (late 1954 to mid 1957), and investment in the later stages of the latter upturn had already stagnated. Not until 1962 did private business investment surpass its level of 1957.[11]

9   Indeed, incumbent corporations may have over-invested—intentionally or unintentionally maintained excess capacity—thereby further discouraging the entry of new competitors into their markets. See R. E. Hall, 'Chronic Excess Capacity in US Industry', National Bureau of Economic Research, Working Paper, no. 1973, Cambridge, Mass.,July 1986.

10   Of course, entrants who could make the average rate of profit at prices so low as to prevent some incumbents from making the average rate of profit even on their circulating capital could not be deterred from coming into the line.

11   See Vatter, *The US Economy in the 1950s*, pp. 84–6, 110, 147.

Producers' reluctance to expand their productive base during the later 1950s was manifested in their allocation of an ever decreasing proportion of investment to new plant and an ever increasing proportion to equipment. Between 1950 and 1958, the average annual growth of manufacturing investment in equipment, at a low 2.2 per cent, was still some 50 per cent higher than in plant, at a mere 1.1 per cent; for the private business economy as a whole, equipment investment grew at an average annual rate of 4.2 per cent, compared to only 1.75 per cent for plant. These figures show that, while US producers were willing to try to defend their place in the market by adding new machines presumably embodying at least some advance in technology, they lacked the incentive required to build the new plants that were needed to underpin really major increases in output and qualitative transformations in productive technique.[12]

The slow growth of investment may well have been partly responsible for the reduction in the growth of labour productivity in manufacturing. During the years 1950–58, labour productivity in manufacturing grew at an average annual rate of only 1.85 per cent—compared to 5.5 per cent between 1946 and 1950. Capital productivity in manufacturing (the real manufacturing output-capital ratio) fell at an average annual rate of 1.8 per cent at the same time.

While the powerful surge of manufacturing productivity growth of the immediate postwar period petered out in the 1950s, wage growth failed to follow suit. The 1950s was the true golden age for the American worker. From 1950 through 1958, the growth of real wages in manufacturing averaged 3.6 per cent per annum. In the same period, the manufacturing product wage grew somewhat more slowly, increasing at an average annual rate of 2.7 per cent, but it still increased faster than did manufacturing net labour productivity, which rose at an average annual rate of just 1.8 per cent per annum, with the result that the manufacturing profit share fell at an average annual rate of 2.4 per cent. *If there was a major squeeze on profits by the action of labour at any point during the postwar epoch, it took place in manufacturing in the course of the 1950s.*

US Labour in the 1950s

The US labour movement of the 1950s was still a force to be reckoned with. During the 1930s, while authoritarian and fascist regimes were destroying labour organizations in Germany and Japan, US labour won historic victories with the triumphs of the CIO, and secured an unprecedented position in American life for unskilled, industrial workers. It is true that, by the end of the 1940s, the movement had dissipated much of the power and the momentum it had derived from the historic battles and conquests of the 1930s. Decay had set in as a consequence of the rapid bureaucratization of the trade unions (accelerated by the wartime period of state-regulated labour-management relations), of the containment of the huge (but at best moderately successful) strike wave of 1946, of the government-backed assault on the trade-union Left and the union movement in general during the Red Scare of the late 1940s (highlighted by the passage of the Taft-Hartley Act in 1948), and of the generally reactionary turn of US politics with the onset of the Cold War and McCarthyism. Yet even in the early 1950s, labour still retained a surprising degree

12   Ibid., pp. 282–94, especially 284.

of power and militancy and remained well positioned to exploit the favourable conditions for struggle of those years.

Probably most crucial in opening the way for the trade unions, the Korean War boom tightened up the labour market, the rate of unemployment falling from an average of 5.6 per cent for 1949 and 1950 to an average of just over 3 per cent for 1951–53. Since US corporations had, during the immediate postwar period, further improved their already dominant position internationally, organized labour as yet had little reason to take account of international competition in making its demands. US unions were therefore able to flex their muscles and revive some of the militancy that they had displayed at the end of World War II. They continued to win a high percentage of NLRB (National Labor Relations Board) union recognition elections, further increasing the proportion of the labour force unionized, and union density reached its historic peak in 1953–54.[13] They also displayed a higher propensity to strike than they would do at any other time in the postwar epoch. Taking either the decade 1946–56 or the half decade 1949–54, a greater proportion of workdays was lost to work stoppages than in any other comparable periods between 1946 and the end of the century (see p. 116, Figure 8.2).[14] At the level of the shop floor, in traditional strongholds like car manufacturing, workers continued to resort routinely to direct action, especially wildcat strikes, to defend their conditions.[15] On the basis of this continuing militancy, the labour movement was, until the later 1950s, able to prevent manufacturing wage growth from adjusting to the slowdown in manufacturing productivity growth. The economic consequences were significant, not only domestically, in terms of the squeeze on profits, but also internationally, in terms of declining US competitiveness.

With wages rising, with slow investment growth helping to push down both labour and capital productivity growth, and with capacity utilization declining, the 1950s understandably witnessed a very major decline in manufacturing profitability. Between 1950 and 1958, the manufacturing profit rate fell by 41 per cent, with some of this reflecting a significant fall in capacity utilization after mid-decade, particularly in the severe recession of 1957–58.[16]

Growing Competition from Abroad

The trend toward rising costs in absolute terms, with the resultant squeeze on profits, was made more serious by the emergence of a problem unprecedented in the US economy during the twentieth century: the growth of competition from abroad, which further undermined the incentive to invest. The US economy enjoyed

13   For data on union certification elections and levels of unionization, see the fundamental work by M. Goldfield, *The Decline of Organized Labor in the United States*, Chicago 1987, pp. 10, 90–1. I wish to thank Mike Goldfield for many very helpful discussions of the US labour movement in the postwar period, and for providing me with much useful data.

14   'Work Stoppages in the United States, 1927–1980', table supplied by US Department of Labor, BLS, Office of Compensation and Working Conditions, Division of Development in Labor-Management Relations.   15   See the illuminating study by N. Lichtenstein, 'Auto Worker Militancy and the Structure of Factory Life, 1937–55', *The Journal of American History*, vol. lxvii, September 1980.

16   The private business economy outside of manufacturing experienced a much smaller decline in profitability than did the manufacturing sector—of just 21.3 per cent between 1950 and 1958—because it was able to avoid both the extent of increase in the rate of wage growth and the degree of reduction in productivity growth, as well as the extent of reduction in capacity utilization, that affected manufacturing.

far higher absolute levels of productivity than did the German and the Japanese. But this advantage was more than cancelled out by the relatively even higher wages enjoyed by US workers, an expression of both the historic strength of the US economy and the successes of the US labour movement. In 1950, US manufacturing unit labour costs in dollar terms were, on average, 41 per cent higher than Japan's and 37 per cent higher than Germany's, and the gap widened over the course of the decade and beyond, as productivity growth relative to wage growth in both places increased faster than in the US.[17] Especially in the latter part of the decade, the US economy experienced an initial bout of inflation, as employers sought to pass on wage increases in the form of price increases, and US producers had to confront major problems of competitiveness in a number of core manufacturing lines—especially, steel (where us prices rose well above those of Germany), cars, and electrical machinery.[18]

The relatively high rate of growth of costs was reflected in declining export competitiveness. The unit value of manufacturing exports over the course of the 1950s rose by 15 per cent in the US, rose by only 5 per cent in Germany, and *fell* by 11 per cent in Japan.[19] Toward the end of the decade, therefore, US merchandise exports actually decreased, US merchandise imports continued a decade-long acceleration, and the US trade balance, at least for a couple of years, appeared to be dwindling toward zero. From 1953 through 1959, the value of manufactured imports increased at an average annual rate of no less then 10.4 per cent, while real manufactured exports essentially stagnated.[20] Between 1957 and 1959, annual merchandise exports fell from $19.3 billion to $16.2 billion. The merchandise trade balance thus fell, in just the latter two years, from $6.1 billion to only $988 million. The problem was particularly acute in trade between the US and its rising competitors. As late as the mid-1950s, the US had enjoyed a substantial trade surplus with both Germany and Japan. But by 1959, the trade balance had fallen to $50 million with Japan and had actually gone into the red by $40 million with Germany. Reflecting the decline in US manufacturing competitiveness, between 1950 and 1959 the US share of advanced-country manufacturing exports fell sharply from 27.1 per cent to 21.0 per cent.[21] The increased pressure in the world market experienced by US manufacturers could not but have constituted a further disincentive to invest within the US.

As a powerful expression—and, to a growing degree, a cause—of the stagnation of capital accumulation in the US, from the second half of the 1950s US private direct

17   D. J. Daly, *Japanese Manufacturing Competitiveness. Implications for International Trade*, University of Toronto-York University Joint Center for Asia Pacific Studies, Working Paper Series, no. 53, August 1988, p. 35.
18   Sohmen, 'The Dollar and the Mark', in S. E. Harris, ed., *The Dollar in Crisis*, New York 1961, pp. 190–3, where data on relative prices at this time for these industries is presented.
19   Sohmen, 'The Dollar and the Mark', p. 194. Unit labour costs in the US grew by 21 per cent and by about the same amount in Germany, while declining by around 4 per cent in Japan.
20   L. B. Krause, 'The US Economy and International Trade', in K. Kojima, ed., *Structural Adjustment in Asian-Pacific Trade*, Papers and Proceedings of the Fifth Pacific Trade and Development Conference, Vol. ii, The Japan Economic Research Center, Tokyo, July 1973, p. 391; W. H. Branson, 'Trends in United States International Trade and Investment Since World War II', in M. Feldstein, ed., *The American Economy in Transition*, Chicago 1980, p. 198, Table 3.14.
21   Vatter, *The US Economy in the 1950s*, p. 262; T. Liesner, *One Hundred Years of Economic Statistics*, New York 1989, Table US15; Maizels, *Industrial Growth and World Trade*, p. 220.

Figure 4.1. Ratio of foreign to domestic manufacturing investment by US corporations, 1957–93.

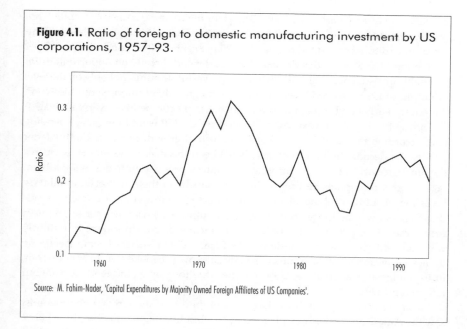

Source: M. Fahim-Nader, 'Capital Expenditures by Majority Owned Foreign Affiliates of US Companies'.

investment overseas grew at the spectacular average annual rate of 10.2 per cent, more than twice as fast as domestic investment was growing.[22] Foreign direct investment never represented more than a small fraction of total investment in the US private business economy as a whole. But for the US manufacturing sector, led by the great US multinationals, overseas investment was very significant, and increasingly so. Between 1957 and 1965, manufacturing investment by majority-owned foreign affiliates of US companies in new plant and equipment overseas grew at an astonishing average annual rate of 15.7 per cent. In just these eight years the ratio of foreign to domestic investment in new plant and equipment made annually by US-based manufacturing corporations thus doubled, growing from 11.8 per cent to a spectacular 22.8 per cent.[23] Just as US manufacturing corporations were deterred from investing in the US domestic economy, they were increasingly attracted to the superior opportunities for profit-making overseas, especially in Europe, where they could combine relatively cheap labour with relatively advanced technology and produce against relatively weak competitors in rapidly growing markets.[24]

During the second half of the decade, as the US economy lost steam as a result of the mutually reinforcing trends towards declining profitability and declining investment, the hugely increased government spending of the postwar epoch—

22   Branson, 'Trends in United States International Trade', p. 238. Foreign direct investment in the US compared to US direct investment abroad in this period was, meanwhile, small and dwindling.

23   M. Fahim-Nader, 'Capital Expenditures by Majority-Owned Foreign Affiliates of US Companies', *Survey of Current Business*, vol. lxxiv, no. 9, September 1994, p. 59.

24   By the early 1960s, Europeans were complaining of the spectacular growth of foreign direct investment by US multinationals, the so-called 'American Challenge'. See J. J. Servan-Schreiber, *Le Défi américain*, Paris 1967.

military spending in particular—was critical for maintaining economic stability, not only within the US but in the world economy as a whole. During the 1950s, government expenditure constituted no less than 25 per cent of GNP, compared to 8–9 per cent in the 1920s.[25] Since this demand did not depend directly on opportunities for profitable investment, it naturally acted as a powerful stimulus, not only on the level of output of US-based producers, but on the magnitude of imports into the North American market by US manufacturers' increasingly competitive overseas rivals.

During the 1950s, approximately 10 per cent of GNP went to military spending and, according to one major study of US industrial growth conducted in the latter part of the decade, 'military demand ha[d] been the major and almost exclusive dynamic growth factor in recent years.'[26] Military production had a major advantage for existing capitals: its output did not compete for their markets. But military investment could contribute relatively little directly to improving the economy's productiveness over the longer run, because its output was used neither to augment firms' means of production nor workers' means of consumption, but simply wasted.[27] Military spending offered US firms, which suffered from declining domestic investment opportunities, an alternative way to make a profit at home; but, in exploiting this alternative, US firms did little to counter the tendency toward retarded growth.

From the vantage point of the last years of the 1950s, more than one economist saw the American economy as plagued by 'continuing stagnation'.[28] In these years, the US economy entered into something of a crisis as the trends toward the slowdown of the growth of output and investment issued in two recessions, in 1957–58 and 1960, and were complicated by the sudden deterioration in the US international position in a way which would later become chronic. From the end of 1940s, when thirty or so countries had devalued versus the dollar, the US had steadily run balance of payments deficits, as an expression of the growth of its international military commitments, its increasing foreign aid, and the rise of private investment overseas. But balance of payments deficits had initially given no cause for worry, since the large US trade surplus had, through the mid-1950s, testified to the competitiveness of US producers and the strength of the dollar. When, however, the trade surplus suddenly collapsed between 1957 and 1959—and was responsible for sending the current account balance into the negative in 1959—declining competitiveness seemed suddenly a reality, especially in view of the fact that much of the deterioration in the trade balance had taken place in periods of recession (1953–54 and 1957–59) when import demand was relatively depressed and export prices rel-

25   R. J. Gordon, 'Postwar Macroeconomics: The Evolution of Events and Ideas', in *The American Economy in Transition*, Chicago 1980, pp. 104–5.

26   R. DeGrasse, *Military Expansion, Economic Decline*, New York 1983, pp. 20–1; S. H. Robock, *Changing Regional Economies*, Midwest Research Institute, MRI-252, 1957, p. 4, quoted in M. Wiedenbaum, 'Some Economic Aspects of Military Procurement', *Current Economic Comment*, November 1960, p. 10.

27   Technological spin-offs from military production did of course make a major contribution to enhancing productivity in some manufacturing lines, notably aircraft. But spending money on military research and development was a highly inefficient way to bring about technical change and productivity increase in the non-military economy. I wish to thank Sam Farber for reminding me of this point.

28   Sohmen, 'The Dollar and the Mark', p. 195.

29   Ibid., p. 191. The export decline would have come sooner and been more acute, had US exporters not enjoyed an artificial surge in sales at the expense of the US's allies during the years 1956–57 because of the Suez crisis.

atively reduced.[29] During the years 1958–60, the overall balance of payments deficit was annually on average about four times what it had been for the years 1951–57. When, in 1960, to pull the economy out of its recession, the Federal Reserve increased the money supply and reduced interest rates, there was a sudden huge outflow of funds which wiped out the gain in the balance of payments that had resulted that year from the improvement in the trade balance. Domestic demand stimulus seemed all at once incompatible with external stability. In October 1960, with worry about US deficits and competitiveness becoming overt and confidence in the dollar declining, a flurry of speculative activity drove up the gold price spectacularly and practically overnight from $35 to $40. Shortly thereafter—as part of the same chain of events, in response to the same sort of speculative pressures—the German government was obliged to revalue the mark.[30] The sequence would, a few years later, become all too typical.

The condition of chronic recession at the end of the decade did soon help to redress the situation by making possible a major reduction in the growth of imports and facilitating a significant decrease in the growth of labour costs. But the ensuing recovery could only be temporary because the underlying problems remained unresolved. Investment growth would, over the longer run, continue to be unsatisfactory, due to the US economy's relatively high costs of production in international terms, and its declining competitiveness in manufacturing. Attempts to stimulate the economy through the subsidy of demand would therefore tend not only to generate relatively little capital accumulation, but also to exacerbate the deteriorating international position by provoking inflation, stimulating imports and foreign direct investment, reducing the trade and current account balances, and putting further pressure on the dollar. Following a brief spell of relief during the first half of the 1960s—when, with costs falling and profitability rising, conditions did become briefly favourable to Keynesian stimulus of demand—the US economy would thus take up in the mid 1960s where it had left off at the end of the 1950s.

2. Short-Term Recovery in the Early 1960s

During the first half of the 1960s, the US economy experienced a significant, though only short term, recovery. Between 1958 and 1965, GNP grew at an average annual rate of 4.6 per cent, faster than in any other period of comparable length after 1950. Manufacturing output grew at an average annual pace of 6.55 per cent, almost triple the 2.3 per cent achieved during the years 1950–58. Behind this spurt lay a spectacular rise in the rate of profit. Between 1958 and 1965, profitability in manufacturing rose by no less than 80 per cent, in the private business economy by 45 per cent. Increased profitability brought about increased growth by spurring a powerful boom in investment. After having barely increased between 1951 and 1961, expenditure on new plant and equipment in manufacturing grew at an average annual rate of 15.6 per cent between 1961 and 1965.

Critical to the revival of profitability was a striking slowdown in the growth of production costs, both absolutely, and relatively to the US's major international rivals. Manufacturers suddenly succeeded in gaining control over labour costs in a

---

30   V. Argy, *The Postwar International Money Crisis*, London 1981, pp. 31–7; Vatter, *The US Economy in the 1950s*, pp. 115, 263.

way they hitherto had found impossible. They unleashed a powerful across-the-board assault on workers and their institutions, and achieved what turned out to be a fundamental shift in the balance of class power and in the character of management-labour relations. In so doing, they demonstrated why workers cannot, as a rule, impose a squeeze on capitalist profitability for very long and thereby cause a real crisis. The fall in manufacturing profitability and competitiveness that had taken place over the course of the 1950s itself set off the ensuing process of adjustment. In response, firms reduced their placements of new capital, so investment stagnated from mid-decade, especially during the serious recession of 1957–58. The resulting rise in joblessness softened up the labour market, opening the way for the ensuing realignment in the balance of class forces and the resulting transformation of industrial relations.

During the mostly boom years that marked the period from the later 1940s through the end of the Korean conflict, employers had maintained an approach to labour that could, *in relative terms*, be described as somewhat accommodating.[31] But, in the course of sustaining a major wages-productivity profit squeeze throughout much of the 1950s and confronting simultaneously an unprecedentedly serious threat from international competition, employers reversed direction and took up what was immediately recognized at the time as a new 'hard line'.[32] Most dramatically, big corporations in manufacturing, not coincidentally in those lines where international competition had increased most, showed themselves willing to confront and defeat labour in a series of decisive battles between 1958 and 1961: the 1958 stalemate in auto bargaining which brought the union unprecedentedly small gains (for the postwar period), the 163-day steel strike of 1959 which won the union virtually nothing, the failed strike of the United Autoworkers and the International Association of Machinists against the United Aircraft Corporation in which the company continued to operate throughout the dispute, and, finally, the epoch-making General Electric strike of 1960 in which the International Union of Electrical Workers struck some fifty plants but after three weeks was forced to accept the widely-publicized terms the company had offered at the start of the strike. In the course of these and other conflicts, managers in car manufacturing began to increase their inter-firm cooperation during negotiations, and, in the newspaper publishing, airline, and railroad industries, companies forged 'mutual assistance pacts' and established strike insurance plans to provide aid to employers hit by strikes.

Management's new look was also evident in its increasing, and increasingly suc-

31   For this generalization, see, for example, T. A. Kochan and M. J. Piore, 'US Industrial Relations in Transition' and J. A. Klein and E. D. Wanger, 'The Legal Setting for the Emergence of the Union Avoidance Strategy', both in T. A. Kochan, ed., *Challenges and Choices Facing American Labor*, Cambridge, Mass. 1985.

32   Around 1960 there was a sudden spate of literature on the employers' new hard line. In this and the following two paragraphs, I depend especially on two lengthy symposia, 'The Employer Challenge and the Union Response', *Industrial Relations*, vol. i, no. 1, October 1961; 'The Crisis in the American Trade-Union Movement', *The Annals of the American Academy of Political and Social Science*, vol. CCCL, November 1963—particularly H. R. Northrup, 'Management's "New Look" in Labor Relations', in the first of these, and G. Strauss, 'Union Bargaining Strength: Goliath or Paper Tiger?' in the second. I also draw upon N. Lichtenstein, 'UAW Bargaining Strategy and Shop-Floor Conflict: 1946–70', *Industrial Relations*, vol. xxiv, no. 2, Spring 1985; D. J. B. Mitchell, 'Recent Union Contract Concessions', *Brookings Papers on Economic Activity*, no. 1, 1982, p. 174; D. J. B. Mitchell, *Unions, Wages, and Inflation*, Washington, DC 1980, pp. 45–7. Compare G. Strauss, 'The Shifting Power Balance in the Plant', *Industrial Relations*, vol. i, no. 3, May 1962.

cessful, resistance to the extension of unionization, particularly in newly constructed plants, many of them 'runaways' relocated in the south and south-west.
Especially by exploiting new, pro-business interpretations of the already fiercely
anti-labour Taft-Hartley Act of 1948—which were handed down by the National
Labor Relations Board that was appointed by the Eisenhower administration—
firms began to interfere with union organizing efforts much more openly and
powerfully than hitherto. Beginning in the mid to late 1950s, the number of illegal
actions committed by management in the course of union recognition campaigns,
after declining for years, began to rise rapidly, and unions found it significantly
harder to win recognition.[33] The proportion of union victories in NLRB elections
fell from 73.5 per cent in the years 1950–55 to 63 per cent in the years 1955–60 to 56
per cent in the years 1960–65. Unions had been able to organize 2 per cent of all
private wage and salary workers in the year 1950 and 1 per cent in the year 1955,
but by the year 1960 only 0.7 per cent. Between 1955 and 1961 the percentage of the
private- sector labour force that was unionized fell from its peak of 34.5 per cent in
1954 to 29.8 per cent in 1962—from 38 per cent to 33 per cent in manufacturing.[34]
All of these trends have continued to the present, and one cannot but conclude that
the decade from the mid 1950s to the mid 1960s marked a turning point for the US
union movement, the beginning of a long and precipitous process of decline.[35]

Employers became as intransigent at the level of the plant as at the level of the
union. Urged on by a phalanx of newly hired, college-trained labour relations
professionals, employers sought to reverse a relatively loose regime of supervision
on the shop floor, under which foremen had been allowed considerable leeway in
keeping the peace with rank and filers. At the same time, employers suddenly began
to stand firm against unofficial strikes. From this time onward, most notably in the
auto industry where shop-floor organization had been relatively strong, the number
of wildcats dropped precipitously.[36]

The results were dramatic. Contrary to received wisdom, there was never anything approaching an 'accord' between capital and labour in the US at any time
during the postwar period. But, to the extent that even a temporary modus vivendi
had emerged during the late 1940s and early 1950s, US employers, especially in
manufacturing, were now able to achieve major gains by breaking rather than by
perpetuating it.

First, employers significantly lowered the rate of wage growth, especially in
manufacturing. During the period 1958–65, the average annual growth of manufacturing real wages fell by 40 per cent, to only 2.2 per cent compared to 3.6 per
cent for 1950–58, and this despite the fact that accelerating economic growth was

33   Klein and Wanger, 'The Legal Setting for the Emergence of the Union Avoidance Strategy', passim;
R. B. Freeman, 'Why Are Unions Faring Poorly in NLRB Representation Elections?', in Kochan, ed., *Challenges
and Choices Facing American Labor*, pp. 46, 53.

34   Goldfield, *Decline of Organized Labor*, pp. 10, 90; R. B. Freeman, 'Contraction and Expansion: The
Divergence of Private Sector and Public Sector Unionism in the United States', *Journal of Economic
Perspectives*, vol. ii, Spring 1988, p. 64.

35   The stage for this turnaround had already been set, of course, by labour's organizational and
political failures during the Cold War decade between 1945 and 1955. See the sophisticated account by
N. Lichtenstein, 'From Corporatism to Collective Bargaining: Organized Labor and the Eclipse of Social
Democracy in the Postwar Era', in S. Fraser and G. Gerstle, ed., *The Rise and Fall of the New Deal Order 1930–80*,
Princeton 1989.

36   Lichtenstein, 'UAW Bargaining Strategy and Shop-Floor Conflict', pp. 376–7.

Figure 4.2. US unionization and employer opposition to unions as reflected in violations of National Labor Relations Act, 1945–95.

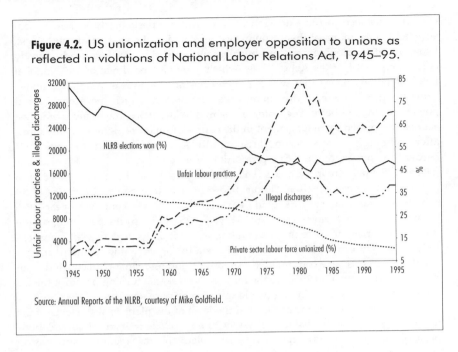

Source: Annual Reports of the NLRB, courtesy of Mike Goldfield.

bringing about a reduction of unemployment by 45 per cent in these years, from 6.6 per cent to 3.7 per cent.[37] Employers were, in addition, able to secure striking gains in productiveness, as both labour productivity and capital productivity (the real output-capital ratio) in manufacturing grew at what for the US were spectacular average annual rates of 4.1 per cent and 3.5 per cent respectively. Faster investment growth leading to more rapid technological advance was surely in part responsible for this increase. But, in view of the fact that the amount of plant and equipment *per worker hour* grew so slowly between 1958 and 1965—the net capital-labour ratio increasing significantly less rapidly than in any other comparable period in the postwar epoch—much of the gain in productiveness registered in this new era of employers' offensive may well have been achieved by a combination of shedding less productive plant and equipment and compelling workers to labour more intensely.[38]

The reduction in the growth of manufacturing unit labour costs made possible a significant recovery of export competitiveness. After deteriorating rapidly in the latter half of the 1950s, US relative costs did a major turnaround. Between 1960 and 1965, unit labour costs (expressed in dollars) in manufacturing in the US actually *fell* by 5.2 per cent, while those in Germany and Japan rose by 24.7 per cent and 22.9 per cent respectively. US export prices thus grew at an average annual rate of only

37   It should be noted that the reduction in wage growth that took place in these years in the private business economy as a whole was much smaller than in manufacturing—only 11 per cent—because wage growth outside of manufacturing actually rose very slightly.

38   The average annual rate of growth of the net capital-labour ratio was 0.6 per cent for 1958–65, 3.5 per cent for 1950–58, and 2.7 per cent for 1950–73.

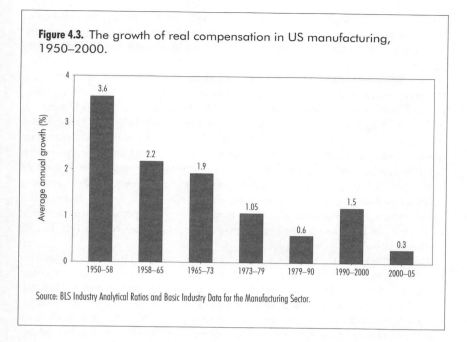

Figure 4.3. The growth of real compensation in US manufacturing, 1950–2000.

Source: BLS Industry Analytical Ratios and Basic Industry Data for the Manufacturing Sector.

1.3 per cent between 1960 and 1965 (only 0.6 between 1960 and 1964), more slowly than Germany's 1.4 per cent over the same period, although still not as slowly as Japan's 0.3 per cent (0.5 per cent between 1960 and 1964).

On the basis of capital's renewed capacity to control costs, the economy achieved a new export boom. Between 1958 and 1965, the average annual growth of exports increased to 7.1 per cent, from 4.4 per cent between 1950 and 1958. The US merchandise trade balance had drifted downward during the 1950s to an average of slightly under $3 billion for the years 1958–60. But it increased to $7 billion by 1964 and was still at $5.3 billion in 1965, and it recovered particularly well with respect to Germany and Japan.

The fact remains that the boom of the first half of the 1960s marked no definitive break from the long-term postwar trend. Between 1958 and 1965, falling wage growth opened the way for rising profitability, which set off the increased growth of investment; the latter, by helping to raise productivity growth, reduced the growth of costs further and thereby spurred increased exports, making, in turn, for higher profitability. But this virtuous circle could not sustain itself beyond the mid 1960s, and the reason, especially in light of subsequent events, is clear: the US manufacturing economy was unable to sustain the favourable trend in relative international costs which made it so successful in this era. Manufacturing had been able to achieve impressive cost improvements between 1958 and 1965, in part because capacity utilization rose so sharply, but this trend obviously could not continue indefinitely. Employers had succeeded in raising profits particularly rapidly because they had been able to sharply reduce wage growth and intensify work at the point of production, but these processes could be carried only so far. Finally,

US exporters had been able to fare especially well because, during the first half of the 1960s, their leading competitors in Germany and Japan were experiencing short-term difficulties in reducing costs, but those troubles could not be expected to persist.

Even during this period of dynamism, when US competitiveness was improving far more rapidly than at any other time between 1950 and 1971, intensifying international competition was imposing evident limits on US economic achievement. Although US manufacturers raised their prices more slowly between 1958 and 1965 than in any other period after 1950, the US still saw its share of world manufacturing exports fall from 18.7 per cent to 15.8 per cent. US and foreign corporations left little doubt, moreover, where they believed capital investment would yield its best return. US corporations increased their direct investment in manufacturing overseas in these years 50 per cent faster than in the US; in parallel manner, the value of the stock of foreign direct investment in the US as a percentage of the value of the stock of US direct investment abroad fell from 28.8 per cent in 1950 to 17.5 per cent in 1966.[39]

During the 1950s, the slow growth of domestic investment had helped make for the slow growth of productivity, and the latter, in combination with rapidly rising wages, had brought about rising relative costs, chronic difficulties with the balance of trade, and the rapid growth of direct investment in manufacturing overseas. Despite the slowdown in wage growth that took place after 1958, and the further slowdown of wage growth that would take place after 1965, that pattern turned out to characterize the economy's postwar evolution through the length of the boom. Just how vulnerable it would leave the economy to intensifying international competition will be seen shortly.

---

39 Branson, 'Trends in United States International Trade', p. 196, Table 3.13; Fahim-Nader, 'Capital Expenditures by Majority-Owned Foreign Affiliates of US Companies', p. 59; R. E. Lipsey, 'Foreign Direct Investment in the US: Changes Over Three Decades', in *Foreign Direct Investment*, Chicago 1993, p. 117, Table 5.3. Compare Maizels, *Industrial Growth and World Trade*, p. 220; A. D. Morgan, 'Export Competition and Import Substitution', in *Industrialization and the Basis for Trade*, Cambridge 1980, p. 48, Table 5.3.

Chapter 5

GERMANY: THE EXPORT-DRIVEN BOOM

The path taken by the German economy over the course of the postwar boom was both the reverse, mirror image of the path assumed by the US economy, and significantly dependent upon the US economy. The key to Germany's impressive growth during this epoch was thus its export dependence and its extraordinary export dynamism. The rapid growth of exports was initially made possible by its very low wage costs in international terms relative to skill, and by its competitiveness in the production of goods disproportionately in demand by a fast-growing international economy, especially a recovering and newly booming Europe, as well as the US. It was maintained by virtue of the economy's ability to prevent the too rapid rise of production costs, attributable, on the one hand, to its ability to moderate the growth of wages in the face of hyper-full employment, and, on the other hand, its exploitation of the opportunities for the growth of productivity provided by an unusually large and fast-growing manufacturing sector, heavily dependent upon exports. Crudely put, the German economy succeeded so unusually well over the first part of the postwar epoch because it could use its very cheap labour and historical endowment of very highly skilled labour to emulate, and in some cases surpass, US production methods and, on that basis, seize markets formerly held by US manufacturers.

1. The 1950s 'Miracle'

By 1951, German manufacturing labour productivity had reached 95 per cent of its 1938 level, but the manufacturing product wage only 80 per cent. The manufacturing rate of profit therefore surpassed even the very high rates achieved under Nazi rule. While labour productivity in manufacturing was about one-third the US level, wages were one-fifth. Thus average unit labour costs in manufacturing stood at only 64 per cent the US level. The conditions for a decade long investment boom had been set in place.[1]

The basic prerequisite for the restoration of Nazi-era profitability levels was the subordination of labour. The Nazis had of course destroyed the interwar

---

1 Daly, *Japanese Manufacturing Competitiveness*, pp. 35, 37, 39; W. C. Carlin, 'The Development of the Factor Distribution of Income and Profitability in West Germany, 1945–73', D.Phil. dissertation, Oxford University, 1987, pp. 192–3. I wish to express my gratitude to Wendy Carlin for making her thesis available to me, and to acknowledge my great indebtedness to this work. See also W. C. Carlin, 'West German Growth and Institutions, 1945–90', in N. Crafts and G. Toniolo, eds, *Economic Growth in Europe Since 1945*, Cambridge 1996.

labour movement, but in the immediate aftermath of World War II, the Occupation authorities favoured the restoration of strong unions and, in the British zone, the establishment of a high degree of state control over the economy. In this environment, even the Christian Democrats advocated a new socialist ordering of society and several *Länder* passed laws favouring the right of co-determination at all levels of economic decision-making for unions and works councils with CDU/CSU assent. Indeed, 'some form of socialization seemed inevitable in every one of the zone *Länder*.'[2] German workers were thus able to move quickly to establish factory councils, which often maintained production in the absence of the former owners. But, when Hamburg workers organized a politically radical Socialist Free Union, the Occupation quickly suppressed it—by early 1946. In 1947–48, under conditions of extreme deprivation due to economic disruption and food shortages, German workers began mass strikes in which the demand for socialization of part or all of the economy was salient. But this movement was quickly either defeated or side-tracked, under the combined pressure of the Occupational authorities, the German government, and private employers. The last of these, having weathered the Occupation's ephemeral commitment to de-Nazification and to the dismantling of the great corporations, were soon allowed to revive the same business associations that had served them in the Weimar years and under the Nazis.[3]

In 1947, the US imposed its recently adopted Cold War perspectives upon the occupied lands, Germany as well as Japan. It made clear, in particular, that Marshall Plan aid was conditional upon the restoration of a free-market economy, confirming a definitive shift in the balance of power in favour of capital. The German authorities immediately fell into line, establishing, in the course of less than two years, the characteristic patterns and structures of the new German political economy, in which industry was at once provided with low costs and high potential profits and made dependent upon successful exports. In June 1948, on the advice of the Americans, the new bi-zonal administration (of the now merged US and British zones) introduced a hard-line currency reform, which aimed to provide the foundations for a free-enterprise system, transcending the combination of black market and Occupation-administered economic controls through which production, allocation, and distribution had hitherto been carried out. While ending price and wage controls, the currency reform sought to create favourable conditions for businesses by preserving the real value of firms' assets, wiping out their debts, and shifting the burden of the tax system from property and profits to lower income groups. Although the currency reform allowed production to grow much more rapidly than before, inflation immediately threatened to get out of hand due to the easy credit conditions provided by the central bank and firms' ability to band together to keep prices up. In response, the German and allied authorities imposed a draconian monetary squeeze in November 1948, which had the effect not only of undercutting intercapitalist collusion and reducing prices, but, in compensation, of driving the

---

2   Carlin, 'Profitability in West Germany', p. 168–70 (quotation from J. Gimbel, *Origins of the Marshall Plan*, Stanford 1976, p. 205).

3   See the account in Armstrong et al., *Capitalism Since 1945*, pp. 18, 35, 50–1, 95–9.

rate of unemployment up from about 4.5 per cent in the second half of 1948 to a peak of about 12 per cent in 1950.[4]

The upward spiral of unemployment at the end of the 1940s dramatically weakened working-class resistance, which was further depressed by the wiping out of the unions' treasuries by the currency reform. A highly conservative trade union leadership had from the end of the war played a major role in restraining mass militancy, and it now moved to consolidate its power. Dismissive of the radical alternatives espoused by some elements at the base, it was anxious to seize the carrot of economic growth and saw little choice for labour but to fall into line.[5] Soon, a centralized, highly integrated union movement had emerged—consisting of just sixteen unions nationwide—which saw as one of its central tasks to ensure that workers' demands were made to cohere with the requirements for profitability and competitiveness. The successful containment of working-class resistance immediately manifested itself in a steep decline of the share of wages in national income. Between 1948 and 1951, labour productivity increased by a spectacular 50 per cent, but product wages grew by just one-quarter.[6]

The high, and rapidly growing, levels of productivity achieved by German manufacturing from the early postwar years were made possible, in the last analysis, by Germany's highly skilled labour force, the product of long-established industrial traditions. Germany's postwar economic 'miracle' must therefore be interpreted, to an important degree, as the economy's recovery of its historical pre-eminence in manufacturing. In the 1920s and 1930s, Germany held a share of world manufacturing exports equal to those of the UK and the US, and was the world's leader in the overseas sale of chemicals and other manufactures. In the postwar epoch, the German economy was able to base its resurgence directly on its earlier achievements. In 1952–53, 80 per cent of exported branded articles were sold using international trademarks valid before the war.[7]

Productivity could grow rapidly and smoothly from 1948 because losses of capital stock during the war had been limited and could be made up relatively easily. Wartime destruction in Germany was significant, but wartime investment compensated for it. Between 1938 and 1945, Germany's capital stock thus grew by 14 per cent. It embodied, moreover, more advanced techniques—including new, mass-production methods—and in many cases elicited an increase in workers' skills. Major gains in productivity could therefore be quickly achieved after the war

4   W. Carlin, 'Economic Reconstruction in Western Germany, 1945–55: The Displacement of "Vegetative Control"', in I. D. Turner, ed., *Reconstruction in Post-War Germany*, Oxford 1989; H. Giersch, K.-H. Paque, and H. Schmieding, 'Openness, Wage Restraint, and Macroeconomic Stability: West Germany's Road to Prosperity 1948–59', in R. Dornbusch, W. Nolling, and R. Layard, eds, *Postwar Economic Reconstruction and Lessons for the East Today*, Cambridge, Mass. 1993.

5   Armstrong et al., *Capitalism Since 1945*, pp. 50, 94–5. As Carlin notes, 'Despite the fact that works councils had often taken quite radical steps in the months immediately following the collapse, the emergent trade union leadership did not take up an oppositional stance but sought rather to gain as many concessions as possible from the military authorities on the basis of common interests.' 'Profitability in West Germany', p. 171.

6   Carlin, 'Economic Reconstruction in Western Germany', p. 56. See also Giersch et al., 'Openness, Wage Restraint, and Macroeconomic Stability', p. 8.

7   Maizels, *Industrial Growth and World Trade*, pp. 192–3; H. Giersch, K.-H. Paque, and H. Schmieding, *The Fading Miracle. Four Decades of Market Economy in Germany*, Cambridge 1992, p. 164; Carlin, 'West German Growth and Institutions', p. 465.

through the relatively cheap and simple process of rebuilding the infrastructure, especially the totally demolished transportation system.[8]

While the intent of the deflationary policy imposed in 1948 had been to weaken labour, intensify competition, and reduce domestic demand so as to force German industry into dependence upon exports, its initial effect was to throw the economy into deep recession and apparent crisis. But, like Japan at the same juncture, Germany was fortuitously rescued by the outbreak of the Korean War. With the mark having been sharply devalued in 1949—to allow sufficient exports to avoid chronic trade deficits and further overcome the so-called dollar shortage and enable the large-scale import of US goods—German industry could not have been better positioned to respond to the surge of orders that now came from the US. The first of a long series of export-led cycles, catalyzed by US demand, which would drive German postwar industrial growth, had begun.[9]

The Process of Growth

Between 1951 and 1961, with high levels of profitability and competitiveness providing both the means and motivation, the growth of manufacturing investment averaged 11.1 per cent per annum, of the manufacturing capital stock 8 per cent per annum. The rapid increase of investment brought the rapid growth of both output and productivity, as well as high capacity utilization. During the 1950s, the growth of manufacturing output averaged 10 per cent per annum, and GDP 8 per cent per annum, the fastest in Europe. Over the same period, labour productivity leapt forward at an average annual rate of 7 per cent in manufacturing and 5 per cent in the private business economy as a whole, benefiting not only from the application of the most advanced technology available, but also from the transfer of workers into industry from Germany's still large agricultural sector. Capacity utilization averaged 90 per cent for the decade.[10]

The German economy was able to sustain its dynamism because, throughout the 1950s, it was able to ward off the trends towards rising costs that tend to accompany bursts of capital accumulation of such proportions. The key here was its capacity to keep down the price of labour, which prepared the way for the rapid growth of manufacturing exports and a resulting amplification of the rate of capital accumulation and productivity growth. The expansion of industry thus brought with it a major increase in the size of the labour force and a steep decline in unemployment. Between 1950 and 1955, the unemployment rate fell from 10.4 per cent to 5.2 per cent, and by 1960 to 1 per cent. But full employment failed to bring about the squeeze on profits that might have been predicted by the supply-side theorists. Between 1950 and 1955, while unemployment was cut in half, profitability rose, in Kaleckian fashion—by 13 per cent in manufacturing and by a whopping 48.5 per cent in non-manufacturing. In 1960, profitability outside manufacturing still maintained its high level of the mid 1950s, and the profit share was actually higher than

8　W. Abelshauser, 'West German Economic Recovery, 1945–51: A Reassessment', *The Three Banks Review*, no. 135, September 1982; Carlin, 'Profitability in West Germany', pp. 151–62; Carlin, 'West German Growth and Institutions', pp. 463–4.

9　Carlin, 'Economic Reconstruction in Western Germany', pp. 60–2.

10　Carlin, 'Profitability in West Germany', pp. 192–4, 200–1, 311–14; Van Der Wee, *Prosperity and Upheaval*, p. 168; Hennings, 'West Germany', p. 480.

in 1955. Manufacturing profitability did fall during the second half of the 1950s, but was in 1960 still only about 10 per cent lower than it had been in 1950 when the unemployment rate had been eight times higher.[11]

The relatively slow growth of wages was made possible, in the first instance, by large reserves of labour in the countryside and abroad, which kept the labour supply up with demand. In 1950, the agricultural sector comprised 29 per cent of the labour force and even in 1960 the figure was still as high as 14 per cent. Mass immigration of highly skilled labour from East to West Germany also played a key role in keeping the labour market loose.

It has sometimes been argued that slow wage growth (in relation to productivity growth), and thus sustained capital accumulation through the 1950s, was ultimately dependent upon the forging of an implicit deal between capital and labour, in which unions held down wage demands in exchange for employers' commitment to invest.[12] But this implies that, had they wished to, unions could have imposed more rapid wage growth on the employers, a dubious proposition. As Carlin has argued, it is more realistic to explain wage restraint in terms of the unions' growing weakness and owners' increasing power and cohesion, as manifested especially in the strengthening of their employers' associations. Employers, aided by the US Occupation authorities, had already begun to tip the balance of class forces in their favour in the later 1940s by exploiting high unemployment and the temporary weakness of the unions' treasuries. In 1951–52, they further consolidated their advantage, especially by largely getting their way in the framing of the Works Constitution Act. This Act, despite the unions' expectations, failed to extend parity co-determination beyond the iron, coal, and steel industries. It had, moreover, the effect of reducing the influence of the unions, for it limited them to negotiating what were in effect minimum national wage increases, while assigning to the works councils, from which the unions were officially excluded, the task of working out the all-important increments above the minimum increase, in accord with firms' profitability and thus ability to pay, as well as local labour market conditions. Between 1951 and 1955, moreover, union density fell from a peak of 36 per cent to 32 per cent. It was capital's increased power to rebuff labour, not labour's self-restraint with respect to capital, which made possible high rates of profit throughout the 1950s, and capitalists' high rates of profit and inability to escape intense competition, not any commitment to labour, which induced high rates of capital accumulation over this period.[13]

11   Carlin, 'Profitability in West Germany', pp. 146, 141; Semmler, 'Economic Aspects of "Modell Germany"', in A. S. Markovits, ed., *The Political Economy of West Germany. Modell Deutschland*, New York 1982, p. 31. According to Hennings, during the 1950s, 'the share of wages in national income actually fell if corrected for the declining number of self-employed.' ('West Germany', p. 484.) '[T]he 1950s were a time of decreasing labour costs and widening profit margins … both the first and the second halves of the decade.' (Giersch et al., *Fading Miracle*, pp. 71–2.) For an analysis of the fall in manufacturing profitability between 1955 and 1960, see above, pp. 71–3.

12   For the interpretation of German growth in the 1950s in terms of unions' voluntary wage restraint and, more generally, of the forging of a 'cooperative game' between management and labour to refrain from consumption in the interest of the growth of investment and productivity, see B. Eichengreen, 'Institutions and Economic Growth: Europe after World War II', in *Economic Growth in Europe Since 1945*, pp. 44–5, 47–8.

13   Carlin, 'Profitability in West Germany', pp. 314–16; Carlin, 'West German Growth and Institutions', p. 467. 'It is union weakness in this period more than a conversion to the "politics of productivity" which accounts for wage moderation.' For further evidence and argument in support of this view, see J. Bergmann

Employers' ability to keep down the growth of costs made possible the powerful 1950s wave of capital accumulation largely by making possible the exceptionally fast growth of exports. Between 1950 and 1960, Germany increased its exports at the impressive average annual rate of 13.5 per cent. It was able to do so, because, despite rapid growth, it succeeded in improving its international competitive position. Over the course of the decade, German relative unit labour costs in manufacturing—with respect to those of France, Italy, the UK, and the US—fell by about 6 per cent.[14]

Export success was not merely an expression of the immediate strengths of the economy, it was also a function of policy. Far from adopting a Keynesian approach, the government curtailed the growth of domestic demand by running state budget surpluses and by enforcing tight credit leading to high interest rates. It thereby forced a search for overseas sales, while facilitating this by limiting upward pressure on prices. The government also implemented a vigorous policy of trade liberalization, opening the way to the untrammelled growth of imports and thus cheaper inputs for German industry, while imposing increased pressures upon it to improve competitiveness.

Still, German economic policy is incomprehensible in strictly laissez-faire terms. Especially in the early years of postwar development, the government sought to assist German producers in coping with trade liberalization by directly subsidizing exports through granting exporters favoured access to imported inputs, as well as cheap export-promotion loans. It also allowed firms generous tax write-offs for depreciation. Moreover, starting from the time that the mark was devalued in 1949 and extending through the later 1960s, German exporters were able to profit from an effectively under-valued exchange rate.[15]

If the initial capacity to increase productivity and to control the growth of costs made possible rapid exports, rapid export growth itself made for more rapid productivity growth. Exports enlarged the manufacturing sector and thus expanded the opportunities for economies of scale and learning by doing. The spectacular growth of exports during the 1950s made possible a doubling of the share of exports in German manufacturing output[16] (the increase of export dependence being especially pronounced in the critically important chemical, automobile, and machinery industries)[17] and, in turn, the maintenance of an unusually high share of manufacturing in the total economy. Manufacturing export growth was thus, in important respects, self-reinforcing. Both manufacturing output and the manufacturing labour force as a percentage of the total, after rising slightly in the 1950s, averaged close to 40 per cent for the entire period up to 1970, the industrial sector as a whole almost 50 per cent. Because manufacturing was the site of the best

and W. Muller-Jentsch, 'The Federal Republic of Germany: Cooperative Unionism and Dual Bargaining System Challenged', in S. Barkin, ed., *Worker Militancy and Its Consequences, 1965–75*, New York 1975, pp. 235, 241–2, 248–56.

14   Carlin. 'Profitability in West Germany', pp. 218, 220.

15   Ibid., pp. 193–8, 316; Carlin, 'Economic Reconstruction in West Germany', p. 63.

16   Henning, 'West Germany', p. 481.

17   These three industries accounted for about 40 per cent of industrial employment and a similar share of total industrial production—20 per cent of the total labour force and of GNP—during the period of the postwar boom. Henning, 'West Germany', p. 480.

opportunities for technical change, the German economy's enlarged manufacturing sector made for greater productivity growth and competitiveness and thus higher export growth, as is indicated by the fact that while manufacturing labour productivity grew by 96.5 per cent over the decade of the 1950s, labour productivity outside manufacturing grew by only 45.5 per cent.[18]

The sharp increase in the export share of manufacturing output during the 1950s was ultimately made possible by a rapidly growing world economy in which output for export among the advanced capitalist economies was growing 50 per cent faster than output for the domestic market. But another side of the story was even more significant. German producers were able to achieve such high rates of export growth only by taking a growing *share* of that growing market, not only at the expense of, but also with the help of the governments of its leading competitors, especially that of the US. During the 1950s, Germany nearly *tripled* its share of the manufacturing exports of the advanced industrial countries, its quotient increasing from 7.3 per cent to 19.0 per cent.[19] No less than 59 per cent of the increase in German manufacturing exports during the decade was thus made possible by Germany's taking an increasing share of the market, compared to only 41 per cent made possible by the growth of the market per se. And almost all of that increase in share came at the expense of the economies of the US and UK.[20]

German export-led growth was not only facilitated by the declining competitiveness of US producers in the world market, but was directly stabilized, indeed driven forward, by the call for German imports from the enormous US market itself.[21] Over the course of the 1950s, exports to North America as a share of German exports increased by almost 60 per cent, from 5.7 per cent to 9.0 per cent.[22] Between 1950 and 1965, moreover, every upturn of the German business cycle was set off by a surge in exports which was given its impetus by an increase of US demand associated with a US cyclical upturn. At the start of the 1950s, it was only the Korean war and the wave of speculative buying that it incited that allowed the German economy to overcome its deflationary crisis of the late 1940s and initiate the first of these cyclical booms. Cyclical upswings in the American economy also set off the second, third, and fourth of these cycles, in 1955, 1960, and 1963, respectively.[23] In effect, the growth of demand in the US economy, and particularly the stabilization of demand there by means of large-scale military spending,

18   Carlin, 'Profitability in West Germany', p. 220.
19   Maizels, *Industrial Growth and World Trade*, p, 220; Morgan, 'Export Competition and Import Substitution', p, 48.
20   Put another way, had Germany failed to increase its share of the world market, its exports during the 1950s would have been only 41 per cent of what they turned out to be. Maizels, *Industrial Growth and World Trade*, p, 201. The 'world export market' is here taken to be the total exports of the twelve leading economies.
21   'The foreign locomotive for postwar Europe certainly was the US as a source of demand and as a pacemaker for domestic supplier activities,' H. Giersch, 'Aspects of Growth, Structural Changes, and Employment. A Schumpeterian Perspective', in H. Giersch, ed., *Macroeconomic Policies for Growth and Stability. A European Perspective*, Tubingen 1979, p. 189.
22   Giersch et al., *Fading Miracle*, p. 91.
23   H. Giersch, *Growth, Cycles, and Exchange Rates. The Experience of West Germany*, Stockholm 1970, p. 15.

Table 5.1. Germany: share of exports in output (per cent).

	1950	1958	1967	1970	1974
Cars	11.5	36.3	40.7	40.6	46.1
Machines	20.3	30.2	38.0	35.5	43.5
Iron-prodcing machinery	16.4	17.8	30.3	24.0	35.2
Chemical	12.3	22.5	29.0	31.1	36.0
Non-metal industry	11.4	14.9	24.4	18.3	22.9
All manufacturing	8.3	15.1	18.7	19.3	24.2

Source: W. Semmler, 'Economic Aspects of "Modell Germany" ', p. 31.

helped drive an export-oriented economy in Germany which was itself founded on anti-Keynesianism.[24]

2. Contradictions of Internationalization, Late 1950s to Mid 1960s

During the late 1950s and early 1960s, while the US economy temporarily broke from its long-term pattern of relatively slow growth, the German economy sustained an interruption of its momentum. The drop-off in growth began from a high level and, from the mid 1960s, the economy regained some of its former dynamism. Nevertheless, the problems behind the economy's short-term hesitations were hardly superficial; they manifested profound structural problems which would turn out to plague not only the German economy, but also the advanced capitalist economies taken together, and would ultimately bring about the shift from long boom to long downturn.

The slowdown began around 1960. Between 1960 and 1965, the average annual growth of manufacturing output fell to 5.8 per cent, having averaged just under 10 per cent during the years 1955–60 and just about 12 per cent for the whole decade of the 1950s. The average annual growth of GDP, at 5.1 per cent, was down by about one-third from that of the previous five (and ten) years. Part and parcel of the deceleration in the growth of output was a major reduction in investment growth, the average annual growth of investment in manufacturing falling to 4.1 per cent between 1960 and 1965 from the spectacular average annual rate of 15 per cent between 1950 and 1955 and the still quite impressive average annual rate of 8.4 per cent between 1955 and 1960. Over the same period, the average annual growth of the manufacturing capital stock also fell, but only slightly.

Finally, there was a decisive fall in profitability in manufacturing, originating in the mid 1950s. Manufacturing profitability in 1960 was only about 10 per cent below its 1950 level. Still, the not insubstantial fall of 20 per cent between 1955 and 1960

---

24   On Germany's export-led, export-based growth from the 1950s to the early 1970s, see Hennings, 'West Germany', pp, 480-3, 486-90. 'That again and again the initial stimulus for an upswing came from export demand is explained by the low rate of inflation together with high productivity growth and lagging increases in wages.'

turned out to initiate a longer-term trend. Between 1960 and 1965, manufacturing profitability fell by a further 30 per cent.[25] What had occurred to force down the rate of profit and, in turn, the rate of growth of investment and output? Just as the US temporary recovery between 1958 and 1965 had stemmed to an important degree from a major improvement in relative international productive costs that had issued in an export boom (making possible a major increase in manufacturing profitability and investment), the German slowdown from the later 1950s through to the mid 1960s resulted largely, though not entirely, from a decline in competitiveness, which undermined the capacity to export and resulted in a downward price squeeze on the profit rate. Declining competitiveness derived from two trends which were to become ever more pronounced over the period before 1973, one external, the other internal: first, the rise of manufacturing producers across the advanced capitalist world prepared to challenge German producers for markets and, second, the self-limiting character of a German form of economic development that was structured to stimulate the growth of manufacturing exports at the expense of the domestic market.

Between 1955 and 1960, although the German economy's relative costs continued to decline in relation to the US, the UK, and the whole world, they ceased to do so with respect to its increasingly competitive continental European rivals France and Italy, or to Japan.[26] From 1960 onwards, moreover, the problem of relative costs intensified. In 1961, the revaluation of the mark brought an immediate increase of 4.8 per cent in Germany's relative unit labour costs. And between 1961 and 1965, Germany's relative unit labour costs compared to its five leading competitors grew by another 2.4 per cent, a total of about 7 per cent for the five years.[27] During the second half of the 1950s, German manufacturing productivity growth had been significantly higher than that of France and Italy, but thenceforth there was a remarkable reversal, with both French and Italian manufacturing productivity growth out-distancing that of Germany by more than 50 per cent between 1960 and 1973.[28]

Rising relative costs, representing both the intensification of competition from abroad and upward pressure on costs from within, brought a steady and increasingly sharp reduction in Germany's capacity to export, and to garner share of advanced-country manufacturing exports, while opening the way to growing import penetration. Between 1950 and 1955, Germany's exports grew at an average annual rate of 15.2 per cent and its share of advanced-country manufacturing exports increased spectacularly from 7.3 per cent to 15.3 per cent. Between 1955 and 1960, Germany's exports were still increasing at an average annual rate of 11.8 per cent, and its share of advanced-country manufacturing exports grew to 20.3 per cent. Nevertheless, in these latter years, only one-third of the gain in share was due to the increased competitiveness of German goods, the remainder deriving from disproportionately inflating demand for the products which Germany exported. Between 1960 and 1965, Germany's export growth fell to an average annual rate of

25   Carlin, 'Profitability in West Germany', p. 146.
26   Ibid., pp. 320–1; Sohmen, 'The Dollar and the Mark', p. 194.
27   Carlin, 'Profitability in West Germany', p. 327.
28   Carlin, 'West German Growth and Institutions', p. 457; AGH; OECD, *Historical Statistics 1960–95*, Paris 1997, p. 52, Table 3.6.

only 6.1 per cent per annum, and by 1965, its share of advanced-country manufacturing exports had declined slightly, to 19.2 per cent. Over the years 1955–65, import penetration increased from 19 per cent to 32 per cent.[29]

The close correlation between declining competitiveness and declining profitability in manufacturing suggests that the former had an important role in determining the latter. To what extent can this relationship be demonstrated more directly?

During the second half of the 1950s, rising international competition, manifested in downward pressure on manufacturing prices, was responsible for at least half of the fall in manufacturing profitability.[30] Between 1955 and 1960, the average annual growth of unit labour costs in manufacturing, at 3.2 per cent, was about 12.5 per cent lower than that in non-manufacturing, at 3.6 per cent. Nevertheless, the manufacturing profit share declined by almost 8 per cent (and the profit rate by 20 per cent), while the non-manufacturing profit share increased by 8 per cent (and the profit rate remained the same) for the simple reason that, while manufacturers could raise their output prices at an annual average rate of just 1.6 per cent, non-manufacturers could raise theirs at an average annual rate of 3.6 per cent. Manufacturers' inability to sufficiently mark up prices over costs was evidently their problem. Since manufacturing output consists largely of tradables, while non-manufacturing output consists mainly of non-tradables, it seems reasonable to conclude that manufacturers' relative inability to mark-up over costs can be attributed to their vulnerability to intensifying international competition. By the same token, it was the effective immunity of non-manufacturing producers from international competitive pressure that allowed them to raise their prices sufficiently over their costs to avoid a wages-productivity squeeze on profits.

Between 1960 and 1965, German manufacturing profitability continued to fall largely, though certainly not exclusively, as a consequence of declining competitiveness. In 1961, the mark was revalued by 5 per cent against the dollar, bringing about an increase in its effective exchange rate of 4.5 per cent, with an immediate effect on manufacturing profitability, which fell by 12 per cent in just that one year.[31] Between 1961 and 1965, manufacturing profitability fell further, at an average annual rate of 5.3 per cent (or 21 per cent over the period). This time, unlike between 1955 and 1960, profitability outside manufacturing did fall; even so, the decline was 60 per cent less steep than in manufacturing, at an annual average of just 2.05 per cent. In part, manufacturers' problem remained what it had been in the second half of the 1950s: their inability to mark up over costs to the extent non-manufacturers did, due to their exposure to the relentless downward pressure on prices emanating from their overseas competitors.

Unit labour costs in manufacturing, at 2.8 per cent, grew even more slowly than in the previous period relatively to those in non-manufacturing, at 4.5 per cent.

29   Maizels, *Industrial Growth and World Trade*, p. 220; Morgan, 'Export Competition and Import Substitution', p. 48; Carlin, 'Profitability in West Germany', pp. 320–1, 327–8. When manufacturing profitability finally rose again between 1965 and 1969, the rate of growth of exports increased by two-thirds compared to 1960–65, and German manufacturing regained the share it had lost during that period.

30   This analysis follows Carlin, 'Profitability in West Germany', p. 320.

31   Ibid., pp. 320–1. 'Though only very small, the 1961 revaluation appears to have checked the country's export performance.' Llewellyn and Potter, 'Competitiveness and the Current Account', in A. Boltho, ed., *The European Economy. Growth and Crisis*, Oxford 1982, p. 142.

Table 5.2. Costs, prices, and profitability in Germany, 1955–60.
(Average annual per cent change.)

	NPR	NPSh	PW	LPy	NW	ULC	PPri
Mfgr	-4.5	-1.6	6.3	5.7	8.0	3.2	1.6
Non-mfgr	0.0	1.7	2.3	3.2	5.9	3.6	3.6

Source: See Appendix I on Profit Rates. Key to legend on p. xiii.

Similarly, while the manufacturing output-capital ratio expressed in nominal terms fell at an average annual rate of 3.3 per cent, it fell in real terms by just 1.8 per cent. The root of the divergence appears to have been the same in both cases: that manufacturers selling mostly tradables could raise their prices at an average annual rate of just 2.4 per cent, whereas their counterparts in non-manufacturing and in construction (producing capital stock, specifically structures) selling mainly non-tradables could raise their prices at average annual rates of 4.05 per cent and 4.0 per cent, respectively. As a result, between 1961 and 1965, the non-manufacturing profit share fell at an average annual rate of just 0.5 per cent, the output-capital ratio only 1.5 per cent. More than three-quarters of the 2.1 per cent average annual fall in the profit share and almost one-half of the 3.3 per cent average annual fall in the output-capital ratio are thus attributable to declining German competitiveness.[32]

The first half of the 1960s was the period when the postwar German labour market was at its tightest, since immigration from East Germany had just been closed and the systematic recruitment of *Gastarbeiter* would not begin for another year or two. Unemployment was under 1 per cent. Yet the German labour movement failed to take much advantage of these favourable conditions to increase its political or institutional power and economic leverage. Instead, by all accounts, it was placed ever more on the defensive by increasingly well-organized employers, the pressure from whom, in Carlin's words, 'contributed to a realignment of the centre of gravity in the union movement toward moderation'.[33] While employers' pressure was one factor, there is not much evidence that the trade union movement even tried to exploit the scarcity of labour. With the economy booming, it seems to have implicitly accepted the principle that the wage share should be kept roughly constant to facilitate ongoing capital accumulation. The trade unions thus sought wage gains roughly in accord with productivity. Up to 1958, there had usually been at least one major strike each year; after that date, official strike action pretty much disappeared—until 1969–70. The really decisive steps in determining wages seem to have occurred largely at the local level, where negotiations in the works councils made for increments over the nationally negotiated agreements in accord

---

32   Somewhat more than half of the fall in the output-capital ratio is accounted for by the falling productivity of capital.

33   Carlin, 'Profitability in West Germany', pp. 332–3; A. S. Markovitz and C. S. Allen, 'Trade Unions and the Economic Crisis: The West German Case', in *Unions and Economic Crisis. Britain, West Germany and Sweden*, London 1984, pp. 124–6.

with profitability. It was, then, only in the decade from the end of the 1950s to the end of the 1960s, *after* capital had succeeded in largely imposing a basic framework for labour relations in accordance with its needs, that the 'politics of productivity' came into its own—an expression of the progressive bureaucratization of the trade unions in the context of labour-movement weakness and economic prosperity.[34]

Over the years 1960–65, the average annual growth of nominal compensation in manufacturing, at 8.6 per cent, was not all that much higher than the 8.0 per cent recorded for 1955–60. And, compared to that for 1955–60, the average annual growth of real compensation actually fell somewhat, to 5.2 per cent from 6.1 per cent for 1955–60—and 6.0 per cent for the entire decade of the 1950s. The tight labour market was no doubt responsible for German producers having to absorb the not insignificant cost of the revaluation of the mark in 1961. But to attribute part of the squeeze on profits to capitalists' inability to force labour to adjust to a fall in profitability (caused by declining competitiveness due to large current account balances and revaluation) is not the same thing as to attribute that fall directly to an increase in pressure from labour—for which, again, evidence is lacking.[35] It was the decline in competitiveness, not the pressure from labour, that was 'the moving part'. As even conservative German economists have been obliged to admit, with some amazement, until the end of the 1960s, the German labour movement was, by design or necessity, a model of sensitivity to the requirements of capitalist profitability. 'Despite the early visible indications of labour shortage and despite recurrent waves of immigration, [unions] did not immediately press for long-term real wage increases above productivity growth.' 'To explain union restraint in the 1960s is very difficult … [But] for the time being, unions apparently took their assigned active role as corporatist guardians of stability seriously enough to keep wage increases in check.'[36]

As has already been emphasized, the weakening of the export-led growth that was largely responsible for declining manufacturing profitability over the decade 1955–65 resulted, in part, from the increasing potency of Germany's international rivals, but it also had domestic roots. Export-led growth was thus, in tendency, self-limiting. Because it was systematically buttressed by macroeconomic policy aimed at restricting the growth of demand so as to keep down prices, major current account surpluses were unavoidable, and these were bound to create strong pressures to revalue the mark. Mark revaluations, of course, undermined competitiveness, for they translated into higher relative unit labour costs—unless employers could somehow counteract their effect by correspondingly reducing wage growth or increasing productivity. During the second half of the 1950s, German current account balances grew to about 2.5 per cent of GDP. Yet external surpluses of this

---

34   J. Bergmann and W. Muller-Jentsch, 'The Federal Republic of Germany: Cooperative Unionism and Dual Bargaining System Challenged', in S. Barkin, ed., *Worker Militancy and Its Consequences 1965–75*, New York 1975, pp. 248–53, 257; W. Muller-Jentsch and H.-J. Sperling, 'Economic Development, Labour Conflicts and the Industrial Relations System in West Germany', in C. Crouch and A. Pizzorno, eds, *The Resurgence of Class Conflict in Western Europe Since 1968*, London 1978, Vol. 1, pp. 261–3, 281–2.

35   Carlin, 'Profitability in West Germany', pp. 326–7.

36   Giersch et al., *The Fading Miracle*, pp. 154–6. Wage growth may well have played some indirect role in bringing down the profit rate in these years, especially in manufacturing. It appears to have induced the 'premature' substitution of capital for labour, and thereby at least some of the marked decline in the productivity of capital (though the fall in the real output-capital ratio was paradoxically greater outside manufacturing than within, despite manufacturing's much faster rate of product wage growth).

Table 5.3. Costs, prices, and profitability in Germany, 1961–65.
(Average annual per cent change.)

	NPR	NPSh	RW	PW	LPy	NW	ULC	PPri	NY/NK	NY/NK real	NKPri
Mfgr	-5.3	-2.2	5.2	5.7	5.4	8.3	2.8	2.4	-3.3	-1.7	4.0
Non-mfgr	-2.1	-0.5	5.3	3.8	3.8	8.4	4.5	4.4	-1.5	-2.9	3.0

Source: See Appendix I on Profit Rates. Key to legend on p. xiii.

magnitude could not be sustained unproblematically, and, by the end of 1950s, they had issued in increases the money supply that were threatening to push up prices and undermine competitiveness. The German monetary authorities initially sought to counteract inflationary pressure through monetary stringency, but this only encouraged an inflow of speculative capital aiming to profit from the increase in the rate of interest.

Germany's competitiveness thus threatened to self-destruct by bringing about an increase in German relative prices, either through the inflation caused by the increase in the supply of money that was the counterpart of current account surpluses, or directly through the revaluation of the currency. In the end, an appreciation of the currency could not be avoided, and the revaluation of 1961 led directly to a major fall in manufacturing (and non-manufacturing) profitability. That revaluation did, though, also help to reduce the current account surplus and thus to alleviate further upward pressure on the mark for the next half decade.[37]

Developments in Germany during the late 1950s and early 1960s represented a phase in a longer-term evolution that would reach its culmination between 1969 and 1973, when Germany, and the other advanced capitalist economies, would experience the end of the boom and the onset of the long downturn. At that point, a further sudden decline in international competitiveness—which manifested both the specifically German tendency to exploding current account deficits leading to currency revaluations and the broader international trend of intensified competition resulting in system-wide over-capacity and over-production—would put unbearable pressures on manufacturing profitability and investment from which neither the German economy, nor the other advanced capitalist economies, would soon recover. In this sense, the slowdown of the first half of the 1960s prefigured the crisis that was to come.

---

37 Llewellyn and Potter, 'Competitiveness and the Current Account', p. 142.

Chapter 6

JAPAN'S 'HIGH-SPEED GROWTH'

At the beginning of the postwar period, Japan's economy lagged far behind Germany's; its industrial development had begun later and had come less far. Japan's producers, like Germany's, were initially able to compensate for their relatively low productivity by paying wages that were relatively even lower. The fact remains that the Japanese economy's extraordinary postwar growth process is incomprehensible without reference to its specific economic, organizational and political forms, forms that, as a late developer, it was able to put in place in a way that would have been impossible for the US or UK. Only by virtue of its economic institutions and the intervention of the state was the Japanese economy able to exploit the extraordinary opportunities offered by the world market, and particularly US demand, throughout the length of the postwar boom.

Initial Conditions

In 1950, at the end of its postwar reconstruction process, Japan's manufacturing productivity was, on average, 11 per cent that of the US and about 35 per cent that of Germany. But hourly wages in manufacturing were, at this point, just 6–7 per cent that in the US and 33 per cent that in Germany. This left Japanese manufacturing unit labour costs 40 per cent below those of the US, although only slightly lower than those of Germany.[1] It was Japan's favourable relative cost position in international terms that constituted the point of departure for its postwar economic development.

Technical know-how and skilled labour. Although well behind the leading industrial economies at the start of its postwar development, Japan was hardly starting from scratch. More than a half-century of factory industrialization, initially in textiles, then in the heavy and chemical industries, had enabled the Japanese economy, beginning from a very low base, to steadily narrow the technology and skills gap between itself and the capitalist powers of the West. Japan's prewar and wartime military build-up had accelerated this process: its rate of technological advance had increased, and, by virtue of the technical training provided by the military industries, the workforce had further raised its level of skill. The educational standards of the working class, already fairly high as a consequence of the provision of universal primary education in the prewar period, were further elevated when middle school and high school education were made compulsory after the war.[2]

---

1   Daly, *Japanese Manufacturing Competitiveness*, pp. 35, 37, 39.
2   M. Itoh, *The World Economic Crisis and Japanese Capitalism*, London 1990, pp. 143, 145–7. I am much indebted to this important work.

Low-waged labour. Japanese employers were able to get away with paying very low wages for their relatively skilled labour. As in Germany, during the 1930s a highly authoritarian regime had destroyed what had been a rather weak union movement. But, following Japan's defeat in World War II, the initially pro-labour policies of the US Occupation (SCAP) had opened the way for the vertiginous rise of a militant, politically radical, mass working-class movement. By the end of 1946, Japanese labour had engaged in strikes costing six million person days, many of them 'production control' struggles, in which employees occupied workplaces and continued production under their own management to defend wages and working conditions and to prevent layoffs. Less than two years after the war had ended, unionization had risen to an extraordinary 46 per cent of the labour force. The labour movement had, moreover, quickly assumed a directly political character and, in addition to protesting the lack of food, was seeking by direct action to bring in a more left-wing government.[3]

With the onset of the Cold War in 1946–47, however, US Occupational authorities, as in Germany, reversed gears and moved to quell the rising tide of labour resistance. Having already dispersed a major direct-action movement against the food distribution system in May 1946, on 1 February 1947 General Douglas MacArthur invoked the full power of the Occupation to put a stop to a strike of government employees in which 2.6 million people had been expected to participate. In the succeeding period, in collaboration with the Japanese government, SCAP imposed a ban on government workers' right to strike, announced it would refuse to approve wage increases that led to price increases, and levied devastating defeats on militant unions in the newly established public corporations for the railways and for tobacco and salt production.

At the end of 1948, again as in Germany, the Occupation authorities and the Japanese government implemented a harshly deflationary programme, the Dodge Plan, one purpose of which was to soften up the labour movement. Japanese employers exploited the ensuing recession, in which unemployment rose above four million, to sack 750,000 workers. With the workers' movement seriously weakened, the US Occupation authorities, the Japanese government, and Japanese corporations worked hand-in-hand to roll back labour's conquests of the previous years. Under the protective umbrella of the 1949 amendments to the Trade Union Act, employers imposed new collective agreements that prescribed employers' untrammelled right to manage and deprived unions of hard-won influence over personnel matters. They also carried out a huge purge of communist labour leaders from the factories and the unions and, urged on by SCAP, sought to have the Communist-led All-Japan Congress of Industrial Unions (Sanbetsu Kaigi) replaced by a newly formed General Council of Trade Unions of Japan (Sohyo). Even so, corporations still had to defeat a long series of bitter strikes to demolish the very substantial power Japanese workers had managed to establish at the level of the shop floor. In this way they prepared

3 For this and the following paragraph, I have relied upon the discussion in Armstrong et al., *Capitalism Since 1945*, pp. 17–18, 32–3, 44–6, 90–4, supplemented by Kosai, *The Era of High-Speed Growth*, Tokyo 1986, pp. 27–8, 49–53, 64–5; H. Shimada, 'Japan's Industrial Culture and Labor Management Relations', in S. Kumon and H. Rosovsky, eds, *The Political Economy of Japan*, Stanford 1992, Vol. 3, pp. 270–1; and Itoh, *Japanese Capitalism*, pp. 147–9. For an account of the labour upsurge, see Joe Moore, *Japanese Workers and the Struggle for Power 1945–47*, Madison 1983.

the ground for their newly adopted rationalization and modernization pro-grammes—at Toshiba (1949), Hitachi Electrical Machine Company (1950), Toyota (1951), Nissan (1953), Nihon Steel Muroran Works (1954), Oiji Paper (1958), and, finally, Miike Coal Mines (1960).[4] Only from the mid to late 1950s were they able to consolidate Japan's distinctive postwar system of cooperative labour relations, pow-erfully harnessing the Japanese labour force to the requirements of capital accumulation and competitiveness.[5] Although this system has been heralded as con-secrating a 'capital-labour class compromise', it is better understood as manifesting the subordination of labour to capital, resulting from the destruction and consequent transformation of the militant postwar Japanese labour movement.[6]

How Growth Occurred

Between 1950 and 1960, Japanese manufacturing output grew at an average annual rate of 16.7 per cent, and GNP at about 10 per cent—the highest rates among the advanced capitalist economies. The key to this extraordinary expansion was an investment boom of historic proportions. Private investment in new plant and equipment in the economy as a whole rose at the spectacular average annual pace of 15.6 per cent for the decade, 22.6 per cent for the years between 1955 and 1960. After a hesitant start in the early 1950s, investment in manufacturing increased at the unheard of average annual rate of 33 per cent between 1954 and 1961, the capital stock 9.5 per cent. The ratio of plant and equipment investment to GNP almost doubled over the period, increasing from 7.7 per cent to around 14 per cent.[7] Such extraordinary investment growth naturally brought about an extremely rapid increase in the economy's productiveness. Between 1950 and 1960, labour produc-tivity in manufacturing grew at an average annual rate of 10.8 per cent, in the private business economy at 7.5 per cent.[8]

What made it possible to sustain such rapid growth, was, as in Germany, the Japanese economy's ability to prevent the investment boom from bringing about the too rapid growth of costs. Over the years 1950–60, the huge growth of the demand for labour brought about the doubling of the industrial labour force.[9] Nevertheless, even while manufacturing labour productivity accelerated over the period, wage pressure remained minimal. Between 1952 and 1961, the real consumer wage

4   At Nissan, for example, workers had established a shop-floor system whereby each group of ten workers elected delegates to a shop committee, and these committees assumed the authority to grant or refuse overtime requests. 'In the summer of 1953 the union carried out strikes and go-slows in support of a wage claim, but were locked out. The management had the financial support of the Industrial Bank of Japan, the Employers Federation ensured that Nissan's contractors would receive alternative orders, and its rivals guaranteed that they would not steal its markets while the firm was out of production.' Eventually, after the union leadership was fired, the workers were cajoled into a 'second union', started by the white collar staff who wanted to cooperate with the company. Armstrong et al., *Capitalism Since 1945*, p. 132. See also M. A. Cusumano, *The Japanese Auto Industry*, Cambridge, Mass. 1985, p. 148.

5   Shimada, 'Japan's Industrial Culture', pp. 272–4; S. Tokunaga, 'A Marxist Interpretation of Japanese Industrial Relations, with Special Reference to Large Private Enterprises', in T. Shirai, ed., *Contemporary Industrial Relations in Japan*, Tokyo 1983, pp. 314–17; Armstrong et al., *Capitalism Since 1945*, pp. 92–4, 132–5.

6   See, for example, M. Kenney and R. Florida, *Beyond Mass Production. The Japanese System and its Transfer to the US*, New York 1993, pp. 27–32.

7   Kosai, *Era of High-Speed Growth*, pp. 7, 9, 112; Armstrong et al., *Capitalism since 1945*, p. 354, Table A3.

8   Kosai, *Era of High-Speed Growth*, pp. 7, 9.

9   Itoh, *Japanese Capitalism*, p. 146; AGH.

increased at an average annual rate of 4.7 per cent, the real product wage at an average annual rate of 6.1 per cent—*only two thirds as fast as labour productivity*. The manufacturing profit share thus rose at an average annual rate of 6.6 per cent during these years. With the output capital-ratio increasing at an average annual rate of close to 5 per cent, the profit rate in manufacturing *tripled* between 1952 and 1961.[10]

The Institutional Foundations of the Japanese 'Miracle'

The rise of the profit rate through 1961 and—after a brief hiatus between 1961 and 1965—its further rise through 1970, goes a long way to explain the magnitude of the boom. But the spectacular trajectory of the profit rate itself needs to be accounted for, and is quite inexplicable in purely market terms. In view of the extraordinary rates of capital accumulation and of the growth of the labour force over such an extended period, upward pressure on wages might have been expected, if not to squeeze profitability, at least to prevent profitability from much increasing. But the profit share and output-capital ratio were able to grow continually (with only very brief breaks) for close to two decades.

According to neoclassical economic expectations the plentiful supply of cheap labour should have led the economy towards a labour-intensive path. But, while nurturing major labour-intensive industries such as textiles and clothing, the Japanese economy focused from the outset upon basic capital-intensive industries such as iron, steel, and petro-chemicals, despite initially low efficiency and high relative costs, and, from very early on, upon machinery. It became, moreover, almost immediately, not merely a successful borrower of technology, but a technological innovator, embarking upon a strongly capital- and (soon) technology- intensive trajectory. How can this evolution be explained? The 'Japanese miracle' is explicable only in terms of the specific political and institutional forms through which the economy developed, forms whose main raison d'être was precisely to transform the pattern of relative prices that would otherwise have prevailed. Only by reference to these forms can one account for the cheap capital, the reduced level of investment risk, the high levels of information (at reduced cost), the enhanced degree of protection from international rivals, the relative upward inflexibility of wages, and the enhanced opportunities to invest in human capital, which were made available to Japanese firms. And these forms alone can account for Japanese firms' exceedingly productive, because so highly disciplined, exploitation of their extraordinary cost advantages.

In the years immediately following World War II—marked as they were by the implementation of de-concentration policies, inflation, a mass labour uprising, and the recession brought on by the severely deflationary Dodge Plan—even large manufacturing firms found themselves desperately short of capital and often on the verge of collapse. To make matters worse, with the opening of the economy to the world market at the end of the 1940s, the strategically pivotal heavy and chemical industries, possessed of plant and equipment for the most part of ancient vintage, revealed themselves to have high relative and absolute costs, and thus incapable either of competing internationally or of achieving a sufficient level of

10   Armstrong et al., *Capitalism Since 1945*, p. 352, Table A1.
11   Kosai, *Era of High-Speed Growth*, pp. 80–1.

profitability to generate the funds needed for technological modernization.[11] All else equal, capital should have been highly costly, and large-scale and long-term fixed-capital investment should have been extremely risky. However, because the Japanese growth process was structured from the start by close interrelationships among networks of interlinked manufacturers, great banks that were deeply involved in industry, and a highly interventionist state, these problems were never allowed to materialize.

Horizontal networks in manufacturing and the merger of finance and industry. At the end of World War II, the US Occupation authorities formally dissolved the great *zaibatsu* that had dominated the prewar economy, destroying the holding companies that had formed their core and selling the shares of what had been their constituent manufacturing firms to the general public. But in so doing, they helped prepare the ground for the emergence of a new form of equally big-business-dominated economic structure that brought together in a new pattern the basic elements of the old system.

The leading manufacturing firms that had formerly been subsidiaries of the *zaibatsu* holding companies emerged as autonomous entities, under the direction of a new layer of professional managers, recruited from within their ranks and possessing close, and critically important, ties to the firms' pivotal layers of technical and skilled workers. Almost immediately, however, these firms began to collaborate with the other subsidiaries of their old *zaibatsu* so as to create horizontally linked industrial networks, initially on the informal basis of meetings between their company presidents. These so-called groups (or horizontal *keiretsu*), composed as they were of firms that had been in the possession of the now-dissolved *zaibatsu* holding companies, typically contained a large number of major enterprises, representing an enormous range of different sorts of productive activity. Their members served to an important degree as one another's customers, kept one another abreast of their technical changes and investment plans, and committed themselves to offering mutual aid to keep one another afloat. They thereby vastly increased their ability to plan, to reduce risk, and to react to changes in the market by altering their product mix, bringing in new products, and adopting new technologies.[12]

These developments were complemented by the emergence unscathed from the Occupation of the old *zaibatsu* 'lead banks'. These banks were actually highly favoured by the postwar reforms, and they quickly acquired positions at the core of the horizontal *keiretsu*, providing their generally money-starved members a great part of their investment funds in the form of loans and acquiring a significant bloc of each of their stocks. Dependent for their own success upon the success of the firms of their group, the banks typically found that it made sense both to support

---

12   For the previous two paragraphs, see I. Nakatani, 'The Economic Role of Financial Corporate Grouping', in M. Aoki, ed., *The Economic Analysis of the Japanese Firm*, Amsterdam 1984; H. Miyajima, 'The Transformation of Zaibatsu to Postwar Corporate Groups: From Hierarchically Integrated Groups to Horizontally Integrated Groups', *Journal of Japanese and International Economies*, vol. viii, 1994; T. Kikkawa, 'Kigyo Shudan: The Formation and Functions of Enterprise Groups', *Business History*, vol. xxxvii, April 1995; Y: Miyazaki, 'Rapid Economic Growth in Postwar Japan: With Special Reference to Excessive Competition and the Formation of Keiretsu', *The Developing Economies*, vol. v, June 1967; Y. Miyazaki, 'The Japanese-Type Structure of Big Business', in K. Sato, ed., *Industry and Business in Japan*, White Plains 1980; R. P. Dore, *Flexible Rigidities*, London 1986.

and supervise them, and adopted the practice of sending representatives to the members' boards of directors to monitor the firms' activities and to provide information and advice, as well as funds.

Because the banks were so deeply involved with their manufacturer-debtors, the latter were able to finance themselves to an unusual extent on the basis of debt rather than equity. Because stocks standardly require higher rates of return than loans (because of the greater risk with which they are usually associated) Japanese manufacturers were thereby enabled to operate at lower rates of profit on total assets (loans plus stocks) than could many of their international competitors, yet still accumulate capital at the same rate. They could also charge lower prices than could their competitors and make the same rate of profit on equity. Equally, because the banks' own fate was so closely tied to that of their manufacturing debtors and because they so closely monitored their debtors' economic activities, they found it both possible and in their own interest to actively commit themselves, on an informal basis, to their debtors' economic success. They were therefore well-disposed to provide large injections of funds when potentially profitable projects suddenly emerged. They were, moreover, able and willing to come up with money to keep their debtors strong and solvent through hard times that were not of their own making, allowing Japanese producers to maintain investment levels, even through recessions, that were an impossibility for most of their rivals in the West.[13]

With debt playing such a big part in corporate finance, equity could assume a different role for Japanese manufacturers than in much of the rest of the capitalist world. By the early 1960s, many leading manufacturers, especially but not only from the groups, had begun implementing a policy whereby they would buy one another's stocks, with the understanding that they would both hold these over the long run and refrain from interfering in one another's operations. The idea was to prevent 'outsiders', possibly American investors, from purchasing shares and thereby to secure the managers' own long-term freedom of action. Firms were thereby relieved from the need to pay large dividends; payments to stockholders out of profits were in fact tiny, especially in comparison with those of the average US firm. They were thus able to invest a greater proportion of their profits than their rivals elsewhere. They were allowed, moreover, to orient their operations to long-run returns, subject only to their ability to satisfy their banker-financiers. The arrangement whereby banks' monitoring and commitment functioned effectively in place of the stock market gave Japanese producers further scope to charge lower prices and accept lower short-term profit rates in the interest of increased market share and higher profit rates in the long run. This provided a big advantage for Japanese manufacturing in the drive for increasing shares of world exports upon which its prosperity ultimately rested.[14]

The Crucial Role of the State

Even given these powerful arrangements for mutual support within manufacturing and between manufacturing and finance, the banks could never have contemplated

---

13   J. C. Abegglen and W. V. Rapp, 'Japanese Managerial Behavior and "Excessive Competition"', *The Developing Economies*, vol. viii, December 1970, 427-30; J. C. Abegglen and G. Stalk, Kaisha, *The Japanese Corporation*, New York 1980, pp. 149-50; Dore, *Flexible Rigidities*, p. 68.

14   Dore, *Flexible Rigidities*, pp. 69-72.

what would have been the exceedingly demanding and perilous task of financing the across the board transformation of industry on their own. The state was therefore, from the start, obliged (and able) to assume a strategic position in shaping the economy. Largely at the expense of workers and consumers, it provided desperately needed investment funds, either directly or through the banks, to Japan's leading corporations and effectively guaranteed their continuing existence. By making financial advances contingent on how these funds would be used, the state was able to go far in determining the direction of the explosive process of growth that its patronage made possible.[15]

During the initial epoch of Japanese manufacturing development, banks found themselves not only incapable of sustaining on their own the enormous risks required, but found themselves chronically short of funds. The government stepped in, formally and informally, to fill the breach, generally with the proviso that the money be used in ways of which the government explicitly approved. Knowing that the government would back them up in case of emergency, banks were thus able to stretch their lending capability through entering into a permanent condition of 'overloan', effectively lending more money than they possessed to their manufacturing customers on the assumption that the Bank of Japan would provide the funds to cover. To make up for the shortfall that remained even so, the state established a series of new lending institutions of its own, notably the Export-Import Bank of Japan and the Japan Development Bank. Under the Fiscal Investment and Loan Program (FILP), the Ministry of Finance, in close collaboration with the Ministry of International Trade and Industry (MITI), funnelled money from the postal savings accounts maintained by households all over the country, through the Export-Import Bank and the Japan Development Bank, into favoured industrial and infrastructural projects. Even as late as the 1970s, the FILP supplied nearly one-third of all bank loans made in Japan, and, over the postwar epoch as a whole, loans under FILP accounted for 15 to 20 per cent of the nation's gross fixed-capital formation.[16]

The state maintained tight control of the credit market, with the goal of keeping interest rates low for the great manufacturing corporations. To that end, during much of the postwar epoch, it protected capital markets from foreign penetration and directly rationed credit, preventing interest rates from reaching the levels they would have done had the market been allowed to operate—and all agents allowed to bid for funds. The authorities thereby ensured that the privileged few were adequately supplied with cheap loans, accomplishing this through their famous 'window guidance', whereby they saw to it that the great 'city' banks at the core of the major horizontal *keiretsu* got most of the money and in turn lent it to their constituent firms. By the same token, consumers were largely deprived of credit,

15   C. Johnson, *MITI and the Japanese Miracle. The Growth of Industrial Policy 1925–75*, Palo Alto 1982, especially ch. 6.
16   T. Okazaki, 'The Evolution of the Financial System in Post-War Japan', *Business History*, vol. xxxvii, April 1995; Y. Noguchi, 'The Role of the Fiscal Investment and Loan Program in Postwar Japanese Economic Growth', in H.-K. Kim et al., eds, *The Japanese Civil Service and Economic Development*, Oxford 1995; W. Hatch and K. Yamamura, *Asia in Japan's Embrace: Building a Regional Production Alliance*, Cambridge 1996, pp. 64–5; K. Nagatani, 'Japanese Economics: The Theory and Practice of Investment Coordination', in J. A. Roumasset and S. Barr, eds, *The Economics of Cooperation. East Asian Development and the Case for Pro-Market Intervention*, Boulder 1992, especially pp. 192–5; Johnson, *MITI and the Japanese Miracle*.

and thereby obliged to put aside money in their bank and postal savings accounts over many years at low interest rates before they could buy big-ticket items, especially housing. The price of housing was intentionally pushed up by the government (for instance, through zoning regulations restricting the number of floors in residences) in order to force savings, further repress consumption, and thereby free up additional funds for investment. Similarly, utilities rates discriminated against consumers and in favour of industrial corporations. The Japanese economy thus secured the highest household savings rate among the advanced capitalist economies, and the government saw to it that much of the money amassed in savings accounts was recycled into industry. Industrial credit was therefore cheap, and became less costly over the whole period to 1970.[17]

The government did not confine itself to the indirect and passive role of ensuring adequate financial resources for industrialization. It used its power to provide loans, tax breaks, and other favours to banks and industrial corporations as a lever to influence the specific direction, as well as the level, of investment. As in Germany, the increase in demand generated by the Korean War fortuitously pulled the Japanese economy from the deep recession precipitated by the implementation of the Dodge Plan. When the Korean War boom petered out, the government stepped in to catalyze a mammoth planned modernization process directed towards the development of heavy industry. It made huge investments in infrastructure—roads, railways, port facilities—which were carefully planned to enable Japanese producers to get their output from their plants to ships for export as cheaply as possible. It allowed, moreover, huge tax breaks on capital investment— accelerated depreciation and the like—and *directly* provided close to 40 per cent of the loans assumed by the steel, coal, electric power, petro-chemical, cement, and shipping industries in the course of the 1950s. The enormous advances it made to fund-starved banks were forwarded on the condition that they would be directed to these priority industries. Gigantic—and otherwise inconceivable—investments in the import of machinery were thus made possible, and further facilitated by government rationing of foreign exchange, which it largely limited to those firms that showed themselves capable of exporting. Over the course of the decade, this programme brought major reductions in the prices for the output of basic industry, paving the way for the emergence, especially from the later 1950s and early 1960s, of a new phase of industrial development, marked by the rise of dynamic new 'processing' sectors which used the outputs of heavy industry, especially the burgeoning transportation (car) and machinery industries. The state gave powerful support to the latter through the Machinery Industry Promotion Temporary Measures Law of 1956 and the Electronics Industry Promotion Provisional Measures Law of 1957, under which it offered extensive loans and other forms of subsidy to the large sector of small, under-capitalized engineering firms that supplied parts and services to the great exporting corporations at the core of the manufacturing economy. To make sure all of these sectors had time to mature, the

17   H. T. Patrick, 'Finance, Capital, and Economic Growth in Japan', in A. Sametz, ed., *Financial Development and Economic Growth. The Economic Consequences of Underdeveloped Capital Markets*, New York 1972; E. Sakakibara, 'The Japanese Financial System in Transition', in T. Agmon, R. Hawkins, and R. Levich, eds, *The Future of the International Monetary System*, Lexington, Mass. 1984.

government provided an umbrella of trade protection across manufacturing, treating virtually the whole sector, in defiance of neoclassical orthodoxy, as 'infant industry' for an extended period, and prohibited most direct investment in Japan by foreign multinational corporations.[18]

The government sought not only to stimulate the most rapid possible growth of investment, especially in those sectors it deemed most strategic, but to control its effects by regulating its level through the organization and sanction of investment cartels. In so doing, it aimed to avoid the 'ruinous' price competition that tended to result from cost-cutting and that threatened to undermine profits on the huge fixed-capital investments required for development. The problem with cartels, of course, is that, in the process of reducing risk and guaranteeing profits, they also reduce the competitive pressure to improve. The government went some distance to overcome this drawback by forcing firms to compete for the right to invest. Under its 'administrative guidance', firms were allowed to invest only in proportion to their share of the market. To increase their investment quotas, firms were thus obliged to struggle to raise their market share, and—given the at least formal absence of price competition—they were obliged to accomplish this through making the fullest utilization of their capacity, introducing new cost-cutting techniques, and improving the quality of their goods, while carrying out mergers and acquisitions. Investment skyrocketed leading to rapid improvement, with ever greater economies of scale further facilitated by a powerful trend to industrial concentration across manufacturing.[19]

Even in the presence of investment cartels, the market tended to become flooded and to put downward pressure on prices. But the government made sure that overproduction caused minimal damage by establishing recession cartels, which, by more firmly setting prices and quantities, allowed firms to maintain profits despite over-stocked markets, again at the expense of consumers. Japanese big businesses could thus have it both ways, as their leading rivals overseas could not: they were able to lay down great quantities of fixed capital embodying the best technology at a dizzying pace and thereby rapidly increase productivity; but they could largely avoid the premature obsolescence and reduced profitability that might result from their competitors' introduction of lower-cost, lower-priced goods and/or overproduction in the line. They thereby increased their already enhanced ability to maintain their levels of investment through recessions. With domestic prices artificially inflated, moreover, they were enabled to more easily increase international market share by reducing their prices on exports below what they charged on sales at home.[20]

---

18   Johnson, *MITI and the Japanese Miracle*, pp. 202–18; Kosai, *Era of High-Speed Growth*, pp. 80–90; Y. Kosai, 'The Reconstruction Period', in R. Komiya, ed., *Industrial Policy of Japan*, Tokyo 1988; K. Imai, 'Japan's Changing Industrial Structure and US–Japan Industrial Relations', in K. Yamamura, ed., *Policy and Trade Issues of the Japanese Economy*, Seattle 1982; K. Imai, 'Japan's Industrial Organization', in *Industry and Business in Japan*; M. Shinohara, *Industrial Growth, Trade, and Dynamic Patterns in the Japanese Economy*, Tokyo 1982, pp. 22, 29–30, 50, 113.
19   For this and the following two paragraphs, K. Yamamura, 'Success that Soured: Administrative Guidance and Cartels in Japan', in *Policy and Trade Issues of the Japanese Economy*; Imai, 'Japan's Changing Industrial Structure', p. 49; Imai, 'Japan's Industrial Organization', pp. 81–3; C. Johnson, 'Japan: Who Governs? An Essay on Official Bureaucracy'. *Journal of Japanese Studies*, vol. ii, Autumn 1975.
20   Yamamura, 'Success that Soured', p. 101.

In sum, with the help of the banks and their associated networks of manufacturing firms, the state placed giant investment funds into the hands of Japan's large corporations, which it believed were the economic agents best equipped to carry out the growth process, while making sure that money flowed most freely to enterprises in those sectors it saw as strategic—initially heavy industry, then the processing industries. At the same time—and indispensably—it *disciplined* the corporations by obliging them to enter into intense competition for market share, both at home through imposing investment quotas and abroad through requiring export performance as a condition for financial support. Finally, with its implicit guarantee against the business failure of the leading corporations, the state offered Japanese capital the most secure possible environment for profit-making, thereby facilitating, for close to two decades, what would otherwise have been the hazardous process of investing 'in advance of the market'.

The Slow Growth of Wages

It remains to explain why, in view of the unprecedented rates of accumulation of capital, wages failed to increase so as to place greater pressure on profits. During much of the 1950s, the slow growth of real wages compared to labour productivity was, in part, due to the presence of the huge population of semi-employed labour and labour of low productivity that remained in agriculture and the small business sector. As late as 1950, half the labouring population was in agriculture; self-employed people in small businesses, plus small farmers and their workers, made up 60.6 per cent of Japan's labour force.[21] By drawing upon this huge pool of workers, the industrial economy could at once secure productivity gains by transferring labour into manufacturing and keep wages down by keeping labour supply up with labour demand. Even so, by the end of the 1950s, unemployment had fallen to 1 per cent. Given this much pressure in the labour market, labour's share would surely have been higher, had it not been for the intervention of a Japanese labour movement oriented to the needs of capital accumulation.

Japanese unions were organized on a firm-by-firm basis. This type of 'enterprise union' structure had not prevented their functioning as powerful weapons of struggle in workers' temporarily successful efforts of the immediate postwar years to win a measure of control over the labour process and over hiring and firing. But management had reversed labour's gains and, by the middle to late 1950s, achieved virtually unchallenged hegemony on the shop floor. New, more moderate trade-union federations had risen to prominence on the ruins of their more militant predecessors, and, in just a few years, Japanese unionists had transformed themselves from among the most strike-prone to among the least strike-prone in the world.[22]

With prospects for further successful resistance so profoundly reduced, many workers saw little choice but to hitch their fate to that of their firms, and to seek to improve their condition by improving their firms' profitability. The significance of enterprise unions was thus transformed. Far from taking workers out of competition with workers in other firms in the same industry—the basic function of standard trade unionism—Japanese enterprise unions yoked their members to the competitive

---

21 Itoh, *Japanese Capitalism*, p. 145.
22 Armstrong et al., *Capitalism Since 1945*, p. 263, Table 15.1.

process. Enterprise unions in Japan thereby came to provide the perfect institutional framework for eliciting the collaboration of the labour force in the tumultuous processes by which new technology was rapidly introduced and production radically reorganized, allowing for the intensification of labour and increasing flexibility in the allocation of labour on the shop floor. At the same time, employees were made acutely conscious of the need to keep their wage demands in line with productivity growth and the requirements of their firms' profitability.[23]

While the emergence of this new system of collaborative labour relations had as its historical precondition the persistent application of great force against labour, its relatively smooth reproduction is incomprehensible without reference to the gains it provided the labour force, especially those sections employed in the great manufacturing corporations. These workers accrued steady wage increases, which were very substantial in absolute, if not in relative, terms. More significantly perhaps, they were able to win guaranteed 'lifetime employment'—an assured job with their firm until enforced retirement at about the age of fifty-five. Still, the great corporations derived a great deal of benefit from 'lifetime employment', because its obverse side, so to speak, was a system of promotion by seniority that effectively confined employees to the same company throughout their careers by stipulating that employees who left their firm would lose their seniority. With the likelihood that their employees would leave thereby reduced, Japanese corporations could safely invest in and profit from their employees' skills and education to a degree unimaginable for the typical capitalist employer dependent upon the market in mobile wage labour. Because firms could not fire their employees, employers were obliged to treat them as one more, very major, fixed cost, thereby acquiring a powerful incentive to keep investment up during the course of recessions and, in extremis, to diversify into new lines rather than to cut back when the market would no longer absorb their output at former levels.

In view not only of the dynamism but also the stability of the accumulation process during the first two postwar decades, the great Japanese corporations could hardly have been much inconvenienced financially by the grant of permanent employment. Intentionally or not, moreover, the labour movement effectively compensated capital for this privilege by refraining from extending its organization beyond the 30 per cent or so of the labour force employed by the leading manufacturing companies (union density, it will be recalled, had risen above 45 per cent during the postwar labour upsurge, but had then fallen by a third in the wake of the ensuing employers' offensive). Workers employed in the myriad small shops which supplied the great corporations were left un-unionized. Corporations therefore had an especially powerful incentive to 'contract out' production to these firms, and to constitute and expand those vertical networks of subordinated, but nonetheless formally independent, suppliers (vertical *keiretsu*) which provided a great proportion of their semi-finished inputs. By this means, the major companies could both enhance their own profits, since their suppliers paid lower wages than they did themselves, and cushion themselves from the business cycle, since they could oblige these sup-

---

23   Tokunaga, 'A Marxist Interpretation of Japanese Industrial Relations', pp. 315–17. Having ceded to management a virtual monopoly on the shop floor, unions had little role but to organize the annual 'Spring Offensive' on wages.

pliers and their workers to absorb the unused capacity and the unemployment which accompanied business downturns. While the great corporations at the core of the economy thus dominated and exploited their suppliers, they also maintained very close, long-term relationships with them, helping them to improve their technology and productive organization with the aim of making them maximally competitive precisely so that there would be no need to replace them.[24]

Investment-Led, Export-Oriented Growth

Japan's rapid growth process during the 1950s and beyond was 'investment-led' and based heavily on the home market. Demand grew rapidly as a result of the rapid growth of investment, the sharp increase of the labour force, and the vigorous real wage growth facilitated by the large increases of labour productivity. But Japanese growth was also, from the start, export-oriented, indeed fundamentally dependent upon exports. The ability to rapidly raise productivity allowed the Japanese economy to increase its competitive advantage and its share of the world market with respect to its leading overseas rivals in a growing range of manufacturing lines. But, as for the German economy, rapid export growth was for the Japanese economy itself a basic condition for maintaining such rates of productivity increase. It was also indispensable for maintaining the high levels of capacity utilization required to cover the enormous fixed costs that resulted from the economy's fast growth of capital stock, its dependence on debt financing, and its commitment to permanent employment.[25]

For the Japanese economy, as for the German, successful export growth was not only a manifestation of its producers' ability to keep costs down, but also an artefact of policy. Both fiscal and monetary policy were keyed to controlling inflation in general and promoting exports in particular. Until the mid 1960s, the Japanese government, like Germany's, always maintained a balanced budget, eschewing any sort of Keynesian fiscal policy, and in this way actually repressed home demand.[26] Monetary policy was formulated so as to maintain the balance of payments. Throughout the length of the long upturn, the mechanism of the Japanese business cycle was thus driven by government action. Until the mid 1960s, each investment boom would eventually threaten to send the balance of payments into deficit. In response, the government would deliberately tighten the money supply so as to engineer a recession, reducing imports and lowering pressure on export prices. 'When the recession had sufficiently redressed the payments imbalance … monetary policy was shifted toward ease, encouraging growth to resume at its own pace until the need for restriction again became clear.' Domestic expansion, in particular the growth of domestic demand, was thus subordinated to the requirements of export growth, in particular the need to control export prices, and domestic production costs were kept in line with the requirements of international competition. The state was of course also giving the strongest possible support to the drive to

---

24 On the 'relational contracting' (neither vertical integration nor arm's length contracting) that characterized the links between the core firm and their vertical network of suppliers, see Dore, *Flexible Rigidities*, pp. 77–8.

25 See Shinohara, *Industrial Growth*, p. 23.

26 On fiscal policy, see G. Ackley and H. Ishi, 'Fiscal, Monetary, and Related Policies', in H. Patrick and H. Rosovsky, eds, *Asia's New Giant*, Washington, DC 1976.

increase exports by subsidizing investment in export industries and providing a high degree of protection to Japan's largely export-oriented manufacturers.[27]

Japan enjoyed the lowest rate of manufacturing price increase of all the advanced industrial economies throughout most of the two decades after 1950. The wholesale price index for the manufacturing sector grew by a *total* of 1 per cent between 1955 and 1960. Japan's international competitiveness thus improved steadily and significantly over the course of the 1950s. Manufacturing unit labour costs in Japan remained virtually level between 1950 and 1960, while those of the US grew by about 40 per cent and those of Germany by a little less than 20 per cent. Export prices for Japan actually declined at an average annual rate of 1.9 per cent over that period, while those for Germany and the US increased at average annual rates of 0.5 per cent and 2.2 per cent, respectively. Japan's exports could thus increase at an average annual rate of 14.9 per cent between 1951 and 1960 (15 per cent between 1951 and 1965), 50 per cent faster than the growth of output.[28]

The Japanese economy, like the German, took advantage of its rapid export growth to secure otherwise unachievable productivity gains, both by securing economies of scale in particular lines and by constructing an exceptionally large manufacturing sector, the locus of accelerated processes of technical change that could not have been matched in other sectors. Between 1952 and 1960, Japanese exports as a share of GDP rose by 14 per cent. But this aggregate figure does more to obscure than illuminate the central place of export growth in postwar Japanese development, because it distracts attention from the fundamental role of exports in underwriting the pivotal, and extraordinarily dynamic, Japanese manufacturing sector. By 1960, the share of manufacturing exports in manufacturing output had grown to 28 per cent, and contributed significantly to the increase of the share of Japanese manufacturing output in total output from 19.5 per cent to 26.4 per cent and of the manufacturing labour force in the total labour force from about 15 per cent to 22 per cent during the previous decade.[29]

The rapid growth of international trade during the 1950s and the 1960s was for Japan, as for Germany, an enabling condition for export expansion. Still, like Germany, Japan could not have increased its exports anywhere near as energetically as it did except by appropriating an increasing share of world exports. Between 1950 and 1959, Japan doubled its share of the manufacturing exports of the twelve leading capitalist economies, from 3.3 per cent to 6.6 per cent (and to 7.6 per cent by 1963); in this way it accounted for no less than 75 per cent of the total increase in its exports in this period (1950–59). Had Japan merely maintained its market share, its exports would have increased in these years by only a quarter of the amount they actually did. Japan's was the only economy besides Germany's to substantially increase its share of the world market over this period. The two countries' gains, taken together, accounted for almost the total loss sustained by the US and the UK.[30]

27   Ibid., pp. 178–9, 181ff, 219 (quotation); Kosai, *Era of High-Speed Growth*, pp. 100–1, 104–5, 106.

28   Daly, 'Japanese Manufacturing Competitiveness', p. 39; L. Krause and S. Sekiguchi, 'Japan and the World Economy', in *Asia's New Giant*, p. 401; Ackley and Ishi, 'Fiscal, Monetary, and Related Policies', p. 175.

29   Itoh, *Japanese Capitalism*, p. 146.

30   Maizels, *Industrial Growth and World Trade*, pp. 189, 200–1; A. D. Morgan, 'Export Competition and Import Substitution: The Industrial Countries 1963–71', in R. A. Batchelor et al., eds, *Industrialization and the Basis for Trade*, Cambridge 1980, p. 48.

The high degree of confidence that allowed manufacturers to unleash Japan's extraordinary postwar wave of investment is, in the last analysis, incomprehensible apart from their ability to virtually count on being able to invade the markets of their main overseas competitors. Japanese manufacturing thus developed through hot-housed 'excessive competition', bringing about debt-financed over-investment, leading systematically to manufacturing over-production. The tendency to over-production had a major potential for disruption because of the economy's unusually high reliance on fixed costs—inevitable interest payments on the loans taken out to cover the huge investments in plant and equipment and invariant wage bills for a labour force that could not be laid off. Cartels were constructed to cope with the tendency to over-production, but they could be only partially effective. Japanese manufacturers therefore had no choice but to sell abroad, and it made sense to do so as long as the prices they could secure exceeded their costs for variable capital. The unavoidable outcome were those 'concentrated downpourings of exports' for which the Japanese economy became famous—or infamous.[31] It is hardly surprising that, in pursuing this course, the Japanese economy, even more than the German, cramped the growth potentials of its leading competitors, and, in the longer run, as we shall see, threatened the stability of the entire international system.

---

31   Yamamura, 'Success that Soured', pp. 99–100; Shinohara, *Industrial Growth*, pp. 110–14.

Chapter 7

ACCOUNTING FOR THE LONG BOOM

From the late 1940s into the mid 1960s, the advanced capitalist economies experienced a boom of historic proportions. But the trajectories of the US, Japanese, and German economies in this period provide little basis for concluding that this extraordinary spurt of growth was attributable to the emergence of new institutions making for the steady increase of effective demand through the welfare state, the 'capital-labour accord', and Keynesian demand management. The increased steadiness in the growth of demand, resulting from the permanently increased size of the state sector in most of the advanced capitalist economies, must have helped endow these economies with greater stability than in the past. It may also have made for increased confidence on the part of capitalists, encouraging them to invest and innovate. But in Germany and Japan, where the most rapid growth took place, supply-side conditions were clearly responsible for economic dynamism. In the US, by contrast, the economy grew slowly during the 1950s, despite the subsidy of demand by public deficits and the growth of the wage share, and its brief takeoff during the first half of the 1960s was made possible largely by holding down the growth of wages and increasing productivity by means of intensifying labour.

Where the autonomous growth of demand *did* operate powerfully to augment investment, growth and stability, it did so, paradoxically, less within national boundaries than across them. German and Japanese manufacturers derived much of their dynamism by means of appropriating large segments of the fast-growing world market from the US and UK, while beginning to invade the US domestic market. This redistribution of market share—the filling of orders (demand) by German and Japanese manufacturers that had formerly been supplied by US producers—gave a powerful boost to their investment and output, while detracting somewhat from the growth prospects of the US and the UK. The resulting pattern of development was highly uneven, but it made for a boom of historic proportions.

Even in the early to mid 1960s, the process of international competition leading to the redistribution of export shares appeared not only inevitable, but to be welcomed. The game's big winners had been Germany and Japan, recently economic basket cases, and its losers were the old wealthy hegemons, the US and the UK, and then only in relative terms. From a global standpoint, moreover, the effects of international competition in terms of the redistribution of world export shares were clearly subordinate to those arising from the growth of the international division of labour. It is true that improvements in the relative cost position of manufacturing production in Germany and elsewhere had been detrimental to the manufacturing sector in the US to the degree that it attracted investment overseas and away from

Table 7.1. Exports of manufactures as a percentage of manufacturing output.

	1913	1950
Germany	31	13
Japan	40	29
France	33	23
US	45	23
Total for advanced industrial economies (including US)	18	10

Source: Maizels, *Industrial Growth and World Trade*, p. 223.

the domestic economy. Nevertheless, the increasing of competitiveness of German and Japanese manufacturing exports in this period appears to have had relatively little direct negative effect on US production or profits for the simple reason that goods produced abroad remained as yet to only a limited extent able to compete in the US market itself and because US producers as yet depended to only a small degree on overseas sales. Because the German and Japanese economies were still so small relatively to that of the US, the appropriation of relatively minor shares of the US market could have a major positive impact on the growth of their exports while having little negative effect on US producers. Uneven development was thus even at the start of the 1960s still to a surprising extent separate development, unmediated by world trade and the world division of labour.

At the start of the 1950s, reflecting the collapse of world trade in the interwar period, advanced capitalist countries' manufactured exports constituted just 10 per cent of manufacturing output (in constant prices), about half the proportion in 1913.[1] Over the following decade, the growth of trade was quite rapid. Still, even by the early 1960s, trade represented a very restricted part of total output, especially in the US.[2] As late as 1965, imports constituted a mere 3.1 per cent of the US market and manufacturing imports just 5.4 per cent. US exports at this point constituted just 5.1 per cent of GDP and manufacturing exports only 8.8 per cent of manufacturing output. Up to that point, Japanese and German exports were unable to much affect US manufacturing profitability by forcing down the prices of goods in relation to their costs. Prices rose just as rapidly in the manufacturing sector as in non-manufacturing in the years between 1950 and 1958, when manufacturing profitability fell substantially. This was the case even though the former sector produced mostly tradables and was therefore subject to the pressure of international competition, whereas the latter sector produced mainly non-tradables and was therefore mostly invulnerable to it. It was because US-based manufacturers founded their

1   Glyn et al., 'Rise and Fall of the Golden Age', p. 43; Maizels, *Industrial Growth and World Trade*, p. 223.
2   Due to the rapid growth of output for the home market, between 1950 and 1960 the proportion of GNP that was exported (in current prices) actually declined in both Europe and Japan—from 22.3 per cent to 21.0 per cent for the former, and from 12.7 per cent to 10.5 per cent for the latter, although it increased substantially in constant prices. Glyn et al., 'The Rise and Fall of the Golden Age', p. 43, 50–2, 87.

growth to such a great extent on the US domestic market, and because their foreign rivals were only just beginning to compete strongly in that market, that US manufacturers' loss of world export share had so little impact on their profitability.

The fact remains that the intensification of international competition retained the potential for undercutting profitability more directly. The same processes of technical innovation leading to cost- and price-cutting that enabled some to improve their shares of world trade could undermine the ability of others, not only to attract investment funds, but to realize their investments at their former rates of return, threatening profitability not only in particular economies but in the advanced capitalist world as a whole. It would not indeed be long before just such processes would reveal their potential for disruption, not only of the world's leading economy, that of the US, but of the international system as a whole.

PART THREE
From Boom to Downturn

Chapter 8

DESCENT INTO CRISIS

During the brief period between 1965 and 1973, the advanced capitalist world was suddenly projected from boom to crisis. Profitability for the G-7 economies, taken individually and in aggregate, fell sharply, especially in manufacturing, initiating a long epoch of reduced rates of profit on capital stock. With some lag, investment growth fell sharply and in secular fashion, leading to severe reductions in the growth of output, of productivity, and of real wages, as well as sharply higher rates of unemployment and much more severe recessions.

As I shall try to demonstrate, the onset of the long downturn across the advanced capitalist world is comprehensible in terms of the mechanisms leading to profitability decline sketched earlier.[1] Between 1965 and 1973, German and especially Japanese manufacturers combined relatively advanced techniques and relatively low wages to reduce costs sharply relative to those of their competitors; they dramatically seized increased shares of the world market and imposed on it their relatively reduced prices. Their competitors found themselves facing reduced prices for their output with the same production costs as before. Some had to withdraw. Others, to hold on to their markets, had no choice but to accept significantly reduced profit shares, output-capital ratios, and profit rates since they could not raise prices above costs as much as they had previously. As a result of the unplanned-for irruption of lower-priced Japanese and German goods onto the market, US manufacturing producers in particular turned out to have over-invested, in the sense that they were unable to secure the established rate of return on their placements of capital and labour. Over-capacity and over-production leading to falling aggregate profitability in the manufacturing sector of the G-7 economies was the result. Between 1965 and 1973, US manufacturers sustained a decline in the rate of return on their capital stock of over 40 per cent. Because the US manufacturing capital stock represented such a large share of the G-7 total, the G-7 economies sustained a fall in their aggregate manufacturing profitability of about twenty-five per cent in those same years.[2] Well before the oil crisis, then, the advanced capitalist economies as a whole were facing a significant problem of profitability.

Still, a fall in profitability, even a sharp one, does not necessarily create longer term economic difficulties. Such problems emerged in this case because, in response to their reduced rates of profit, higher-cost—mainly US—manufacturers failed to redirect their investments sufficiently into other lines. Instead, they sought to

---

1   See above, Chapter 2.
2   Armstrong et al., *Capitalism Since 1945*, p. 351, Table A1.

maintain their output and retain their markets by lowering their prices and accepting reduced profit rates, reproducing in the process system-wide over-capacity and over-production. Because they possessed great masses of fixed capital that was sunk, already paid for, these firms had every reason to try to retain their place in the market so long as they could make at least the average rate of profit on their new advances of circulating capital. This was all the more the case, given their vast accumulation of proprietary intangible assets—most especially technical knowledge, but also ties to suppliers and customers and the like—as well as their ability to take on debt to make possible modernization investments and tide them through recessions. A long economic downturn thus began because the stereo-typical process of adjustment—whereby firms suffering reduced profit rates cut back production and move into new lines, bringing supply and demand back into line and restoring average profitability—failed to take place.

Falling profitability was not long confined to the US economy, but soon enveloped all of the leading capitalist economies, including Germany and Japan. In attempting to sustain their position on the market, US producers were obliged to accept their fixed-capital costs as given. But they had other ways to respond. They could try themselves to improve efficiency by bringing in new techniques. They could attempt to reduce wage growth and intensify labour. They could turn to their government to secure currency and trade policies that would improve domestic firms' competi-tiveness by increasing their overseas competitors' relative costs. In fact, US manufacturers achieved some success on all these fronts. They repressed labour and the growth of wage costs to an extent that their competitors found impossible to match. They also unleashed a major wave of investment designed to update their plant and equipment. But what was ultimately most decisive, by triggering a pro-found crisis of the international monetary system, the US government forced a very major devaluation of the dollar, which sharply reduced the relative costs of US man-ufacturers at the expense of their main overseas rivals in Germany and Japan.

The international monetary crisis was itself prepared by the same processes of over-investment resulting from uneven development and intensifying international competition that had precipitated the initial fall in profitability in the US. Japanese and German manufacturers based the final stages of their postwar booms in large part on the accelerated penetration of a US home market that was rapidly expanding in response to the precipitate rise of US federal deficits. But the unavoidable con-comitant of the stepped-up subsidy of US domestic demand, and the ongoing repression of German and Japanese domestic demand, was the emergence of record-breaking US current account deficits and record-breaking Japanese and German current account surpluses. The rise of such deficits and surpluses could not but pre-cipitate a fundamental revision in international exchange rates, in favour of US and at the expense of German and Japanese competitiveness. Between 1970 and 1973, US producers were thus able to markedly improve their international competitive posi-tion and thereby shift, to some degree, the weight of the overall international decline of profitability in manufacturing on to their leading overseas rivals, extending the profitability crisis to both Japan and Germany but without resolving it at home.

In what follows, I shall attempt to provide evidence and argumentation for the foregoing interpretation. In the process, I shall try to demonstrate that the rise of working-class resistance in the three economies in this period was more a consequence than a cause of the problems of profitability, a response to the offensives unleashed by employers to restore their rates of return. I take as my point of departure an empirical critique of what remains today the dominant view, that of the supply-side theorists.

1. The United States: A Falling Rate of Profit

The origins of the long downturn in the advanced capitalist world are to be found in the US economy in the years after 1965. Between 1965 and 1973, the rates of profit in the manufacturing and private business sectors fell by 40.9 per cent and 29.3 per cent, respectively. Put another way, from the business cycle that marked the height of the long postwar upturn, which ran from the second quarter of 1960 through to the third quarter of 1969, to the first business cycle of the long downturn, which ran from the fourth quarter of 1969 through to the third quarter of 1973, the average rates of profit in the manufacturing and private business sectors fell by 31 per cent and 18.5 per cent, respectively. Profitability in the US economy thus began a downward trajectory that would not bottom out until the early 1980s. The fact that the profitability decline predates 1973 is significant, because it implies that the fall in profitability that set off the long downturn, coming as it did *before* the onset of the oil crisis, could not have been caused by it. What, then, lay behind the fall in profitability?

According to advocates of the consensus, supply-side view, the fall in profitability was the result of the out-running by wage growth of productivity growth, which was itself an expression of labour's enhanced market and socio-institutional power and pressure. I will try to refute this interpretation by showing that profits were squeezed, not so much by increased upward pressure on costs resulting from the exercise of increased power by workers, as by increased downward pressure on prices reflecting intensified international competition leading to over-capacity and over-production in the market for manufactures.

In criticism of the idea that workers squeezed profits by pushing up costs, I make three main points to prepare the ground for my own analysis. First, the growth of real wages, a rough-and-ready indicator of workers' influence, fell not only in the short run but in the long term—first during the period of rising profitability from 1958 through 1965, then during the period of falling profitability from 1965 through 1973. A fifteen-year slowdown in the growth of real wages would seem to bespeak the opposite of increasing workers' power. Second, there is no trend toward declining productivity growth before 1973, since the growth of manufacturing productivity actually increased in this period, while that of the private business economy as a whole failed to fall. It is therefore hard to see how increased workers' resistance and slacking on the shop floor could have brought down profitability by undermining productiveness. Third, in the non-manufacturing private business economy—the entire private business economy excluding manufacturing—the effect of workers' upward pressure on costs to the detriment of the profit rate could have manifested itself only with relation to the profit share, since there was no decline whatsoever in the productivity of capital; moreover, the fall of the profit share was limited and the proportion of that fall attributable to increasing pressure from workers even more so.

The fall in profitability was disproportionately great in the manufacturing sector. But, neither the substantial declines in the manufacturing profit share nor the manufacturing output-capital ratio which together determined the decline in the manufacturing profit rate can be shown to be attributable to pressure from labour on wages or productivity. On the contrary. Manufacturing profitability fell because producers were unable to mark up prices over costs sufficiently to maintain their established rates of return. It is the central role of downward pressure on prices in determining the fall in the US profit rate between 1965 and 1973 that constitutes the point of departure for the interpretation of the onset of the long downturn in terms of the unforeseen irruption of low-cost Japanese and German products onto the world market and the onset of manufacturing over-capacity and over-production that this brought about.

Wages, Labour Productivity, and the Power of Labour

It has become something of a commonplace that a 'wage explosion', conditioned by rapidly falling unemployment and driven by an increase in workers' power and militancy, was responsible for the initial squeeze on profitability in the US economy which began in the latter half of the 1960s. The prima facie basis for this view is twofold. First, there was a major increase in strike activity in these years. Second, during the period 1965 through 1973 when profitability initially declined, the average annual growth of nominal compensation in the private business economy, at 6.8 per cent, was more than 40 per cent greater than that during the period 1950 through 1965. Nevertheless, if the apparent explosion of militancy and of the nominal wage from 1965 through 1973 are placed in context—by reference to the longer-term evolution of profitability, unemployment, and the growth of workers' purchasing power—they may be seen to represent no autonomous wage push, conditioned by tight labour markets and reflecting enhanced workers' power, but understood as what they actually were: a lagging response on the part of labour to a spectacular increase in profitability between 1958 and 1965, to an extended decline in real wage growth between 1958 and 1973, and to an acceleration of inflation from 1965.

By the time that nominal wages began to accelerate in the period from the mid 1960s, the US was in the midst of the longest period of uninterrupted expansion in its history (1961–69). During this period, the rate of unemployment fell from an average of 5.8 per cent over the recession-plagued years from 1958 through 1961 to an average of 4.4 per cent for 1966–73, from a peak of 6.7 per cent in 1961 to a low of 3.5 per cent in 1969. Were profits squeezed and real wage growth enhanced as a result of falling unemployment? The data would appear to confirm the opposite hypothesis.

Almost all of the decline in the rate of unemployment that occurred during the 1960s boom took place between 1961 and 1966, when unemployment fell from 6.7 per cent to 3.8 per cent; yet, during these years, the rate of profit *rose* by 46.6 per cent and 46.3 per cent in manufacturing and the private business economy, respectively. Between 1966 and 1969, the unemployment rate did fall a bit further, from 3.8 per cent to 3.5 per cent; but it is difficult to see how such a small decline could have played a major role in determining the substantial fall in profitability that began in those years, especially in light of the fact that profitability fell significantly further after 1969 when unemployment rose. The relationship between the state of the labour market and profitability over the course of the 1960s is more in line with the theory of Kalecki—who expected that falling unemployment would maintain or increase profitability by raising capacity utilization and sales so as to compensate for any accompanying increase in wage growth compared to productivity growth—than with that of his followers-cum-revisers.

Nor did workers benefit in terms of their real wages during the period of declining unemployment, as might have been expected according to the supply-side argument. In 1966, when nominal wage growth began to accelerate, workers both in manufacturing and outside it had been watching their real wage increases steadily shrink. During the period 1950–58, the average annual growth of real compensation in manufacturing and in the private business economy as a whole was higher than for any other comparable period of time after 1945, averaging 3.6 per cent and 3.1 per cent, respectively, and precipitated a major wages-productivity squeeze on profits, especially in manufacturing. In the years 1958–65, the period in which the US economy established its greatest postwar momentum, average annual real wage growth nonetheless fell off markedly—by 40 per cent in manufacturing and by 12 per cent in the private business economy as a whole. A period in which profitability soared and the growth of real compensation, especially in manufacturing, was reduced, despite falling unemployment, thus forms the longer-term context for the acceleration of nominal wage growth from the mid 1960s onwards.

Nor did the trend in real wage growth shift upward thereafter. From late in 1965, under the impetus of stepped-up Vietnam War spending, inflation suddenly accelerated, the consumer price index growing at an average annual rate of 4.8 per cent between 1965 and 1973, compared to 1.4 per cent between 1958 and 1965 (and 1.6 per cent for the whole period 1950–65). This acceleration of the increase in prices more than cancelled out the increase in the growth of nominal compensation that took place during this period. Between 1965 and 1973, while the profit rate in the private business economy fell by a total of 29.3 per cent, the average annual growth of real compensation declined to 2.3 per cent, compared to 2.8 per cent for the years 1950–65 (2.6 per cent for 1958-65, and 3.1 per cent for 1950–58), a fall of 19 per cent. In the same period, while profitability dropped by a total of 40.9 per cent in the manufacturing sector, the average annual growth of manufacturing real compensation fell by 34 per cent, averaging 1.9 per cent, compared to 2.9 per cent for the years 1950–65 (2.2 per cent for 1958–65, 3.6 per cent for 1950–58). On the face of it, these long-term developments would seem to indicate the opposite of growing labour strength during the period of falling profitability. The question posed by this data would seem rather to be why profitability could not be better maintained in view of the significant limitation on real wage growth.

In fact, advocates of the supply-side approach to the long downturn in the US have tended to attribute the squeeze on profitability much more to a decline in labour productivity growth—the onset of a 'productivity crisis'—than to an increase in real wage growth. In the words of Jeffrey Sachs, a 'rising labor share came about because productivity growth slowed without a commensurate slowdown in real wages'.[3] The authors of *The Golden Age of Capitalism*, as well as representatives of the US Social Structure of Accumulation School and of the French Regulation School, hold the same position, arguing that, beginning in the later 1960s, workers were able to take advantage of high employment and the

---

3   Sachs, 'Wages, Profits, and Macroeconomic Adjustment', pp. 275, 280.

reduced cost of job loss made possible by unemployment insurance to reduce the amount of effort put forward per unit of wages, while increasing their resistance on the shop floor. What, then, is the evidence that an increase in workers' pressure leading to a decline in the rate of productivity growth was behind the decline in the rate of profit?

The experience of the manufacturing sector provides a critical test. It is not just that this sector is economically central. It is the place where one would have expected workers' shop floor resistance to be most in evidence, both most marked and easiest to detect. Yet, annual labour productivity growth in manufacturing actually increased during the period of profitability decline, averaging 3.3 per cent between 1965 and 1973, compared to 2.9 per cent between 1950 and 1965.[4]

Nor did labour productivity growth in the private business economy as a whole fall noticeably in the period of profitability decline. Between 1965 and 1973, it increased at an average annual rate of 2.7 per cent, compared to 2.8 per cent between 1950 and 1965.[5] Indeed, were one to adjust for the business cycle—to allow for the fact that when the economy turns down, productivity initially falls simply as a consequence of businesses' failure to immediately shed labour in proportion to the reduced output resulting from reduced demand—the growth of productivity in the private economy between 1965 and 1973 would undoubtedly be shown to have increased.[6]

Nevertheless, the foregoing data would, in itself, be unlikely to convince advocates of the supply-side approach to the long downturn. Defenders of that perspective would respond to the data on the growth of real wages by pointing out that, in accounting for trends in profitability, what counts is not the real wage (which refers to the money wage expressed in terms of the bundle of consumer goods it can purchase—that is, the nominal wage adjusted by the consumer price index) but rather the product wage (which refers to the money wage expressed in terms of the amount of output—in its own industry or sector—that it can purchase, that is, the nominal wage adjusted by the product or output price deflator). It is, after all, the nominal wage expressed in terms of the prices of what they sell, rather than of what their workers buy, which is of concern to employers. Advocates of the supply-side perspective would point out further that whether or not a given trend in productivity can be said to represent an increase in the power of labour cannot be determined until that trend is directly related to the

---

4   Manufacturing labour productivity growth did fall briefly, though sharply, in the last years of the 1960s, when the economy went through successive periods of over-heating and recession, both of which were almost certainly characterized by (cyclical) over-manning. But the initial fall was more than offset by the subsequent sharp rise in labour productivity from 1970, making for the overall increase in productivity growth, compared with 1950–65.

5   Between 1965 and 1973, total factor productivity in manufacturing averaged 1.36 per cent per annum, almost the same as the average annual rate of 1.42 per cent between 1950 and 1965. Similarly the rates for the private business economy over the same periods were 1.6 per cent and 1.8 per cent, respectively. 'Multifactor Productivity Trends, 1995 and 1996', in US Department of Labor, BLS, *News*, 6 May 1998, Tables 5, 6.

6   As R.J. Gordon concludes, 'It was during the 1967–73 period that concern first surfaced about the behavior of US productivity growth … It now appears, however, that this slow-down mainly reflects cyclical phenomena … a tendency that seems to surface in the last stage of every business cycle for firms to allow themselves to become overstaffed.' 'Postwar Macroeconomics: The Evolution of Events and Ideas', p. 144 and p. 161, n.41.

parallel trend in the product wage—the evolution of the profit share. Finally, they would say, it is not only through affecting the growth of labour productivity relative to the growth of product compensation that workers can affect the profit rate, but also through affecting the growth of the productivity of capital. To understand the fall in profitability that took place between 1965 and 1973, we are therefore obliged to analyze the experience not only of the profit share, but also of the output-capital ratio.

The Profit Share

The Non-Manufacturing Private Business Sector. Between 1965 and 1973, the average annual growth of the product wage in the private business economy outside of manufacturing, at 2.75 per cent, was roughly the same as between 1950 and 1965, at 2.65 per cent. But, the average annual growth of non-manufacturing labour productivity fell in these years to 2.4 per cent from 2.7 per cent (to 2.3 per cent from 2.7 per cent in net terms), and the profit share did decline, at an average annual rate of 2 per cent, or by 15.6 per cent over the initial period of profitability decline.

The fact remains that increased pressure on the part of labour caused hardly any of the fall in the non-manufacturing profit share. What was mainly behind it was increasing indirect business taxes, mainly at the state and local levels. If no adjustment is made for the growth of indirect business taxes, the profit share fell at an average annual rate of just 0.7 per cent between 1965 and 1973. Put another way, even on the assumption that labour was responsible for the entire decline, rising labour resistance would have brought about a fall in the profit share of just 5.9 per cent in total between 1965 and 1973. Since there was, in fact, as shall be seen, no fall in the productivity of capital in these years in the non-manufacturing private economy, the latter represents ʾthe maximal negative impact of labour on profitability in this sector.[7]

Manufacturing. Between 1965 and 1973, the profit share in the manufacturing sector fell sharply at an average annual rate of 2.7 per cent, or a total of 22.9 per cent. Nevertheless, this decline cannot support the supply-side interpretation of the fall in profitability that took place in those years, because it cannot plausibly be attributed to increased pressure from labour.

Although the fall in the profit share in manufacturing was thus somewhat greater than in non-manufacturing between 1965 and 1973, the growth of unit labour costs in manufacturing was actually very much lower than in non-manufacturing, putting significantly less pressure on the manufacturing profit share and profit rate.[8]

---

7   As a proportion of net output, indirect business taxes were, on average, 4 per cent higher in the years 1965–73 than they had been in 1965. State and local indirect business taxes constituted about 75 per cent of the total of indirect business taxes collected in 1965 and about 83 per cent in 1973. State and local indirect business taxes doubled between 1965 and 1973, accounting for well over 90 per cent of the increase in total US indirect business taxes during this period, with state and local property taxes and sales taxes each accounting for about half of the rise. US Department of Commerce, Bureau of Economic Analysis, National Income and Product Accounts (henceforth NIPA), Tables 3.2 and 3.3.

8   To maintain consistency, adjustment is always made for indirect business taxes, unless otherwise stated. Indirect business taxes as a percentage of net manufacturing output actually *fell* slightly between 1965 and 1973, so that there was a slightly greater fall in the profit share and profit rate in this sector before than after adjustment for taxes.

The average annual growth of the nominal wage was 10 per cent slower in manufacturing than in non-manufacturing (6.4 per cent compared to 7.1 per cent) and the average annual growth of labour productivity was 50 per cent higher (3.3 per cent compared to 2.3 per cent), with the result that the average annual growth of unit labour costs in non-manufacturing was 57 per cent faster than in manufacturing—4.7 per cent compared to 3.0 per cent. Since the growth of labour costs was so much slower in manufacturing than in non-manufacturing, how could the manufacturing profit share have ended up falling faster than that of non-manufacturing, or even at all?

What accounts for the greater fall of the profit share in the manufacturing sector than in non-manufacturing—indeed, for the entire fall of the profit share in the manufacturing sector—is the much lesser ability of manufacturers to increase the rate of increase of their prices to keep up with the increase in the growth of their costs. Between 1950 and 1965, each sector's unit labour costs and prices increased, respectively, at pretty close to the same average annual rates as the other's—1.91 per cent and 1.86 per cent in manufacturing, 1.92 per cent and 1.73 per cent in non-manufacturing. Because the respective rates of growth of unit labour costs and prices within both manufacturing and non-manufacturing had been so close to one another, there was not much change in the profit share in either sector over the period. Between 1965 and 1973, however, the growth of unit labour costs in non-manufacturing suddenly accelerated, increasing, as just noted, at an average annual rate of 4.8 per cent, 150 per cent faster than it had in the years between 1950 and 1965. Nevertheless, the fall in the non-manufacturing profit share was limited to 16 per cent in this period because prices accelerated to almost as great an extent as did unit labour costs, increasing at an average annual rate of 4.25 per cent, 146 per cent faster than it had in the years between 1950 and 1965. In sharp contrast, in manufacturing, the average annual growth of unit labour costs between 1965 and 1973, at 3.0 per cent, was only 57 per cent greater than it had been between 1950 and 1965. The problem for manufacturers, however, was that the increase in the growth of their prices did not remotely match even that (relatively small) increase in the growth of their costs. Manufacturing prices grew at an average annual rate of just 2.3 per cent, 53 per cent slower than did non-manufacturing prices, and only 24 per cent faster than they had increased between 1950 and 1965. Had manufacturers been able to raise the rate of growth of their prices to anything like the extent that their counterparts in non-manufacturing had, they would obviously have been able to prevent any fall in their profit share, and might even have been able to raise it.[9] An explanation as to why manufacturers could not do this thus becomes central to explaining the fall in profitability in manufacturing, and I shall return to this question shortly.

---

9   Another way of making the same point is to note that the average annual growth of the manufacturing real wage between 1965 and 1973, at just 1.9 per cent, failed to keep up with the growth of manufacturing labour productivity, at 3.3 per cent, because the average annual growth of consumer prices, at 4.4 per cent, was of the same order of magnitude as that of non-manufacturing product prices. Yet, because manufacturing product prices grew so slowly, the average annual growth of the manufacturing product wage, at 4.2 per cent, turned out to be more than double that of the real wage, bringing about a sharp squeeze of the manufacturing profit share.

The Output-Capital Ratio

Advocates of the supply-side approach who argue that reduced productivity growth, brought on by workers' slacking and resistance, was one factor behind the fall in profitability that took place between 1965 and 1973 have emphasized the need to refer, not only to the growth of labour productivity, but also the path of the productivity of capital. As they point out, output-capital ratios did fall significantly during this period. Does this development support their argument?[10]

Non-Manufacturing. Between 1965 and 1973, the non-manufacturing output-capital ratio fell at an average annual rate of 1.1 per cent, or a total of 8.8 per cent, making a contribution to the overall fall in non-manufacturing profitability rather smaller than that of the fall in the profit share. The decline in the non-manufacturing output-capital ratio cannot, however, be taken to support the supply-side interpretation, because it cannot properly be interpreted as representing a decline in productivity growth, let alone one resulting from increased labour resistance or slacking. If the output-capital ratio is to express capital productivity, it must be expressed in terms of *real* output compared to *real* capital input, in terms, that is, of constant output and capital stock prices, so as to take into account changes in relative prices. Expressed in constant prices, the average annual decline in the non-manufacturing output-capital ratio between 1965 and 1973 turns out to be zero. The fall in the non-manufacturing output-capital ratio cannot, then, be understood to have been the result of a decline in capital productivity resulting from increased workers' resistance and slacking for the simple reason that non-manufacturing capital productivity did not fall.

Manufacturing. Between 1965 and 1973, a fall in the manufacturing nominal output-capital ratio—at an average annual rate of 3.2 per cent, or 23.4 per cent in total—contributed about the same amount as did the fall in the manufacturing profit share to the decline in manufacturing profitability. The decline in the output-capital ratio in manufacturing cannot, however, be taken to support the supply-side interpretation any more than can the fall that took place outside of manufacturing. This is because, like the fall in the output-capital ratio in non-manufacturing, it fails to represent a decline in capital productivity. Adjusted for prices so as to express capital productivity, the (real) output-capital ratio in manufacturing fell barely at all between 1965 and 1973.[11]

What then did lie behind the substantial fall in the output-capital ratio in manufacturing? The answer is made clear, once again, when its trajectory is compared with that in non-manufacturing. Prices for capital stock in manufacturing grew more slowly, though only slightly so, than in non-manufacturing, at an average annual rate of 5.2 per cent, compared to 5.6 per cent in non-manufacturing. The reason that the output-capital ratio in non-manufacturing nonetheless fell less than one-third as fast as did that in manufacturing was that (as with respect to unit labour costs and the profit share) non-manufacturers could raise output prices 85 per cent faster. Had manufacturers been able to raise their prices to the same degree—at an average

---

10   See Glyn et al., 'Rise and Fall of the Golden Age', p. 114; Lipietz, 'Behind the Crisis', pp. 22ff.
11   At an average annual rate of 0.4 per cent, or a total of 4 per cent, a negligible amount, which would disappear if adjustment was made for capacity utilization.

Table 8.1. Costs, prices, and profitability in the US, 1965–73.
(Per cent rates of change.)

	NPR	NPSH	RW	PW	LPY	NW	ULC	PPri	NY/NK	NY/NKreal	nkpri
Mfgr	-5.5	-2.7	1.9	4.0	3.3	6.4	3.1	2.3	-3.2	-0.4	5.2
Nmfgr	-3.0	-2.0	2.7	2.8	2.4	7.2	4.7	4.3	-1.1	0.0	5.6

Adjusted for indirect business taxes

	NPR	NPSH	RW	PW	LPY	NW	ULC	PPri	NY/NK	NY/NKreal	nkpri
Mfgr.	-6.0	-2.8	1.9	4.2	3.3	6.4	3.1	2.1	-3.4	-0.4	5.2
Nmfgr	-1.7	-0.7	2.7	2.7	2.4	7.2	4.7	4.4	-1.0	0.0	5.6

Not Adjusted for indirect business taxes

Source: See Appendix I on Profit Rates. Key to legend on page xiii.

annual rate of 4.25 per cent, rather than 2.3 per cent—their output-capital ratio would have fallen less than 20 per cent as much as it did. Put another way, it was the inability of manufacturers to raise their prices sufficiently that accounted for more than 80 per cent of the fall in their output-capital ratio. As with the manufacturing profit share, to understand (most of) the contribution of the fall in the manufacturing output-capital ratio to the fall manufacturing profitability between 1965 and 1973, it is necessary to understand why manufacturers were so much less able to mark up over costs than were their counterparts outside manufacturing.

What Caused the Decline in Profitability?
The foregoing analysis works against the supply-side thesis, and points toward my alternative interpretation, that the fall in profitability originated in the inability of US manufacturers to fully realize their investments because of the increased downward pressure on prices that resulted from the unanticipated entry into the market of lower-cost producers, especially from abroad. To begin to make this case, two conclusions of the foregoing analysis must be emphasized: first, just how much greater was the fall of profitability in manufacturing than in non-manufacturing between 1965 and 1973; second, to just how great an extent the fall in profitability in manufacturing was the result, not of an increase in upward pressure on costs, but an increase in downward pressure on prices. Only in the manufacturing sector did the fall in profitability reach crisis proportions, amounting to 40.9 per cent between 1965 and 1973. At 23.1 per cent, the fall in the rate of profit in the non-manufacturing private sector was barely half that in manufacturing. Indeed, if no adjustment is made for indirect business taxes, the decline in non-manufacturing profitability is just 13.1 per cent, compared to 41.9 per cent in manufacturing. The declines in the profit share and the output-capital ratio that determined arithmetically the fall in manufacturing profitability did not result from an increase in pressure from workers, as the supply-side theorists contend. They were, on the contrary, almost entirely the result of the slow rate of increase of manufacturing output prices. Not the growth of costs in themselves, but the inability of US manufacturers

Figure 8.1. US manufacturing and non-manufacturing private net profit rates, 1949–2001.

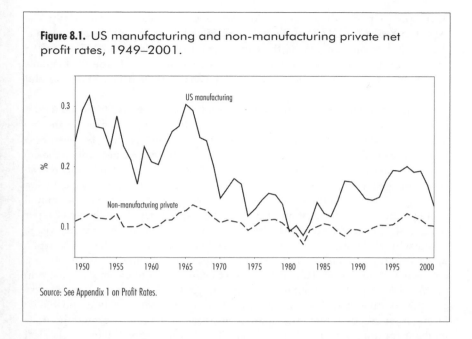

Source: See Appendix 1 on Profit Rates.

to sufficiently mark up prices over costs, accounts for almost all of the fall in manufacturing profitability (see p. 109, Figure 8.1).

During the years between 1965 and 1973 when profitability first fell, US manufacturers were, in terms of *their own* cost effectiveness, actually performing as well as they had over the course of the boom between 1950 and 1965: the growth of labour productivity was up by about 10 per cent, capital productivity maintained itself, and real wage growth continued its fall. The cause of the US manufacturers' profitability problems was thus to be found, not in the rate of growth of their costs in absolute terms, but the rate relative to the prices that were now being imposed on the world market by their leading competitors. What had occurred to bring this predicament about? Following the establishment of currency convertibility in the advanced capitalist world at the end of the 1950s, the growth of world trade accelerated, with far-reaching, though contradictory, consequences for the international economy. Between 1963 and 1973, with the volume of both world exports and world manufacturing exports increasing 42 per cent faster than between 1953 and 1963, the growth of exports began to outrun the growth of domestic production in a truly radical fashion. Already growing 50 per cent faster than world manufacturing output between 1953 and 1963, world manufacturing exports were suddenly increasing almost *twice* as fast. Between 1960 and 1974, in the advanced capitalist economies, the average annual rate of growth of manufacturing exports was two-thirds faster than that of manufacturing output—9.9 per cent compared to 5.9 per cent.[12]

Part and parcel of the same development, from the early to mid 1960s, exports as a proportion of output (the export share) for the OECD as a whole, as well as for

12   Glyn et al., 'Rise and Fall of the Golden Age', p. 111.

its component parts, was suddenly growing at *twice* the pace it had previously. The export shares of the OECD as a whole, and of its European and US components, thus grew the same amount in the eight years between 1965 and 1973 as in the fifteen years between 1950 and 1965. The increase in the rate of growth of Japan's export share began a bit earlier, and was even sharper (see p 111, Tables 8.2 and 8.3).

The rapid acceleration of the growth of trade from the early 1960s had a dual effect on the economic evolution of the advanced capitalist economies. On the one hand, it provided an additional impetus to rapid economic growth. Between 1965 and 1970, as world trade grew faster, the G-7 capitalist economies, minus the US and Canada—that is, Germany, Japan, France, Italy, and the UK—reached the zenith of their postwar boom, with manufacturing output and manufacturing labour productivity in those five economies taken together increasing at annual average rates of 8.0 per cent and 6.3 per cent, respectively, compared to 7.0 per cent and 4.4 per cent, respectively, between 1955 and 1965. In the same five years, manufacturing investment growth for those five economies accelerated sharply, increasing at an annual average rate of 13.2 per cent, compared to 7.9 per cent between 1955 and 1965. Behind this growth spurt lay a major improvement in profitability, the rate of profit in manufacturing in Germany, Japan, Italy, France, and the UK taken together increasing by 21.4 per cent between 1965 and 1969.[13] From one standpoint, then, the dramatic increase in the rate of growth of international trade apparently had just the effect it was supposed to: in classical fashion, it helped make possible the accelerated economic expansion of the advanced capitalist economies by means of the growth of the international division of labour.

On the other hand, due to such precipitous growth in world trade, new producers, without warning, began to supply radically increased fractions of the world market, supplanting long-ensconced incumbents. Such radical uncoordinated and unplanned-for shifts could not be expected to be, and were not in fact, effected without disruption. The relatively great concentration on home markets and the relatively separate growth that characterized the postwar boom into the early 1960s had been paralleled by a relatively high level of diversification within regions and nations. The technologically-following, later-developing, hegemonized—and fast-growing—economies were thus producing bundles of goods which were quite similar to those already being produced by the technologically-leading, earlier-developing, hegemonic economy. It was therefore inevitable that they would develop their export potential by increasing the output of such goods. As the OECD notes, 'the industrial countries' patterns of trade and output tended to converge, with most countries increasingly producing and exchanging similar commodities.'[14] Indeed, the manufacturers of the follower economies had every reason to increase their exports of goods that they were already producing for the domestic market, since they could often do so at a lower cost than could the earlier-developing incumbents. The newer, lower-cost producers, based in the follower regions—notably Germany and, above all, Japan—thus expanded their exports largely by invading

---

13   AGH.
14   OECD, *Structural Adjustment and Economic Performance*, Paris 1987, p. 269.

Table 8.2. World exports and world output.

| | Annual growth rates | | Ratio of annual growth rates |
	1953–63	1963–73	1963–73/1953–63
World Exports	9.2%	13.1%	1.42
World Output	6.7%	8.0%	1.19
Exports/Output	1.4	1.63	
World Mfgr. Exports	12.7%	18.0%	1.42
World Mfgr. Output	8.5%	9.7%	1.14
Mfgr.Exp./Mfgr.Out.	1.49	1.86	

Source: Van Der Wee, *Prosperity and Upheaval*, p. 260.

Table 8.3. Percentage growth of export shares of GDP (constant prices).

	1950	1965	Increase	1965	1973	Increase
OECD Total	9.0	12.4	37.7	12.4	16.8	35.4
OECD Europe	12.7	18.1	42.1	18.1	25.6	42.9
US	4.3	5.1	35.0	5.1	6.9	36.0
	1950	1960		1960	1973	
Japan	4.7	5.6	19.0	5.6	7.9	38.0

Source: Glyn et al., 'The Rise and Fall of the Golden Age', p. 43.

markets hitherto dominated by producers of the leader regions, especially the US, but also the UK. This trend was, of course, already evident during the 1950s, but now the process was very much accelerated.

During the second half of the 1960s, the German and Japanese economies regained their earlier vitality, after slowdowns in the first half of the 1960s. In these years, the Japanese economy reached the peak of its postwar dynamism, achieving unprecedented rates of investment and productivity advance and on that basis posing a wide-ranging challenge to US manufacturing supremacy. Between 1960 and 1965, the ratio of Japanese to US average annual labour productivity growth in manufacturing had been about two to one (8.7 per cent to 4.4 per cent); between 1965 and 1973, this ratio grew to about four to one, 13.1 per cent to 3.3 per cent.

US manufacturing's problem of increasingly slow productivity growth in relative terms was exacerbated by the renewed outbreak of inflation after 1965, provoked by the rapid rise of government deficits, accommodated by loose money. The sharp increase in the rate of growth of the nominal wage that took place did not, of course, force up prices; indeed, it was insufficiently rapid to prevent real wage growth from falling. Nevertheless, in attempting (unsuccessfully) to keep up with the increase in the rate of growth of consumer prices brought on by government fiscal and monetary policies, workers raised the nominal wage so as to create a rising floor on prices and thereby helped to further fuel inflation. Between 1965 and 1970, the growth of manufacturing unit labour costs in the US in dollar terms was double that in Germany and Japan.

A comparison of cost *levels* in US manufacturing with those of Germany and Japan indicates the sort of competitive pressures to which US producers were being subjected. According to data provided by the US Bureau of Labor Statistics, by 1970 average labour productivity in German and Japanese manufacturing had only reached 75 per cent and 50 per cent of the US level, respectively. But since manufacturing wages in Germany and Japan were 60 per cent and 25 per cent, respectively, of those in the US, manufacturing unit labour costs in Germany and Japan turned out to be 80 per cent[15] and less than 50 per cent those in the US.[16] Representing as it does an industry-wide average, even this unit labour cost figure understates the potency of the Japanese challenge, because the great corporations that were responsible for the preponderance of Japanese exports had achieved much higher than average levels of productivity. In the large, usually modern, plants— those with more than 500 employees—that produced a disproportionate share of the country's exports, labour productivity was about 50 per cent above the average; in the small, generally older, plants, it was about 50 per cent below the average.[17] In their comparative study of the evolution of costs in the US and Japan, Jorgenson and Kuroda were able to conclude that, 'in 1970, on the eve of the Smithsonian Agreements ... *almost all Japanese industries were more competitive internationally than their US counterparts. By this we mean that they could provide products to the international marketplace at prices below those available from their US competitors.*'[18]

The sharp relative increase in US costs of production stimulated a further acceleration of manufacturing investment overseas by US multinational corporations, accentuating the already established trend. By 1965, the ratio of investment by majority-owned foreign affiliates of US corporations in manufacturing overseas to corporate manufacturing investment in the US had grown to 21.4 per cent, up from 11.4 per cent in 1957. By 1973, this figure had increased to 31.3 per cent.[19] In 1973 US corporations were therefore investing about one dollar abroad for every three

15   Germany's competitive position had been significantly undermined by the major revaluation of the mark in 1969.

16   Daly, 'Japanese Manufacturing Competitiveness', pp. 35, 37, 39. These figures may exaggerate the average manufacturing productivity gap between the US and Japan. According to the Japan Productivity Center Report on International Comparison of Labor Productivity (Tokyo 1981), in 1974 US labour productivity was just 38 per cent higher than that in the Japan. (M. Bronfenbrenner, 'Japanese Productivity Experience', in W. J. Baumol and K. McLennan, eds, *Productivity Growth and US Competitiveness*, Oxford 1985, p. 71.) According to Denison and Chung, moreover, Japan achieved its labour productivity level with capital inputs (stock, equipment, and inventories) per person that were, in 1970, 40 per cent or more below that in the US. This would imply that taking into account all inputs, the Japanese productivity level was a good deal closer to that of the US than the relative labour productivity figures would indicate. (E. F. Denison and W. K. Chung, *How Japan's Economy Grew So Fast: The Sources of Postwar Expansion*, Washington, DC 1976, pp. 104–7, 250, 255–7.)

17   Daly, 'Japanese Manufacturing Competitiveness', p. 11.

18   D. W. Jorgenson and M. Kuroda, 'Productivity and International Competitiveness in Japan and the United States, 1960–85', *The Economic Studies Quarterly*, vol. xliii, December 1992, p. 314 (emphasis added).

19   Fahim-Nader, 'Capital Expenditures by Majority-Owned Foreign Affiliates of US Companies', p. 59.

they invested in the US. There could hardly be a clearer sign of the relative cost problem confronting manufacturing investors in the US economy at this point (see p. 59, Figure 4.1).

As a consequence of US manufacturers' growing inability to match the costs of their chief overseas rivals, the US experienced a crisis of trade in the later 1960s and early 1970s. The recovery of export price competitiveness achieved by US manufacturers over the first half of the 1960s thus turned out to be only temporary. Between 1965 and 1973, export prices grew at an average annual rate of 4.5 per cent in the US, compared to 3.2 per cent in Germany (1.4 per cent between 1965 and 1969), and 2.1 per cent in Japan, with negative consequences for US producers' competitive position. Having stabilized itself at around 24 per cent over the years 1958–65, the US share of the manufacturing exports of the main industrial countries fell sharply by a third, to around 18 per cent, in the short period from 1965 to 1973.[20] Simultaneously, there was a major invasion of manufactured imports, as foreign-made steel, autos, machine tools, machinery, consumer electronics, and the like quickly grabbed a significant share of the US market. Until this point, the twentieth-century US economy had been remarkably self-enclosed, a reflection of its superior competitiveness, as well as the costs of trans-oceanic transport. But change came suddenly and dramatically from the mid 1960s. Between 1965 and 1970, manufacturing imports grew at an average annual pace of 19.1 per cent, twice as fast as during the comparable period of the 1950s when competitiveness was also plummeting. The manufacturing import penetration ratio, still averaging only 6.9 per cent over the years 1959–66, grew to an average of 11.9 per cent in 1966–69 and to an average of 15.8 per cent in 1969–73.[21]

US manufacturers' loss of markets abroad and at home represented only the tip of the iceberg, and provides only a partial indication of the decline in US manufacturing competitiveness in this era, and of the damage visited by declining competitiveness on the economic health of US manufacturers. To the degree that they avoided ceding market share, and as a condition for retaining it, US manufacturers had to refrain from raising prices to as great an extent in proportion to costs as they had been accustomed to doing, with unavoidable consequences for profitability. It is the accelerated injection of lower-cost, lower-priced manufactures onto the world market—manifested in the rise of over-capacity and over-production on an international scale—that therefore constitutes the key to the puzzle of the relatively slow growth of manufacturing prices in this period, and therefore to the

20   B. R. Scott, 'US Competitiveness: Concepts, Performance, and Implications', in B. R. Scott and G. C. Lodge, ed., *US Competitiveness in the World Economy*, Cambridge, Mass. 1985, p. 27. For a close analysis of the spectacular increase in the Japanese share of advanced industrial country trade in this period, see especially A. D. Morgan, 'Export Competition and Import Substitution: The Industrial Countries 1963 to 1971', in R. A. Batchelor et al., eds, *Industrialization and the Basis for Trade*, Oxford 1980, pp. 48ff. Morgan has the US share of total exports of the twelve leading industrial countries falling from 20.1 per cent in 1967 to 16.4 per cent in 1971 and the Japanese share increasing in this period from 10.6 per cent to 14.7 per cent. The US share of world exports decreased from 17.24 per cent in 1963 to 12.58 per cent in 1973, while that of Japan increased from 5.98 per cent to 9.92 per cent. Van Der Wee, *Prosperity and Upheaval*, p. 265.

21   Scott, 'US Competitiveness', p. 22; Krause, 'US Economy and International Trade', p. 395; T. Weisskopf, 'Sources of Profit Rate Decline in the Advanced Capitalist Economies: An Empirical Test of the High-Employment Profit Squeeze Theory', unpublished manuscript, University of Michigan, December 1985, Table 10.

resulting fall in the manufacturing rate of profit. Because its output was composed largely of tradables, the manufacturing sector was highly exposed to intensifying international competition. In contrast, despite sustaining increases in unit labour costs and capital costs that, taken together, were substantially higher than those in manufacturing, the private business economy outside of manufacturing, which was largely immune from international competition, experienced a much more limited fall in its profit rate because its firms could raise prices in line with much faster growing costs almost as easily as before.

Labour Resistance and the Onset of the Downturn

Against this background, we can specify the economic significance of action by labour in the years of declining profitability between 1965 and 1973. A quite major eruption of labour militancy did take place. But that outbreak should be understood much more as an indirect effect of the fall in profitability than as a cause. It represented an attempt on the part of an organized labour movement, already in retreat, to reverse its decline and counter an ongoing employers' offensive. That offensive, while dating back to the last years of the 1950s, increased in intensity from the mid 1960s, to compensate for the fall in profitability.

Employers had initiated their assault in order to hold down wages and to increase shop-floor discipline in aid of rationalization so as to both reverse the wages-productivity squeeze on profits that had overtaken the manufacturing sector in the period leading into the recession of 1957–58, and to respond to the simultaneous rise of international competition. Even during the subsequent period of improving competitiveness, US manufacturers had faced unrelenting price pressure from abroad. By the mid 1960s, they were therefore seeking to reduce wage growth even further than the 40 per cent it had already been brought down in the years between 1958 and 1965 (compared to 1950–58), while attempting to further raise output per hour by increasing the pace of work. Apparently reflecting the speed-up, the industrial accident rate was, on average, almost 20 per cent higher between 1965 and 1970 than between 1960 and 1965.[22]

To prevent workers from interfering in their campaign to cut costs, employers intensified their resistance to unionization. From the early 1950s up to 1965, employers had consistently and voluntarily accepted about 42 per cent of all petitions to hold union representation elections; but, from that point on, their willingness to accept such petitions dropped precipitously. The proportion of petitions voluntarily accepted fell to 26.5 per cent by 1970 and 16.3 per cent by 1973. Meanwhile, there was a remarkable increase in employers' illegal efforts to interfere with union organizing. Between 1965 and 1973, the number of charges against employers which involved firing workers for union activity rose by 50 per cent, the number of workers awarded back-pay or reinstated to their jobs after having been illegally fired almost tripled, and the number of all unfair labour practices charges against employers doubled (see p. 64, Figure 4.2).[23]

For an extended period, the highly bureaucratized official labour leaderships

---

22   US Department of Commerce, *Historical Statistics of the United States*, p. 182.
23   R. L. Seeber and W. N. Cooke, 'The Decline in Union Success in NLRB Representation Elections', *Industrial Relations*, vol. xxii, Winter 1983, pp. 42–3; Freeman, 'Why Are Unions Faring Poorly in NLRB Representation Elections?', p. 53.

failed to respond to the employers' growing pressure. While profitability soared during the first half of the 1960s, they accepted with barely a murmur both the major reduction in the growth of compensation in manufacturing and the employers' moves to rationalize production, as official strikes fell to postwar lows. Whereas the loss of total work time resulting from stoppages had averaged 0.23 per cent during the years 1950–58, it averaged 0.16 per cent during the years 1958–65. Whereas the proportion of the labour force involved in work stoppages had averaged 4.44 per cent during the years 1950–58, it averaged 2.63 per cent during the years 1958–65. Rank and file unionists were thus left to face the employers largely on their own. As one knowledgeable observer summed up a widely held opinion at the time, 'the trend here at the moment is quite clear. Unions have lost much of their vitality and forward motion; they are playing an essentially conservative role in the plant community, seeking to preserve what they have rather than make gains. Management, on the other hand, is on the offensive and has acquired a new sense of sureness in dealing with industrial relations.'[24]

In the absence of a response from above, rank-and-file resistance seems to have begun to stiffen from the onset of the employers' 'hard line' at the end of the 1950s. Between 1960 and 1966, workers resorted to wildcat strikes increasingly frequently, the percentage of strikes during the term of the agreement rising from 22 per cent of all strikes in 1960 (the first year of reporting) to 36.5 per cent in 1966. They also increasingly voted down contracts negotiated by their leaders, with the percentage of rejections growing steadily and increasing by more than 60 per cent between 1964 and 1967, and leading industrial unions like the machinists, the auto workers, and longshore especially affected.[25] At the same time, to try to secure a more militant and effective leadership, rank and filers supported a series of successful campaigns to replace insufficiently militant local officers, as well as long-entrenched top union bureaucrats, notably David MacDonald in steel, James Carey in electrical and, later, Tony Boyle in coal.[26]

To maintain control, the official union leaderships had to act and, beginning in 1966 and 1967, they organized a major wave of strikes. In the years 1966–73, the percentage of total work time lost due to work stoppages grew to 0.23, compared to 0.18 for the years 1958–66. Meanwhile, the proportion of the employed labour force annually involved in work stoppages grew to an average of 3.6 per cent, almost a third higher than the average of 2.6 per cent for 1958–66. These figures did represent a major increase in labour resistance, but the magnitude of the revolt should not be overstated. Although more workers in terms of absolute numbers

24   G. Strauss, 'The Shifting Power Balance in the Plant', *Industrial Relations*, vol. i, May 1962, pp. 94–5.

25   J. Barbash, 'The Causes of Rank-and-File Unrest', in J. Seidman, ed., *Trade Union Government and Collective Bargaining*, New York 1970, pp. 41, 45, 51–3; W. E. Simkin, 'Refusals to Ratify Contracts', *Industrial and Labor Relations Review*, vol. xxi, July 1968, p. 520. There are no statistics on unofficial strikes per se, so data on strikes during the period of the contract—not the same thing, but hopefully a decent surrogate—are used to stand for them.

26   S. Weir, 'USA: The Labor Revolt', *International Socialist Journal*, vol. iv, nos. 20–21, April–June 1967. In the single year 1963, more than one-third of the top officials in United Auto Worker Union (UAW) auto production locals were voted out of office. N. Lichtenstein, 'The Treaty of Detroit: Old Before its Time', unpublished paper presented at the American Historical Association Annual Convention, January 1995. I wish to thank Nelson Lichtenstein for allowing me to make reference to this paper in advance of publication.

Figure 8.2. US strike activity, 1940–80.

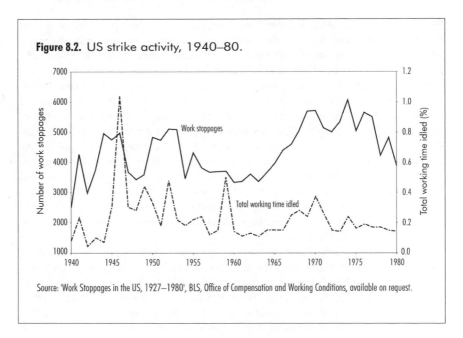

Source: 'Work Stoppages in the US, 1927–1980', BLS, Office of Compensation and Working Conditions, available on request.

were annually involved in strikes in this period than at any other time in the postwar period, in terms both of the proportion of days lost through strikes and the proportion of the labour force annually involved in strikes—not to mention economic gains—the militancy of this period fell notably short of that of the late 1940s through the mid 1950s (see p. 116, Figure 8.2).

Judging from its results, the rise of union militancy in the private economy appears to have represented less the flexing of muscles of an increasingly powerful labour movement than a defensive struggle for survival provoked by the assaults of an increasingly well-organized and aggressive class of capitalist manufacturing employers. Real wage gains in manufacturing between 1965 and 1973 were about one-third lower than between 1950 and 1965, although they fell only slightly in the private business economy as a whole. Even more telling, despite the much increased number of strikes, unions were decreasingly able to hold their place within the labour force. During the years 1965–73, the proportion of union victories in NLRB elections fell to 56.4 per cent, compared to 60.4 per cent in the early 1960s, and the proportion of the private sector labour force that was unionized fell by 15 per cent, from 32 per cent in 1966 to 27 per cent in 1973.[27]

Unions' declining leverage against employers, even when they took militant action, is illustrated by the fact that, between 1964 and 1971, union workers secured wage gains that were at best equal to, and most likely somewhat less than, those won by non-union workers. Union clout did once again begin to make a clear difference around 1971, after which point non-union workers saw their real wage

---

27   Goldfield, *The Decline of Organized Labor*, pp. 90–1; Freeman, 'The Divergence of Private Sector and Public Sector Unionism', p. 64.

growth plummet to near zero. Still, while union workers began to do much better in relative terms than did their non-union counterparts, they were able to do no more than maintain their real wage growth at the level of the later 1960s, at which point it had fallen substantially compared to the 1950s and early 1960s.[28] In the absence of pressure from labour, real wage growth would certainly have fallen significantly faster than it did, and the fall in profitability would have been correspondingly reduced. But to argue that increased labour resistance prevented a better adjustment by capital to the decline in profitability is a long way from seeing it as at the root of that decline.

2. The Boom's Final Phase in Japan

The reduction of relative costs and prices on the part of Japanese and German— and perhaps other overseas—producers that was responsible for so much of the fall in the rate of profit in US manufacturing between 1965 and 1973 determined a reduction in the aggregate rate of return in manufacturing for the G-7 economies taken together of the order of 25 per cent. The fall in profitability initially experienced by less cost-effective US producers was therefore an expression of the rise of over-capacity and over-production for the advanced capitalist economies considered in aggregate. Even so, the same renewed dynamism in German and Japanese manufacturing that put downward pressure on US and aggregate G-7 manufacturing profitability initially brought increased profit rates to Japanese and German manufacturing. (See p. 142, Figure 9.1.)

Towards the end of 1965, at virtually the exact moment at which the onset of the profitability crisis in the US began to initiate the long downturn on a world scale, the Japanese economy took off, transcending a brief deceleration during the years 1961–65, and in particular its most serious postwar recession up to that point in 1964–65. The fifty-seven month boom that ran from the autumn of 1965 to the summer of 1970 represents the zenith of the spectacular expansion enjoyed by the Japanese economy throughout the postwar boom. During these years, GNP grew at an average annual rate of 14 per cent, while manufacturing output increased at an average annual rate of 15.8 per cent. These figures were impressive even by the extraordinary standards already set by the Japanese economy between 1950 and 1961.[29]

As before, unprecedentedly high rates of investment drove the economy forward. Between 1965 and 1970 investment in new plant and equipment in the private business economy grew at an average annual rate of 21.1 per cent, just about matching the rate obtaining between 1955 and 1961.[30] This extraordinary rate of investment growth was motivated by high, and increasing, rates of profit, which were themselves an expression of the economy's extraordinary capacity to secure, with the growth of investment, unusually high rates of productivity advance combined with relatively low wage growth. Between 1965 and 1970, the Japanese growth paradigm was operating at its peak effectiveness.

If ever conditions seemed ripe for wages to squeeze profits in the manner envi-

---

28   D. J. B. Mitchell, *Unions, Wages, and Inflation*, Washington, DC 1980, p. 40, Table 2–4, as well as pp. 48–53.
29   Kosai, *Era of High-Speed Growth*, pp. 159, 161.
30   Ibid., p. 144.

sioned by the supply-side theorists, they seemed so in Japan in the later 1960s. The Japanese economy had reached full employment by the end of the 1950s. Having dropped to an average of just 1.3 per cent during the years 1960–65, the unemployment rate fell even further between 1965 and 1970. The ratio of job openings to applicants, at 0.64:1 in 1965, rose to 1:1 in 1967 and escalated to 1.41:1 in 1970, making for truly hyper-full employment.[31] Workers naturally won major wage gains, with real wages growing between 1965 and 1970 at the very high average annual rates of 8.6 per cent and 6.2 per cent in manufacturing and the private business economy, respectively, and product wages increasing at average annual rates of 11.1 per cent and 7.6 per cent, respectively. These rates of wage growth turned out, however, to manifest the continued subordination of Japanese workers to the requirements of capital accumulation.

The Japanese economy had no trouble accommodating such high rates of wage growth because the parallel rates of productivity growth were even higher. Between 1965 and 1970, the average annual rates of labour productivity growth in manufacturing and the private business economy, were 12.5 per cent and 10.75 per cent, respectively. The profit share thus rose during this period 9.6 per cent in manufacturing and a spectacular 31.3 per cent in the private business sector. At the same time, the output-capital ratio also rose a little, growing annually, on average, by 0.5 per cent and 1.9 per cent in manufacturing and the private business economy, respectively. Far from falling in an epoch of super-full employment, the rates of profit in manufacturing and the private business economy rose more than 20 per cent and 66.5 per cent respectively (see p. 7, Figure 0.3 and p. 8, Figure 0.4).

A major structural transformation of Japanese industry, taking place during the decade or so before 1973, lay behind the enormous productivity gains achieved in this era. Having focused during the previous decade on raw-material processing industries (prominently including steel, petro-chemicals, cement, and electricity generation) Japanese manufacturing came to concentrate on 'machinery industries' (broadly defined to include transportation, electrical machinery, and all other types of machinery equipment), which made use of the raw-material processing industries' outputs.[32] In so doing, it achieved much of its productivity growth by way of the fuller application of technological advances first implemented during the previous decade. The later 1950s and early 1960s had witnessed a major technological revolution—the initial introduction of new consumer durables such as televisions and electric refrigerators, new producer durables such as silicon, steel plates, and polyethylene, and new methods of production such as thermal-electric power plants, strip mills, and transfer machines. Over the second half of the 1960s, record rates of productivity increase could thus be achieved by increasing the proportion of the technologically advanced sectors within the economy, by rationalizing already implemented technical gains, by improving plant layout and quality control, and, especially, through economies of scale.[33]

The rapid growth of investment could bring such extraordinary gains in labour

---

31   Ibid., p. 158.
32   Imai, 'Japan's Changing Industrial Structure', pp. 47–53.
33   'The controlling factor [in economic growth over the years 1965–70] was the interaction [of the big growth of investment] with expansions in scale.' Kosai, *Era of High-Speed Growth*, pp. 161–4 (quote p. 163).

productivity because it embodied such rapid technical progress. It could embody such rapid technical progress because it occurred in the context of such accelerated *internationalization*. Between 1965 and 1970, Japanese exports grew at an average annual rate of 17.2 per cent. Such rapid export growth was obviously made possible by the high rate of productivity increase, but it was also a critical *condition* for that productivity increase. The acceleration of export growth thus made possible both the major economies of scale achieved in this era, and the especially rapid expansion of those manufacturing lines that were enjoying the fastest productivity growth.

Fast-growing Japanese exports were made possible in part by the unusually rapid growth of world trade. But, had Japanese producers had to depend solely on the growth of the market, they could not have increased exports at anything like the rate they did. As in the previous period, they thus continued to rely for most of their gains in overseas sales on grabbing an ever larger share of the world market. Between 1963 and 1967, Japan doubled its exports, and doubled them again between 1967 and 1971. It did so by spectacularly increasing its share of the manufacturing exports of the twelve leading capitalist economies from 7.6 per cent to 13.0 per cent (at current prices). Over the period 1963–71, no less than 54 per cent of Japan's total gain in exports derived from the increase in its share of the world market, compared to only 46 per cent made possible through the growth of the market itself. Since, in this same period, the US share of advanced-country manufacturing exports fell from 20.8 per cent to 17.0 per cent, while the UK share fell from 15.4 per cent to 10.9 per cent, and since no other national economy beside Japan's very significantly increased or decreased its share, it can be concluded that virtually the entirety of the Japanese gain was made at the direct expense of the US and UK.[34]

Japanese exports hit particularly hard in the US domestic market. Between 1964 and 1971, Japanese exports to the US quadrupled in value, with the share of exports to the US in total Japanese exports growing from 27.6 per cent to 31.2 per cent. Japanese manufacturing exports as a share of total US manufacturing imports thus grew rapidly from 17 per cent to just under 25 per cent. The intensification of Japanese pressure on US markets came mostly from the transport equipment and machinery industries, which were also developing most rapidly at home, with intermediate metals and intermediate chemicals also figuring prominently.

The Japanese economy succeeded in so dramatically increasing its market share at the expense of the US in this period by virtue of its ability to hold down costs. In this respect it widened its lead in spectacular fashion over the second half of the 1960s, holding the rate of growth of unit labour costs and of export prices to one-half and one-fourth, respectively, that of the US economy. The growth of federal budget deficits leading to inflation in the US in this period made this development that much more pronounced. The combination of the growth of demand in and the decline in competitiveness of the US economy between 1965 and 1970 was thus a fundamental condition for the Japanese boom. By the same token, the downward

---

34   Morgan, 'Export Competition and Import Substitution', pp. 48, 50, 54, Tables 4.1, 2, 3. In these years Italy (1.3 per cent) and Canada (1.5 per cent) were the only other countries of the leading twelve to increase their share by as much as 1 per cent. 'From 1967 to 1971 Japan secured no less than 90 per cent of the $7.3 billion shift in market shares.' Morgan, p. 53.

price pressure exerted by Japanese producers on US manufacturing output prices played a central role in the squeeze on US manufacturing profitability that set off the international crisis.

3. The Boom's Final Phase in Germany

During the second half of the 1960s, Germany's manufacturing economy followed a path rather analogous to Japan's, though in far less spectacular fashion. After a half-decade of reduced dynamism between 1960 and 1965, German economic authorities, in collaboration with employers and labour, implemented a series of policies designed to contain production costs, especially in relative international terms, and these had the desired effect.

In 1966–67, the Bundesbank consciously engineered a slowdown with the explicit purpose of reducing the inflationary trend that had resulted from a period of unusually expansionary fiscal policy. Manufacturing firms had, of course, already been experiencing an extended period of declining profitability, though from very high levels. The outcome was the first serious recession of the postwar epoch—the first year of negative growth—and it turned out to constitute something of a turning point.[35]

In a serious effort to reverse the negative trend in profitability, firms ruthlessly reduced capacity in accord with changes in demand and rapidly introduced new technology, while pushing hard to reduce wage costs. As part of this broad process of rationalization, firms shed labour to a much greater extent than in previous recessions. While generally intensifying labour, they also introduced new systems for job evaluation and performance appraisal. In some plants, moreover, they held back from workers the expected non-contractual bonuses and company benefits. Meanwhile, from 1966–67, they began to recruit foreign workers on a large scale, and, by the end of the decade, had thereby done much to alleviate the labour shortage.[36]

Despite the employers' attacks, the trade-union movement did its part to restore the economy's vitality. In the wake of the formation of the Grand Coalition in 1966 and the entry of the Social Democrats into the government, the unions explicitly agreed to refrain from exploiting the increased bargaining power that would accrue to them when the economy once again turned upward, and pledged to hold down wage increases so as to restore profitability.[37]

Taken in combination, these initiatives proved fairly successful. Between 1965 and 1969, manufacturing labour productivity grew at an average annual rate of 5.7 per cent (5.6 per cent net), somewhat faster than during the first half of the decade, while nominal wages grew sufficiently slowly to bring down average annual product wage growth to 5.4 per cent from 5.7 per cent between 1960 and 1965. On the basis of the resulting reduction in the growth of unit labour costs, German manufacturing exporters were able to partially reverse the previously prevailing trend to declining international competitiveness, and launch a new export boom. They

---

35   Giersch et al., *The Fading Miracle*, pp. 143–6.

36   Hennings, 'West Germany', pp. 490–2; Carlin, 'Profitability in West Germany', pp. 330, 337–42; Carlin, 'West German Growth and Institutions', p. 471; Muller-Jentsch and Sperling, 'Economic Development', p. 471.

37   Hennings, 'West Germany', pp. 491–2; Carlin, 'Profitability in West Germany', pp. 337–8, 342.

were much aided in this by the new trend toward rising costs and prices in the US. Between 1965 and 1969, exports grew at an average annual rate of 10 per cent, two-thirds faster than between 1960 and 1965. German manufacturers were thus able to regain the share of advanced-country manufacturing exports that they had lost between 1961 and 1965.[38] By 1969 the manufacturing rate of profit had made a very partial recovery, rising by 7.5 per cent over its level of 1965.

For Germany, then, as for Japan and the other European G-7 economies, the final stage of the postwar boom paralleled the onset of the profitability crisis in the US. The transition to international economic downturn can thus be said to have begun, somewhat paradoxically, at a point when most of the advanced capitalist world was in full expansion, at the height of its postwar dynamism.

38   Carlin, 'Profitability in West Germany', pp. 336–8.

Chapter 9

THE CRISIS SPREADS

The German and Japanese manufacturing economies could secure the final phase of their economic boom only by destroying essential conditions for its continuation. During the second half of the 1960s, the German and Japanese manufacturing economies expanded rapidly by sharply increasing their export growth, mainly by taking over, or at least profoundly threatening, the markets of US manufacturers. The emergence of major US current account deficits and major German and Japanese current account surpluses was the unavoidable result. These external deficits and surpluses were driven up further by the US's reliance on growing federal deficits and loose credit to keep the economy turning over in the face of falling profitability, and the corresponding German and Japanese persistence with policies that restricted the increase in domestic demand in the interest of export-based growth.

In effect, the leading rivals of the US granted it advances so that US purchasers could continue to buy their products and keep their export-driven manufacturing sectors growing, while the US government sped up the borrowing process with its stepped-up subsidies to demand through fiscal deficits and easy money. But, as the prospects of the US fully paying its debts declined—because of its declining competitiveness, as manifested in its decreasing capacity to export and increasing propensity to import and invest abroad—these credits had, ultimately, to be discounted. Dependent as they were upon the maintenance of increasingly under-valued currencies for their economic dynamism, the Germans and Japanese were willing to accept increasingly over-valued dollars without limit. But a world money crisis, precipitated by one speculative run after another on the dollar, could not be avoided, and the dollar inevitably lost much of its value with respect to the yen and the mark between 1971 and 1973. US manufacturers' leading overseas rivals thus saw their effective costs of production rise sharply with respect to those of US producers, and could no longer sell at the old rates of profit. The outcome was not only a major redistribution of the gains from international trade among the advanced capitalist countries, but a shift of a significant part of the burden of the fall in the profit rate of the leading advanced capitalist economies taken together from the US to Germany and Japan. Even so, as profitability and the rate of accumulation in Germany and Japan declined, it failed to recover very much in the US.

1. The US Counter-Offensive and the World Money Crisis
During the boom of the first half of the 1960s, the US economy had partially restored its international position by increasing export growth and reducing import growth.

Having fallen precipitously during the later 1950s, the US current account balance, swelled by the rapidly rising merchandise trade surplus, had reversed itself over the following half-decade, and reached a peak of $5.8 billion in 1964. Still, the facts that the US failed to recover any of the international market share that it had lost in the 1950s and that US manufacturing corporations continued to direct an ever-increasing portion of their total investment to production overseas, showed that the US economy had secured no really decisive self-transformation. Even by mid-decade, the US economy began to experience, in intensified form, much the same set of domestic and international problems that had plagued it in the later 1950s.

From the start of the 1960s, US policy makers adopted a series of increasingly comprehensive measures aimed at slowing down the accelerating outflow of capital to prepare for a programme of Keynesian stimulus to restore economic dynamism in the wake of the economy's stagnation during the later 1950s.[1] They were, no doubt, less reluctant than they might otherwise have been to restrict the activities of US international bankers and multinational corporations in view of the rise, beginning in the late 1950s, of the essentially unregulated Eurodollar market, which US authorities had decided *not* to control. Through the Eurodollar market, despite increased domestic capital controls, US banks were largely enabled to continue their foreign lending from their overseas bases, and US multinational corporations enabled to meet both their borrowing and investment needs throughout the period.[2] The fact remains that, between 1960 and 1964, even in the face of the growing controls on the outflow of capital from the US, the increase in the net export of long-term capital outran the increase in the current account surplus, with the result that the basic balance of payments stayed negative. From 1965 its fall accelerated, as the trade balance began once again to decline while net overseas investment kept rising.[3] Already in early 1965, well before any major step-up in government spending, a new run on the dollar in response to news of the decline in the trade surplus manifested the failure of US domestic manufacturing to have overcome its problems in competing and in attracting investment funds, and signalled the economy's entry into a new era of economic instability.

During the second half of the 1960s, US manufacturers experienced, as has been seen, major falls in competitiveness and profitability, which could not but seriously undermine US economic dynamism. In this context, when, to keep the economy moving, the government stepped up what was already a substantial stimulus programme, it was bound to call forth accelerated price increases and invite growing international imbalances. Faced as they were with declining rates of profit, and thus

---

1   The government's measures to restrict overseas investment included 'Operation Twist', which involved keeping short-term interest rates relatively high to attract short-term capital from overseas but long-term rates relatively low to stimulate investment spending and relieve unemployment; the Interest Equalization Tax which was designed to discourage portfolio investment abroad by imposing a tax on purchases of foreign securities by US residents; and the Voluntary Foreign Credit Restraint Program and the Foreign Direct Investment Program, which, respectively, imposed ceilings on loans to foreigners by US financial institutions and restricted the availability of funds from US non-financial corporations, notably multinational corporations, to their overseas affiliates. Argy, *Postwar International Money Crisis*, pp. 39–40.

2   E. Helleiner, *States and the Reemergence of Global Finance. From Bretton Woods to the 1990s*, Ithaca 1994, pp. 84–91.

3   Argy, *Postwar International Money Crisis*, pp. 39–40.

reduced surpluses and a deteriorating business climate, US manufacturers naturally responded to any given increase in demand with relatively lower rates of growth of output and investment than previously, as, for example in the period of rising profitability between 1961 and 1965. The increased demand that resulted from rising government deficits was thus predictably unable to stimulate a corresponding increase in domestic supply, and called forth instead more rapidly rising prices and imports. The results were devastating for the US international position and the dollar, and led inevitably to remedial deflationary policies that could not but bring on recession. It was a go-stop progression that would repeat itself with numbing regularity over the next fifteen years.[4]

In 1964, and again in 1965, the Johnson administration, backed by Congress, had implemented major tax cuts—originally planned by the Kennedy administration—even though the economy had already begun to grow quite rapidly in 1962 and 1963. The stage was therefore set for economic over-heating when Johnson refused to propose a tax increase to pay for sharply rising expenditure on the Vietnam War because he feared that Congress would exploit the opening to cut his Great Society programmes. In late 1965, the Federal Reserve stepped into the breach, raising the discount rate and tightening up the supply of credit. By mid 1966 a credit crunch had begun to materialize which threatened to precipitate a cyclical downturn. But the Fed eased up once again to prevent recession and, as military spending continued to rise rapidly, it pursued an accommodating, highly expansionary monetary policy until the last quarter of 1967. In January and August 1967, Johnson finally did propose first a 6 per cent, then a 10 per cent, tax surcharge to slow the economy down but, despite the powerful stimuli already in place and increasing inflationary pressures, Congress failed to enact it. By the end of the year, the Fed was once again having to worry about inflation, but it failed to tighten credit for fear it would bring down the very shaky British pound—a futile consideration, as things turned out. In spring 1968, the government finally did pass the tax surcharge (a case of too little, too late since it seems to have had little effect in depressing consumption demand) and the Fed raised interest rates. But by this time a major crisis was maturing.[5]

At almost exactly the same moment that the US economy was avoiding a cyclical downturn but also fuelling inflation by means of increased federal deficits and easy money, both the German and Japanese economies were experiencing serious recessions—Germany in 1966–67 and Japan in 1965. These cyclical downturns sharply slowed the growth of costs and prices in both countries. With competitiveness thus improved, both economies immediately entered into dynamic, export-led booms, which brought record-breaking current account surpluses (especially at the expense of an increasingly inflation-bound US economy) and, ultimately, the massive increase in imported inflationary pressure (especially from the US).

During the first half of the 1960s, consumer prices in the US had not risen faster than 1.7 per cent in any year. But with the sudden step-up of spending for the

---

4   For further discussion of the relationship between subsidies to demand, falling profitability, and rising inflation, see below, pp. 174–6.

5   Calleo, *Imperious Economy*, pp. 12–14, 25–8; Gordon, 'Postwar Macroeconomics', pp. 136–40; Eckstein, *Great Recession*, pp. 25–7.

Table 9.1. The US trade balance with Germany, Japan, and the world.

	1963	64	65	66	67	68	69	70	71	72	73
Japan	0.3	0.2	-0.5	-0.8	-0.3	-1.2	-1.6	-1.4	-3.3	-3.9	-1.3
Germany	0.6	0.4	0.3	-0.1	-0.3	-1.0	-0.5	-0.4	-0.8	-1.4	-1.6
Japan & Germany	0.9	0.6	0.2	-0.9	-0.6	-2.2	-2.1	-1.8	-4.1	-5.3	-2.9
World	5.2	6.8	4.9	3.8	3.8	0.6	0.6	2.6	-2.3	-6.4	0.9
Current Account	4.4	6.8	5.4	3.0	2.6	0.6	0.4	2.3	-1.4	-5.8	2.3

Sources: Kosai, *The Era of High-Speed Growth*, p. 177; Liesner, *One Hundred Years of Economic Statistics*, p. 104, Table US.15; ERP 1983, p. 76, Table B-101.

Vietnam War from the second half of 1965, they suddenly doubled to 3.4 per cent in 1966. Following the appearance in 1967 and 1968 of the largest federal deficits since the Korean War, inflation accelerated further, reaching 4.2 per cent and 5.4 per cent in 1968 and 1969. In parallel manner, beginning in 1965, US trade balances with Japan and Germany—quite healthy and positive from 1960 through 1964— fell rapidly. In 1966, the trade deficit with Germany and Japan combined reached close to $1 billion; by 1968 and 1969 it exceeded $2 billion; and in 1971 and 1972, as the trade crisis hit its nadir, it grew to (what at that point were considered) the colossal levels of $4.1 billion and $5.3 billion respectively (see Table 9.1).

The decline of the combined trade balance with Germany and Japan was the dynamic factor determining the collapse of the overall US trade balance. Between 1960 and 1964, merchandise imports had increased by 27 per cent, exports by 29.7 per cent; between 1964 and 1971, imports grew by 144 per cent; exports by 66.5 per cent. By 1966, the trade balance had already declined by close to 50 per cent with respect to its 1964 peak; by 1968 and 1969, undercut by the accelerating inflation, it had fallen to new postwar lows and, at $635 and $607 million, respectively, was heading toward disappearance. In 1971, the US experienced its first trade deficit of the twentieth century. The merchandise trade balance went into the red by $2.72 billion in 1971 and by $6.99 billion in 1972—down by a spectacular $13.7 billion in the eight years from 1964. Meanwhile, the trade balance in manufactured goods fell to zero in 1971 and to $2 billion in deficit in 1972. These merchandise trade deficits were far too large to be counterbalanced by surpluses on trade in services and returns on foreign investment and in 1971 and 1972 the balance on current account also went negative, by $1.4 billion and $5.8 billion.

As US external balances fell and those of Germany and Japan rose, the money market inevitably placed renewed downward pressure on the dollar and upward pressure on the mark and the yen. In early 1968, after having undermined the pound—despite US support for it—speculators once again attacked the dollar, threatening to bring down the whole dollar-based international monetary system. The US was able to prevent the collapse of the Bretton Woods system only by partially dismantling it. It ceased to honour its commitment to sell gold to private parties at $35 per ounce, thereby ending dollar convertibility and putting the system on a purely dollar basis.[6]

But the matter did not end there. As Germany's international competitiveness improved, its current account balance took off once again, rising spectacularly from DM1.7 billion in 1966 to DM13.2 billion in 1968. With the currency implicitly strengthened, speculative inflows, emanating largely from the eurodollar market reached record proportions, leading to pressures to revalue the mark quite analogous to those of the end of the 1950s. Dollars thus poured into the country in search of marks, massively swelling the money supply. Hardly had the economy emerged from recession, than it began, bit by bit, to experience imported inflation. By autumn 1968, the Bundesbank had decided to advocate a revaluation. The German government put off taking this step for another year, but ultimately could not avoid it. Following a new wave of speculation in September 1969, the government raised the value of the mark by 9.3 per cent in late October 1969, posing an immediate problem for the continued growth of German exports and, in turn, for the extension of the German boom.[7]

In Japan, too, the rapid growth of the current account surplus from 1968 and 1969 attracted a huge influx of dollars, the beginning of imported inflationary pressure, and a growing demand for yen revaluation. Unlike the Germans, however, the Japanese sought to avoid at all cost the revaluation of their currency, inviting a wave of inflation that would eventually dwarf that of Germany.

The US government made one last attempt to turn the tide. In the latter part of 1968, the Johnson administration finally began to combine fiscal austerity and tight money, with the goals of preventing further prices rises and of heading off renewed international monetary instability. From early 1969, the newly elected Nixon administration extended the 10 per cent tax surcharge initiated in mid 1968, reduced the investment tax credit, and cut federal spending, while the Fed maintained a tight rein on credit. With US interest rates continuing high, international monetary turmoil briefly subsided, as short-term money poured back into dollars. Meanwhile, a credit crunch developed, leading to the recession of 1970, and the first full year of negative growth since 1958.[8]

Nevertheless, the combined economic and political costs of sustaining a serious anti-inflationary policy quickly proved unacceptable to the Nixon administration, especially in the wake of an alarming fall in the stock market and a lengthening string of business failures highlighted by the collapse of the Penn Central Railroad. Well before the defeat of the Republicans in the congressional elections of November 1970, and as high interest rates threatened to choke off the recovery, the government turned once again to fiscal stimulus and the Fed accommodated with

6　Calleo, *Imperious Economy*, pp. 56–7. The US maintained a formal, hypothetical commitment to pay out gold at the official price to central banks, thereby constituting the so-called two-tiered system. But this pledge had already been emptied of substance by the combination of US power and economic weakness. 'America's hegemony over its allies was no longer to be mocked by the private market. Gold was effectively demonetized. The world was on a de facto dollar standard.'

7　Giersch et al., *The Fading Miracle*, pp. 148–51; O. Emminger, 'The D-Mark in the Conflict Between Internal and External Equilibrium, 1948–75', *Princeton Essays in International Finance*, no. 122, June 1977, pp. 24–6.

8　For this and the following paragraph, see Eckstein, *Great Recession*, pp. 40–1; Calleo, *Imperious Economy*, pp. 58–9.

a policy of easy credit. As Nixon was to put it several months later, 'We are all Keynesians now.' Even under the pressures of declining competitiveness, rising prices, and the deterioration of the US balances of trade and payments, the Nixon administration thus showed itself unwilling to take remedial action. By its refusal to act, it signalled to its trading partners that it would take no responsibility for the export of inflation; countries wishing to avoid the flooding in of dollars and the resulting rise of domestic prices should revalue their currencies. Currency revaluations by the US's trading rivals, as Nixon of course understood, would improve US competitiveness, raise profitability on US exports, and reduce the pressure from imports on the US economy.

Once the US authorities had turned toward macroeconomic expansion in mid 1970, the international monetary order was as good as dead. In Germany, the respite provided by the revaluation of the mark in autumn 1969—as well as by temporarily high interest rates and recession in the US—turned out to be very brief. In response to the continued increase of inflationary pressures, the Bundesbank progressively tightened credit from March 1969, taking the discount rate to the record level of 7.5 per cent in March 1970. It also began a two-year tightening of fiscal policy. In Japan, where no revaluation took place despite the fast-rising current account surplus, the authorities also restricted the money supply and raised interest rates to try to contain prices. But, when interest rates fell in the US while they remained high or were increased in Germany, in Europe more generally, and in Japan, short-term speculative money fled the dollar, and the US overall payments deficit (short and long term together) exploded to $10 billion in 1970 and $30 billion in 1971. World reserves in these two years thus rose by no less than 18 per cent and 32 per cent, respectively, laying the foundations for uncontrollable international inflation. By 1971, the US's gold reserves represented less than a quarter of its official liabilities. In 1971, as the US federal deficit reached its highest level of the postwar epoch up to that point, the US trade deficit hit a twentieth-century record.[9]

The pressures for a reordering of international rates of exchange had now become unbearable. The Bundesbank had raised the discount rate with the purpose of cooling down the economy, but from the point that the US had begun to loosen, money had flooded into Germany in search of marks to exploit the interest-rate differential, and inflation continued to soar. This is exactly what had happened in 1960, but it now occurred on a much greater scale. The US was exporting inflation with a vengeance—it increased in Germany from 3.8 per cent in 1970 to 5.2 per cent in 1971—and by May 1971, the German government, along with the Dutch, saw no choice but to allow their currencies to float upward. The Swiss and Austrians revalued their currencies. The US government seemed to be getting its wish. Speculative dollars now, however, flowed into France and Belgium, where they were converted to gold, and US gold reserves fell towards the symbolically critical $10 billion mark. Japan, under huge pressure from the US to revalue in the face of trade and current account surpluses that in 1970–71 smashed all previous records, nonetheless stood pat, announcing that it would maintain its currency at 360 yen to the dollar, the level at which it had been fixed in the late 1940s. In August 1971, however, Nixon introduced his 'New Economic Policy', by which he

9 Argy, *Postwar International Money Crisis*, p. 62; Giersch et al., *Fading Miracle*, pp. 149–54, 178–9.

suspended the convertibility of dollars into gold and imposed a 10 per cent surcharge on imports, while, not coincidentally, introducing new fiscal stimuli into the
economy in the form of an increased investment tax credit, the repeal of excise taxes
on cars and trucks, and personal income tax reductions. This was an open declara-
tion of war on the US's economic rivals and an implicit demand that they revalue
their currencies. In December 1971, the signing of the Smithsonian Agreement
brought a devaluation of the dollar by 7.89 per cent against gold and the revaluation of other currencies against the dollar, the mark by a total of 13.5 per cent and
the yen by a total of 16.88 per cent.[10]

The new international monetary dispensation, which continued to feature fixed
exchange rates, failed to stabilize itself and lasted little more than a year. It was
well-known that the Smithsonian rates had only emerged after hard bargaining,
that the US had maintained that larger changes in exchange rates would be needed
to restore equilibrium, and that key US officials regarded the new parities as only
provisional. Already in February and March 1972, the dollar was again in trouble
and the US government and its partners had to bail it out by means of currency
purchases. But with a presidential election coming up in the autumn, the Nixon
administration placed renewed pressure on the dollar by enacting still another
round of stimulus. The ensuing budget deficit accommodated by easy credit helped
bring a tripling of the previous record trade deficit in 1972 and, with it, a new round
of capital flight from the dollar. By the end of 1972, mainly as a consequence of the
rocketing US balance of payments deficits, world reserves had doubled their total
of 1969, increasing as much in the intervening three years as in all previous cen-
turies of recorded history.[11] With Germany and Japan accumulating dollars at rates
that made it impossible to control liquidity and inflation, the Smithsonian parities
were not long for this world.[12]

Prices were now ready to go through the roof. Nixon's wage-price controls had
briefly restrained inflation. But in January 1973, these controls were unexpectedly
lifted, and the annual rate of increase of consumer prices exploded from 3.9 per
cent in the last quarter of 1972 to 6.2 per cent in the first quarter of 1973. By February
1973, the acceleration of inflation in the US had detonated a new foreign-exchange
crisis, and the US and its allies quickly agreed to a further devaluation of the dollar
of 10 per cent. Even so, the US authorities made clear that they were in no way
committed to support the new parities or, by implication, even to the maintenance
of a fixed-rate regime, almost inviting further instability. Between January and
March 1973, DM27.8 billion flooded into Germany, and after a brief attempt to
defend the new parities, the advanced capitalist countries formally abandoned the
fixed-rate system of exchange, resorting to the float.[13] During 1973, the mark was
revalued by 20.4 per cent against the dollar, making for an extraordinary total of
appreciation of the German currency against the dollar between 1969 and 1973 of

10   Giersch et al., *Fading Miracle*, pp. 178–9; Eckstein, *Great Recession*, p. 41; Calleo, *Imperious Economy*,
pp. 60–2; T. Uchino, *Japan's Postwar Economy*, Tokyo 1983, pp. 179–86.
11   R. Triffin, 'The International Role and Fate of the Dollar', *Foreign Affairs*, vol. lvii, Winter 1978/1979,
pp. 270–1.
12   B. Tew, *The Evolution of the International Monetary System, 1945–1981*, London 1982, pp. 161–2.
13   Argy, *Postwar International Money Crisis*, pp. 65–6; Eckstein, *Great Recession*, p. 43; Uchino, *Japan's
Postwar Economy*, pp. 192–6; Giersch, *The Fading Miracle*, pp. 179–80.

50 per cent. The yen was revalued a further 12 per cent in 1973, making for a total appreciation since December 1971 of 28.2 per cent.

In the space of a few short years, the US manufacturing sector secured by dollar devaluation the kind of turnaround in relative costs that it had been unable to achieve by way of productivity growth and wage restraint, even when it was performing at its postwar best during the first half of the 1960s. This gain did not, of course, come without a cost: dollar devaluation meant an increase in the price of imports and thus a decline in living standards, but reducing relative wages in aid of improving competitiveness was obviously its purpose. Between 1970 and 1973, unit labour costs in manufacturing (expressed in dollars) grew at an average annual rate of 0.6 per cent in the US, compared to 17.6 per cent in Germany and 19 per cent in Japan. Over the same period, US relative unit labour costs in manufacturing fell on average by 9.9 per cent per year.[14] The average annual growth of US export prices between 1971 and 1973, at 9.5 per cent, could therefore achieve rough equality with those of Japan, at 9 per cent, and Germany, at 8.7 per cent—after having grown at double Germany's and at close to five times the rate of Japan's between 1965 and 1970.

The reductions in US relative costs made possible by the devaluation of the dollar, along with the gains in capacity utilization secured with the recovery from recession, had a galvanizing effect on the US economy. After having averaged -2.8 per cent per annum between 1966 and 1971, investment growth in manufacturing suddenly hit 9.7 per cent and 14.7 per cent in 1972 and 1973 respectively. Between 1970 and 1973, labour productivity growth in manufacturing also increased impressively, at an average annual rate of 5.2 per cent (5.3 per cent net), and outran the average annual growth of product compensation, at 4.5 per cent for these years. In the same period, capital productivity also slightly increased. Manufacturing profitability, which had dropped precipitately, by 50 per cent between 1965 and 1970, ceased to fall and staged something of a comeback, increasing by 20 per cent in the subsequent three years, leaving the total decline between 1965 and 1973 at 40.9 per cent. Meanwhile, by 1973, the US trade balance, on a downward trajectory from the mid 1960s until 1972, was suddenly restored to surplus, as merchandise exports hit an all-time high.

The outcome of the international monetary crisis, set off by intensifying international competition leading to declining profitability and rising external deficits in the US, was thus a partial recovery of US competitiveness, leading to somewhat improved profitability and international balances. The impact, however, on the German and Japanese economies of the revaluations of the mark and yen that marked the disintegration of the Bretton Woods system was just the opposite—and they now began to shoulder the burden of the world crisis of profitability.

2. The Crisis of the German Economy, 1969–73

From 1969, profitability in the German economy, especially its manufacturing sector, declined sharply, continuing the pattern whereby German manufacturing profitability mirrored that of the US but in reverse—rising through much of the 1950s

14   Expressed in a common currency by reference to the trade-weighted average of the seventeen leading international competitors. 'Unit Labour Costs in Manufacturing Industry and in the Whole Economy', *European Economy*, no. 11, March 1982, Table 11.

while it fell in the US, falling from the latter part of the 1950s through the mid 1960s while it was recovering in the US, and then rising again between 1965 and 1969 as US profitability plunged. The decline in German manufacturing profitability in the years immediately before the onset of the oil embargo represented, in important respects, a continuation, and a serious worsening, of the decline in German manu-facturing profitability of the late 1950s and early 1960s. Like the earlier decline, it was largely an irrepressible by-product of Germany's particular form of export-oriented pattern of development as well as the intensification of international competition. Germany's descent into crisis at the end of the 1960s was thus the consequence both of the vertiginous rise of the mark and of the simultaneous and closely related exacerbation of international over-capacity and over-production in manufacturing. Between 1969 and 1973, the German economy thus joined the whole of the advanced capitalist world in entering the long downturn, driven by the inter-national profitability crisis in manufacturing.

Manufacturing profitability had fallen by 12 per cent in 1961 and at an average annual rate of 5.3 per cent between 1961 and 1965, before recovering at an average annual rate of 2.6 per cent between 1965 and 1969. Between 1969 and 1973, it fell again, at an average annual rate of 8.35 per cent, or by 30 per cent in total. At the same time, profitability in the private business economy as a whole fell at an average annual rate of 5.1 per cent.

A rising demand for labour no doubt conditioned the squeeze on profitability, but cannot be said to have caused it, since the labour market had actually become looser than it had been in the early 1960s. Following the large-scale introduction of immigrant workers in 1966–67, and the policy decision to integrate them and their dependants on a long-term basis, the labour force was never again as fully employed as it had been at the start of the decade.[15] But the fact remains that increased labour militancy did in these years express the growing organized power of German workers, and *did* bring serious downward pressure to bear on the profit rate. Between 1969 and 1973, the manufacturing real wage increased at an average annual rate of 6.6 per cent, compared to 4.9 per cent between 1965 and 1969, and 5.7 per cent between 1960 and 1965. Average annual labour productivity growth in man-ufacturing fell to 3.9 per cent, compared to about 5.2 per cent for the years 1960–69.

During the mid 1960s, following the Social Democrats' entry into the Grand Coalition and the government's adoption of a voluntary incomes policy and wage-price guidelines, the unions had continued to accommodate the requirements of capital accumulation, deliberately adopting a policy of restraint in the hope of enabling the economy to firmly re-enter a solid path of growth following the severe recession of 1966–67. But wage growth dropped below and profitability rose above even the levels recommended by the semi-official Council of Experts.[16] In autumn 1969, a series of major wildcat strikes, emanating not from the official

15   Carlin, 'Profitability in West Germany', pp. 340–1.
16   'The main impact that might be ascribed to [the incomes policy and wage-price guidelines that accom-panied concerted action] was an outstandingly long wage lag after 1967 ... wages had lost contact with sharply rising profits in the upswing of 1968 and 1969 ... curiously, the real wage increase realized in 1968 was even less than the council had suggested as realizable in its guideline for 1968.' G. Fels, 'Inflation in Germany', in L. B. Krause and W. A. Salant, eds, *Worldwide Inflation. Theory and Recent Experience*, Washington, DC 1977, p. 620.

unions but from the rank and file, shook German industry—employers and union bureaucracy alike. The unions were thus obliged to try to make up for the losses sustained by their members during the previous period as a consequence of their concessions to the employers, as well as to protest the intensification of work introduced after the cyclical downturn of 1966–67. In this they were highly successful. Whereas during the period from January through August 1969, wage gains had fallen within the 6.0–7.1 range, from September through December they reached the 8.5 per cent–12.1 per cent range, smashing the guidelines set at 5.5–6.5 per cent. To regain control, union officialdom henceforth adopted a more aggressive bargaining stance, securing an especially large real wage increase in 1970.[17]

The rise of worker militancy and the so-called 'wage explosion' was thus a *compensatory reaction* to the previous 'profit explosion'. As Hennings puts it, 'The profit explosion generated high wage demands.'[18] In the end, the average annual growth of the manufacturing real wage over the two periods taken together— between 1965 and 1973—was thus, at 5.7 per cent, almost exactly the same as the 5.6 per cent registered between 1960 and 1965, while the average annual growth of manufacturing labour productivity, at 4.7 per cent, was only slightly lower than the 4.9 per cent registered between 1960–65.

Given domestic factors alone, the resulting fall in profitability would have been minor. This is evident from the fact that, although the average annual growth of unit labour costs between 1969 and 1973 in the private sector outside manufacturing was, at 9.4 per cent, actually higher than that in manufacturing, at 8.0 per cent, the non-manufacturing sector was able to avoid a serious decline in its profit rate because it was able to raise its prices at an average annual rate of 8.5 per cent, compared to just 5.8 per cent in manufacturing. Between 1969 and 1973, therefore, the average annual decline of the non-manufacturing profit share was just 2.05 per cent, that of the profit rate 2.3 per cent, for a total of 9.1 per cent over the four years. The fall in the manufacturing profit rate in this period was, by contrast, 30 per cent. It was only because the profit rate decline in manufacturing was more than three times as great as in non-manufacturing that there was, in these years, a significant decline in the profit rate in the private business economy as a whole, of about 20 per cent.

It was an increase in relative costs in international terms that determined that German manufacturing profitability would, by 1973, fall significantly below not only its level of 1969, but also that of 1965. Throughout the long boom, Germany had, of course, based its economic growth on the rapid increase of exports. It had done so by restraining the growth of domestic costs by political and socio-economic means, and by exploiting its historic comparative advantage in the production of capital goods, chemicals, and the like at a time in which international demand for these products was rapidly rising. Between 1960 and 1973, exports grew at an average annual rate of 7.5 per cent, while domestic absorption grew only half as rapidly, at an average annual rate of 3.6 per cent.[19] But, as repeatedly stressed, the fact that the German economy's ability to export was so dependent upon the repression of

---

17   Muller-Jentsch and Sperling, 'Economic Development', pp. 265–7, 269–72, 285–8.
18   Hennings, 'West Germany', p. 491.
19   Giersch et al., *Fading Miracle*, p. 132.

domestic demand to keep costs down meant that trade and current account surpluses were, in the medium run, an inevitable by-product of export dynamism
—and, sooner or later, a barrier to it. This structural limitation of export-oriented
German development, in combination with the growing threat posed by Germany's
overseas competitors, had already proved an impediment to German growth in the
late 1950s and early 1960s, and declining German competitiveness had been heavily
responsible for declining manufacturing profitability in that period. The same syndrome manifested itself once again in the tumultuous economic environment of the
late 1960s and early 1970s.

The reduction in the growth of costs following the government's deflationary
measures and the recession of 1966–67 had made possible, as we have seen, a new
boom in exports, an associated rise of external surpluses, an implicit strengthening
of the currency, speculative upward pressure on the mark, and ultimately a
revaluation of the currency by 9.3 per cent. But the revaluation of autumn 1969
could not stabilize the international monetary order, for it could not prevent the
intensification of the same trends that had brought it about. Between March 1969
and December 1971, although the German current account fell, the combination of
US loosening to stimulate growth and German tightening to control inflation produced intolerable pressure on currencies that forced first the float and ultimately
the further 16 per cent revaluation of the mark that came with the Smithsonian
Agreement of December 1971. Of course, the Smithsonian Agreement itself soon
fell apart, bringing about the final collapse of Bretton Woods and still another round
of revaluation in February–March 1973. All told, between 1969 and 1973, the effective or trade-weighted exchange rate of the mark increased at an average annual
rate of 6.1 per cent.

Faced with such a sizeable increase in the mark's value, German manufacturers,
heavily dependent as they were upon exports, were obliged to choose between two
routes. Were they to attempt to maintain their profit rates by accepting higher relative prices, they could not but sustain declining export growth and declining shares
of the world market. Were they to try to maintain their export growth by holding
down their prices, they could not but sustain declining profit rates.

In fact, as Carlin has demonstrated, German manufacturers took the latter route.
Between 1969 and 1973, Germany's relative unit labour costs grew at the very large
average annual rate of 6.1 per cent, a development entirely attributable to the
increased value (effective exchange rate) of the mark. Nevertheless, German exporters
held down the increase of their export prices in terms of marks to an average annual
rate of only 3.7 per cent. Even though the revaluation of the mark imposed a further
average annual effective increase in their selling price of 6.1 per cent, they were thus
able to keep the selling price of their goods competitive, as world export prices were
increasing in these years at an average annual rate of 9.1 per cent. German manufacturers were therefore actually able to slightly increase their share of world exports
and world manufacturing exports between 1969 and 1973, although it should be noted
that, because the growth of world trade was already slowing, the average annual
increase of German exports, at 7.2 per cent, represented a significant fall-off from the
boom levels of 10 per cent achieved between 1965 and 1969.[20]

20   Branson, 'Trends in US International Trade', p. 196, Table 3.13.

Table 9.2. Costs, prices, and profitability in Germany, 1969–73.
(Percentage rates of change.)

	NPR	NPSh	PW	LPy	NW	ULC	PPri	NY/NK	NY/NK real	NKPri
Mfgr	-8.4	-7.7	5.9	3.5	12.0	8.0	5.8	-0.8	-0.8	5.7
Non-mfgr	-2.3	-2.1	3.7	2.9	12.5	9.4	8.5	-0.3	-2.6	6.6

Sources: See Appendix I on Profit Rates. Key to legend on page xiii.

German producers, to retain their markets, were thus obliged to refrain from raising their prices in marks in accord with increased costs, and even so had to accept declining export growth. But holding down prices in the face of rising costs had an inevitable result: while protecting in the short term its capacity to export and thus its main engine of growth, the German manufacturing sector could not but sustain a major decline in its rate of profit on capital stock, and thus a profound blow to its longer-term prospects for growth.[21] In the non-manufacturing sector, because the (relatively restricted) fall in profitability represented only a short-term out-running of labour productivity by product wage growth, there was no reason to expect it to precipitate irresolvable longer-term problems. Adjustment to the fall in the profit share could—and did—take place through the subsequent restraint of wage growth. But in manufacturing, because the fall in profitability represented not so much a local problem of rising wages relative to productivity, as a system-wide problem of over-capacity and over-production resulting from intensified international competition, the road to recovery was far less direct, and would turn out to be very much more difficult to negotiate.

3. The Crisis of the Japanese Economy, 1970–73

After 1970, profitability in Japanese manufacturing—and in the economy in general—turned down, suddenly and sharply. In so doing, it continued to track the evolution of profitability in German manufacturing, while mirroring in reverse that of the US, as it had done throughout the postwar era. Japanese profitability thus tripled over the course of the 1950s (through 1961), fell back temporarily during the first half of the 1960s, then exploded upward from 1965 to 1970. In Japan, the culminating rise in profitability over the second half of the 1960s was far more spec-tacular than that in Germany, bringing the profit rate to its highest level for the postwar period, and was made possible by a much more powerful explosion of exports. The Japanese export boom, like the German, was fed by the US government's fiscal and monetary expansion—and the Japanese government's ongoing fiscal and monetary moderation—and brought about enormous current account surpluses. Like the German expansion, therefore, it ultimately proved self-undermining, as it placed irresistible upward pressure on the yen. With the fall of the dollar and the

---

21   Carlin, 'Profitability in West Germany', pp. 346–9.

revaluation of the yen over the years 1971–73, the Japanese manufacturing economy lost much of its cost advantage in the world market, suffered a substantial fall in profitability, and sustained a definitive reduction in its potential for growth.

The fall in the profit rate and the descent into crisis of the Japanese economy took place in two stages. The first downward step in profitability occurred during 1970–71, and resulted from the petering out of the massive wave of investment undertaken by Japanese industry in the second half of the 1960s, the Japanese government's sharply deflationary measures of 1969–70, and Nixon's 10 per cent import surcharge and de facto move to devalue the dollar in August 1971. The second downward step in profitability took place over the subsequent two years, 1972 and 1973. Beginning in 1971, the government applied a massive monetary and fiscal stimulus designed to counteract the shock to business confidence that had followed the revaluation of the yen, to raise domestic demand so as to compensate for the sudden fall in exports, and, above all, to force the value of the yen back down so as to revive export dynamism. But this policy ended in failure. In the face of the intransigent pursuit of expansion, inflation, and international deficits by US policy-makers, the stoking of demand was unable to bring down the yen. Nor, alternatively, could the subsidy to demand precipitate the very difficult, if not impossible, domestic structural adjustment that was required to maintain the economy's momentum: specifically, the substitution for the loss of opportunities to profit from sales overseas by the creation of opportunities to profit from sales at home, through the creation of a domestic market that could grow dynamically with only limited help from exports. The result was runaway inflation and ultimately a further squeeze on profits.

Step 1. Deflation and Contraction

After a brief slowdown in the early 1960s, Japanese real exports had, from 1964 or so, once again begun to grow at annual rates of close to 20 per cent. Even so, as late as 1967, the Japanese trade surplus stood at only $800 million dollars, no threat to international stability. But, as US federal deficits suddenly leapt higher, US external balances abruptly deteriorated and Japanese external balances exploded upward. For Japan, as for Germany, the years 1968–69, when the US economy sustained accelerating inflation and an accompanying fall in the trade balance, seem to have marked the turning point. In 1968, the Japanese trade surplus tripled, reaching $2.5 billion, and averaged $3.75 billion in 1969 and 1970. Japanese foreign currency reserves which, at around $2 billion, had changed little from 1961 to 1968, reached $4.4 billion at the end of 1970 and $7.6 billion in June 1971.[22]

The sharp increases in the trade and the current account surpluses introduced, as they had in Germany, major imported inflationary pressures into the Japanese domestic economy. Starting in 1968, for the first time since the start of the boom, not only consumer but also wholesale prices grew rapidly. From the standpoint of its overseas rivals, and most notably the US government, Japan should have attacked inflation, as did Germany, by bringing down its external surpluses by revaluing the currency. But the Japanese government did roughly the opposite. It

---

22   For this and the following paragraph, see Uchino, *Japan's Postwar Economy*, pp. 171–9. In these years, Japan and Germany were the only advanced industrial economies running substantial trade surpluses.

Table 9.3. The Japanese trade surplus ($ billions).

1961	62	63	64	65	66	67	68	69	70	71	72	73
-0.1	0.5	0.0	1.0	1.9	2.2	0.8	2.5	3.6	3.9	7.7	8.9	3.7

Sources: Kosai, *The Era of High-Speed Growth*, p. 177; Uchino, *Japan's Postwar Economy*, p. 174.

adopted a series of cosmetic trade-liberalization measures to quiet foreign critics. At the same time, to quell inflation in a fashion that would make possible the continuation of export-oriented growth, it implemented a policy of tight credit.

The turn to deflationary policy in 1969–70 proved remarkably successful in its own narrow terms, for the economy immediately turned down and the growth of prices for manufactures and exports came to a halt by the end of 1970.[23] Its ultimate impact, however, was precisely the opposite of that intended by the authorities. In 1971, the Japanese trade surplus broke all records: its global total doubled, reaching $7.7 billion and accounting for more than 75 per cent of the total trade surplus accrued by the OECD countries taken together; in manufactures it reached $17.1 billion; and with the US, it grew by almost two-and-a-half times.[24] By cooling down the Japanese economy at the very moment at which the US was heating up, the Japanese authorities had thus brought the simmering international monetary crisis to a boil, creating unstoppable pressures for yen revaluation/dollar devaluation. Next came Richard Nixon's New Economic Policy, and, with it, the effective end of the 'era of high-speed growth'.

The 'Nixon Shock' occurred on 15 August 1971. Before the month was out, it had precipitated the float of yen and the worst stock-market crash in Japanese history, deepening and extending the recession which, having begun in the middle of 1970, lasted until the end of 1971. In 1971, the growth of manufacturing output and of GDP fell drastically from average annual rates, respectively, of 15.8 per cent and 12.3 per cent for the period 1965–70 to 6.2 per cent and 4.7 per cent, respectively. Behind the recession was a spectacular collapse of investment which, after having grown at an average annual rate of well over 20 per cent in both manufacturing and the private business economy between 1965 and 1970, actually *fell* in 1971 by 10 per cent in manufacturing and by 3.1 per cent in the private business economy. Capacity utilization fell by about 6 per cent in manufacturing and half that in the private business economy. In the space of this one year, the rate of profit declined in manufacturing by 16 per cent and in the private business economy by 22 per cent.

The cause of the fall in the rate of profit during 1971 was not, as in the supply-side story, an autonomous acceleration of wages or slowdown of productivity, but quite obviously a fall in demand. The latter may have had its origins in an exhaustion of the cyclical investment boom of the second half of the 1960s. The extraordinary expansion of new plant and equipment that took place in those years

23   Krause and Sekiguchi, 'Japan and the World Economy', p. 401.
24   Uchino, *Japan's Postwar Economy*, pp. 173–4; Kosai, *Era of High-Speed Growth*, p. 177.

was not indefinitely sustainable and it seems to have begun to falter in 1970, in much the same manner as its equally impressive predecessor of the second half of the 1950s had in 1961. In any case, the government's tightening of credit in 1969–70 intentionally reduced the growth of demand, which was further slowed by the Nixon Shock with its import surcharge on US imports and by yen revaluation. Reduced demand brought down profitability in both manufacturing and the private business economy as a whole by causing major falls in both the profit share and the output-capital ratio, as well as capacity utilization.

A sharp decline in measured productivity growth was the main source of the decline in the profit share. But this formal reduction in productivity increase represented no decline in the efficiency of production. It was rather an artefact of the reduced growth of demand. Japanese business was committed to avoiding layoffs unless absolutely necessary. Despite the sharp slowdown in growth and the accompanying fall in capacity utilization that took place during the 1971 recession, unemployment therefore failed to increase. Labour productivity fell because there was no downward adjustment of labour inputs in keeping with the reduction in output. That no autonomous downward trend in labour productivity growth was behind the Japanese economy's slipping into crisis is confirmed by the fact that, after having increased at average annual rates of 13.4 per cent and 10.7 per cent in manufacturing and in the private business economy, respectively, over the years 1965–70 (and by 11 per cent and 12 per cent in these sectors, respectively, in 1970), labour productivity suddenly plunged to 5.3 per cent and 3.9 per cent, respectively, in the recession year of 1971, but immediately returned to 11 per cent and 9.4 per cent in manufacturing and the private business economy, respectively, in 1972.

The growth of nominal and real wages in 1971 was actually slightly lower in both manufacturing and the private business economy than it had been in the previous several years. Nevertheless, in both sectors, increased product wage growth was sufficiently high to squeeze profits because in 1971 firms in manufacturing and the private business sector could raise their product prices at average annual rates of just 0 per cent and 2.6 per cent respectively, whereas they had been able to raise them at average annual rates of 3.55 per cent and 4.7 per cent respectively, between 1965 and 1970. Wage growth brought down profitability because, due to the fall in demand, manufacturers could not mark up over costs to the degree they had previously.

The final factor depressing profitability in 1971 was a reduction in the output-capital ratio, which fell by 5.7 per cent and 11.6 per cent in manufacturing and the private business economy respectively—after having performed impressively in both sectors between 1965 and 1970. Reduced demand was still again the main determining factor. If the manufacturing output-capital ratio is adjusted for capacity utilization, the registered fall is virtually eliminated.

Step 2. Inflation and the Failure of Recovery

The Japanese economy had experienced slowdowns precipitated by the government's macroeconomic tightening in 1957–58, 1961–62, and 1965, but had in each case quickly regained its momentum. The cyclical downturn of 1971 was distinctive in two major respects. First, it went on a good deal longer than any previous one. Second, and most significant, even after it ended, the economy never regained its former momentum. The question is why.

What discouraged economic revival was mainly the narrowing of Japanese export prospects, resulting from the revaluation of the yen, as well as the dramatic reduction in the growth of world demand and world trade that was part and parcel of the generalized slowdown of growth of the advanced capitalist economies. In the years 1972 and 1973, the average annual growth of exports (in yen terms) was 4.6 per cent, a reduction of almost three-quarters from the average annual increase of 17.2 per cent between 1965–70 and clear-cut evidence of the suddenly transformed conditions facing Japanese producers. When the government's record-breaking stimulus programme of these years failed to restore the economy's dynamism by shifting its foundations to the domestic market, there could be little doubt that an historic turning point had been reached for the Japanese economy.

As early as autumn 1970, the government had begun to back off from its restrictive monetary policy, because manufacturing and export price inflation had been just about brought under control. During 1971, the government had eased up further to counter the unexpectedly severe slowdown, sharply increasing the supply of credit while taking fiscal policy in a stimulative direction. In the wake of the Nixon Shock, meanwhile, the state had sought to prevent businesses from suffering losses from dollar devaluation by buying up an enormous quantity of dollars at the old exchange rate for several weeks in August before going to the float. Finally, with export prospects so profoundly reduced by the yen revaluation of December 1971, the government unleashed a monetary and fiscal stimulus of historic and (some would say) foolhardy proportions. The 1972 budget called for spending increases that amounted to 22 per cent (and the supplementary budget approved later in the year added expenditures amounting to a further 1.4 per cent of GNP). The money supply, having already grown by a stunning 24.3 per cent in 1971, increased by 24.7 per cent in 1972.[25]

In embarking on its inflationary course, the government had several ends in mind. Because of the enormous investment in fixed capital made by Japanese producers during the second half of the 1960s, much of it debt-financed, a really serious recession threatened huge realization problems and devastating losses. The government hoped to preclude these effects by substituting its own expenditures for lost export demand. Because the initial yen revaluation had failed to dissipate Japan's large current account surplus, international pressure mounted to force the yen up further. Rather than accede to this pressure, the government sought through subsidizing demand to suck in more imports, correct the current account balance, and force the yen back down.

By the end of 1972, the historically unprecedented government stimulus had failed to restore the economy's momentum. The growth of manufacturing output for 1972, at 10.6 per cent, was still at only 60 per cent of the average for 1965–70, while the growth of output for the economy as a whole (real GDP), at 8.2 per cent, was not much better. Investment growth fell another 7.2 per cent, making for a total reduction of 18 per cent over two years, and capacity utilization failed to recover,

---

25   Ackley and Ishi, 'Fiscal, Monetary, and Related Policies', p. 230. Japan's 1972 budget called for spending increases that were 20–30 per cent over the original budgets for 1971 and which amounted to 18 per cent of GNP.

and by some measures fell further. In December 1972, the OECD *Economic Outlook* described business investment as weak, referred to sizeable over-capacity, and characterized the growth of GNP during 1972 as 'insufficient to reduce the margin of slack'.[26] Manufacturing profitability fell another 4 per cent in 1972 beyond the 16 per cent it had fallen in 1971.

There had been at best a partial recovery because the government-generated subsidy to demand had been unable to compensate for the collapse of exports. In 1972, export growth in nominal terms had fallen to 4.1 per cent, down from the 16 per cent increase in 1971, which was pretty close to the average for the previous five years. Profits were squeezed by much increased product wage growth, combined with somewhat reduced productivity growth, along with a further reduced output-capital ratio—developments which were themselves reflective of increased competitive pressure on prices, as well as the further fall in investment growth and the still reduced level of capacity utilization.

Money wage growth in manufacturing in 1972 returned to the average annual level achieved between 1965 and 1970—15 per cent—and turned out to be a major factor forcing down profits. But a 15 per cent increase in the nominal wage in 1972 would have meant no increased pressure on profitability had it not represented a product wage increase of 14 per cent, up 40 per cent from the 10.1 per cent average annual increase in the product wage which that same nominal wage figure had represented during the years between 1965 and 1970. It was the reduction in the rate of growth of manufacturing output prices that brought the increase in product wage growth. In 1972, the manufacturing output price deflator rose by a scant 0.9 per cent, less than a quarter its average rate of increase between 1965 and 1970, and the reason is not hard to find.

With the appreciation of the yen, Japanese manufacturers suddenly faced intensified competition from abroad. In 1972, unit labour costs in manufacturing in terms of the national currency rose by just 1.1 per cent, but in terms of a trade-weighted currency by no less than 11.8 per cent,[27] and in terms of the dollar by a stunning 20.3 per cent. Like their German counterparts in the same period, Japanese manufacturers had two possible responses to their reduced competitiveness: to maintain the profitability of their exports by keeping prices up and accepting the resulting reduction in export sales; or, to maintain the level of their export growth and their share of international export markets by keeping price increases down and accepting the implied fall in profitability. Like their German counterparts, Japanese exporters generally chose the second route. In an effort to maintain exports in the face of the revaluation, Japanese manufacturers limited their export price increases in dollar terms to only 8 per cent, which required a *reduction* in their export prices in yen terms of 3 per cent, compared to an average annual increase of almost 2 per cent over the previous five years. Given that manufacturing exports made up about 30 per cent of manufacturing output, the sharp increase in costs of Japanese production in international terms was evidently behind the squeeze on prices, thus on mark-ups and profits.[28] Even so, Japan sustained, as noted, a 75 per cent fall in

26   Ackley and Ishi, 'Fiscal, Monetary, and Related Policies', p. 209, n. 43 (quotation).

27   'Unit Labour Costs in Manufacturing Industry and in the Whole Economy', *European Economy*, no. 11, March 1982, p. 106.

28   Krause and Sekiguchi, 'Japan and the World Economy', pp. 401, 420.

export growth.

Labour productivity growth in 1972 was 10.8 per cent, which was insufficient to counteract the huge product wage increase and was still noticeably below the average annual labour productivity increase of 13.4 per cent between 1965 and 1970.[29] Nevertheless, in terms of the increase in actual efficiency of production that it denoted, the labour productivity performance of 1972 may have been at least as good as that of the second half of the 1960s. It was achieved despite the fact that, while capacity utilization remained at its low 1971 level, the jobs open to jobs wanted ratio actually rose to 1.4/1, while the unemployment rate grew only very slightly (from 1.2 per cent to 1.4 per cent), as employers continued largely to refrain from layoffs. In other words, employers honoured their commitment to retain labour, despite their inability to make full use of it.

In early 1973, following the new explosion of prices in the US which finally brought down Bretton Woods, the yen was allowed to float and by March had increased its value against the dollar by a further 8 per cent. By July 1973, the yen was worth 280/$, a total revaluation of 22 per cent for the two years since the Nixon Shock.[30]

At the beginning of 1973, with the economy's recovery still to be secured and the yen's value still to be stabilized, the Japanese authorities extended their stimulus programme, providing for even greater annual expenditures than in 1972. But the outcome was not what they had intended. The accretion of foreign currency that was the inevitable concomitant of sharply increasing current account surpluses since the later 1960s had already been placing strong upward pressure on prices. Liquidity had also been increased by the huge influx of foreign exchange in the run up to the yen revaluation. To this was added the gigantic private borrowings that were stimulated by much-lowered interest rates. A huge inflationary surge, beginning in autumn 1972 with manufacturing output prices and spreading to consumer and export prices by the end of the year, could not be avoided. In 1973, the consumer price index and the wholesale price index grew by 11.8 per cent and 22.6 per cent respectively, up from 4.6 per cent and 3.2 per cent respectively in 1972.[31]

The most immediate manifestation of the runaway inflation was the explosion of land prices, a trend exacerbated by rising speculative investment, itself encouraged by lenders' increasing ability to borrow by making use of increasingly valuable land as collateral. The stock-market boom had a similar dynamic. Both were facilitated by plummeting real interest rates, as nominal rates which had already been forced down by government action were at first unable to keep up with inflation. With interest rates down and prices rising uncontrollably, some corporations were placed in an extraordinarily favourable position. Through purchases and delayed sales, but also by way of a certain amount of productive investment, they could exploit yawning gaps that had temporarily opened up between costs and prices.[32]

Nevertheless, even inflation-based capital gains could not restore the health of

29   The output-capital ratio also fell in 1972 by 3.51 per cent, but this reduction disappears when adjustment is made for prices.
30   Uchino, *Japan's Postwar Economy*, pp. 192–6.
31   Ibid., pp. 196–200, 222; Kosai, *The Era of High-Speed Growth*, pp. 184–7.
32   Ackley and Ishi, 'Fiscal, Monetary, and Related Policies'; Uchino, *Japan's Postwar Economy*, pp. 190–2.

Japanese producers. Manufacturing investment did increase sharply, by 19.4 per cent in 1973, and it was accompanied by a further increase in annual manufacturing output growth to 13.8 per cent (almost comparable to the annual average during the 1965–70 boom), although also by a falling back of GDP growth to 7.5 per cent. Still, the level of manufacturing investment growth remained below what it had been in 1970. It was therefore inadequate to bring about either increases in productiveness compared to product wage increases or to stimulate gains in capacity utilization sufficient to raise profitability.

Under the impact of the enormous stimulus, the economy overheated and the ratio of jobs wanted to jobs open reached 1.9:1 in November 1973. With inflation out of control, workers in manufacturing won nominal wage increases of 21.3 per cent in 1973. Nevertheless, the rise in manufacturing prices cancelled out much of the negative effect of wage growth on profitability. At 10.3 per cent, product wage growth in 1973 was actually around 25 per cent less than it had been in 1972. But this was not enough of a reduction to allow for any increase in profitability since the growth of labour productivity was 9.1 per cent. Because capacity utilization, though still not fully recovered, did increase by 4 per cent and because the output-capital ratio did grow slightly, manufacturing profitability did not drop significantly further, but, on the other hand, it failed even slightly to improve.[33]

In sum, between 1970 and 1973, there was something of the appearance, but little of the reality, of a wages-productivity squeeze on profits caused by tight labour markets and the power of labour. The achievement of full and hyper-full employment had not caused Japan's economic problems. Between 1965 and 1970, the jobs available to jobs wanted ratio had gone well above unity, but both profit shares and profit rates had risen impressively in manufacturing and actually skyrocketed in the private business economy as a whole. Neither an acceleration of nominal wage growth nor a problem of productivity growth had brought the squeeze on profits in manufacturing between 1970 and 1973. Manufacturers had sustained a fall in profitability because they were unable to mark up over costs as they had in the past. Mark-ups had fallen in 1971 as a consequence of the government's contractionary macroeconomic policy, which had issued in recession and reduced demand across the board; they had failed to sufficiently recover in 1972 and 1973 as a result of the rise of Japanese relative costs in manufacturing in international terms brought on by the sharp revaluation of the yen.

It is true that, following the recession of 1971, in the business economy as a whole, unlike in manufacturing, the growth of the nominal wage was sufficient to bring about a squeeze on profits, despite producers' relative immunity from international competition. But such rapid money wage growth is itself incomprehensible apart from the profoundly stepped up pressure on the labour market caused by the historically unprecedented subsidy to demand. And the latter can itself be understood only as a response to an *already ongoing* crisis, set off *not* by heightening pressure from labour, but by the yen revaluation. It was the government's attempt to reverse yen revaluation and its disastrous impact on Japanese international competitiveness, as well as to compensate domestically for the resulting loss of overseas

---

33   The manufacturing rate of profit actually fell by a further 1.3 per cent in 1973 (after declines of 19.2 percent in 7.75 per cent in 1971 and 1972 respectively).

demand for Japanese goods, that explains its unprecedented stimulus programme, and the latter that explains the subsequent overheating and (very temporary) outrunning by wage growth of productivity growth outside manufacturing.[34]

Even those large nominal wage increases could most probably have been accommodated, as had the wage explosion that had followed the analogous (if less extreme) anti-recessionary measures in 1965, if the stimulus had been more successful in raising capacity utilization or in bringing about the growth of investment. That the stimulus failed was not due to the appearance of difficulties in either raising productivity or in holding down wage demands, but of the general depression of investment prospects that had come with the sharply deteriorated international situation. Had the Japanese economy not had to face yen revaluation and the slowing of the growth of the world market—not, of course, a realistic counterfactual—it would have accommodated the growth of wages and maintained its established growth trajectory.

4. The Deepening Crisis: A Summary

To sum up my argument on the onset of the long downturn, in both its negative and positive aspects: between 1965 and 1973, aggregate manufacturing profitability in the G-7 economies declined by about 25.5 per cent. Considering the US, Japanese, and German cases, there is little evidential basis for the supply-side argument that the increased power of and pressure from labour leading to the outrunning of productivity growth by wage growth was responsible for this fall. This conclusion can be extended to cover the G-7 economies taken together. From the middle 1960s through the early 1970s, for the G-7 economies in aggregate, the average annual growth of the product wage, at about 5.45 per cent, barely exceeded that of labour productivity, at about 5.15 per cent, while the average annual growth of capital productivity (the real output-capital ratio) was about -0.2 per cent. Since labour did not therefore bring down either the profit share or the output-capital ratio to any significant degree, it can hardly have brought down the profit rate.

Rather, aside from the increased growth of the costs of raw materials, the fall in G-7 aggregate profitability in manufacturing was determined entirely by a fall in the nominal output-capital ratio. Since what lay behind that fall was the inability of output prices to keep up with the growth of capital stock prices, it seems reasonable to advance the hypothesis that what caused a good part of the decline was, once again—as in the cases of the US, Japan, and Germany, taken individually—the inability of manufacturers to mark up sufficiently over costs due to international manufacturing over-capacity and over-production. That proposition is given further credence by the fact that, between 1965 and 1973 aggregate profitability in the G-7 economies outside of manufacturing fell by only about 19 per cent—compared to 25.5 per cent in G-7 manufacturing—despite the fact that unit costs of production

---

34   '... yen revaluation and, by extension, the "Nixon shock" resulted in enormous losses for Japan, not only in terms of their direct impact on private industry but also in terms of their influence in distorting the efficient management of fiscal and monetary policy.' Uchino, *Japan's Postwar Economy*, p. 188.

35   For the previous two paragraphs, Glyn et al., 'The Rise and Fall of the Golden Age', p. 80, Tables 2.7 and 2.12. The rate of profit in G-7 non-manufacturing was extrapolated from the rate of profit in G-7 manufacturing and G-7 private business, using the G-7 gross capital stock (constant) of each sector as weights. Armstrong et al., *Capitalism Since 1945*, data appendix, Tables A1, A2, A5, A6.

Figure 9.1. G-7 manufacturing and non-manufacturing private net profit rates, 1952–90.

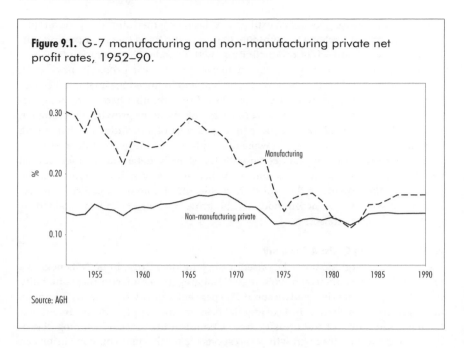

Source: AGH

seem to have risen considerably faster outside manufacturing than within it.[35]

By 1973, the advanced capitalist world had, in a sense, come full circle. The massive injection of low-cost Japanese, as well as German, manufactures into the world market during the second half of the 1960s had precipitated international over-capacity and over-production, forcing down manufacturing profitability in the advanced capitalist economies taken in aggregate, with US producers initially bearing the brunt of the fall. Nevertheless, the very form in which that crisis had developed—characterized by Japanese and German expansion at the direct expense of US manufacturing, leading to German and Japanese external surpluses and US external deficits—had forced dramatic revaluations of the yen and mark against the dollar that soon brought about a major realignment of relative costs. Since there was rather little movement out of manufacturing to other lines, the underlying system-wide problem remained the same—an over-supply of manufacturing capacity and output resulting in downward pressure on product prices that lowered the rate of return on capital stock. But, with the realignment of relative costs that came with the movement of currencies, it was now Japanese, as well as German, producers who had to sacrifice their rates of return if they wished to maintain their sales. The world economy had thus failed to recover between 1969 and 1973, but the effects of its slide had now become more evenly proportioned in international terms.

PART FOUR
The Long Downturn

Chapter 10

WHY THE LONG DOWNTURN? AN OVERVIEW

The advanced capitalist world entered into crisis well before the end of 1973, experiencing falling profitability, especially in manufacturing, and increased rates of inflation. The oil crisis of 1974–75 could not therefore have been the original source of its economic difficulties. It did, however, exacerbate them. The cost of oil rose everywhere, although with uneven effects—very great in oil-dependent Japan, relatively mild in the oil-rich US and in fiscally disciplined Germany. Since wages and technology did not immediately adjust to the rise in energy costs, rates of profit fell further, and inflation accelerated. At this point, governments had little choice but to put on the brakes, raising interest rates and limiting the supply of credit. A sharp deflation thus followed immediately upon the inflationary crisis, bringing about another step down in profitability and the greatest recession since the Depression of the 1930s.

But that was only the beginning. During the next two decades, neither manufacturing nor private business profitability in the US, Germany, Japan, or in the G-7 economies in aggregate surpassed the level to which it had fallen by 1973, let alone recovered the peak level it had reached during the boom; investment growth fell sharply with the reduction in profitability, especially in manufacturing; and the capitalist world experienced a long economic downturn that continues to this day.[1] Between 1973 and 1990, the manufacturing gross capital stock of the G-7 economies in aggregate grew at an average annual rate 35 per cent below that between 1950 and 1973, and for the years between 1980 and 1990, 50 per cent below.[2] With the capital stock growing so slowly, the growth of labour productivity naturally fell off in tandem: between 1973 and 1990, the average annual growth of labour productivity in manufacturing for the G-7 economies taken together was about 30 per cent below what it had been between 1950 and 1973—and the drop-off was more like 50 per cent for the whole economy.[3] Given the reductions in productivity growth and profitability, real wage growth was bound to be constrained and fell far more rapidly than did output per person. With the growth of both investment demand, especially in manufacturing, and consumer demand so much reduced—as an expression of the slowdown of the growth of the capital stock and of the growth of

---

1   For a comprehensive account of the quantitative dimensions of the long downturn, see Armstrong et al., 'The Great Slowdown', in *Capitalism Since 1945*, pp. 233–61. See also below, p. 240, Table 13.1.

2   Armstrong et al., *Capitalism Since 1945*, p. 356, Table A5.

3   OECD, *Historical Statistics 1960–95*, Paris 1997, pp. 53–4, Tables 3.7, 3.10; AGH for 1950s. The fall in manufacturing productivity growth after 1973, from what it had been during the years 1960–73, was more than 40 per cent.

wages—the growth of output had to fall too; as it did, the manufacturing sector shed much labour, and unemployment increased precipitously. Between 1973 and 1995, the unemployment rate in the G-7 economies averaged 6.5 per cent, more than double the average of 3.1 per cent for the years 1960–73.[4] With output and demand suppressed, the growth of international trade had to fall as well: between 1973 and 1990, the average annual growth of world trade was just 3.9 per cent, compared to 7.1 per cent between 1950 and 1973.[5] Meanwhile, the advanced capitalist world was subjected to a series of cyclical downturns substantially deeper and longer than any it had experienced since the 1930s.

1. Success and Failure of the Employers' Offensive

There was, from the start, one force, one trend, which tended to bring about the restoration of profitability and thereby recovery. As was entirely predictable, employers throughout the advanced capitalist world, backed up by their governments, sought to offset the fall in profitability at the expense of workers. Almost everywhere, employers attacked unions, in some instances—most notably the US—profoundly crippling them. Almost everywhere, they also assaulted bastions of workers' strength on the shop floor, seeking to revise traditional work rules and speed up production. To reduce indirect labour costs, as well as to soften up labour resistance, governments across the advanced capitalist world launched severe austerity drives—tight credit to drive up unemployment and reduced social services to weaken workers' safety net. At least in appearance, moreover, employers realized their goal to a significant degree, achieving an ever greater shift in the balance of class forces in their own direction.

The apparent success of the employers' offensive must constitute the point of departure for any attempt to explain the long downturn. For if ever-intensifying assaults on working-class economic and political organizations, in the context of high and growing unemployment, did profoundly weaken labour resistance and bring about decisive reductions in the growth of workers' private and social wage, why did profitability fail to recover and the long downturn continue? The foregoing issue is particularly acute for advocates of the supply-side approach. If employers did succeed in reasserting their power over workers, it would follow from the supply-side thesis that they should also have restored the conditions for successful capital accumulation. Does the fact that they failed to accomplish this contradict the theory?

To this question, advocates of the supply-side approach have replied, in essence, that the appearance of a definitive shift in the balance of class forces in favour of capital was just that, an appearance. The long downturn continued because labour forced capital to pay too high a price for what turned out to be a Pyrrhic victory. Employers, with the help of their governments' tight-money and austerity policies, certainly achieved reductions in the growth of wages and social services; but they did not actually succeed in sufficiently reducing workers' power, for they lost as much from reduced employment and capacity utilization, as well as declining revenues from sales, as they gained from the reduced growth of wage and social

---

4   OECD, *Historical Statistics 1960–95*, p. 45, Table 2.15.
5   A. Maddison, *Monitoring the World Economy 1820–92*, OECD, Paris, 1995, p. 239, Table 1–4.

welfare costs. Had governments stimulated the economy to bring down unemployment, employers would have found themselves having to pay for direct and indirect wage increases at the levels that got them into trouble in the first place. In the formulation of the Social Structure of Accumulation school, because the trade-off between increased capacity utilization and sales, on the one hand, and increased labour costs, on the other, did not improve; whatever was gained from the subsidy of demand in terms of an increase in profitability would have been more than counterbalanced by what was lost from the outrunning of productivity growth by wage growth. In the formulation of mainstream macroeconomics, because the NAIRU (the non-accelerating inflation rate of unemployment) did not fall, whatever could be gained from a stimulus to demand in increased output and employment would have been more than offset by the return of wage-driven inflation to unacceptable levels.[6]

The consensus of economists, from Right to Left, has therefore been that, just as it set off the long downturn, labour's institutionally based power perpetuated it by standing in the way of the proper functioning of the labour market. Either unions succeeded, by directly preventing the growing masses of non-union or unemployed 'outsiders' from affecting the wage bargain; or, the level of welfare state support allowed the unemployed to refrain from entering the labour market at an insufficiently reduced wage; or a combination of both. They thereby prevented wage growth from falling to its 'equilibrium' rate, as was indicated by the apparent rise, across the advanced capitalist world during the 1970s and 1980s, of 'wage gaps'—that is, of the wage share adjusted to what its level would have been at full employment.

Now, as is universally acknowledged, wage gaps are notoriously hard to measure, and calculations thereof have been highly controversial.[7] But, even if it could be successfully shown that labour's share of the product, however measured, increased over the period, it seems exceedingly difficult to see how this could be attributed to the perpetuation of workers' power.

The notion that capital failed to reassert its hegemony during the 1970s and 1980s flies in the face of common knowledge, especially of the US, where, by every standard measure, labour's power plummeted catastrophically during these years, or of Japan, where workers' efforts to assist capital to respond to the fall in profitability by means of restraining real wage growth and increasing productivity are almost legendary. In those cases, it strains credulity to assert that workers' power and pressure prevented the recovery of profitability over the course of two decades. Yet, in both these places, the profitability crisis continued, at least into the 1990s.

Still, the really fundamental point is that, in the wake of the generalized fall in profitability between 1965 and 1973, labour was obliged to, and did, adjust its returns downward, not slowly and continuously, but sharply, virtually instantaneously, and ever increasingly, just as it was supposed to have done. Having averaged nearly 4.4 per cent per annum in the years 1968–73, the growth of hourly real wages in

---

6   Bowles, Gordon, and Weisskopf, 'Business Ascendancy and Economic Impasse', *Journal of Economic Perspectives*, vol. iii, Winter 1989, p. 111, 118, and passim; P. Krugman, 'Slow Growth in Europe: Conceptual Issues', in R. Z. Lawrence and C. L. Schultze, eds, *Barriers to European Growth. A Transatlantic View*, Washington, DC 1987, pp. 57–64.

7   See, for example, Krugman, 'Slow Growth in Europe', p. 62–3.

Table 10.1. The growth of real social expenditures.
(Average annual per cent change.)

	1960–75	1975–80	1980–85
US	6.5	2.0	2.7
Germany	4.8	2.0	0.7
Japan	8.5	8.2	3.2
G-7	7.6	4.2	2.6

Sources: OECD, *Social Expenditure 1960–89*, Paris 1985, p. 28; OECD, *The Future of Social Protection*, Paris 1988, p. 11.

Table 10.2. The growth of real government final consumption expenditures.
(Average annual per cent change.)

	1960–73	1973–79	1979–89	1989–95
US	2.3	1.7	2.5	0.1
Japan	5.9	4.9	2.7	2.0
Germany	4.5	3.0	1.3	1.8
G-7	3.2	2.4	2.2	0.9

Source: OECD, *Historical Statistics 1960–95*, p. 61. The G-7 and US figures for the 1980s are inflated by the huge increase in US military spending in that decade.

manufacturing in the G-7 economies taken together averaged only 1.4 per cent per annum in the years 1973–79 and 0.5 per cent per annum in the years 1979–89.[8] Having averaged about 5.5 per cent per annum in the years 1960–73 and about the same amount between 1965 and 1973, manufacturing product wage growth in the G-7 economies taken together averaged only 2.7 per cent per annum between 1973 and 1979.[9] Having averaged 7.6 per cent per annum between 1960 and 1975, the growth of real social expenditures in the G-7 economies averaged only 4.2 per cent per annum in the years between 1975 and 1981, and about 2.6 per cent per annum for the 1980s. Having averaged 3.2 per cent per annum between 1960 and 1973, the growth of real government final consumption expenditure averaged only 2.4 per cent per annum between 1973 and 1979 and 2.2 per cent between 1979 and 1989.

In light of these immediate, very substantial reductions in private and social wage growth which took place from 1973 and which continued through the 1980s—and into the 1990s—it seems question begging to locate the source of the long down-turn's perpetuation in an ongoing squeeze by labour on profits. On the contrary, to explain why the downturn has been so extended, what must be explained is why

---

8   OECD, *Historical Statistics 1960–84*, Paris 1986, p. 91; OECD, *Historical Statistics 1960–95*, p. 100.
9   Glyn et al., 'The Rise and Fall of the Golden Age', p. 80, Table 2.12.

the advanced capitalist economies were suddenly unable to accommodate real wage growth, product wage growth, social spending growth, and state spending growth that was, respectively, less than one-quarter, less than one-half, less than one-half, and about two-thirds what it had been during the boom.

The supply-side theorists do have an explanation for the sharply reduced capacity of the advanced capitalist economies to accommodate increases in returns to labour over the course of the 1970s and 1980s. They account for it in much the same terms as they do the long downturn's origins—as a function of a major reduction in the underlying rate of growth of labour productivity below even the reduced rate of growth of product wages. It was the intensification of the productivity crisis, from this standpoint, that is the ultimate source of the long downturn's extension through the 1970s, 1980s, and beyond.

There can be no doubt that a sharp fall in productivity growth after 1973 made a recovery of profitability significantly more difficult, but the question is, how can the advocates of the supply-side approach explain this? It is hard to see how it can be covered by their fundamental thesis of 'labour inflexibility', or the failure of the power of labour to decline sufficiently. This is, in the first instance, because there is little evidence that pressure from labour brought down productivity growth sufficiently to squeeze profitability even in the period when profitability first fell between 1965 and 1973, when militancy and assertiveness on the part of labour were palpably on the upswing. Having been insufficient to do so in that period of high boom and cresting workers' struggle, could pressure from labour really have *increased* sufficiently to have done so in the subsequent period of apparently accelerating labour retreat?

Workers' resistance and slacking could not have caused much decline in labour productivity growth in the years when profitability first fell (before 1973) for the simple reason that, during that period—despite an undeniable growth in labour militancy and assertiveness—labour productivity growth, at least in manufacturing, failed to drop. In the US, manufacturing labour productivity growth was maintained during the initial period of profitability decline (1965–73) and in Japan it also failed to fall (once the decline in capacity utilization and the retention of labour in the face of that decline is taken into account).[10] Nor, in either of these countries can labour productivity growth be shown, all else equal, to have been insufficiently high to keep up with workers' upward pressure on wages. In the G-7 economies taken together, hourly labour productivity growth in manufacturing maintained itself at a steady rate through the height of the boom and into the period of profitability drop-off, increasing at the average annual rates of 5.4 per cent in the early 1960s, 4.7 per cent in the later 1960s, and 5.6 per cent in the early 1970s (through 1973).[11] As has been emphasized, moreover, it was high enough to match the accompanying increase in product wage growth for the G-7 economies in aggregate and thereby to prevent any aggregate G-7 wages-productivity squeeze on the profit share before 1973. Yet by the time that manufacturing labour productivity growth did fall—and it fell by almost half, to an average annual rate of 3.0 per cent, between

10   There was a decline in the average annual growth of hourly manufacturing labour productivity in Germany from about 6.5 per cent between 1960 and 1969 to about 5.0 per cent between 1969 and 1973.
11   Glyn et al., 'The Rise and Fall of the Golden Age', p. 80, Table 2.12.

1973–79—the level of labour resistance was well past its peak.[12] The fall in manu-facturing labour productivity after 1973 was discontinuous and precipitous: but was there really a corresponding increase in resistance from labour—or even a maintenance of existing pressure—to account for it?

What makes the supply-side interpretation's inability to account for the sharp, discontinuous decline in productivity growth in the years after 1973 in terms of workers' power and resistance so very problematic is precisely the fact that the pro-ductivity growth decline took place at the very same time that individual and social wages were falling so dramatically. Since direct (and indirect) wage costs to employers were so sharply reduced in the period after 1973, the profit share could obviously have been significantly higher than it actually was had the rate of produc-tivity growth been maintained at anything like the level which prevailed between 1960 and 1973. Indeed, had a wages-productivity squeeze driven by the power of labour actually been at the root of the profitability problem in the period 1965–73, the sharp reduction in wage growth after 1973, in combination with the failure of the power and resistance of labour to increase, should have prepared the ground for a solution. With wage growth so reduced after 1973, the way was open for employers to sharply raise their profit shares and profit rates by maintaining productivity growth at even close to the same level as before 1973. Since they had prevented pro-ductivity growth from falling for the thirteen-year period right up to 1973, it is hard to see why they should suddenly have been unable to do so in the immediately suc-ceeding period, had they been willing to keep up former levels of investment growth. That they failed to maintain their former levels of investment growth would seem to indicate that something other than the power and pressure of labour was behind not only the initial fall in profitability, but also the failure of profitability to recover, and would therefore appear extremely damaging for the supply-side interpretation.

Because there turns out in fact to be such a close temporal correlation between the sharp and discontinuous decline in labour productivity growth which took place after 1973 and the correspondingly sharp and discontinuous decline in the growth of investment, it is difficult to believe that the latter was not largely responsible for the former.[13] Just as average annual manufacturing productivity growth for the G-7 economies taken together fell by 42 per cent, from about 5.2 per cent to 3.0 per cent between 1960–73 and 1973–79, over the same interval the average annual growth of gross capital stock for these economies fell by 35 per cent, from 5.5 per cent per annum to 3.6 per cent per annum. While average annual manufac-turing labour productivity growth for these economies failed to recover but also failed to fall further during the years 1979–89, during the same interval, the average annual growth of the gross capital stock for these economies also failed to make a comeback and even fell somewhat further.[14] In a similar manner, in both Germany

12   Ibid.

13   A version of the supply-side account which has recently become prominent abjures the explanation of the fall in productivity primarily in terms of the increased power of labour, and seeks to account for it in terms of a putative exhaustion of technological potential, associated with the depleted opportunities for catch-up. There are, however, fundamental problems with such a view. These are discussed below, see pp. 241–49.

14   Armstrong et al., *Capitalism Since 1945*, pp. 239, 241; Glyn et al., 'The Rise and Fall of the Golden Age', p. 80, Table 2.12; Glyn, 'The Costs of Stability', p. 86. It is true that these aggregate figures conceal a great deal of complexity and variation among national economies.

Table 10.3. Labour productivity as against manufacturing capital/labour ratio. (Average annual per cent change.)

	Germany		Japan	
	K/L	LPy	K/L	LPy
1960–73	6.2	4.8	10.9	10.0
1973–79	3.7	3.5	7.5	4.3
1979–90	1.5	1.8	4.2	3.2

Sources: OECD, *Historical Statistics 1960–1995*, 1995, p. 54, Table 3.10; AGH. Key to legend on page xiii.

and Japan, the decline in the average annual growth of manufacturing labour productivity closely traced the simultaneous fall in the growth of capital with respect to labour inputs (the capital-labour ratio), as can be seen in Table 10.3 above.[15]

Since the decline in the growth of the capital stock was largely determined by the ongoing problem of reduced profitability, which was not itself explicable in terms of an outrunning by wage growth of productivity growth resulting from the power and pressure of labour, *the fall in productivity growth must be seen as a result, not a cause, of the economic downturn*. While the sharp fall in productivity growth no doubt helped to perpetuate and exacerbate the fall of profitability, it was itself a consequence of that fall.

Finally, and perhaps most tellingly from the standpoint of this text, the advanced capitalist economies *did*, in one important respect, make a more or less immediate—although *partial*—adjustment to the fall in profitability, despite the sharp reduction in productivity growth. The manufacturing sectors of the G-7 economies taken in aggregate, as well as individually, having already been hit by sharp reductions in their profitability between 1965 and 1973, could not prevent a further major fall in profitability over the course of the 1970s, despite the immediate, steep, fall in manufacturing real and product wage growth that took place in those years. But, symptomatically, the private business economies *outside* of manufacturing, *were* able to respond fairly successfully to the (less severe) fall-off in profitability that they had suffered before 1973, warding off all but very minor further falls in profitability during the 1970s precisely by holding down real and product wage growth. They thereby succeeded in stabilizing themselves in a way the manufacturing sector could not. Equally significant, after 1973, in the manufacturing sector, the growth of output, the labour force, and the capital stock fell drastically and increasingly, clear evidence of the over-capacity and over-production that had gripped that sector and led to falling profitability. But in the non-manufacturing sector, the growth of output, of the labour force, and perhaps most crucial, of the capital stock maintained themselves for the most part at or above their pre-1973 rates throughout the whole period of the long downturn, as that sector avoided the over-capacity and over-production that prevailed in man-

---

15   The pattern of productivity growth in the US during the years 1973–79 is less clear-cut and more difficult to interpret, for a variety of reasons.

ufacturing, and responded to improving profitability.

The diverging trajectories of the manufacturing and non-manufacturing profit rates and, in turn, of the growth rates of manufacturing and non-manufacturing output, labour force, and capital stock before and after 1973 reflected what I have argued to be the fundamental source of the long-term systemic crisis of profitability—downward pressure on prices resulting mainly from over-capacity and over-production in manufacturing, itself deriving from the intensification of international competition. Because the non-manufacturing private economy was largely immune from the intensification of international competition, it had, up to a point, a fairly clear-cut path to recovery. This sector *was* seriously held back by the secular fall in the growth of demand for its output that resulted from the slowed growth of the manufacturing sector. But, over time, it could go at least a good distance toward securing its own recovery simply by holding down wage growth. Because, in contrast, the source of the profitability decline in manufacturing was for the most part systemic over-capacity and over-production, the reduction of wage growth could offer at best a partial solution. For there to be a full recovery of the manufacturing profit rate, not only had the growth of output, the labour force, and the capital stock to slow to a crawl over an extended period, exerting in the process a strongly depressing effect on the growth of demand for the economy as a whole; in addition, much of the redundant, higher-cost, less profitable capital stock, output, and labour force that was the expression of manufacturing over-capacity and over-production had somehow to be eliminated, opening the way to much increased instability.

In the G-7 economies taken in aggregate, then, sharp declines in productivity growth hit both the manufacturing and non-manufacturing sectors after 1973: but, whereas the manufacturing profit share for the G-7 economies in aggregate fell by a further 14.5 per cent between 1973 and 1978, then made up more than half that loss by the end of the 1980s, the non-manufacturing profit share for the G-7 economies failed to fall at all between 1973 and 1979, then increased to a point 8 per cent above its level of 1973 by the end 1980s. The G-7 manufacturing profit rate was hard hit in the deep international recession of 1974–5, fell by a total of 25 per cent between 1973 and 1978, and did not improve appreciably during the 1980s—despite the profound reduction of employers' direct and indirect wage costs. But, in contrast, the non-manufacturing profit rate, dipping only slightly in the oil crisis recession, declined by only 4 per cent in total between 1973 and 1978, and had, by the later 1980s, actually risen slightly above its 1973 level, precisely by virtue of the profound reduction of employers' direct and indirect wage costs. (See p. 142, Figure 9.1.)

The divergent trajectories of the manufacturing and non-manufacturing profit rates and profit shares were reflected in the divergent rates of increase of output and inputs in these sectors. Between 1960 and 1973, in the G-7 economies taken in aggregate, the average annual rate of growth of output in manufacturing, at 6.4 per cent, was substantially higher than in services, at 5.2 per cent. But, with the appearance of manufacturing over-capacity and over-production in the late 1960s and early 1970s, these trends were suddenly, sharply reversed, as the average annual growth of output in manufacturing fell precipitously to 2.5 per cent between 1973 and 1979 and 2.1 per cent between 1979 and 1989, while that in the service sector actually increased to 6.5 per cent between 1973 and 1979, before falling back to 3.0 per cent between 1979 and 1989.[16] Similarly, between 1960 and 1973, in the G-7 economies taken in aggregate, the average annual growth of the capital stock was about

20 per cent higher in manufacturing, at 5.5 per cent, than in non-manufacturing, at 4.5 per cent. But, between 1973 and 1979, and between 1979 and 1990, the average annual growth of the manufacturing capital stock fell to 3.8 per cent and 3.25 per cent, respectively, while that of the non-manufacturing sector rose above it to 4.5 per cent and 4.3 per cent, respectively. *Virtually all of the decline in the rate of growth of the capital stock for the G-7 economies in aggregate after 1973 was thus the result of the reduction that took place in manufacturing.*[17]

As shall be seen, the same pattern that obtained in the G-7 economies taken together also largely held good in the US, German, and Japanese economies taken individually. Had the performance of the manufacturing sector after 1973 compared to its performance before that date been remotely as good in relative terms as that of the non-manufacturing sector, the long downturn would have been very mild indeed. Because the performance of the manufacturing sector after 1973 could not stabilize itself, unless and until there was a profound reallocation of its productive power, the downturn turned out to be long and difficult to resolve.

To conclude in the simplest terms, the employers' offensive, which was provoked by the fall in profitability from 1965 through 1973, was very powerful and very successful in its own terms. Indeed, it appears to have brought a surprising level of stability to the non-manufacturing sector of the advanced capitalist economies from 1973 onwards, despite the fall in demand for that sector's goods which resulted from the stagnation of the manufacturing sector. But the employers' offensive had limited ability to bring the long downturn to a conclusion because the source of the profitability problem was not, at root, a maldistribution of power or income in favour of labour, but rather the continuation of that same failure of adjustment to over-capacity and over-production in the manufacturing sector that was responsible for its onset.

2. Why Did Over-Capacity and Over-Production Persist?

Nevertheless, my invocation of an ostensibly continuing, long-term failure of adjustment to over-capacity and over-production in manufacturing to explain the persistence of the downturn would seem to raise problems and paradoxes as formidable as those confronting the supply-side argument. I have, of course, explained the initial descent into crisis as resulting from the failure of the decline in profitability, precipitated by the over-capacity and over-production that resulted from the intensification of international competition from around 1965, to set off the standard processes of adjustment. Incumbent high-cost manufacturers, first in the US,

---

16   OECD, *Historical Statistics 1960–95*, p. 52, Tables 3.5 and 3.6. The growth of the labour force followed the same pattern. Whereas the average annual growth of employment in manufacturing in the G-7 economies fell sharply from 1.3 per cent between 1960 and 1973 to 0.3 per cent between 1973 and 1979, and to minus 1.2 per cent between 1979 and 1989, that for services remained pretty stable, at 2.4 per cent between 1960 and 1973, 2.6 per cent between 1973 and 1979, and 2.2 per cent between 1979 and 1989. OECD, *Historical Statistics 1960–95*, pp. 32–3, Tables 1.10 and 1.11

17   Armstrong et al., *Capitalism Since 1945*, pp. 355, 356, Tables A5, A6.

then in Japan and Germany, maintained production in their lines, despite the reduced rates of return on their total (sunk) capital stock, because they could still make a satisfactory rate of return on their circulating capital. But, even if this account were correct, and this mechanism of maladjustment actually did explain the initial phase of long downturn of the advanced capitalist economies, a question would still immediately impose itself: how could that same mechanism explain the downturn's perpetuation? That mechanism ostensibly began to operate in the period when profitability first fell, from the mid to late 1960s through the early to mid 1970s; but the downturn continued long after that point. Firms might very well have continued producing at a lower than average rate of profit on their capital stock, while profiting on their circulating capital, *for a limited period of time*. But eventually, most would presumably have either seen their fixed capital wear out, or discovered better opportunities to profit in other lines, or have gone out of business. In these ways, the original problem of over-capacity and over-production should have been resolved. It is one thing, in other words, to explain a 'medium term' profitability decline in terms of the aforementioned maladjustment mechanism, but quite another to account for a downturn lasting more than two decades.

Why, then, did the crisis persist beyond the point that could be explained by the initial failure of adjustment? It did so, I would argue, because the *further* strategies individual capitalists found it best to adopt to restore their own profits, like the initial ones, continued to bring about an insufficiency of exit and too much entry, exacerbating the initial problem of manufacturing over-capacity and over-production.

Insufficient Exit

The standard notion that incumbent firms saddled with low profitability and high relative costs on their fixed capital stock can be counted on to leave their line once investment in circulating capital ceases to be profitable turns out to be an over-simplification. The corporations that dominated manufacturing across the advanced capitalist world had, through years of experience, built up invaluable proprietary *intangible* assets in their own line but not others—information about markets, relationships with suppliers and customers, and above all technical knowledge. These assets offered them advantages in continuing to produce where they were already located of which they could not avail themselves in any other industry. They could therefore hardly have been expected to close up shop merely because the returns on their existing fixed tangible stock suffered decline.

In fact, over the course of the 1970s, in the face of reduced profit rates, US manufacturers launched an all-out counterattack, designed to hold their place in the market by accelerating technical change through refusing to reduce the rate of growth of investment and, on this basis, increasing the rate of growth of their exports. But their leading competitors, in Germany and especially Japan, far from backing off, responded in kind. To compensate for the slower growth of global demand, they sought to increase their share of international export markets. To accomplish this, they showed themselves not only willing to absorb the same sort of reductions in their profit rates that US manufacturers had initially sustained, but able to do so successfully by virtue of their capacity to elicit the requisite financial support from understanding banks and stockholders. The unavoidable outcome of this widespread attempt to maintain the growth of output in over-subscribed manufacturing lines was an exacerbation of the very tendency to over-capacity and over-production that had set off the downturn in the first place.

Firms stuck to their lines not only because of the incentive provided by their intangible assets, but because of the barriers against their entering new lines. With the growth of profits—and thus of investment and wages—suppressed, aggregate demand grew more slowly. The rapid increases in discretionary income that had hitherto facilitated the easy reallocation of means of production into new industries through most of the postwar epoch thus came to an end, and alternative lines yielding adequate rates of return became correspondingly scarce. The problem was made all the more formidable because it had a major structural aspect. A disproportionate part of the fall in demand resulted from the disproportionately large slowdown in growth of the manufacturing sector. Obliged to confront a new pattern of economic needs, firms faced greater difficulties in discovering just where the slower growing demand was to be found, or, indeed created, a problem made much more onerous by their reduced capacity to fund research and development.[18]

For the German and Japanese and many other economies, the problem of eliminating redundant productive forces from over-subscribed manufacturing lines was made all the more difficult to the degree that this entailed transferring means of production into the service sector. On average, levels and rates of productivity growth in manufacturing lines were significantly higher than in services. So if a reallocation of investment from manufacturing into services was to be undertaken with no loss of profitability, reductions in wage levels and wage growth would tend to be required. But employers in Germany and Japan, and elsewhere, found it no easy task either to further reduce wage growth in services or to increase the disparity in wages received by manufacturing and service workers in an era in which returns to labour were already being slowed very substantially. In fact, in Germany wage dispersion (wage inequality) actually declined in the 1970s and 1980s. One therefore witnesses in both economies (as in the US) a striking shift into finance, insurance, and real estate, where productivity and profitability were evidently on the rise, but difficulties of profitable entry into service-sector lines where productivity was low, such as retail trade and hotel and restaurants. By contrast, in the US, where wage inequality grew very strikingly, employers were able to take advantage of historically unprecedented downward flexibility not only of real wage growth, but of real wage levels, and, in this important respect, ultimately found the path to adjustment—the recovery of profitability and the reduction of unemployment—easier than most of their counterparts throughout the advanced capitalist world.

---

18   Note also: 'On the one hand, stagnation and shrinkage in some traditional growth industries have been apparent since 1973/1974 and have destroyed a great number of jobs. On the other hand, not enough new activities have emerged to meet the job demands of all the labour force participants ... Transitional difficulties involved in changes of the output and input structure [thus] contribute to current employment problems ... full employment can be regained only if new, and, at the moment possibly unknown, patterns of production and technology can be found.' G. Fels and F. Weiss, 'Structural Change and Employment: The Lesson of West Germany', in H. Giersch, ed., *Capital Shortage and Unemployment in the World Economy*, Tubingen 1979, p. 31

Increased Entry: The Rise of East Asia

While the struggle of manufacturers in the leading capitalist economies to hold their places within over-subscribed world manufacturing markets, combined with their difficulty in finding suitable alternatives, perpetuated the problem of over-capacity and over-production from the exit side, the challenge by new producers, especially those based in East Asia, exacerbated the problem from the entry side. Like their Japanese predecessors, manufacturers in Korea, Taiwan, Singapore, and Hong Kong—and later Southeast Asia—combined cheap but relatively skilled labour with relatively advanced techniques, often under the auspices of Japanese-style state intervention and Japanese-style structures of bank-manufacturing, inter-firm, and capital-labour relations to secure even more rapid rates of growth of manufacturing exports than had the Japanese and to seize comparable shares of the world market in a similar length of time.

Like Japan in the postwar epoch, these economies premised their development on the destruction (or absence) of landlordism, as well as on preventing the emergence of an autonomous class of financiers. The East Asian states were therefore freed to foster, much as had their Japanese predecessors, the development of an export-oriented manufacturing capitalism, and to do so, like Japan, on the basis of institutional arrangements that made for the closest links between financiers and manufacturers and among manufacturers. Operating through government-owned or government-dominated banks, as well as on the basis of government-owned giant firms and/or great private corporations organized in conglomerates, the East Asian states, like the Japanese, saw to the provision of cheap investment funds, either through overseeing highly regulated lending from Western and Japanese banks or through encouraging high rates of domestic savings, or both. They meanwhile went to great lengths to socialize the risks entailed by huge fixed-capital investments, offering a high degree of protection to nascent manufacturers through quotas, tariffs, subsidies, and limitations on direct foreign investment, giving special support to industries with the capacity for high rates of productivity growth and for whose products the income elasticity of demand was high. On the other hand, again as in Japan, they made access to their multiple forms of assistance conditional on firms' performance, demanding that they subject themselves to the price-cost discipline of the world market through exporting. The export-dependence of the East Asian statist 'organized capitalisms' reached extraordinary proportions and was one of the central foundations of their ability so rapidly to raise productivity, for it allowed them to nurture large manufacturing sectors, where the best opportunities to raise productivity were to be found. Finally, the East Asian states made sure not only to provide public goods at high levels—infrastructure, education of workers and technicians, and research and development—but also to deliver, through a combination of repression and material gains, relatively 'cooperative' labour forces. Unheard of rates of capital accumulation, growth of output (especially in manufacturing), and technological advance ensued, which made possible the seizing of huge shares of the world market for exports.[19]

---

19   See A. Amsden, *Asia's Next Giant*, Oxford 1989; R. Wade, *Governing the Market. Economic Theory and the Role of Government in East Asian Industrialization*, Princeton 1990.

Even by the years 1965–1973, the East Asian economies were making a palpable impact on the advanced capitalist world, and probably contributed not insignificantly to the initial rise of international over-capacity and over-production in manufacturing. Between 1963 and 1973, the share of exports from the East Asian 'Gang of Four' in total US imports quadrupled, rising from 1.6 per cent to 6.7 per cent, and in total German imports doubled, increasing from 0.9 per cent to 2.2 per cent.[20] Over the course of the long downturn, these economies would expand their share of world exports to a greater extent than had the Japanese during the long boom, and would thereby make a substantial contribution to the international problem of over-capacity and over-production in manufacturing that the Japanese had helped bring into being.

3. The Growth of Debt

It was, however, one thing for firms to refrain from exiting increasingly over-subscribed manufacturing lines, and to show themselves willing to sustain, on average, further reduced profitability even as other firms were entering; it was quite another for them to be *able* to follow such a course over an extended period and still survive. The system might, in other words, fail to adjust by means of the smooth reallocation of resources across lines; but, to the extent it did so fail, it invited rising business failures and serious crisis. As the average rate of profit, especially in manufacturing, declined sharply across the G-7 economies between 1965 and 1973, and further between 1973 and 1979, an ever greater proportion of firms found themselves on the brink of bankruptcy, vulnerable to the sort of shock that generally catalyzes cyclical downturns or even depressions. Economic instability thus became the order of the day, with a full-fledged crash a real possibility, as the economy grew ever more susceptible to the sort of domino effect that results from multiple bankruptcies bringing about large scale defaults on debts. In 1974–5, 1979–82, and in the early 1990s, the advanced capitalist world did indeed sustain a series of recessions more severe than any since the 1930s, after each of which the level of unemployment was generally higher and the rate of growth of output lower than following the previous ones. Had it not been for the unprecedented expansion of both public and private debt in response to these recessions, the world economy could not easily have avoided a depression. Yet, the same expansion of credit that ensured a modicum of stability also held back recovery. For, by cutting recessions short—and more generally making possible the survival of those high-cost, low-profit firms that perpetuated over-capacity and over-production and prevented the average rate of profit from recovering—the subsidy to demand through Keynesian debt creation prolonged the downturn. Keynesianism made the downturn both milder and longer.

Staving Off Depression

In the late 1960s and early 1970s, Keynesian deficit spending accommodated by loose money had been the initial response to the onset of crisis. Keynesian subsidies to demand were, moreover, largely responsible for bailing the world economy out of the severe recession of 1974–75 and keeping it turning over through the

20   Giersch et al., *Fading Miracle*, p. 224.

remainder of the decade. The turn to monetarism at the end of the 1970s—as a response to the ever worsening stagflation that accompanied the implementation of Keynesianism—was, it is true, supposed to put an end to the subsidy of demand, and government authorities in Germany and Japan, as well as in most of the other advanced capitalist countries, did make a more or less permanent commitment to tight money and fiscal austerity. The fact remains that the dual process of debt deflation and industrial shakeout that was detonated in 1979 by the introduction of unprecedentedly restricted credit by Paul Volcker in the US and Margaret Thatcher in the UK, turned out to be indiscriminate in impact and uncontrollable in extent, with the result that the large-scale subsidy of demand could not, in the end, be discontinued. In 1981–82, as business failures and unemployment hit levels unmatched since the Great Depression, the US Federal Reserve eased its draconian monetary regime, and the Reagan administration undertook the greatest programme of Keynesian pump priming that the world had ever seen. Through its record budget deficits, the US federal government massively raised demand so as to bail out yet again not just the US, but also the Japanese and German, economies from the recession of 1979–82 and to keep the whole system turning over during the 1980s. In addition, by making it clear that it would intervene decisively to counteract any liquidity crisis that might threaten to precipitate depression, as for example at the time of the stock-market crash of 1987, it helped reduce risk and thus maintain favourable conditions for the expansion of private borrowing. Both corporations, strapped for funds as a result of reduced profits, and consumers, in need of money to offset radically reduced wage growth, could and did sharply increase their borrowing. It was the unprecedented growth of debt of all types—government, corporate, and consumer—which kept up employment and capacity utilization and ultimately secured stability throughout most of the length of the downturn.

Preventing a Shakeout and Slowing Recovery

But while the growth of debt, both public and private, was helping to stave off depression, it was also slowing down that recovery of profitability which was the fundamental condition for economic revitalization. What the advanced capitalist economies needed to found a new boom was a rollback of that redundant manufacturing capacity and output which had resulted from the intensification of international competition and which had been made all the greater by debt creation—specifically the elimination of that great ledge of high-cost, low-profit means of production which stood in the way of the recovery of the aggregate rate of profit in manufacturing. The series of severe recessions that occurred from the end of the 1960s through the early 1990s constituted the world economy's main instrument for accomplishing this task, and they certainly did much to wipe out redundant productive capacity. But the increased demand created by rising debt tended to cut short the processes of destruction unleashed by recession, to pave the way for greater entry, especially from East Asia, and to soften the impact of competition. Higher-cost/lower-profit firms were thus able to long occupy economic positions that could, in the abstract, eventually have been assumed by more productive, higher-profit, and more dynamic enterprises. But allowing the less productive, less profitable firms to go out of business by letting the business cycle take its natural course would quite possibly have turned the long downturn, with its relatively serious but nonetheless limited recessions, into outright depression. Simply put, the precondition for restoring the system to health was a debt-deflation, leading to what Marx called 'a slaughtering of capital values'. But since the only systematic way to achieve this was through deeper and longer recession or perhaps depression, the only real alternative was continuing debt expansion, which contributed both to stagnation and financial instability.

Stimulating Inflation

While the successive rounds of Keynesian stimulus, and the growth of debt that these facilitated, staved off depression, they also exacerbated inflation, at least through the end of the 1970s. *Because the rate of profit on capital stock had been reduced*, especially in over-subscribed manufacturing, firms were, on average, left with reduced surpluses available for investment. Put another way, assuming that the dispersion of profit rates remained constant, with profitability reduced, many more firms found themselves impoverished or barely on the edge of survival, with little or nothing in the way of funds for capital accumulation. In this situation, firms were, as a rule, less able than previously, when the rate of profit was higher, to meet the rising demand created by Keynesian fiscal deficits and the private loans that those deficits facilitated with increased supply; they could invest less, thus raise productivity less, and therefore raise output less. By the same token, firms were generally more obliged than previously to meet that rising demand by simply purchasing labour power and making greater use of existing capacity. Indeed, for those firms that were just saved from going out of business by Keynesian deficits, the growth of demand could do little more than allow survival, making possible little or no increases in output at all. The outcome was that any given stimulus to demand tended, all else being equal, to bring about relatively smaller increases in supply than hitherto, and, correlatively, greater increases in price ('less bang for the buck'). Put another way, firms raised prices rather than output relatively more than they had previously when profitability was higher. Keynesian increases in demand could not, then, restore the economy's dynamism because the fundamental problem was not that of realizing high potential profits through greater investment and employment of unused capacity and unemployed workers; it was, instead, over-capacity and over-production in manufacturing which brought about falling profitability in that sector by making for prices that were too low in relation to costs. Increases in aggregate demand did not then tend to cause inflation by bringing about tighter labour markets leading to higher wage costs and, as a result, higher prices, as in the supply-side story. They did so, rather, because, while failing to evoke greater supply and lower costs by stimulating greater investment and growth of productivity and output, they made it possible to raise prices.

4. The Deepening Downturn

At the end of the 1970s, easy credit, and Keynesianism in particular, gave rise to its opposite. Throughout the advanced capitalist world, monetarism became the order of the day, even if its impact was somewhat diluted by massive deficit spending in the US. Over the course of the 1980s and through the 1990s, governments steadily reduced the growth of their spending, sought increasingly to balance their budgets, and had recourse more readily to tight credit.

Ever more restrictive macroeconomic policy was supposed to restore profitability and thereby the economy's dynamism by undoing the inertial effects of Keynesian debt creation by flushing from the system redundant, high-cost means of production, and by reducing direct and indirect wage costs via higher unemployment. Nevertheless, like Keynesianism, while accomplishing part of what it set out to do, monetarism ultimately proved inadequate, largely because it operated only through changing the level of aggregate demand, when the fundamental problem was over-capacity and over-production in a particular sector, manufacturing, resulting from the misallocation of means of production among economic lines. To the extent that major restrictions on the availability of credit were seriously undertaken, they tended to prove counterproductive, as the sudden, sharp reductions of aggregate demand that they provoked struck over-stocked and under-stocked lines indiscriminately and brought down both well-functioning and ill-functioning firms without distinction. The reduction of aggregate demand also caused problems by making the reallocation of means of production into new lines that much more difficult. In a sense, the problem with monetarism as a solution to the problem of international over-capacity and over-production in manufacturing was the opposite of that with Keynesianism. Keynesianism, by subsidizing aggregate demand, slowed exit from over-supplied lines, but it did create a more favourable environment for the necessarily risky and costly entry into new ones; monetarism, by cutting back aggregate demand, did force a more rapid exit from over-supplied lines, but it created a less favourable environment for entry into new ones.

Against a background of increasing demand for loans and declining rates of saving, monetarist policies depressed growth prospects by making for exceedingly high real interest rates on a quasi-permanent basis. The call for loans grew discontinuously and rapidly from the start of the 1980s, mainly as result of the record deficit spending by the Reagan administration, but also the steady rise of government debt in Europe, which grew by about 25 per cent as a proportion of GDP between 1980 and 1986, as a function of the sharp rise of unemployment and of expenditures related to it.[21] The demand for credit was also pushed up by the growth of private borrowing by straitened workers attempting to keep consumption up in the face of stagnant wages, by capitalists seeking leverage for mergers and acquisitions, and by profit-starved firms seeking funds to invest. At the same moment, the supply of credit was restricted as a consequence of a sharp decline in corporate retained earnings and a major fall in the personal savings rate in the US and throughout most of the advanced capitalist world,[22] as well as the Federal Reserve's refusal to accommodate increased deficit spending by easing up on the money supply. The Fed was, it should be said, probably limited in its ability to loosen credit, because it had to maintain high interest rates and to keep the dollar from falling to make possible the borrowing from abroad that was needed to cover

---

21   T. Helbling and R. Wescott, 'The Global Real Interest Rate', IMF Staff Studies, September 1995; G. Davies, 'A Mountain of Reasons to Reduce Public Debt', The Independent (London), 9 October 1995. I wish to thank Robin Blackburn for calling my attention to the latter article.

22   B. M. Friedman, Day of Reckoning. The Consequences of American Economic Policy under Reagan and After, New York 1988, pp. 156–8; Armstrong et al., Capitalism Since 1945, p. 235. Germany and Japan are exceptions to this trend.

the fiscal deficit. During the 1980s, real interest rates thus skyrocketed from their 1970s levels to reach historic highs for periods of comparable length—especially in the US, where the change from what were essentially negative rates in the previous decade was most severe.[23]

Because the turn to more or less permanent macroeconomic restrictiveness at the aggregate level was limited in its capacity to alleviate the over-capacity and over-production that was focused on the manufacturing sector of the international economy, it could not significantly raise profitability. As a result, the surge of investment that was supposed to follow from the slowdown in the growth of costs never appeared. On the contrary. In the context of still reduced profitability and exceedingly high real interest rates, the growth of investment in over-supplied manufacturing plummeted, and the growth of investment outside of manufacturing failed to compensate. The reduced growth of investment demand was thus added to the dampened growth of consumer demand that followed from the slowed growth of wages, as well as the more sluggish growth of government demand that came with the cuts in state expenditures, to make for the diminished growth of aggregate demand and, by the same token, of output. The advanced capitalist economies of the 1980s and 1990s, weighed down by the deceleration of economy-wide purchasing power that resulted from reduced profitability, were even less vital—grew significantly more slowly—than in the 1970s.

As the economies of the advanced capitalist world lost steam over the course of the 1980s, uneven development proved, in certain respects, self-limiting. But, far from helping to resolve the underlying problem of over-production and over-capacity in manufacturing, the achievement of more even development exacerbated it. This was because the relative revival of the US economy which had the effect of evening out development—though only within the traditional core of world economy—was largely secured through a limiting of the growth of the US market and, ultimately, the world market.

The forms of development taken by both the Japanese and German economies in the postwar epoch featured the restriction of the growth of domestic demand in the interest of export growth. The dynamism of both economies was thus ultimately dependent upon the growth of the world market and, as stressed, predicated especially upon their ability *to appropriate growing shares of that market*. The quite different form of development assumed by the US economy proved for this reason to be the perfect—and indispensable—complement to those of Japan and Germany, for it instantiated both relatively slow-growing productivity and ever greater reliance on the Keynesian subsidy to demand through federal deficits in the interest of domestic (and international) stability. The US offered to Germany and especially Japan, not only a huge, but also an easily permeable, market.

Nevertheless, the operation of this symbiosis tended, as has been stressed, to undermine the conditions for its own perpetuation. First, the export-oriented growth of the German and Japanese economies in combination with the domestically oriented production and foreign direct investment of the US economy—highlighted by subsidy to demand and slow growth of productiveness—issued in

23   A. Knoester and W. Mak, 'Real Interest Rates in Eight OECD Countries', *Revista Internazionale di Scienze Economiche e Commerciali*, vol. xli, no. 4, 1994, especially pp. 325–30.

ever greater US external deficits and Japanese and German external surpluses. These deficits and surpluses brought about the devaluation of the dollar and thus the decline of US purchasing power. Moreover, while German and Japanese living standards tended to rise with their currencies, so also did German and Japanese production costs, leading to declining competitiveness. Second, especially under the stress of intensified overseas competition, US firms were obliged to push ever more fiercely to reduce wage growth. As they did, the growth of the US market was further slowed. Third, eventually US budget deficits had to be reduced, for, given the reduced profitability of US manufacturing, they could provide only limited stimulus to investment and growth, and tended to keep real interest rates up. The increase of US demand was thereby reduced still more. But with the US market providing a declining stimulus to world demand because of the devaluation of the dollar, reduced wage growth, and falling federal deficits, the Japanese and German economies saw their growth prospects doubly undermined: whereas they had derived their dynamism from increasing competitiveness and fast-growing productivity in the context of rapidly expanding markets for manufactures, they were obliged to confront not only rising relative costs and slower-growing markets for manufactures, but also the limitations on the potential growth of productivity in their non-manufacturing sectors.

Throughout the 1970s, despite the falling value of the dollar, rising US deficits continued to subsidize the German and Japanese manufacturing economies. Both Germany and Japan found it increasingly difficult to export profitably, suffered downward pressure on manufacturing profit rates, and engaged in much increased foreign direct investment. US producers slightly improved their performance, making noticeable gains in export growth and sharply reducing the growth of their foreign direct investment. But, especially in the face of domestic inflation and the refusal of their chief overseas rivals to yield export share despite reduced profitability, they were unable to create the conditions for restoring manufacturing profitability and dynamism.

During the first half of the 1980s, on the basis of Reagan's record federal deficits, along with the skyrocketing dollar that resulted from the accompanying high interest rates, the German and Japanese economies secured further, if meagre, extensions of the same sort of export-led growth that they had experienced in the 1970s. Over the same period, in some contrast, the US economy, thrust into crisis by Volcker's extreme monetary tightening and then the high dollar, began a major process of self-transformation. Largely by ridding itself of a great mass of high-cost, low-profit plant and equipment and labour (downsizing), a very much slimmed-down manufacturing sector began to improve its productivity sharply and, in the long run, to make a comeback. By achieving in these years an *historically unprecedented* repression of wage growth, US capital was also able to make profitable a large-scale transition into low-productivity services that their rivals in Germany and Japan found difficult to duplicate. Perhaps most spectacular of all, the US financial sector underwent an accelerated expansion—both domestically and internationally—benefiting massively from an array of state policies designed to subsidize and support it.

From the mid 1980s, with the very large-scale and long-term revaluations of the yen and the mark that followed upon the signing of the Plaza Accord, US producers began to achieve major gains in competitiveness and, especially as the 1990s progressed, significant improvement in their profitability. Nevertheless, since the US rise in competitiveness came by means of dollar devaluation (especially against the yen and the mark), the reduction of wage growth in relative (and absolute) terms, and government macroeconomic austerity, its effect on the evolution of the advanced capitalist economies was not only to undermine the growth prospects of Germany and Japan, but to further depress the already slowed growth of demand system-wide. In the absence of a major investment boom in the US (or anywhere else), improvements in relative costs which allowed US producers to maintain or increase their export shares were experienced by their overseas rivals as a loss of markets. This was obviously a zero-sum game.

But what made matters decisively worse for the system as a whole, was the US's definitive turn in 1993 to fiscal austerity, not just monetary tightness, with the ascendancy of Clinton. This removed what had been perhaps the most important remaining counter-tendency to the contractionary trend unleashed with the turn to monetarism—the ongoing experiment by Reagan and Bush in military Keynesianism for the rich. Much of the world had been progressively restricting the growth of domestic demand through the repression of wage growth and increasingly tight fiscal and monetary policy through the 1980s in the interest of reducing costs and raising profitability. But when the US, too, turned to budget balancing, international disinflationary tendencies were increased qualitatively. In response, most economies had little choice but to radically step up their dependence on manufacturing exports, but this only exacerbated already intensifying international competitive pressures.

By the midpoint of the 1990s, a certain recovery of the US economy had therefore been purchased at the cost of exacerbating international stagnation. Neither Europe nor Japan had definitely transcended their early 1990s recessions. International over-capacity and over-production had been made even more threatening through the shrinkage of market growth and the resulting intensification of downward pressure on profits by slow-growing, or even falling, prices of tradable goods. It is true that an investment boom was finally beginning to materialize in the US in response to the creeping growth of profitability. But whether it would be great enough and sufficiently long-lasting to pull the world economy definitively from its doldrums remained an open question.

Chapter 11

THE FAILURE OF KEYNESIANISM, 1973–79

To surmount the deep recession of 1974–75, set off by runaway inflation and the consequent recourse to tight credit, and to keep the world economy turning over throughout the remainder of the 1970s, the governments of the advanced capitalist countries, led by the US, incurred steadily greater budget deficits, accommodated by easy money. Nevertheless, by the end of the decade, the advanced capitalist economies had returned to much the same point at which they had started it, although to get there they took a rather different route than previously.

During the second half of the 1960s, the entry of lower-cost German and Japanese producers and the subsequent failure of higher-cost US producers to leave their lines, had brought about over-production and over-capacity and a falling rate of profit on an international scale, focused on the manufacturing sector. Likewise, over the course of the 1970s, over-production and over-capacity was perpetuated and exacerbated, when a counter-offensive by US-based capital, designed to bring about lower costs of production and re-establish profitability, competitiveness, and the hegemonic position of US production, was met by the refusal of higher-cost German and Japanese—as well as higher-cost US—manufacturers to retire from the field, despite their own reduced profitability. This large-scale failure to exit was made possible in the last analysis by Keynesian deficits which allowed for the parallel growth of private debt, but also by the willingness and the ability of manufacturers, especially in Germany and Japan, to accept ever lower rates of profit.

Because profitability failed to recover, the subsidy to demand that kept the system turning over could not but bring about the same succession of developments as in the late 1960s and early 1970s: the build-up of increasing numbers of high-cost, low-profit firms that in the absence of the subsidy would have gone under; a reduction in the growth of output that could be obtained by any given increase in demand due to firms' reduced access to surpluses and correspondingly reduced ability to invest; the corresponding acceleration of inflation, as any given increase in demand brought a smaller response in terms of supply than previously when profit rates were higher; rising interest rates and tight credit policies to combat inflation; and, ultimately, a new cyclical downturn. Another round of the same sort of go-and-stop cycle that had issued in the recessions of 1970–1 and 1974–5 thus culminated in the recession of 1979–82 and testified to the persistence of the economy's underlying problems.

1. The US Economy in the 1970s

Ensuring Demand

In response to the onset of the Great Depression of the 1930s and the accompanying federal budget deficits, the Republican Hoover administration had sought to reduce spending to balance the budget. But, in response to the oil crisis recession of 1974–75, the Republican Ford administration, following the precedent set by the Republican Nixon administration, effected the largest tax reduction in US history, implementing the first in a series of stimulus packages that were adopted annually by the US federal government through the remainder of the decade.[1] During the second half of the 1970s, the Ford and Carter administrations incurred deficits, which, as a percentage of GDP, rose to triple the level of the later 1960s. They thereby signalled to the private economy that they would do whatever was necessary to prevent the economy from falling into depression and helped to create the conditions for a parallel increase of borrowing in the private sector. Between 1975 and 1979, public and private annual borrowing taken together reached record levels, averaging 19.2 per cent of GDP, almost double that for the Vietnam years between 1965 and 1970, and provided the foundations for a brief period of stability and growth.[2]

US Manufacturing's Counter-Offensive

Beginning about 1971, rather than cede the field in the face of sharply intensified international competition, US manufacturers, strongly supported by the state, launched a sustained counter-attack. Already by the end of 1973, they had achieved significant gains in competitiveness by means of a major devaluation of the dollar, by preventing real wage gains as large as those secured by German and Japanese workers, and by the elevation of productivity growth in manufacturing, at least for a few years. During the oil crisis of 1974–75, US producers were able to further improve their position, since their dependence on imported oil was much smaller than that of their main competitors. In the years that followed, they were able to make even greater gains through launching new assaults on labour domestically and on their main manufacturing rivals internationally.

Reducing Labour Costs

Having suffered progressive decline under the accelerating attacks of capital from the end of the 1950s, the trade-union movement, under pressure from its rank and file, had launched a major comeback in the late 1960s and early 1970s. But, with the oil embargo recession, which brought unemployment to 8.5 per cent in 1975, firms were able to bring this upsurge to an end, opening the way to a further

---

1   Calleo, *Imperious Economy*, pp. 139–45.
2   The data on the growth of borrowing come from the US Federal Reserve, Flow of Funds Accounts. If, following J. Gurley and E. Shaw, one divides the years between 1897 and 1970 into four 17–18 year phases, one finds that, before the 1970s, the proportion of borrowing to GDP remained remarkably stable at only about 9 per cent for each long phase. 'Financial Intermediaries and the Saving-Investment Process', *Journal of Finance*, March 1956, pp. 257–76, as reported and extended by R. Pollin in 'Financial Intermediation and the Variability of the Saving Constraint', unpublished manuscript, July 1995, p. 6, n. 5. I am grateful to Bob Pollin for providing this material to me.

dramatic reduction in the growth of labour costs, both direct and indirect.

During the latter part of the 1970s, employers virtually ceased to accept without resistance petitions from their workforce for union representation elections filed under the National Labor Relations Act. As late as 1965 they had acceded to 42 per cent of such petitions, but that figure had already fallen to 16 per cent by 1973, and it dropped further to 8 per cent by 1978. The number of illegal actions committed by management against workers in the course of union organizing drives also continued to increase: between 1973 and 1979, charges against employers for unfair labour practices rose by 60 per cent, the number of workers awarded back-pay or ordered reinstated to their jobs as a result of employers' illegal actions increased by about two-thirds, and the number of illegal firings for union activity rose by about 50 per cent. Whereas unions had won 60.4 per cent and 56.4 per cent of union representation elections in the periods 1960–65 and 1965–73, respectively, they won just 48.3 per cent of union representation elections between 1973 and 1979. In the same period, union density fell precipitously, in the private sector from 27 per cent to under 22 per cent, in manufacturing from 38.8 per cent to 32.1 per cent (in 1980). Strike action also fell off noticeably in these years, with the percentage of work time lost to strikes decreasing by almost a quarter compared to 1966–73.[3] (See p. 64, Figure 4.2 and p. 116, Figure 8.2.)

As worker resistance waned and the political influence of the labour movement collapsed, employers secured remarkable reductions in the growth of their labour costs. Between 1973 and 1979, the growth of real compensation decelerated sharply, averaging 1 per cent per annum in manufacturing and 0.4 per cent per annum in the non-manufacturing private business sector, compared to 1.9 per cent per annum and 2.6 per cent per annum respectively for 1965–73, and 2.9 per cent per annum and 2.8 per cent per annum respectively for 1950–65. The growth of real social expenditures simultaneously plummeted, averaging just 2 per cent per annum between 1975 and 1980, compared to 6.2 per cent per annum between 1960 and 1975.[4]

The Further-Weakening Dollar and the Falling Cost of Credit

US manufacturers also gained at the direct expense of their international rivals. With the collapse of the short-lived Smithsonian regime in February–March 1973, the US had made clear its preference for floating rates and opposition to any return to a fixed-rate system, however flexible. Under the new regime, with the dollar continuing as the key currency, US governments were left free to pursue the politically preferable option of keeping the economy moving through rising federal deficits and could finance the rising trade and current account deficits that would inevitably ensue, simply by increasing the supply of money. In fact, as Nixon had,

---

3   Seeber and Cooke, 'The Decline in Union Success in Representation Elections', pp. 42–3; Freeman, 'Why Are Unions Faring Poorly in NLRB Elections?', p. 53; Goldfield, *Decline of Organized Labor*, pp. 90–1; Freeman, 'Contraction and Expansion', p. 64; H. Farber, 'The Extent of Unionization in the United States', in Kochan, ed., *Challenges and Choices Facing American Labor*, p. 16; H. Farber, 'The Recent Decline of Unionization in the United States', *Science*, vol. ccxxxviii, 13 November 1987, p. 916; L. Troy and N. Sheflin, *us Union Sourcebook*, West Orange 1985, p. 3–15; 'Work Stoppages in the United States, 1927–80', table supplied by US Department of Labor, BLS, Office of Compensation and Working Conditions, Division of Development in Labor-Management Relations.

4   OECD, *The Future of Social Protection*, Paris 1988, pp. 11–12.

Ford and Carter actually invited what turned out to be the record current account deficits that resulted from their record federal budget deficits because the former inevitably brought down the dollar's value and improved US export competitiveness. During the oil crisis recession, the US had run current account surpluses, which reached 1.1 per cent of GDP in 1975. But with the further turn to Keynesianism, external deficits came back with a vengeance, the current account deficit reaching $14.5 billion and $15.4 billion, respectively, in 1977 and 1978, about 0.7 per cent of GDP, and about three times the level of 1972.

The rise of external deficits, accompanied as they were by the parallel growth of Japanese and German surpluses, did put heavy downward pressure on the dollar. Between 1975 and 1979, the dollar fell by 26 per cent and 27 per cent against the yen and mark respectively, with the result that manufacturing wages in Japan and Germany, expressed in dollars, grew in this period almost twice as fast as in the US, increasing at annual rates of 16.4 per cent and 17.1 per cent respectively, compared to 9.3 per cent in the US. The average annual rate of growth of manufacturing unit labour costs in dollar terms in the US was, similarly, only half that in Japan and Germany—5.9 per cent in the US, compared to 11.2 per cent in Japan and 11.4 per cent in Germany.

In addition to reduced real wage growth and improved relative costs in international terms, US producers were able to benefit from a sharp reduction in the real cost of borrowing. The fall in the cost of credit was the intended effect of the government's policy of easy money. It was amplified by the sudden increase in the international supply of loanable funds resulting from the recycling of petrodollars from the oil-exporting states of the Middle East as well as the declining demand for credit from the now slower-growing advanced capitalist world. For the years 1973–79, real interest rates fell below zero, averaging -0.1 per cent, compared to 2.5 per cent for 1960–73, and allowed manufacturers to sharply increase the degree to which they financed investment on the basis of debt at minimal cost. During most of the postwar period, manufacturers had barely relied on debt to finance production: between 1950 and 1965, interest payments had constituted a mere 1 per cent of profits, although net interest as a percentage of profits had jumped to 11 per cent between 1965 and 1973, as profitability fell sharply. Between 1973 and 1979, with profits down and the cost of credit reduced, that figure increased by another one-third to 15 per cent.

The Growth of Investment, Output, and Productivity

Encouraged by these improvements in their cost position, US manufacturers made a concerted effort to maintain or even raise investment in aid of increased output and productivity growth, even in the face of reduced profitability. Between 1973 and 1979, to help increase investment out of profits, manufacturing corporate managers reduced annual dividend payments as a proportion of profits to just 16 per cent, compared to 26 per cent for 1950–73. In so doing, they helped allow the manufacturing sector to increase its investment in these years at an average annual rate of 5.6 per cent, about the same rate as between 1950 and 1973, when it was 5.8 per cent, and simultaneously its net capital stock at an average annual rate of 3.8 per cent, which was just about the same as between 1950 and 1973, when the figure had been 3.9 per cent.[5] The results, moreover, were not unimpressive. Between 1975 and 1979, manufacturing output rose at the average annual rate of 7.2 per cent, about the same rate as during the high boom years of 1958–65. In the same period, following a disastrous drop-off during the oil crisis recession, manufacturing labour productivity grew at the average annual rate of 2.6 per cent, not all that far below the average annual increase of 3.0 per cent for 1950–73 (especially considering that the figure for 1979 was in the negative, due to the onset of the new recession).

The improvement in US relative costs made possible quite respectable export growth in the face of the slowdown of the growth of world trade. During the years 1973–79, US exports increased at the average annual pace of 5.8 per cent. This figure was only a bit higher than the 5.3 per cent achieved between 1965 and 1971, but, since world trade grew in this period at only half the rate of the later 1960s and early 1970s, it must be seen to represent a significant improvement. It was achieved through a very major increase in US dependence on world trade, with exports increasing as a proportion of GDP by 35 per cent, manufacturing exports as a proportion of manufacturing output by almost 50 per cent.

Just as increasing US competitiveness made for a significant improvement in the US capacity to export, it dramatically reduced the incentive to invest overseas. By 1970–73, as a reflection of secularly declining US competitiveness, US manufacturing corporations were investing almost 30 per cent as much abroad as they were at home, up from 11 per cent in 1957. But by the second half of the 1970s (1975–79), that figure had fallen back to just 21 per cent.[6]

Nevertheless, the fact remains that by the eve of the second oil crisis in 1979, despite the not insignificant reductions in input costs and the decent performance of investment, productivity, exports, and growth, there was little sign that the US economy was on its way to revival, mainly because profitability in the manufacturing sector had fallen further. Outside of manufacturing, capital's ability to stamp out wage growth stabilized the profit rate. The average annual growth of product compensation was thus reduced by 75 per cent to just 0.7 per cent between 1973 and 1979—from 2.8 per cent between 1965 and 1973—with the result that the average level of the profit share between 1975 and 1979 rose 15 per cent above its level in 1973. In those four years, therefore, the rate of profit outside manufacturing was, on average, 8 per cent above that in 1973, with the result that profitability in the private business economy as a whole was able to maintain itself at slightly above its 1973 level, despite the further drop-off in profitability that took place in manufacturing. In manufacturing, profitability fell during the oil crisis of 1974–75 by a further 25 per cent or so from its level in 1973, when it was already more than 40 per cent below its peak level of 1965. Between 1975 and 1979, profitability in manufacturing remained, on average, perhaps 15 per cent above its level at the bottom of the oil crisis, but by 1978 was still about 12 per cent below its 1973 level.

5   The BLS's measure for capital inputs in manufacturing between 1973 and 1979 averaged 4.7 per cent per annum, compared to 4.15 per cent per annum between 1950 and 1973. 'Multifactor Productivity Trends, 1995 and 1996,' Table 6.

6   Fahim-Nader, 'Capital Expenditures by Majority-Owned Foreign Affiliates of US Companies', p. 63. Similarly, whereas the value of the stock of foreign direct investment in the US as a percentage of the value of the stock of US direct investment abroad had, as an expression of the declining relative profitability of the US, fallen from 28.8 per cent in 1950 to 17.5 per cent in 1966, it rose again to 23.5 per cent in 1977. R. E. Lipsey, 'Foreign Direct Investment in the US: Changes over Three Decades', in K. A. Froot, ed., *Foreign Direct Investment*, Chicago 1993, p. 117, Table 5.3.

In 1979, as the economy re-entered recession, manufacturing profitability fell back to its levels of the first oil crisis on its way to even more debilitating lows (see p. 7, Figure 0.3).

Why had the apparently positive combination of cost improvement and subsidy to demand failed to yield better results in terms of manufacturing profitability? The answer would seem to lie, largely if not wholly, in the paradoxical persistence of over-capacity and over-production in the manufacturing sector in the face of reduced profitability, a phenomenon to which the Keynesian subsidy to demand contributed mightily. The expansion of manufacturing which took place during the 1970s thus encompassed the output not only of that segment of firms that had improved their productiveness in aid of better profits, but also that segment of firms that had failed to reduce costs. Firms with high costs and/or low productivity growth stayed in business, despite their low profit rates, by virtue of the unprecedented level of deficit spending, as well as ultra-low interest rates. The large-scale failure of exit of low-profit firms was not, moreover, confined to the US; it was an international phenomenon. US expansionary policy was critical therefore not only in keeping the economy of the US turning over during the 1970s, but in providing indispensable demand for export-dependent firms in Germany and Japan too. Meanwhile, the striking ability of manufacturers in both Germany and Japan to attract support from financiers and stay in business, despite their much reduced profitability, only exacerbated the systemic problem of manufacturing over-capacity and over-production.

The Failure of Exit

Despite reduced profitability, relatively few manufacturing firms appear to have reduced their means of production or transferred them out of over-supplied manufacturing lines or gone out of business. During the period 1973–79, manufacturing output as a percentage of total private business output stayed level, and manufacturing investment as a percentage of total private investment actually grew by about 10 per cent. But what may be most telling—especially in light of the major fall-off in profitability, which must have sharply raised the proportion of firms on the edge of bankruptcy—is the fact that, far from increasing, as might have been expected, the annual rate of business failure sharply *declined*, averaging 20 per cent less between 1973 and 1979 than between 1960 and 1973.[7] That the proportion which survived actually increased seems inexplicable apart from the record stimulus to demand. By contributing to the economy's stability during the 1970s, through keeping in business large numbers of low-profit firms, Keynesianism helped to perpetuate the economy's underlying lack of dynamism by preventing greater increases in the growth of productivity and prices, and thus, of course, of profitability.

When the US federal government began to incur ever greater deficits from 1975, it helped to revive not only the US, but the world economy as a whole. The oil crisis

---

7   I wish to thank Bob Pollin for forwarding to me the time series on business failures, which was constructed from the May issues of the *Survey of Current Business* and the *Statistical Abstract of the United States*. See also A. B. Frankel and J. D. Montgomery, 'Financial Structure: An International Perspective', *Brookings Papers on Economic Activity*, no. 1, 1991, p. 264.

struck the Japanese and German economies much harder than that of the US. The Japanese and German economies were held back, moreover, by their governments' overriding concern to control inflation in the interest of export growth, and their consequent reluctance to stimulate demand through budget deficits and reliance on tight money. It was only the deficit-driven expansion of US demand that allowed these economies to emerge from their recessions. Both Japan and Germany based their recoveries almost entirely on the growth of exports so the rise of the US trade and current account deficits was therefore the key to their revival.

It remains the case that the US external deficits that emerged, determined as they were by US budget deficits, seem even larger than they 'should' have been, larger, that is, than would seem to have been warranted by the evolution of relative costs in international terms. Manufacturing unit labour costs in the US in dollar terms grew only half as fast as did those in Japan and Germany between 1975 and 1979. One can reasonably ask how Japanese and German producers were able to raise imports into the US so rapidly in this period and, beyond that, by what means they were simultaneously able to maintain, or even slightly increase, their share of the international market, while the US share declined.[8]

As we shall shortly see in some detail, the German and Japanese manufacturing economies were able to undertake export-led expansions only by accepting much reduced rates of profit. One need only note here that, while Japanese and German manufacturers sustained average annual increases in their unit labour costs that were in both cases 5 per cent higher than those of the US between 1975 and 1979, they charged export prices that rose at average annual rates that were, respectively, 7 per cent and 4.5 per cent *lower* than those charged by US producers. On the basis of their improved relative costs, largely facilitated by the falling dollar, US manufacturers were able to mark up over costs to an extent that had been long impossible. But they would have succeeded in raising prices over costs even further had Japanese and German producers not been so willing and able to sustain such reduced rates of return in order to increase their export dependence by expanding their shares of the world market.

With the failure of profitability to recover, the record federal deficits of Carter and Ford could not bring increases in supply that were in any way commensurate with the growth of demand, and accelerating inflation was the inevitable result. By 1977 and 1978, the rate of increase of the GDP price deflator, at 6.3 per cent and 7.7 per cent, respectively, had risen above its pre-oil crisis peak of 5.7 per cent, registered in 1973. In the same two years, the exchange rate of the dollar fell by 11 per cent in trade-weighted terms and by about 25 per cent and 35 per cent against the mark and yen, respectively. It was 1965–68 and 1971–73 all over again. Interest rates had to rise or the US government would intervene to raise them. As it turned out both occurred, setting off an epoch-making US-led international reorientation of state policy, away from Keynesianism and toward a more or less permanent anti-inflationary approach.

---

8   The US share of the exports of the leading eleven capitalist economies fell from 17.7 per cent in 1975 to 15.9 per cent in 1979, while Japan's and Germany's remained stable. *National Institute Economic Review*, no. 96, May 1981, p. 75, Table 23. For a similar result, see B. R. Scott and G. C. Lodge, *US Competitiveness in the World Economy*, Boston 1985, p. 27.

2. Japan in the 1970s

In the wake of the twin disasters of yen revaluation and the oil crisis, the Japanese economy emerged with radically reduced prospects. It is hard to see how its subsequent process of adjustment could have been improved upon. But, despite its impressive response to the new, unfavourable structure of international costs, the Japanese economy could secure no recovery of profitability, and could relaunch no sustained investment boom, because it proceeded along the same manufacturing-focused, export-oriented trajectory as hitherto. As a consequence of the exceedingly slow growth of its prices, attributable in part to its restrictive, anti-inflationary macropolicy, and the extreme difficulty of penetrating its import market in manufactures due largely to the multiple networks that linked its firms as one another's semi-permanent customers, Japan tended to run ever greater trade and current account surpluses, which, sooner or later, would drive up the yen and raise Japanese productive costs in international terms. Because, moreover, of the already existing international over-capacity and over-production in manufacturing lines, the improvement of US competitiveness, and the rise of new adversaries in East Asia, Japanese manufacturers found themselves under increasing pressure from their rivals in international markets. The Japanese economy was therefore able to maintain its manufacturing export-oriented path only by accepting much-reduced levels of manufacturing profitability, levels which would have been even lower had not the growth of Japanese wages slowed so drastically. During the oil crisis, Japanese manufacturing was badly set back by the temporary collapse of the world market. After that, its expansion was frustrated not only by the slow growth of world demand for manufactures in general, but especially by its inability to grow in the manner that it had previously, by appropriating great chunks of market share from less competitive rivals, above all the US.

In large part as a reaction to the international and domestic inflationary booms through which the advanced capitalist governments in general and the Japanese government in particular had sought between 1971 and 1973 to sustain the long postwar expansion, Japan experienced the sharpest recession anywhere in the advanced capitalist world at the time of the first oil shock. At the start of 1973, to stem the inflationary tide, the Japanese government turned to increasingly tight credit and, when the oil embargo struck at the end of the year, the economy plunged into crisis. By early 1975, both industrial output and capacity utilization were down more than 20 per cent from their levels of early 1973. By the end of 1975, manufacturing employment (in terms of hours) had fallen by no less than 12 per cent from its level of 1973.[9]

It was only the stepped-up growth of manufacturing exports that kept the Japanese economy turning over during the recession.[10] Accelerated export growth appears paradoxical in light of the sharply reduced growth of world demand that accompanied the international crisis. It was to be expected, however, of the Japanese manufacturing sector, given its unusually high fixed costs. Because of their tendency

---

9   T. Nakamura, 'An Economy in Search of Stable Growth: Japan Since the Oil Crisis', *Journal of Japanese Studies*, vol. vi, no. 1, Winter 1980, pp. 156–8.

10   'There is no denying that exports were the prime-mover which nudged Japan out of the recession.' Ibid., p. 163.

to rapidly build up fixed capital and to do so on the basis of debt, as well as their difficulty in shedding labour, Japanese firms had to maintain output and capacity utilization at almost any price. During the two years 1974–75, export growth averaged 11 per cent and the share of exports in Japanese GNP increased by 28 per cent. The trade surplus therefore provided the leading source of the increased demand that kept the economy going and prevented even worse depression.

The fact remains that export growth could be secured only at the cost of the spectacular collapse of manufacturing profitability. In 1974, with wage demands still keyed to a hyperinflation that was in the process of vanishing, nominal wages grew by about 25 per cent in manufacturing and in the private economy as a whole; in 1975, with deflation now a fact of life, they increased a further 13.5 per cent. In the private economy outside of manufacturing, these increases were not a serious problem. Firms could raise prices almost as much as they had raised wages; despite zero productivity growth, they were therefore able to keep product wage growth in line and limit the fall in profitability over the two years to a total of 'only' about 25 per cent. In manufacturing, however, despite the fact that the growth of costs was almost identical to that in non-manufacturing, firms could not prevent profitability from plunging by 60 per cent. Up against a suddenly stagnant world market and intensified international competition, but needing to sell at just about any price in order to make use of the capital stock that they had only recently so vastly expanded and a labour force that they could not easily lay off, Japanese manufacturers simply had no choice but to keep a lid on the prices of their mostly tradable goods to maintain output and sales. Whereas in the non-manufacturing private sector firms raised prices at an average annual rate of 18.3 per cent, in manufacturing they could raise prices at an average annual rate of just 7.5 per cent. Even so, firms in the manufacturing sector could not prevent capacity utilization from dropping a staggering 22 per cent over the two years, compared to only 4.6 per cent in the non-manufacturing private business sector. With capacity utilization and price increases so much reduced, profits had to plummet.

But Japan's economic difficulties did not end with the transcendence of the oil crisis. Even by 1979, manufacturing profitability had failed much to recover, remaining considerably lower than it had been in 1974, only about 12 per cent higher than it had been at the depths of the oil crisis in 1975, and 40 per cent below its level in 1973, when it had already fallen 22 per cent below its 1969–70 peak. Over the intervening years, the manufacturing profit share had improved by a scant 10 per cent and the output-capital ratio failed to do much better, increasing by less than 15 per cent. As the direct expression of the sharp deterioration in the rate of profit in manufacturing in these years, the average annual rate of growth of new plant and equipment spending fell to zero, compared to more than 20 per cent for the years 1965–70, and of gross capital stock to 5.6 per cent, compared to around 17 per cent for 1965–70. With investment growth so reduced, it was to be expected that the increase of output would also drop dramatically, and between 1975 and 1979 the average annual growth of real output fell to around 6.6 per cent in manufacturing, compared to 20 per cent between 1965 and 1970. Nor was there any increase in those four years in the size of the manufacturing labour force (measured in hours), which remained in 1979 about 12 per cent per cent below its 1973 level. The question that is raised, therefore, is what prevented a better recovery of the manufacturing rate of profit and of investment after the oil crisis?

The Cost and Quality of Labour

As early as the oil crisis of the years 1974 and 1975, the growth of real wages was plunging, averaging only 2.8 per cent in manufacturing (and 3.4 per cent in the private business economy). Then, with the average annual growth of the manufacturing nominal wage falling to 7.7 per cent, from about 19 per cent for the years 1970–75, the manufacturing real wage ended up growing at an average annual rate of just 3.0 per cent for 1973–79 (2.65 per cent in private business).[11] Manufacturing and private business real wages in Japan had increased, on average, at about 8.5 per cent per annum over the years 1970–73, approximately the same rates that had obtained between 1965 and 1970. In thus accepting reductions in the growth of their real wages of some two-thirds, Japanese workers could hardly have been much more accommodating in terms of their pay.

The performance was analogous in terms of labour productivity. Between 1975 and 1979, manufacturing labour productivity grew at an average annual rate of 6.4 per cent (5.1 per cent between 1973 and 1979), a bit less than half as fast as it had grown in the years of high boom between 1965 and 1970. But this figure is highly misleading. It is not adjusted for the sharply reduced capacity utilization of the years 1973–79, which was, on average, about 15 per cent below its level in the later 1960s and early 1970s, nor, equally important, for employers' retention, in the face of that unutilized capacity, of almost the entirety of their old labour force—the level of unemployment in Japan even by 1979 was only 2.1 per cent. Nor does it take into account the profoundly diminished rates of growth of the capital-labour ratio for the years 1973–79 and 1975–79, which were, respectively, one-half and one-quarter those for the years 1965–73. In the context of reduced capacity utilization, increased labour hoarding, and slowdown in equipping workers with new plant and machinery, the growth of Japanese labour productivity in this era actually turns out to be rather good.

The relatively impressive performance of Japanese labour productivity was made possible through the more efficient and more intensive application of labour. In what was termed at the time 'operation scale-down', firms stopped replacing retired personnel, reduced overtime, dispatched redundant workers to related units (often within the same 'group'), and replaced male by lower-paid female labour. There was also intensified use of 'quality circles' to elicit more committed and careful labour, or to facilitate plain and simple speed-up.[12] Adjusted for capacity utilization, though not for labour hoarding or the reduced growth of the capital-labour ratio, the average annual growth of manufacturing labour productivity for these years reached 7.05 per cent, not all that much below the figure of 9.3 per cent for whole period 1955–73 (although substantially below the especially high average rate of 12.5 per cent achieved in the later 1960s).[13]

The question thus raised by Japanese economic performance during these years

---

11   The reduction is even more extreme when measured on an hourly basis, as manufacturing hourly wages grew at only 1.31 per cent per annum between 1975 and 1979.

12   Itoh, *Japanese Capitalism*, p. 171; Nakamura, 'Japan Since the Oil Crisis', pp. 159–60; H. Shimada, 'The Japanese Labor Market After the Oil Crisis: A Factual Report I', *Keio Economic Studies*, vol. xiv, no. 1, 1977, pp. 60–4.

13   Baily, 'What Has Happened to Productivity Growth?', *Science*, vol. ccxxxiv, 24 October 1986, p. 444.

is not why the measured growth of labour productivity fell substantially, but why more investment funds were not forthcoming to take advantage of the combination of sharply reduced rate of growth of wages and palpably stepped-up effort and efficiency of Japanese labour so as to raise productiveness and thereby the profit share and profit rate. This issue is made all the more acute, given the extraordinary transformation of the structure of Japanese industry that took place at this time.

The Recomposition of Industry

Japan's impressive productivity growth performance was achieved as part and parcel of a vast restructuring of Japanese industry, designed to respond to the upward turn in Japanese production costs in international terms that took place during the 1970s. Declining competitiveness was the consequence of the radical increases in relative wage costs that were brought on by successive waves of yen revaluation, of the sharply increased energy costs that resulted from two major oil price explosions, and of the entry into the world market of low-priced manufactures originating in East Asia. In response, in the space of less than a decade, the Japanese economy dramatically reduced its commitment to, or profoundly rationalized, the 'heavy', energy-intensive and labour-intensive lines that had played such a central role during in the high-growth era. At the same time, it came to concentrate ever more exclusively on high value-added industries (especially cars), and in particular 'mechatronics' lines—that is, high technology industries that combined electronics and machinery (such as numerically controlled machine tools or electrical machinery containing programmed integrated circuits).[14]

The speed with which the process of economic restructuring was accomplished was without parallel within the advanced capitalist world and was only made possible by the specific institutional framework through which the Japanese economy was organized. It is true that in these years, as firms increased their capacity to finance themselves and secured greater access to alternative sources of funds, the state intervened far less in the investment process and did far less to directly administer the economy than previously. Still, its role in facilitating coordination among firms and influencing the economy's direction remained substantial. At the start of the 1970s, the government issued a 'vision' for reorienting the economy toward high value-added, high-technology lines, and away from labour-intensive and heavy industries. It also provided incentives to bias investment in that direction by granting low interest loans and tax breaks, by organizing consortia of private companies to cooperate in carrying out research and development, and by offering a significant degree of protection for new industries. Beginning in 1978, the government also organized a series of 'depression cartels' in labour-intensive, energy-intensive industries, such as aluminium refining, shipbuilding, and petrochemicals, designed to allow firms in these industries to keep up their profits by

---

14   This and the following two paragraphs depend on Imai, 'Japan's Changing Industrial Structure', pp. 58–9, along with three OECD analyses of Japanese 'structural adjustment' to the higher yen, higher energy costs, and competition from the NICS, in *Economic Survey of Japan 1980–81*, Paris, July 1981, pp. 37–61; *Economic Survey of Japan 1984–85*, Paris, August 1985, pp. 54–77; *Economic Survey of Japan 1988–89*, Paris, December 1989, pp. 67–82; as well as Yamamura, 'Success that Soured', pp. 91–4 and Dore, *Flexible Rigidities*, pp. 73–6 on the 'depression cartels'. Compare Hatch and Yamamura, *Asia in Japan's Embrace*, especially ch. 4.

artificially maintaining prices, while they reduced their productive capacity. Throughout the period, it should be added, the government continued to devote a substantially higher proportion of state expenditure to investment than did that of any other advanced capitalist country.

Of course, it was private industry that directly carried out the transformation. Here, Japanese labour was, again, extraordinarily accommodating, reducing the growth of wage demands and facilitating technical and organizational change. At the same time, as a result of their commitment to eschewing layoffs, Japanese firms were very willing not only to make huge investments in modernization—as they did for example in the steel industry, where they raised the proportion of production carried out by continuous casting methods from 20.7 per cent to 86.3 per cent in the decade after 1973—but also to diversify production into new lines where they could make use of what would otherwise have been superfluous workers. This naturally sped up the process of adjustment.

The organization of much of the economy into horizontal and vertical networks linking banks to firms and firms to one another also played a major role in the transformation. Since firms within the groups constituted to a large degree one another's markets and since they informed one another of their investment plans, they were able to reallocate investment toward new lines with a high degree of security and speed. The close ties maintained between great firms within and between the groups with their subsidiary suppliers contributed to the same effect.[15]

Perhaps most crucial, by virtue of their close relationships with their banks, Japanese firms enjoyed an enormous advantage in terms of access to finance over their main overseas rivals. Despite their sharply reduced profitability, they could still be sure of ample funds from their bank creditor-partners to carry out new projects, and could count on the banks and firms which held their stock to be understanding when they reduced dividends. They were therefore able to sustain investment plans in the face of declines in corporate profitability that would probably have provoked the cut-off of funds from outside investors in much of the rest of the advanced capitalist world, notably in the US. They could, moreover, expect to be able to borrow at very low interest rates by international standards, as households' high propensity to save continued to yield a steady supply of cheap funds.

Although Japanese annual gross investment in new plant and equipment failed to increase during the five or six years following the onset of the oil crisis, it remained, as a proportion of GDP, the highest among the advanced capitalist economies by a good margin. Even in the depressed years between 1973–79, Japanese manufacturing increased its gross capital stock at an average annual rate which was 34 per cent higher than that of its US counterparts in the same period (5.6 per cent compared to 4.2 per cent).

By virtue of their extraordinary transformation, Japanese manufacturing firms were, by the start of the 1980s, able to present their international competitors with a new look. In the space of just six years, between 1975 and 1981, the share of total manufacturing investment allocated to technology-intensive lines grew by 42 per cent (from 38 per cent to 54.1 per cent) while the share apportioned to other

---

15   For this and the following paragraph, Nakatani, 'Economic Role of Financial Corporate Grouping'; Dore, *Flexible Rigidities*, pp. 66–8.

manufacturing investment fell accordingly. Over the years 1973–80, output in the advanced electrical machinery and precision instruments industries and in other 'processing' industries (including other machinery, transport equipment, and metal products) grew at average annual rates of 15 per cent and 6.2 per cent, respectively, compared to just 4.6 per cent in the 'heavy' chemical, petroleum, and metal industries and 3.6 per cent in the labour-intensive textile and food industries. By 1984, the consumption of raw materials per unit of manufacturing output had, remarkably, been reduced to 60 per cent of its level in 1973. Between 1971 and 1981, the shares of general machinery, electrical machinery, and transport equipment in total exports increased by 50 per cent, 25 per cent, and 20 per cent, respectively, while those of textiles, chemicals, and primary metals fell by 60 per cent, 30 per cent, and 25 per cent respectively.[16]

Despite such spectacular change, the Japanese economy could achieve only a limited recovery in the years after the oil crisis. This was because its expansion became even more reliant than previously on the growth of manufacturing exports, in a period in which international over-capacity and over-production were increasing as a consequence of the sharp deceleration of world trade and in which Japan's own overseas sales were proving increasingly self-undermining because inextricably bound up with the build-up of Japanese external surpluses. The gains in competitiveness secured in this period through keeping down wages, keeping up productivity growth, and reorienting production were thus, to a significant degree, nullified by the halving of the growth of world trade and the effective revaluation of the yen by more than one-third. While Japanese firms could grow during the latter half of the 1970s by increasing their exports, they could not make export growth the basis for the restoration of their former dynamism because they could not make it the basis for the recovery of their profitability.

The US cyclical recovery from 1975, driven by record budget deficits, detonated Japan's cyclical upturn. Between 1973 and 1979, Japanese exports increased at an average annual rate of 9 per cent. This rate of growth was barely half that of the period of the boom, and gives an indication of what export-oriented Japanese producers were up against. It was, however, in itself rather impressive, for it entailed an increase in the Japanese share of world exports of better than 10 per cent, from 9.9 per cent to 11.1 per cent (and 13.7 per cent in 1980), in the space of just half a decade. Between 1973 and 1979 meanwhile, exports as a share of Japanese GDP rose from 10.0 per cent to 11.6 per cent (and 13.7 per cent in 1980) while manufacturing exports as a share of manufacturing output rose from 27.1 per cent in 1973 to 38.6 per cent in 1979 (45.7 per cent in 1980). Such stepped-up export-dependence was, however, only made possible on the basis of rising US budget and external deficits and record Japanese surpluses, and the unavoidable concomitant of these deficits and surpluses was an enormous revaluation of the yen.

Between 1975 and 1978, the yen's effective exchange rate increased at the average annual rate of 12.4 per cent (7.6 per cent between 1975 and 1979). Now, when figured in terms of *national* currencies, the relative unit labour costs of Japanese manufacturing *fell* at the extraordinary average annual rate of 6.7 per cent between 1975 and

16   OECD, *Economic Survey of Japan 1984–5*, Paris, August 1985, pp. 55–7, 69, 74; OECD, *Economic Survey of Japan 1981–82*, Paris, July 1982, p. 50.

1978, by reference to the trade-weighted average for nineteen main competing countries. But, adjusted for yen revaluation, that is, expressed in a common currency by reference to the weighted average of these same competing countries, this figure *rose* by 4.9 per cent![17] By the same token, whereas, in terms of the yen, Japanese manufacturing unit labour costs fell at an average annual rate of 2.3 per cent between 1975 and 1978 (1.9 per cent through 1979), in terms of the dollar they increased at an average annual rate of no less than 16.9 per cent (11 per cent through 1979), while those in the US rose at an average annual rate of just 3.8 per cent (5.4 per cent through 1979). To make possible the rate of export growth that they achieved, therefore, Japanese manufacturers were obliged to *reduce* export prices in yen terms at an average annual rate of 2.6 per cent between 1975 and 1978 (0 per cent per annum between 1975 and 1979)! Only by doing so could they hold down the average annual increase in their export prices in international terms to about 10 per cent (-2.6 per cent plus 12.4 per cent for yen revaluation) between 1975 and 1978 and about 7.6 per cent (0 plus 7.6 per cent for yen revaluation) between 1975 and 1979. This was no doubt necessary to make sales, since average export prices for the twelve members of the European community and for the US rose at average annual rates of 9.2 per cent and 5.6 per cent, respectively, between 1975 and 1978 (and 9.4 per cent and 7.5 per cent respectively, between 1975 and 1979).[18]

The inability of the Japanese manufacturing sector to achieve a greater recovery in profitability in the years following the oil crisis was thus largely the result of its inability to impose greater mark-ups, the consequence, in turn, of its declining ability to maintain competitiveness while it increased its export dependence in an epoch of international manufacturing over-capacity and over-production. Put another way, to prevent even greater reduction in their output and export growth, Japanese manufacturers had to accept much reduced manufacturing profitability. Had there been no yen revaluation—a highly unrealistic counterfactual—Japanese manufacturers would have been able to raise prices in yen on the 35–40 per cent of the output that they exported at an average annual rate of 10 per cent between 1975 and 1978 and still maintain the same export volume, rather than having to lower these prices at an average annual rate of 2.6 per cent. As it was, in order to transcend the barriers to profit-making at home that they had increasingly to confront from the time that the currency began to ascend in 1971, Japanese corporations radically stepped up their investment overseas, aided in so doing by the same rising yen that was depressing their exports and domestic rates of return. Having amounted in total to a mere $ 1.45 billion for the entire period between 1951 and 1967, Japanese foreign direct investment leapt from $0.85 billion in 1971 to nearly $5 billion in 1979.[19]

Clearly the Japanese manufacturing export growth machine was having to run ever harder just to stay in place. The intensity of the international pressures on the Japanese manufacturing sector is set in sharp relief, when the trajectory of the man-

---

17 'Unit Labour Costs in Manufacturing Industry and in the Whole Economy', *European Economy*, no. 19, 1984, p. 124, Table 15.

18 'Statistical Annex', *European Economy*, no. 58, 1994, Table 28.

19 OECD, *International Investment and Multinational Enterprises. Recent International Direct Investment Trends*, Paris 1981, p. 81, Tables 30, 31. Inward flows of foreign direct investment in this period were derisory, peaking at $520 million in 1979 (Tables 31, 32).

ufacturing sector during the 1970s is contrasted with that of the economy outside it. By 1978–79, the rate of profit in manufacturing remained no less than 35–40 per cent below its level of 1973. In contrast, profitability outside had risen by around 13 per cent above its 1973 level.[20] The average annual growth of unit labour costs in non-manufacturing was actually about 25 per cent higher over the period than in manufacturing. Nevertheless, largely immune to the downward pressure on prices that plagued manufacturing, firms outside of manufacturing could translate the very sharp reduction in the growth of wages into higher profits because they could raise prices to an extent impossible for manufacturers. With its better profitability recovery, the non-manufacturing sector was able to attract investment so as to increase its capital stock at an average annual rate of growth almost 25 per cent higher than in manufacturing, and this despite the fact that any given increase in capital stock in non-manufacturing was much less effective in raising labour productivity than in manufacturing. While the manufacturing labour force (in terms of the number employed) fell by 7.8 per cent between 1973 and 1979, the non-manufacturing industrial labour force as a whole grew slightly and service sector employment grew by a striking 15 per cent.

Nevertheless the recovery outside manufacturing was a very long way from making up for the reduction in manufacturing dynamism. By 1979, the profit rate in the private business sector as a whole still remained 22 per cent below its already sharply reduced level of 1973, with the result that investment remained flat in the intervening period, while the average annual increase of business sector gross capital stock and output fell sharply to 7.3 per cent and 3.2 per cent respectively, compared to about 12.5 per cent and 10.5 per cent respectively between 1960 and 1973.

Because Japanese manufacturing export growth took place under such inauspicious price-cost conditions, it was insufficient by itself to pull the economy fully out of recession, and had to be supplemented by a major government subsidy to demand. Having been burned at the start of the decade by runaway inflation, the government long delayed any attempt to jump-start the economy. However, from 1977–78, under intense pressure from the US, the Japanese authorities finally implemented a major stimulus programme—as did their German counterparts—featuring high levels of public investment and sharply increased budget deficits. Responding to this fiscal jolt, the Japanese economy, and especially its manufacturing sector, gathered momentum, and investment increased sharply in 1979 and 1980.[21]

Nevertheless, the brief and transitory nature of this boom brought home the profound structural problems faced by the Japanese economy. The descent back into recession at the end of the decade followed the pattern charted during the initial entry into crisis between 1971 and 1973. As earlier, when the yen rocketed in the face of exploding US international deficits (and Japanese surpluses), Japanese

---

20   The profit rates for the non-manufacturing sector have been extrapolated from those of the manufacturing and private business sectors, weighting each by its net capital stock. The non-manufacturing profit rates must therefore be seen as fairly rough, but their rates of change should not be too inaccurate.

21   Itoh, *Japanese Capitalism*, p. 170; Nakamura, 'Japan Since the Oil Crisis', pp. 163–5; Still, the level of investment never reached even the 1970 level at any time during the decade, nor did annual GDP growth rise above 5.3 per cent.

export growth plummeted, as it had previously under similar circumstances, averaging 2 per cent per annum during 1978 and 1979. When the US authorities then implemented a deflationary policy in response to those same deficits from 1979, and a new round of oil price increases soon followed on, the Japanese government saw little choice but to follow suit. They had, in any case, already begun to put on the brakes of their own accord in 1979 in response to their perception that rapidly rising government deficits were inducing inflationary pressures that would threaten export growth. In 1980, domestic demand slowed sharply and, somewhat later, export growth fell sharply as the US market collapsed with the onset there, and throughout the advanced capitalist economies, of a new, serious recession. The Japanese economy entered a cyclical downturn of even greater length, though significantly lesser depth, than that of 1974–75.[22]

3. Germany in the 1970s

The German economy, like the Japanese, emerged from revaluation and oil crisis in straitened circumstances. Unlike the Japanese, it had, under the pressure of intensifying international competition and an irrepressible mark, been experiencing a gradual secular slowdown, in both relative and absolute terms, from the later 1950s and early 1960s, although that slowdown had begun from extremely high levels. The German economy, perhaps even more than the Japanese, remained dependent upon manufacturing exports. For this reason, the enormous revaluation of the mark of the years 1969–73, and the fall in profitability that it had entailed, profoundly weakened the foundations of German growth. By 1975, German hourly wages in manufacturing, in dollar terms, had reached the level of those in the US, having been one-half the US level as recently as 1970, with the unsurprising result that significant sections of German manufacturing, mainly in standardized and labour-intensive lines, ceased to be viable.[23] To transcend their difficulties—which were, more broadly, due to international over-capacity in manufacturing—German producers were obliged to pursue one, or a combination, of three options: move sharply 'up the product cycle' so as to produce new, higher-technology manufactures that would face less intense international competition than had the standardized and labour-intensive ones in which they had hitherto heavily specialized; radically transform productive techniques in standardized and labour-intensive lines; or, shift into services. None of these was a simple task. The already very major fall in profitability tended to make it more difficult to allocate funds to research and development. The reduction in the growth of investment and consumer demand, disproportionately steep in the manufacturing sector, made the introduction of new goods especially problematic. The restricted potential for the growth of productivity in services compared to that in manufacturing implied lower profitability in services, unless wage growth could somehow be further slowed or skills or technology could be upgraded. As it was, the 1970s saw little in the way of a German economic revival.[24]

Because the German authorities had put on the brakes at the start of 1973, the oil crisis struck the German economy with less force than elsewhere. Over the two

---

22   OECD, *Economic Survey of Japan 1980–81*, Paris, July 1981, pp. 29, 33; OECD, *Economic Survey of Japan 1981–82*, Paris, July 1982, p. 32; OECD, *Economic Survey of Japan 1982–83*, Paris, July 1983, pp. 7–10.

23   BLS, *International Comparisons Among the G-7 Countries: A Chartbook*, May 1995, Table 11.

24   Fels and Weiss, 'Structural Change and Employment', pp. 32–6.

years 1974–75, profitability outside manufacturing fell hardly at all, so that profitability in the private business economy as a whole fell by 'only' 15 per cent. Still, largely because German exports actually *fell* with the collapse of world growth and demand, manufacturing profitability dropped 23 per cent. It is true that by 1978–79, the manufacturing sector had made up more than two-thirds of that loss, so that profitability stood just 9 per cent below its level of 1973. But by 1973, the manufacturing profit rate had already fallen 30 per cent below its level of 1969, 47 per cent below its level of 1960, and 54 per cent below its level of 1955. Unable to transform itself, the German manufacturing sector could not but grow much more slowly or, in certain respects, contract, given the trends to rising costs domestically and intensifying downward pressures on prices emanating from abroad.

Between 1973 and 1979, the manufacturing gross capital stock grew *less than one-third* as fast as it had during the 1960s and early 1970s, plunging to an average annual rate of just 2 per cent (1.85 per cent between 1975 and 1979), compared to 6.4 per cent between 1960 and 1973, and manufacturing investment stagnated, continuing a trend that had begun between 1969 and 1973.[25] Such a profound drop in the growth of capital stock and investment sapped the economy's vitality. It prevented the recovery of manufacturing labour productivity, which grew at roughly the same rate between 1973 and 1979 as it had between 1969 and 1973; it set off a major decline in the average annual growth of manufacturing output, which plummeted to 1.8 per cent, compared to 5.0 per cent between 1960 and 1973; and it precipitated a sharp fall in the manufacturing labour force. In just five years between 1970 and 1975, the manufacturing labour force (in terms of hours) fell an astounding 18 per cent, and by 1979 it was 20 per cent below its 1970 level (again in terms of hours) and 10 per cent (in terms of numbers employed). Meanwhile, in the wake of the deep recession of 1974–75, largely as a consequence of the profound shrinkage of manufacturing employment, unemployment became a significant fact of life in Germany for the first time since the 1950s, averaging 4.4 per cent between 1974 and 1979.

In view of the huge long-term decline in the manufacturing profit rate, the parallel plunge in the growth of manufacturing investment is all too understandable. Still, one question concerning that investment fall-off requires further clarification. Between 1973 and 1979, manufacturers succeeded in cutting real wage growth almost by half, to an average annual rate of 3.7 per cent, from 6.6 per cent between 1969 and 1973. Although hardly investing at all, they managed to elicit sufficient effort and quality of work from the labour force to maintain labour productivity growth in those years at almost the same average annual rate as between 1969 and 1973 (3.45 per cent, compared to 3.8 per cent). Since manufacturers had maintained average annual productivity growth at close to 5.5 per cent throughout the 1960s, it is hard to believe that they could not have raised it substantially above the levels achieved in the 1970s, had they been willing to maintain anything like normal levels of investment. Why did they lack the motivation to attempt this?

What clearly prevented profitability prospects from improving was the further intensification of international competition, reflecting ongoing over-capacity and over-production in worldwide manufacturing, especially as manifested in contin-

25   Manufacturing gross investment increased at an average annual rate of 0.7 per cent between 1973 and 1979.

uing downward pressure on output prices. Between 1973 and 1979, unit labour costs rose at pretty close to the same average annual rates in both manufacturing and non-manufacturing—4.8 per cent versus 4.4 per cent—with labour productivity growth significantly higher in the former than the latter, but nominal wage growth rising proportionally even more in the former than the latter. But German producers outside of manufacturing were able to raise their prices 23 per cent faster than were their counterparts in manufacturing. They were thereby able to raise their profitability slightly over the period between 1973 and 1979, beginning a long-term trend to profitability recovery. Manufacturers, by contrast, were not able to prevent their profitability from falling at an average annual rate of 1.4 per cent over the same period—although it levelled out after the first year of the oil crisis. That manufacturers could not mark up as non-manufacturers did seems attributable once more to conditions in the world market, by which firms outside of manufacturing were largely unaffected. Given the inability to mark up, manufacturing product wage growth outran labour productivity growth, keeping the profit share and, thereby the profit rate, from rising.[26]

The relatively slow increase of manufacturing, compared to non-manufacturing, prices with respect to unit labour costs gives an initial indication of the profound increase in the international competitive pressures that German manufacturers were having to confront. The German economy, like the Japanese, was initially able to surmount the oil crisis largely through the growth of exports, and it increased its dependence upon exports through the rest of the decade. Again, the US economy, with its vast budget and trade deficits and easy-money regime, served as the major locomotive, though other advanced capitalist economies also helped out by inflating. Yet in these years, growth through trade proved as difficult for Germany as for Japan.

Between 1975 and 1979, the German manufacturing sector proved quite capable of keeping costs down, as relative unit labour costs *expressed in terms of the national currency*, actually *fell* at an average annual rate of 3.1 per cent, with respect to nineteen competing countries. It did so, however, not through any marked rise in productiveness—its rate of labour productivity growth was at the European Community average—but rather through particularly slow nominal wage growth, made possible by the government's restrictive, export-promoting, low pressure macroeconomic policy. The upshot was therefore not only relatively low inflation but also a new round of current account surpluses, which together drove up the mark's effective exchange rate at an average annual rate of 6.2 per cent for the years between 1975 and 1979. Relative unit labour costs, expressed in terms of a trade-weighted common currency, with respect to the same nineteen competing countries, thus *rose* at an average annual pace of to 3.2 per cent.[27]

Over the years 1975–79, German export prices in terms of the mark increased at an average annual rate of just 2.95 per cent. But in view of the fact that the average annual increase of the trade-weighted value of the mark was 6.2 per cent in these years, this barely allowed them to remain competitive, since the average

---

26   For a similar analysis, see Giersch et al., *The Fading Miracle*, pp. 197–8.
27   'Unit Labour Costs in Manufacturing Industry and in the Whole Economy', *European Economy*, no. 19, March 1984, p. 115.

Table 11.1. Costs, prices, and profitability in Germany, 1973–79.
(Average annual per cent change.)

	NPK	NPSh	PW	LPy	NW	ULC	PPri
Mfgr	-1.4	-2.7	4.0	3.5	8.4	4.8	4.2
Non-mfgr	0.4	1.5	1.6	2.3	6.8	4.4	5.2

Sources: See Appendix I on Profit Rates. Key to legend on page xiii.

annual export price increase of the fifteen members of the European Community in these years was 9.1 per cent. Despite their self-imposed restraint on prices and profits, therefore, German producers could increase their exports at an average annual rate of just 5 per cent, which was slower than the average annual growth of world exports, at 6.4 per cent. By comparison, US producers succeeded in increasing their exports at an average annual rate of 5.8 per cent in these years, even though they raised their export prices in terms of their own national currency at an average annual rate of 7.5 per cent, two-and-a-half times as rapidly as did their German counterparts.[28] Although German manufacturers continued to sacrifice both price and profitability to maintain export growth and markets, they were now so profoundly hemmed in by their declining relative cost position that they could not begin to restore the export drive that had propelled German growth forward, if with slowly decreasing power, during the first postwar quarter century. One major consequence was that, aided by the same revaluation of the mark that limited exports, foreign direct investment sharply accelerated—as in Japan. Whereas German net foreign direct investment had averaged $4.6 billion per annum between 1970 and 1975, by 1979 and 1980, it was averaging $8.3 billion.[29]

Profitability and prospects declined nowhere near as much outside manufacturing as within it, and the non-manufacturing sector displayed, in relative terms, much greater vitality than manufacturing. Between 1973 and 1979, the average annual increase of the non-manufacturing gross capital stock, at 4.6 per cent, was more than twice that of manufacturing, and the average annual increase of non-manufacturing output, at 2.85 per cent, was 55 per cent faster. Between 1970 and 1980, the number of those employed in services increased by 22.8 per cent, while it fell by 10 per cent in manufacturing. Clearly, the German economy was in part responding to the profitability crisis in manufacturing lines by reallocating means of production to services. But, the relative success achieved in non-manufacturing was far from sufficient to make up for the problems in manufacturing and restore the vigour of the economy as a whole. Within the private business sector, profitability fell a further 4 per cent between 1973 and 1979 and the rate of capital stock and output growth fell, respectively, by 40 per cent and 50 per cent, compared to that of the late 1960s and early 1970s. Moreover, as the average annual growth of GDP declined to just 2.4 per cent between 1973 and 1979, from 4.2 per cent between

28   'Statistical Annex', *European Economy*, no. 58, 1994, Table 28.
29   OECD, *Economic Survey of Germany 1981*, Paris, June 1981, p. 68.

1960 and 1973, the total civilian labour force dropped in absolute terms by about 3 per cent in those years. With the growth of demand that had once come from manufacturing lines plunging so sharply, it was clearly out of the question for the economy to elicit the large-scale investment and technological innovation that would have been necessary to raise productivity and thus profitability sufficiently outside of those lines so as to counteract the contraction taking place within them.[30]

By 1977, output was already beginning to stagnate and unemployment continued high, at least by German standards. The German government sought to improve the conditions for growth by way of exports by driving down the mark through a policy of easy credit. But, with the US trade deficit spiralling out of control, US authorities were pushing in another direction, demanding that Germany, as well as Japan, shoulder some of the responsibility for keeping the world economy turning over by subsidizing demand through fiscal expansion. By 1978, the Germans, like the Japanese, had agreed to implement a major stimulus programme, with the budget deficit supposed to reach 1 per cent of GNP. The results of the German essay in Keynesianism were, however, at best mixed. Growth and investment did pick up in the short run, in the last couple years of the decade. But the rate of inflation doubled and export growth, as noted, continued to slip. Perhaps most symptomatically, while profitability outside manufacturing did return to the (reduced) levels of 1973, manufacturing profitability stagnated.[31] The German economy was caught in a bind from which there was no easy exit. International over-capacity in manufacturing and the rise of German manufacturing costs in international terms had made it ever more difficult for the German economy to continue to base its growth on manufacturing, via the increase of manufacturing exports. As has been seen, each apparent solution to this problem entailed significant costs. Increasing aggregate demand through deficit spending helped capitalists set up production in new lines. But it had the drawbacks both of allowing high-cost, low-profit firms to remain in manufacturing and of making it more difficult to control wage costs. Restricting the growth of demand would force more rapid exit from manufacturing, but it would make entry into new lines more risky and therefore more difficult. It would also tend to reduce wage growth and improve manufacturing competitiveness, as well as ease the shift into services by helping to make up for the generally more limited potential for any given investment to bring about productivity growth outside manufacturing than within it. Given their traditional attachment to anti-inflation and 'sound finance', it was not at all surprising that, like their Japanese counterparts, the German authorities soon gave up on their brief experiment with Keynesianism—basically imposed upon them by the Americans—in favour of what turned out to be a long-term com-

30   A greater increase in service employment through the creation of low-wage, low-productivity jobs was prevented, it should be emphasized, by the ability of the German labour movement to extend its purview to include the service sector and more generally to resist this trend. Virtually all of the increase of service sector employment between 1973 and 1979 took place in FIRE (finance, insurance, and real estate) and virtually none of it in low-productivity retail trades, and the same pattern would persist through the 1980s. Giersch et al., *The Fading Miracle*, pp. 199, 201–2; M. C. Burda and J. D. Sachs, 'Assessing High Unemployment in West Germany', *The World Economy*, vol. xi, no. 4, 1988.

31   Giersch et al., *Fading Miracle*, 189–92.

32   See Giersch, 'Aspects of Growth, Structural Change, and Employment', pp. 197–9. For a critique of German austerity policy, see W. Carlin and R. Jacob, 'Austerity Policy in West Germany: Origins and Consequences', *Economie Appliquée*, vol. xlii, 1989, 203–38.

mitment to austerity and tight credit.[32] With the US turn to monetarism from 1979, and the onset of the second oil crisis at about the same time, Germany, too, put on the brakes, sharply limiting the supply of credit and entering, with the rest of the world economy, once again into recession.

4. Recession Once More

The process that precipitated the international recession of 1979–82 attested to the persistence of the manufacturing over-production and over-capacity that lay behind the long downturn, and demonstrated how little distance the world economy had come toward recovery. Over the course of the 1970s, the growth of US federal deficits, accommodated by easy money, and supplemented toward the end of the decade by German and Japanese government deficits, made possible the explosive growth of private debt and thereby a whole new phase of otherwise unsustainable manufac-turing-centred growth along the lines established at the end of the 1960s. In thus maintaining, both in the US and internationally, a growing mass of redundant high-cost, low-profit firms that would otherwise have gone out of business, this further expansion of credit kept the economy turning over in the short term, but also pre-vented that reduction in aggregate costs of production and improvement in mark-ups over costs that were needed to restore profitability in the longer term.

Manufacturers in all three leading capitalist economies took advantage of the new phase of debt-based subsidy to demand to improve and grow. With the help of reduced real wage growth, dollar devaluation, lower real interest rates, and lower dividends, US producers launched a decade-long drive to strengthen man-ufacturing competitiveness and restore manufacturing profitability. At the same time, German and Japanese producers pursued new expansions along the old, export-based lines, although to accomplish this, even with the artificial inflation of markets, they were obliged to directly exacerbate systemic over-capacity and over-production by accepting reductions in manufacturing profitability. Symptomatically, between 1973 and 1979, whereas profitability in the manufac-turing sectors of the G-7 economies taken in aggregate fell by another third, it fell by less than 8 per cent in the non-manufacturing sectors; over the same period, the average annual growth of the capital stock, compared to that between 1965 and 1973, fell by one-third in aggregate G-7 manufacturing (to 3.8 per cent from 5.8 per cent), but barely at all in non-manufacturing (to 4.5 per cent from 4.95 per cent).[33] The recovery of the economy outside manufacturing was clearly limited by the sharp fall in the demand for its goods that resulted from the slowdown of growth and investment in the manufacturing sector. Non-manufacturers could neverthe-less do much to overcome the earlier (relatively limited) reduction in their profitability, simply by holding down the growth of wages. For those within manufacturing, however, the conditions determining their profitability were in crit-ical respects beyond their control: all were undermined in their individual pursuit of better returns by the general refusal to significantly reduce commitment to one's line of production despite sharply reduced profitability.

Because its macroeconomic policy was more stimulative than that of its chief rivals, its labour productivity growth slower, and the tolerance of rival capitalists abroad

33   AGH.

Figure 11.1. Relative unit labour costs: US, Germany, and Japan, 1975–95.

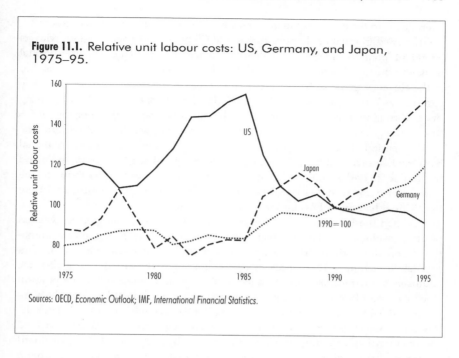

Sources: OECD, *Economic Outlook*; IMF, *International Financial Statistics*.

for reduced profitability apparently greater, the US economy was obliged, over the years 1975–79, to incur record trade and current account deficits. The resulting debts, like the earlier ones, could never be paid back. As they had at the end of the 1960s, and again in the early 1970s, the German and Japanese manufacturing economies in the mid to late 1970s accepted payments in dollars for their exports that could neither be made good in purchased US imports, nor redeemed at the exchange value at which they had been purchased. Further dollar devaluation was thus inevitable.

The fact remains that few major economic players outside the US could regard a new collapse of the dollar with equanimity. As holders of enormous dollar reserves, built up through years of current account surpluses and of interventions to buttress the US currency in the interest of the competitiveness of their own manufacturing sectors, the German and Japanese governments stood to sustain enormous losses, as did many of their private citizens. To make matters worse, with every new decline of the dollar, the manufacturing sectors of the export-dependent German and Japanese economies saw their economic prospects darken. At the time of the collapse of Bretton Woods, neither of these surplus-accruing economies had much of a basis for protesting the devaluation of the dollar, for both had profited mightily from years of under-valued currencies and had little choice but to accept some adjustment to the system. Yet, neither Japan nor Germany nor Germany's European trading partners—nor the oil exporting economies who did their business in dollars—could afford to accept dollar devaluation indefinitely, and, by the last years of the 1970s, in the wake of the dollar's precipitous decline, were seeking

34   Tew, *The International Monetary System*, pp. 195–214.

alternatives to the dollar as the main currency for international transactions.[34]

The rising international opposition to the US policy of benign neglect, with its attendant inflation and dollar devaluation, coincided with that of US international bankers, who not only disliked—as did US multinationals—the growing instability in the currency markets, but regarded any threat to the dollar's status as the key currency as a threat to their business. US domestic financiers, hard-hit by rising prices throughout the 1970s, also naturally joined the ranks of opponents of US 'fiscal irresponsibility'. The US government, for its part, had throughout the postwar period placed a high priority on defending the interests of its international bankers. Even while it had, during the 1960s, restricted capital exports to defend the dollar, it had sought to compensate them by neglecting to regulate the Eurodollar market, and, as business conditions had become more difficult during the 1970s, it had moved to eliminate all capital controls.

Still, had the US government's expansionary macroeconomic policies yielded positive results, it is quite conceivable that even the powerful coalition of international and domestic interests arrayed against it would have failed. But, with profitability failing to recover and wages stagnating in the face of rising inflation, enthusiasm for traditional demand-side policies was waning, while the political clout of its most fervent advocates, namely the labour movement, was rapidly evaporating. The way was open for a major change of perspective. Almost unbelievably, it was now the US which was obliged to accept a programme of 'stabilization', and the result was something of a revolution. Led by US Federal Reserve Board chairman Paul Volcker, the advanced capitalist governments gave up on Keynesianism and turned instead to monetarist tight credit and so-called supply-side measures aimed at cutting costs. In a sense, the new macroeconomic austerity retracted the debt-based subsidy to demand that had been keeping the world economy turning over in the face of manufacturing over-capacity and over-production, and made renewed deep recession unavoidable.[35]

35   Helleiner, *States and the Reemergence of Global Finance*, pp. 119–22, 131–5.

Chapter 12

THE US COUNTER-OFFENSIVE

At the start of the 1980s, the international economy had not begun to transcend the long downturn, held back as it was by further reduced profitability resulting from ongoing over-capacity and over-production, focused on the manufacturing sector. The Reagan–Thatcher revolution advertised itself, in this context, as confronting the underlying economic problems that Keynesianism had papered over and perpetuated. Through a policy of restriction of credit and of government borrowing, it proposed not only to bring down wage growth, but also to destroy that ledge of high-cost, low-profit firms that had been maintained by the Keynesian-based explosion of credit in the 1970s, and which stood in the way of the restoration of average aggregate profitability. By removing the supply-side burdens on capital ostensibly constituted by over-powerful trade unions, excessively high wages, burdensome taxes, and too much government regulation, it sought to further raise profitability for the firms that remained. The strength of Reaganism–Thatcherism was located in its at least implicit attack on the international economy's very real problem of over-capacity leading to reduced profitability. But its weakness was to be found in the inherent crudeness of its methods for accomplishing this, in particular its ability to affect the economy only at the aggregate level. Its results were therefore rather different from what its advocates had intended.

From 1979–80, the advanced capitalist countries implemented an unprecedented curtailment of the growth of credit, while simultaneously committing themselves to a long-term programme of reducing state expenditures in the interest of reduced state deficits. This programme did precipitate a sharp intensification of competition and, in so doing, put out of business many of those high-cost, low-profit firms which had hung on through the 1970s. But in making for such a drastic and undifferentiated reduction in the growth of demand in the aggregate, monetarist measures could not but create problems that were the opposite of those of Keynesianism. Because they reduced demand in the aggregate, they indiscriminately eliminated the purchasing power required for the survival of all firms (whether cost-ineffective or not), and set off a downward deflationary spiral that was hard to control. For the same reason, they also failed adequately to confront the problem of over-capacity and over-production which was essentially confined to the manufacturing sector: in contrast to Keynesianism, by restricting demand and credit they reduced the ability of high-cost, low-profit producers to survive, but made it more difficult for producers to establish themselves in new lines.

Monetarism could, in the end, save the economy only by destroying it. By the summer of 1982, eighteen months of ultra-tight government credit had set in motion a large-scale and extended process of industrial shakeout, and the resulting weeding-out process and its sequels ultimately did work to rationalize the US manufacturing sector. But, in striking an international economy profoundly vulnerable to shocks due to its much reduced profitability, this same deflationary binge also precipitated the worst recession since the 1930s, pushing the US economy in particular to the brink of collapse, and forcing the authorities to back off from their draconian policies. Disillusioned by their previous (in their own view, misguided) attempts to augment domestic demand, the German and Japanese governments (with a number of major lapses) persisted through the 1980s and beyond with tight credit and fiscal austerity. Their goal, as in the past, was to reduce domestic costs so as to revive the economy through increased exports. Most of the other governments in the advanced capitalist world followed suit. But the US Federal Reserve did the opposite: to bail out the economy, it began to make up for the attempts by its counterparts abroad by at least partially easing up on the supply of credit, ending the monetarist experiment in its pure form. Most dramatic, the Reagan administration, which had come to office on a programme of balancing the budget, launched what turned out to be the greatest experiment in Keynesianism defecit spending in the history of the world.

The supply-side programme which accompanied monetarism in the US, highlighted by record tax cuts, did succeed in transferring enormous sums of money into the hands of capitalists and the rich from the pockets of almost everyone else. But it did not lead to the upsurge of investment and entrepreneurship expected by its advocates for the simple reason that, given the generally poor investment climate, tax reductions could not create the anticipated incentives. Yet, precisely because the tax cuts totally failed to vindicate their advocates' predictions that they would pay for themselves by bringing about higher growth and thus higher tax revenues, they produced the highest federal deficits of all time. This was in a way fortunate, for major deficits were evidently necessary to bail out the US, and revive the rest of the world economy. As had been the case with every recovery from recession from the start of the long downturn in the later 1960s, economic revival in the 1980s was ultimately secured through a dose of deficit spending substantially larger than the one before. Monetarism, it turned out, could not be implemented unless supplemented by Keynesianism; yet Keynesianism could not but, once again, weaken the thrust of monetarism, increasing stability but prolonging the downturn and slowed growth.

Reagan's record Keynesian deficits, combined with the Fed's partial relaxation of its policy of tight money, like the stimulus programmes that preceded them, did bring about a new and lengthy cyclical upturn. But they could do little to restart dynamic capital accumulation because they could not address the underlying difficulties of the international economy. The advanced capitalist economies remained burdened by manufacturing over-capacity and over-production and thus mired in what continued to be a heavily zero-sum struggle for over-supplied manufacturing markets. This problem manifested itself in the failure of manufacturing profitability to recover in the US, Germany, Japan, or the G-7 economies taken in aggregate, and also in the continuing inability of the German and Japanese manufacturing sectors to improve their profitability except at the expense of the US, and vice versa. It was expressed as well in the greater recovery of both profitability and investment in the non-manufacturing sectors of all three capitalist economies, as well as the G-7 economies taken together, than in their manufacturing sectors (see p. 142, Figure 9.1). As it had in the 1970s, the stepped-up commitment to Keynesian credit creation in the US continued to slow down—though it did not prevent—that destruction of redundant high-cost, low-profit manufacturing producers required to restore profitability. Moreover, it exacerbated the underlying problem of reduced returns on investment, since the government's massive accumulation of debt to fund its record deficits, in combination with the rise of public borrowing throughout the advanced capitalist world, naturally led to record high real interest rates. This was because the rise in demand for credit coming from governments was very much amplified by that coming from corporations and workers, and was accompanied by the slowdown in the supply of credit that resulted from monetarist restrictiveness, as well as the reduced rates of savings that were the unavoidable result of low profitability and low wage growth.

During the first half of the 1980s, ascending real interest rates, plus the soaring dollar that these interest rates induced, spelled disaster for broad sections of US manufacturing. Exports fell, imports rocketed, the current account deficit broke all records, and manufacturing profitability temporarily collapsed. Still, the US manufacturing sector did begin to rationalize itself and, with the closing down of many of its least productive units and the large-scale shedding of labour, its labour productivity growth began to recover. As part and parcel of the same evolution, the service sector exploded through a vast expansion of low-productivity, low-waged jobs, facilitated by the unmatched 'flexibility' of the increasingly union-free US labour market. Meanwhile, with low returns on capital stock discouraging long-term placement of funds in new plant and equipment, money went increasingly to finance and speculation, as well as to luxury consumption, the way being paved by an undisguised lurch in state policy in favour of the rich in general and financiers in particular.

By serving to raise international demand and reduce US competitiveness, record US budget deficits and the high dollar once again pulled the German and Japanese economies from their recessions and created the basis for new export-led cyclical upturns. Yet the high real interest rates in the US and worldwide that went hand-in-hand with sharply increased government borrowing ensured that the international economic recovery displayed little dynamism. In particular, funds flowed en masse away from Japan to fund the US budget deficits. One witnessed the extraordinary spectacle of Japanese financiers providing the credit needed by the US government to subsidize the continuing growth of Japanese exports. US Keynesianism drove the Japanese boom, but was itself made possible only by Japanese loans; without advances from Japan, interest rates would have gone through the roof. It was difficult to determine who was more dependent upon whom—the US Treasury on Japanese lenders or Japanese manufacturers on US borrowers and their demand. What was crystal clear, however, was the degree to which the two leading capitalist economies—and thus the world economy as a whole—were dependent upon the historically unprecedented growth of debt in the US and the willingness of the Japanese to help fund it. What should perhaps have been equally obvious was that this process was self-limiting. The subsidy of US demand made possible by Japanese loans was bound to stimulate the growth of Japanese exports, undermine US production, further drive up the US external deficit, and push down the dollar. This would decrease the value of Japanese loans to the US, undermine the ability of Japanese goods to compete in the US and world market, and reduce the ability of US purchasers to buy Japanese products.[1]

By the middle of the decade, the inflated dollar was thus again proving self-undermining, with momentous results. Its eventual collapse set off what turned out to be a major shift in the pattern of growth among the three leading capitalist economies. With US current account deficits and German and Japanese surpluses hitting record levels by the mid 1980s, the exchange rate of the US currency was poised to take a fall, much as it had between late 1971 and 1973 and again from 1975 through 1978. In the Plaza Accord of September 1985, the leading capitalist states agreed joint action to force down the dollar. When the relative level of US interest rates compared to those abroad began to fall soon after, the dollar—which had already peaked earlier in the year and begun to drift downward—plummeted and the yen and mark took off, bringing about a major reversal in competitive advantage and a concomitant realignment of the loci of export growth away from Japan and Germany and towards the US. This development was further aided by the effective capping of real wage growth in the US.

US manufacturers, though retaining a much reduced labour force, were now better able to defend and even improve their position on the world export market; even so, during the decade of the 1980s they could only very partially restore profitability in the face of relentless international competition expressed in ongoing international over-capacity and over-production. By contrast, faced by sharply increased relative costs and the much slowed growth of the US market caused by dollar devaluation, the German and Japanese economies found themselves once more largely deprived of their export motors, but no more able than previously to reorient toward the home market and services. The US economy, it should be emphasized, did not decisively improve its relative performance in international terms during the decade or so following the Plaza Accord—quite the opposite. But improved US competitiveness, and the increase in profitability that accompanied it, were paralleled—as they had been in the analogous periods of the early 1960s and early 1970s—by intensifying difficulties for the German and Japanese economies.

The Intrusion of East Asia

The problems that resulted from ongoing over-capacity and over-production in manufacturing among the advanced capitalist economies were exacerbated during the decade of the 1980s by the accelerated intrusion of the four Asian NICs, and East Asia more generally, into the world market. East Asian exports became particularly disruptive at this juncture, because they continued to grow very rapidly at a time when the growth of the world economy in general and of world trade in particular was slowing, and when the leading capitalist economies were already struggling with over-supplied manufacturing markets. Whereas Japan had increased its share of world exports from 0.9 per cent to 6.0 between 1950 and 1975, the four Asian NICS increased their combined share from 1.2 per cent to 6.4 per

---

1   On the US-Japanese economic relationship in this era, see the account in R. T. Murphy, *The Weight of the Yen*, New York 1996, to which I am much indebted.

cent between 1965 and 1990. By 1990, the share of world exports of goods held at this point by all of non-OPEC, non-Japanese Asia had risen to 13.1 per cent, higher than that of the US (11.7 per cent), Germany (12.7 per cent), or Japan (8.5 per cent). In the immediately preceding years, the four East Asian NICS had not only stepped up their export of heavy industrial, capital-intensive commodities, but also begun to venture into technology-intensive lines. They therefore levied a particularly heavy toll on US manufacturing in the period up to about 1986, when the latter was crippled by the revalued dollar; when the dollar fell and the yen rose after 1985, it was Japan's turn to feel the pressure.[2]

Because their currencies were generally pegged to the dollar, the Asian Gang of Four, as well as the newly emerging economies of Southeast Asia, particularly benefited from the precipitous decade-long rise of the yen against the dollar following the Plaza Accord of 1985. Indeed, by moving into markets previously held by the Japanese, both in North America and in Asia itself, they were able to achieve, for a full decade from 1985 through 1995, otherwise inconceivable gains in exports that made possible otherwise inconceivable gains in manufacturing output, as well as the attraction of otherwise inconceivable flows of overseas loans and foreign direct investment. Yet much of the increase in exports from East Asia actually came from Japanese multinationals, which, sparked by the high yen, relocated significant portions of their production facilities in Southeast Asia, bringing with them their networks of suppliers. Indeed, by continuing to progress up the product cycle and by improving technology even in supposedly standardized manufacturing lines, the Japanese economy was able to make good use of East Asia's dynamism to aid in its own process of adjustment to what was in effect much higher priced labour. By gaining markets in East Asia for its technology-intensive capital and intermediate goods, Japanese manufacturers more than compensated for losing to Asian-based producers some of their former share in the trade in labour- (and to an extent capital-) intensive goods. Meanwhile, they profited handsomely in the latter trade through the rising exports of their multinationals based in Malaysia, Thailand, the Philippines, and Indonesia into the North American market.

By the time a new cyclical downturn hit the international economy in 1990–91, neither the US, nor Germany, nor Japan, nor the G-7 economies taken together, had come close to transcending the long downturn, because the problem of over-capacity and over-production in manufacturing remained unresolved. Profitability in manufacturing failed to rise much above its level of the later 1970s (at which point it had fallen below its already sharply reduced rate of 1973) in the US, German, and Japanese economies, and in the G-7 economies taken together. As a result, profitability in the private business sectors of these economies was kept from recovering as well. In keeping with the failure of manufacturing profitability to rebound, the growth of both manufacturing output and capital stock fell substantially further, by about 33 per cent and 25 per cent respectively in the G-7 economies in aggregate during the years 1979–90, compared to the years 1973–79.[3] (See p. 142, Figure 9.1.)

2   OECD, *Economic Outlook*, no. 60, December 1996, p. A49, Table 46.
3   Armstrong et al., *Capitalism Since 1945*, p. 365, Table A5; OECD, *Historical Statistics 1960–1995*, p. 52, Table 3.5.

A US Comeback?

During the cyclical recovery of the first half of the 1990s, the divergence that had begun to open up during the second half of the 1980s in the economic trajectories of the US economy, on the one hand, and those of Germany and Japan, on the other, was accentuated, with potentially far-reaching implications, not only for their own subsequent developmental patterns, but for the world economy as a whole. But the fact remains that the economic performance in these years of the three leading capitalist countries, and of the advanced capitalist world more generally, was even worse than it had been during the comparable upturn of the 1980s, which had itself been somewhat less good than that of the 1970s.[4]

In the US, the sharp cyclical downturn and slow recovery of the early 1990s precipitated a new round of industrial shakeout, which continued the work of the deep recession and overvalued dollar of the early 1980s. Through ongoing downsizing, outsourcing, reorganization of the labour process, and speed-up— and only in small part through investment growth—the US manufacturing sector was able not only to maintain, but actually to step up, its already improved rate of productivity growth. Meanwhile, on the basis of a decade-long stagnation of wages and a stunning collapse of the dollar against the mark and the yen, it also achieved a major long-term improvement in competitiveness, making possible a substantial increase in the growth of exports. The outcome was of major significance: during the first half of the 1990s, US manufacturing secured a decisive improvement in its profitability, the rate of profit on its capital stock rising above the level of 1973 for the first time since the start of the long downturn, though falling short of its 1950s and 1960s peaks. The way was thus opened for a true recovery of the profit rate in the economy as a whole, for, outside of manufacturing, profitability had not fallen all that much initially, had made certain gains in the later 1970s and first half of the 1980s, and, as long as wages remained so immobile, had a clear path toward restoration by way of even modestly increasing productivity. For the years 1990–95, the major macroeconomic indicators—output, investment, productivity, and wage growth—were even worse than for the years 1979–90. Nevertheless, because a revival of profitability had been set in motion, there beckoned the possibility that investment growth could be sustained and the level of economic performance, at least in the US, decisively improved. (See p. 109, Figure 8.1.)

In sharp contrast, the still very large and central manufacturing sectors maintained by both the Japanese and German economies, which by virtue of the vertiginous rise of the dollar had managed during the first half of the 1980s to partially avoid the reckoning with international over-production that had begun to be imposed on their US counterpart, faced deepening crisis. When the mark and the yen began their long, steep ascent following the Plaza Accord—while wages continued to creep up—they were obliged to confront even more serious threats to their fundamental, export-driven mechanisms of growth than during the previous periods of dollar devaluation between 1969 and 1973, and 1975 and 1978. In Japan, the introduction of a new phase of ultra-easy credit from 1986 was supposed to compensate for the fall in international demand and turn the whole

---

4   See below, p. 240, Table 13.1.

economy towards the domestic market. But what it actually precipitated was something like a re-run, in even more accentuated form, of the progression from speculative boom to bust that one had witnessed in the early 1970s—a half-decade 'bubble economy' through 1990–91, which issued in Japan's longest and deepest recession from 1991 through 1995 and beyond. In Germany, the collapse of oil prices, the short-term easing up on credit and on fiscal stringency in the wake of the crash of October 1987, and the huge increase in state spending to integrate the former GDR brought about an analogous, though less spectacular, chain of events to those in Japan—particularly an ultimately inflationary boom from the end of the 1980s through 1991, followed by what was also Germany's worst postwar cyclical downturn.

In this context, the refusal of the US government under Clinton to resort to deficit spending to reflate the US and world economy following the recession of the early 1990s, breaking a pattern going back to the 1960s, constituted a turning point. Not only did it very much exacerbate the economic problems facing Germany and Japan, but, by profoundly intensifying the already existing, long-standing and powerful, systemic trends toward the reduction in the growth of demand, it could only, in the absence of a sufficient countervailing trend to increased investment growth, exacerbate the problem of systemic over-capacity and over-production in manufacturing.

From the start of the long downturn, real wage growth throughout the advanced capitalist world had progressively decelerated, and shrank toward disappearance as the 1990s progressed. Wage repression was supposed, of course, to raise profitability to prepare the ground for a new investment boom. But that investment boom never appeared, in part because the problem of over-capacity and over-production in international manufacturing persisted, in part because gains in profitability were counterbalanced by rising real interest rates. As a result, the macroeconomic tightening unleashed throughout most of the advanced capitalist world by monetarism was bound to intensify the problem of demand that was resulting precisely from slower investment and slower growth. Over the course of the 1980s and the first half of the 1990s, as wage growth and then unemployment growth fell, public credit was increasingly restricted and the increase of government spending and the size of government deficits were progressively reduced, tending to strangle the world economy.

During the 1980s, thanks to Reagan's record-smashing budget deficits, the US virtually single-handedly prevented the ever more bitter monetarist medicine from taking full effect. Through the length of the downturn, the expansion of government credit had fallen steadily. Having ranged from 12 to 18 per cent between 1973 and 1979, the annual increase of the money supply for the US, Germany, Japan, the UK, and Canada taken in aggregate had ranged from 7 to 12 per cent between 1982 and 1990, and from just 2 to 6 per cent between 1992 and 1997.[5] However, in telling contrast, the average annual growth of real government final consumption expenditure for the G-7 economies in aggregate pretty much maintained itself, slipping to 2.2 per cent between 1979 and 1989 from 2.4 per cent between 1973 and 1979. The

5   W. Wolman and A. Colamosca, *The Judas Economy: The Triumph of Capital and the Betrayal of Work*, New York 1997, p. 154, Figure 7.2.

limited extent of this decline was made possible entirely by the US, where, as a result of Reagan's runaway military spending and tax reductions, a new round of Keynesianism reduced the bite of monetarist austerity. In the US, the average annual growth of real government final consumption expenditure thus *increased* by almost 50 per cent between 1979 and 1989, compared to 1973–79, making up for the substantial reductions in the other six G-7 economies (outside of Italy), where the fall-offs ranged from around 33 per cent in Canada and France to 47 per cent and 57 per cent respectively in Japan and Germany. But, when the US under Clinton joined the international consensus behind fiscal as well as monetary constriction— at the very time when Europe was further tightening the noose both on the supply of credit and the growth of state expenditures in the run-up to monetary union— demand emanating from governments throughout the advanced capitalist world collapsed. Between 1989 and 1995, monetarist austerity thus finally took full effect, as the average growth of real government final consumption expenditure in the US fell almost to the point of disappearance, to 0.1 per cent per annum, with the result that the average annual growth of real government final consumption expenditure for the G-7 economies in aggregate in these years, compared to that for 1979–89, fell 60 per cent to 0.9 per cent.[6]

Taken in combination with the longer term trends toward reduced profitability and slowed investment growth, the macroeconomic squeeze had predictable consequences. During the years 1990–96, the average annual growth of GDP in the US and G-7 economies taken together fell by 25 per cent and 45 per cent, respectively, by comparison with the years 1979–90. Largely as a consequence of the fall in aggregate demand, all of the world's leading manufacturing economies found themselves obliged to sharply step up their manufacturing exports, to seek an exit from the recession. In the eight-year economic upturn of the 1980s (1982–90) that followed the early 1980s recession, the growth of GDP in the OECD economies in aggregate averaged 3.7 per cent per annum, while the increase of exports averaged 5.0 per cent per year. But in the five-year upturn (1992–97) that followed the recession of the early 1990s, whereas the average annual growth of GDP in the OECD economies in aggregate fell to just 2.4 per cent, the average annual growth of merchandise exports jumped to 7.1 per cent, undoubtedly exacerbating the already existing trend toward over-capacity and over-production in manufacturing. In view of the impressive rebound in profitability secured by US firms during the first half of the decade, a US-led international recovery could not be ruled out. But, unless a boom in investment materialized and sustained itself in the US during the second half of the 1990s, the world economy risked deeper stagnation, and perhaps worse.

1. From Reagan to Clinton: Transcending the Long Downturn?

From the end of the 1970s right through to the present, the US economy has pursued a complex and profoundly contradictory path. Despite the much ballyhooed Reagan and Clinton 'booms', actual economic performance has been poor: each of the long cyclical expansions, first of the 1980s and then of the 1990s (through 1997), was less vibrant than the one that preceded it. Nevertheless, the US economy underwent a major transformation, with far-reaching positive implications for capital. The

6   OECD, *Historical Statistics 1960-95*, p. 61, Table 4.7.

business climate was profoundly improved by the long-term weakening of labour and two decades of close to zero real wage growth, an exceptionally long period of ever-deeper devaluations of the dollar against the currencies of US producers' leading overseas rivals, and a series of administrations more unapologetically pro-capitalist in every aspect of policy than had been seen since the 1920s. In the wake, moreover, of two serious recessions and extended periods of tight money, a great mass of redundant means of production, especially in manufacturing, was finally forced out by gales of 'creative destruction', better known as downsizing. Above all, as the decade of the 1990s passed its midpoint, profitability finally rose decisively above its highest previous levels of the long downturn, surpassing the point to which it had fallen in 1973 and trending upwards.

Reaganomics

By the summer of 1982, the US economy, subjected to the monetarist medicine since 1979, was reeling from the resulting recession. Pulled down by record high real interest rates, capacity utilization plummeted and manufacturing profitability fell 50 per cent below its level of 1978, leaving it 54 per cent below its level of 1973 and more than 70 per cent below its level of 1965. Unemployment (at 11 per cent), bankruptcies, and bank failures reached levels hitherto unapproached during the postwar epoch. With the Latin American debt crisis threatening the viability of American's biggest banks and a collapse into depression a real possibility, Paul Volcker unceremoniously put an end to the experiment in what might be called pure monetarism, and let the growth of credit accelerate.[7] One year previously, Ronald Reagan had morphed himself into the greatest Keynesian in history. With the enthusiastic support of the Democrats, he had initiated a series of enormous cuts in taxes for the rich and combined these with major increases in military spending, setting off a record increase in federal borrowing. Meanwhile, with its repression of the air-controllers' strike (effectively destroying their union, PATCO), the government gave the go ahead for the still further ratcheting up of the employers' assault against labour, and real compensation ceased to grow until the second half of the 1990s. With demand and thus capacity utilization growing rapidly, labour costs held down and tax payments reduced, the economy entered a new and lengthy cyclical upturn.

Over the course of the 1980s and beyond, the economy of the US continued to display its superiority over those of other advanced capitalist countries most decisively in its capacity to control wage growth, as the employers' offensive against labour, originating as far back as the end of the 1950s, reached something of a culmination. Employers had been stepping up their very long-term assault on workers and unions from the time of the deep, oil crisis recession of 1974–75, immensely aided by the government's programme of deregulation in such industries as trucking, airlines, railroad, and telecommunications, where regulated prices had hitherto generally allowed higher wages. But the repression of PATCO, coming as it did in the midst of the worst US slump since the 1930s, represented a turning

---

7   B. M. Friedman, *Day of Reckoning: The Consequences of American Economic Policy Under Reagan and After*, New York 1988, pp. 148-9, 173; W. Greider, *Secrets of the Temple: How the Federal Reserve Runs the Country*, New York 1987, pp. 495–534ff.

point, as was immediately recognized at the time.[8] During the years 1975–81, the number of union recognition elections organized by the labour movement had averaged about 7,100 per annum (6,858 in 1980), but in 1982 that number nose-dived to 3,561 and failed to recover during the remainder of the decade, averaging 3,463 between 1982 and 1987. By 1982, moreover, approximately one-third of firms in which a majority of workers voted to unionize were refusing to sign a collective contract, effectively reversing the supposedly lawful election. Whereas the absolute number of union members had held up reasonably well into the mid-1970s, despite the ongoing decline in the percentage unionized, it now plummeted at average annual rates of 817,000 between 1979 and 1983 and 361,000 between 1983 and 1987. In 1982, meanwhile, despite—or perhaps as one major cause of—the sharp decline in the number of union elections, unfair labour practices committed by management during organizing drives continued to massively increase, reaching an average of 7.45 per election, compared to 4.0 just five years previously in 1977 and 1.8 in 1960. Almost unbelievably, over the second half of the decade, the ratio of the number of individuals fired in campaigns to win union recognition to the number voting at the end of those campaigns reached 14 per cent, or about one in seven. During the years 1982–90, the average number of strikes annually involving 1,000 or more workers fell to around 60, compared to 142 for the years 1979–83, 280 for the years 1973–79, and 325 for the years 1950–73. Workers involved in these strikes represented, on average, just 0.04 per cent of the labour force's total work time, compared to 0.11 per cent for the years 1973–79 and 0.16 per cent for the years 1950–73. Unionized workers as a percentage of the private sector and manufacturing labour forces, at levels of 28.5 per cent and 38.8 per cent, respectively, as recently as 1973, declined, by 1990, to 12.1 per cent and 20.6 per cent, respectively (see p. 64, Figure 4.2).[9]

Slipping downward more or less continuously from the late 1950s, wage growth plumbed new depths in the 1980s. Between 1979 and 1990, real hourly compensation in the private business economy grew at an average annual rate of 0.1 per cent. The trend in these years for hourly real wages and salaries alone (excluding benefits) for production and non-supervisory workers was worse, *falling* at an average annual rate of 1 per cent. At no time previously in the twentieth century had real

8   Note the following contribution by Paul Volcker, then head of the Federal Reserve, to a National Bureau of Economic Research roundtable on American economic policy in the 1980s, held in 1990: 'Volcker added that, in his view, the most important single action of the administration in helping the anti-inflation fight was defeating the air traffic controllers' strike. He thought that this action had had a rather profound, and, from his standpoint, constructive effect on the climate of labor-management relations, even though it had not been a wage issue at the time.' M. Feldstein, ed., *American Economic Policy in the 1980s*, Chicago 1994, p. 162.

9   G. N. Chaison and D. G. Dhavale, 'A Note on the Severity of the Decline in Union Organizing Activity', *Industrial and Labor Relations Review*, vol. xliii, April 1990, p. 369; H. S. Farber, 'The Recent Decline of Unionization in the United States', p. 919; R. B. Freeman and M. M. Kleiner, 'Employer Behavior in the Face of Union Organizing Drives', *Industrial and Labor Relations Review*, vol. xliii, April 1990, p. 351; *Handbook of Labor Statistics*, BLS Bulletin 2340, August 1989, p. 543, Table 140; E. E. Jacobs, ed., *Handbook of US Labor Statistics*, Lanham 1997, p. 287 (After 1980, government strike data is available only for walkouts involving one thousand or more workers; after 1989, the Bureau of Labor Statistics discontinued publication of the *Handbook of Labor Statistics*, which was revived by private publishers in 1997); Leo Troy and Neil Sheflin, *MS Union Sourcebook. Membership, Finances, Structure, Directory*, West Orange 1985, Table 3.63; BLS, *Employment and Earnings*, vol. xxxix, January 1992, p. 229; and vol. xliv, January 1997, p. 211. I wish to thank Mike Goldfield for supplying me with the data on the numbers voting in union elections and the numbers illegally discharged.

wage growth been anywhere near so low for anywhere near so long.

While upward pressure from wages on profits was thus reduced, downward pressure on profits from taxes was also alleviated. Tax cuts were, of course, the centrepiece of the supply-side revolution. High tax rates ostensibly reduced the incentive to invest and to work; lowering them was supposed to unleash a new era of accumulation and innovation. The Economic Recovery Act of 1981 reduced tax rates on corporations and greatly liberalized depreciation benefits. After falling as a proportion of profits from 47.5 per cent to 35 per cent during the Kennedy-Johnson administrations, the rate of taxation on non-financial corporations had averaged around 40 per cent between 1967 and 1980. But between 1980 and 1990, as the effect of more accelerated depreciation allowed by the new tax legislation, as well as the sharp increase in the proportion of (tax deductible) interest payments in total profits, taxes as a proportion of profits fell far lower, averaging just 26 per cent.[10]

As a result of the cuts in taxes and the simultaneous increases in military spending, the federal budget deficit as a proportion of GDP broke all records, averaging 4 per cent over the course of the 1980s (over 5 per cent for 1982–87), compared to 2.3 per cent for the 1970s and 1.1 per cent for the 1960s. The explosion of the federal deficit established the basis for an historic increase in private borrowing of all types—an increase much facilitated by the profound deregulation of financial markets that had begun to take place in response to the inflation of the 1970s. During the years 1982–90, total annual borrowing (public plus private) as a percentage of GDP rose to an unprecedented peacetime level of 22.1 per cent, compared to 17.4 per cent for the years 1973–80, 11.8 per cent for the years 1960–73, and 8.5 per cent for the years 1952–60.[11]

On the basis of the major turn to federal deficits, as well as the parallel expansion of private indebtedness, the US economy, and the world economy more generally, succeeded during the 1980s in achieving the longest peacetime expansion in history. But, it was one thing to make use of the tried methods of federal debt creation to secure a modicum of growth of output, given the huge amount of unused capacity and high unemployment that initially prevailed; it was quite another to achieve a new secular boom. Transferring enormous sums of money to the wealthiest owners of the means of production turned out to be easy; but inducing these capitalists to accumulate and innovate proved exceedingly difficult.

Although during the course of the expansion, the rate of profit for the private business economy rose substantially from its deeply depressed levels of 1982, it failed, even at its height in 1989, to quite reach its previous post-oil crisis peaks, attained during the cyclical upturn of 1975–79, or to rise above its level of 1973. But this was only part of the story. Federal deficits were so huge that US lenders could not come close to funding them. It was only the fortuitous and unexpected entry by the Japanese into the money market that bailed out the

10   L. Mishel et al., *The State of Working America 1996–97*, Economic Policy Institute, Armonk 1997, pp. 121–4.

11   I wish to thank Bob Pollin for providing me with the time series on US borrowing, derived from the Board of Governors of the Federal Reserve System, Flow of Funds Accounts, that underlie these numbers.

government and prevented a bond-market crash. Japanese lenders funded perhaps one-third of the federal debt throughout the 1980s.[12] Even so, real interest rates hit their highest levels for a period of comparable length in at least a century, rocketing to an average of 5.8 per cent for the years 1982–90, from an average of *minus* 0.1 per cent for the years 1974–79 and about 2.5 per cent for the years 1960–73.[13] The actual incentive to invest was thus significantly lower than indicated by the profit rate itself.

With the profit rate so reduced and the interest rate so elevated, investment growth was bound to fall. Between 1982 and 1990, the average annual growth of the net capital stock in the private business economy fell to 2.9 per cent from 3.4 per cent between 1973 and 1979 and 4.3 per cent between 1965 and 1973. Net investment as a percentage of GDP, having averaged 3.3 per cent between 1950 and the end of the 1970s, fell to just 2.3 per cent.[14]

Productivity growth in the private business economy had already fallen substantially in the crisis-ridden 1970s. With investment growth declining, it failed to recover in the 1980s, averaging 1.5 per cent, compared to 1.2 per cent between 1973 and 1979. At no time during the previous century had productivity growth been so slow for so long as it was between 1973 and 1990 and beyond. Nor did the growth of output itself improve. Between 1979 and 1990, private business value added increased at an average annual rate of 3.1 per cent, which was actually slightly lower than the 3.2 per cent registered between 1973 and 1979 despite the two oil crises.

In the 1980s, there was much talk of a 'Reagan Boom' and economic turnaround. In reality, the economy showed less vitality than in the much-maligned 1970s, especially when one takes into account the two major waves of high oil prices that undermined growth in the 1970s and the collapse of oil prices that promoted growth in the later 1980s.

Clinton's Deflation

Nor, when viewed in all its aspects, was the economy's performance over the length of the cyclical upturn that extended through Bill Clinton's first administration and into his second better than that of the Reagan-Bush years. The fact remains that during the middle third of the 1990s, profitability did begin to rise above its previous highs of the period of the long downturn, and the economy did begin to accelerate noticeably in terms of a restricted number of key indicators, particularly the growth of investment. Whether, and for how long, it would maintain this momentum was the question of the day.

When Clinton assumed the Presidency at the start of 1993, the fierce if short reces-

---

12   R. Taggart Murphy, *The Weight of the Yen*, New York 1996, pp. 33–4, 147–50. It was widely believed at the time that, when the financial markets became cognizant of the combined programme for spending increases, tax reductions, and (inevitably) federal deficits planned by the government, they would sharply raise interest rates. As Federal Reserve Chairman Paul Volcker later commented, 'The shortage of domestic savings was compensated in substantial part by an enormous inflow of mainly borrowed capital from abroad. That inflow was at one point running at a greater rate than all the personal savings in the United States and *turned out to be far larger than I had thought possible.*' (p. 148, Murphy's emphasis.)

13   R. Pollin, 'Destabilizing Finance Worsened this Recession', *Challenge*, vol. xxxv, no. 2, March–April 1992, pp. 18, 22. According to Pollin, real interest rates averaged 3.4 per cent between 1890 and 1929 and 0.7 per cent between 1947 and 1979.

14   Friedman, *Day of Reckoning*, pp. 198–9.

sion that had gripped the economy in the middle of 1990 had been over for eighteen months. Nevertheless, the economy still showed little life, with output at that point growing at less than half the average rate of the previous five business cycles at analogous points back to 1959.[15] But, as a legacy of the years of deficits under Reagan and Bush, the national debt was at an all-time high. Net government debt as a proportion of GDP, at 21.8 per cent as recently as 1980, had climbed by 1993 to 46.4 per cent and, in combination with similar mountains of government debt accrued in most of the other leading capitalist economies, was placing strong upward pressure on interest rates.[16] There is more than a touch of irony in the fact that, whereas it had been mainly Republican presidents from Nixon through Bush who incurred the Keynesian budget deficits that kept the US and world economy turning over during the length of the long downturn, it was a Democratic chief executive who made the first major effort since the 1950s to balance the federal budget, ignoring the deflationary consequences. Still, the fact remains that Clinton did confront a potential double bind. Unless he sustained federal deficits to stimulate demand, the cyclical upturn could be expected to limp along. But, if he took on more government debt by incurring major budget deficits, interest rates might go through the roof. This was especially so since, at the very moment Clinton assumed office, Japanese investors, facing mounting obligations at home as the Japanese economy fell into deep recession, were withdrawing their funds from the US market for Treasury Bonds, ceasing for the time being to fund the long-term government debt.[17]

Clinton initially proposed a very mild stimulus package of $16 billion, but even this largely symbolic attempt at Keynesian demand management failed to pass Congress. Making a virtue of necessity, Clinton made balancing the budget the central goal of his administration, as legislation passed during the summer of 1993 ensured that there could be no increase in expenditures for any programme that was not elsewhere counterbalanced by an equal decrease. Between 1992 and 1996, the federal budget deficit as a percentage of GDP fell from 4.7 per cent for 1992–93, to 1.4 per cent, and virtually to zero in 1997.[18] Over the same period, Alan Greenspan and the Federal Reserve complemented Clinton's fiscal austerity by maintaining a tight hold on the supply of credit. To fight the recession of 1990–91, the Fed did introduce very major cuts in interest rates, which brought the real cost of short-term borrowing close to zero and overcame the slump. But the economy had barely begun to take off when the Fed turned to tightening once again, raising interest rates on four occasions between February 1994 and February 1995—by no less than 3 per cent—because growth was thought to be gaining 'excessive momentum', even though the unemployment rate was still above 6 per cent.[19] A turning point had clearly been reached. For the first time since the days of Dwight Eisenhower, the federal government failed to make full use of the Keynesian macroeconomic arsenal to overcome recession and assure more rapid growth. Especially since long-term interest rates failed to fall very much, it was hardly surprising that the ensuing

---

15 OECD, *Economic Survey of the United States 1992–93*, Paris, November 1993, p. 11.
16 OECD, *Economic Outlook*, no. 61, June 1997, p. A38, Table 35.
17 Murphy, *Weight of the Yen*, pp. 272–4.
18 *Economic Report of the President 1997*, Washington, DC 1997, p. 390, Table B-377.
19 *Economic Report of the President 1996*, Washington, DC 1996, p. 46. The growth of GDP in 1993 was a vigorous 2.3 per cent.

Figure 12.1. US strike activity, 1947–95 (stoppages involving 1,000 or more workers).

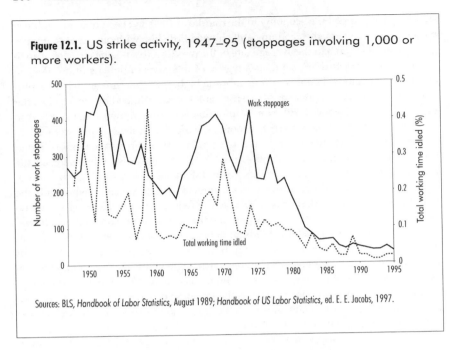

Sources: BLS, *Handbook of Labor Statistics*, August 1989; *Handbook of US Labor Statistics*, ed. E. E. Jacobs, 1997.

cyclical recovery in the US—and on a world scale—was, by any standard, rather feeble at least to 1996 or 1997.

Labour continued in retreat, as union density fell to 10.2 per cent and 17.2 per cent, respectively, in the private economy and in manufacturing by 1996, and strike activity declined still further, the number of strikes involving 1,000 or more workers averaging just 37 between 1990 and 1995.[20] Between 1990 and 1996 the average annual growth of real compensation in the private business economy was less than zero.

Even in the face of a decade's worth of the failure of wages to grow, the response of investment continued, on average, to be sluggish. Between 1990 and 1996, as a proportion of GDP, net investment averaged just above 2.0 per cent.[21] Over the same period, the average annual growth of the private business net capital stock fell, on average, to just 2.2 per cent, compared to 2.8 per cent between 1982 and 1990. It took until 1993 for annual investment to exceed its level of 1989, although from that point on it grew rapidly, opening the way to greater economic dynamism in the second half of the decade.

With the capital-labour ratio growing at an average annual rate of 0.9 per cent between 1990 and 1996, compared to an already-low 1.4 per cent between 1979 and 1990, output per labour input could hardly have been expected to take off. Between 1990 and 1996, private business sector labour productivity growth averaged only

---

20   BLS, *Employment and Earnings*, vol. xliv, January 1997, p. 213; *Handbook of US Labor Statistics*, p. 287. In 1997 private sector unionization fell below 10 per cent.
21   OECD, *Economic Survey of the United States 1994–95*, Paris 1995, p. 70.

1.8 per cent per annum, not much higher than the meagre 1.5 per cent it had averaged between 1979 and 1990 and, of course, far lower than the 2.8 per cent it averaged between 1950 and 1973.

A mild economic expansion was, however, just what the political and economic establishment wanted. Clinton's budget balancing and the Fed's monetary stringency constituted a slow-growth policy, consciously designed to fit the quite specific needs of the very much altered US economy that had been slowly emerging over the 1980s and early 1990s. During this period, US capital had become profoundly dependent on close to zero real wage growth, as well as low inflation. Employers required the repression of wage growth inside manufacturing to help counter intense competition from their leading international rivals; they required it outside of manufacturing, so that they could increase their profit shares and profit rates, despite the snail-like pace of non-manufacturing productivity growth. US capitalists needed low price increases as well as low wage increases, because they had profoundly increased their involvement in finance and in speculation on the stock market, and thereby had become exquisitely sensitive to rises in prices that would undercut their returns from lending, or further push up their costs of borrowing for purposes of financial manipulation. Not only did the rate of price increase plummet but, as emphasized, real wage increases continued to average around zero. More than any other single factor, it was the stagnation of wages for well over a decade that opened the way for profitability in the private business economy as a whole to transcend, for the first time since the onset of the oil crisis recession, its levels of 1978 and 1989 and, by the second half of the 1990s, to rise above its level of 1973.

To understand the far-reaching changes that lay behind the palpable improvement in US economic prospects, if not actual performance, manifested in the revival of profitability, and to grasp the meaning of the newly arisen framework of US state policy, viewing the economy as a whole can take US only so far. An aggregate perspective conceals the very different trajectories of the manufacturing and non-manufacturing sectors in this period, a divergent evolution that was caused by the major upheavals that were transforming the economy's character from the end of the 1970s. Furthermore, it cannot illuminate the decisive lurch toward finance that also took place in these years. It was the profound rationalization of the manufacturing sector, the rise of a labour-extensive low-wage economy outside manufacturing, and the turn to finance which shaped the economy that emerged in the mid 1990s.

Transformation Within the Downturn

During the 1970s, it will be recalled, US manufacturing corporations, encouraged by a devalued dollar and sharply reduced wage growth, as well as declining real interest rates, had launched an impressive wave of investment aimed at restoring competitiveness and profitability. Their failure to bring about significant improvement in the rate of profit by the end of the 1970s must have done much to discourage the continuation of such a strategy. In any case, under the combined impact of the deep recession of 1979–82, the very high real interest rates which largely persisted throughout the decade and into the next, and a new, if temporary, rise of the dollar, US manufacturing corporations were left with little choice but to cut back and change their modus operandi if they wished to survive.

Volcker's recession marked the turning point. Between 1979 and 1982, interest rates rocketed in real terms from less than 1 per cent to 6.5 per cent, and the resulting collapse of demand delivered a decisive shock to the manufacturing sector, setting it on a new trajectory. Over these three years, manufacturing output decreased by 10 per cent and capacity utilization fell from 85 per cent to a postwar low of 72.8 per cent; at the same time, manufacturing employment, which had managed to grow, albeit slowly, during the 1970s to reach its postwar high of 21.2 million, dropped by a stunning 10.5 per cent to 18.95 million. The economy now paid the price for its success in fending off bankruptcies during the Keynesian 1970s. By 1982, the annual bankruptcy rate was almost double that of 1979 and it continued to increase past the middle of the decade.[22]

Meanwhile, during the years between 1978 and 1985, driven by the rise in interest rates, the value of the dollar rose at an average annual rate of 1.75 per cent against the yen and 5.0 per cent against the mark, helping to bring about an average annual increase in unit labour costs (in dollar terms) of 4.6 per cent, compared to minus 1.4 per cent for both Japan and Germany. Already reeling from record costs of borrowing, US firms faced unbearable competitive pressure when the record federal deficits plus the high dollar opened the way for the explosive growth of imports from all over the world.

Having increased at an annual average rate of 5.8 per cent between 1973 and 1979, exports grew at an average annual rate of just 2 per cent between 1978 and 1985, actually falling by a total of 13 per cent in the years 1982 and 1983. Over the same period, having increased from about 15 per cent to 19.2 per cent between 1973 and 1978, manufacturing import penetration leapt to 33.75 per cent, a jump of more than 70 per cent, but manufacturing exports as a proportion of manufacturing output managed to grow by only 16 per cent, from 18.1 per cent to 21 per cent. By 1985, the US current account, in surplus by $5 billion or 0.2 per cent of GDP in 1981, was in deficit by $124 billion or a record 3 per cent of GDP.[23]

With the yen so low and the demand for imports so inflated by the rising federal deficit, Japanese exports to the US took off once again: between 1979 and 1986, they grew at an average annual rate of 18.2 per cent and increased their share of total US imports from 12.5 per cent to 22.2 per cent. But that was only half the story, for this was the period in which the four dynamic Asian manufacturing economies made their mark on the US market. Between 1970 and 1980, Korea, Taiwan, Singapore, and Hong Kong, taken together, had increased their share of US imports by a not unimpressive 50 per cent, from 5.1 per cent to 7.6 per cent. But over the subsequent seven years, they raised the latter figure by an astonishing 100 per cent to 15.3 per cent, more than double the share of US imports held by Germany and higher than the share held by all of the European economies combined. These incursions were made all the more devastating because not only Japan, but also the East Asian NICS, were in these years sharply increasing the proportion of high-technology goods in their exports to the US.

With downward pressure on US prices now reaching unparalleled intensity as

---

22   See above, p. 187, footnote 31.
23   OECD, *Economic Outlook 1996*, pp. A53–A54, Tables 50–1.

a result of deep recession combined with sharpened international competition, manufacturing profitability could not but cave in, especially given the profound fall in capacity utilization. Between 1977–78, when it hit its post-oil crisis peak, about 11 per cent below its level of 1973, and 1982, when it hit its recession low, the rate of profit in manufacturing fell by 43 per cent; by 1986, after four years of cyclical recovery, manufacturing profitability still remained about 19 per cent below its pre-recession peak. By comparison, profitability in the private business economy outside of manufacturing, fell by 33 per cent between 1978 and 1982, and by 1986 it had recovered its pre-recession peak. It is by now a familiar story: profitability in non-manufacturing could rebound because non-manufacturing firms were largely immune from the international competition that held down prices in manufacturing. Between 1978 and 1986, costs in non-manufacturing once again rose a good deal faster than in manufacturing, but these could be offset by increasing product prices. The revaluation of the dollar, which sharply limited US producers' ability to raise prices over costs on their tradables, was therefore heavily responsible, along with worsening international over-capacity, for US manufacturers' profitability problems through the middle of the 1980s.

During the 1970s, corporate managers had sharply cut back dividend payments and tried to invest their way out of the profitability crisis. Firms had benefited, moreover, from extraordinarily low real interest rates. But, from the start of the 1980s, the trends were reversed. Stockholders ran out of patience and secured radically increased dividend pay-outs. At the same time, encouraged by the new tax breaks, which ensured higher returns on unearned income and capital gains, by the loose enforcement of anti-trust laws, by the deregulation of finance, by the lure of higher dividend payments, and by the vulnerability of labour, financial manipulators borrowed heavily to purchase controlling interest in companies in expectation of wringing increased returns from them—especially by way of the stepped up exploitation of labour, the speeding up of depreciation and refusal to invest, the shedding of manpower, and downsizing in all forms. Especially in order to pay for mergers and aquisitions, firms ended up financing themselves to a much greater extent than previously through debt rather than equity in a period of sharply increased real interest rates, and the weight of interest payments on company profits grew accordingly. The outcome was that average annual retained earnings (the residue after interest and dividends are subtracted from profits) in the manufacturing sector fell to just 37 per cent of profits between 1982 and 1990, and 40 per cent between 1990 and 1996, compared to 69 per cent between 1973 and 1979, and 75 per cent between 1950 and 1965 (see p. 214, Figure 12.5).

With interest rates and dividend payments so high, retained earnings out of profits so low, and the investment climate so unpropitious, manufacturing corporations were obliged to deeply cut investment. Between 1979 and 1990, the average annual growth of manufacturing net capital stock fell to 1.8 per cent, from 3.6 per cent during the years 1973–79. Between 1990 and 1996, it fell a bit further, to just 1.6 per cent.

It remains the case that, during this extended period of stress and stagnation of investment for the manufacturing sector, manufacturing labour productivity growth actually *improved very markedly*, especially with respect to its reduced levels of the oil crisis-plagued 1970s. Between 1979 and 1990, it averaged 3.0 per cent per annum, just about its average for the years 1950–73. Between 1990 and 1996, it further increased its momentum, growing at an average annual rate of 3.8 per cent, a speed of improvement surpassed during the postwar epoch only between 1958 and 1965, when manufacturing productivity growth averaged 4.1 per cent.[24]

In the context of the major reduction in the growth of manufacturing capital stock, the achievement of significantly increased growth of productivity appears paradoxical. But it becomes immediately less puzzling once it is understood to have resulted as much from the removal from operation of outdated and inefficient plant and equipment—along with the workers who had manned it—as from the putting into play of state-of-the art plant and equipment, and also as much from unmeasured increases in labour input achieved through the intensification of work as from actual gains in efficiency, that is, output per unit of labour input.

The revival of manufacturing productivity growth was prepared during the recession years between 1979 and 1982. In these three years, manufacturing labour input, in terms of hours, fell by no less than 13.4 per cent and, as a direct expression of this decline, the average annual growth of the capital-labour ratio leapt to 8.9 per cent. On this basis, labour productivity began to rise at what was in fact an impressive average annual rate of 2.7 per cent, given that capacity utilization in manufacturing in these years fell by about 15 per cent.[25] Since manufacturing output and investment *fell* at average annual rates of 0.5 per cent and 2.05 per cent, respectively, and since bankruptcies doubled, it was evidently much more by shutting down old, inefficient facilities than by opening up new, efficient ones that US manufacturing got its labour productivity recovery started.

During the remainder of the 1980s and the first half of the 1990s, manufacturers kept labour productivity growing steadily, despite the continuing stagnation of manufacturing investment, expressed in a manufacturing net capital-labour ratio that grew at an annual average rate of just 1.1 per cent between 1982 and 1996, compared to 3.4 per cent between 1973 and 1979 and 2.7 per cent between 1950 and 1973. How was this made possible? Part of the answer clearly lies in more or less continuous 'downsizing'. On the eve of the recession of 1990–91, after the longest peacetime expansion in US history, the absolute size of the manufacturing labour force, in terms of hours, was still 4 per cent below its 1979 peak and, by 1996, it had fallen further, standing almost 10 per cent below that peak. Between 1978 and 1995, the top 100 US companies laid off, on a net basis, no less than 22 per cent of their labour force.[26] Part of the answer also must lie in the accomplishment of significant, efficiency-increasing technical advance—secured, for example, by means of robotization and the application of computer-aided production and design. Even so, possibly contributing as much to productivity increase as any other factor was a new form of 'improvement' that came into its own in this era. Known by the omnibus term 'lean production', this represented the (partial) adoption in the US of Japanese

---

24   As to the 1970s, if one confines one's view to the brief, inter-oil crisis years 1975–78, manufacturing productivity growth, at an average of 3.6 per cent per annum, was high; but, if one looks at the years 1973–79, which included the two oil-crisis recessions, manufacturing productivity growth, at an average of 0.4 per cent per annum, must be seen to have fallen off drastically.

25   And despite the fact that productivity failed to grow at all in 1980.

26   M. J. Mandel, 'Economic Anxiety', *Business Week*, 11 March 1996, p. 50.

methods of making labour input more intense, continuous, and effective.

On the shop floor, under the justificatory umbrella of the 'team concept'—and with the putative aim of raising productivity by means of increasing employees' skills and their control over the labour process—employers carried out the de-skilling of jobs by breaking them down into their simplest parts. This secured both the maximum 'flexibility' (or interchangeability) of the shop-floor labour force and the greatest possible labour input per unit of time. The technique has been illuminatingly termed 'management by stress', the goal of which is not only to remove, as far as possible, all 'specialist' labour coming from 'reserve' off the assembly line (maintenance, repair, housekeeping, quality checking, and the like) and all excess materials at work stations, but also to make sure all workers labour constantly when materials are at their station. Initially, teams of managers and group leaders work on each job and provide, from above, a highly detailed specification of the tasks making it up. Workers then carry through the same tasks under conditions in which, to the greatest possible extent, all 'safety nets' in the form of surplus materials and adjunct workers have been removed. Workers and their teams are not allowed to let defects pass, to be dealt with at the end of the line—as on the traditional assembly line—but are required to take responsibility for quality control by fixing each when it is discovered and, in particular, by tracing the problem back to its source. By these means, workers, as well as managers, are able to discover which tasks can be allocated in less time and which jobs need to redesigned, so that the labour force can be reapportioned in the most effective possible manner. Workers' enhanced ability to carry out an ever greater proportion of the now-simplified tasks—which can be called 'polyvalence' only if the most attenuated meaning of term is intended—is conducive to the same effect. The outcome is neither to substantively re-skill labour nor increase workers' control (although jobs might become more varied and less boring), but rather to augment employers' power over production, with the specific goal of increasing the number of seconds of every minute on the job that workers are actually working.[27] It is often, in addition—precisely due to the simplification of tasks—to pave the way to further mechanization.

Employers also sought more and more effective labour input through outsourcing operations formerly done in-house. Here the goal, again following the Japanese example, was to be able to pay lower wages than those paid to unionized workers, as well as to get around union work rules, by farming out tasks to (often quite large and technologically advanced) independent suppliers unburdened by union contracts and work rules. Indeed, the new ideal was, as much as possible, to employ, directly or indirectly, what have come to be known as 'contingent workers'—non-union employees who, because hired for a limited period of time

---

27   For a path-breaking account of the Japanese-style labour process and team production, see M. Parker and J. Slaughter, *Choosing Sides. Unions and the Team Concept*, A Labor Notes Book, Boston 1988, especially ch. 3. See also J. P. Womack, D. T. Jones, and D. Roos, *The Machine That Changed the World*, New York 1990, especially chs 3 and 4. These two studies, despite their very different attitudes toward team or lean production, offer very similar, mutually corroborating accounts of just what it entails, heaping scorn on those who wishfully believe that the new system is bringing about the rise of some sort of skilled, autonomous neo-artisanate. See also M. Parker, 'Industrial Relations Myth and Shop-Floor Reality: The "Team Concept" in the Auto Industry', in N. Lichtenstein and H. J. Harris, eds, *Industrial Democracy in America*, The Ambiguous Promise, New York 1993; H. Shaiken et al., 'The Work Process under More Flexible Production', *Industrial Relations*, vol. xxv, Spring 1986.

or to complete a particular job, will be maximally exploitable, having the least possible leverage to negotiate decent terms of employment. Allowing for the accelerated adoption of these processes in the 1980s was the new availability of telecommunication and computer technologies that made possible unprecedented levels of coordination between geographically separated productive units (as in just-in-time production).[28] It should be added that, since some of the jobs farmed out by manufacturing companies were low-productivity services previously counted within the manufacturing sector, the sector was able to further raise its rate of productivity advance simply by shedding service jobs to the service sector.

The recovery of productivity growth in US manufacturing did mean the transcendence of the manufacturing 'productivity crisis' of the 1970s but its scale should not be exaggerated nor its significance misconstrued. Its contribution was a relatively minor one to the quite major increase in US competitiveness that took place during the decade following the Plaza Accord. From the middle of the 1980s, the US manufacturing sector did, then, achieve a decisive reduction in its relative costs of production in international terms, making possible a marked acceleration in the growth of exports and a corresponding increase in its share of world exports. But this improvement was attributable barely at all to productivity growth, and almost entirely to the repression of real wage growth and the profound decline in the value of the dollar. Between 1985 and 1995 (and between 1990 and 1995), average annual US manufacturing productivity growth was slightly lower than that of Japan, Italy, and the UK, and somewhat above that of Canada and Germany, but in all cases (except for Canada) the difference between the US figure and that of the others was minimal, no more than 0.5 per cent.[29] During the same period, the average annual increase of real hourly compensation in the US manufacturing sector was, on the other hand, the *lowest* among the G-7 economies, averaging 0.15 per cent per annum, compared to 2.9 per cent in Japan and 2.85 per cent in Germany. While real wages in manufacturing in Germany and Japan thus both grew by about 35 per cent during the decade, in the US they grew by 1 per cent!

What mattered most, though, was the value of the currency. Between 1985 and 1990, and then between 1990 and 1995, the exchange rate of the yen and mark appreciated against the dollar at the extraordinary average annual rates of 10.5 per cent and 12.7 per cent, respectively, and then 9.1 per cent and 2.5 per cent, respectively. The way was thus prepared for an enormous gain in US manufacturing competitiveness. Between 1985 and 1995 US nominal wages expressed in dollars rose at an average annual rate of 4.65 per cent, while those of Japan and Germany rose respectively at the average annual rates of 15.1 per cent and 13.7 per cent. Over the same ten-year period, manufacturing unit labour costs expressed in dollars rose at an average annual rate of just 0.75 per cent in the US, compared to 11.7 per cent and 11.3 per cent in Japan and Germany respectively. By 1995, therefore, hourly wages for manufacturing production workers were $17.19 in the US, $23.66 in Japan, and $31.85 in Germany. (See p. 209, Figure 12.4.)

On the basis of such extraordinary advances in relative costs, US producers could

---

28   For these aspects of 'lean production', as applied in both the manufacturing and service sectors, see S. Head, 'The New, Ruthless Economy', *New York Review of Books*, 29 February 1996.

29   C. Sparks and M. Greiner, 'US and Foreign Productivity and Unit Labor Costs', *Monthly Labor Review*, February 1997, p. 29.

Figure 12.2. The growth of real hourly compensation in manufacturing in Germany, Japan, and the US, 1973–2004.

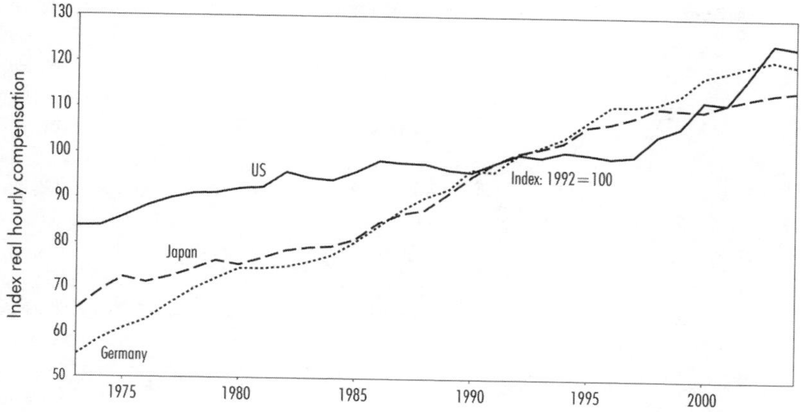

Source: BLS, 'International Comparisons of Manufacturing Productivity and Unit Labor Cost Trends,' Table 13, available at BLS website.
Note: lines indicate only change in real hourly compensation, not relative levels.

make major gains in overseas sales. US exports grew impressively, at their fastest rate during the postwar period, shooting up at an average annual rate of 10.6 per cent in the wake of the Plaza Accord between 1985 and 1990, and at an average annual rate of 7.4 per cent between 1990 and 1995, compared to 2.1 per cent between 1979 and 1985, 5.8 per cent between 1973 and 1979, and 6.5 per cent between 1950 and 1973. By the early 1990s, the US had raised its share of world exports back to the levels of the end of the 1970s.

The Plaza Accord marked, then, a major watershed, the opening of a new era in which, in relative terms, the fortunes of the manufacturing economy of the US would dramatically improve, while those of the Germany and Japan would deteriorate. Even so, through the 1980s and even through the first half of the 1990s, the US manufacturing sector achieved only a limited recovery, attesting to the continuing barriers to manufacturing dynamism anywhere within the advanced capitalist world. The striking fact is that, while US manufacturing productivity growth in this period was nearly as high as it had been in any other period of comparable length during the postwar epoch, and manufacturing real wage growth was at unprecedented lows, US manufacturing profitability fell significantly short of its levels of the boom. At the high point of the Reagan boom in 1989, manufacturing profitability did reach its level of 1973, but this was still some 40 per cent below its level of 1965. After collapsing again during the ensuing recession, manufacturing profitability did rise impressively throughout the cyclical upturn of the 1990s. Still, only in 1994 did it again reach its level of 1973 and only in 1995 did it climb substantially higher. Even by this juncture, it remained one-third below its 1965–66 peaks, and about one-

Figure 12.3. Exchange rates against the dollar: the mark and the yen, 1968–2005.

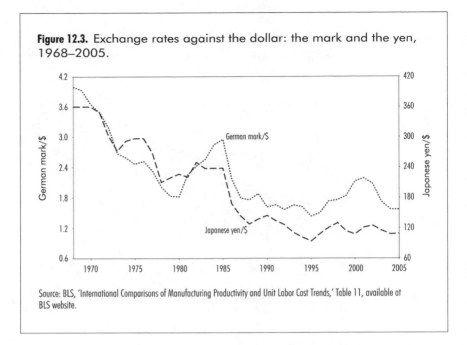

Source: BLS, 'International Comparisons of Manufacturing Productivity and Unit Labor Cost Trends,' Table 11, available at BLS website.

quarter off its average for the 1960s. But, the fact remains that the rebound achieved was in long-run terms substantial. It must have been a significant factor in the new acceleration of investment growth that began at this time, again from very low levels, and it opened up the potential for a decisive US economic turnaround. Whether that potential would be realized, however, would be determined by developments not only in the US, but in the world economy as a whole. (See p. 7, Figure 0.3 and p. 8, Figure 0.4.)

The Rise of the Non-Manufacturing Sector and Deepening Decline

As the size of the manufacturing labour force hit its ceiling and began to decline from 1979, the place of manufacturing employment within the economy shrank sharply. Whereas the manufacturing labour force as a percentage of the total (measured in hours) had remained roughly constant between 1950 (at 25.5 per cent) and 1973 (24.3 per cent) and fallen only relatively little between 1973 and 1979 (to 22.2 per cent), thereafter it declined sharply, to 19.2 per cent in 1985, 17.4 per cent in 1990, and 15.9 per cent in 1996. The reverse side of this decline was, of course, the rapid rise of service employment. While the manufacturing labour force (in terms of number employed) fell by 1.1 million between 1979 and 1990 and a further 830,000 between 1990 and 1996, service employment grew by 20 million between 1979 and 1990 and an additional 8.6 million between 1990 and 1996.

But, far from an expression of economic rejuvenation, the rapid net increase in the number of US jobs during the 1980s and first half of the 1990s, all of them outside manufacturing, was a manifestation of US economic decline. While the non-manufacturing labour force came to constitute an ever larger proportion of the

Figure 12.4. The growth of hourly compensation in manufacturing in dollars, Germany, Japan, and the US, 1970–2004.

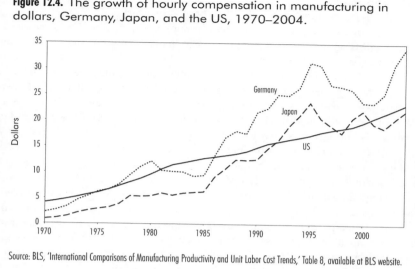

Source: BLS, 'International Comparisons of Manufacturing Productivity and Unit Labor Cost Trends,' Table 8, available at BLS website.

total—84.3 per cent in 1996 (measured in hours)—non-manufacturing labour productivity grew at what were by far the lowest rates in recorded US history. Between 1979 and 1990, labour productivity growth in the non-manufacturing private business sector averaged a shockingly low 0.6 per cent per annum, compared to 2.6 per cent per annum for the years 1950–73, and was not that much better between 1990 and 1996, at 1.1 per cent.

The key to the collapse of productivity growth outside manufacturing can be found in the emergence of the low-wage economy, which began to emerge as early as the first part of the 1960s, with the turning point located sometime in the middle to late 1970s. We have seen that the sharp recession of 1974–75 dealt a powerful blow to labour, and worker resistance thenceforth rapidly declined, virtually collapsing in the 1980s. In the labour force outside manufacturing, the level of unionization was negligible. Workers had to take what they could get, and this was steadily less. Between 1979 and 1995, the average annual growth of the product wage in the non-manufacturing private sector was just 0.4 per cent, and there were only four years in which product wage growth rose as high as 1 per cent. Real wage growth was even worse in this period, averaging just 0.2 per cent per annum.

But aggregate figures do not begin to tell the story of the rise of the low-wage economy. Between 1979 and 1995, average annual real wage growth for the bottom 40 per cent of the labour force fell by almost 12 per cent, for the bottom 60 per cent by 9.8 per cent. (Even workers in the 80th percentile saw their wages fall by 0.4 per cent between 1979 and 1995).[30] Put another way, over the course of this sixteen-year

---

30   Mishel et al., *State of Working America*, p. 143, Table 3.6.

period, the bottom 60 per cent of the US labour force worked for progressively lower real wages and, by the end of the period, was working for real wages that were, on average, 10 per cent lower than they had been at the start.

In light of the collapse of real wages, the supposedly baffling US 'productivity puzzle' is less mysterious than it might appear. In manufacturing, there is really not much to explain: as has been emphasized, excluding the oil crisis recession years of 1974 and 1975 and of 1979 and 1980 (or, alternatively, the whole period 1973–80), the average annual growth of manufacturing labour productivity more than held its own, from the boom of the early 1960s, through the initial years of falling profitability from 1965 through 1973, right through to the middle of the 1990s. Outside of manufacturing, it is not hard to see why productivity growth should have fallen sharply. During the period 1950–73, the product wage in the private non-manufacturing sector had grown at an average annual rate of 2.7 per cent, and the net capital-labour ratio in this sector grew at an annual rate of 2.0 per cent. But between 1979 and 1996, with the average annual growth of the product wage growth collapsing to just 0.4 per cent, the average annual growth of the capital-labour ratio fell to just 1.0 per cent. With average annual product wage growth reduced to near-zero, and no pressure from foreign competitors, firms outside of manufacturing found it more profitable to add workers increasingly fast as against machines, so that the growth of output per unit of worker input could not but fall sharply. In addition, because more than half of the labour force was available for work at decreasing real wages, firms could, with profit, increasingly expand employment in jobs where productivity growth was very low and slow, like restaurant services, and wholesale and retail sales. These lines absorbed at least a third of those added to the workforce in this period.[31]

The slowdown in the growth in plant and equipment available to each worker does not just explain the reduction in the growth of output per unit of labour input. It would also seem to explain the simultaneous reduction in the growth of output per unit of labour input and capital input combined (total factor productivity). This is because the reduced speed of equipping each worker would have had as one of its by-products a slowdown in the pace of *improvement* in the machinery available to each worker and thus a slowdown in the gains in output from any given sum of labour and capital inputs.

The 'great American jobs machine' of the 1980s and 1990s was, then, almost literally just that: the growth of employment taking place outside of manufacturing with hardly any parallel increase in the equipment at the disposal of each worker and hardly any resulting increase in each worker's productivity. Because there was

---

31   A comparison of US developments with those in Germany in this period tends to confirm the foregoing analysis. In Germany, between 1979 and the early 1990s, because product wages continued to grow, though more slowly than before (at around 1.1 per cent per annum), and because continuing union strength outside of manufacturing prevented any increase of wage inequality—wage dispersion actually fell—German employers were much more motivated to adopt labour-saving techniques than were their counterparts in the US. At the same time, because German employers did not get access to increasingly low-wage labour, they could not profitably add employees, as did US employers, in lines with low productivity, such as wholesale and retail trade, restaurants and hotels, and the like. Between 1979 and 1990 the number of employees in wholesale and retail trade in the US grew by 30 per cent, from 17.6 million to 22.7 million, in Germany, by 8 per cent, from 3.35 million to 3.73 million. The result was that productivity growth in non-manufacturing was much higher in Germany than in the US in this period, averaging 2.5 per cent per annum, compared to 0.2 per cent per annum. OECD, *National Income and Product Accounts*, Vol. ii, Detailed Tables (various issues). See also Burda and Sachs, 'Assessing High Unemployment'

essentially no real wage growth on average, and for much of the labour force declining real wage growth, employers could profit even while productivity barely edged up. For the same reason, they could profit while precipitously increasing the numbers hired and bringing down aggregate unemployment. In the latter part of the 1980s and in the 1990s, the US had the lowest unemployment rate in the advanced capitalist world outside of Japan, but, given the terms of employment, this was not much to boast about. The upshot has been a truly vicious circle, in which low wages have made for low labour productivity growth which has in turn rendered 'unrealistic' any significant growth of wages and thereby provided the basis for continued low productivity growth.[32] So much for the Reagan-Bush-Clinton 'morning in America'.

A Golden Age for Finance and the Rich

The other side of capitalists' refusal to place much of their capital in production was their search for alternative ways to make money.[33] With profitability down, interest rates up, and instability heightened, investors had increasing incentive to avoid the risks associated with longer-term placements of new plant and equipment. Still, to profit merely by buying cheap and selling dear is normally no simple task: for every gain there is an equivalent loss, for every winner a loser. Capitalists and the wealthy accumulated wealth with such success during the 1980s largely because the state intervened directly to place money in their hands—enabling them to profit from their own business failure through lucrative bail outs, offering them giant tax breaks which played no small part in the recovery of corporate balance sheets, and providing them with an unprecedented array of other *politically constituted* opportunities to get richer faster through fiscal, monetary, and deregulation policies—all at the expense of the great mass of the population.

The pattern was clearly established under the Carter administration, which initiated union-busting industrial deregulation in airlines, trucking, and the like. Most definitive of the new trend, though, was the bail out of Chrysler in 1980. When Chrysler threatened bankruptcy, the government not only intervened, at taxpayers' expense, to save the company, but also as part of the bail out agreement, extracted extensive concessions from the Chrysler workers, both to ensure the company a more profitable future and to set a pattern for the labour force as a whole.

By the Economic Recovery Act of 1981, taxes on individuals were cut by 20 per cent over three years, with the top bracket on unearned income—rents and interest—reduced from 70 per cent to 50 per cent. The Tax Reform act of 1986 further reduced that rate to 28 per cent. The capital gains tax, which had already been reduced from 49 per cent to 28 per cent under Carter in 1978, was slashed to 20 per cent. By contrast, the social security tax, which falls disproportionately on working-class families, was increased by about 25 per cent over the course of the decade.[34]

---

32 The trend towards the low-wage economy was not confined to non-manufacturing. Between 1970 and 1992, the degree to which US manufacturing exports were specialized in high-technology and high-wage lines actually fell somewhat. OECD, *Industrial Policy Annual Review 1994*, Paris 1994, p. 134.

33 I wish to thank Bob Pollin for many helpful discussions on the material in this section, concerning both the data and its interpretation.

34 K. Phillips, *The Politics of Rich and Poor. Wealth and the American Electorate in the Reagan Aftermath*, New York 1990, pp. 76–86.

Between 1981 and 1992, personal and corporate taxes as a proportion of GDP thus fell by almost 2 per cent, but the benefits were very unequally distributed. Because the explicit objective of the supply-side tax reduction was to lower marginal rates, and since only the well-off saw their incomes increase during the 1980s, only well-off families saw any significant reduction in their taxes. According to the Congressional Budget Office, between 1977 and 1989, the effective tax rate fell by 6.0 per cent on persons with income in the top 1 per cent, by 2.6 per cent on those in the top 5 per cent, and by 1.7 per cent on those in the top 10 per cent, with effectively no gain for the rest of the population.[35]

The 1980s tax cuts not only benefited the rich directly, but were largely responsible for record federal deficits, which had to be covered by federal borrowing. Those with great wealth naturally did most of the lending. They were able to do so at record-smashing real interest rates, helped out by the Federal Reserve's failure to accommodate with easier credit the unprecedented pressure on the money markets that resulted from the government's elevated demand for loans. Between 1950 and 1980, the share of interest payments in the federal budget had averaged under 7 per cent, averaging 7.6 per cent between 1974 and 1979. But between 1982 and 1990, it almost doubled to 13.4 per cent. Of the total federal debt owned by US individuals in 1983, the richest 10 per cent held nearly 80 per cent and the richest 1 per cent about one-third, with the distribution even more skewed if only the larger denomination, marketable Treasury securities are considered.[36] The interest payments accrued by the rich had, of course, to be directly covered by tax revenues largely paid for by working-class citizens. As the conservative columnist George Will observed, 'To pay the interest component of the 1988 budget will require a sum ($210 billion) equal to approximately half of all the personal income tax receipts ... a transfer of wealth from labour to capital unprecedented in American history. Tax revenues are being collected from average Americans (the median income of a family of four is slightly under $30,000) and given to buyers of US government bonds—buyers in Beverly Hills, Lake Forest, Shaker Heights and Grosse Point, and Tokyo and Riyadh.' Not always such a keen student of exploitation, Will might well have added that by 1990, the size of the interest component of the federal budget was equal to almost 60 per cent of total corporate profits, up from around 10 per cent in the mid 1960s before the long downturn began.[37]

With secularly reduced profitability sinking further in the wake of the deep recession of 1981–82, the market value of assets compared to their replacement cost collapsed; investors began therefore to have reason to believe that the time was right to buy, because stock prices could only go up. The authorities removed almost all reason for doubt when they moved first to cut taxes in 1981 and then, from the summer of 1982, to loosen the supply of credit. With taxes on capital gains and unearned income sharply reduced, the value of stocks to their owners automatically went up. With the cost of borrowing suddenly down somewhat, the purchase

35   P. Krugman, *Peddling Prosperity*, New York 1994, pp. 155–6.
36   R. Pollin, 'Budget Deficits and the US Economy: Considerations in a Heilbronerian Mode', in R. Blackwell et al., ed., *Economics as Worldly Philosophy. Essays in Political and Historical Economics in Honour of Robert L. Heilbroner*, London 1993, pp. 124–5, 135.
37   Phillips, *The Politics of Rich and Poor*, pp. 89–91 (quotation). NIPA Table 6.16 (corporate profits adjusted); *Economic Report of the President 1997*, Washington, DC 1997, Table B-80 (government net interest).

of assets was made easier. Reagan made certain, moreover, that the subsequent stock-market boom would have a real, if strictly limited, material foundation, when he incurred record federal deficits to ensure that output, thus capacity utilization, thus profitability would rise sharply, if for the most part only cyclically, from their depressed levels of 1981–82.[38] Like the increase in return on government bonds, the stock-market rise benefited the wealthy almost exclusively, since (in 1989) the top 1 per cent of wealth holders owned about 46 per cent of all stock, while the top 10 per cent owned 90 per cent.[39]

Those with money not only cashed in on the expanded opportunities offered by Republocratic tax, spending, and credit policies to profit without producing; as the government let it be known that it would no longer enforce anti-trust laws as in the past, and found itself unable or unwilling to prevent insider trading, financiers made huge killings by discovering creative new ways to squeeze higher returns from existing assets, manifesting in the process their disdain for productive investment. Although retained earnings out of profits were, as noted, at very reduced levels between 1982 and 1990, non-financial corporations found them more than sufficient to cover *all* of the capital investment that they undertook in those years because, as stressed, that capital investment was so restricted. Meanwhile, they assumed record levels of debt either to repurchase shares from stockholders or to gain a controlling interest in another firm, with the goal in both cases of profiting by transforming the rules of the corporate game, especially in manufacturing.[40] Manufacturing corporations' interest payments as a proportion of profits, having grown to 15 per cent during the years 1973–79 compared to just 3.8 per cent for the years 1950–73, increased to 35 per cent between 1982 and 1990 and 24 per cent between 1990 and 1996.

On the basis of their buy-backs, mergers, and takeovers, the financial tycoons forced huge increases in dividends. In an effort to keep up investment levels, corporate managers had cut dividend pay-outs as a proportion of profits from an average of 25 per cent in the years 1950 to 1973 to an average of 16 per cent between 1973 and 1979. In contrast, their successors boosted dividend payments to 27 per cent between 1982 and 1990 and to an extraordinary 36 per cent between 1990 and 1996. They exploited, moreover, already existing creditors of the firm whose lending terms had been set when risk was much lower because debt dependency was much lower. Above all, they carried through, with a thoroughness and viciousness perhaps unimagined by their predecessors, that 'corporate downsizing'—the weeding-out of all but the most productive and profitable means of production— which was in fact demanded by redundant, often obsolete, productive capacity and profoundly reduced profitability, especially on manufacturing capital stock. To do so, they simply ignored their firms' implicit and explicit contracts with their labour

---

38   Greider, *Secrets of the Temple*, pp. 537ff; Pollin, 'Destabilizing Finance', p. 18. For the years 1973–81, the ratio of market value of equities to replacement cost of assets of all non-financial corporations fell to an average of 42 per cent (44 per cent in 1981) from 83.6 per cent in the years 1970–73 and 96.1 per cent in the 1960s.

39   Mishel et al., *State of Working America*, pp. 279–80.

40   Pollin, 'Destabilizing Finance', p. 18. '[I]n addition to their ... internally generated funds, corporations have borrowed in record amounts ... [and] ... have used an unusually large part of these funds for purposes other than productive new investment. Companies have increasingly distributed their cash flows outside the corporate sector, mostly through payments made to individual and institutional shareholders ...'. Friedman, *Day of Reckoning*, pp. 264–5.

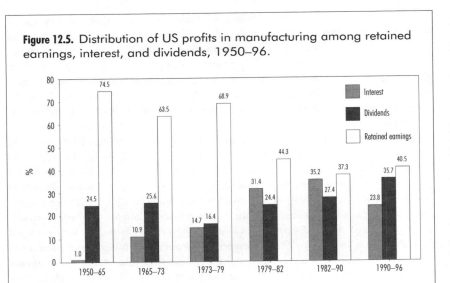

Figure 12.5. Distribution of US profits in manufacturing among retained earnings, interest, and dividends, 1950–96.

Source: BEA NIPA 6.16.

forces, and imposed the sort of mass layoffs, wage reductions, benefits cuts, and speed-ups at work that hitherto had been largely forced off the corporate agenda during the postwar epoch. As has been seen, the application of this approach did accomplish a major rationalization of the manufacturing sector over the course of the 1980s and early 1990s, raising productivity growth and ultimately profitability.[41]

This is not the place to attempt an in-depth analysis of the foregoing much-chron-icled trends. But two of their effects do need emphasis: first, the sheer size of the movement away from production and toward unproductive expenditure that they involved; second, the extraordinary redistribution of income and wealth that they helped to accomplish.

Between 1980 and 1989, there were 31,105 mergers and acquisitions, totalling in value $1.34 trillion. This figure was roughly equal to one-third the amount spent in the US on non-residential fixed investment over the decade.[42] It is sometimes argued

41   In this light, *both* of the main competing interpretations of the wave of mergers and acquisitions and leveraged buy-outs that began in the early 1980s—that by Jensen, which understands them as aiming to increase profits by increasing efficiency, and that by Schleifer and Summers, which understands them as aiming to increase profits by breaking commitments so as to increase exploitation—can be seen to be correct. But both are marred by their failure to see the determinants to which they correctly point as themselves emerging from the crisis of profitability in manufacturing and by their consequent over-concentration on the subjective attitudes of economic agents—Jensen with his preoccupation with the irresponsibility of corporate managers beyond the control of stockholders, and Schleifer and Summers with their preoccupa-tion with the greed of the money men. Both see as causes what are in reality effects. See M. C. Jensen, 'Takeovers: Their Causes and Consequences', *Journal of Economic Perspectives*, vol. ii, no. 2, 1988; A. Schleifer and L. H. Summers, 'Breach of Trust in Hostile Takeovers', in A. J. Auerbach, ed., *Corporate Takeovers: Causes and Consequences*, Chicago 1988, pp. 33–67.

42   R. Pollin, 'Borrowing More but Investing Less: Economic Stagnation and the Rise of Corporate Takeovers in the US', unpublished manuscript, December 1994, p. 4.

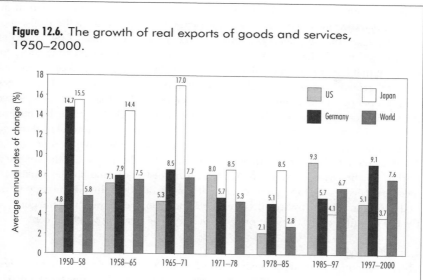

Figure 12.6. The growth of real exports of goods and services, 1950–2000.

Sources: 'Statistical Annex', *European Economy*, Autumn 2005, Table 37; IMF WEO Database.

that such figures have little or no meaning for the productive economy, since they represent no using up of real resources, just the transfer of paper claims. Over the years 1975–90, however, the proportion of the total investment on plant and equipment in the private business economy annually devoted to finance, insurance and real estate (FIRE) doubled, from about 12–13 per cent to about 25–26 per cent. Between 1982 and 1990, almost a *quarter* of all the plant and equipment investment that took place in the private business economy was devoted to FIRE, more than to any other sector, including manufacturing. During the first half of the 1990s, with about 16 per cent of the private sector's labour force, FIRE deployed more than 23 per cent of the private sector's total net fixed capital stock, more than any other industry. This was up by almost 50 per cent (from 16 per cent in 1977. The shuffling of paper through which so many fortunes were enhanced over the course of the 1980s and 1990s added nothing directly to consumption or the productive power to raise consumption, but that did not stop it from wastefully absorbing massive real resources, including a significant share of the computer power that was put into play over the decade. Between 1980 and 1990, FIRE made use of some 35 per cent of the net stock of office, computing, and accounting equipment employed by the total economy; by contrast, manufacturing's share was around 25 per cent.[43] Ironically, then—but all too understandably in view of the fortunes made there— the most technologically dynamic of US industries during the 1980s and 1990s probably contributed less than any other to raising US living standards by means of its own immediate output.

43   D. E. Sichel, *The Computer Revolution. An Economic Perspective*, Washington, DC 1997, pp. 44–5.

Since productivity growth in the private business economy proceeded at an historically low rate, not much new wealth could be created during the 1980s, and, over the years 1977–89, average family income increased by just 11 per cent. But the 'Reagan Revolution' was still able to work miracles for the very wealthy by ensuring that they received the lion's share of the little wealth that was created. Of the total growth in average family income that occurred between 1977 and 1989, the top 1 per cent of all families (by income) received no less than 70 per cent, while the top 10 per cent received virtually the entire increase. On this basis, the income going to the top 1 per cent (averaging $800,000 per annum) more than doubled during the decade, while that of the median family increased by just 4 per cent.[44] Nor was the trend toward inequality discontinued in the 1990s. On the contrary, during the first two years of the Clinton Administration, the share of national income earned by the top 5 per cent grew at a faster rate than during the eight years of the Reagan administration. Between 1992 and 1996, the share of income going to the top one-fifth of the population increased from 46 per cent to 49 per cent.[45]

Toward Recovery?

The US economy entered the second half of the 1990s performing qualitatively less well than it had in the later 1970s. Still, there was a bright side to this bleak picture, at least for capital. *On the condition that they could continue to prevent product wage growth from increasing*—as they were into the second half of the decade—US firms outside of manufacturing could count on continuing to raise their profit shares and thus their profit rates, so long as could they achieve even quite small increases in productivity. They could, in addition, continue to mark up over prices to an extent not feasible for their counterparts in manufacturing who were faced with withering international competition. During the second half of the 1980s, non-manufacturing profitability had actually fallen somewhat from its high points of mid-decade. But by 1996, with wages continuing to stagnate, it had crept back up past its level of 1973 and was approaching its levels of the later 1960s. Manufacturing profitability was still more than 30 per cent below its heights of the boom, but it had made a major comeback, increasing at an accelerating rate over the course of the 1990s, and contributing decisively to the overall profitability revival. The upshot was that, by 1996, profitability in the private economy as a whole had, for the first time, definitively surpassed its level of 1973, and stood about 20–25 per cent below its boom-time peaks. If wage growth could continue to be held down as the labour market continued to tighten and if manufacturing profitability (only partially, but still dramatically, recovered) could at least maintain itself as international competition intensified—both big ifs—the US economy had at last opened the way toward a new boom in investment and thus the potential transcendence of the long downturn. (See p. 7, Figure 0.3; p. 8, Figure 0.4 and p. 109, Figure 8.1.)

2. Japan in the 1980s and 1990s: From Bubble to Bust and Beyond

During the second half of the 1980s and the first half of the 1990s, the Japanese

---

44   Krugman, *Peddling Prosperity*, pp. 134–8.
45   S. A. Holmes, 'Income Disparity Between Poorest and Richest Rises', *New York Times*, 20 June 1996; S. A. Holmes, 'New Reports Say Minorities Benefit in Fiscal Recovery', *New York Times*, 30 September 1997.

economy faced its greatest challenge of the postwar epoch, as the price it had to pay to preserve its distinctive relationship with the world economy, and especially the US market, grew ever greater. Between 1979 and 1985, emerging from the second major international recession in less than a decade, it derived its energy as usual from a deficit-driven economic expansion in the US. Japan's export-oriented road had already become rockier during the late 1970s, as the US dollar plunged in value, and it did not become much easier in the first half of the 1980s, even when the dollar ballooned under the impact of high US interest rates. But traversing it proved a truly gargantuan task in the decade following the Plaza Accord of 1985, as the yen rose constantly and the US proved ever less willing to assume its old role of creating demand for the world economy.

Weak Recovery, 1980–85

The Japanese recession of the early 1980s was far less serious than that which took place simultaneously in the US and Germany, or in Japan itself in 1974–75. Between 1980 and 1983, the manufacturing and private business sectors experienced falls in profitability of 20 per cent and 15 per cent respectively, as against their post-oil crisis peaks of 1978. But these reductions were not remotely as great as those experienced in 1974–75, nor were their effects anywhere near so severe. Nominal and real wage increases that were respectively less than a quarter and less than a half of those of 1974–5 helped prevent profits from falling dramatically. So did the maintenance of high rates of growth of exports, helped by the new fall of the yen from 1979, at least through 1981. Whereas both GDP and manufacturing output had actually fallen somewhat, and manufacturing investment had decreased very sharply at the time of the first oil shock, during the cyclical downturn of 1980–83, both GDP and manufacturing output continued to grow fairly well and manufacturing investment at least stayed positive.

From 1982–83, as from 1974–75, a combination of record US government deficits and a fast-rising dollar pulled the Japanese economy from recession and drove a new cyclical upturn, led by exports but limited in its dynamism. Between 1982 and 1986, the obverse side of those record-smashing US trade and current account deficits, Japanese exports to the US grew at the spectacular average annual rate of 23 per cent (in nominal terms). In just these four years, Japanese exports to the US as a percentage of total Japanese exports grew by almost 50 per cent, from 26.4 per cent to 38.9 per cent. By 1985, Japanese exports as a percentage of GDP, at 11.1 per cent as recently as 1979, had grown to 14.5 per cent, while manufacturing exports as a percentage of manufacturing output, at 35.6 per cent in 1979, had grown to 47.7 per cent. The current account surplus, at 0.4 per cent of GDP in 1981, had risen to 4.2 per cent of GDP in 1986.

Despite the boom in exports, the Japanese cyclical upturn was weak. Fixated on spurring exports and horrified by the build-up of state debt that had accompanied its essay in Keynesianism in the late 1970s, the Japanese government, taking the opposite course to that of the US, repressed the growth of domestic demand by embarking on an extended campaign to reduce spending and balance the budget. Between 1980 and 1985, Japan reduced its government deficit from 4.2 per cent of GDP to 0.8 per cent of GDP. At the same time, in response to the record-high US interest rates that had brought about the super-high dollar, Japanese money poured into US Treasury instruments, and was thereby rendered unavailable for productive use in Japan itself. Given the still unresolved problem of reduced profitability in manufacturing on a world scale, stimulating demand was clearly becoming an ever more contradictory and difficult process. By incurring record deficits, the US government powerfully increased the demand for Japanese exports; but it could finance those deficits only by raising domestic interest rates and tapping into Japanese surpluses, thereby undercutting Japanese (as well as US) domestic investment. During the first half of the 1980s, Japanese capital formation, particularly in manufacturing, grew significantly only in 1984 and 1985. The rate of growth of GDP and especially labour productivity achieved in that period thus fell far short of that of the second half of the 1970s. By 1985, when it once again peaked, Japanese manufacturing profitability was still slightly below its level of 1978 and barely half its average level for the years 1965–70. (See p. 7, Figure 0.3 and p. 304, Figure 15.6.)

The Plaza Accord and the Bubble Economy, 1985–91

Nor could the increase of exports be counted on to power the Japanese economy for very long. Export growth entailed the build-up of enormous US current account deficits and giant Japanese current account surpluses; it was bound to undermine itself. With the Plaza Accord, the dollar collapsed and the yen took off, subjecting the Japanese economy to unprecedented stress. Between 1985 and 1988, the yen's value increased by 56 per cent in trade-weighted terms and 93 per cent against the dollar, a much greater appreciation than those of either 1971–73 or 1975–78. In fact, the yen-dollar exchange rate, at 260/$ as late as March 1985, had reached 120/$ by 1988, almost double the value of its previous peak of 210/$ in the late 1970s and triple its value before December 1971 when the rate was 360/$. By 1990, the effective exchange rate of the yen had fallen back slightly, by 14 per cent, with its value in terms of dollars dropping to 145. But, in the face of what remained a truly radical realignment in relative international costs, the Japanese economy could no longer proceed as before.

By 1986, with the effective (trade-weighted) exchange rate of the yen already down by 46 per cent, the Japanese economy was obliged to confront what was potentially its worst crisis since the end of the long boom. In that year, exports fell in real terms by 4.9 per cent, private business growth slipped to 1.2 per cent, manufacturing output actually declined, and the economy seemed headed for another major recession. To turn the tide, over the course of 1986, the government launched a policy of extreme monetary ease, sharply reducing the interest rate from 5 per cent to 3 per cent and, in 1987, to a postwar low of 2.5 per cent. This programme staved off an extended cyclical downturn and helped to force-feed a new boom, which lasted through 1990–91. But it signally failed to achieve its central goal, which was to provide a new, more solid, foundation for Japanese capital accumulation.

The Japanese economy had suddenly entered an unprecedentedly difficult phase. Yet from a longer-term perspective, what was transpiring was hardly novel, but merely the deepening of a long-established trend. The institutional and political arrangements that structured postwar Japanese development had, from the start, biased the economy in favour of the growth of investment at the expense of the growth of consumption, domestic demand, and imports. With the growth of domestic demand thus held back, the economy was thus ultimately dependent on the growth of exports and tended to create external surpluses that could not but continually drive the yen upwards. The trend toward a rising current account balance had its origins in 1968, bore its first fruits with the upward correction in the value of the yen in 1971–3, continued with the further yen revaluation between 1975–76 and 1979, and reappeared in the mid 1980s. But, to the degree it continued—and was not counterbalanced by offsetting improvements in costs of production—it could not but bring about the progressive narrowing of Japanese growth prospects.

What the government was thus attempting to accomplish with its loose money regime was to fundamentally reorient the whole pattern of Japanese economic evolution. It intended to increase radically the assets of Japan's leading industrial firms— which possessed mammoth quantities of one another's shares, as well as huge holdings of land—so as to enable them to carry through sufficient investment to accomplish the formidable tasks not only of raising export competitiveness by another order of magnitude, but also of reorienting the Japanese economy away from exports toward the home market. The banks were supposed to channel increasing supplies of credit to financial investors who could be expected to buy stocks and land, driving up the value of these assets and enriching the corporations in the process.[46] And this is exactly what happened. As in the government's attempt to bring down the rising yen through inflation during the early 1970s, ultra-cheap money led, as was hoped, to runaway speculation. Land prices rocketed, with residential and commercial property prices doubling between 1986 and 1989. Meanwhile, share prices on the Tokyo Stock Exchange reached their historic high at the end of 1989, also having doubled in price over the previous two years.

From one standpoint, then, the government's essay in easy money did have pretty much the intended outcome, for the economy did enter a new and powerful cyclical upturn, which lasted through the end of the decade. Real-estate companies borrowed massively to buy land with the intent to sell at a higher price. Consumers reduced their savings rate and stepped up their spending, and residential construction boomed. Corporations appear at first to have used the enormous increase in the value of their stocks and land to reduce their reliance on debt finance, as well as to engage in financial manipulation ('zaitech'), raising funds very cheaply on the money market and depositing them at higher rates of return in interest rate deposits. But eventually, as had been hoped, the corporations took advantage of the growth of consumer demand, as well as the enormous increase in their wealth—which derived from the explosion of the prices not only of their stocks, but also of the large holdings of prime Tokyo land that many of

---

46   As one high-ranking Bank of Japan official summarized the government's strategy in 1988, 'We intended first to boost both the stock and property markets. Supported by this safety net—rising markets—export-oriented industries were supposed to reshape themselves so they could adapt to a domestically-led economy. This step then was supposed to bring about enormous growth of assets over every economic sector. This wealth-effect would in turn touch off personal consumption and residential investment, followed by an increase of investment in plant and equipment. In the end, loosened monetary policy would boost real economic growth.' Quoted in T. Taniguchi, *Japan's Banks and the 'Bubble Economy' of the Late 1980s*, Princeton University, Center of International Studies, Program on US-Japan Relations, Monograph Series, no. 4, Princeton 1993, p. 9.

them had bought up decades before at bargain basement prices—to carry through a wave of plant and equipment investment on a scale not seen since the 1960s. Between 1986 and 1991, the economy boomed, as private business plant and equipment investment shot up at an average annual rate of 10.5 per cent and the growth of GDP averaged 4.8 per cent per annum.[47]

Benefiting from the huge financial assistance that they were able to secure by way of the state-sponsored bubble, Japanese manufacturers made Herculean efforts to improve and transform manufacturing so as to maintain exports in the face of the new rise of the yen after 1985, much as they had during the years of currency revaluation of the mid to late 1970s. Between 1985 and 1991, they maintained an average annual rate of growth of the gross capital stock of 6.7 per cent. US manufacturers, who were simultaneously benefiting from a collapsing dollar, increased their gross capital stock in this period less than one-third as fast. In the same years, Japanese producers raised their expenditures on research and development as a percentage of GDP by about a quarter, compared to that for the years 1980–85 (from about 1.75 per cent to about 2.2 per cent), while US producers were reducing theirs by about the same amount (from about 2.1 per cent to about 1.75 per cent). The average annual growth of manufacturing labour productivity in these years in Japan thus reached 5.4 per cent, compared to 2.2 per cent in the US. As a result of its developmental push, Japan had succeeded by the end of the 1980s in increasing the proportion of its manufacturing output that was either high-tech or mixed high-tech and capital-intensive to about 85 per cent, catching up in the process with the US in its degree of specialization in high-tech and high-wage lines, and becoming even less specialized than was the US in low-wage and low-tech production.[48]

Still, to have a hope of remaining competitive by improving technology and moving up the product cycle, Japanese manufacturers were obliged to carry through a decisive restructuring of their international operations. The high yen obviously made it more difficult to export, but it also made it easier to invest overseas. In response, Japanese producers radically altered the directions of their trade, in close connection with a major turn to foreign direct investment. At the heart of the problem faced by Japanese manufacturing was their declining ability to access the critically important US market. Already in 1981, as part of a pervasive protectionist thrust by governments throughout the advanced capitalist world aimed at stemming the tide of Japanese imports, the Reagan administration had introduced so-called 'voluntary export restraints' (VERs) on a number of Japanese goods, particularly automobiles. When the dollar fell against the yen at the time of the Plaza Accord, therefore, Japanese producers found themselves with much more costly exports confronting a protected US market. Between 1985 and 1990, Japanese nominal exports to the US grew by only 37 per cent in dollars terms, with the result that Japanese exports to the US as a proportion of total Japanese exports fell from a peak of 40 per cent in 1986 to 31.6 per cent in 1990.[49]

In part, Japanese producers responded to their declining ability to export to the US simply by seeking markets where they were less disadvantaged by yen revalu-

---

47   Murphy, *Weight of the Yen*, pp. 209–18; Taniguchi, *Japan's Banks*; Y. Noguchi, 'The "Bubble" and Economic Policies in the 1980s', *Journal of Japanese Studies*, vol. xx, no. 2, Summer 1994.

48   OECD, *Industrial Policy in OECD Countries*, Paris 1994, pp. 117, 134.

49   OECD, *Economic Survey of Japan 1990–91*, Paris 1991, p. 172, Table J.

ation. Since the yen rose so much less against European currencies than against the dollar, Japanese exporters were able to increase their exports to Europe by 168 per cent in dollar terms between 1985 and 1990, with the result that the percentage of all Japanese exports that went to Europe grew from 13 per cent to 22 per cent.[50] But their really decisive new departures were tied to stepped-up foreign direct investment.

Before the 1970s, Japanese direct foreign investment was small, and mostly for developing overseas supplies of raw materials in Southeast Asia and establishing subsidiaries of trading companies in North America. But following successive trade liberalization measures after 1969, and especially the yen revaluations of 1971–3 and 1975–78, foreign direct investment surged, as Japanese manufacturers sought to get around their newly increased domestic labour costs by moving labour-intensive production to East Asia. Even so, in the years between 1973 and 1980, Japan's cumulative foreign direct investment amounted to only about one-seventh that of the US. Nevertheless, as in so many other respects, the Plaza Accord turned out to be the turning point for Japan's investment overseas. Between 1985 and 1989, Japanese foreign direct investment tripled in terms of the yen and grew by a factor of six in terms of the dollar. Between 1981 and 1990, it was more than 10 per cent greater than that of the US, and almost double that of the US between 1987 and 1990.[51]

One fundamental thrust of Japan's foreign investment offensive was to relocate production in the US, both to get around import barriers and to make use of the US's increasingly cheap labour. Whereas the export of autos to the US peaked in 1985, due to the growth of US-based production, overall sales of Japanese cars in the US continued to increase by more than 5 per cent a year in the later 1980s. Even more significant in the longer run was the invasion by Japanese manufacturers of East Asia, by means of which they sought to gain maximum benefit from the emergence of a new set of triangular trades linking Japan, East Asia, and the US. By developing this commerce, Japanese manufacturers aimed not only to secure indirect access to the US market, circumventing restrictions on Japanese imports and exploiting cheaper Asian labour to do so, but also to tap into the new dynamism of the East Asian economies themselves. Japanese manufacturers thus supplied the East Asian Gang of Four's increasingly sophisticated producers with ever more advanced means of production and intermediate goods, which they used to produce textiles, consumer electronics, and as time went on, higher-tech items like computer memory chips for the US market, and to some extent the growing Asian markets. At the same time, they established increasing numbers of foreign affiliates in Southeast Asia—Thailand, Malaysia, the Philippines and Indonesia—to which they also shipped capital goods and intermediate goods for assembly and (re-) export, mainly again to North America.[52]

Japanese producers did have to cede a certain share of the North American and

---

50   Ibid.

51   OECD, *Economic Survey of Japan 1981–82*, Paris, July 1982, p. 43; OECD, *Economic Survey of Japan 1987–88*, Paris, August 1988, pp. 65–7; OECD, *Economic Survey of Japan 1989–90*, Paris, December 1990, p. 52, Table 14; OECD, *Industrial Policy Annual Review 1994*, Paris 1994, p. 146, Table 31.

52   OECD, *Economic Survey of Japan 1989-90*, pp. 51–4; Park and Park, 'Changing Japanese Trade Patterns with the East Asian NICS', p. 94.

the Japanese markets to increasingly competitive East Asian-producers able to combine relatively cheap labour with relatively high technology in clothing, appliances, and consumer electronics. This was especially because the East Asian currencies were for the most part pegged to the dollar in the decade after the Plaza Accord, and followed the dollar downward against the yen, vastly improving East Asian competitiveness. While the Japanese share of imports into the US thus fell from 22.2 per cent to 18.3 per cent between 1986 and 1991, the proportion held by the East Asian NICs grew by about the same amount, from 11.75 per cent to 15.3 per cent. In the same period, East Asian exports to Japan grew perhaps three times faster than did those of the US. Nevertheless, Japanese manufacturers were able to gain much more through stepping up their exports to East Asia than they lost as a result of East Asian incursions into their US and domestic markets. Japanese exporters supplied East Asian producers with the ever higher-tech capital goods needed to produce the labour- and capital-intensive consumer goods that they were exporting to the US and, to some extent, to Japan itself. Between 1985 and 1990, Japanese exports to East Asia in dollar terms thus grew by 148 per cent, with the result that Japanese exports to East Asia as a percentage of total Japanese exports grew in these years from 18.7 per cent to 28.9 per cent. In particular, Japanese machinery exports to the Gang of Four economies quadrupled between 1985 and 1992, while those to the ASEAN-4 quintupled. Japan's dominance of the whole process of East Asian growth was manifested in its growing bilateral trade surpluses with all of the leading economies of the region. East Asia's industrial-commercial dynamism thus turned out to provide a crucial enabling condition for the Japanese to improve domestic production to counter the high yen.[53]

Nevertheless, the fact remains that, even despite their multifaceted effort at adjustment, and the enormous assistance they received from their government, Japanese manufacturers proved unable to use the growth of exports to transcend the structural problems inherent in their particular form of export-oriented development. The increase in costs entailed by the massive revaluation of the yen was simply too great to offset—even by means of increasing manufacturing efficiency, entering new, technology-intensive manufacturing lines where competition was less intense, and refashioning their overseas commercial and production networks. In the end, Japanese producers could neither avoid a sharp fall in the rate of growth of manufacturing exports nor achieve a significant recovery of manufacturing profitability.

Between 1985 and 1990, the yen's effective (trade-weighted) exchange rate rose at an average annual rate of 6.9 per cent. The response of Japanese producers was impressive. During this same period, in terms of yen, they were able to reduce manufacturing unit labour costs at an average annual rate of 0.7 per cent. Nevertheless, even this effort could not prevent a decline in competitiveness, as the average annual growth of unit labour costs among their trading partners was 2.6 per cent. Japanese producers were thus obliged to reduce the yen prices of their exports at an average annual rate of no less than 3.5 per cent, making for an average annual

53   OECD, *Economic Survey of Japan 1992–93*, Paris, November 1993, p. 64, Table 16; p. 141, Table J.; P. A. Petri, 'Market Structure, Comparative Advantage, and Japanese Trade under the Strong Yen', in P. Krugman, ed., *Trade with Japan*, Chicago 1991, pp. 57–65; Park and Park, 'Changing Japanese Trade Patterns', pp. 93–6; Hatch and Yamamura, *Asia in Japan's Embrace*, pp. 177–80.

increase in international terms of about 3.4 per cent.

During the years 1985–91, then, Japanese exports could grow at an average annual rate of only 3.95 per cent, compared to 7.7 per cent for 1980–85 and 9.9 per cent for 1973–79, and they would have grown even more slowly had they not been so strongly subsidized by gargantuan US budget deficits. In the same period, imports shot up at an average annual rate of 11 per cent, compared to 0.8 per cent in the years 1980–85 and 4.1 per cent in the years 1973–79. As a share of the world total, Japan's exports fell from a peak of 10.3 per cent in 1986 to 8.5 per cent in 1990.[54]

With export prices held down so low, profitability on manufacturing exports was naturally squeezed. According to the OECD, Japanese exporters could pass through as price increases only about 75 per cent on average of the increased costs brought about by the higher yen. Since, in these years, the share of manufacturing exports in manufacturing output had risen to around 45 per cent, one can see what Japanese producers were up against.[55] Understandably, by 1990, the manufacturing rate of profit had failed to rise at all above its levels of 1985 or 1978.

The difficulties of a manufacturing sector hemmed in by over-production and by intensifying international competition loomed especially large because they could not, despite the best efforts of the Japanese government, be easily resolved by redirecting production towards the domestic market. Japanese exports were highly concentrated in (relatively few) manufacturing lines with the potential for fast-growing labour productivity. Any given investment would generally raise productivity in these lines substantially more rapidly than in most others, especially lines outside manufacturing. During the years 1986 and 1991, in accord with the hopes of the authorities, investment in non-manufacturing did rise significantly faster than in manufacturing, with the non-manufacturing capital stock increasing at an average annual rate of about 8 per cent, compared to about 6.5 per cent in manufacturing. Nevertheless, the average annual growth of labour productivity per person in manufacturing, at 4.6 per cent, was still higher than in non-manufacturing, at 4.0 per cent. Because it cost so much in terms of the growth of capital stock to raise labour productivity outside of manufacturing, the non-manufacturing sector had been no more able to raise its profitability above its level of the end of the 1980s than had the manufacturing sector.

Japanese producers could thus raise profitability by means of transferring resources out of over-subscribed manufacturing lines into many (low-productivity growth) service lines only to the extent that, in the process, they could decrease wage growth even faster than they sustained reduced productivity growth with

54   By comparison, US exporters, enjoying a 50 per cent devaluation of the dollar against the yen in these years, were able to increase their prices at an average rate of 2.3 per cent and still achieve a rate of growth of exports that was triple that of their Japanese counterparts.

55   OECD, *Economics Survey of Japan 1988–89*, pp. 93, 95. OECD, *Economic Survey of Japan 1987–88*, pp. 55–7.

56   Hatch and Yamamura, *Asia in Japan's Embrace*, p. 71. In this period, the Japanese case appears to have fallen somewhere between the US and German cases with respect to the expansion of service employment. The Japanese economy raised service employment significantly more rapidly than did Germany but less rapidly than the US; it reduced service sector relative wage growth, as Germany did not, but not as much as the US; and it raised non-manufacturing productivity growth faster than did the US, but not as fast as did Germany. The upshot appears to have been that the non-manufacturing economy of Japan had greater difficulty in raising profitability than did those of either Germany or the US, because it could not tolerate German levels of unemployment or impose US levels of wage restraint. See also *Economic Planning Agency of Japan, Economic Survey of Japan 1995-96*, Tokyo 1995, pp. 214–20.

respect to both labour and capital inputs. Japanese employers do appear to have succeeded in imposing some increase in wage dispersion between manufacturing and service industries in this period, but nowhere near as much as their US counterparts—or was apparently necessary for profitability to further recover.[56] It is no wonder, therefore, that the government's programme of strengthening domestic demand at the end of the 1980s failed to succeed much better than had its predecessors in reorienting the economy.

From Slump to Transformation?

By 1990–91 profitability in Japan's private business economy as a whole had still failed to rise above its level at the peaks of the previous expansions in 1985 and 1978. At the end of 1989, in order to gain control over the bubble, the Japanese government began slowly to raise interest rates. Following the start of another cyclical downturn in the US in the second quarter of 1990, the Japanese economy entered a new recession which turned out to be the longest and deepest of the postwar epoch, GDP growing at an average annual rate of just 0.8 per cent between 1991 and 1995. Clearly the investment boom detonated by the bubble had failed to reduce costs sufficiently to ensure its own perpetuation, let alone set the Japanese economy on new foundations.

The deep recession that began at the end of 1991 and continued into the second half of 1995 was, in part, a reaction to the bubble itself. After engaging for almost half a decade in the most massive accumulation of capital stock, inventories, and labour without succeeding in raising their rate of profit, Japanese corporations could not but, sooner or later, cut back compensatorily on the growth of new plant and equipment, inventories, employment, and wages. The reductions had to be that much more severe because so much of the previous spurt of capital accumulation had been financed through the accumulation of debt. When years of record-low interest rates were suddenly replaced by sharply higher ones—6 per cent in September 1990, up from 2.5 per cent a year before—Japanese firms could not but impose across-the-board cuts. The resulting, extended collapse of both investment and consumer demand was at the root of the recession. Moreover, just as the positive wealth effect of sharply rising stock and land prices had fuelled the boom, the negative wealth effect of collapsing stock and land prices could not but exacerbate the downturn, further reducing investment and consumer demand. Finally, when land prices collapsed, many real-estate companies were unable to pay their debts, leaving many banks overwhelmed by non-performing loans. Their consequent difficulty in making new loans impeded any movement towards recovery.[57]

Yet, the cyclical aspects of the recession only exacerbated the economy's underlying structural difficulties, which the government had failed to overcome and which were responsible for the unusual severity of the ensuing crisis. It was an old story: despite the enormous changes wrought during the bubble, the Japanese economy was faced in 1991 with the same predicament as in 1986, but it had now exhausted its options, at least for the time being. Given the economy's dependence on manufacturing exports and the particular form which that dependence took,

---

57   OECD, *Economic Survey of Japan 1992–93*, pp. 9, 14.

manufacturers confronted an insurmountable task in restoring manufacturing profitability in the face of the secularly rising yen and the continuation of international over-capacity and over-production in manufactures. Yet, there was no easy solution to the profitability problem by means of the reallocation of resources out of over-subscribed manufacturing lines, in view of how costly in terms of investment it was to raise labour productivity in other manufacturing industries and in the non-manufacturing sector in general.

From 1991 through 1995, the yen once again took off. During the late 1980s, encouraged by the government, Japanese investors had propped up the dollar by means of the most extensive accumulation of US assets; but, with the onset of the recession of the 1990s, they were obliged to liquidate properties, reduce or cease their purchases, and bring their money home. Purchases of US Treasury instruments, US securities, and other sorts of US assets fell sharply. At the same time, with the collapse of demand at home and the earlier recovery from recession in the US, the relative growth of imports as against exports slowed. The relative demand for yen could not then but increase (and for dollars fall): between 1990 and 1995, the currency's effective exchange rate grew at an average annual rate of 9.5 per cent, even faster than in the previous five years, and its value against the dollar grew by a total of 54 per cent.[58]

To make matters worse, the US was refusing to play its assigned role of bailing out the Japanese, and the world, economy. The Clinton administration, as noted, failed to resort to deficit spending to speed recovery from the US recession of 1990–91, with the result that the US market was relatively slow to grow. Over the four years following this slump, real US imports grew at an average annual rate of 9.4 per cent, compared to 12.6 per cent in the four years following the recession of 1979–82.

Pressed on both the domestic and international fronts, Japanese manufacturers faced their greatest crisis. Due to the over-investment of the previous years, and the resulting over-accumulation of productive capacity and of labour that was hard to lay off, as well as firms' deep indebtedness and banks' difficulties in lending, domestic demand stagnated. Especially with the bursting of the bubble, it was impossible to once again ratchet up capital accumulation so as to raise productivity growth sufficiently to compensate for the rise of the yen. Between 1991 and 1995, investment as a proportion of GDP fell from 20 per cent to 14 per cent and the average annual increase of the capital stock fell by more than one-third, compared to that for 1985–91. These reduced figures were still higher than the comparable ones for the US in the same period, but they were entirely inadequate to the formidable task of maintaining competitiveness or profitability.[59]

By 1995, Japanese manufacturers had managed to raise the technological level of their exports still another notch. They had increased the share in total exports of high-technology-intensive products—including sophisticated capital goods (such as industrial robots), components (such as liquid crystal displays and other devices for computers and telecommunications equipment), and industrial intermediate materials (such as ceramics)—to 80 per cent, from just 55 per cent in

58 Murphy, *Weight of the Yen*, pp. 287–8; OECD, *Economic Survey of Japan 1993*, p. 9.
59 OECD, *Economic Survey of Japan 1994–95*, Paris 1995, p. 9, Figure 5.

1985, while cutting back the share of capital-intensive but medium-technology products, such as steel, automobiles, and home electronics. They had, in the same period, raised the share of capital goods in total exports to 62 per cent from 48 per cent, while reducing the share of lower value-added consumer goods correspondingly.[60] The government, meanwhile, had helped offset their cash flow problems by stepping up subsidies for research and development. Nevertheless, in contrast to the years 1985–91, when, by virtue of their increased productiveness and ability to control costs, Japanese manufacturers had come close to maintaining their international competitive position despite the vertiginous rise of the yen, during the years 1990–95, they were unable to prevent relative unit labour costs, which grew at the extraordinary annual average rate of 11 per cent, from rising even faster than the effective exchange rate, profoundly reducing Japanese export competitiveness.

Between 1991 and 1995, Japanese producers managed to increase their exports at roughly the same very reduced rate as between 1985 and 1991—3.1 per cent— while maintaining their share of world exports; but they could do so only at great cost. To maintain export growth and share, they were obliged to reduce their export prices at an average annual rate of 3.9 per cent, but, given the huge increase in their costs, doing so implied an enormous squeeze on the profitability of their overseas sales.[61] Between its 1980s peak, achieved in 1988, and 1995, the rate of profit of non-financial corporations dropped by 37 per cent, and that for manufacturing a stunning 55 per cent.

Limited in their ability to respond to the pressures of the high yen and slower-growing markets through stepped-up investment in manufacturing, and restricted in their capacity to raise profitability through productivity increase outside manufacturing, Japanese producers sought to maintain their established, export-oriented production system by further expanding it into East Asia, where relative costs, during the first half of the 1990s, were made even lower by devaluations of the local currencies against the yen of the same order of magnitude as that of the dollar. This process had, of course, been well under way since the second part of the 1980s, but it was now radically accelerated, with the government once again playing a critical role, by making possible improved coordination and the dissemination of information. The idea was to take advantage both of relatively low-waged East Asian labour and improving Asian know-how and infrastructure so as to increase efficiency through the growth of the division of labour. It was to be implemented by rapidly expanding the triangular trade, centred on newly-emerging Japanese production in the Asian continent. Manufacturers in Japan would be enabled to further expand their export markets in high-tech capital and intermediate goods needed by Asian producers, while Japanese manufacturing plants relocated in Asia would be enabled to secure the otherwise unachievable cost improvement needed to further penetrate both the North American and rapidly growing Asian markets. But relatively limited

60   M. Yoshitomi, 'On the Changing International Competitiveness of Japanese Manufacturing Since 1985', *Oxford Review of Economic Policy*, vol. xii, no. 3, 1996; OECD, *Economic Survey of Japan 1995–96*, Paris 1996, p. 31.
61   For the difficulties of passing through the cost increases resulting from yen revaluation in higher export prices, and consequent downward pressure on profitability, see OECD, *Economic Survey of Japan 1992–93*, p. 31; OECD, *Economic Survey of Japan 1993–94*, pp. 22, 27.
62   For the foregoing paragraph, I have relied especially on M. Bernard and J. Ravenhill, 'Beyond Product Cycles and Flying Geese: Regionalization, Hierarchy, and the Industrialization of East Asia', *World Politics*, vol. xlvii, January 1995, as well as Hatch and Yamamura, *Asia in Japan's Embrace*.

amounts of Asian-produced manufactures would be allowed to come back to Japan, which would hold on, as much as possible, to advanced manufacturing production as the basic condition for developing manufacturing technology, even in supposedly 'mature' lines.[62]

At the core of this effort was a further huge increase of foreign direct investment in Asia, centred on subsidiaries of Japanese multinationals but also including many members of vertical *keiretsu* in Japan, which relocated to Asia to join newly emerging production networks organized roughly on the old lines. In just the four years between 1991 and 1995, annual foreign direct investment in manufacturing by Japan grew by almost 50 per cent, from $12.3 billion to $18.9 billion, with almost all of the increase absorbed by Asia, where Japanese manufacturing annual direct investment almost tripled, from $2.9 billion to $8.1 billion.[63] Over the same period, therefore, the share of manufacturing output produced abroad by Japanese firms rose from 6.4 per cent to over 10 per cent (to 15 and 20 per cent, respectively, in general machinery and transport equipment), by Japanese multinationals from 17 to 25 per cent. The dizzying ascent of Japanese production in Asia brought a continuing reorientation of trade in that direction. By 1995, the share of Japanese exports going to Asia had climbed sharply to 44 per cent, up from 31.1 per cent in 1990 and just 18.7 per cent in 1985. Imports from Asia into Japan grew less rapidly; still, between 1982 and 1995, reverse imports from Japanese multinationals' foreign subsidiaries increased at over 40 per cent per annum, and by 1995 accounted for 14 per cent of total imports.[64]

The ultimate impact on the domestic economy of Japanese corporations' spectacular reorientation toward Asia remains to be seen. Even so, because Japanese corporations see their fate as tied to their ongoing accelerated improvement of manufacturing technology across many lines, and view such improvement as possible only by actually engaging in manufacturing production, they have been at great pains to nurture production in Japan itself. They have therefore done their best to make their expansion into Asia aid improved productivity at home by facilitating the overall 'Japanese' manufacturing division of labour, and allowed the substitution of Asian-based for Japanese-based lower-waged, lower-technology production only to the extent that the latter could be compensated by the expansion of Japanese-based higher-technology, higher-waged production.[65] After an 11 per cent fall from 27.8 per cent to 24.6 per cent between 1973 and 1979, the Japanese manufacturing labour force as a proportion of the total, in sharp contrast to that of the US, ceased to fall through 1991. By 1996, it had declined to 22.5 per

63   OECD, *Economic Survey of Japan 1995–96*, Table 3, p. 19. It is estimated that in 1996 alone annual foreign direct investment increased by $19 billion to $70 billion. Of this increase, by far the greater part, something like $16 billion, was composed of manufacturing foreign direct investment, which doubled to $35 billion. More than half of the increase in manufacturing direct investment went to Asia, where FDI increased by about 80 per cent to $18 billion. W. Dawkins, 'Moving Abroad', *Financial Times*, 12 May 1996.
64   OECD, *Economic Survey of Japan 1995–96*, pp. 30, 32, 229; OECD, *Economic Survey of Japan 1994–95*, pp. 23–5. In some sectors the share of overseas investment was much higher. For large manufacturing companies that already had at least one overseas plant, foreign investment rose to about 40 per cent of domestic investment (38.5 per cent in Fiscal Year 1995 for 158 manufacturing firms in the Tankan survey and 39 per cent of 170 firms in the survey by the Export-Import Bank of Japan). OECD, *Economic Survey of Japan for 1996*, p. 185, n. 3.
65   Hatch and Yamamura, *Asia in Japan's Embrace*, pp. 31, 97–114.

cent, but, in view of the extremity of the Japanese crisis, and especially of the yen revaluation of that period, it would be premature to reach the conclusion that Japan is 'hollowing out'.

Towards Recovery?

The course and depth of the Japanese depression must be kept in perspective. The highest level of unemployment in Japan during the downturn has been lower than the lowest level achieved by the US during its parallel boom. Between 1991—when the recession began—and 1996, manufacturing hourly real wages increased by 12 per cent in Japan, compared to 2 per cent in the expanding US. Throughout the 1990s, Japanese investment per employee continued to exceed that of the US. Finally, despite the well-known proclivity of Japanese firms to retain labour during recessions, Japanese productivity in manufacturing has not done too badly, growing at an average annual rate of 2.7 per cent between 1991 and 1996, despite two years of zero growth (although the figures are probably much worse outside manufacturing).

The fact remains that the Japanese crisis has been extremely serious, especially because recovery has been so very difficult, and because a Japanese failure to recover (or worse) would jeopardize the world economy. Beginning in 1992, the government launched repeated rounds of major public spending increases, while continuing to bring down interest rates. But the stimulative effects of the macroeconomic expansion were, on each occasion, more than counterbalanced by the depressive impact of a new rise in the value of the yen. In the spring of 1995, in the wake of the crisis in Mexico, a flight from the dollar pushed the yen's exchange rate to the unprecedented height of 80/$, threatening the economy with collapse. It was only at this point, when the G-3 governments intervened decisively to reverse the decade-long decline of the dollar and force down the value of the yen, that the Japanese economy began to right itself. Even then, it took the largest fiscal stimulus in Japanese history in the late summer of 1995 to keep the upturn progressing.

Japan's transcendence of its long recession has thus remained very much in doubt, with major consequences for the system as a whole. As soon as the yen began to fall, Japan's leading manufacturing firms, generally capable of at least breaking even at an exchange rate of 100 yen/$, succeeded in launching a major new export-driven expansion. In part through exports and in part as a result of the earlier stimulus package, Japan thus enjoyed a major revival of growth in 1996. But, by 1997, Japan's cyclical upturn had run out of steam, with rising exports unable to catalyze a sustained recovery beyond manufacturing.

In part, Japan's stalled recovery was clearly attributable to government policy, specifically to the state's over-anxiety to make up for the enormous increase in its indebtedness during the previous half-decade. In early 1997, to begin to rebalance the books, the government implemented a major tax increase, despite widespread predictions that it would undercut the nascent business revival. To compound the problem, the government was long reluctant to incur new deficits to jump-start the economy, even as it slid back toward serious recession in 1997 and 1998. The fact remains that the government policy could hardly have proved so negative in its impact had the domestic economy possessed greater vitality and less fragility in the first place. As it was, when the government turned to reduced interest rates, rather than fiscal stimulus, to get the economy moving, the increased lending that resulted financed not so much increased domestic investment, as the accelerated flow of money out of the country into US Treasury Bonds and US securities. This put ever greater downward pressure on the yen, not to mention the Japanese stock market.

In the past, of course, a falling yen had generally been sufficient to generate a recovery, because it had made possible access to the huge, absorptive US market. But, since the time of the previous export-led expansion driven by a devalued yen, which had taken place between 1979 and 1985, Japan had been obliged to reorient its commerce, away from the US and toward East Asia. The switch to Asia, however, came with a catch. Whereas a rising dollar with respect to the yen had automatically improved Japanese export prospects in the US market, rising East Asian currencies with regard to the yen could very well end up undercutting Japanese export prospects in East Asian markets because they could easily undermine the growth prospects of heavily export-dependent East Asian economies. When the yen fell, that is exactly what happened. Korea and most of the other economies of Northeast and Southeast Asia immediately ran into difficulties exporting, which eventually cut short their expansion—with vast repercussions for Japanese exporters, Japanese multinational investors, and banks, and the world economy as a whole.[66]

3. Germany in the 1980s and 1990s: Monetarism in the Name of Exports

Like the Japanese, the German economy faced, from the start of the 1980s, unprecedented barriers to maintaining its economic momentum. Over the course of the 1960s and 1970s, it had already found it progressively more difficult to make its export-oriented form of development bear fruit. During the 1980s and 1990s, the prospects narrowed further, as fiscal austerity and tight money became the order of the day, as the mark hesitantly but relentlessly continued its upward ascent, as the growth of world output and world trade fell below their levels of the 1970s, and as the US ultimately reneged on its commitment to provide the demand needed for international economic growth and stability. In this situation, responding to what they saw to be a failed experiment in Keynesianism at the end of the 1970s, the German economic authorities, unlike their more interventionist (and more adventurous) counterparts in Japan turned resolutely, and more or less permanently, to their traditional remedy, the pursuit of balanced budgets and relatively tight money.[67]

Perhaps more than ever before, the prospects for German economic growth came to depend on holding back the growth of domestic demand, with the goal of keeping down costs and prices, and intensifying competitive pressure on domestic producers, so as to spur rationalization and improvement, in the interest of promoting the growth of exports and thereby investment. This policy had, of course, a certain logic, since major sections of the German manufacturing plant had clearly become redundant in international terms, and required trimming, rationalization, upgrading, and supersession. The authorities thus left it to the

---

66   See below pp. 262–6.
67   Giersch et al., *Fading Miracle*, pp. 194–5. 'All in all, demand management virtually disappeared from the policy agenda ... in the 1980s.'

market to pressure the economy for change, and to Germany's capitalist institutions—its banks linked to manufacturers and especially its unmatched labour force—to fabricate the required transformation. Yet, to pose such a challenge to the German economy was hardly to ensure a successful response, especially since the deep roots of the problem were not by any means mostly German, but lay fundamentally in the over-capacity and over-production in manufacturing that plagued the advanced capitalist world. Government policy was certainly successful in securing its immediate end, the control of costs and prices, but deflation proved, in itself, no panacea.

Growth Through Stagnation?

The German recession of the early 1980s was precipitated, much like that of 1974–75, by a combination of runaway oil prices and a coordinated international turn to tight money. It struck the German economy, at the peak of its deficit-driven boom, very hard. During the three years 1980, 1981, and 1982, capacity utilization fell sharply, the average annual growth of GDP fell to 0 per cent, and the rate of profit in manufacturing, though not outside it, dropped to very low levels, on average 50 per cent below its level of 1979. Nor, with the end of the wrench of the recession, did the authorities much relax their pursuit of 'sound finance'. Not only did they fail to significantly loosen the supply of credit until 1987, they also, like the Japanese, reduced the budget deficit as a fraction of GDP, from 3.1 per cent in 1980 to 1.1 per cent in 1985.[68] Meanwhile, with the record-setting deficits and borrowing of the US government, on the one hand, and the continuing tight credit imposed by the US Fed, on the other, the US authorities induced radically higher interest rates on a world scale, and Germany saw its real interest rates rise from an average of about 2.5 per cent in the 1970s, to an average of 5.1 per cent for the years 1980–84 inclusive and of 4.1 per cent for the years 1985-89 inclusive.[69]

Under pressure first from recession, then from highly restrictive macroeconomic policy, the economy certainly sustained a major reduction in the growth of costs. With the growth of their output failing to rise even to 2 per cent in any year before 1986, manufacturers were able to reduce the average annual increase of the nominal wage between 1982 and 1990 to 4.2 per cent, from 8.4 per cent between 1973 and 1979. They thereby cut average annual real and product wage growth in those years to 2.4 per cent and 0.6 per cent respectively, from 3.7 per cent and 4.0 per cent respectively, between 1973 and 1979. In this context, inflation was pretty much brought under control, as the growth of the consumer price index fell from 6.2 per cent in 1981 to 0.6 per cent in 1987 and 1.3 per cent in 1988. Rationalization and downsizing now proceeded apace, bringing, virtually on their own (with the benefit of little investment growth) a certain growth of productivity through the reduction of outmoded plant and the shedding of labour. Between 1979 and 1985, as in the analogous period of crisis between 1970 and 1975, the manufacturing labour force fell precipitously, by 10.2 per cent in terms of hours. Between 1982 and 1990, the average annual growth of unit labour costs in German manufacturing fell by more than half, to 2.1 per cent, from 4.8 per cent between 1973 and 1979.

68   Giersch et al., *Fading Miracle*, pp. 192–5.
69   Ibid., p. 212.

On the basis of these reductions in the growth of costs, the growth of exports succeeded in bringing about a new cyclical upturn and in returning the economy to very full capacity utilization by the end of the decade. But export growth could not durably restore the economy's dynamism. In 1989, the return to full capacity utilization was thus accompanied by an 8.4 per cent rate of unemployment, almost double the 4.8 per cent rate that prevailed at the end of the 1970s. The reason was that the growth of the manufacturing capital stock had almost ceased in the intervening period.

The expansion of exports was insufficient to revivify the economy for the simple reason that it could not stimulate the required major increase in the accumulation of capital. The increase of the manufacturing capital stock, already sharply reduced in the 1970s, fell significantly further, to an average annual rate of just 1.4 per cent between 1979 and 1990, from an already low 2.0 per cent between 1973 and 1979. It is therefore not surprising that manufacturing labour productivity growth also went down, increasing at an average annual rate of less than 2.0 per cent between 1979 and 1990, compared to 3.45 per cent between 1973 and 1979. During this period, Germany had the lowest rate of manufacturing labour productivity increase among the G-7 economies, except for Canada.

Given the intensity of international competition, unless productivity growth could be raised significantly, German manufacturing could not increase competitiveness sufficiently to found a real boom in exports. But the catch was that there was no way to raise productivity growth substantially because the prospects of raising profitability through exports were nowhere near promising enough to sufficiently stimulate the growth of investment. As the stimulus from the US economy under Reagan reached its peak, exports did, as in Japan, grow impressively in 1984 and 1985, at an average annual rate of 7.9 per cent. But, because this boom was driven by a combination of US deficits and a high dollar and of German macroeconomic restrictiveness plus a low mark, it could not last. German domestic demand was, of course, intentionally limited to keep down prices. But precisely because this policy 'worked', it could not but give rise to a new round of German current account surpluses and US deficits. Upward pressure on the mark thus quickly materialized, and following the Plaza Accord, the German currency appreciated sharply in 1986–87 and 1990, its effective exchange rate increasing at an average annual rate of 4.6 per cent between 1985 and 1990. Since wage growth could, for the time being, be reduced no further, and productivity could be made to grow no faster, German manufacturing had to absorb almost all of the cost increase caused by the currency appreciation, its relative unit labour costs in international terms increasing at an average annual rate of 4.2 per cent in those years.

As usual, German producers went out of their way to keep export price increases down so as to keep export growth up, actually *reducing* export prices, in terms of the mark, at an average annual rate of 1.1 per cent between 1985 and 1990. This was undoubtedly necessary to maintain and increase sales but obviously it was also heavily to blame for the squeeze on export, and thus manufacturing, profitability. Even so, the gain secured in export growth through price restraint was not all that great. Under the stimulus of an international expansion fuelled by universally easy money in 1987–88, a major fall in oil prices, and the opening of the market to the East with German unification, exports boomed again at the end of the decade, increasing by 10 per cent and 11 per cent, respectively, in 1989 and 1990. Over the decade of the 1980s, moreover, Germany slightly increased its share of OECD manufacturing and world exports. The fact remains that between 1979 and 1990, export growth averaged only 5.3 per cent per annum, and even between 1985 and 1990, no more than 5.5 per cent. These figures were not significantly higher than those of the 1970s, and of course one-third to one-half off those of the 1960s, not surprising given that the rate of growth of world trade remained, as in the 1970s, at half what it had been in the years 1960–73, and that the manufacturing rate of profit for the G-7 economies taken in aggregate remained more than one-third below its, quite reduced, level of the late 1970s. It was not only the secular rise of relative German production costs in international terms, but ongoing over-capacity and over-production on a world scale, which rendered prospects for profitability, and thus investment, in German manufacturing distinctly bleak.

The counterpart of the stagnation of manufacturing investment at home was the explosion of investment overseas. Until 1985, German foreign direct investment had been stable at around 10 billion marks per annum, and largely offset by an influx of foreign investment into Germany. But, following the Plaza Accord, in just the five years between 1985 and 1990, German foreign direct investment more than *tripled* to 30 billion marks, while investment in Germany from abroad stagnated.[70] That the economy lacked opportunities for profitable investment in domestic man- ufacturing could hardly have been more obvious.

That the problems facing German manufacturing were fundamentally systemic, inherent in the condition of the world manufacturing economy and the form of Germany's relationship to it, is evident not just from the stagnation of manufac- turing profitability at a low level, and from the rise of investment overseas, but also from the *relative* dynamism of the non-manufacturing economy. Manufacturing profitability had fallen sharply in the recession of 1979–83 and, by the end of the 1980s, had barely recovered its pre-recession levels of the late 1970s, when it was already some 10 per cent below its much reduced level of 1973. But non-manufac- turing profitability, which had already climbed slightly above its 1973 level at the end of the 1970s, and had barely fallen during the recession of 1979–83, had by the later 1980s reached its 1973 level and by 1990 had actually risen by 15 per cent above it, attaining its level of the end of the 1960s.[71] Part of the same process, between 1979 and 1990, the non-manufacturing capital stock rose almost three times as fast as did the manufacturing capital stock. What made for the difference? (See p. 7, Figure 0.3 and p. 8, Figure 0.4.)

As in manufacturing, wage growth outside of manufacturing was cut sharply during the 1970s and 1980s. Between 1982 and 1990, the real wage and product wage grew, respectively, at average annual rates of 1.4 per cent and 1.25 per cent, compared to 2.2 per cent and 1.6 per cent, respectively, between 1973 and 1979 and 5.65 per cent and 4.05 per cent, respectively, between 1960 and 1973. But, because producers outside of manufacturing were largely immune from both the upward

---

70   P. Norman, 'Savage German Shake-Out as Industrial Jobs Go Abroad', *Financial Times*, 7 February 1997.

71   The profitability recovery in the service sector alone was probably significantly greater than that of non-manufacturing more generally, for the latter also includes the construction, mining, and utilities indus- tries, all of which were in varying degrees of difficulty during the 1980s.

pressure on relative costs resulting from the mark's revaluation and downward pressure on prices from intensifying international competitors, they could continue to exploit the repression of wage growth in a way that manufacturers could not. Were they to maintain the rate of growth of investment, they could raise productivity growth above product wage growth, and thereby begin to recover their profit rate. And this is exactly what they did. Between 1982 and 1990, non-manufacturers increased the average annual growth of the capital stock at more than twice the rate that manufacturers did, 3.6 per cent compared to 1.7 per cent. Non-manufacturing labour productivity rose at an average annual rate of 2.85 per cent, compared to 2.1 per cent in manufacturing, despite the inherently greater difficulty of raising productivity outside than within manufacturing. Non-manufacturers were thereby enabled consistently to increase their profit share, and thus their profit rate. Had the power of workers and pressure of wage growth relative to productivity growth been the main problem facing manufacturers, they, too, could have pursued this route. That they did not is a further indication that this was far from the main problem that the manufacturing sector was up against.

By the years 1989–92, the steady rise in non-manufacturing profitability had made a major contribution to the restoration of profitability in the economy as a whole. In these years, the rate of profit in the private business economy hauled itself, for the first time since the start of the long downturn, back to—indeed slightly above—its level of 1973. Nevertheless the recovery of profitability in the German economy outside of manufacturing remained limited in its capacity to dynamize the German economy. Above all, it was insufficient to compensate for the still very reduced rate of profit in manufacturing. Even in regaining its level of 1973, the private sector rate of profit still remained, respectively, one-fifth and one-third below its levels of the second half and first half of the 1960s. Moreover, the very same macroeconomic tightening that helped bring down wage growth and raise the profit rate contributed significantly to increasing real interest rates and thereby to undercutting the impact of the gain in profitability: in effect, the 2.5 per cent rise in the real interest rate in the second half of the 1980s over that of the 1970s reduced the effective profit rate for private business as a whole and for the non-manufacturing sector in these years by more than by 15 per cent and 12 per cent respectively.

Despite the marked recovery of non-manufacturing and private business profitability over the course of the 1980s, therefore, the non-manufacturing and private business capital stocks grew respectively 18.5 per cent and 20 per cent more slowly between 1979 and 1990 than they had between 1973 and 1979. By the same token, the growth of the service sector labour force, at 17.2 per cent for the decade of the 1980s, was more than 25 per cent slower than during the decade of the 1970s, and was insufficient to prevent unemployment from sharply increasing. While the German authorities' sound finance thus contributed significantly to the shakeout of over-extended German manufacturing lines in these years, it also very much

72   Giersch et al., *Fading Miracle*, p. 199. As in the 1970s, FIRE accounted for virtually all of the growth in service sector employment over the course of the 1980s. Again, because the strength of the German labour movement prevented the sort of radical increase in wage dispersion that took place in the US, employment could not expand in low-productivity, low-wage services. Indeed, employment in retail and wholesale trade actually fell by 6.6 per cent between 1980 and 1986. Burda and Sachs, 'Assessing High Unemployment', pp. 555–9.

fettered the entry of means of production into other lines. Over the course of the 1980s, the private sector labour force increased by a scant 311,000, with the service sector increase of 1,146,000 in those years barely enough to compensate for the decline of 390,000 in agriculture, 398,000 in manufacturing, 206,000 in construction, and 21,000 in mining and utilities.[72] Between 1982 and 1990, there appeared in Germany for the first time since the late 1940s what could be properly called mass unemployment, the rate of unemployment over that period averaging 8.5 per cent, twice that of the second half of the 1970s.

The Crisis of German Manufacturing

The structural difficulties that the German manufacturing sector had failed to over-come were concealed by the brief boom at the end of the 1980s and the beginning of 1990s. In this short period between 1988 and 1991, not only did exports take off, but investment boomed, and the growth of capital stock began to accelerate from its low level. Nevertheless, when the conditions that had set off the boom proved ephemeral, the German economy fell back into stagnation and worse.

From late 1987 through the latter part of 1988, the advanced capitalist countries went all-out to make sure that the crash of October 1987 did not issue in a liquidity crisis, flooding the world economy with credit. But, when the danger of collapse quickly passed, they promptly backed away from their temporarily expansionary stance. Not long after, in the middle of 1990, the US economy entered into a short but sharp recession, which further reduced the growth of demand. The enormous transfer of state funds from West to East Germany that accompanied unification had, meanwhile, given West German firms a major shot in the arm, pumping up the call for their goods in 1990 and 1991. But, by 1991, a compensatory reaction had set in. In that year, to counteract the inflationary effects of the huge government deficits that had financed the East German subsidies, the German authorities cut spending and raised taxes. They also initiated an extended period of high interest rates to ensure long-term price stability. Rising German interest rates had a doubly depressing effect: first, they further undercut growth in Europe, contracting the market for German products at the very moment that the stimulus from the East began to peter out; second, they drove up the mark. Once again, therefore, the German authorities sought, through macroeconomic probity, to keep prices down in the interests of anti-inflation and cheaper exports but ended up undercutting German competitiveness. To make things worse, as the brief boom had strength-ened, German wages had finally begun to shoot up rapidly, to compensate for many years of very slow growth. The German economy yet again came face to face with the problem of relatively high costs in international terms, under conditions of system-wide manufacturing over-capacity and over-production, and entered its worst and longest recession since 1950. Between 1991 and 1995, GDP grew at an average annual rate of just 0.9 per cent, the slowest for any comparable period since 1950.[73]

With the return to austerity at home, the German economy was from 1991 thrust back into its standard dependence upon exports to mitigate recession and to secure

73   OECD, *Economic Survey of Germany 1990–91*, Paris 1991, pp. 15, 19–20; OECD, *Economic Survey of Germany 1992–93*, Paris 1993, p. 10.

its recovery under even more difficult conditions than previously. The basic problem remained that investors continued to doubt the ability of significant sections of German manufacturing to profit via exports. The growth of the capital stock thus fell back, capacity utilization declined, and productivity growth languished, increasing at an average annual rate of only 1.5 per cent between 1991 and 1995. At the same time, partly as an effect of the high interest rates that had been imposed to keep domestic costs down, the effective exchange rate of the mark rose at an average annual pace of 4 per cent. Because the manufacturing sector was totally incapable of increasing investment to reduce costs so as to compensate for the rise of the currency, relative unit labour costs grew even faster than did the exchange rate, at an average annual rate of 5.35 per cent.

West German manufacturers, for still another time, sought to keep up overseas sales by keeping down the growth of prices, which increased at an average annual rate of just 1.5 per cent between 1991 and 1995, far below the growth costs.[74] Even so, exports *fell* by 0.3 per cent in 1992, then fell again by 4.7 per cent in 1993, so that, by 1995, they were only 6 per cent above their level of 1991. In the latter year, the German share of world exports was down to 10.4 per cent, from 12.1 per cent as recently as 1990 and 12.4 per cent in 1987.

The combination of domestic austerity and export crisis brought a day of reckoning to the West German manufacturing sector. The German economy had, of course, by virtue of its export success, maintained an extraordinarily large manufacturing sector, constituting close to 40 per cent of both output and the labour force, right up to 1970. It had done so partly on the basis of its strong manufacturing competitiveness in a period of rising demand for the goods in which it specialized, partly on the basis of the increasing under-valuation of its currency. But with the rise of German relative costs, especially from 1969, the viability of an ever greater portion of this sector's productive power was undercut. In the crisis years culminating in the oil embargo of the early to mid 1970s and, then again, in the crisis years of the early 1980s, the German manufacturing sector had lost 18.4 per cent and 10.25 per cent respectively of its labour force (in terms of hours).

The deep recession of the 1990s brought still another phase in this trimming-down and weeding-out process. Starting in 1990, by which point it had risen only to its level of the end of the 1970s (when it was 30 per cent below the already reduced level of 1969), the manufacturing profit rate *fell by three quarters* by 1993. By 1995, moreover, it appears to have come back to no more than 50 or 60 per cent of its 1990 level.[75] With manufacturing profitability so depressed, the growth of manufacturing capital stock averaged 0.4 per cent for 1992 and 1993 (the last years for which data is available), while investment fell by 7.75 per cent and 23.7 per cent respectively in those years. By 1995, the level of manufacturing output was 10 per cent below that of 1991, and, in the intervening years, the manufacturing labour force had fallen by 16 per cent.

That the crisis was firmly rooted in the manufacturing sector could not have been clearer, and was evidenced in the continuing rapid growth of foreign direct invest-

---

74 OECD, *Economic Survey of Germany 1995–96*, Paris 1996, p. 9.
75 Ibid., p. 15, Figure 6.
76 Norman, 'Savage German Shakeout'.

ment, which averaged DM25–30 billion per annum between 1991 and 1994, then leapt to DM50 billion in 1995.[76] Meanwhile, the non-manufacturing sector continued to perform creditably. After peaking in 1992, a full 23 per cent above its level of 1973 and close to its level of the mid 1960s, non-manufacturers' profitability appears to have fallen only to a small degree, and was, by 1995, at most 11 per cent below its early 1990s levels. Clearly, the immunity of non-manufacturing producers from international competition continued to leave them a breathing space that was typically unavailable to their counterparts in manufacturing.[77]

Towards Recovery?

As with the Japanese economy, the precipitous rise of the currency in early 1995 brought the German economy to new depths, while its subsequent fall, largely engineered through the joint intervention of the German, Japanese, and US governments, made possible a new cyclical upturn. Nevertheless, again as in Japan, while exports responded promptly and vigorously to devaluation, the economy failed dismally to respond to exports, and one does not have to look far to find the reason. Even as the manufacturing sector began to revive, the rationalization of industry and the relocation of production abroad continued apace, while a new investment boom failed to materialize. 'Faced with high costs at home and stiff competition from abroad, companies have decentralized, stepped up foreign investment, and adopted lean techniques', while seeking to radically revise traditional collective-bargaining arrangements.[78] In 1996 alone, the manufacturing sector shed another 4 per cent of its workforce (in terms of hours), and, largely as a result of the continued shrinking of manufacturing, unemployment in West Germany in 1997, rose close to 10 per cent, a postwar record. Put simply, the manufacturing sector, even more than previously, could not get the economy turning over because, with productivity rising largely through labour-shedding and speed-up, investment failing to take off, and wages growing very slowly, it could not generate much in the way either of investment demand or consumer demand for the rest of the economy. Nor would a German government—more convinced than ever that the market had to be allowed to work freely to bring down German costs—step in, especially as the need for greater austerity and monetary tightening to prepare the way for European monetary unification became ever more pressing. To note that, in 1996, average hourly wages for German production workers stood at $31.87, compared to $17.74 for their counterparts in the US, gives a crude idea of what German manufacturing was up against. In any case, while the prospects for German manufacturing seemed to steadily improve as the process of slimming continued, the same could not be said for the German economy as a whole. The German economy, in short, was still in the process of adjusting to, and resolving, a problem of system-wide international over-capacity and over-production in manufacturing that remained, even after a quarter of a century, to be transcended.

---

77   OECD, *Economic Survey of Germany 1996*, p. 15, Figure 6. 'Low Deutschmark import prices reduced the scope for price increases by domestic competitors to foreign exporters. As a consequence, there has been a widening gap between the profit-markups in the tradable and non-tradable goods sectors.' (p. 9)

78   P. Norman and G. Bowley, 'Turmoil and Paralysis', *Financial Times*, 29 May 1997.

PART FIVE
Prosperity Regained?

Chapter 13

THE LONG DOWNTURN AND THE 'SECULAR TREND'

Since the victories of Reaganism-Thatcherism at the end of the 1970s, capital has greatly deepened its domination, especially in the US. Wage growth has been effectively repressed. Fiscal austerity, combined with tight credit, has brought universal disinflation. The rich have benefited from several rounds of tax reduction. Industry after industry has been deregulated so as to weaken unions. The global flow of capital has been progressively unfettered so that multinational corporations and banks can better scour the world to find the most profitable location for their multifarious activities. Finance has been unshackled, to create ever more baroque means to squeeze more money from money. The brutal stabilization programmes of the World Bank and the IMF have been accepted as gospel. What is more, the statist regimes of the former Soviet Union and Eastern Europe have collapsed, and China has taken the capitalist road. Yet, despite all this, things are not going smoothly for the world capitalist economy.

Ironically, there has been a very close correlation between the extent to which capital has got its way and the extent to which the performance of the advanced capitalist economies has deteriorated, cycle by cycle, since the 1960s. During the 1960s, when ostensibly over-strong labour movements, bloated welfare states, and hyper-regulating governments were at the height of their influence, the global economic boom reached historic peaks. Since then, as the neoclassical medicine has been administered in ever stronger doses, the economy has performed steadily less well. The 1970s were worse than the 1960s, the 1980s worse than the 1970s, and 1990s have been worse than the 1980s. Speaking only of results, and not for the moment of prospects, the long downturn has continued to defy capital's remedies. (See p. 240, Table 13.1.)

Faced with this dismal trajectory, mainstream economics has recurred to its standard theory of last resort, but now in its purest form. For many years, supply-side theorists located the source of secular stagnation in a crisis of productivity, which they attributed to the slacking and resistance of undisciplined and rebellious workers, emboldened by the social safety net, who precipitated and perpetuated the long downturn by refusing to reduce the growth of their wages in line with reduced output per person. But, with the downturn extending into the mid 1990s, and with only a few signs of let up, orthodox economists—having little choice but to recognize how profoundly labour's power has been reduced over the last two decades, and with how little positive effect on the economy—have implicitly relinquished their sociologized and politicized versions of Malthusianism, and reverted to its most pure classical rendering. The economy has not grown more vigorously,

Table 13.1. Declining economic dynamism, 1960–2005.
(Average annual per cent change.)

	1960–69	1969–79	1979–90	1990–95	1995–2000	1990–2000	2000–05
GDP							
US	4.2	3.2	3.2	2.5	4.1	3.3	2.6
Japan	10.1	4.4	3.9	1.5	1.3	1.4	1.2
Germany	4.4	2.8	2.3	2.1	2.0	2.1	0.7
Euro 12	5.3	3.2	2.4	1.6	2.7	2.2	1.4
G-7	5.1	3.6	3.0	2.5	1.9	3.1	–
GDP per capita							
US	3.3	2.5	1.9	2.5	4.1	3.3	2.6
Japan	9.0	3.4	4.0	1.5	1.7	1.6	1.3
Germany	3.5	2.8	1.9	2.5	1.9	2.2	0.8
G-7	3.8 (60–73)	2.1 (73–79)	1.9	2.1	2.8	2.5	1.7
Non-Residential Capital Stock (private business economy)							
US (net)	4.5	4.0	3.2	2.3	3.8	3.1	2.1
Japan (gross)	12.5	9.4	6.2	5.4	3.6	4.5	2.8
Germany (gross)	8.4	4.9	3.0	3.2	1.7	2.5	1.6
Industrial countries	5.0	4.2	3.1	5.3	3.6	3.3	2.1
Labour Productivity Total Economy (GDP/worker)							
US	2.3	1.2	1.3	1.4	2.0	1.7	2.2
Japan	8.6	3.7	3.0	0.8	1.3	1.0	1.5
Germany	4.2	2.5	1.3	2.8	2.4	2.5	1.5
Euro 12	5.1	2.9	1.8	2.1	1.3	1.7	1.4
G-7	4.8 (60–73)	2.8 (73–79)	2.6	1.7	–	–	–
Real Compensation Total Economy (per employee)							
US	2.7	1.0	0.8	0.6	0.6	2.4	1.6
Japan	7.5	3.9	1.7	0.9	0.3	0.6	0
Germany	5.7	3.0	0.8	3.0	1.6	2.3	0.2
Euro 12	5.8	3.2	0.6	1.2	0.8	1.1	0.4
Unemployment Rate							
US	4.8	6.2	7.1	6.5	4.6	5.6	5.4
Japan	1.4	1.7	2.5	2.6	4.1	3.3	5.0
Germany	0.8	2.1	5.8	7.2	8.3	7.7	8.7
Euro 15	2.3	4.6	9.1	9.3	9.0	9.2	7.7
G-7	3.1 (60–73)	4.9 (73–79)	6.8	6.7	6.4	6.6	–

Sources: OECD, *Historical Statistics, 1960–1995, 1995*, Table 2.15, 3.1, 3.2; 'Statistical Annex' *European Economy*, Autumn 2005, Tables 11 and 31; OECD, *Economic Outlook Database*, IMF, World Economic Outlook Database; Andrew Glyn, 'Imbalances of the Global Economy,' *New Left Review* 34 (July–August, 2005); Armstrong et al, *Capitalism Since 1945*, p. 356, Table A6.

many now contend, simply because its technological potential has, for the most part, been exhausted.

On the eve of the long downturn, in the late 1960s and early 1970s, economic orthodoxy, still under the sway of the neoclassical-Keynesian synthesis, saw no reason why the postwar Golden Age of growth and prosperity could not continue forever. Since the only potential problem for ongoing expansion was thought to be insufficient aggregate demand, and since aggregate demand could always be subsidized (and presumably reduced when necessary to control inflation), there was no reason to doubt that the economy could remain perpetually dynamic. Scientists and technologists, supported by ever greater expenditures on research and development, would provide an endless array of technological possibilities; capitalists, assured of growing markets, would adapt these discoveries to production and implement them at accelerated rates. As the OECD expressed the received wisdom in its early 1970s report: 'the industrial and commercial exploitation of the existing body of scientific and technical knowledge will continue to generate increases in productivity for a long time to come.'[1]

Today, however, economic orthodoxy has changed to adopt precisely the opposite viewpoint. After a quarter-century marked by snail-like growth of investment, productivity, and wages, more severe cyclical crises, weaker cyclical upturns, and rocketing unemployment, mainstream economists cannot—any more than could their boom-time predecessors—even consider the possibility that the individual profit maximizing and the competitive market mechanisms that drive the capitalist economy might themselves be responsible for secular economic problems. That the capitalist system might, by its very modi operandi, actually breed crises and long (though not permanent) downturns, as well as long booms, is simply not thinkable, despite the fact that long booms and long downturns have been chronic, if not cyclical, throughout capitalism's history from the start of the nineteenth century. According to the newly purified Malthusian consensus, the economy proved dynamic in the early postwar period and stagnant in the later postwar period for exogenous, essentially technological reasons. In the early postwar period, the economy boomed because stocks of unused technological knowledge allowed for preternaturally high rates of productivity growth on the part of both followers and leaders; but, as those stocks were used up, productivity growth slowed down. The long downturn has manifested no underlying economic problems, but merely a return to the technologically-determined norm after a period of abnormal dynamism. The US leader initially availed itself of the backlog of apparently powerful techniques left unused during the Great Depression but, as it did so, its growth naturally slowed down.[2] The follower economies in Europe and Japan initially had available to them the enormous shelf of unused technology already in use in the US, but, they used this up to make possible their postwar booms. As they caught up, their growth naturally fell back to the 'secular trend'. Indeed, as the propo-

---

1   OECD, *The Growth of Output*, p. 166. For official confidence in Keynesian demand subsidies as the solution to the economy's problems well into the 1970s, see P. MacCracken et al., *Towards Full Employment and Stability. Summary of a Report to the OECD by a Group of Independent Experts*, Paris, June 1977.

2   The locus classicus for this argument is W. J. Baumol, 'Productivity Growth, Convergence, and Welfare: What the Long-Run Data Show', *The American Economic Review*, vol. lxxvi, December 1986, especially pp. 1081–2. It is buttressed, for instance, by Krugman, *Peddling Prosperity*, pp. 59–63.

nents of this standpoint conclude, 'If seen in a broad secular perspective, the *explanandum* ... appears to be not so much the slowdown of the 1970s as the growth spurt of the previous two decades.'[3] On the premise that the US economy could grow at a *maximum* annual rate of 2.5 per cent, the US Federal Reserve committed itself during the first half of the 1990s to essentially permanent tight money, and is literally cheered on in so doing by leading mainstream economists, who urge the Fed not to give in to irresponsible politicians, unions, and publicists demanding looser credit and state subsidies to demand in the interests of impossible-to-secure higher rates of growth.[4] We do live in the best of all possible worlds, these economists tell US, it's just not as good as we hoped it would be.

Not all elements within the political and intellectual establishment, it must be said, are entirely pleased by this Panglossian prognosis. More right-wing and less politically insulated advocates of the free market are unable to accept so restrained an endorsement of capitalism. After all, the implementation of Thatcherism–Reaganism, given a massive ideological and material fillip by the fall of communism, was supposed to unleash entrepreneurial energies previously restrained by high taxes, inflexible labour markets, too large a welfare state, and too much state regulation of business. But if, after more than two decades of wage-cutting, tax-cutting, reductions in the growth of social expenditure, deregulation, and 'sound finance', the ever less fettered 'free market' economy is unable to perform half as well as in the 1960s, there might be some reason to question the dogma that the freer the market, the better the economic performance.

Unable to admit the feeble results so far achieved by close to two decades in the saddle of what could hardly be more profoundly pro-capitalist policy regimes, the publicists in charge of the *Economist* and the *Wall Street Journal*, as well as business economists of various political stripes, point to the striking advances in science and technology that have undoubtedly taken place in recent decades and conclude that growth and productiveness just *must* have been occurring at a rapid rate, especially in that paragon of the free market, the US economy.[5] The low growth of measured output and thus productivity, they conclude, is a statistical artefact, resulting from the inability to properly gauge the national product, especially in the service sector where the growth of output is notoriously difficult to measure.

The representatives of each of these standpoints, both the economists and the publicists, have an important point to make with respect to the other. But the focus of each is misplaced. Both mistake effect for cause, since both entirely ignore the long-term crisis of capital accumulation, manifested in the near-universal, radical and sustained slowdown in the growth of the capital stock—itself deriving from a crisis of profitability in manufacturing—which has been at the root not only of the sharply reduced growth of output and of productivity, but also cyclical instability and elevated unemployment.

The publicists of capitalist revival are on strong ground when they call into question mainstream economists' blithe accounting for sharply reduced productivity

---

3   N. Crafts and G. Toniolo, 'Postwar Growth: An Overview', in Crafts and Toniolo, eds, *Economic Growth in Europe Since 1945*. In 'the perspective of secular trends in "modern economic growth"... the period 1950–73 was truly exceptional ... [and] the subsequent growth record can hardly be regarded as unsatisfactory' (pp. 2, 25).

4   See, for instance, P. Krugman, 'Stay on their Backs', *The New York Times Magazine*, 4 February 1996.

5   See especially P. Woodwall, 'The Hitchhikers Guide to Cybernomics', *The Economist*, 28 September 1996.

growth after 1973, and for the quarter-century economic downturn more generally, as a return to normalcy—as the expression of the exhaustion of abnormally elevated postwar technological potentials and the reversion to a supposed 'secular trend'. The very idea of a 'normal' growth path for capitalism, to which the economy can be expected to return, as if to an equilibrium, appears speculative at best, in light of the long periods of either strongly above average or significantly below average growth that have marked the whole of capitalism's history, as well as the extraordinary transformations in the conditions under which capitalism has developed over the last century or century and a half.[6] In view of the succession from the long boom of the years 1850–73, to the 'Great Depression' of the early 1870s to the mid 1890s, to the prewar upturn of the later 1890s through World War I, to the Great Slump of the interwar period, to the boom of the quarter-century following World War II—why should one expect a return to an 'average' between 1973 and the present? Given, moreover, the extraordinary qualitative changes that have taken place in the advanced capitalist world over the last century—with respect to the nature of scientific and technical knowledge, the size of the agricultural and small-business sector, the level of demographic growth, the role and place of the state in the economy, the nature of firms, the degree of education of the labour force, and levels of expenditure on research and development (to name just a few important variables)—why should we expect the economy to tend to anything like a constant, or 'trend', rate of growth? Afterall, it is not the same economy as it used to be.

Far from appearing slow and stagnant, the scientific and technical progress of the past quarter-century gives the impression to many analysts of having been as rapid as before. It is not easy to determine the level of technological potential at any given juncture, or the rate of improvement in technology over any given period of time. Still, by the necessarily crude yardsticks by which technical change is measured, virtually all of the systematic studies point in the direction of the maintenance of past levels of improvement right through the long downturn, while virtually none supports the opposite conclusion.[7] Continuity of technical change, but a reduction in the ability to make use of it, which has resulted from the appearance of manufacturing over-capacity and over-production, the consequent fall in profitability, and the ensuing declines in the growth of investment and aggregate demand would of course be congruent with the argument of this text.

Most directly telling, however, against the interpretation of postwar boom and downturn in terms of technological potentials is that the actual historical path that the growth of productivity—let alone of investment, wages, or employment—has taken does not conform to what should have been expected, had productivity growth acceleration and deceleration been determined primarily by the appearance and exhaustion of technological possibilities. Had the decline in productivity growth been primarily driven by the using up of technological potentials, one would have expected the following: first, paths of productivity growth on the part of both the leader and the follower economies that declined both continuously and relatively

6 Crafts and Toniolo 'see the period from 1913 to 1973 as being an exceptional one in the history of "modern economic growth", in that it departed from the secular trend first (1913–45) by under- and then (1945–73) by over-performing it'. 'Postwar Growth', p. 1.

7 See, for instance, Z. Griliches, 'Productivity, R&D, and the Data Constraint', *American Economic Review*, vol. lxxxiv, March 1994.

slowly over the long term; second, a generalized process of catch-up mainly located in the manufacturing sector, where the pressures to compete internationally in tradable goods are particularly intense; third, the onset of a productivity growth slowdown only as the technological catch-up process by the followers in relation to the leaders approached completion. But in neither temporal nor sectoral terms do the postwar trends of productivity advance conform to the predicted patterns. Nor did the onset of the postwar productivity growth slowdown await the closing of the gap between followers and leader.

The US leader should have enjoyed its greatest productivity growth in the period immediately following the Great Depression or World War II, and seen its productiveness steadily decline thereafter. But there is virtually no correspondence between what was theoretically the technologically-driven and the actual path of productivity growth.

In US manufacturing, the course of productivity growth simply bore no relationship to the theory. Indeed, in this sector there is little sign that technological potential declined at all over the period. Between 1938 and 1950, when it should have been at its peak, average annual manufacturing productivity growth, at 2.7 per cent, was slightly below that for the whole period between 1938 and 1973.[8] Then, between 1950 and 1958, it fell sharply, to under 2.0 per cent, only to accelerate dramatically in the years between 1958 and 1973, to 3.5 per cent, when it should have been slowing down. Nor is there evidence of an exhaustion of technology in the subsequent period. In the years around the two oil crises of the 1970s, the average annual growth of manufacturing productivity did fall sharply. But from 1979 it once again accelerated markedly, and from that point until the present has proceeded at better than its average rate for the boom years of the long boom—at over 3 per cent per annum. Over the course of the 1990s, manufacturing productivity growth has been more vigorous than at any time since the early 1960s.

The productivity trend outside of manufacturing, or for the economy as a whole, is as problematic as that for manufacturing from the standpoint of the thesis of technological exhaustion, but for the opposite reason. Whereas the drop-off supposedly driven by the exhaustion of technology is non-existent within manufacturing, outside manufacturing the decline is far greater than could possibly be explained by such an exhaustion. For the long period from 1938 through 1973, productivity growth for the private business economy, as well as for the non-manufacturing sector, was fairly steady, except for modest fall-offs between 1950 and 1958 and 1965 and 1973, and averaged 2.6–2.7 per cent per annum. There is little evidence for much of a slowdown before 1973—especially once capacity utilization is taken into account. Yet, when private business and non-manufacturing productivity growth did fall, after 1973, the decline was not gentle, as in theory it should have been, but catastrophic. If what lay behind the productivity growth decline after 1973 was the using up of the exceptionally large backlog of major technological opportunities that had been left unused following the Great Depression, the rate of productivity growth outside of manufacturing, or in the private business economy as a whole, should surely have fallen no lower than the twentieth-century historical average. But, for almost a quarter of a century,

---

8   US Department of Commerce, *Historical Statistics of the United States*, Washington, DC 1970, Series D 685, p. 162.

Table 13.2. US productivity growth, 1890–1996.
(Average annual per cent change.)

	1890 –1913	1913 –29	1929 –38	1938 –50	1950 –58	1958 –65	1965 –73	1973 –79	1979 –90	1990 –95	1995 –2000
Mfgr	–	–	–	2.7	2.0	4.1	3.3	0.4	2.9	3.7	5.7
Nmfgr	–	–	–	2.7	2.5	2.5	2.4	1.9	0.6	0.9	2.2
Private business	–	–	–	2.7	2.2	3.3	2.6	1.2	1.5	1.7	2.6
GDP/hr	2.2	2.4	1.4	2.2	2.5	3.0	2.4	1.1	1.35	1.2	2.2
Total economy TFP	1.1	1.7	0.3	3.2	–	–	–	–	–	–	–
Private business TFP	–	–	–	–	1.1	2.5	1.6	0.5	0.3	0.7	0.9

Sources: for GDP/hr before 1950 and total economy TFP: A. Maddison, *Dynamic Forces in Capitalist Development*, Oxford 1991, p. 71, Table 3.13; For manufacturing and private business TFP: BLS, 'Multifactor Productivity Trends.' See also Appendices I and II.

between 1973 and 1996, labour productivity in the private business economy and that for the economy outside manufacturing has averaged 1.5 per cent and 1.0 per cent, respectively. These rates were far below those which prevailed in any other periods of comparable length since 1890—leaving aside the years of the Great Depression.[9] Obviously, the productivity growth decline that has taken place between 1973 and 1996 for the whole economy, as well as that outside of manufacturing, has been anything but a 'return to trend'. (See Table 13.2.)

The follower economies diverged as sharply from the predicted pattern as did the US leader. These economies should, according to the theory, have had the greatest potential for catch-up at the start of the period, and seen it decline thereafter. But, in the G-7 economies outside the US, taken both in aggregate and individually, productivity growth, far from pursuing a relatively continuous downward path as technological potentials were used up, actually accelerated during the 1960s compared to the 1950s and, neither in manufacturing nor in the private business economy, slowed down in any clear way before 1973. When the productivity growth decline occurred, moreover, it took place not in relatively continuous fashion, but drastically and all at once, falling by at least half in the years 1973–79, compared to the years 1960–73. It did so, moreover, in all of the follower advanced capitalist countries at almost exactly the same point in time. It is very difficult to see how a process of using up technological potential could have brought about a pattern of sharp, discontinuous, and universal fall in productivity growth such as that which occurred after 1973.

Nor does the sectoral pattern of productivity decline among the followers conform to the exhaustion of technology thesis any better than the temporal pattern. According to the theory, the force that theoretically drives catch-up—the pressure imposed by competition upon the followers to emulate the leader's technology—

9   For the period before 1938, see A. Maddison, *Dynamic Forces in Capitalist Development*, Oxford 1991, p. 71; A. Maddison, *Monitoring the World Economy 1820–92*, OECD, Paris 1995, p. 41. Between 1973 and 1992, total factor productivity in the total economy has crept up at an average annual rate of 0.18 per cent, compared to 1.72 per cent between 1950 and 1973 and 1.50 per cent between 1913 and 1950. (p. 42).

is mainly applicable to the manufacturing sector, constituted mostly by tradables, and not really to non-manufacturing, relatively untouched as it is by international trade and competition. But, against the expectations of the theory, catch-up has gone significantly less far in the manufacturing sector. In manufacturing, in the period of the long downturn since 1973, the drive to catch up has been slow and patchy at best; this is because US manufacturing productivity growth since 1979 has actually been as fast or faster than that of Germany, France, and Canada, though somewhat slower than that of Japan, Italy, and the UK. In contrast, in the private business economy as a whole, the closing of the gap has continued apace between 1973 and the present, as the G-7 follower economies have continued to maintain their superiority in their productivity growth rates over that of the US much better outside of than within the manufacturing sector. In fact, by 1992, in terms of output per hour for the whole economy, West Germany, France, and Canada had actually surpassed the US, and the US ranked only ninth in the world.[10]

Nevertheless, one should be wary of attributing this closing of the gap outside of manufacturing to any great vitality of the catch-up process during the period of the long downturn. This is because the followers have caught up to the US in this sector in spite of the *sharp slowdown* in their own rates of non-manufacturing productivity growth from 1973, and only because non-manufacturing productivity in the US in this era has barely grown at all. Had US productivity growth achieved even its average rate between 1890 and 1973, catch-up outside of manufacturing in the period since 1973 would have been minimal to non-existent.[11]

Finally—and perhaps most disconfirming of the thesis that the exhaustion of the opportunities for catch-up can explain the decline in productivity growth—the deep, discontinuous, and simultaneous drop-off in productivity growth that took place after 1973 occurred at a point when productivity levels in the G-7 economies (aside from Canada) were still only 45–55 per cent of the US level in manufacturing and 55–70 per cent of the US level in the economy as a whole.[12] It encompassed, moreover, the US leader and the G-7 followers, and did so at precisely the same time and more or less to the same degree. It is impossible to see how the exhaustion of opportunities for closing of the gap could have brought about such a pattern.

The idea that productivity growth should be understood as taking place primarily by way of followers' adoption of the leaders' technology, and leaders' ever slower pushing back of the technological frontier is so schematic as to be positively misleading. Over the long period between 1890 and 1950, the US actually *extended* its lead over virtually all followers.[13] By the same token, in the postwar half-century,

---

10   N.F.R. Crafts, 'Economic Growth in East Asia and Western Europe Since 1950: Implications for Living Standards', *National Institute Economic Review*, no. 4, October 1997, p. 81, Table 6.

11   Average annual growth of GDP per hour worked in the US between 1890 and 1973 was 2.4 per cent. Between 1973 and 1987 it was 2.6 per cent in Germany, 3.5 per cent in Japan, 2.3 per cent in the UK, 2.6 per cent in Italy, 3.2 per cent in France, and 1.8 per cent in Canada. S. N. Broadberry, 'Convergence: What the Historical Record Shows', in B. van Ark and N. Crafts, eds, *Quantitative Aspects of Post-War European Growth*, Cambridge 1996, p. 330, Table 8.1.

12   Broadberry, 'Convergence', pp. 336–7, Tables 8.3 and 8.4; Hulten, 'From Productivity Slowdown to New Investment Opportunities', in H. Siebert, ed., *Capital Flows in the World Economy*, Tubingen 1991, p. 68.

13   'From 1870 to 1950, 13 of the [16] advanced capitalist countries which Baumol examined [to demonstrate catch-up and convergence after 1950] were falling behind US productivity levels.' Maddison, *Monitoring the World Economy*, p. 45.

Table 13.3. Labour productivity growth of G-7 economies excluding the US.
(Average annual per cent change.)

	1951–58	1958–66	1966–73	1973–79
Private business	3.6	5.1	5.2	2.3
Manufacturing	3.4	5.7	6.2	3.5

Source: AGH.

Japanese manufacturing productivity has not just caught up, but forged ahead of that of the US in many key lines of production. By 1992, according to McKinsey Associates, Japanese manufacturing productivity surpassed that of the US in five of the nine industries studied (steel, automotive parts, metalworking, cars, consumer electronics), was ahead by at least 50 per cent in metalworking and steel, and was approximately equal in two others (computers, and soap and detergent). On the other hand, in the two industries studied in which Japan lagged behind, indeed very far behind, the US (food and beer), the explanation clearly had nothing to do with technological potentials and everything to do with economic regulations and protection that allowed, even encouraged, those industries to avoid adopting readily available labour-saving techniques.[14]

The notion that there is a given armoury of technology, which the leader is best at improving, but which the followers can draw on to increase productivity more rapidly than the leader can through innovation, is too simple to grasp the actual processes of technical change. In the first place, levels of expenditure on research and development and on human capital (including the education of technicians or engineers, skilled workers, and unskilled workers), will certainly have a significant effect on technological advance, and thus productivity growth, yet these can be quite independent from technological leadership or followership. In addition, technological advance usually takes place in the course of capital accumulation itself through learning by doing, economies of scale, and so forth. Technical advances achieved in the process of production will, moreover, often stimulate breakthroughs in the laboratory, as well as vice versa. It follows that the speed-up of economic growth, made possible by rapid capital accumulation, *itself* tends to lead to the *acceleration* of productivity growth, making it possible for the leader to stay ahead or the follower to leap ahead.

The point is obviously not to challenge the proposition that, all else being equal, a greater availability of unused technology will allow for faster growth. It is rather, to point to the need, in explaining the postwar growth process, to expand the focus beyond the degree of unused technology to include the economy's *capacity to adopt* what technology exists and, in particular, its *capacity to create* new technology, as well as to maintain cognizance of the idea that technological advance may be as much a function of economic growth—and thus the (not-immediately-technological) conditions making for growth—as vice versa.

14 McKinsey Global Institute, *Manufacturing Productivity*, Washington, DC, October 1993.

Catch-up was thus certainly critical in explaining the accelerated growth of the period of the boom between 1950 and 1973. But it could assume such a central role only because of certain, historically quite specific, conditions that came to prevail in the postwar epoch: first, the dramatic increase in the capacities for capital accumulation and technical change accrued by the European and Japanese economies as a result of the internal socio-economic, political, and institutional transformations that took place in these economies in the wake of World War II; second, the corresponding reduction in the capacity for capital accumulation and technical advance which affected the US economy, not only as a result of domestic socio-economic and institutional developments, but especially the stepped-up orientation to overseas investment of its leading manufacturers and financiers; and third, the dramatic reduction in barriers to the free flow of goods and investment, which was itself fed, and overseen, by a US hegemon that, at least for a time, appreciated the necessity to nurture the economies of its partners and rivals in order to realize the interests of its own leading capitalists and its state. Catch-up did not, moreover, work by itself to power accelerated productivity growth; it was heavily supplemented by large-scale, 'indigenous' technological improvements in the follower economies themselves, advances that emerged from learning by doing which was itself a by-product of their unusually high levels of investment in new plant and equipment. In line after line—textiles, cars, steel, consumer electronics, machinery and so on—the followers did not just match the state of the art established in the US, they surpassed it by introducing major technological advances of their own.

As to the period of the long downturn from 1973 to the present, the exhaustion of opportunities for catching up is incapable of explaining the productivity decline, let alone the long downturn itself, because, as emphasized, the pattern of sudden, sharp, universal, and simultaneous productivity growth drop-off during the years 1973–79, which followed upon an extended period of quite high, universal, and steady productivity growth increase, simply cannot be explained in terms of the exhaustion of backlogs of technological opportunities—especially since so much of that backlog was still available and unused in the follower economies when the productivity growth decline began.

That pattern is, however, explicable in terms of the reduction in the advanced capitalist economies' capacity to realize and develop their technological potentials, which resulted, as I have argued, from the sudden, sharp, universal, and simultaneous falls in growth of the capital stock, especially in manufacturing, that took place across the advanced capitalist world. The reduction of capital accumulation was a function of the decline in the rate of profit, especially in manufacturing, that took place between 1965 and 1973—and also between 1973 and 1982—in all of the advanced capitalist economies, taken individually and in aggregate. Sharply reduced manufacturing profitability and investment growth brought about sharply increased instability, manifested in three recessions more serious than any that had occurred between 1950 and 1973, as well as unemployment at Great Depression levels (outside the US). It is impossible to see how a reduction in technological potential could have universally occurred in such a sharp and discontinuous way as to have accounted for such developments. But, the sharply reduced growth of investment—as well as the increased instability, decreased capacity utilization, and elevated unemployment that accompanied that reduced growth of investment—must surely account for a great part of the productivity drop-off, as must also (in the US at least) the growing use of labour relative to capital in production that followed from the holding down of wage growth that was itself the direct, immediate response to the fall in profitability. An exhaustion of opportunities for catch-up cannot account for the secular decline of productivity growth, let alone the long downturn; but the long downturn is itself largely responsible for the secular decline in productivity growth. By the same token, were the conditions that have held profitability down and that precipitated the long downturn to be transcended, the economy would find no overriding technological barriers to very substantially raising investment, and on that basis, productivity growth and economic dynamism.

Chapter 14

A NEW LONG UPTURN?

While the long downturn is inexplicable in terms of the exhaustion of technological opportunities, its great length, specifically its extension through the middle of the 1990s, certainly cries out for further explanation. After all, the processes of wage repression resulting from the success of capital in class conflict, and of the shakeout of high-cost, low-profit means of production resulting from the sharpening of intercapitalist competition and periodic recession, have been proceeding for quite a long time, with a good deal of intensity, especially in the US, but also in Germany and Japan. Why have these processes failed to bring about a reduction of production costs sufficient to restore the rate of profit, particularly in manufacturing, and found a new boom? To this question, a broad range of commentators in the business press, the mass media, and multifarious journals of opinion have been saying, in effect, that in fact *they have*—that the international economy has suddenly entered an era of 'turbo-charged capitalism' and that the performance of the US economy in particular, going back at least to the start of the 1990s, if not the 1980s, and most especially in the last few years, manifests an economic revolution that has opened up a 'new era'. Even the normally cautious head of the US Federal Reserve, Alan Greenspan, has allowed that the US economy just might be going through a 'once in a lifetime' spurt in productiveness. Have we finally transcended the long downturn and entered a new secular boom? And, if not, why not?

1. A New Age of US Growth and Hegemony?

Although the view that the US economy has entered a 'new age' has become something of a commonplace, the empirical foundations for this claim are, as has been emphasized, remarkably hard to find in the basic macroeconomic data for the cyclical upturn of the 1990s. What, then, has been behind the view's increasing acceptance?

The fundamental, intuitive basis for the idea that a new economic epoch has arrived, requiring a 'new paradigm' to understand it, is unquestionably the spectacular performance of the stock market. Between the second half of 1989—when it recovered its level on the eve of the crash of October 1987—and October 1997, the stock market tripled in value. From the end of 1994 through October 1997, it somewhat more than doubled. In the two years ending April 1998, it rose by 60 per cent. Between the cyclical trough of March 1991 and July 1996, the financial net worth of the US public mushroomed by over $5.5 trillion, the equivalent of the total amount of new saving which American households had accumulated over the previous twenty-five years.[1] Such spectacular gains, it is widely assumed, just must be indicative of a positive transformation of the real economy.

Yet it should be obvious that, in itself, the performance of the stock market in the short and even medium run is at best a gross indicator of the performance of the underlying economy. As recently as 1991, a boom in the Japanese stock market of roughly the same order of magnitude—which accompanied, moreover, a half-decade or so of economic growth that was rather more impressive than that which the US has recently experienced—issued, unceremoniously, in deep recession. True, the analogy with Japan is, in important respects, off the mark, since the US economy's upturn in the 1990s has brought significantly greater gains in profitability than did Japan's of the second half of the 1980s. Still, there can be little doubt that the bull run of the 1990s has far out-distanced any parallel gains in the underlying economy.

By spring 1998, the ratio between stock prices and earnings had soared into the high 20s, well above its pre-crash level in October 1987, more than double its average of 13.7 between 1871 and 1992, and an all-time high. The so-called 'Tobin's Q', which measures the ratio of companies' stock-market value to their net assets at current cost of replacement was, at 130 per cent of underlying corporate net worth, higher than at any time since 1920, double its long-run average, and about three times higher than a decade ago. There are two possible responses to these figures. One is to believe that the US economy has entered a 'new era'. The other is to conclude that the stock market has overshot the recovery of the economy. It is true that the profit picture has improved significantly for US firms in recent years—between 1989 and 1997, corporate profits increased by about 82 per cent and a gain in profits. Yet such a gain in profits cannot justify the tripling in stock prices that took place in the same period, and gains in actual economic performance over the 1990s that parallel the gain in profits are, as emphasized, hard to locate.

The main direct argument for the notion that there has been a qualitative improvement in US economic performance is that the fundamental macroeconomic statistical series denying the reality of such a qualitative improvement—namely, that for the growth of output and thus productivity in the private business economy—is fatally flawed. US productivity growth, it is argued, exploded upwards, but the statistical evidence documenting this explosion has eluded the data gatherers because it has occurred in new lines within the service sector, where the growth of output is difficult or impossible to measure. Nevertheless, the fact remains that, while some gains in productivity outside manufacturing over the past quarter-century or so may well have gone unregistered in the official statistics, it appears to be *statistically impossible* that even their full incorporation in the data could much alter the official picture. The point is that those who argue that productivity growth outside manufacturing has gone so under-recorded as to account for the recorded (but in their view non-existent) productivity crisis cannot explain how productivity growth outside manufacturing could possibly have been *so much more* under-recorded in the quarter-century following 1973 than in the quarter-

1   M. Wolf, 'On a Wing and a Prayer', *Financial Times*, 17 September 1996; M. Wolf, '1929 and All That', *Financial Times*, 7 October 1997.

century before as to have determined the enormous *fall-off* that occurred between these two periods. The reason that they cannot is that the *increase* in size of the sectors where productivity growth is plausibly under-recorded was far too small to have accounted for more than a fraction of the *change for the worse* in aggregate productivity growth that took place, even on the most generous assumptions about the degree of under-recording that took place.

According, then, to Zvi Griliches, a leading contemporary student of US productivity growth, the 'unmeasurable sector' of the economy—where productivity growth either cannot be properly gauged or is at least subject to legitimate doubt—could very well include all of the service sector (aside from the transportation and utilities industries, which are tolerably well-measured) plus the construction industry. By this definition, the output of perhaps half of the private business economy was measurable with a good degree of confidence in the immediate postwar period, whereas the fraction today may be under one-third.[2] Still, as D.E. Sichel has pointed out, the *growth* of this 'unmeasurable sector' was limited to just 5.6 per cent for the years 1973–79 as against 1950–72 and another 3.8 per cent for the years 1980–90 compared to the years 1973–79. For this reason, even if the *amount* of unmeasured productivity growth that took place in the 'unmeasurable sector' is assumed to have been (an extreme maximum) of 2.4 per cent for the years 1973–90—so that productivity growth in the 'unmeasurable sector' averaged 3.4 per cent, rather than the 1.0 per cent that was recorded—only a fairly trivial 0.23 per cent of the total productivity growth *drop-off* of 1.5–2 per cent that took place in the years 1973–90 from the years 1950–73 would be accounted for.[3] The point, again, is that the only unrecorded productivity growth relevant to the explanation of the change for the worse in measured productivity growth that took place after 1973 occurred in the *addition* to the 'unmeasurable sector that was made after that date; this is because all other unmeasured productivity growth, whatever its estimated size, would presumably apply equally to, and thus raise the productivity growth totals equally for, the periods both before and after 1973.'[4]

To reach the same conclusion another way: even on the extreme assumptions, first, that, before 1973, all of the non-manufacturing labour productivity growth that occurred was perfectly recorded and, second, that after 1973, 50 per cent of the non-manufacturing productivity growth that actually took place went unrecorded, the average annual rate of US labour productivity growth outside manufacturing from 1973 to the present, at 0.75 per cent rather than 0.5 per cent as recorded, would still have been less than one-third its level of something over 2.5 per cent for the period 1968–73, and still at record lows.[5]

2   Griliches, 'Productivity, R&D and the Data Constraint'.

3   D. E. Sichel, 'The Productivity Slowdown: Is a Growing Unmeasurable Sector the Culprit?', The Brookings Institution, unpublished manuscript, November 1995.

4   It should be noted that if to take account of hypothetically unmeasured productivity growth that took place in the years 1948-73, one were to accept an upward adjustment of the rate of productivity growth that was symmetrical with one for the years 1973 to the present sufficient to significantly raise the rate of productivity growth and thus output growth for those years, it would have the effect of lowering levels of productivity and output in 1948 far below the lowest levels that could possibly have obtained. It would, for example, suggest very implausible levels of poverty.

5   Robert J. Gordon suggests that at most one-third of post-1973 productivity growth is unmeasured. 'Comments and Discussion', in *Brookings Papers on Economic Activity*, no. 2, 1994, p. 327.

In fact, much reduced productivity growth outside of manufacturing is just what was to be expected, given the greatly reduced rate at which workers have been equipped with new plant and equipment over the course of the long downturn, especially since the start of the 1980s. Between 1982 and 1996, labour productivity in non-manufacturing grew at the feeble average annual pace of 0.5 per cent. But this was hardly surprising since in these days the non-manufacturing net capital-labour ratio grew at an average annual rate of 0.3 per cent. Between 1950 and 1973, when non-manufacturing labour productivity was growing at an average annual rate of 2.6 per cent, the net capital-labour ratio grew at an average annual rate of 2.0 per cent.

Those who believe productivity growth has been greatly under-measured in recent years might point out, in response, that investment in computer and peripheral equipment, as well as other sorts of information-processing technology has been growing extremely rapidly, and might therefore suggest that under-measurement of its contribution may account for a significant part of ostensibly unmeasured productivity growth. The capital stock of computers and peripheral equipment increased at the phenomenal average annual rate of 30 per cent between 1975 and 1985, and near 20 per cent between 1985 and 1993. The fact remains that, even by 1993, the share of computer and peripheral equipment in net capital stock was just 2 per cent. This was more than triple its level of 1975, but, even granting huge productive powers to computers, clearly too small to make much of a dent in aggregate private business productivity.[6]

Beyond unjustifiable deductions from the stock-market boom and unsubstantiated claims about unmeasured productivity growth and the impact of computers, it is the combination of low rates of price increase and low unemployment that has been most vaunted as indicative of the emergence of a so-called 'new paradigm'. In recent years, the average annual increase of the consumer price index, at under 3 per cent, has fallen to levels not seen since the mid 1960s, while unemployment has fallen below 5 per cent for the first time since 1970. Had all else been equal, these might have been significant achievements. As it is, they are hardly a cause for celebration, for the *costs* of their achievement far outweigh the gains that they represent for the great majority of the working population.

It should be noted first that even contemporary economic orthodoxy has failed to establish that inflation rates of up to 8 per cent have *any* negative impact on the economy's vitality. As even the International Monetary Fund has been obliged to admit, there is no evidence that reducing inflation below 8 per cent yields any gains whatsoever in terms of growth or living standards.[7] For this reason, there are strong grounds for believing that the grand crusade to control inflation, while very costly to most people, has had little positive effect, except, of course, for the owners and lenders of capital.

The low rates of inflation and unemployment of the recent period are unremarkable, for they are the direct result of the extraordinarily slow growth of both demand and wage costs. The slow growth of aggregate demand is evident in the slow growth of GDP. Following the recession of 1990, the US economy experienced 'the most

6 S. D. Oliner and D. E. Sichel, 'Computers and Output Growth Revisited: How Big is the Puzzle?', *Brookings Papers on Economic Activity*, no. 2, 1994, pp. 276, 279.

7 IMF, *World Economic Outlook*, October 1996, pp. 120–1. See also M. Sarel, 'Non-Linear Effects of Inflation on Economic Growth', *IMF Staff Papers*, vol. xliii, March 1996.

sluggish recovery in modern times'.[8] Even by the end of 1996, the average annual rate of growth for the six years of cyclical upturn from 1990 through 1996 was 2 per cent (2.4 per cent in 1996). Nor is the slow growth of aggregate demand a mystery; it is the direct expression of the slow growth of investment demand, arising from low profit rates and secularly high real interest rates, the stagnation of consumer demand resulting from the long-term stagnation of wages, and the collapse of governmental demand stemming from the sharp turn to budget balancing under Clinton.

If the growth of demand pulling up prices has been muted, the growth of costs pushing up prices, especially as represented by the growth of wages, has been all but non-existent. Between 1990 and 1996, the average annual growth of the real wage in the business economy was 0.2 of 1 per cent. By the end of 1996, as one consequence, median income for a family of four was still 3 per cent below its level of 1989 and just 1.6 per cent above the level of 1973.[9] It is true that such very low wage growth as has prevailed throughout the 1990s has not always been compatible with the relatively low rates of unemployment that have recently been achieved. But it can hardly be surprising in light of recent economic history. It is not only that workers' organizations have been profoundly weakened under the decades-long assault of employers. It is also that conditions in the labour market itself, specifically high levels of job insecurity and intensified competition for falling numbers of decent jobs, have powerfully and directly depressed wage aspirations. While the proportion of jobless has been low, the proportion of those laid off has been extremely high. In the 1990s, the share of workers losing jobs (held a year or longer) jumped significantly, to 15 per cent for the three years ending 1995. This rate of job loss was higher than at any other time since the Bureau of Labor Statistics began gathering data on job loss in 1981—including the recession years of the early 1980s and early 1990s—and is especially significant in light of the fact that displaced employees who find new jobs earn on average 14 per cent less in their new posts. Nor has the pace of downsizing shown any sign of slowing down.[10]

Similarly, while the size of the unemployed population putting downward pressure on wages has been relatively small, the size of the *employed* population putting downward pressure on wages has been very great. The rise of a low-wage economy has been a central theme of this text, and it has been noted that over half of the labour force experienced wage declines of between 8 per cent and 12 per cent during the period between 1979 and the present. One of the manifestations of this trend is that, today, 'nearly a third of all workers are stuck in lower-skilled jobs paying less than $15,000 a year. So employers can find plenty of eager applicants willing to jump ship and trade up to fill well-paying jobs that don't require a college degree—a category that ... covers three-quarters of all jobs.'[11] Put another way, at least a third of the employed labour force, though actually holding jobs, constitute a huge 'surplus army of employed', functioning along with the unemployed to place powerful downward pressure on wages.

8   *Business Week*, 14 July 1997.

9   Fiore and Brownstein, 'All But the Poor Got Richer in '96' *Los Angeles Times*, 30 September 1997.

10   As G. Koretz summed up his report on the most recently reported data on job loss early in 1997, '... the downsizing trend continues unabated.' 'The Downside of Downsizing', *Business Week*, 4 April 1997.

11   For the material in this paragraph, and much else of interest on current economic conditions, see A. Bernstein, 'Sharing Prosperity', *Business Week*, 1 September 1997.

Table 14.1. The cost of controlling inflation in the US: comparing 1950–65 to 1990–97.

(Average annual per cent change.)

	Consumer price index	Unemployment rate	GDP	Real hourly wages
1990–97	3.0	6.2	2.8	0.5
1950–65	1.8	5.0	4.0	3.1

Sources: See Appendix II Sources for Main Variables.

The US government, along with those of all the other advanced capitalist countries, has, of course, for almost two decades, made the reduction of price, and especially wage, increases the supreme goal of policy, and has, to this end, consciously and intentionally traded off economic growth and the living standards of the vast majority for reduced inflation. But just how modest has been its achievement can be grasped when the 1990s numbers on unemployment and the rise of prices are juxtaposed to the corresponding figures for the growth of output and of wages, and then compared with their counterparts for the years 1950–65.

The fact remains, however, that, in terms of its own *raison d'être*, the unending campaign against 'inflation' has been an unmitigated success. The control of inflation has been manna from heaven—or perhaps, more precisely, from the Federal Reserve—for the leading capitalist interests in today's economy. The benefit for the 'finance industry' in particular has been enormous, its loans retaining virtually all their nominal worth and the flow of its investments to the stock market eased by stable interest rates. Still, the overriding significance for capital of the misleadingly termed 'fight against inflation' is to be found in the repression of wage growth; it is only the stagnation of wages that has made possible the continued making of profits in a private business economy outside of manufacturing that has been unable to raise average annual productivity growth much above 1 per cent a year during the period from 1990 through 1996—or in fact over a quarter of a century. Most indicative of the real condition of the US economy, then, has not been its ability to control prices, but its dependence on controlling the price of labour, its *incapacity* to accommodate virtually any real wage growth. Alan Greenspan made clear how much confidence he has in the view that the US economy has entered a new era when in October 1997, in the wake of little more than a year of 3–4 per cent growth of GDP, he warned that he might soon have to raise interest rates. This was not, as he made explicit, to keep down the growth of prices, which had in fact been decreasing, but to control the increase in wages. Greenspan admitted that there was still 'little evidence of wage acceleration'.[12] What he failed, however, to point out was that the real wage in the

12   In Greenspan's words, '… the performance of the labor markets this year suggests that the economy has been on an unsustainable track … Short of a marked slowing in the demand for goods and services and, hence, labor—or a degree of acceleration of productivity growth that appears unlikely—the imbalance between the growth in labor demand and the expansion of potential labor supply of recent years must erode the current state of inflation quiescence.' 'Excerpts From Fed Chief's Statement', *New York Times*, 10 September 1997.

business economy had succeeded in reaching its level of 1988, and that in the manufacturing sector its level of 1986, only by the middle of 1997.[13]

2. A New Global Boom?

It is, however, one thing to demonstrate that actual US economic performance during the 1990s has shown little sign of a decisive economic turnaround; it is quite another to demonstrate that a new secular boom is off the agenda. From the standpoint of this text, the fundamental condition for a definitive transcendence of the long downturn is the overcoming of the secular problem of manufacturing over-capacity and over-production, as manifested in a *system-wide* recovery of profitability. Has such a recovery occurred, or is it in the offing?

The decade of the 1990s has been mostly one of crisis for both the Japanese and German economies, with the rate of profit in their private business sectors falling by mid-decade below their levels at the end of the 1980s, largely due to steep declines of profitability in their manufacturing sectors. For these one-time economic miracles, recoveries in profitability sufficient for the restoration of their former dynamism would require major turnarounds. (See p. 7, Figure 0.3 and p. 8, Figure 0.4.)

In the US, in sharp contrast, profitability *had* rebounded significantly. Despite the weakness of the cyclical upturn, the rate of profit in the private business sector had increased steadily over the course of the 1990s. By 1996, it had, for the first time since the start of the long downturn, decisively surpassed its level of 1973, achieving its level of 1969, 20–25 per cent below its boom time peaks, and, by 1997, it had risen 7 per cent further. Making this recovery possible was, in part, the resiliency of the non-manufacturing sector. There profitability had never fallen all that greatly, had made significant recoveries in both the late 1970s and the early to mid 1980s, and had risen over the course of the 1990s above its 1969 level, to within 15–20 per cent of its heights in the boom. But the truly dynamic element was obviously the manufacturing sector: rising by 25 per cent above its average for the second half of the 1980s, 100 per cent above the terrible lows of the early 1980s, and about a third above the levels registered at the end of the Keynesian 1970s, the manufacturing profit rate managed by 1995 and 1996 to exceed its level of 1973 for the first time and to come to within about 30 per cent of its level at the peak of the boom.

The practical significance of this recovery was considerably amplified by corporations' success during the 1990s, first, in reversing the trend of the 1980s toward the accumulation of debt and, second, in exploiting the tax breaks that they had secured with the massive shift in political power in favour of capital that had taken place since the 1960s. Net interest payments had taken 35 per cent of manufacturing corporate profits between 1982 and 1992, up from just 15 per cent between 1973 and 1979. But they consumed only 17 per cent of corporate profits between 1992 and 1996. Between 1965 and 1973, after-tax profitability in corporate manufacturing fell 41.6 per cent to set off the long downturn, a couple of points *more* than pre-tax profitability had fallen in the same period. But by 1996, whereas the recovery of pre-tax

---

13   The BLS's indices of real hourly compensation in the business economy and manufacturing stood, respectively, at 99.1 in 1988 and 100.6 in 1986, and 99.7 and 100.8, respectively, in early to mid 1997.

profitability had left it still 30 per cent short of its boom-time peaks of 1965–66, that of after-tax profitability left it only 16 per cent below that high point.

Very recent positive developments in the US economy, notably in its manufacturing sector, have not only reflected the rise in profitability, but have helped to carry it further. Above all, year-on-year increases in investment in new plant and equipment, which were almost non-existent between 1985 and 1992, have suddenly become very large indeed, averaging approximately 10 per cent between 1993 and 1997 in both the private business economy and in manufacturing.[14] This new and rapid investment growth had a positive impact on already rising manufacturing productivity growth, which averaged an impressive 4.4 per cent between 1993 and 1996, contributing centrally to the parallel rise in the manufacturing profit share, and thereby the manufacturing profitability revival. Moreover, coming on top of a decade-long fall of the dollar against the mark and yen, the acceleration of manufacturing productivity growth, in combination with still stagnant wages, made it possible for manufacturing exports to rise sharply, at 11 per cent per annum between 1993 and 1997, thereby enhancing the growth of manufacturing output, feeding back into the revival of profitability, and making for a virtuous cycle of a sort last seen in the early 1960s. Outside manufacturing, there is still little sign of a break from the long-term stagnation of productivity. Nevertheless, the profitability rise that has taken place there has made for an even greater increase in investment growth than in manufacturing, and brought about a major increase in the expansion of output. Indeed, in 1997, the US economy finally achieved—for the first time during its supposedly miraculous recovery—a true boom year, securing outstanding gains in just about every significant variable: GDP, investment, productivity, wages, and employment.

The ultimate issue, of course, is whether the economy can sustain its momentum. This amounts to the question of whether or not it can extend and consolidate its recovery of profitability by continuing to ward off or counteract both upward pressures on costs resulting from rising wage growth (or falling productivity growth) at home, and downward pressures on prices, resulting from intensifying competition from its leading international rivals. This question takes on special urgency in light of the fact that the US recovery was built precisely upon historically unprecedented wage repression and dollar devaluation.

In 1997, for the first time in five years, real compensation rose noticeably, by 1.5 per cent, and was growing much faster than that in the second half of 1997 and the first half of 1998. Clearly, ever lower rates of unemployment and recent rapid growth, as well as the lengthening expansion, have begun to hit home. Even now, however, the pressures militating against the *disruptive* growth of wages are extraordinarily powerful, and provide perhaps the strongest basis for believing that the ongoing US revival can continue. Even in 1997, the growth of unit labour costs for the private business economy as a whole was still lagging behind price increases. This is not to deny that wage growth could conceivably undercut profitability. It is rather to contend that the limits of the US recovery in the medium to long run are likely to be found more in limitations on the broader capacity of the US economy

---

14 Though these are not yet large enough to bring about a decisive increase in the rate of growth of the capital stock.

to maintain its vitality, and thereby to accommodate increased wage growth, than in any autonomous push from wages beyond productivity and prices. What will, in the last analysis, determine the fate of the upward trend of profitability in the US will not be domestic economic developments alone, but those developments in relationship to systemic and international ones. The fundamental question is whether, in the course of its current halting cyclical economic recovery, the world economy can finally transcend the over-capacity and over-production in manufacturing which have fettered economic growth in the advanced capitalist economies since the long downturn began at the end of the 1960s.

Slowing Demand, Accelerating Exports

From the start of the long downturn, of course, the advanced capitalist economies sought to restore economic dynamism by imposing ever greater restrictions on the growth of wages, direct and indirect, as well as, from the end of 1970s, on the supply of credit and the size of government deficits. This programme was supposed to raise profitability in aid of revived capital investment and thereby renewed dynamism, directly by holding down costs and indirectly by intensifying intercapitalist competition so as to weed out less productive, less profitable means of production. Nevertheless, it failed to accomplish its purpose, mainly because the underlying problem behind reduced profitability was not so much generalized upward pressure from direct and indirect wage costs, as downward pressure on prices resulting from over-investment leading to over-capacity and over-production in manufacturing. Since the required investment surge never materialized, the accelerating reduction in the growth of wage and social spending costs and in the availability of credit throughout the period could not but issue in the ever declining growth of aggregate demand, exacerbating manufacturing over-capacity and slowly strangling the economy.

The Keynesian subsidies to demand that marked the era from the mid to late 1960s to the end of the 1970s were helpless to alleviate manufacturing over-capacity and over-production because they facilitated the survival of precisely those redundant means of production that most needed to be eliminated. The monetarist macroeconomic restrictiveness that came in the 1980s did, no doubt, somewhat help to resolve the problem by forcing the more rapid expulsion of high-cost, low-profit firms from over-subscribed lines; but it also exacerbated it by making it more difficult to set up new establishments outside those lines. Monetarism might have 'worked' better had capitalist governments been willing to sustain more severe recessions in aid of more severely reduced wages and the more extensive (and indiscriminate) destruction of capital. As it was, the increased assumption of credit especially by Reagan's military-Keynesian state, as well as by consumers suffering decreased income growth, by corporations hit by reduced retained earnings, and by financial operators undertaking leveraged buy-outs and mergers and acquisitions, made for a certain degree of stability, but slowed the shakeout. Coming on the heels of severe monetarist restrictions on lending, they also caused a sharp rise in real interest rates. Since profitability did not much recover, investment growth actually fell during the 1980s, as against the 1970s, intensifying the slowdown in the growth of aggregate demand that was the result of severe wage repression and (in most places) greater limits on the growth of state expenditures and deficits.

The launching near the start of the 1990s of Clinton's budget-balancing campaign in place of Reagan's record deficit spending and the parallel commitment by the European governments to ever-increasing austerity in preparation for monetary unification further tightened the noose around the neck of the world economy. For the first time during the long downturn, virtually all of the advanced capitalist economies were systematically tightening both fiscal and monetary policy in unison. Since investment growth fell still further, domestic markets stagnated even more, leaving the world's economies with little choice but to step up their reliance on exports to spur growth. But, as the ratio between the growth of exports and the growth of domestic output reached record levels for the postwar epoch, the contrast between the booming 1960s and 1990s could not have been starker: whereas in the earlier period the acceleration of trade had amplified rapidly growing domestic markets, in the latter it sought to compensate for declining ones. (See p. 265, Table 14.2.)

Since the growth of output of (mostly manufactured) tradables was accelerating discontinuously as domestic markets stagnated, over-capacity and over-production were made worse. When Germany and Japan, on one side, and the US, on the other, once again went in opposite directions in response to a further and unprecedentedly drastic reversal in the value of their currencies, the divergence was more extreme than before. Germany and Japan suffered what were by far their longest and deepest economic downturns of the postwar epoch. In contrast the US manufacturing sector, helped by the declining competitiveness of its leading rivals, succeeded in expanding its overseas sales at rates that it had long been unable to approach. Largely on this basis, it achieved a significant recovery of manufacturing profitability and dynamism. Nevertheless, this bifurcated evolution was hardly symmetrical in its nature, since, over the first half of the decade the reductions in manufacturing profitability and the consequent damage to the German and Japanese economies were by no means compensated for by US gains, and the world economy was exhibiting less dynamism than for any comparable period since 1950. (See p. 240, Table 13.1.) Is there any reason to foresee an escape from this pattern during the second half of the decade and in the years to come?

The Optimistic Scenario

From autumn 1996 to autumn 1997, the advanced capitalist world would appear to have been following a textbook pattern of growth through the expansion of the division of labour. During that year, the US merchandise exports surged spectacularly by 24 per cent, accounting for no less than 42 per cent of the economy's growth and thereby for the first really major annual increase in economic growth, of 4.3 per cent, during the highly restrained cyclical upturn of the 1990s. The US boom contributed substantially, moreover, to setting off more robust export expansions in both Europe and Japan.[15] It has therefore held out the possibility that the advanced capitalist economies are finally ready to follow a Smithian recipe of mutually self-reinforcing growth through specialization and the gains from trade.

In this classic scenario, a US economy—in which profitability had finally been restored by means of wage repression and painful, very large-scale processes of

---

15   G. Koretz, 'America's Edge in Capital Goods', *Business Week*, 22 September 1997; G. Koretz, 'All Eyes on the US Economy', *Business Week*, 29 September 1997.

rationalization and technical change in manufacturing—would lead the world economy out of its doldrums. It would do so by accelerating the growth of the US market not, as before, through Keynesian deficits and declining competitiveness, but by sustaining and stepping up its nascent investment boom. The latter, by taking advantage of economy's newly won competitiveness on the world market and its highly exploitable labour force, would bring about the increase of output and productivity at rates not seen since the long postwar upturn. For their part, the US's chief trading rivals, having profited from the huge shakeouts of redundant means of production that took place during their 1990s recessions, would now grow through providing cheaper goods for the US (and world) market, while soaking up ever greater quantities of US exports.

This new and optimistic scenario certainly cannot be ruled out, for the US profitability recovery has been major and its positive economic effects real. Even so, there are grounds for doubting that the international conditions are in place to realize it, for we may be on the verge of still another, perhaps even more brutal, round of that heavily zero-sum battle for world markets in manufacturing, under conditions of slow-growing demand, that has for so long stood in the way of renewed international economic dynamism. The fundamental point is the obverse of the Smithian hypothesis just referred to—that since virtually all of the world's leading economies are seeking to emerge from their difficulties through major, simultaneous increases in their reliance on the world market, based on still another and deeper phase of wage repression and macroeconomic austerity, the inevitable flood of exports is more likely to issue in redundancy of output, intensified competition, and over-supplied markets than in the mutual gains from trade.

Most strikingly, even the US economy was able to secure its first whiff of boom conditions during the current extended cyclical upturn only on the basis of extraordinarily accelerated export growth. At the end of 1997, the growth of manufacturing capacity in the US was increasing at 4.3 per cent per annum, well ahead of the growth of consumption, and expenditures on business investment more generally were expected to rise at double the rate of consumer spending.[16] Barring the unlikely appearance of massively increased wage growth, the growth of consumer spending can hardly grow much faster, because so much of it has been powered by a precipitous decline of savings—justified by consumers' reference to the vastly increased personal wealth that has ostensibly been created by the rocketing of stock- market values.[17] It would seem then that much of the recent expansion in US productive power will be realizable only if sales on the world market can be substantially increased. Yet the international conditions required to make this possible seem unlikely to materialize for all-too-familiar reasons.

Barriers to Systemic Recovery

US economic success and the weaknesses of its leading rivals have already issued in yet another adjustment of currency values, with the result that US manufacturing is already seeing eroded perhaps the single most significant prop of its

16   M. Mandel et al., 'The Threat of Deflation', *Business Week*, 10 November 1997.
17   G. Koretz, 'The Uncertain Wealth Effect', *Business Week*, 20 October 1997. Since 1992, savings as a percentage of disposable personal income has fallen by more than one-third, from 6 per cent to under 4 per cent, the latter being the lowest rate registered in fifty years.

decade-long export boom. Since the 'reverse Plaza Accord' of spring 1995, agreed to by the G-3 governments to prevent the collapse of the Japanese economy, the dollar has appreciated substantially against the mark and the yen (by 20 and 50 per cent, respectively). The conditions are thus being been created, not only for yet another reversal of the loci of competitive advantage, but, in addition, for the further exacerbation of manufacturing over-capacity and over-production. For, while both the German and Japanese economies are relying on the growth of exports as the basis for their recoveries, their overseas sales have, less than on any previous occasion, succeeded in catalyzing economy-wide expansions. The outcome can only be even slower-growing domestic demand and even greater reliance on exports.

In Germany, as stressed, the radical programme of cost-cutting that has prepared the way for a new and vibrant export boom has proceeded largely through various forms of rationalization and the slowing of the growth of direct and indirect wage costs, and *not* through growing investment or employment. So the revival of man-ufacturing through exports has provided little demand pull on the rest of the economy. Despite increasing unemployment, moreover, the German authorities have not budged from their long-held conviction that subsidies to demand only cover up the underlying, 'structural' cost problem. To underscore the point, they sharply raised interest rates in the summer of 1997. The upshot has been predictable: the German economy has recovered only slowly; the other European economies, in lieu of the German market, have depended much more than usual on the US; and Germany itself will look even more to exports.

In Japan, the situation is analogous, though far worse, with much more serious implications for the world economy. The export boom that followed the initial fall of the yen proved even less successful in providing impetus for the economy than in Germany. The Japanese government meanwhile demonstrated its determination to make sound finance the basis for revived growth with a spectacular essay in deflationary hubris—a 2.5 per cent increase in indirect taxes—and thereby put a quick end to the weak upturn, opening the way to the worst recession of the postwar epoch. To prevent recession becoming depression, the government did finally launch, in the first part of 1998, a new, very major round of fiscal stimulus; yet it is hard to see how this can do much more than secure some temporary stability. Especially with the yen at lows not seen since the start of the 1990s, and with no apparent alternative force to drive the economy forward, the Japanese economy continues to look to exports to revive. Even so, there are grounds for believing that it has already, precisely by securing through yen devaluation the conditions appar-ently necessary for the revival of its manufacturing sector, ended up actually undercutting the foundations of its recovery by undermining its manufacturers' markets.

It has been a central theme of this text that, under the prevailing conditions of international over-capacity and intensified competition, competitive advantages secured by one major economy have tended to imply losses for others. It need hardly be added that, in this situation, where even the strongest of the developing economies have been vulnerable, the weaker ones—such as Mexico or Argentina or India—have 'survived' in competition only by inflicting major reductions of living standards on their populations. It was thus the reduction in the value of the yen beginning in spring 1995, so vital for keeping the Japanese economy afloat, which propelled the Asian economies into their current profound crisis and ended up threatening not only Japanese recovery but that of the entire system.

The East Asian Crisis

The economies of Northeast Asia and Southeast Asia had exploited the super-high yen of the post-Plaza Accord decade to grow impetuously, initially by invading markets previously held by Japanese producers, particularly in North America. Japanese multinationals, of course, played a central role in underwriting the Asian economies' export boom through substantial direct investment in relatively low-cost production facilities, made all the more attractive by local currencies which, because pegged to the dollar, fell against the yen by 40 per cent or more between 1990 and 1995. What appeared to be the unlimited possibilities for the growth of manufacturing through exports allowed these economies access to apparently unlimited supplies of capital which fed enormous building booms, as well as the construction of ever greater productive capacity in manufacturing sectors that began to cater not only to North America, and to a lesser extent to Japan, but to growing domestic markets on the Asian continent.

With the fall of the yen, however, the continuation of the super-fast growth that had come to be taken for granted throughout the region was put in jeopardy. Nevertheless, the general response throughout most of Northeast and Southeast Asia to intensified competition and weakening demand for their goods was to pour even more money into new plant and equipment. This appears paradoxical, but, in view of their overwhelming dependence on exports, and the impossibility of reorienting to the home market in the short term, manufacturers in the region had little choice but to try to improve their export competitiveness through greater investment. Existing over-capacity, the consequence of years of investment growth at 20 per cent per annum, was thus made worse. Inevitably, virtually all of these economies suddenly suffered sharp reductions in their export growth and/or profits, especially under the impact of intensified Japanese, as well as Chinese, competition, not only in other markets but in Japan itself, as the growth of overseas sales in the region as a whole (excluding Japan) fell from 20 per cent in 1995 to 4–5 per cent in 1996–97. As current account deficits suddenly rose, it became obvious that the region's growth prospects had been significantly reduced—even though local construction and stock-market booms temporarily continued, driven by over-valued currencies. The influx of outside funds soon slowed, however, and speculative attacks on local currencies mounted, ultimately forcing very major, competitive devaluations across the region.[18]

In this situation, Western and Japanese banks, which had recently been pouring in money to finance both manufacturing over-production and domestic over-building, suddenly began a rush to withdraw their mostly short-term capital, precipitating a run on the money markets. East Asia found itself suffering from the

---

18   P. Lewis, 'Export Growth Slows for Asia's Tiger Economies', *New York Times*, 3 August 1996; P. Montagnon, 'Overcapacity Stalks the Economies of Asian Tigers', *Financial Times*, 17 June 1997; J. Ridding, 'Chilled by an Ill Wind', *Financial Times*, 23 October 1997; B. Bremner, 'Who's Really Pounding Asian Economies?', *Business Week*, 22 September 1997; 'Is The East Asian Juggernaut Sputtering?' *Business Week*, 26 August 1997.

familiar domino effect that marks an accelerating debt crisis, the same sort of downward spiral that is experienced in a stock-market panic. Each foreign lender feared that all the others might withdraw their money, and tried to get out as quickly as possible. The result was the self-fulfilling disappearance of almost all overseas credit from the economy of the region, which made it impossible for producers, used to routinely rolling over their loans, to honour their commitments. The situation was made much worse by the fact that Asian manufacturers generally operated on the basis of high levels of debt and that Asian borrowers were having to repay their loans with currencies that had lost much of their value.

It was here that the IMF stepped in. The IMF might have attempted to get the international banks to agree formally to act together to keep their money flowing into Asia so as to counteract the panicky withdrawal of credit, for pouring in money is the normal remedy for a liquidity crisis. After all, the underlying problem facing many Asian firms was the insufficient international demand for their goods, not the inefficiency of their production, let alone their dependence upon (non-existent) government deficit spending. Some firms would no doubt have had to be trimmed back; others would have had to go under. But the whole regional economy did not have to go down. As it was, the IMF, mainly concerned that European, US, and Japanese banks be repaid in full, demanded, in Hoover-like fashion, that credit be tightened and austerity imposed, radically exacerbating the debt crisis and ensuring a devastating depression.[19]

In less than a year, the fall of Northeast and Southeast Asian currencies against the dollar has been in the range of 35–40 per cent and the broader destruction of values has been much greater. Since June 1997, stock markets have fallen by 89 per cent in Indonesia, 75 per cent in South Korea, 73 per cent in Malaysia, 71 per cent in Thailand, 57 per cent in the Philippines and 47 per cent Hong Kong. 'This is no orderly reversal; it is a panic-led rout', and it cannot but bring about a very major reduction of global demand vis-à-vis supply and consequent intensification of international competition.[20] First, Asian goods will obviously be much cheaper, given the size of the currency devaluations.[21] Second, Asian markets, in the grip of depression, will be able to absorb far fewer capital and consumer goods, thus far fewer imports.[22] Third, since a smaller proportion of Asian-produced goods will be sold within the region, Asian economies will depend to an even greater extent on exports to the rest of the world. Finally, the flood of Asian exports into markets outside Asia will be all that much greater, since so much of recently constructed plant and equipment was predicated on the continuing growth of the Asian economies at their former rates of expansion and will therefore have to find outlets at lower prices beyond the region.[23]

19 This is not the place to discuss the other terms imposed by the IMF, to break down and open up the East Asian statist and organized capitalisms, notably in Korea. But see R. Wade and F. Veneroso, 'The Asian Crisis: The High Debt Model Versus the Wall Street-Treasury-IMF Complex', NLR 228, pp. 3–23.
20 M. Wolf, 'Flight to Quality', Financial Times, 13–14 June 1998.
21 P. Lewis, 'For Asia, Austerity and Exports', New York Times, 9 September 1997.
22 For example, in Southeast Asia as a whole, car sales grew by 20 per cent a year between 1993 and 1995, but by only 6 per cent in 1996 and a forecast 5 per cent in 1997. 'The Downpour in Asia', The Economist, 1 November 1997.
23 See, for instance, M. L. Clifford and O. Port, 'This Island is Crazy for Chips', Business Week, 16 September 1996; 'The Downpour in Asia'.

The sudden squeeze on the East Asian economies, it must be stressed, has come not just from Japan, but from the growing presence of China on the world market. When China devalued its currency in 1994, it sharply increased its cost competitiveness in low-end production, just as Japan was to do in high-end production in 1995. In recent years, moreover, there has been a major slowdown in the growth of consumer demand in China, which has reduced capacity utilization to 58 per cent, while bringing down inflation from 30 per cent in 1994 to less than 2 per cent presently, obliging Chinese producers to orient to an ever greater extent toward the world market. The decision by the Chinese authorities to shrink the enormous state-owned industrial sector can only bring about an even greater fall in the growth of domestic employment and consumption. But, given the devaluations in Southeast Asia, Chinese producers will face fiercer competition in mainstay exports like apparel and textiles, and will thus find it sensible and obligatory to accept lower prices; indeed, the Chinese government may ultimately have little choice but to further devalue its currency, thereby increasing the downward pressure on Northeast and Southeast Asian manufacturing prices.[24]

It can be too easily forgotten that, over the past decade and a half (through 1996), Northeast and Southeast Asia was the *only* centre of dynamic capital accumulation within a stagnant world capitalism. Some indication of the depressing impact that the struggling region could have on the world economy is conveyed by the fact that in 1996 the Asian economies combined (excluding Japan) invested no less than $914 billion, almost exactly the same amount as did the very much larger US economy in the same year.[25] Given, moreover, that these economies are already responsible for perhaps 20 per cent of the world's exports, the inevitable decisive increase in their export orientation is bound to be strongly felt everywhere on world manufacturing markets. It is conceivable that, were the East Asian economies the only ones in the process of sharply stepping up their overseas sales and experiencing the slowed growth of domestic purchases, the increased supply could be absorbed without too much disruption to the system. But in view of the fact that Japan, Germany, and Europe, as well as the US, have been pursuing analogous patterns of export-dependent growth with slow-growing domestic markets, it is not easy to see how the world economy will avoid a further major worsening of manufacturing over-capacity and over-production, with rising exports in the face of stagnant domestic demand pushing down profit rates.[26]

In particular, it is difficult to see how the depressing impact of the Asian crisis can fail to communicate itself, and be very much amplified, as a consequence of its effect on Japan. The Japanese economy, it has been emphasized, has sought for more than a decade to extricate itself from the profound crisis of its export-oriented form of development, mainly through a very rapid and profound reorientation to Northeast and Southeast Asia. By 1996, Asia was absorbing 45 per cent of Japan's

24   T. Walker, 'Slack Demand Mars China Outlook', *Financial Times*, 30 July 1997; J. Harding, 'Jitters in Beijing', *Financial Times*, 10 November 1997; G. Koretz, 'Low Price: Bad Omen for China', *Business Week*, 10 November 1997.

25   Mandel, 'The Threat of Deflation.'

26   The US current account deficit has already been exploding throughout 1997, under the impact of Japanese and Chinese exports, and will undoubtedly get much worse quickly, as the effects of the dollar's revaluation kick in fully.

Table 14.2. Exports accelerate as output stagnates.
(Average annual percent change.)

	1960–74	1970–80	1980–90	1990–97
OECD exports	8.8	5.4	4.9	6.5
OECD output	4.9	3.2	3.0	2.2
Ratio of exports to output	1.8	1.7	1.5	3.0

Sources: Glyn et al., 'Rise and Fall of the Golden Age', p. 111, Table 2.22; OECD, *Economic Outlook*, no. 62, pp. A4 and A43, Tables 1 and 39.

exports and approximately the same percentage of its foreign direct investment in manufacturing. Japan's banks were responsible, moreover, for between 30 and 40 per cent of all of East Asia's outstanding loans from the advanced capitalist economies. There can not be much doubt therefore that the Asian collapse has been an absolutely pivotal factor in undermining the Japanese recovery. Not only has the depression in Asia reduced Japan's export growth, while exacerbating its banks' already major problem with bad loans and thereby further restricting credit; it has profoundly darkened the overall outlook for the economy by blocking what has long been viewed as the most promising pathway to renewed Japanese economic dynamism. Simply put, the crisis in East Asia has at least partially enveloped the world's second largest economy, and in so doing must exacerbate already deepening international difficulties with shrinking demand growth and the over-supply of manufactures.

It could possibly still be the case that, with a sufficiently sustained expansion of investment and employment, the US economy can provide the growing market which the international economy needs to offset and absorb its emerging explosion of exports. In this—again optimistic—scenario, the flood of low-priced goods coming from Japan and the rest of Asia would mainly serve, like those coming from the rest of the export-oriented advanced capitalist economies, not so much to force down US producers' prices and profits as to reduce their production costs, enhancing their competitiveness, increasing their mark-ups, and stimulating further capital accumulation. They would, by the same token, revive the local economies, making possible the greater absorption of US imports. Complementarity would, in other words, override competition, setting off a virtuous upward spiral, with the US pulling along the world economy toward a new boom.

Given, however, how rapidly and discontinuously the growth of world exports is likely to increase and how sharply the growth of world markets is likely to contract, the perpetuation and exacerbation of longer-term trends toward international over-capacity and over-production seems more likely than their transcendence. In particular, because East Asia, including Japan, has been absorbing one quarter to one third of the US economy's manufacturing exports during the latter's boom, it is not easy to see how the growth of US overseas sales can fail in the coming period to be very significantly reduced. Given, moreover, the radical devaluation of Asian currencies, it is difficult to understand how Japan's manufacturers, who have prepared themselves to compete at an exchange rate of 100 yen/$, can fail, in tandem with their Asian counterparts, to place excruciating downward pressure on US manufacturers' prices with the exchange rate at 130 to 140 yen/$. But, in view of the absolutely crucial role that has been played by the reviving US manufacturing sector in the broader recovery of US capital, any substantial reduction in that sector's prospects must have major consequences for the sustenance of the US boom. Yet, given the emerging conditions on the world and US market, such a narrowing seems unavoidable.

Intensifying competition seems almost certain, then, to squeeze manufacturing profits especially by reducing US exports to Asia and increasing the pressure from especially Asian tradables on US import markets and US prices. But if manufacturing profitability falls, the ramifications will be extensive indeed. Investment growth would fall, but then so would productivity growth, opening the way for further pressure on profits from wage growth. The stock market would have to fall too, sustaining the long-expected downward adjustment, but, if stocks did fall, the growth in consumer demand required to make up for falling export and investment growth could not easily materialize. In this more probable scenario, redundant production would for still another time undermine the gains from trade *and competition would end up trumping complementarity*. The accelerating supply of world exports in the face of shrinking markets, far from fuelling US profits and sustaining the boom, would undercut them and thereby the recovery, in this way cutting short a system-wide secular upturn and risking a serious new turn downward of the world economy.

Afterword

DEEPENING TURBULENCE?

Almost eight years have passed since the original publication of *The Economics of Global Turbulence*. Written at the height of the 'New Economy' boom, it questioned the foundations of the upswing of the late 1990s, suggesting that the persistence of chronic over-capacity in the international manufacturing sector would continue to prevent the advanced capitalist economies from transcending the long downturn. The emergence of new data and the perspective of historical distance since then have, I believe, both confirmed that analysis and allowed for a deeper and more detailed account of the recent period. In what follows, I briefly retrace the transition from long boom to long downturn between the mid 1960s and mid 1970s and the initial responses by the advanced capitalist economies to the accompanying crisis of profitability, as the newly industrializing East Asian economies entered the stage. From that point of departure, I review the significant revival achieved by the US economy between the mid 1980s and mid 1990s, its trajectory and foundations, and go on to locate its ultimate limitations in the factors making for the declining economic dynamism of the world economy *as a whole* during this period. On that basis, I explain why the very forces that unleashed the New Economy boom and stock-market bubble could not but issue in the stock-market collapse and recession of 2000–01. I conclude by analyzing the hesitant cyclical expansion that has marked the first half-decade of the twenty-first century with the goal of confronting the fundamental but still-unresolved question of the future of the long downturn. What forces are making for its transcendence? What factors are contributing to its still further perpetuation? [1]

The fact remains, however, that, according to the official story, the disconcerting economic developments of 1997–98, 2000–01, and since represent no more than minor glitches in an ongoing story of US economic progress. In this account, during the second half of the 1990s, the US economy, by virtue of its freed-up markets and its unmatched entrepreneurial-cum-financial institutions, achieved a breakthrough unavailable to its stodgier counterparts in Western Europe and Japan, who remained mired in the slowed growth that had plagued the advanced capitalist economies for more than two decades. Taking advantage of epoch-making

---

1 I here build on, and sometimes borrow from, a series of studies that I have completed since the publication of *The Economics of Global Turbulence*. See in particular: *The Boom and the Bubble*, London 2002, along with the 'Postscript' to the paperback edition published in 2003; 'New Boom or New Bubble?', *New Left Review*, no. 25, January–February 2004; 'The Capitalist Economy, 1945–2000', in D. Coates, ed., *Varieties of Capitalism, Varieties of Approaches*, Basingstoke 2005; and 'After Boom, Bubble and Bust: Where is the US Economy Going?', in M. Miller, ed., *Worlds of Capitalism: Institutions, Economic Performance, and Governance in the Era of Globalization*, London and New York 2005. Compare. 'Toward the Precipice', *London Review of Books*, 6 February 2003.

advances in information technology, the US stock market was able to hothouse a production revolution and economic boom on the basis of its ability to single out those companies that promised the best profits by virtue of their technological dynamism. Institutional investors piled into those firms' equities, driving up their prices, and signalling to bond markets, banks, and equity markets the desirability of lending to them and buying their shares. On the basis of the increased borrowing and stock issuance thereby made possible, these same corporations—disproportionately in high-tech industries, but also to be found throughout the manufacturing durable goods sector and related industries—were enabled to accelerate investment *in advance of profits*, making for faster productivity growth and even greater potential returns. Higher 'expected profits' made for still more elevated equity prices, which enabled further stepped-up borrowing and stock issues, allowing still more rapid capital accumulation, making for further leaps forward in technology, enabling productivity growth to rise even higher, making possible even higher expected profits ... issuing in what Fed chairman Alan Greenspan celebrated as a 'virtuous cycle' of economic expansion.[2]

But this analysis proved topsy-turvy for the simple reason that expected profits failed to materialize as actual profits. During the long expansion of the 1990s, the average rate of profit rate in the private economy remained 15–20 per cent below that for the 1950s and 1960s, and a good deal more depressed than that in Germany and Japan. From 1997, moreover, profitability plummeted in the US and across the world economy, even as the New Economy boom ascended to its zenith. Rather than setting the US and world economy on a new course, the forces driving the New Economy actually exacerbated the fundamental problem making for long-term slowed growth—namely, persistent chronic over-capacity in manufacturing and related sectors making for secularly reduced profit rates for the economy as whole. As a consequence, they ensured the still further extension of the long downturn, rendering unavoidable the equity price crash and sharp cyclical fall-off that brought a dramatic climax to the long expansion of the 1990s and opened the way to a new period of turbulence opening in the early years of the new millennium.[3] To explain this dénouement and its sequels is the ultimate goal of this Afterword.

The US Recovery and Its Limitations

Between 1985 and 1995, the US economy, led by its manufacturing sector, initiated a very real and, in its own terms, well-founded recovery. This was based upon the spectacular, if ultimately incomplete, reversal of the deep decline in manufacturing profitability that was heavily responsible for driving the US and the advanced capitalist world from long boom to long downturn. Nevertheless, the resurgence

---

2 'Testimony of Chairman Alan Greenspan Before the Committee on Banking, Housing, and Urban Affairs', US Senate: The Federal Reserve Board's semi-annual monetary policy report, 21 July 1998, Federal Reserve Board website. Compare 'Annual Report of the Council of Economic Advisers', *Economic Report of the President 2001*, Washington, DC 2001; A. S. Blinder and J. L. Yellen, *The Fabulous Decade*, New York 2001. For Greenspan's retrospective reiteration of this standpoint, see, for example, 'The Economy: Remarks by Chairman Alan Greenspan at the Bay Area Council Conference', 11 January 2002 and 'The US Economy: Remarks by Chairman Alan Greenspan Before the Independent Community of Bankers of America', 13 March 2002, both at the FRB website.

3 For US, German, Japanese, and G-7 net profit rates, see p. 282, Table 15.1; p. 240, Table 13.1; p. 304, Figure 15.6.

of the US manufacturing sector and the private economy as a whole ultimately proved abortive, because the profit rate revival on which it was founded turned out to be unsustainable in the context of a world economy that remained fettered by reduced rates of return and ever weaker economic growth.

The advanced capitalist economies had originally been projected from long boom to long downturn as a consequence of the extension and intensification of the same process of uneven development that had underpinned the postwar expansion. Exploiting the potential advantages of coming late, the statist and organized capitalist manufacturing economies of Japan and Germany achieved unprecedented rates of development between 1950 and 1970, especially by focusing on exports and the appropriating of large chunks of the world market from the US hegemon. The latter managed, however, to perform quite creditably by defending its own domestic market, while its leading corporations turned to foreign direct investment in manufacturing and the internationalization of finance. But the operation of this initially symbiotic relationship between earlier and later developers ultimately proved self-limiting, because it took place increasingly by way of the accelerating growth of redundant output. By the middle 1960s, manufacturers of the later-developing blocs were not only succeeding in imposing their relatively low prices on, so as to swell their shares of, the world market, but were simultaneously able, by virtue of their relatively reduced costs, to maintain their old rates of profit. US producers thus found themselves facing slower growing prices for their output, but caught with inflexible costs as a result of being weighed down by outdated plant and equipment, as well as relatively high wage levels that could not quickly be squeezed downward. The outcome was the emergence of manufacturing over-capacity system-wide.

Over-capacity struck the US first during the second half of the 1960s, and, owing to the US economy's preponderant place within the advanced capitalist world, it made for the reduction of profitability in both manufacturing and the private economy as a whole for the G-7 economies taken together. But Japan and Germany did not long remain immune. With the deep devaluation of the dollar, and corresponding appreciation of the yen and the mark, that resulted from the international monetary crisis of 1969–73, Japan and Germany also came to shoulder a significant share of the overall profitability decline. Symptomatically, non-manufacturers in the US, and across the G-7 economies, shielded as they were from the pressures of international competition, experienced the crisis of profitability to only a relatively small extent, despite sustaining higher increases in unit costs than their counterparts in manufacturing; this was because, unlike the latter, they were able to raise prices sufficiently to protect profits. (See p. 108, Table 8.1 and p. 109, Figure 8.1.)

The initial response by US manufacturers to the intensification of international competition leading to sharply falling profitability was to try to invest their way out of its crisis. This they sought to accomplish by falling back on their proprietary capital, especially their capacity for technical change, in order to raise productivity growth so as to restore their competitiveness and rate of return. Between 1969 and 1979, despite their reduced profit rates they accumulated capital almost as rapidly as between 1959 and 1969. The US government provided all-out support for this effort by forcing down the dollar and erecting major new protectionist barriers, while unleashing a macroeconomic stimulus of historic proportions. But US producers' Japanese and German rivals refused to yield ground. They accepted lower prices and further reduced profit rates in order to retain their shares of the world market, rather than gracefully ceding the field in textbook fashion, thereby thwarting the efforts of US producers to restore their rates of return.

Simultaneously, the processes of uneven development that had initially driven the world economy from long boom to long downturn extended themselves further, as the manufacturing economies of the Northeast Asian NICs exploded onto the scene, making for still fiercer competition and greater over-capacity in international manufacturing during the 1970s and after, in much the same way as had their Japanese and European predecessors in the 1960s and early 1970s. South Korea and Taiwan led the way, matching the record rates of growth achieved by Japan by recurring to Japanese-style state intervention, organized capitalism, and export orientation, as well as by tying their trajectories of development very closely to that of Japan.[4] As Japanese manufacturers rose rapidly up the technological ladder and faced ever higher wage costs, they sloughed off industries where technique was less advanced and less skill was required. South Korea and Taiwan took up these same industries, accelerating the process of technical advance through the purchase of Japanese capital and intermediate goods, participation with Japanese multinationals in joint ventures, and reliance on Japanese distribution facilities, so as to penetrate the US market with remarkable rapidity. By nurturing South Korean and Taiwanese manufacturing, Japan's government and its manufacturers cultivated fast-growing markets for Japan's own high-tech inputs for manufacturing production and gained indirect access for Japan's producers to the US market in a period of rising protectionism. The triangle trade thus constituted among Japan, the Northeast Asian NICs, and the US—with only restricted exporting back to the Japanese market—would constitute the elementary model or template for the spectacular development of East Asian manufacturing that ensued, although subsequent variations on this basic theme of regional economic integration would become ever more complex, soon entailing large-scale foreign direct investment for the relocation of manufacturing as well as trade. By ascending by these means the product cycle with unexpected speed, South Korean and Taiwanese producers— and their East Asian successors—exacerbated the problem of international over-supply by duplicating rather than complementing already-existing production and seizing market share at the expense of their competitors in the advanced capitalist economies as rapidly as had the Japanese themselves.

By the end of the 1970s, due to the combination of an insufficiency of exit from over-supplied manufacturing industries by producers in the core economies and a surfeit of entry by producers in the emerging periphery, manufacturing over-supply vis-à-vis demand was exacerbated, and manufacturing and private sector profitability in the advanced capitalist economies taken individually and in aggregate fell even lower than in 1973. (See p. 142, Figure 9.1.) In this context, Keynesian deficits, along with the increases of private borrowing that they facilitated, provided the additions to demand that made it possible for the economy to sustain

---

4   For the inextricable interdependence of Korean and Taiwanese development and that of Japan, see R. Castley, *Korea's Economic Miracle. The Crucial Role of Japan*, New York 1997; V. Chibber, 'Building a Developmental State: The Korean Case Reconsidered', *Politics and Society*, vol. xxvii, September 1999; T. B. Gold, *State and Society in the Taiwan Miracle*, New York 1986.

worsening over-capacity yet avoid crisis and continue to expand. But they also held back the shakeout of high-cost, low-profit means of production that was needed to restore profitability. Against this background, inflation exploded out of control and current account deficits reached historic highs, precipitating runs on the currency that demanded decisive action if the dollar's very status as international key currency was to be preserved. The Federal Reserve found itself with little choice but to impose 'structural adjustment' upon the American economy itself.

The turn by the Federal Reserve to monetarist tight credit at the start of the 1980s was aimed, in the first instance, to force up unemployment so as to further reduce wage pressure and break the back of inflation. But it was also intended, with the help of big tax breaks for the corporations and a major dose of financial deregulation, to detonate a major restructuring of the US economy—by eliminating the huge overhang of high-cost low-profit means of production that continued to hold down manufacturing profit rates, by dealing a death blow to unions so as to make increases in real earnings ever more difficult, and by opening the way for a reallocation of means of production out of industry into financial services. In fact, the cataclysms and shifts that were detonated by the Volker quake did set the US economy on a new course—toward manufacturing revival, the expansion and consolidation of a low-wage economy outside of manufacturing, and the dramatic ascent of finance.

Manufacturing. The Fed's historic tightening brought real interest rates to their highest level of the twentieth century, and, in turn, an ultra-high dollar. As a consequence, during the early 1980s, as the US and world economy sank into their deepest recession since the 1930s and the dollar ascended to unprecedented heights, the US manufacturing sector entered into its most severe crisis of the postwar epoch. Not only did already-serious system-wide over-capacity in international manufacturing get much worse as a consequence of the collapse of global demand, but US manufacturing competitiveness plummeted, with the consequence that both exports and profitability plunged. When the Reagan administration invited record Keynesian deficits in the face of already ascending real costs of borrowing, it forced up interest rates further, encouraging the real effective exchange rate of the dollar to rise into the stratosphere. It thereby supplied the demand to drive the domestic economy and that of the rest of the world from its cyclical downturn, but at the same time incited a crisis of US trade. Between 1980 and 1985, the explosion of federal borrowing in the context of an ascending dollar enabled US purchasers to suck in manufacturing imports at a pace unprecedented during the twentieth century; but meanwhile export growth virtually disappeared. For the first time in the postwar epoch, therefore, the US current account balance, in surplus as late as 1982, went deeply negative. This descent was almost entirely accounted for by the parallel reversal of the manufacturing trade balance, which went from a surplus of $27 billion in 1980 to a deficit of $124 billion in 1987. In that turnabout, exporters from Japan and the Northeast Asian NICs played the leading role, as they appropriated hugely increased shares of the US import market. The resulting increase of the trade deficit with East Asia (including Japan) accounted for the entirety of the increase in the US manufacturing trade deficit in this interval. It was a sequence that would be repeated several times over the next quarter-century—with the explosion of debt, the elevation of asset prices, and the rocketing of the dollar leading, on successive occasions, to record-

breaking current account deficits, major jumps forward for East Asian manufacturing, and devastating hits to the US manufacturing sector.[5]

In 1981–82 the US manufacturing profit rate dropped to its postwar nadir, and,
even by 1986, remained 20 per cent below its level of the late 1970s. Under this
degree of stress, the manufacturing sector had little choice but to contract in order
to cut costs, sloughing off a great mass of redundant high-cost, low-profit means
of production—both labour power and plant and equipment. In 1982, the business
failure rate reached its highest level since the Great Depression of the 1930s, and it
continued to rise past the middle of the decade.[6] The resulting gargantuan shakeout
constituted a turning point. For it established the necessary, if not sufficient,
condition for the revival of the manufacturing profit rate and thereby that of the
private economy as a whole. (See p. 273, Figure 15.1.)

Over the next ten years, between 1985 and 1995, US manufacturers were able to
achieve a dramatic turnaround, which set the US private economy as a whole on a
path toward revitalization. They held down the growth of real compensation
(wages plus benefits) to near zero, benefiting meanwhile from steadily falling real
long-term interest rates, which declined from a peak of 8.7 per cent in 1984 to 4.65
per cent in 1990, as well as the substantial reduction of corporate taxes.
Rationalization, moreover, continued apace, as the growth of manufacturing capital
stock between 1979 and 1990 fell off by more than half compared to that of the 1970s,
while manufacturing employment (in terms of hours) stagnated between 1985 and
1990. Out of the resulting processes of capital and labour shedding, the rate of manufacturing productivity growth rose impressively with the benefit of little
investment, surpassing that for the postwar boom. Most important of all, with the
Plaza Accord of 1985, the G-5 powers (the US, Germany, Japan, the UK and France),
acting in response to the devastation of US manufacturing wreaked by record high
interest rates and the rocketing currency, detonated a decade-long plunge of the dollar.

The huge resulting improvement in relative international costs made possible a
great leap forward in US international competitiveness, and US exports increased at
their highest rate since World War II. On this basis, the US manufacturing sector was
able to achieve an extraordinary 65 per cent increase in its rate of profit between 1985
and 1995 of 65 per cent. In the same interval, profitability outside manufacturing
failed, in effect, to rise at all. The ascent of the manufacturing profit rate was therefore entirely responsible for the parallel comeback in the profitability of the private
economy as a whole, lifting its rate of profit above its level of 1973 for the first time
in two decades. (See p. 274, Figure 15.2.)

Because it was achieved mainly by means of rationalization and the reduction of
costs, the recovery of profitability in manufacturing failed, for an extended period,
to lead to any improvement in manufacturing dynamism to speak of, let alone any
contribution by manufacturing to economy-wide growth. Manufacturing corporations rendered themselves that much less capable of inciting economic revitalization
when they assumed a vanguard role in the great leveraged merger and buyout mania

5   UNCTAD, *Trade and Development Report, 2005*, New York 2005, p. 18, figure 1.2.

6   Time series on the business failure rate and liabilities of failed businesses, 1950–97, were constructed
by M. Naples and A. Arifaj. I am grateful to Michele Naples for making them available to me. Compare
Naples and Arifaj, 'The Rise in US Business Failures: Correcting the 1984 Discontinuity', *Contributions to
Political Economy*, vol. 16, 1997.

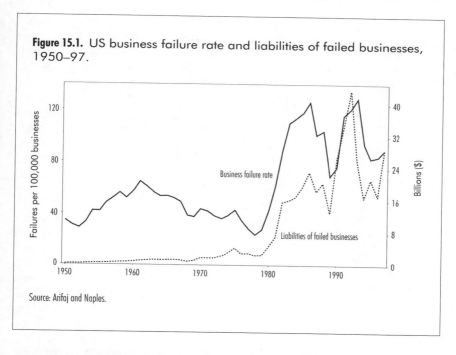

Figure 15.1. US business failure rate and liabilities of failed businesses, 1950–97.

Source: Arifaj and Naples.

of the 1980s. This entailed record-breaking borrowing by manufacturing corporations for the purpose of purchasing the equities of other corporations, and left manufacturers by the end of the 1980s saddled with previously unheard-of levels of debt. When the economy entered into a new recession in 1990, manufacturing corporations across the economy confronted still another life-threatening crunch, and between 1990 and 1993, the business failure rate reached and exceeded the postwar records set in the recession of the first half of the 1980s.

Had it not been for the bail-out engineered at this point by the Federal Reserve Board, the debacle in manufacturing might well have been worse, as financial institutions, especially commercial banks, were themselves weighed down by mountains of bad debt and in no position to come to the aid of crippled manufacturers. Between 1989 and 1993, the Fed reduced the Federal Funds rate—the rate of interest that banks charge one another, by six percentage points, bringing the real cost of short-term borrowing in the US close to zero. The real cost of long-term borrowing had, meanwhile, continued its extended slide, falling from 4.65 per cent in 1990 to 3.6 per cent in 1993. Under these favourable conditions, simply by effectively ceasing to borrow, as well as by selling equities rather than purchasing them as they had persisted in doing throughout the previous decade of mergers and acquisitions, manufacturers were able, in a relatively short space of time, to repair their balance sheets, preparing the way to finally translate their profit rate recovery into economic expansion.

Beginning in the fourth quarter of 1993, with profitability on the rise and balance sheets righted, the manufacturing sector was finally ready to shake off its lethargy. Manufacturing investment, output, and exports all suddenly thrust forward,

Figure 15.2. US net profit rate indexes, 1978–2001.

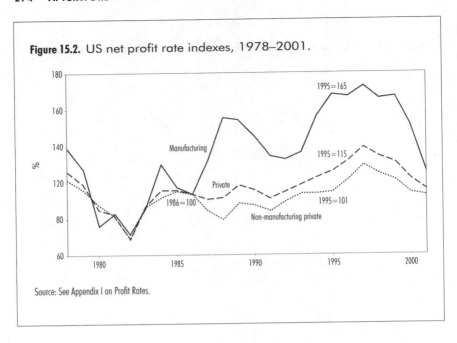

Source: See Appendix I on Profit Rates.

initiating an extended acceleration and providing a major stimulus to the rest of the economy. Non-manufacturing industries in general, and the financial sector in particular, evinced new life and, during the middle third of the decade, the private economy as a whole appeared to be verging on a new era. (See Figure 15.2.)

Non-Manufacturing. While the manufacturing sector laid the foundations for a US economic resurgence by means of a process of self-transformation achieved primarily through slimming down, cost-cutting, dollar devaluation, and, only late in the day, stepped-up GDP growth and capital accumulation, most of the non-manufacturing sector did something like the opposite—achieving fairly rapid growth but with virtually no development, consolidating in the process what was in effect a vast, and ever-expanding, low-wage economy. This process had its origins as far back as the early 1960s, but came into its own in the 1970s, with employers' stepped-up assault on unions and the government's deregulation of a number of industries, which also had the primary purpose of reducing union power. It was brought to fruition in the 1980s when, under the approving eye of the Reagan administration, employers engaged in systematic violations of the National Labor Relations law so as, in effect, to obliterate private sector unionism, especially outside the manufacturing sector. The implicit or explicit goal was to bring down wage growth—indeed absolute wage levels—especially in those industries where these had hitherto been relatively high due to union strength.

Employers' cutbacks of wage growth in response to the fall in the rate of profit and economic slowdown had been—and continued to be—powerful, and lasting. As early as 1972–73, the sudden rise in the rate of inflation, which doubled in the latter year, had begun to suffocate the increase of salaries and benefits. But employers sustained the downward pressure on earnings even as the rate of price increase fell back, and by 1995 in the private sector as a whole they had succeeded in reducing the *level* of real wages (excluding benefits) for production and non-supervisory workers 8.5 per cent below their level in 1973. The carnage was particularly extreme in such industries as construction, transportation, and mining, where workers had hitherto been relatively well-organized and well-paid, but were now subjected to enormous cuts, the result of systematic employer attacks—by way of carefully planned union-busting, deregulation, or radical shifts in location and technology, or a combination of these. As the manufacturing sector entered into crisis, this revolutionary reduction in earnings growth, indeed absolute earnings levels, opened the way for a huge redirection of capital and labour, enabling the giant sector of the US economy outside of manufacturing to expand impressively, and on an entirely new basis.

From the early years of the 1980s, the jolt to demand imparted by the Reagan administration's record budget deficits pushed the non-manufacturing economy forward. With real wages falling, firms in non-manufacturing industries found it easy to add jobs, and they increased employment at breakneck speed, at twice the average annual rate of the postwar boom. Meanwhile, in view of the decline of real earnings, employers had every incentive to substitute labour for capital, and, the growth of output per unit of labour input collapsed. Contrary to received opinion, labour productivity in the economy outside of manufacturing had grown about as fast as that in manufacturing during the long period between 1939 and 1965 and decelerated only to a small degree as profitability declined between 1965 and 1973. But in the wake of the sustained onslaught on real earnings that followed, the rate of growth of productivity in the non-manufacturing sector between 1979 and 1995 plunged to levels previously unheard of during the twentieth century. (See p. 245, Table 13.2.) Employers thus turned to labour-using techniques to exploit the lack of wage growth; by the same token the snail-like pace of productivity growth meant that they could not afford to allow wages to rise much. The US had emerged as a low- wage economy par excellence.

Employers' success in forcing down real wages of production and non-supervisory workers for the better part of a quarter-century did not however enable them to restore the indispensable basis for sustained dynamism, viz a satisfactory rate of profit. The non-manufacturing economy, producing mostly non-tradables and therefore largely shielded from international competition, sustained nothing remotely like the deep fall in profitability that struck manufacturing in the later 1960s and 1970s. Henceforth, however, the situation darkened considerably. The non-manufacturing sector was hard hit by the Volcker shock, and the elevated real interest rates that subsided only gradually during the remainder of the 1980s. Perhaps most decisive, between 1985 and 1995, while the manufacturing sector was relying heavily on the deep decline of the dollar to restore its competitiveness and help found its profitability recovery, industries outside manufacturing were undercut by the rising costs of imported goods that resulted from that same dollar devaluation. During the decade, the average rate of profit for the non-manufacturing sector as a whole fell to 20 per cent below that of the postwar boom. (See p. 109, Figure 8.1.)

From its postwar nadir in the recession of 1990–91, the non-manufacturing rate of profit did begin to float upwards, although it was not until 1995 that it reached even its level of 1986. Shortly before this point, moreover, in response to the impetus imparted by the revitalization of the manufacturing sector, as well as falling costs of borrowing and perhaps the start of the ascent of its own profitability, the non-manufacturing sector began to revive. Industries such as construction, retail trade, and wholesale trade were suddenly expanding at annual rates of between 6 per cent and 7 per cent, and would continue to do so, enabling the non-manufacturing sector as a whole to assume ever-increasing vitality across the middle years of the decade and thereby to complement the takeoff in manufacturing. (See p. 274, Figure 15.2.)

Finance. When the manufacturing sector entered into deep crisis at the start of the 1980s, there began a major reallocation of capital in the direction of financial activity. This shift had been delayed during the length of 1970s especially by the government's expansionary macroeconomic economic policies, which issued in fast-rising prices, the reduction in the value of the dollar, and the deep decline of real interest rates. The latter trends were supposed to help bring about the revival of manufacturing, but were obviously the opposite of helpful to the financial sector. Nevertheless, when the effort to sustain the expansion of manufacturing ended in unambiguous and ignominious failure, the late Carter and especially the Reagan administrations sought to make up for lost time. They moved decisively toward financial deregulation, breaking down hitherto existing barriers that confined financial institutions to specialized functional and geographic spheres. They also adopted a series of policies designed to raise the rate of return on financial activity. But the fact remains that lenders, promoters, and speculators, as well as the government, still faced an overriding problem. How could firms in financial services make a killing by doing business with companies and households in a situation in which non-financial corporations were producing such sharply reduced surpluses with respect to their capital stock and when wage earners were so hard pressed? How could the financial sector succeed when the real economy struggled, not really to take off again until 1993–94?

The Reagan regime, in its early years, could hardly have catered more directly to the needs of financiers. The imposition of unprecedentedly tight credit, certainly the defining policy departure of the period, was designed to break the back of inflation and in that way raise returns on lending. Commercial banks saw their profits soar almost immediately. The deep reduction of corporate tax rates in 1981, followed by the Fed's partial easing of interest rates in 1982, ensured that the stock market, and thus returns to investors in equities, would escalate, especially once the government's deficit spending on the military brought about the more rapid growth of aggregate demand. Finally, with a growing gap between federal tax revenues and federal expenditures producing record-breaking federal deficits that had to be financed, with real rates of interest at historic highs, and with the value of the dollar rising inexorably, investors in financial assets from the US and abroad could for an extended period make enormous profits on the purchase of US Treasury bonds, and money poured into US financial markets.

The Reagan administration's novel policy package was designed, apparently for the first time during the postwar epoch—though certainly not the last—to intentionally directly stimulate *both* the macroeconomy *and* the financial sector, though it would certainly not be for the last time. Nevertheless, the contradictions entailed by such decided government support for finance, both domestic and international—as well as, implicitly, for overseas exporters into the US—manifested themselves immediately. During the first half of the 1980s, record high real interest rates, a runaway dollar, and historic federal deficits not only buttressed financial sector earnings, but also nourished the manufacturing sectors of the US's leading rivals and partners, making for record-breaking external deficits and the decimation of the US manufacturing sector. By 1985, chief executive officers (CEOs) of some of the greatest US manufacturing corporations were organizing an unprecedented political campaign to defend US industry against foreign competition by bringing down the dollar, and Congress was clamouring for protectionist legislation. The administration was compelled to back off its campaign to make America 'the investment capital of the world', as Ronald Reagan had put it in his State of the Union address of January 1995, and reverse course.

Nevertheless, the Plaza Accord and the new protectionist measures that accompanied it, designed to defend US manufacturing, entailed contradictions of their own. As the G-5 drove down the currency and US interest rates fell relative to those abroad, the value of US assets in international terms declined in tandem. Just as international capital had hitherto flowed inexorably toward the US as interest rates and the dollar had risen, it now began to recoil from the US as interest rates and the dollar descended, threatening US equity and bond markets with disaster. US policy makers were caught in a bind, needing relatively low interest rates and a low dollar to spur the manufacturing sector and the opposite to prop up finance. This was a conundrum that they were never able to solve, and the outcome, sooner rather than later, was the stock-market collapse of 1987, soon to be followed by the mini-crash of 1990.[7]

The difficulty of profiting from financial investment through purely private initiatives in a period of powerful downward pressure on profits in international manufacturing had already been forcefully brought home to private investors over the course of the 1970s. Facing the drying up of opportunities in the advanced capitalist economies, where the demand for credit had declined as growth slowed and real interest rates had gone negative in the face of easy money and runaway inflation, commercial banks from the US and the advanced capitalist economies more generally piled into lending to the newly industrializing countries, which were themselves dependent for their own growth on the continued expansion of markets for their exports in the US and Europe. When Thatcher, Volcker, and Reagan put a violent end to the inflationary 1970s, these banks were caught in the maelstrom of the LDC (less developed country) debt crisis, holding the debt obligations of Third World states that had little or no hope of fulfilling their obligations in the face of record high borrowing costs on a world scale and contracting purchasing power in the core of the global economy. The flooding of US savings and loan institutions into commercial real estate, which came in the wake of the deregulation of the savings and loans in 1980, followed a similar pattern. Over-lending led inexorably to bubble, and then collapse, by the end of the decade.

Nor did the leveraged buyout craze turn out much differently. At the start,

---

7   For this, and the previous paragraph, see C. R. Henning, *Currencies and Politics in the United States, Germany, and Japan*, Washington, DC 1994, pp 273–87.

during the early 1980s, the financial engineers in charge did net impressive returns through huge layoffs, refusing to invest, and running down the capital stock, as well as by breaking contracts with unions and cutting off long-standing relationships with suppliers. Indeed, at this juncture, their approach made a certain amount of sense, as manufacturing corporations faced mammoth over-capacity and the collapse of demand, so had little choice but to impose upon themselves the harshest of austerity measures. But the fact remains that the resulting gains, achieved by once-and-for-all increases in productivity and reductions in input costs, were soon wiped out by the rising price needed to play the game. As ever more investors tried to get in on the action, stock values rose ever higher, and as the cost of buyouts rose correspondingly, corporate debt and interest obligations skyrocketed.

Nor is there much evidence that the 'discipline of finance' served to increase the efficiency of manufacturing production by facilitating technological advance or reallocating capital from unprofitable to profitable lines. On the contrary, freed-up financial markets opened the way for an enormous allocation of credit to non-financial corporations, which made possible in turn an orgy of speculation in the form of mergers and acquisitions. Manufacturers thus stepped up their borrowing to historically unprecedented levels, not to fund investment in new plant and equipment, but for the most part to buy up the equities of other corporations. As a consequence, by the time the decade was over, the non-financial corporate sector was immobilized not only by rates of profit that had failed to rise above their depressed levels at the end of the 1970s, but also by unprecedented, paralyzing levels of debt. Meanwhile, commercial banks, which had sought to profit by financing the booms in leveraged mergers and buyouts, as well as commercial real estate, found themselves in their worst condition of the postwar epoch. Over the course of the 1980s, the ostensible decade of financial takeoff, their returns on both equity and assets fell to the lowest levels of the postwar epoch, and as the decade drew to a close they experienced their greatest wave of bank failures since the Great Depression (see p. 298, Table 15.7).[8]

The US financial sector, and particularly its commercial banks, entered the 1990s in deep trouble. But the Fed's decisive intervention at this juncture made for an even more astonishing turnaround for the financial sector than for manufacturing. During the recession of 1990–91, Alan Greenspan not only brought short-term interest rates down dramatically, enabling banks to pursue with ever-improving results their standard policy of borrowing cheap short-term and lending dear long-term. In addition, he allowed banks, in violation of government regulations, to hold onto enormous quantities of long-term bonds without setting aside funds to cover the associated risk. These appreciated spectacularly as long-term interest rates declined precipitously, miraculously restoring the banks' balance sheets.[9] Between 1993 and 1995 inclusive, commercial banks' rate of return on both equity and assets

8   W. F. Long and D. J. Ravenscraft, 'Decade of Debt: Lessons from LBOs in the 1980s', and M. M. Blair, 'Financial Restructuring and the Debate about Corporate Governance', both in Blair, ed., *The Deal Decade. What Takeovers and Leverage Buyouts Mean for Corporate Governance*, Washington, DC 1993; J. R. Crotty and D. Goldstein, 'Do US Financial Markets Allocate Credit? The Case of Corporate Restructuring in the 1980s', in G. Dymski et al., eds., Transforming the US Financial System, Armonk, NY 1983; R. E. Litan, *The Revolution in US Finance*, Washington, DC, p. 6 and passim; L. White, *Why Now? Change and Turmoil in US Banking*, Group of Thirty, Washington, DC 1992, p. 13.
9   J. Stiglitz, 'The Roaring Nineties', *Atlantic Monthly*, October 2002.

shot up by almost 100 per cent with respect to 1989 through 1991, to their highest levels of the entire postwar epoch. The financial sector thus emerged from its worst crisis of the postwar epoch more than well-placed to make the most of any break toward economic growth. When the non-financial economy finally entered upon its long-delayed revival during the middle years of the decade, the financial sector took off in epoch-making fashion (see p. 298, Table 15.7).

In late 1993 and early 1994, as the manufacturing sector gathered steam, GDP was suddenly rising at a rate of 4.5 per cent, and 'expectations for real GDP growth … were continuously revised upward'.[10] Had the economy been left to its own devices, the expansion of the 1990s would have gained momentum uninterruptedly from that point onwards. However, the newly installed Clinton administration could not regard economic growth without ambivalence, for it was committed to sustaining the economy by enforcing what might be called a low-pressure regime, its top priority the control of prices. Instead of falling back on public deficits and consumption-led growth, the administration would depend on holding down costs across the board in aid of increased competitiveness, profits, and sales abroad and in that way increased investment, employment, and productivity growth, not to mention lower interest rates, reduced inflation, and higher returns to the financial sector.

In the event that the administration's first lines of defence were somehow breached, the Federal Reserve, led by Alan Greenspan, was prepared to fill the gap. The Fed was fully committed to Milton Friedman's doctrine that views accelerating inflation as resulting from wage-price spirals, in which rising wages drive up prices that in turn force up wages and so on. It therefore stood poised to intervene the moment unemployment threatened to fall below its 'natural' level. In early 1994, 'full employment was generally thought to be achieved' but 'the economy was still picking up steam'. As a consequence, the Fed launched 'an aggressive path of tightening monetary conditions'. In reality, the cyclical recovery had in effect only just begun and the unemployment rate had barely reached 6 per cent. Nevertheless, between February 1994 and February 1995, the Fed raised interest rates by three percentage points, setting off an international bond market crisis and interrupting the upturn for a full year.[11]

It was testimony to the transformation that had been wrought by the resurgence of profitability over the previous decade, as well the recent righting of corporate balance sheets, that the economy was able to regain its momentum almost immediately, as the manufacturing sector steamed ahead. Manufacturing GDP and investment had grown at average annual rates of 1.9 per cent and 1.3 per cent respectively between 1979 and 1992. But between 1993 and 1997, they jumped ahead at average annual rates of 5.7 per cent and 9.5 per cent. With the growth of the manufacturing capital stock doubling in the same interval, manufacturing labour productivity accelerated, jumping ahead at 4.4 per cent per annum between 1993 and 1997, while capital productivity also grew smartly.

During the middle years of the 1990s, the economy assumed a new pattern of growth, rooted in the recovery of profitability and competitiveness. Between 1979

---

10   OECD, *Economic Survey. United States 1995*, Paris 1995, p. 14.
11   Ibid., pp. 48–9.

and 1990, it had been the increase of consumption, itself heavily dependent upon government deficits, that was primarily responsible for economic expansion, explaining in growth accounting terms 71 per cent of the increase of GDP, with investment responsible for just 12.4 per cent. But between 1993 and 1997, the contribution of investment to GDP growth jumped to 30.5 per cent, while that of consumption declined to 63 per cent. Exports continued to account for between 25 and 30 per cent of GDP increase, as they had since the Plaza Accord, compared to zero during the years of crisis for manufacturing and trade between 1980 and 1985. For the first time in a quarter-century, the economy was functioning on all cylinders, with the manufacturing, non-manufacturing, and financial sectors mutually supportive. Based on the recovery of profitability and competitiveness, this was the *real* boom of the 1990s. Had its foundations held up, it could well have brought an end to the long downturn.

A Tightening Noose around the Global Economy

Nevertheless, the US economy was in the end unable to prolong its economic revival on a satisfactory basis much past the mid-1990s, because it could not sustain, let alone extend, that rise of profitability that had served as its indispensable enabling condition. The ultimate reason was that the US economy remained profoundly imbricated within, and powerfully limited by, an advanced capitalist world that, *as a whole*, remained fettered by reduced profitability and mired in quasi-stagnation, evincing ever-decreasing vitality, business cycle by business cycle, between 1973 and 1995. In such an interdependent global economy, it turned out to be impossible for the US segment to sail ahead while most of the rest of the world fell back.[12]

As a consequence of the continuous, precipitous fall in profit rates that resulted from the worsening of global over-capacity and intensifying international competition between the later 1960s and early 1980s, there emerged, in classical fashion, a dual problem of weakening aggregate demand and weakening productivity growth, which tended to be self-perpetuating. In order to restore profit rates, firms across the advanced capitalist economy moved immediately and decisively to reduce the growth of real wages, while governments cut back sharply on the increase of social spending. Because, as an expression of reduced profitability, firms could secure only declining surpluses for any given increase in their capital stock, they were simultaneously obliged to reduce the growth of investment, as well as employment. As a result, the growth of consumption, investment, and government demand were all forced down, leading to the reduced growth of purchasing power economy-wide. Meanwhile, because firms, in the face of declining profits and prospects, neither wished to nor could expand their plant, equipment, and software as rapidly as before, a decline in the rate of growth of productivity naturally resulted. Of course, the slower growth of productivity further threatened profits, leading firms to exert further downward pressure on wages and, thereby, aggregate demand, especially as each additional person hired brought a declining addition to aggregate purchasing power. Slower growth of aggregate demand itself undermined profit rates further and firms responded by reducing capital accumu-

---

12   On the declining economic dynamism of the advanced capitalist economies over the length of the long downturn, see p. 240, Table 13.1.

lation and wage growth even more, leading to the further reduction of productivity and aggregate demand growth, and, in turn, profitability ... a self-sustaining, indeed self-intensifying, process. Between the late 1960s and 1995, as profit rates fell and failed to recover on a system-wide basis, private investment (capital stock) for the US, Japan, Germany, the eleven members of the EU taken together, and the G-7 grew ever more slowly, business cycle by business cycle, as also did productivity, employment, and real wages, as well as private consumption and government demand, along with GDP. (See pp. 282–83, Tables 15.1–15.6.)

Against the background of the ever-increasing downward pressure on the growth of productivity and aggregate demand, the advanced capitalist economies were obliged to rely, as they had already begun to do in the middle to late 1960s, on ever larger government deficits to keep them expanding. From the mid-1970s, US federal deficits were responsible for pulling the world economy out of every cyclical downturn. By contrast, the US's partners and rivals turned ever more systematically to macroeconomic austerity, reducing government deficits and tightening credit, restricting the growth of the domestic market and becoming perforce ever more dependent upon exports for growth. The outcome was that the US government ended up providing an increasingly large fraction of the macroeconomic stimulus required by an international economy that came to depend upon it to provide the market of last resort.

Nevertheless, recourse to Keynesian deficits, and the increased private borrowing that they tended to facilitate, proved counter-productive with respect to the system's fundamental underlying problem—viz, to restore profitability. Deficits buttressed employment and thereby wage growth. Above all, they slowed the shakeout of that huge mass of redundant means of production that continued to hold down profit rates system-wide. To complicate matters, the high-cost low-profit firms sustained by Keynesian deficits were obliged to respond to greater demand less by raising output than increasing prices. Government stimulus therefore stoked inflation but secured decreasing output per dollar of deficit, ever less bang for the buck. By failing, moreover, to address in any decisive manner the underlying problem of reduced rates of profit, it appeared to consign the economy to worsening stagnation.

The Volcker shift to monetarism at the start of the 1980s was intended to break beyond the foregoing syndrome by directly confronting over-capacity and reduced profitability, so as to pave the way for the inauguration of a new liberal order in which markets for manufacturing exports, short-term capital, and financial services would be forced open, especially in the developing world. Nevertheless, the Reagan administration was unprepared to give up dependence on Keynesian deficits, with the result that although the economy was stabilized for the remainder of the decade, the shakeout of high-cost, low-profit firms was slowed system-wide. By the end of the 1980s, the aggregate private business rate of profit for the G-7 economies taken together, or for the US, Japan, and Germany taken together, was, at best, only slightly above its already much-reduced level at the end of the 1970s, while real interest rates were still an order of magnitude above what they had been at that juncture. The investment climate remained discouraging. (See p. 8, Figure 0.4; p. 142, Figure 9.1; p. 282, Table 15.1; p. 312, Figure 15.8.)

It was only during the early 1990s, with the Clinton administration's epoch-

Table 15.1. US, Japan, Germany, and G-7: manufacturing and private sector net profit rates, 1949–2000.

	US MFGR	US Private	Japan MFGR	Japan Non-financial Corporate	Germany MFGR	Germany Private	G-7 MFGR	G-7 Private
				(per cent)				
1949–59*	25.0	13.5	31.6	17.3	30.3	23.4	26.8	16.9
1960–69	24.6	14.2	36.2	25.4	19.8	17.5	26.3	18.3
1970–79	15.0	11.5	24.5	20.5	13.4	12.8	17.8	14.0
1980–90	13.0	9.9	24.9	16.7	10.1	11.8	13.9	12.4
1991–2000	17.7	11.9	14.5	10.8	5.2	10.5	–	–

*Japan 1955–59 only, Germany 1950–59 only; German figures are for West Germany through 1990 and for United Germany for 1991–2000.

Sources: See Appendix I on Profit Rates; G-7 Armstrong et al, *Capitalism Since 1945*, 1991, p. 352–53, Tables A1 and A2.

Table 15.2. The growth of private sector real non-residential capital stock, 1960–2005.

	Industrial Countries	US	Japan	†Germany	France	Italy	Korea	China
1960–69	5.0	4.5	*12.5	8.4	11.6	8.0	8.9	1.9
1970–79	4.2	4.0	9.4	4.9	8.3	6.0	14.6	7.2
1980–90	3.1	3.2	6.2	3.0	4.6	3.5	11.2	8.4
1991–2000	3.3	3.1	4.5	2.5	3.3	2.5	9.6	10.9
2001–05	–	2.1	2.4	1.4	3.2	2.6	–	–

†Germany 1960–90 is West Germany; 1990–present is United Germany; *Japan 1960–69 is actually 1965–69.

Sources: OECD Database; A. Glyn, 'Imbalances of the Global Economy,' *New Left Review*, no. 34, July–August 2005, p.14.

Table 15.3. The growth of labour productivity, 1960–2005.
(GDP per employee.)

	US	Japan	Germany	Euro-12
1961–70	2.3	8.6	4.2	5.1
1971–80	1.2	3.7	2.5	2.8
1981–90	1.3	3.0	1.3	1.7
1991–2000	1.7	1.3	1.6	1.5
2001–05	2.4	1.9	0.9	0.8

Source: 'Statistical Annex,' *European Economy*, Autumn 2005, Table 11.

Table 15.4. The growth of private sector employment and real compensation per employee, 1960–2005.

(Average per cent change.)

	US		Japan		Germany		Euro-12	
	Employ	**Comp**	**Employ**	**Comp**	**Employ**	**Comp**	**Employ**	**Comp**
1960–69‡	2.5	2.7	3.9	7.5	0.7	5.7	–	5.8
1970–79	2.3	1.0	1.5	3.9	0.3	3.0	–	3.2
1980–90	1.9	0.8	2.1	1.7	0.6	0.8	–	0.6
1991–2000	2.0	1.6	0.9	0.6	0.0	1.8	–	1.1
2001–05	-0.7	1.7	*0.4	0	†-0.6	0.2	–	0.4

Employ = Employment, Comp = Compensation; ‡Average of period 1960–69 is actually 1961–69;
Japan employment 2001–05 is actually 2001–02; †Germany employment 2001–05 is actually 2001–03.

Sources: OECD STAN, on line; 'Statistical Annex,' *European Economy*, Autumn 2005, Table 31.

Table 15.5. Private sector employees' total real compensation.

(Average annual per cent change.)

	US	Japan	Germany
1960–69	5.1	11.1	5.9
1970–79	3.5	6.8	4.7
1980–90	2.8	3.5	2.0
1990–2000	3.6	0.9	0.5
2000–05	1.6	-1.3	-0.5

Adjusted by OECD private consumption expenditure deflator; West Germany 1960–1991; United Germany 1991–present; Japan and United Germany 2000–05 = 2000–03 only.

Sources: BEA GPO By Industry; OECD National Accounts, II, Detailed Tables; OECD Data Base; OECD online.

Table 15.6. The growth of real private and government consumption expenditures, 1960–2005.

(Average annual per cent change.)

	US		Japan		Germany		Euro-12	
	Private	**Government**	**Private**	**Government**	**Private**	**Government**	**Private**	**Government**
1961–70	4.4	3.5	9.0	4.8	5.1	4.4	5.5	4.3
1971–80	3.2	1.0	4.7	4.8	3.4	3.8	3.6	3.9
1981–90	3.5	3.0	3.7	3.5	2.2	1.4	2.3	2.4
1991–2000	3.5	0.9	1.5	3.3	2.1	1.9	2.0	1.8
2001–05	3.1	3.1	1.0	2.3	0.4	0	1.4	1.8

Source, 'Statistical Annex,' *European Economy*, Autumn 2005, Tables 16 and 18.

making move to balance the budget and Europe's macroeconomic tightening in the run-up to Maastricht, that the advanced capitalist countries shifted in earnest toward governance by way of the free market. The core of the world economy was now obliged, as the neoliberal advocates of free enterprise had long been demanding, to operate to an ever-increasing extent on the basis of private sector initiative. It was left to its constituent firms to increase capital accumulation and employment and in that way raise investment and consumption and thereby drive aggregate demand and economic growth.

But as the advanced capitalist economies came during the first half of the 1990s to eschew the subsidies to demand that had hitherto kept them turning over and to rely more exclusively on purchases of plant and equipment and labour power by private businesses, they became that much more urgently dependent upon the revival of profitability. Yet, there was no evidence that, by this juncture, profit rates had achieved a sufficient recovery system-wide to underpin a new expansionary spurt. On the contrary. As a consequence, in the face of declining public stimuli to demand, firms across wide swathes of the advanced capitalist world were obliged to seek ever more systematically to restore their rates of profit not by stepping up investment and employment so as to raise aggregate demand and productivity, but by accelerating the scrapping of high-cost, low-profit means of production, while sharply downsizing labour and further suppressing wage growth. Their so doing made for the weakening of purchasing power system wide and deepening recession in much of the world economy between 1991 and 1995, and risked detonating a downward spiral in which declining investment and job creation and decelerating aggregate demand fed upon one another.

The situation was rendered that much more precarious by the fact that, in the face of the slowed growth of domestic purchasing power, producers everywhere could not but ratchet up their orientation to exports even more. During the first half of the 1990s, the ratio of the growth of exports to the growth of GDP reached its highest point during the postwar epoch. Since manufacturers were [thereby,] for the most part, simply directing a greater proportion of what they had been producing away from the domestic market and toward the world market, the increase of redundant production was the unavoidable result.

The main exception to the rule of ever slower growth was, of course, the emerging manufacturing economies of East Asia. The Northeast Asian NICs had led the way, but Southeast Asia's Little Tigers had followed in their footsteps, their political economies not so much modelled after that of Japan, as made a subordinate part of it, when Japanese corporations launched a massive process of relocation into the region from the middle 1980s in the wake of the revaluation of the yen. Just a short time later, the Chinese behemoth began to stir. The East Asian economies, virtually alone within the developing world, had managed to sustain their momentum through the deep recession of the early 1980s and the international debt crisis. Over the subsequent decade, they reached the zenith of their postwar dynamism, very much aided by financial developments in the core. Because their currencies were, for the most part, tied to the dollar, both NICs and Little Tigers enjoyed rising manufacturing competitiveness between 1985 and 1995 as the automatic result of the US currency's decade-long decline against the yen. When the advanced capitalist economies entered into recession in 1990–91—triggering a stock-market mini-crash, financial crisis, and the Fed's move to sharply reduce short-term   interest   rates—financiers from the core, in search of higher returns, detonated the so-called 'emerging markets' boom. According to the IMF, portfolio capital flows to the LDCs totalled $350 billion between 1990 and 1995; of this amount, no less than $261 million, or 74.5 per cent, went to East Asia.[13]

Following in the footsteps of the Japanese, South Korean producers had already moved up the technological ladder into steel, petrochemicals, and shipbuilding. But, in order to maintain their momentum by progressing to the next rung, they faced the imposing task of developing the capacity to produce such technologically sophisticated products as cars, electronics, and semi-conductors in head-to-head competition with the Japanese and the US, while extricating themselves from such labour-intensive lines as footwear and apparel, where they could no longer cope with the intensifying competition of lower-wage producers based in Southeast Asia. In this endeavour, they were able to succeed rather well, at least for the time being, not only by exploiting to the full the declining won, but especially by tapping into the flood of cheap money that suddenly became available on the world market, access to which was opened up to them when the South Korean government took the fateful step to end capital controls.[14]

Meanwhile, under pressure from the yen's unceasing ascent, Japanese corporations further stepped up the level of their specialization in high-end production at home and unleashed a torrent of foreign direct investment in the direction of Southeast Asia, so as to relocate low-end production there in order to take advantage of inexpensive labour made that much cheaper by the rising yen. The outcome was a qualitative deepening of the East Asian triangular trades, as Japanese producers, fully supported by Japanese supplier networks that also relocated to Southeast Asia, sent high-tech capital and intermediate goods to their own processing plants, to be worked up for export, largely to a US market that had been rendered much more difficult to penetrate by rising protectionist barriers, as well as the cheap dollar, but also increasingly to Asia itself. Playing a major role, along with the state, in orchestrating this process, Japanese banks supplied huge loans to Japanese corporations initiating operations in East Asia, as well as to East Asian businesses, and came to constitute the largest external source of bank loans to every country in the region except for Taiwan and the Philippines.[15]

The East Asian economies, like their Japanese precursor, continued to base their economic growth to an important extent on the very rapid appropriation of ever larger shares of the world market, challenging the advanced capitalist economies in an ever broader range of goods of ever higher technological content. Between 1990 and 1995, the Northeast Asian NICs plus the Southeast Asian Little Tigers plus

13   S. Griffith-Jones, *Global Capital Flows. Should They be Regulated?*, New York, St Martin's Press 1998, p. 29, Table 2.2.

14   S. Kim and B. Cho, 'The South Korean Economic Crisis: Interpretations and an Alternative for Economic Reform', in *Studies in Political Economy*, no. 60, Autumn 1999.

15   See W. Hatch and K. Yamamura, *Asia in Japan's Embrace. Building a Regional Production Alliance*, Cambridge, Cambridge University Press 1996; M. Bernard and J. Ravenhill, 'Beyond Product Cycles and Flying Geese: Regionalism, Hierarchy, and the Industrialization of East Asia', *World Politics*, vol. xlvii, January 1995; R. Bevacqua, 'Whither the Japanese Model? The Asian Economic Crisis and the Continuation of Cold War Politics in the Pacific Rim', *Review of International Political Economy*, vol. v, Autumn 1998.

China raised their fraction of world goods exports from 11.7 per cent to 16.4 per cent, while those of the US and Japan stagnated and those of the European Union and Germany fell. In so doing, the emerging East Asian economies could not but contribute to the further build-up of that redundant manufacturing productive power that was holding down profitability on a world scale.[16]

With macroeconomic austerity the order of the day across the advanced capitalist economies, the shakeout of high-cost, low-profit means of production pursued ever more relentlessly, and international competition intensifying, economic expansion could not but slow further. Between 1990 and 1995, the growth of world GDP fell to 2.6 per cent per annum, compared to 3.3 per cent per annum between 1979 and 1990 and 4.6 per cent per annum between 1969 and 1979. At the same time, all three of the great capitalist economic blocs experienced their poorest economic performances for any five-year period since 1950. This included not just the European and Japanese economies, but also that of the US, which did not enter decisively into its cyclical upturn until the end of 1993 (see p. 240, Table 13.1).

Against this backdrop of long-term international economic deceleration and market contraction, because the economic pie grew ever more slowly, economic advance tended to take the form of a zero sum game. The advanced capitalist economies could not, therefore escape the grip of a kind of hydraulic dynamic in which the export-based growth spurts of one major country or group of them, secured largely through the devaluation of its currency, found its counterpart in the manufacturing downturns and rapid rises in asset prices of those which revalued. In this process, the US and East Asia, with its currencies tied to the dollar, tended to move together, as did, inversely, Germany and Japan, with the system as a whole dependent for its sputtering growth on the US market. The result was that the US economy was able to put in place the conditions for its manufacturing-based revival of profitability between 1985 and 1995 only at the expense of its leading partners and rivals. From the time of the Plaza Accord, as the flip side of the US recovery, Japan and Germany saw their international competitiveness forced down, not only by the rapid increase of their exchange rates against the dollar, but also by wage growth that was much faster than that in the US. This even as they were obliged to confront the deceleration of the US market for their exports, the growth of which was slowed even further by the refusal, from time of the Clinton administration, of the US government to assume its customary role of incurring federal deficits so as to pump up demand for the world economy.

Both Germany and Japan had, of course, based their postwar dynamism on an orientation to exports, if in different ways. Japan relied on state intervention and its organized capitalism to secure the ongoing restructuring of its manufacturing sector in the direction of ever more technologically advanced production. Germany depended on unending macroeconomic austerity in order to keep prices down and shake out high-cost, low-profit producers, while looking to the continued upgrading of its highly skilled labour force to sustain its competitive position. Yet, as a consequence of their very success, both Japan and Germany were plagued, through somewhat different mechanisms, by the same inherent difficulty—the tendency to build up ever larger trade and current account surpluses and, for that

---

16   World Trade Organization, data set, WTO website.

reason, relentlessly ascending currencies that continually forced down competitiveness and profit rates.

With the transition from long boom to long downturn, both Germany and Japan saw disappear the indispensable condition for their extraordinary dynamism during the first two decades of the postwar epoch—namely the historically unprecedented expansion of the world market. So, as the dollar fell in response to the US government's inflationary policies, they had to run ever harder just to stay in place as their own currencies soared. Reaganomics in its initial finance-oriented phase did offer them a brief reprieve by driving up interest rates and the dollar, thereby opening up the way to the devastation of the US manufacturing sector. But, as the counterpart of the record current account deficits absorbed by the US, both Japan and Germany sustained record current account surpluses, which brought intensifying upward pressure on their own currencies. When the dollar plunged from 1985, while US manufacturing compensation basically ceased to grow, the exchange rates of the mark and yen soared, and both economies experienced excruciating downward pressure on manufacturing profit rates that had already by 1980 sustained very major declines. (See p. 288, Figure 15.3.)

At successive points in the later 1980s and early 1990s, both the Japanese and German economies did secure temporary relief by way of huge, artificial subsidies to demand, which appeared momentarily to offer means by which their dynamic manufacturing sectors might counteract their rising currencies by way of the accelerated improvement of productiveness. In Japan, from 1985 through 1989, the government forced interest rates down and induced banks to offer easy credit to real estate companies and brokerages in order to drive up equity and land prices. By nurturing asset price bubbles, it hoped to swell the treasuries of manufacturing corporations, which possessed large quantities of one another's equities, as well as much land, in order to enable them to step up capital accumulation. Japanese corporations responded as they were supposed to, making use of the enormous windfall profits that fell to them as a result of the rising prices of their assets to unleash a storm of investment of a sort not seen since the 1960s. Productivity surged, and, for a time, it looked as if the historic Japanese bubble was being driven by the Japanese economy's unparalleled dynamism, rather than vice versa. In Germany, on the morrow of unification, the former Federal Republic of Germany (West Germany) provided huge subsidies to the former German Democratic Republic in order to accelerate rebuilding. In the process it created a huge new 'export' market for West German manufacturers, and the economy enjoyed an all too brief surge of growth. But in neither case were these expedients sustainable.

By means of their titanic surge of investment, Japanese manufacturers managed by way of the increase of productivity—and with the help of the moderation of wage growth—to reduce costs sufficiently to make up for the enormous rise in costs that resulted from the ascending yen and thereby to temporarily prevent profitability from falling further. But their doing so, given their already reduced profitability, depended upon their capacity to derive rising income from the revaluation of their land and equity holdings, and the latter could not of course go on forever. By 1990–91, the Japanese government had little choice but to tighten credit so as to rein in equity and land prices, and as the bubble deflated, the economic

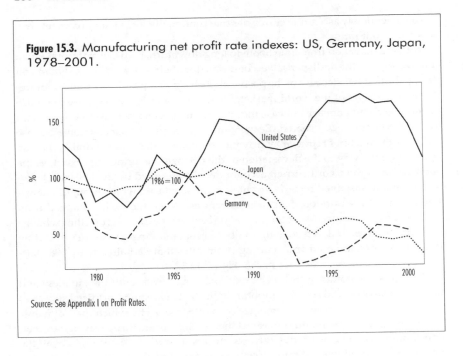

Figure 15.3. Manufacturing net profit rate indexes: US, Germany, Japan, 1978–2001.

Source: See Appendix I on Profit Rates.

expansion expired. About the same time, the East German reconstruction boom was issuing in accelerating price increases, and the German government, permanently intolerant of inflation, put on the macroeconomic brakes. In both places, the ensuing economic slowdowns had the effect of reducing imports, increasing current account surpluses, and inciting still another wave of currency appreciation, which only further depressed profitability and the economy.

From 1991, with costs of borrowing soaring, demand collapsing, and currencies ascending, manufacturing profit rates in Germany and Japan plunged to previously unplumbed depths—averaging 50 per cent and 33 per cent less, respectively, than even during the 1980s—and there would be little revival for either during the remainder of the decade. During the first half of the 1990s, both Germany and Japan, along with Western Europe as a whole, fell into their worst recessions of the postwar epoch, at the very time that US manufacturing was completing its impressive ascent. Right through 1995, in other words, the hydraulic dynamics that expressed system-wide over-capacity in manufacturing and the slowed growth of the global economy remained in force, as the long downturn extended itself still further. (See p. 7, Figure 0.3; p. 282, Table 15.1; p. 288, Figure 15.3.)

A New Economy?

It was out of the international effort to overcome the deep cyclical downturn of the first half of the 1990s that the forces making for the so-called New Economy were unleashed ... asphyxiating in the process the decade-long revival of US profitability that had underpinned the US recovery. By 1995, with the yen reaching an all-time high of 79/$ as a consequence of the devastating run on the dollar set off by the

Mexican peso crisis, the Japanese manufacturing sector was threatening to seize up. With what came to be known as the 'reverse Plaza Accord', the G-3 powers (the US, Germany and Japan) therefore resolved, in the interest of system-wide stability— and to counter the threat of a sudden fire sale of US Treasury bonds by the Japanese—to take collective action to bail out Japan and Germany in a manner pre- cisely analogous to the way the G-5 governments had together rescued the US a decade earlier with the Plaza Accord—by bringing down the value of the yen and the mark and forcing up the value of the dollar, in this way returning the situation, in a rough and ready way, to that of the first half of the 1980s, when the dollar was also revalued and both yen and mark were devalued. In keeping with this agree- ment, the US, the German, and most especially the Japanese government let loose a huge flood of funds onto US money markets, mainly through the purchase of US Treasury instruments. East Asian governments, as well as hedge fund speculators from around the world, followed suit. Meanwhile, the Bank of Japan forced down domestic interest rates, in order to render the purchase of US debt and therefore the US currency that much more desirable.

It was a stunning turnaround of policy, and the Clinton administration could not have made it without due consideration. After all, sustaining the revival of man- ufacturing competitiveness and profitability in order to provide a foundation for investment- and export-led growth had been the centrepiece of its programme for US economic revival, and a low and declining currency was at the heart of that effort. After talking down the currency in its early days, the Clinton administration happily welcomed the further deep decline of the dollar during the first half of 1995 and did not hesitate to exploit the resulting pressure on the Japanese manufacturing sector to threaten to close off the US market to Japanese cars if Japan did not agree to open its market to US auto parts.[17] Nevertheless, with the yen now worth *four times* more with respect to the dollar than it had in 1971 and with the Japanese growth machine seeming to be grinding to a halt, while Germany still languished, the fundamental contradiction of the US growth strategy was made glaringly obvious. Pursuing the low-pressure economy—based on a cheap dollar, budget bal- ancing, and inflation hawks at the Fed—might well pump up US competitiveness, profitability, and exports. Nevertheless, against a background of still-reduced prof- itability and chronic over-capacity system-wide, it threatened in so doing to undermine the leading capitalist economies that were not only the main rivals of the US but also its main markets, not only by seizing their market share and driving down their profits, but also by depriving them of the US market of last resort upon which they ultimately relied. The Clinton administration thus turned on a dime, so as to embrace what was virtually the opposite way forward—a new economic tra- jectory based on cheap imports, rising asset prices, and the influx of foreign money to buy US Treasuries, corporate bonds, and corporate equities.

In broad terms, the Clinton administration was exchanging the low-pressure economy as the road forward for the political economy of the Reagan administra- tion. As in the first half of the 1980s, financiers would be favoured not just by low inflation enforced by inexpensive commodities from overseas, but by asset prices

---

17   R. T. Murphy, *The Weight of the Yen*, New York 1996, pp. 292–5; J. B. Judis, 'Dollar Foolish', *The New Republic*, 9 December 1996; OECD, *Economic Survey. United States 1995*, Paris 1995, pp. 54–8.

that would be driven up in international terms with the value of the dollar. Businesses that relied on imports, either for inputs into production or to sell directly, not least wholesalers and retailers, would also stand to benefit. Still, the fact remains that manufacturers would experience declining competitiveness and the same kind of pressure on corporate earnings that only a decade earlier had impelled the Reagan administration to relinquish the approach that the Clinton administration was now adopting. The administration's economic policy team may have believed that a slimmed-down, toughened-up US manufacturing sector would be able, by this juncture, to withstand a new ascent of the currency. It may have also felt that increasing profitability and economic dynamism in industries outside of manufacturing would make up for declining manufacturing competitiveness and exports. In addition, led as it was by Robert Rubin, former CEO of Goldman Sachs, it could hardly have looked with disfavour on the idea of tying the future of the economy to an ever- increasing extent to financial services, where the US enjoyed a comparative advantage. Still, whatever the calculations behind it and the interests in play, the striking volte-face had to have been viewed as something of a gamble, if a largely unavoidable one.

The reverse Plaza Accord of 1995 turned out to be the turning point for the US economic expansion of the 1990s and thereby the world economy, as it both set off the New Economy boom and ensured that it would have feet of clay. The stepped-up purchases of US Treasury instruments by foreign governments drove down long-term interest rates, even as the Federal Reserve Board simultaneously reduced the short-term cost of borrowing (to stabilize the economy in the wake of the Mexican peso crisis). The stepped up purchases of dollars that these purchases required drove up the dollar's exchange rate against the yen and the mark. Taken together, these two trends—toward cheap credit and an expensive dollar—would persist through the end of the decade and shape the path of economic development on a global scale. There followed, as a consequence, alongside one another, the following epoch-making developments: a new, sharp decline of the US manufacturing profit rate, which immediately found an echo in falling rates of return in manufacturing leading to financial crisis in East Asia; the greatest stock market bubble in American history; an accelerating economic expansion driven by the wealth effect of rocketing equity values; and a radical worsening of already existing manufacturing over-capacity, which resulted from a massive wave of mis-investment in high-tech industries set off by the bubble in New Economy equities. It was an explosive mix, which could persist without self-destructing for only the shortest of intervals.

Between 1995 and 2000, the real effective exchange rate of the dollar shot up at 4.4 per cent per annum, after having declined at 4.6 per cent per annum between 1985 and 1995. As a consequence, the weight of international over-capacity shifted once again away from Japan and Germany and back toward the US as well as East Asia, which, as already mentioned, for the most part, pegged its currencies to the dollar. The US manufacturing sector thus saw brutally cut short that extended rise of international competitiveness and overseas sales that had underpinned the US profitability revival. Between 1990 and 1995, the first five years of the new business cycle, as the dollar persisted in its long descent, US relative unit labour costs had continued to fall briskly at 2.1 per cent per annum (4.8 per cent per year between 1985 and 1995), opening the way for export prices to rise at the rate of 1.8 per cent per year and for the US manufacturing profit rate to increase by one-third, essentially completing its spectacular decade-long ascent. But in 1996 and 1997, as the dollar reversed course, relative unit labour costs exploded upward at 5 per cent per year and export prices declined at almost 1 per cent per year. With its competitiveness thus collapsing, the manufacturing sector could not prevent its rate of profit from flattening out, even though productivity growth rose at a rate of 3.2 per cent per annum and unit labour costs fell at a rate of 1.5 per cent annum. This was because manufacturing prices fell in both 1996 and 1997. They would continue to decline in every year through the end of the century. Indeed, the manufacturing sector avoided an outright decline of its profit rate only by holding nominal wage growth to 1.5 per cent per annum, which worked out to a simultaneous total *fall* of real compensation by 1.5 per cent over the two years 1996 and 1997.

The years between 1995 and 1997 represented the climax of the spectacular recovery of the manufacturing profit rate, but also the beginning of its descent into crisis. Henceforth, the manufacturing profit rate would decline precipitously, depriving the economic expansion of the 1990s of what had hitherto been its main objective foundation. Even at this late date, it must be emphasized, the health of the manufacturing sector was absolutely essential to the health of the economy as a whole. By 1995, manufacturing had come to constitute only 29.3 per cent and 32.7 per cent respectively of corporate and non-financial corporate GDP. But it still accounted for 42.5 per cent of corporate and 50 per cent of non-financial corporate *profits* (before payment of interest). Problems for manufacturing thus implied problems for the whole economy, and, all else equal, a deceleration of investment, job creation, and GDP appeared on the agenda. Nevertheless, thanks to the spectacular take-off of the stock market that now ensued, the expansion actually speeded up.

By 1995, the US stock market had already been enjoying a historic boom, which originated at the time of the Volcker recession of the early 1980s. Yet until that point, its ascent could be said to have been fully justified as, during that interval, the increase of equity prices had found a real basis in the striking restoration of US profits, which rose roughly to the same extent as stocks. Between 1995 and 1997, however, the already rapid equity price rise actually gathered speed and corporate profits fell palpably behind, while between 1997 and 2000 they entered into absolute decline even as share values rocketed to their zenith. A bubble began to inflate, endowing the economic expansion with further life. (See p. 292, Figure 15.4.)

It has become standard to link the stock market takeoff to the stunning returns from Netscape's initial public offering at the start of August 1995, which is routinely viewed as indicative not just of the enormous promise of information technology, but of a contemporary takeoff of productivity. But this view seems at best partial. During the years 1995–1997 inclusive, manufacturing output per hour grew at the very good, but hardly epoch-making, rate of 4.1 per cent, yet in doing so it did not better the rates achieved by its major competitors in the same period— Japan at 5.4 per cent, France at 4.8 per cent, or West Germany, at 4.1 per cent. At the same time, productivity growth for the US private sector as a whole averaged a mere 1.9 per cent. What appears to have played the decisive role in sending equity prices into flight was a much more palpable shift—namely, the major easing of credit brought about at just that moment by the implementation of the reverse Plaza Accord, which provided the fuel for the ensuing fire.

Between April and September 1995, the Bank of Japan cut its interest rate,

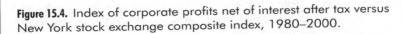

Figure 15.4. Index of corporate profits net of interest after tax versus New York stock exchange composite index, 1980–2000.

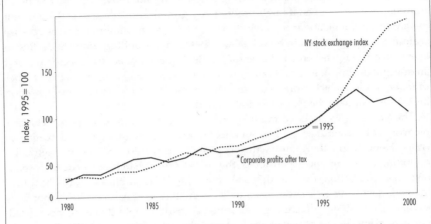

Source: *Economic Report of the President;* see Appendix I on Profit Rates. *With capital consumption and inventory adjustments.

already a very low 1.75 per cent, to 0.5 per cent. This did, as intended, lead to a sharp reduction of the yen's exchange rate, opening the way to a recovery of Japanese competitiveness and exports. But it also had the effect of pumping up the global supply of loanable funds. US investors in particular fabricated a very profitable 'carry trade', borrowing yen at the ultra-low Japanese rate of interest, converting these into dollars, and using the latter to invest in the US stock market.[18] Meanwhile, purchases of US securities by Japanese and East Asian governments, as well as Japanese insurance companies and international hedge funds, skyrocketed, with the result that in the years 1995–1997 inclusive, foreign purchases of US Treasury instruments, totalling more than half a trillion dollars, covered not only the total new debt issued by the US Treasury in this interval, but also a further quarter trillion dollars' worth of Treasuries that was already in the hands of US citizens. The consequence was a dramatic reduction of long-term interest rates, with the interest rate on 30-year bonds diving from 7.85 per cent in January 1995 to 6.05 per cent in January 1996. This 23 per cent drop in the cost of borrowing over the course of 1995 had to have been a further major factor in fomenting the stock market's rapid rise, especially as it detonated a sharp, parallel acceleration in the

18   R. T. Murphy, 'Japan's Economic Crisis', *New Left Review*, new series, 1, January–February 2000, pp. 42–3; Bevacqua, 'Wither the Japanese Model?' p. 415.

19   Board of Governors of the Federal Reserve System, *Flow of Funds Accounts of the United States. Flows and Outstandings* (available at FRB website; hencefore FRB, *Flow of Funds*), Table F.107, Rest of World and Table F. 209, Treasury Securities; OECD, *Economic Survey. United States 1995*, Paris 1995, pp. 55–8; OECD, *Economic Survey. United States 1996*, Paris 1996, pp. 49–51; OECD, *Economic Survey. United States 1997*, Paris 1997, pp.73–5; *Economic Report of the President 2000*, Washington, DC 2000, p. 391, Table B-71.

increase of the money supply, which grew four times faster in 1995 than it had in 1994. So, finally, did the rocketing dollar itself, which brought about, by itself, a corresponding rise in the value of US equities from the standpoint of investors from overseas.[19]

But if the sudden shift toward cheaper long-term borrowing and an increasingly expensive dollar that resulted from the reverse Plaza Accord accelerated the stock-market rise, the US Federal Reserve kept it going, blowing up a bubble. By late 1996, Alan Greenspan was voicing worry, in public, about 'irrational exuberance' in the stock market. But he was clearly more concerned, in private, about the possible stumbling of the real US economy. Thanks to the Clinton administration's move to balance the budget, federal deficits were now drying up and with them the subsidies to demand that had helped to stabilize the US and world economy for most of the previous quarter-century. The problem was exacerbated by Europe's parallel persistence in macroeconomic tightening, even in the face of recession and stagnation through the first half of the 1990s. It is true, of course, that, from 1993, the US economy, led by its manufacturing sector, had evinced impressive vitality. But, as Greenspan was surely aware, the US manufacturing revival had been heavily dependent upon a deep devaluation of the dollar that was now being dramatically reversed. With federal deficits evaporating, the ascent of the dollar threatening profits, and Europe and Japan looking to the US to drive growth, from whence would come the corporate investment or consumer buying power required to keep the expansion going?

Greenspan's answer was to turn to the equity markets and their wealth effect to stimulate demand. Indeed, the strategy that he evolved during the second half of the 1990s—and has continued to implement ever since—might usefully be called 'stock market, or asset-price, Keynesianism'. In traditional Keynesian policy, demand is 'subsidized' by means of the federal government's incurring of rising *public* deficits so as to spend more than it takes in taxes. By contrast, in Greenspan's version, demand is increased by means of corporations and wealthy households taking on rising *private* deficits so as to spend more than they make, encouraged to do so by the increased paper wealth that they effortlessly accrue by virtue of the appreciation of the value of their stocks, or other assets.

In the early 1990s, the advanced capitalist governments had moved to reduce their reliance on traditional Keynesian fiscal stimuli and launched an experiment with unadulterated neoliberal regulation. Governments would resist incurring deficits; private firms would drive demand; central banks, putatively politically neutral, would fine-tune by way of monetary policy. Here was another opportunity, like that of the early 1980s, to allow for the survival of the fittest, expunge the overcapacity that had managed to reproduce itself for more than two decades, and set the economy on a firmer foundation. But the Fed under Greenspan, no more than the Treasury under Reagan, was prepared to let the free market work its restorative magic in the only way it is capable of doing—via deep and 'cleansing' crises. So, when Europe and Japan descended into their worst recessions of the postwar epoch, while the US endured its slowest cyclical recovery since 1950, it felt it had no choice but to ride to the rescue, quickly restoring the subsidies to demand to which a profit-short world economy had been addicted since the late 1960s. This time however it would be private businesses and the rich who did the borrowing and the spending, not the government, thanks to the rapid rise in the value of their equities courtesy of the Fed. Having been suitably supplemented by a new and politically more acceptable—if also radically more destabilizing—form of Keynesianism, the free market could be allowed to continue its nominal governance of the economy.

Although the stock-market's rise actually speeded up in the wake of his warning, Greenspan henceforth refrained from mentioning irrational exuberance. Far from seeking to dampen investor enthusiasm or control the emerging bubble, the Fed nourished them both. Greenspan has been lauded for his supposed wisdom and courage in breaking at this juncture from both the orthodox belief in a 'natural rate of unemployment' and his earlier incarnation as an inflation hawk and allowing the economy to gather steam even as unemployment fell sharply.[20] In reality, inflation had by this juncture been brought firmly under control by the brutal downward pressure on prices from abroad that resulted from the rising US currency. Nor, as Greenspan himself observed, was there much cause for concern about upward pressure on prices from below, in view, as he put it, of 'the evident insecurity felt by many workers despite the tightest labor markets in decades', due to the 'heightened level of dismissal' that continued to result from a business failure rate that persisted during the later 1990s at levels that were nearly twice the post-war average through 1980 (see p. 273, Figure 15.1). In fact, between 1990 and 1995, the average annual increase of the GDP deflator was already down by about 25 per cent from 1985–90, to 2.45 per cent from 3.2 per cent, and at that point the dollar's exchange rate was still falling. Greenspan's real worry was thus quite the opposite: that the same *disinflation* that was being driven by international over-capacity and the irrepressible dollar was forcing down the manufacturing profit rate at a time when federal deficits were drying up, and that, unless he continued to stoke the wealth effect by keeping equities rising by means of ever-easier credit, the US economic expansion would peter out due to insufficient growth of aggregate demand—government, consumption, and investment. The reverse Plaza Accord had derailed the attempt to drive the recovery via the low-pressure economy—by means of the repression of wages, prices, and currency in aid of increasing competitiveness, exports, investment, and manufacturing profits. Greenspan evidently concluded, not without reason, that stock-market Keynesianism was his best alternative.

Between 1995 and the middle of 1999, Greenspan failed to raise interest rates, aside from a single one-quarter-point increase in early 1997. As a consequence, during the second half of the decade, the money supply increased at quadruple the rate during the first half. Meanwhile, the Fed intervened with ever-easier credit at every sign of instability in the stock markets. Greenspan rationalized the ever greater divorce between runaway equity prices and underlying corporate earnings in terms of the infinite promise of the New Economy, evidenced, he argued, in the ever higher estimates of *expected*, that is, future, corporate profits on the part of secu-

20   See B. Woodward, *Maestro. Greenspan's Fed and the American Boom*, New York 2000.

21   As late as his testimony to Congress of 13 February 2001—on the eve of the corporate scandals that would definitively expose the bent of security analysts and their predictions—Greenspan was citing 'three-to five year earnings projections' 'of equity analysts, who, one must presume, obtain their insights from corporate managers' as a basis for predicting 'continued strength in capital accumulation' ... even as the economy plunged into recession. 'Testimony of Chairman Alan Greenspan before the Committee on Banking, Housing, and Urban Affairs', US Senate: Federal Reserve Board's Semi-annual Monetary Policy Report to Congress, 13 February 2001.

rity analysts (who had every interest, as Greenspan should have known, in over-stating the value of corporate shares for the benefit of the investment banks who employed them as well as their corporate customers).[21] It was equity investors' belief in the so-called 'Greenspan put'—that the Fed would bail out the equity market come what may—that kept the equity price boom going strong in the face of one after another economic disruption right through to the end of the mil-lennium. As a result, as it had through the length of the long downturn, government-supported borrowing continued to drive the US and world economy.

The titanic wealth effect unleashed by the record boom in equity prices allowed the US expansion not only to continue, but to accelerate in the years between 1995 and 2000, even as downward pressure on profit rates deprived it of its initially solid foundation. Although profits became increasingly hard to come by, corpora-tions were able to fund stepped-up capital accumulation with consummate ease on the basis of runaway stock values that bloated market capitalization and thus apparent collateral beyond recognition. Between 1950 and 1995, US non-financial corporations had relied mainly on internal funds to finance their spending on new plant and equipment, with retained earnings covering about 90 per cent of their capital expenditures. But after 1995, their borrowing as a proportion of their GDP climbed to levels previously matched during the postwar epoch only during reces-sions (see p. 317, Figure 15.9). By the end of the decade, they were using borrowing to fund capital accumulation at the highest rates in history. Meanwhile, the less creditworthy among them were able to finance investment to an extent without close precedent through issuing over-priced shares. In 2000, *gross* equity issues by non-financial corporations rose to a level four times their previous peak (in the 1980s).[22]

Households also treated the rapid rise in equity prices as an opportunity for rad-ically stepped-up borrowing and, on that basis, spending. Between 1994 and 2000, the market capitalization of households' shares tripled, rising from $4 trillion to $12 trillion. They thus felt justified in raising their annual borrowing, as well as their debt outstanding, to near record levels as a fraction of GDP (see p. 317, Figure 15.9). As the flip side of the coin, they felt free to sharply reduce their rate of savings as a proportion of consumption, so as to raise their rate of spending. Between 1950 and 1992, the personal savings rate had fluctuated between 11.2 and 7.0 per cent, averaging 9.0 per cent. But between 1992 and 2000, it crashed from 7.7 per cent to 2.3 per cent. The top 20 per cent of the population by income was almost entirely responsible for this collapse of savings and rise of spending, which is hardly sur-prising since they own 95 per cent or more of all financial assets. As one pundit put it, the boom of the later 1990s was the first in US history to be heavily driven by yuppie expenditures.[23]

The equities boom had, it must be stressed, a certain self-perpetuating character,

22   FRB, *Flow of Funds*, Table D.2, Borrowing by Sector; FRB, *Flow of Funds*, Table F.102, Nonfarm Nonfinancial Corporate Business: Line 58, Financing Gap, and Lines 5 and 7, Internal Funds Plus Inventory Valuation Adjustment; Gross Equity Issues by Nonfinancial Corporations, 1984–2000, Federal Reserve Board unpublished time series. I wish to thank Nellie Liang for forwarding the data on gross equity issues to me.
23   FRB, *Flow of Funds*, Table B.100, Balance Sheet of Households and Nonprofit Organizations; D. M. Maki and M. G. Palumbo, 'Disentangling the Wealth Effect: A Cohort Analysis of Household Saving in the 1990s', Federal Reserve Finance and Discussion Series, April 2001, Federal Reserve website.

because the increased collateral it provided for corporations and households could be used for borrowing not only for the purpose of increasing investment and consumption, but for the purchase of more equities. During the second half of the 1990s, non-financial corporations allocated as much of the huge sum that they borrowed to buying shares as to accumulating capital. As a consequence, during this interval, they were the largest *net* purchasers on the stock market. Through share repurchases funded by borrowing, corporations avoided the tedious process of creating shareholder value through actually producing goods and services at a profit, and directly drove up the price of their own equities for the benefit of their stockholders, as well as their corporate executives who were heavily remunerated with stock options. Higher equity values made for still more collateral, further borrowing, greater stock purchases, and so forth.[24] The same sort of process would soon be at work once again in the escalation of housing prices.

Between 1995 and 2000, the New Economy boom thus took flight, underpinned by the wealth effect of rising equity prices on both businesses and households, and GDP rose at an average annual rate of 4.1 per cent compared to 2.5 per cent between 1990 and 1995 and 2.9 per cent between 1973 and 1995 (and 4 per cent between 1948 and 1973). Even as profits fell away, non-residential investment continued to explode upwards, increasing at an average annual rate of about 10 per cent accounting for about one-third of the increase in GDP in the same interval. Employment growth also speeded up and, in the last few years of the century, was accompanied by a significant jump in the rate of growth of real wages, after a very long period of stagnation. With aggregate real compensation (real compensation per employee multiplied by total employees) therefore rising rapidly, while household borrowing levels flew upwards and personal saving simultaneously collapsed, the growth of consumer expenditure naturally also leaped forward—to an average annual rate of 4.4 per cent between 1995 and 2000—and helped in a big way to soak up fast-growing output. All told, according to the Federal Reserve Board and the Council of Economic Advisers, rising equity prices accounted for about one-third of the increase in consumption that took place between 1995 and 2000 and between one-quarter and one-third of the increase in GDP during that interval.[25] In the absence of the wealth effect of rising equity prices GDP growth, at around 3 per cent per annum, would, during this five-year interval, have been no higher than during the 1970s or 1980s.

Constrained as it was by a rising dollar and ultimately dependent for its vitality on escalating aggregate demand generated by runaway equity prices, the expansion of the 1990s could not but assume a distorted and contradictory character and could contemplate only a very limited future. Its vitality was undeniable, but superficial and therefore temporary. As the manufacturing sector's rate of profit flattened and then fell, the sector lost its engine of growth. But, it continued to expand impetuously by tapping into the mountain of virtually costless credit made available by the stock-market rise, its high-tech industries providing a glittering veneer for the

24   Brenner, *The Boom and the Bubble*, pp. 146–52.
25   'The Annual Report of the Council of Economic Advisers', *Economic Report of the President 2001*, Washington, DC, January 2001, p. 61; 'Testimony of Chairman Alan Greenspan Before the Committee on Banking and Financial Services, US House of Representatives: The Federal Reserve's Semi-Annual Report on the Economy and Monetary Policy', 17 February 2000, FRB website.

New Economy boom. Meanwhile, much of the economy outside manufacturing, and especially those of its constituent industries able to cater to the rise of debt-driven consumer spending and/or benefit from cheaper imports made possible by the rising dollar, surged ahead as it had not done since the 1960s, as it also took advantage of easy access to investment funds to accelerate expenditures on new plant, equipment, and software, as well as to expand employment. Between 1995 and 2000, in the non-manufacturing sector both output and the capital stock accelerated remarkably, their average annual rates of growth rising above those of 1979–90 by 60 per cent and 30 per cent respectively, while equalling or bettering those for the long postwar boom. Apparently as a consequence, this huge region of the economy experienced a doubling in the rate of increase of its capital–labour ratio and, in turn, of its labour productivity.

Benefiting from an astonishing, seemingly unending, increase in the demand for homes, construction enjoyed what would turn out to be a decade-long boom, its rate of profit smashing all previous records for the industry. Directly fuelled by the consumer spending spree plus ever cheaper imports, often from East Asia, retail trade and wholesale trade did extraordinarily well too. Both of these industries experienced a major leap forward in output growth, which provided the foundation for remarkable accelerations in their productivity growth, arising in turn largely from economies of scale. In fact, outside of manufacturing, retail trade and wholesale trade were, along with finance and real estate, virtually the only industries to experience increased productiveness, compared to the 1980s and early 1990s, and accounted for the better part of the productivity acceleration experienced by the non-manufacturing sector as a whole. Hotels and restaurants was still another consumer-based industry that prospered. Meanwhile the increasingly corporatized health services sector registered what has come to look like permanent growth, its profits quintupling between the end of the 1980s and beginning of the 2000s.[26]

Last but not least, the financial sector continued to enjoy a historic ascent that was transforming the face of the economy. Every major trend of the period ran in favour of finance. Non-financial corporations expanded their operations as if there was no tomorrow, and radically increased their borrowing. Inflation was suppressed, due mainly to the rising dollar, but also to the ever-increasing insecurity of an American working class being buffeted by intensifying industrial competition, as well as growing threats from overseas imports and US investment abroad, even while union protection was disappearing. The Clinton administration pushed banking deregulation to its logical conclusion, abolishing the landmark Glass-Steagall Act of 1934 so as to open the way to the rise of huge conglomerates that combined commercial banking, investment banking, and insurance, typified by Citicorp and JP Morgan Chase. The stock-market bubble offered historically

---

26 The average annual growth of labour productivity in retail trade and wholesale trade between 1993 and 2000 reached the lofty levels of 4.6 per cent and 5.2 per cent respectively, compared to 2.2 per cent and 3.0 per cent respectively between 1982 and 1990. Productivity growth in finance and real estate also increased notably, to 2.1 per cent between 1993 and 2000, compared to 0.2 per cent between 1982 and 1990. In all the other non-manufacturing industries—including transport and public utilities, communications, construction, mining, and miscellaneous services–productivity growth failed to grow or actually fell. Brenner, *The Boom and the Bubble*, p. 235, Table 9.2. Compare W. Nordhaus, 'Productivity Growth and the New Economy', *Brookings Papers on Economic Activity*, 2002, no. 2, especially p. 233, Table 6.

Table 15.7. US commercial banks: rates of return on equity and assets, 1949–2004 (per cent).

	1949–59	1960–69	1970–79	1980–90	1991–2000	2001–04
Return on equity	9.2	10.5	11.9	9.7	13.2	13.4
Return on assets	0.7	0.8	0.7	0.6	1.1	1.3

Source: Federal Deposit Insurance Corporation, on-line at http://www.fdic.gov/hsob.

unmatched opportunities to rake in fees for superintending share issues and mergers and acquisitions, while simultaneously managing the explosion of household and corporate borrowing. Meanwhile, the nascent run-up in residential housing offered still another huge field for making profits.

During the long business cycle between 1990 and 2000, commercial banks' rate of return on assets rose one-third higher than in any other comparable period in the postwar epoch, on equity about 12 per cent higher. Between 1994 and 2000, profits of the financial sector as a whole, *including interest received*, doubled, and accounted for a stunning 75 per cent of the *increase* in total corporate profits after payment of interest accrued in these years. Already accounting for 30 per cent of total corporate profits net of interest by 1997, financial profits amounted to almost 40 per cent just three years later in 2000. (See p. 299, Figure 15.5.)

The years between 1995 and 1997 constituted a brief era of overlap and transition, between the extended period of manufacturing-led profitability revival culminating in economy-wide revitalization between 1993 and 1997 and the period of stock-market-driven expansion leading to New Economy boom and profitability crisis between 1995 and 2000. Due to the lagged effect of the revaluation of the dollar, the recovery of manufacturing profitability had not yet ceased to impart its momentum to the economy. The wealth effect of the equity price boom was already, moreover, providing its own impetus. As a consequence, the economy displayed a vitality not seen in decades. The manufacturing sector could not prevent its profit rate from ceasing to rise, but managed to keep it from falling. Manufacturing export growth continued to rise impressively, reaching its zenith at 13.5 per cent in 1997, and spurred the ongoing acceleration of manufacturing output. Most fundamental, however, was the major increase in profitability in the non-manufacturing sector, which, after having languished for a decade, bounded upward by 18 per cent as a consequence of the sudden outrunning by productivity growth of real (product) wage growth, made possible by the aforementioned jump-up of non-manufacturing productivity growth against a backdrop of continuing wage stagnation. The rise of non-manufacturing productivity growth at this juncture appears attributable, as noted, to the parallel increases in the rate of growth of the sector's output and its capital–labour ratio, which themselves can most likely be explained, in general terms, by the mutually reinforcing impulses provided by the manufacturing-led recovery and the growing wealth effect of the stock-market boom, as well again as the revaluation of the dollar. To complete the picture, it must be emphasized that the non-manufacturing sector prospered in this interval, even though its produc-

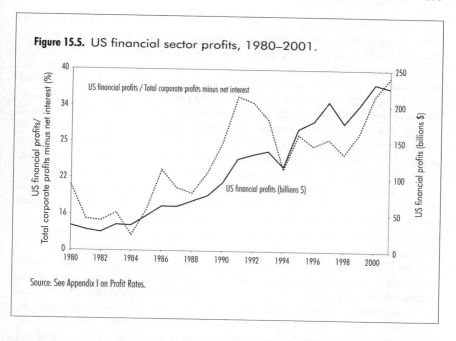

Figure 15.5. US financial sector profits, 1980–2001.

Source: See Appendix I on Profit Rates.

tivity growth was only slightly more than half that of the manufacturing sector, with the consequence that non-manufacturing unit labour costs increased at a rate of 1.3 per cent per annum, while manufacturing unit labour costs *declined* at a rate of 1.5 per cent per year in manufacturing. The non-manufacturing profit rate could nonetheless soar while that for manufacturing stayed flat, because the non-manufacturing sector was unaffected by the intensifying competition that held back manufacturing, while it benefited from the same ascending dollar that was placing downward pressure on manufacturing returns. Thanks especially to dollar revaluation, it was therefore able to raise its prices between 1995 and 1997 at an average annual rate of 2 per cent, while manufacturers were obliged to *reduce* theirs at a rate of 0.45 per cent per year.

In 1997, with the manufacturing profit rate still holding up and the non-manufacturing profit rate rising rapidly, the rate of profit for the private economy as a whole reached its level of 1969 for the first time in almost thirty years. The US economy flourished as it had not in recent memory and pulled the rest of the world with it, out of the doldrums of the first half of the 1990s and into generalized prosperity. For the first time in a long time, all three leading regional capitalist blocks, as well as East Asia, grew rapidly together. The US and the world system seemed on the verge of regaining their 1960s vibrancy. Nevertheless, as it turned out, this was an illusion, for the foundations of the international boom were already crumbling.

From International Crisis to High-tech Mania

As the rising dollar, accompanied by easy credit, enhanced US asset prices and thereby US economic growth from 1995, while shifting the weight of international over-capacity and reduced profitability from Japan and Germany to the US, similar forces brought about similar effects and a similar pattern in the economies of East Asia at the very same time, setting off a chain reaction of crisis that would ultimately engulf the US itself. During the previous half-decade, the East Asian economies had reached the height of their postwar dynamism, their growth amplified by the same declining dollar that was simultaneously paving the way for the recovery of manufacturing profitability in the US, as well as the flood of portfolio investment that poured into the region in search of higher earnings in the wake of the US cyclical downturn. Meanwhile, as Japan's recession deepened while the yen continued its precipitous ascent, Japanese multinationals radically increased foreign direct investment in Southeast Asia and a great swath of Japanese financial capital accompanied it, the latter vastly swelled by cheap credit made available by the Bank of Japan in its attempt to reflate the economy upon the bursting of the bubble (much of which was redirected toward the mainland via the 'carry trade').

By 1996, total capital formation in East Asia (excluding Japan)—the sum of corporate, government, and housing investment—had grown by nearly 300 per cent over its level of 1990, compared to slightly over 40 per cent in Japan and the US and just 10 per cent in Europe. In that year, investment in East Asia (excluding Japan) accounted for more than 18 per cent of the investment in these four regions combined, three times its share just six years earlier. Nevertheless, by this juncture, the foundations of East Asia's long historic boom were (like those of the US) rapidly deteriorating as a result of the sudden huge appreciation of the region's currencies, which rose in tandem with the dollar in the wake of the reverse Plaza Accord, as well as the worsening of international over-capacity in manufacturing to which East Asia itself had made such a signal contribution over the previous decade.[27]

The deep devaluation of the yen, which declined by 60 per cent between 1995 and 1997, coming hard on the heels of the devaluations of the Chinese renminbi in 1994 and the Mexican peso in 1995, placed the East Asian NICs and Little Tigers in a tightening vice—squeezed between intensifying competition from Chinese and Mexican manufacturers, who were accelerating their exports of low-end goods on to the world, market, and newly competitive Japanese producers, who were asserting their accustomed place in high-end goods. The enormous accretions made to the region's plant and equipment over the previous years, which had hitherto yielded fast-rising profit rates, turned out suddenly to manifest over-accumulation, due to the combination of worsening international over-capacity and the precipitate ascent of the region's currencies. Between 1992 and 1995, South Korea, the region's leading economy, had enjoyed a spectacular 67 per cent increase in its annual nominal exports and by 1994–95 its manufacturing profit rate had soared to its highest point since 1988, double the average for 1991–93. But the ensuing turnaround could not have been more abrupt. In 1996, as export prices and export values plunged, the South Korean manufacturing profit rate declined by 75 per cent and plummeted deep into negative territory in 1997 and 1998.[28]

Nevertheless, as in the US, even as manufacturing profitability fell, asset prices rocketed. As the value of their exports soared through 1995, the Northeast Asian

---

27   Bevacqua, 'Whither the Japanese Model?' p. 414.
28   Brenner, *The Boom and the Bubble*, pp. 158–62, Tables 6.1 and 6.2.

NICs had enjoyed rising trade and current account surpluses. When these were converted by governments into local currencies, they tended to swell the domestic money supply, easing the cost of borrowing. As a consequence, land, housing and equity prices were, by 1995, already being forced upwards. Paradoxically, when from that juncture their manufacturing economies sagged under the impact of the sudden revaluation of local currencies, the rise of asset values accelerated, amplified in international terms by the region's rising exchange rates and pumped up further by the ensuing influx of foreign speculative monies. As US equity prices ascended into the heavens, an East Asian asset price bubble blew up alongside it, even as the foundations of the East Asian manufacturing export boom disintegrated.

The growing divergence between falling profits and rising asset prices was unsustainable. As export remittances fell sharply, East Asian producers found it ever more difficult to repay loans. From the beginning of 1997, a succession of South Korea's leading *chaebol*, the great corporate financial–industrial conglomerates that dominated its economy, went bankrupt. In expectation that loans would henceforth be more difficult to collect, funds began to quit the region, and with ever greater speed. As a consequence, asset prices began to crumble, which accelerated the outflow of funds and soon made for downward pressure on the local currencies. But devaluation only raised the dollar value of foreign debts in terms of the local currencies, making them that much more difficult to repay. Central banks raised short-term interest rates to stem the exodus of capital and prevent currencies from collapsing. But, this caused financial institutions, which depended on borrowing from central banks, to go bankrupt, leading to the collapse of asset prices and the panicked flight of capital. Over the course of 1997, East Asia suffered a historic net decline in capital inflows of $105 billion, from an influx of $93 billion in 1996 to a withdrawal of $12 billion in 1997, and the region entered free fall.

The crisis in East Asia, which broke out in the summer of 1997, steadily worsened over the following year. Through much of 1998, asset prices continued to fall and, as money flew out the region, currencies collapsed and the price of East Asian goods fell with them, placing great pressure, direct and indirect, on the rest of the world economy. During the summer of 1998, the East Asian crisis spilled over into the less-developed countries. In August, the Russian government defaulted on its debt. The Brazilian economy started to melt down shortly thereafter. The core of the capitalist world system now came under threat: not only a Japanese economy barely emerging from recession, but also a US economy enjoying an enormous, though highly unstable, boom.

Japan had benefited immediately from the deep yen devaluation set off by the reverse Plaza Accord. Between 1995 and 1997, exports boomed. Hitherto deeply depressed manufacturing profit rates began to rise as a consequence and so too did capital accumulation. Manufacturing investment had plummeted at an average annual rate of 14 per cent in 1992–94 inclusive, but suddenly jumped up at an average annual rate of 11 per cent in 1995–97 inclusive. The economy seemed to be returning to health, driven as usual by rising exports.[29]

Nevertheless, the Japanese recovery turned out to be fragile, and in the end

---

29   OECD, *Economic Survey. Japan 1998*, Paris 1998, p. 154, Figure 32; OECD, *Economic Survey. Japan 1999*, Paris 1999, p. 33.

unsustainable. Anxious to repair government balance sheets that had gone deeply into the red as a consequence of massive deficit spending during the first half of the decade to pull the economy from its doldrums, Japan's economic authorities overestimated the strength of the cyclical upturn. They not only cut back abruptly on the growth of government expenditures but also, in March 1997, imposed a hefty new value-added tax. The resulting shock to demand brought a sharp slowdown of growth, which was made worse by the government's reluctance to incur new budget deficits to jump-start the economy, even as it slid back towards recession. By the same token, in view of the situation by this time facing Japanese corporations, the government's turn to monetary ease to stimulate the economy in place of fiscal deficits was entirely insufficient to restart the expansion.[30]

When the great land and equity price bubble had burst in 1990–91, it had left the Japanese economy burdened with an enormous overhang of excess capacity, the residue of the historic wave of investment that the rapid rise in asset prices had provoked, but then left behind. Yet, with the growth of exports collapsing to 2.5 per cent per annum between 1991 and 1995, over-capacity proved especially difficult for Japan to cope with. The Japanese political economy was designed to repress consumption and imports and to subsidize investment and exports, with the goal of accelerating the growth of productiveness. In this it had succeeded to an historically unprecedented extent, but a tendency to produce more goods and services than the domestic market could absorb was an unavoidable by-product. Surplus output drove Japan's exports systematically upward, which helped to amplify growth, especially by nurturing economies of scale, but it also rendered the economy dependent upon those exports to prevent the emergence of over-capacity. Yet, when exports flagged and over-capacity did arise, the economy was structurally ill-prepared to respond. This was because multiple mechanisms, ultimately defended by the state, tended both to prevent leading corporations and banks from going out of business and to stand in the way of layoffs. In this respect, the Japanese economy was the polar opposite of that of the US, where the politico-legal system rendered bankruptcies both less avoidable and less onerous for corporations, while it placed few if any restrictions on discharging employees. Because, in Japan, the reallocation of means of production and labour from less profitable industries into more profitable ones could not easily be facilitated through defaults and firings, it tended to have to take place through existing firms' and industrial groups' reallocation of resources into new lines via new investment. But the latter could not easily happen against a background of slowed growth, let alone recession—when firms' obligatory retention of redundant means of production and labour would exaggerate the decline in profitability and make investment difficult to undertake. It required the expansion of demand, and this placed a premium, once again, on the growth of exports. It was the Japanese economy's inability either to slough off means of production sufficiently, or to detonate an export boom, that doomed it to stagnation, and worse, through most of the 1990s.

Faced with the build-up of over-capacity during the bubble economy of the later 1980s, no doubt made worse by the burst of investment between 1995 and 1997, Japan's corporations now found themselves hamstrung in their efforts to cut back.

---

30   OECD, *Economic Survey. Japan 1998*, pp. 2–5, 36–45.

To reduce their labour force, they were obliged to depend largely upon retirements, using dismissal very sparingly, with the result that excess labour was, by 1998, running, in some estimates, at over 10 per cent. At the same time, excess plant and equipment was at a postwar high, with capacity utilization in manufacturing far below its average for the previous thirty years. Meanwhile, as the unavoidable concomitant of the rise of industrial over-capacity, firms were hugely burdened by long-term debt, much of it incurred to finance the enormous burst of investment made possible by the bubble but barely reduced in subsequent years because the feeble growth of output and profits had failed to allow it. The outcome was that by 1998 the rate of return on equity, at just 2 per cent, was less than half the average rate for the fifteen years before 1991. According to OECD estimates, in order to bring the rate of return back up to the latter level, Japanese assets would have had to be reduced by 47 per cent.[31]

Against this background of over-capacity making for vastly reduced profitability, it is not surprising that the government's reduced interest rates did little to spur capital accumulation, but rather provoked a huge revival of the 'carry trade', as a great flood of money borrowed at rock-bottom interest rates in yen and converted to dollars left the country for investment in US equities and other assets. The lowered cost of borrowing plus the flight of funds did, however, very much bring down the value of the yen against the dollar, historically the surest way to get the economy turning over. In the not too distant past, yen devaluation had been a reliable route to economic vibrancy because it made it possible for Japanese exporters to gain better access to the US market, and it appeared to have begun to do so again in 1995–97, before the government's precipitate turn to macro-economic austerity. Nevertheless, the fact remains that between 1985 and 1995 the Japanese economy had been countering the irrepressible rise of the yen precisely by reducing its reliance on the US market and reorienting investment, trade, and bank finance to East Asia. In 1985, Japan had sent 40 per cent of its exports to the US market, but by 1996 it sent only 29 per cent. During the same period, Japanese exports to East Asia as a share of the total increased from 19 per cent to 37 per cent. The ironic outcome was that, at the very time when, in the wake of the reverse Plaza Accord, the decline of the yen was restoring competitiveness to Japanese exports and raising hopes of renewed growth, it was destroying the ultimate basis for economic recovery by exacerbating the crisis of East Asian manufacturing. With the aid of the low yen, Japanese exporters undercut East Asian exporters on world markets and Japanese manufacturers stifled East Asian importers in Japan's domestic market. Then, starting in spring 1997, Japanese banks rushed their money out of the region as fast as they had rushed it in, as East Asian manufacturing profits collapsed and the asset price bubbles that had inflated during the previous two years began to deflate. Japan's leading market—which was by now of course East Asia—disinte-

---

31   OECD, *Economic Survey. Japan 1999*, pp. 47–58. 'It would have been no surprise if firms had already engaged in a round of severe cost reductions years ago, in response to disappointing sales and profit outcomes. But this did not occur .... Instead, both personnel and sales and administrative expenses have continued their inexorable rise as a share of sales. The result has been a further dwindling in recurring profit, swamping the rise that occurred in the brief recovery from the post-bubble recession' (p. 55).

32   Murphy, 'Japan's Economic Crisis', pp. 37ff; Bevacqua, 'Whither the Japanese Model?'; OECD, *Economic Survey. Japan 1998*, pp. 2–5, 36–45; OECD, *Economic Survey. Japan 1996*, Paris 1996, p. 181, Table L; OECD, *Economic Survey. Japan 1997*, Paris 1997, p. 229, Table L.

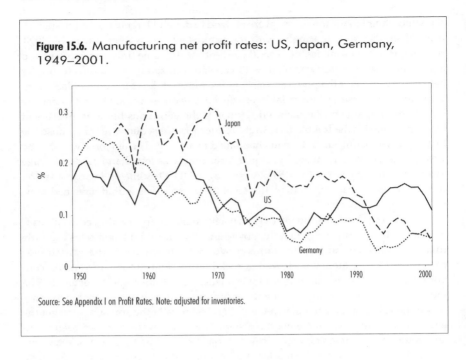

Figure 15.6. Manufacturing net profit rates: US, Japan, Germany, 1949–2001.

Source: See Appendix I on Profit Rates. Note: adjusted for inventories.

grated. In 1998, Japanese exports to the region fell by more than 30 per cent, causing total Japanese exports to decline.[32]

Profitability now fell back sharply, as did capacity utilization and investment growth. With GDP going negative by 2.8 per cent in 1998, the Japanese economy, having never really recovered from the deep cyclical downturn of 1991–95, recoiled into its worst recession of the postwar period, delivering still another crippling blow to the already reeling East Asian economies, a blow that boomeranged back upon Japan itself. Between 1995 and 2000, the average manufacturing profit rate fell a further 15 per cent from its average level between 1990 and 1995, and in 1998, 1999, and 2000 hit its postwar nadir. Not surprisingly, during this half-decade the growth of GDP, capital stock, and real wages in Japan, as well as the level of unemployment, were the worst for any comparable period since World War II. (See Figure 15.6.)

Nor could the US economy escape the East Asian contagion. In 1998, as the dollar continued to ascend, East Asian markets contracted, and East Asian distress sales on the world market increased, the annual increase of US goods exports collapsed virtually to zero (0.6 per cent) after having reached its apex just the year before at above 13 per cent. Corporate profits (net of interest) had begun to decline as early as the last quarter of 1997 and by the second quarter of 1998 had fallen (on an annual basis) more than $90 billion dollars, or about 13 per cent, from their peak in the third quarter of 1997. In acknowledgement of the fall-off in earnings, as well as the looming threat from East Asia, from just after mid-year the S&P500 stock index, having doubled from the end of 1995 to July 1998, suddenly reversed direction and, by the time of the Russian default, had slithered downwards by 20 per cent, threatening to extinguish the wealth effect and thereby terminate the expansion. By late

September a major crisis was unfolding, signalled by the opening up of enormous spreads, or differentials, between interest rates paid on the relatively safe bonds issued by the US Treasury and more risky corporate bonds and loans to Third World governments. Hedge funds and investment banks' investment operations in their own name, both of which tend to be highly leveraged—that is, heavily dependent upon borrowing—were hardest hit, losing untold billions.[33]

The nadir came on 20 September 1998 when the huge Long Term Capital Management (LTCM) hedge fund admitted to the authorities that it was facing catastrophic losses. The international financial system seemed to be freezing up. But, at this decisive juncture the Federal Reserve Board entered the fray, bringing together a consortium of fourteen Wall Street banks and brokerage houses to organize a $3.6 billion rescue of LTCM. The Fed justified this bailout of a non-bank on the grounds that, had it failed to act, the solvency of the international financial system would have been put in jeopardy, with credit markets seizing up.[34] In order to stabilize the situation, the Fed followed up, in short order, with three successive cuts in interest rates. In case anyone failed to get the message, throughout the first half of 1999 Greenspan announced, again and again, in no uncertain terms, that information technology had worked a remarkable transformation of the US economy and, in particular, its capacity to yield profits.[35] In the latter part of November 1999, just to be sure, he used the excuse of the potential breakdown of international computer networks at the turn of the millennium to pump sufficient liquidity into the system to push down the Federal Funds Rate, the interest rate at which banks borrow from each other, from 5.5 per cent to below 4 per cent, accomplishing thereby an unprecedently rapid reduction in the short-term cost of borrowing.[36] This was like throwing gasoline on a raging fire.

The effect of the Fed's series of interventions and Greenspan's supplementary reassurances was electrifying. It did not just rescue the markets but propelled them into orbit. In the short period between the Fed's interest rate reductions of autumn 1998 and spring 2000, the S&P500 index recovered its lost ground from the summer

---

33   For this, and following, paragraph, P. Warburton, *Debt and Delusion. Central Bank Follies that Threaten Economic Diasaster*, London 2000, pp. 263–6; OECD, *Economic Survey. United States 1999*, Paris 1999, pp. 43–55.

34   In the words of William McDonough, President of the New York Fed, who orchestrated the rescue, 'There was a likelihood that a number of credit and interest rate markets would experience extreme price moves and possibly cease to function for a period of one or more days and maybe longer. This would have caused a vicious cycle: a loss of investor confidence, leading to a rush out of private credits, leading to a further widening of credit spreads, leading to further liquidations of positions, and so on.' 'Statement by William J. McDonough, President, Federal Reserve Bank of New York, Before the Committee on Banking and Financial Services, US House of Representatives, 1 October 1998', FRB website. To get a feel for the wave of panic that was enveloping financial circles at this juncture, see the insider's account in M. Mayer, *The Fed*, New York, Free Press 2001, pp. 4–14.

35   'Something special has happened to the American economy ... The synergies that have developed, especially among the microprocessor, the laser, fiber-optics, and satellite technologies, have dramatically raised the potential rates of return on all types of equipment that embody them.' Thus, '[t]he remarkable generation of capital gains of recent years has resulted from a wide variety of technologies that produced crucial synergies in the 1990s'. 'High Tech Industry in the US Economy: Testimony of Chairman Alan Greenspan Before the Joint Economic Committee, US Congress', 14 June 1999 and 'State of the Economy: Testimony of Chairman Alan Greenspan Before the Committee on Ways and Means, US House of Representatives', 20 January 1999, both at FRB website. Compare '[T]he process of *recognizing* the greater value [of our capital stock] has produced capital gains in the equity markets' [emphasis added].

36   IMF, *International Capital Markets. Developments, Prospects, and Key Policy Issues*, Washington, DC September 2000, p. 12; OECD, *Economic Survey. United States 2000*, Paris 2000, p. 69, Table 11.

of 1997 and shot up by 50 per cent. Most spectacular of course was the high-tech-
and internet-dominated NASDAQ index, which doubled between autumn 1998 and
May 1999 and, after a lull during summer 1999, doubled again in the brief interval
from early October 1999 to March 2000. Symptomatically, from October–November
1998 through March 2000, stock values outside the New Economy remained essentially flat, so that the rapid rise in equity prices in the final, most fevered phase of
the bubble was accounted for virtually entirely by technology, media, and telecommunication shares.[37]

The new take-off of the equity markets spurred a climactic acceleration of the
long 1990s expansion. Between, 1997 and mid-2000, GDP growth quickened, driven
to an even greater extent than before by stepped-up capital accumulation that was
itself dependent upon the wealth effect of rampaging equity prices. In this interval,
in both manufacturing and non-manufacturing, the rate of growth of non-
residential investment (that is, investment in plant, equipment and software),
already elevated between 1993 and 1997, reached its highest point of the decade, at
11 per cent and 14 per cent, respectively, and the contribution of non-residential
investment to GDP rose to a postwar high of 37 per cent. As one consequence,
between 1995 and 2000, the manufacturing sector increased its productive capacity
faster than during any other comparable interval in the postwar epoch, at an average
annual rate of almost 7 per cent.

Finally, just as between 1995 and 1997, but with far greater force, the US expansion, now in its culminating phase, pulled the rest of the world from its recession
and motivated a new global expansion, most especially in East Asia. Because the
acceleration of growth in the US took place while the dollar continued to escalate,
US domestic supply fell to an ever increasing extent behind the rise of US demand.
By 2000, the increase of gross domestic purchases was outpacing the growth of gross
domestic product by 25 per cent, and imports had to rise to fill the gap. With US
investment in general and high-tech plant and equipment expenditures in particular leaping skyward, imports of investment goods now rose 20 per cent faster than
imports of consumption goods. East Asian producers, led by Taiwan and South
Korea, as well as Singapore, raised their telecommunications and components
exports in spectacular fashion, transcending their regional crisis with a speed otherwise inconceivable. Japan followed a similar route out of its recession, pulled
upwards not only by US demand for its high-tech capital and intermediate goods,
but also that of the very same East Asian economies whose crisis had initially
plunged it into recession but which were now cresting on the US wave. During the
two years 1998–1999, Japanese exports to the Northeast Asian NICs and the
Southeast Asian Little Tigers had declined at the average annual rates of 17 per cent
and 33 per cent, respectively, compared to 1997. But in 2000, Japanese exports to
both these regions jumped by 20 per cent. Last but not least, Western Europe itself
emerged from stagnation, driven forward by its German dynamo, which was, as
usual, finding its way toward revitalization by way of exports, especially of cars

37   IMF, *World Economic Outlook. Fiscal Policy and Macroeconomic Stability*, Washington, DC, May 2001,
p. 59.
38   UBS Warburg, *US Hard Landing—European Outperformance?* London, July 2000; UBS Warburg, *Global
Economic Perspectives*, London, 19 April 2001; Bank for International Settlements, *71st Annual Report 1 April
2000–31 March* 2001, Basel, 11 June 2001, pp. 12, 13, 43.

and machine tools, to the US market. In the year 2000, the rest of the world rode the US recovery to an enormous global boom, but it was riding the tail of a tiger.[38]

The sucking in of record goods imports at a time when the rest of the world was capable of absorbing only very limited US exports could not but detonate a history-making explosion of US trade and current account deficits. Between 1993 and 1997, as the US economy grew rapidly, the current account deficit had increased, but slowly, because US competitiveness remained relatively strong (especially because the impact of the currency revaluation was felt only with a lag). In 1997, as a percentage of GDP, it was still at only half the record level of 1986. But in the brief period between 1997 and 2000, under the impact of both dollar revaluation and East Asian crisis, the current account deficit *tripled*, its increase totally accounted for by a parallel record-smashing increase of the trade deficit by a factor of 3.5. At the root of this explosion was the takeoff of the manufacturing trade deficit, which rose by two and a half times, accounting for about 70 per cent of the increase in external deficits (the ascent of the trade deficit in oil explaining most of the rest). An increase in the trade deficit is not necessarily problematic, as it can be caused simply by the faster growth of the deficit country than that of its trading partners. However, in this case, as during the first half of the 1980s when analogous rapid increases of debt and asset prices detonated a similar economic pattern, rising trade and current account deficits emerged against a background of worsening over-supply in international manufacturing and were driven by a huge revaluation of the dollar, which, along with the crisis and ensuing currency devaluation in East Asia, led to runaway imports and difficulty in exporting. These external deficits therefore brought with them enormous downward pressure on manufacturing profits, making a crisis for the manufacturing sector unavoidable. As in the early 1980s, the East Asian manufacturing economies (including Japan) were responsible for the greater part of the decline in manufacturing competitiveness and accounted for an overwhelming proportion of the manufacturing trade deficit in the years between 1997 and 2000.

In the end, there was no escaping the fact that the explosion of investment and consumption that drove the last phase of the US expansion—as well as the major uptick in productivity growth to which it gave rise—was heavily dependent upon a historic increase in borrowing, which was itself made possible by a record equity price run-up that was powered by speculation in defiance of actual corporate returns. Rather than discovering and funding the most promising fields for expansion—as in the fables of the Federal Reserve and the Council of Economic Advisers[39]—the deregulated US financial sector ignored the paucity of underlying corporate profits and drove an epoch-making *misallocation* of funds into hi-tech paper assets and, in turn, as a consequence, a parallel, and equally titanic, *misdirection* of new plant, equipment, and software into over-subscribed manufacturing and related lines, especially information technology. The logic behind this behaviour lay in the peculiar constraints under which financial markets operate, which could not be further from the fantasies of orthodox economic theory. As equity prices began to rise

---

39   See 'The Annual Report of the Council of the Economic Advisers' for 2001, which, though completed as late as December 2000, constitutes a triumphalist paen to the New Economy, accepting the trends of both the real and financial economy of the previous five years at face value and attributing to the financial markets a revolutionary role in ushering in a new high tech order. *Economic Report of the President 2001*, especially pp. 65-67, 106—110.

strongly from 1995–1996, fund managers were thus under heavy pressure to buy, even if, in light of the growing gap between stock prices and profits, they doubted the long-term viability of their purchases. This was because the criterion by which they are judged and rewarded by their employers is the (short-term) profitability of their investments. Had fund managers refused to buy equities, especially of New Economy companies, they would have failed to make the (short term) returns that their rivals were in fact netting as share prices rose, and thus risked losing their jobs. At the same time, even if, in the longer run, the assets that they had purchased went sour, as of course they did, they could not be held responsible, since so many of their competitors had done the same thing that they had. Keynes's famous 'beauty contest' dynamic thus drove the inherently speculative process: to maximise profits, financiers had little choice but to base their investment decisions on their best guess as to what assets everyone else would be deciding to buy and sell in the short run, not on their own evaluations as to the intrinsic long-term worth of those assets. These norms constitute, of course, a recipe for the herd behavior so characteristic of financial markets … and the momentum of the ensuing stampede reached epic proportions because the Fed was there to counter the equity markets' every move toward self-correction, while providing a rationale for the markets' apparent irrationality.

The gigantic scale of the misallocation of financial investment was evident in the unprecedented gap that opened up between corporate equity values and corporate earnings, especially in high technology. Between 1997 and 2000, the final frenetic phase of the upward explosion of share values, total corporate profits after taxes net of interest *fell* in absolute terms by a stunning 20 per cent even as the index of the New York Stock Exchange rose by 50 per cent. (See p. 292, Figure 15.4.) In the wake of the Fed's rescue of the economy, between November 1998 and March 2000, prices of stocks in the technology, media, and telecommunications (TMT) sector rose no less than four times faster than profits in that sector.[40] The huge misdirection of plant, equipment, and software was manifested in the intensification of the already-existing problem of overcapacity and falling profitability in the manufacturing sector, especially by its extension deep into the heartland of the New Economy—computers and microchips, as well as telecommunications and telecommunications components. Constituting just 8 per cent of GDP, information technology industries accounted for an amazing—and quite unsustainable—33 per cent of the economy's total GDP growth between 1995 and 2000. Within the information technology sector, the growth of telecommunications and the industries that supplied its components, took on truly gargantuan proportions. Making up at best 3 per cent of GDP, they added a stunning 331,000 jobs between 1996 and 2000, and in 2000 they provided 25 per cent of economy-wide growth of investment in equipment and software. In 1999, expenditures on information technology equipment and software were responsible for more than 11 percentage points of the huge 14 per cent growth in total real equipment and software spending by business. Taken together, between 1995 and 2000, productive capacity in computers, communication equipment, and semi-conductors grew by a factor of *five*, accounting in the

---

40   Bank for International Settlements, *71st Annual Report*, p. 103, Table VI.1, as well as underlying data provided by the Bank for International Settlements. The telecommunications industry is not, technically, located in the manufacturing sector, although the producers of components for it are.

process for more than half of the record-breaking increase of productive capacity in the manufacturing sector as a whole in this quinquennium.

Thanks to the rapid rise of manufacturing investment growth made possible by the last phase of the equity price bubble, the average annual growth of manufacturing productivity, already rapid between 1993 and 1997, at 4.6 per cent, increased still further to 5.5 per cent between 1997 and 2000, compared to 2.9 per cent between 1985 and 1995. On this basis, despite the fact that the growth of nominal manufacturing compensation suddenly zoomed to 5.45 per cent per annum in the same interval, from just 1.6 per cent between 1995 and 1997, manufacturers were able to keep the average annual growth of unit labour costs from rising. Nevertheless, this impressive effort was insufficient to prevent manufacturing profitability from withering under pressure from the runaway dollar, which continued its rise at the average annual pace of 5 per cent, as well as rapidly intensifying US and international manufacturing over-capacity, which was made all the greater by the East Asian financial crisis. Between 1997 and 2000, world export prices measured in dollars declined at the average annual rate of 4 per cent and the average annual increase of US manufacturing exports was limited to 5 per cent, compared to 11 per cent between 1993 and 1997. Even so, one might still have predicted that, with US personal consumption of (manufactured) durable goods rocketing skyward at the astounding pace of 12 per cent per annum in the same period (compared to 5 per cent per annum between 1993 and 1997), the expansion of US demand would have been sufficient to assure the prosperity of the manufacturing sector. In fact, due to the worsening of international competition and further build-up of excess capacity in the US and on a world scale, between 1997 and 2000 capacity utilization in the US manufacturing sector actually *declined* significantly. At the same time, US manufacturing product prices *fell* at an average annual rate of 1.25 per cent, even faster than unit labour costs, thus squeezing profits. As a consequence, the manufacturing rate of profit dropped by 15.5 per cent in that interval.[41] (See p. 310, Figure 15.7 and p. 312, Figure 15.8.)

Due to the amplification of the wealth effect in the last phase of the equity price bubble, the cyclical expansion of the 1990s, which technically originated in March 1991, was able to reach the historically unprecedented length of ten years. With employment growing without cease during this period, at an average annual rate of just about 2 per cent for the nine years between 1991 and 2000, wages eventually had to break from their torpor, and between 1997 and 2000 they finally did. But this could only spell trouble for that huge portion of the economy outside manufacturing. Over the long period between 1973 and 1995, non-manufacturing employers had not only managed to prevent real wages from rising, but had come to depend on doing so, because of the exceedingly slow growth of non-manufacturing productivity. Between 1995 and 1997, thanks to the speed-up in its productivity growth, the non-

---

41   'Thanks to enormous over-investment, especially in Asia, the world is awash with excess capacity in computer chips, steel, cars, textiles, and chemicals … None of this excess capacity is likely to be shut down quickly, because cash-strapped firms have an incentive to keep factories running, even at a loss, to generate economic income. The global glut is pushing prices relentlessly lower. Devaluation cannot make excess capacity disappear; it simply shifts the problem to someone else.' 'Could It Happen Again?' *The Economist*, 22 February 1999. For a very similar account, see Bank for International Settlements, *69th Annual Report 1998–1999*, Basel, 7 June 1999, pp. 5, 146

Figure 15.7. The growth of US manufacturing product prices, US goods export prices, and world manufacturing export prices, 1979–2000.

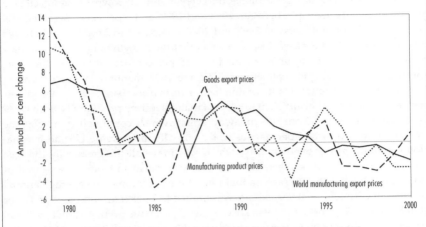

Sources: Courtesy of IMF; BEA NIPA and GPO By Industry. Note: World manufacturing export prices: trade weighted.

manufacturing sector did briefly break free of this syndrome. But because productivity growth in the non-manufacturing sector had hitherto been so very low, the near doubling of its pace of the previous decade during this two-year interval raised it only to 1.7 per cent per annum. This was sufficient to make possible an increase in the non-manufacturing rate of profit by almost one-fifth in this short period, but only because wage growth continued to lag. Between 1997 and 2000, non-manufacturing productivity growth rose a bit further, to almost 2 per cent per annum, thanks to the further speed-up of non-manufacturing output and capital stock growth, which was itself facilitated both by the equity price boom and by declining import prices made possible by the same ascent of the dollar that was simultaneously crushing manufacturing. But during the same period, the unending increase in the demand for labour finally caused wage growth in the non-manufacturing sector to break its bonds. Having languished at 0.25 per cent per annum between 1993 and 1997, non-manufacturing real compensation leaped forward at 3 per cent per annum. Because the rate of growth of non-manufacturing productivity was still so restricted, unit labour costs jumped ahead at 2.8 per cent per annum between 1997 and 2000, 75 per cent faster than during the previous couple of years of rising profits. Although non-manufacturers, benefiting from the rising dollar and mostly exempt from international competition, were able to raise prices at a rate of 1.6 per cent per year, whereas manufacturers squeezed by the same rising currency and by system-wide over-capacity had to reduce them during the same interval at 1.25 per cent per annum, this was not nearly fast enough to prevent their profit rates from falling. Even as the New Economy appeared to be rising into the heavens, the structural limitations of the low-wage economy thus pulled the non-manufacturing sector back to earth. Between 1997 and 2000, the profit rate in the non-manufacturing sector fell by a very major 18 per cent, and this, combined with the 15.5 per cent decline in the manufacturing profit rate, brought about a 16.5 per cent fall-off in the profit rate for the private sector as a whole. With the gap continuing to grow between accelerating economic growth and rocketing equity prices on the one hand and falling profitability on the other, it was only a matter of time till the bubble-led boom would reach its terminus. (See p. 312, Figure 15.8.)

Recession

From July 2000, ever-worsening earnings reported by corporations precipitated a stock-market collapse and, in turn, a sharp cyclical downturn, both by reversing the wealth effect and by revealing the mass of redundant productive capacity and the mountain of corporate indebtedness that constituted the dual legacy of the bubble-driven boom. With their market capitalization sharply reduced, firms found it not only more difficult to borrow or issue new shares, but also less attractive to do so, especially since declining profits and the growing threat of bankruptcy led them to try to repair balance sheets overburdened by debt. Having purchased far more plant, equipment, and software than they could profitably set in motion, they could not think of adding means of production or labour, but were obliged either to reduce prices or leave more capacity unused. Either way, they sustained further reductions in their rate of profit. With not only profits but also loans so much harder to come by, it was inevitable that the growth of jobs and new plant and equipment would be cut back, undercutting both investment and consumer demand, and detonating a self-sustaining downward spiral. The crisis of profitability had, in classical fashion, brought about a crisis of aggregate demand.

The rest of the world followed the US downward. Just as the stock market's last upward thrust had rescued not only the US but also the world economy as a whole from the international financial crisis of 1997–98, setting off a short-lived hyperboom, the collapse of US equity prices and investment reversed the process. As the economy rapidly lost energy, US imports plunged, with the result that the economies of Japan, Europe and East Asia lost steam as fast as the US, while the developing world, notably Latin America, was, after a brief honeymoon, projected back into crisis. A mutually reinforcing international recessionary process was thus unleashed, rendered all the more problematic by the degree to which the rest of the world had, over the previous two decades, in the face of stagnating domestic demand, oriented their economies to exports—and thus perforce to the US domestic market. As the rest of the world, deprived of its US motor, sank ever further into recession, the US could look only to itself to launch an economic recovery upon which most of the global economy depended.

The eye of the storm was to be found in the manufacturing sector, as its overcapacity caught up with it. In the single year 2001, manufacturing GDP, having increased by 4.7 per cent in 2000, plunged a staggering 6 per cent; capacity utilization dropped by 7.1 per cent; and employment in terms of hours plummeted 5.4 per cent. Traditional industries such as apparel, textiles and steel were hard hit, as were closely related non-manufacturing industries such as business services. But the core of the problem was to be found in high-technology lines—microprocessors, computers, and telecommunications components, as well of course as telecommu-

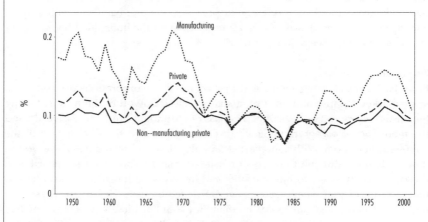

Figure 15.8. US private, manufacturing and non-manufacturing private net profit rates, 1948–2001.

Source: See Appendix I on Profit Rates. Note: adjusted for indirect business taxes and inventories.

nications itself—which saw their ability to make use of the enormous additions to capacity that they had made during the previous half decade suddenly collapse. Capacity utilization in 1999–2000 in computers, communications equipment, and semi-conductors had reached 85.9 per cent; by 2001–02, it had dropped to 59.7 per cent. The extraordinary depth of the crisis in high-tech was revealed in an analysis of the 4,200 companies listed on the NASDAQ Stock Index, home of New Economy industries. The losses these firms reported for the twelve months following 1 July 2000 amounted to $148.3 billion. This was slightly more than the $145 billion in profits that they had realized during the entire five-year boom of 1995 to 2000. As one economist wryly noted, 'What it means is that, with the benefit of hindsight, the later 1990s never happened'.[42] So much for the New Economy boom.

In 2001, the rate of profit in the manufacturing sector as a whole fell by 21.3 per cent, to a level over one-third down from its 1997 peak, while that of the manufacturing durable goods sector, site of all the high-tech lines as well as most of the mainline industries exposed to international competition, dropped by 30 per cent and a breathtaking 46 per cent from 1997. Between 1997 and 2001, as corporate indebtedness soared, manufacturing net interest as a proportion of manufacturing net profits rose from 19 per cent to 40.5 per cent, a postwar record. Partly as a consequence, by 2001, manufacturing profits after payment of interest paid had fallen a total of 44.4 per cent from their high point in 1997.

In telling contrast, the economy outside of manufacturing—neither plagued by systemic over-capacity nor subject to intensifying international competition, yet

42   *Wall Street Journal,* 16 August 2001.

continuing to enjoy the high dollar—largely held its own during the recession. Perhaps most critical in the longer run, non-manufacturing employers took advantage of the sudden sharp weakening of the labour market that accompanied the recession to bring down the growth of real compensation, which fell from 3.2 per cent in 2000 to 1 per cent in 2001. Simultaneously, they succeeded in maintaining productivity growth at around 2 per cent by sustaining the growth of real output at almost 2 per cent, while slightly reducing their labour force. Meanwhile, whereas manufacturing prices fell another 0.4 per cent, non-manufacturing prices rose by 2.4 per cent. The outcome was that the non-manufacturing sector suffered no further fall-off in its profit rate in 2001. Still, because of the profitability decline in the manufacturing sector, the rate of profit for the private economy as a whole did drop by an additional 7 per cent, making for a total decline of 21.5 per cent between 1997 and 2001. (See p. 312, Figure 15.8.)

As was to be expected, employers sought to restore their profitability by making deep reductions in their production costs and expenditures. Manufacturing was the place where over-capacity was mainly focused, so it is understandable that it was also the sector where cutting back for the most part took place. Deep reductions in economy-wide purchasing power were the unavoidable result. Between 2000 and 2003, manufacturing output stayed essentially flat. Capacity utilization fell from 81.5 per cent for 1995–2000 to 73.6 per cent for 2002–3, lower than in any other years in the postwar epoch, except for 1982 and 1975. Manufacturing investment growth also dipped sharply between 2000 and 2003, and in 2004 was still 5 per cent below its 2000 peak. As a result, the manufacturing capital stock failed to grow at all between 2000 and 2004, bringing down the average annual growth of capital stock for the whole of the private economy to 1.9 per cent, less than half its rate during the second half of the 1990s. Above all, manufacturers profoundly reduced employment, eliminating 2.98 million manufacturing jobs between July 2000 and July 2004. This was more than 150 per cent of total private sector jobs lost in the same period, meaning that the economy outside of manufacturing actually gained jobs. Between 1997, its most recent peak, and 2004, manufacturing employment (measured in hours) fell by fully *one-fifth*. After having increased at an average annual rate of 3.8 per cent between 1995 and 2000, aggregate real compensation (real compensation per employee, including benefits, multiplied by employment) in manufacturing thus fell at the average annual rate of 3.1 per cent between 2000 and 2003, thereby accounting for most of the decline in aggregate real compensation that took place in the private economy during that period. Finally, manufacturing exports fell 12 per cent between 2000 and 2002 and remained in 2003 about 10 per cent below their level in 2000; this decrease was responsible for more than 100 per cent of the fall-off of total goods and services exports in these years. Manufacturing *net* exports—exports minus imports—accounted for the entirety of the decline in US net exports during this interval. These major reductions—in the level of manufacturing output, employment, and net exports, as well as the rate of growth of manufacturing investment—delivered a powerful shock to aggregate demand that, all else being equal, would have thrown the economy into deep and extended recession.

Housing Price Bubble Drives the Upturn

Between mid-2000 and mid-2001, GDP and investment growth tumbled to minus 1 per cent and minus 5 per cent, respectively, compared to 5 per cent and 9 per cent, respectively, during the previous twelve months. The growth of economy-wide aggregate real compensation (real compensation per employee, including benefits, multiplied by total employment), which had soared to 4.6 per cent in 2000, fell back below zero in 2001. The growth of real exports of goods and services, at an impressive 8.7 per cent in 2001, collapsed to minus 5.4 per cent in 2001. The economy had entered a tailspin. Conceivably, the Fed could have allowed the deepening recession to run its course, letting the economy purge itself of its enormous over-capacity and allowing asset prices to find their own level. But with the growth of GDP, investment, and exports declining faster than in any other twelve-month period since 1945, the Fed felt it could not take the risk, especially with the stock market and its wealth effect in free fall, the NASDAQ stock index having dived by 40 per cent between September 2000 and January 2001. To stem the tide, beginning in January 2001 the Federal Reserve lowered the cost of borrowing with unprecedented rapidity, reducing short-term interest rates on eleven occasions, from 6.5 per cent to 1.75 per cent, over the course of the year—and then a further total of 0.75 per cent in November 2002 and June 2003, to the level of 1 per cent, where it stayed until the middle of 2004. The outcome was to depress the *real* Federal Funds rate *below zero* for three full years. Nevertheless, as the Fed soon discovered, interest-rate reductions are much more effective in reviving an economy in which the immediate source of recession is a fall in consumption resulting from the tightening of credit—as in all previous cyclical downturns of the postwar period—than in restarting an economy driven into recession by declining investment, employment, and net exports, resulting from over-capacity on a world scale.

Vastly oversupplied with means of production and overburdened by debt, corporations had little incentive to increase hiring or step up the purchase of plant, equipment, and software, let alone to increase borrowing to make these possible, no matter how far interest rates came down. Between 2000 and 2004, private firms eliminated 1.97 million jobs. In the same interval, the average annual growth of non-housing investment remained below that of 2000. Having risen sharply to help power the investment boom of the second half of the 1990s, average annual borrowing by non-financial corporations as a percentage of GDP dropped precipitously, from just under 4 per cent between 1996 and 2000 to just over 1 per cent between 2000 and 2004. Nor could the Fed look to exports to drive the recovery in a world economy reeling from the collapse of US demand and heavily dependent upon the recovery of the US market to regain its own momentum. Even by 2004, real exports of US goods and services were still just 2.2 per cent above where they had been in 2000, whereas real imports of goods and services were 16.5 per cent above that level.

With respect to private business, the Fed was pushing on the proverbial string, its stimulus eliciting little response. It was thus left to rely on households and their consumption. But because jobs were disappearing and wage growth was falling, households had declining capacity to increase their borrowing. Even by 2004, aggregate real compensation (real compensation per employee, including benefits, multiplied by employment) in the private sector had risen only 2.7 per cent above its level of 2000. In order to stimulate the economy, the Fed had little choice therefore but to revert to—or, more precisely, continue with—the 'asset-price Keynesianism' it had been implementing since the second half of the 1990s. But this itself posed a problem: because of the collapse of the stock market in 2000–1, the Fed could not fall back, as it had during the previous decade, upon pumping up corporate equities to spur not only corporate borrowing and thereby corporate investment, but also household borrowing and thereby household consumption. It had to seek instead to force down mortgage rates and inflate the value of residential housing so as facilitate stepped up household borrowing and, in that way, amplify personal consumption. Thanks in large part to the Fed's actions, long-term borrowing costs did fall significantly and housing prices did rise precipitously. Between June 2000 and June 2003, the interest rate on 30-year fixed mortgages fell from 8.29 per cent to 5.23 per cent, a total of 37 per cent. Between 2000 and 2004, housing prices rose, in *real terms* (adjusted by the consumer price index) at the average annual rate of 6.3 per cent, compared to minus 0.6 per cent between 1990 and 1994 (which also encompassed a recession year plus three years of recovery) and just 2.7 per cent in the boom years between 1995 and 2000.[43] These changes together laid the basis for the cyclical upturn.

While the Fed implemented its stimulus by way of the wealth effect of rising real-estate values, the George Bush Jr administration added what had the appearance of a major fiscal stimulus modelled after that of Ronald Reagan, forcing through Congress enormous cuts in taxation and substantial increases in military spending. But these measures were less potent than they appeared. Since most of the reduction in taxation was accounted for by a decrease in the levy on dividends, it benefited the very rich almost exclusively. Its effect was therefore more to increase the purchase of financial assets than to boost expenditures on consumption, or aggregate demand. Then, too, the fact that tax cuts at the federal level had the effect of reducing revenue to money-strapped state governments, forcing them to cut back on spending and in some cases to increase taxation, counteracted much, though not all, of what stimulus they did impart. Military spending amounted to more than three-quarters of the increase in federal expenditures between 2000 and 2004, and did help the economy stay afloat. Even so, it accounted for just 1.1 per cent of the total 9.3 per cent increase in real GDP that took place during that four-year period. With the economy falling into recession, traditional Keynesian policies were no doubt in order, and the Bush administration's spending increases and revenue reductions did bring about a gigantic shift from a hefty federal budget surplus of 3 per cent of GDP in 2000 to a major federal budget deficit of 3.2 per cent of GDP in 2004. But, because they were aimed less to stimulate the economy than to achieve the particular political goals of building up the military and redistributing income to the rich from everyone else, they proved only minimally effective in aiding the economy's revival. The economy would have to continue to rely mainly, as it had been doing since the later 1990s, on asset-price Keynesianism.

Households did assume the vanguard role assigned to them. Between 2000 and

43 'Index of US Housing Prices', Office of Federal Housing Enterprise website.
44 FRB, *Flow of Funds*, Table D.2, Borrowing by Sector.

2004, they took advantage of rocketing housing values and falling interest rates to raise their annual borrowing as a percentage of personal disposable income to an unheard of 11.8 per cent.[44] This was more than double its level at the peak of the equity price bubble in 2000, and almost 20 per cent higher than the previous record, set in 1985. (See p. 317, Figure 15.9.) On this foundation, real personal consumption expenditures, increasing at an average annual rate of 3.0 per cent, drove the cyclical upturn and accounted for *all* the growth of GDP that took place in those four years (See p. 318, Table 15.8.)

Thanks to the huge subsidy to consumption that derived from sharply declining interest rates and the wealth effect of rising residential real estate prices, along with the failure of the dollar to fall all that much, during the first half-decade of the twenty-first century the US economy ended up following a paradoxical and distorted two-track trajectory that had its origins in the last half decade of the twentieth century. The manufacturing sector and related industries experienced a profound contraction, once the stimulus to investment and consumption that had been provided between 1995 and 2000 by the wealth effect of the stock-market bubble ceased to counter the effect of the fall in the manufacturing profit rate. In sharp contrast, due to the rise of housing values, much of the economy outside manufacturing continued to do well. This was especially true of those industries able to respond to the uninterrupted rise of debt-driven consumer spending or to take advantage of falling costs of borrowing or to profit from the build-up of wealth in the form of residential real estate, or to gain from a still relatively high currency. Benefiting from the historically unprecedented ascent in the demand for homes, the construction industry continued to enjoy a record-smashing boom that by 2005 had lasted more than a decade. Retail trade, fuelled by the unbroken rise in private consumption expenditures, also did remarkably well, its real output increasing by 25 per cent in just the four years between 2000 and 2004 and its profits amplified by fast-rising imports, especially from China, themselves puffed up by the undervalued exchange rate of the Chinese currency. Similarly, hotels and restaurants enjoyed ongoing prosperity. Finally, the health services sector continued the meteoric ascent that had begun as long ago as the later 1980s. In the face of the default of manufacturing, it was these industries, plus finance along with real estate, that were mainly responsible for the growth of employment, output, and profits in the real economy throughout the recovery that began at the end of 2001.

The rise of the financial sector had of course already assumed revolutionary proportions and had redrawn the map of the US economy over the course of the 1990s. Amazingly, during the opening years of the new century, the collapse of stock prices and ensuing recession failed to hold it back. On the contrary, the red-hot housing market replaced the equity market and households replaced corporations as generators of business. Less than zero real short term interest rates between mid 2001 and mid 2004, ensured by the Fed, did the rest. By piling up profits in mortgage-related business, as well as in bond trading and underwriting, banks and securities firms were thus able to prosper to an extraordinary degree, even in the face of slowed growth and the huge decline in corporate borrowing. With the Fed effectively *guaranteeing* for an extended period that it would not raise interest rates—and then, when it finally began to raise them, telegraphing the precise speed at which it would do so—financial institutions could not help but make unprecedented profits with little

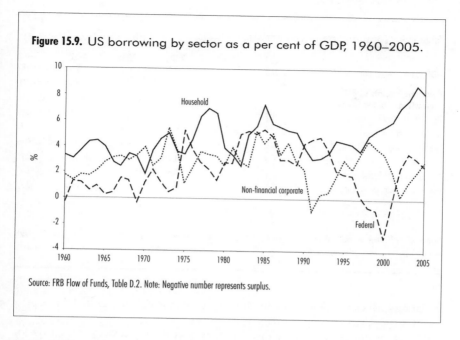

Figure 15.9. US borrowing by sector as a per cent of GDP, 1960–2005.

Source: FRB Flow of Funds, Table D.2. Note: Negative number represents surplus.

or no risk, simply by borrowing short cheap and lending long dear. Between 2000 and 2004, commercial banks' rate of return on equities and assets actually rose above their record levels of the 1990s, and profits for the financial sector as a whole ascended with them (see p. 298, Table 15.7). Indeed, as the non-financial economy languished through 2003, the growth of financial profits far outran non-financial profits and came temporarily to constitute, according to Morgan Stanley, (after the payment of interest) something like 50 per cent of total corporate profits.[45]

A Self-limiting Trajectory

The Fed's turn to ever-easier credit brought a semblance of order to the economy, in much the way it had intended. Between 2000 and 2004 , the US private business sector, in the midst of a titanic process of retrenchment in aid of profits, could contribute precious little to the increase of aggregate demand and thereby economic growth by way of employment, non-residential investment, aggregate real compensation, and net exports. What therefore ultimately proved indispensable in driving the cyclical upturn that began in November 2001 was the ability of the wealth effect of the rapid rise in housing prices, incited by the Fed, to take over from the wealth effect of the equity price bubble of the later 1990s in providing the demand to push the economy forward. Economic growth in the opening years of the new millennium thus continued to follow the same asset-price-, wealth-rather-than-income-, driven trajectory that it had pursued in the closing years of the old one. But it did so, as between 1995 and 2000, by means of—and at the cost of—

45   Steve Galbraith et al., 'Bank of America' and 'Fading Fog' in Morgan Stanley US and the Americas Investment Research, 21 June 2001 and 21 September 2003 respectively.

Table 15.8. Consumption driven growth.

	2001	2002	2003	2004	2005	Total
GDP (Annual per cent change)	0.8	1.6	2.7	4.2	3.5	12.8
Percentage points of GDP growth accounted for by:						
Personal consumption expenditures	1.7	1.9	2.1	2.7	2.5	10.9
Nonresidential Investment	-0.5	-1.1	0.1	0.9	0.9	0.3
Residential Investment	0.0	0.2	0.4	0.6	0.4	1.6
Inventories	-0.9	0.4	0.1	0.4	-0.3	-0.4
Net exports of goods and services	-0.2	-0.7	-0.5	-0.7	-0.3	-2.4
Government consumption expenditures and gross investment	0.6	0.8	0.5	0.4	0.3	2.7
— National defence	0.2	0.3	0.4	0.3	0.1	1.2

Source: BEA NIPA. Note: negative numbers indicate per cent GDP growth reduced by, just as positive numbers indicate per cent GDP growth increased by.

inflating financial asset bubbles and inviting economic imbalances that threatened its very capacity to sustain itself.

As shareholders accumulated wealth by way of the rapid stock market rise of the second half of the 1990s, they were able to demand more expensive houses faster than could be supplied, detonating the rise of real estate values. As their house prices increased, homeowners were enabled to pay ever-increasing sums for their residences, on the assumption that housing values would continue upwards, in the same way as had equity prices. When the stock market crashed and the New Economy boom came to an end in 2000–1, not just the Fed's record interest-rate reductions, but also a major transfer of funds from the equity to the housing market, kept the game going. Like the stock-market bubble, the real-estate bubble fed upon itself, and increasingly so, with increased borrowing facilitated by rising paper wealth and easy credit making for greater housing demand and still higher real estate values, which provided the collateral for still more borrowing making for more demand and higher housing prices, and so on.[46]

Between 1995 and 1999, as household wealth (on an annualized basis) in the form of equities (including mutual funds) rocketed from $5.3 to $12.05 trillion, household wealth in the form of real estate also rose briskly, though somewhat more modestly, from $8 trillion to $12.5 trillion. Between 1999 and 2002, as household equity values tumbled by almost fifty per cent to $7.3 trillion, household real estate continued to rise in value to $13.7 trillion, going a significant distance to compensate for the stock-market decline. Over the next two and a half years, household residential wealth exploded upwards, increasing by more than 30 per cent to $18.4 trillion in the middle of 2005, dwarfing household equity wealth which continued to languish at just under $10 trillion. In just the four years between 2000 and 2004,

46   D. Baker, 'The Run-Up in Home Prices: Is it Real or Is It Another Bubble?', Center for Economic Policy Research, 5 August 2002, CEPR website.

47   FRB, *Flow of Funds*, Table B.100, Balance Sheet of Households and Nonprofit Organizations.

household wealth in the form of real estate increased by more than 50 per cent, and by mid-2005 it was more than 80 per cent greater than household wealth in the form of equities.[47] (See p. 320, Figure 15.10.)

On the basis of this huge on-paper appreciation of the value of their residences, households were able to withdraw dramatically increased funds from their home equity—by selling their houses at prices surpassing their mortgage debt, buying new ones, and still having cash left over; by refinancing and increasing the size of their existing mortgages, extracting cash in the process; and by taking out new home equity loans in the form either of second mortgages or lines of credit. If one adds these three sources together, households were able to raise, by way of mortgage equity withdrawals, the astounding sums of $492 billion, $693 billion, and $734 billion dollars respectively, in the first three years of the recovery, 2002, 2003, and 2004. The *increase* in mortgage equity withdrawals during this period, between 2001 and 2004, at $373 billion, actually outdistanced the increase in private sector disbursements on wages and salaries (that is, excluding benefits), at $321 billion. In the first quarter of 2005, mortgage equity withdrawals, at $794 billion on an annualized basis, amounted to no less than 9 per cent of personal disposable income (see p. 321, Figure 15.11). According to the Federal Reserve, households use roughly fifty per cent of their mortgage equity withdrawals to finance consumer expenditures. All told, taking also into account residential investment and purchases of home furnishings, as well as mortgage equity withdrawals, housing accounted for an astonishing 27.1 per cent of total GDP growth between 2000 and the middle of 2005. By virtue of housing's contribution during this interval, the average annual growth of GDP, which would without it have been 1.7 per cent, reached 2.4 per cent.[48] (See p. 322, Figure 15.12.)

Nevertheless, it is hard to see how housing's huge subsidy to the economic expansion can long sustain itself. This is for the same reason that record borrowing against rising equities leading to stepped-up investment and consumption during the later 1990s was bound, sooner rather than later, to fall back sharply: that is, residential real estate had entered a bubble. Throughout the postwar period, between 1950 and 1995, house prices grew at approximately the same rate as inflation, that is, the consumer price index. This was no less true during the great postwar boom than in the long downturn that followed. But between 1995 and the middle of 2005, house prices rose by more than 45 per cent after taking inflation into account. This historically unprecedented rapid rise in house prices has generated $5 trillion in housing wealth more than would have been created had housing values risen at the same rate as the consumer price index. A sizeable part of the latter should therefore most probably be considered bubble-generated, and thus subject to disappearance via a housing price correction.[49]

---

48   The figures on mortgage equity withdrawals were provided by the Federal Reserve Board. Economy.com calculated the contribution of housing to GDP growth, based on simulation results using its macroeconomic model system. I wish to thank Mark Zandi, chief economist at Economy.com, for kindly making both sets of data available to me. See M. Zandi, 'Through the Roof', *Regional Financial Review*, November–December 2004, p. 16 and note 2.

49   D. Baker, 'The Housing Bubble Fact Sheet', Center for Economic Policy Research, July 2005, CEPR website.

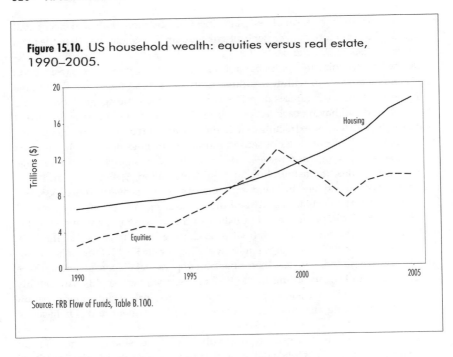

Figure 15.10. US household wealth: equities versus real estate, 1990–2005.

Source: FRB Flow of Funds, Table B.100.

The growth of housing prices compared to that of housing rentals points in the same direction. One would expect these to be the same, since, all else being equal, housing values are merely capitalized rentals. Nevertheless, between 1997 and 2002 the increase of rental prices was already falling behind that of housing prices, and by mid-2005, the ratio of house prices to house rents was 35 per cent above its average level between 1975 and 2000. Put another way, between 1997 and 2005, housing prices increased by 51 percentage points more than did rental prices, an entirely unprecedented divergence. This is a clear indication that housing prices are not being driven up by fundamentals—such as rising incomes, population growth, or a change in consumer preference in favour of housing—which would equally affect rental and housing prices, but by what is in essence speculation. That people are increasingly buying houses for the purpose of reselling them at a profit, or because they expect their values to keep rising, is indicated by the fact that over the last year or two a rapidly rising percentage of house purchases were financed by way of exotic mortgages, requiring zero or negative equity and/or delayed balloon interest payments. According to a study by the National Association of Realtors, one quarter of all houses bought in 2004 were for investment, not owner occupation, and the proportion was no doubt higher in 2005.[50]

Sooner or later the price of residential real estate must be brought into line with rental prices, and this must happen either by way of a rise in rents or a fall in prices,

50   D. Baker and D. Rosnick, 'Will a Bursting Bubble Trouble Bernanke? The Evidence for a Housing Bubble', Center for Economic Policy Research, November 2005, especially p. 7, Figure 1, CEPR website; 'Still Want to Buy? Global House Prices', *The Economist*, 5 March 2005; S. Cecchetti, 'Housing Binge Will Have an Inflation Hangover', *Financial Times*, 19 December 2005.

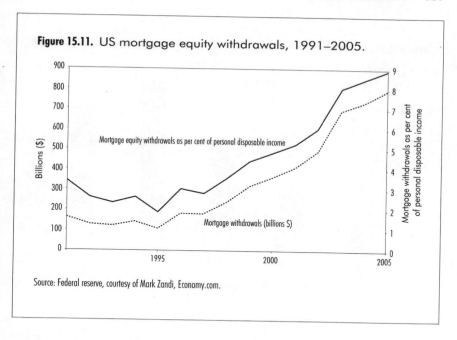

Figure 15.11. US mortgage equity withdrawals, 1991–2005.

Source: Federal reserve, courtesy of Mark Zandi, Economy.com.

or a combination of the two. Were the adjustment to take place entirely by way of the former, rents would have to rise by about one-third. This would make for stepped up inflation of one per cent per year on the best case assumption that it could be spread out over five years. On the other hand, were the adjustment to take place entirely by way of the decline in home prices, the value of residential real estate would have to drop by 25 per cent, or $6 trillion. Since, according to the Federal Reserve, consumption is driven down at the rate of four to six per cent for every dollar of housing price decline, this would imply a $325 billion decline in consumption, which translates into a decrease of GDP growth by 2.6 per cent, a serious blow to the economy even were it to take place over several years. Put another way, were rents to continue to rise at their current annual pace of about 2.5 per cent, house prices would need to remain flat for more than ten years to bring the ratio of house prices to rents back to its long-term norm.[51]

The propensity of homeowners to borrow, in order to buy a home or for any other purpose, seems likely to decline under any circumstances. The equity held by households in their homes has fallen sharply as a percentage of their houses' value. Meanwhile, in 2005, their debt smashed all records, reaching 120 per cent of personal disposable income, 25 per cent higher than it was as recently as 2000, while their interest payments as a percentage of personal disposable income also hit an all-time high. Many US households apparently believe that the appreciation of their houses' values is doing their saving for them, in the same way that they previously

Figure 15.12. Contribution of housing to GDP growth, 2001–05.

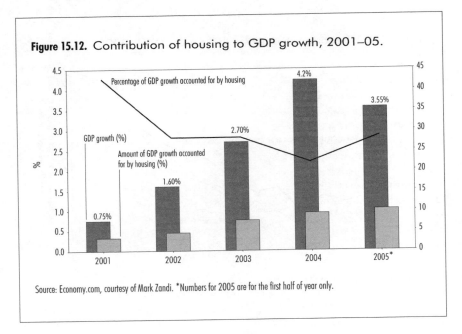

Source: Economy.com, courtesy of Mark Zandi. *Numbers for 2005 are for the first half of year only.

thought the increase in prices of their equities was. As a consequence, in 2005, the US personal savings rate fell to *minus* 0.5 per cent, the lowest since the Great Depression. Should there be any palpable reversal in the trend in house prices, households might very well rapidly reduce their consumption to compensate, in which case the savings rate would shoot up, making for a devastating blow to aggregate demand.[52]

By pumping up the wealth effect of rising residential real estate values and in that way stimulating consumer spending, the Fed not only catalyzed the US cyclical upturn, but also coaxed the rest of the world economy from its slump. The nose-dive of the US economy in 2000–1 was of major proportions and its comeback belated, with the consequence that real goods imports actually dropped by 3.2 per cent in 2001 and rose by just 3.6 per cent in 2002, driving the world economy into recession and keeping it there. Between 2000 and 2003, the average annual growth of world GDP and real merchandise exports was limited to 1.7 per cent and 3.0 per cent respectively, compared to 3.2 per cent and 7.0 per cent respectively between 1995 and 2000.[53]

It was only as the US economy finally accelerated from the latter part of 2003 and especially 2004, with signal assistance from the wealth effect of housing, that US imports once again grew substantially, and it was only from that juncture that US purchases once again detonated an export-driven cyclical recovery throughout the world economy, though with less force than during the later 1990s. Of course, for its part, the rest of the world was unwilling or unable to rely on debt to subsidize demand and thereby spur the growth of GDP to anything like the same extent as the

53   World Trade Organization Database.

US. Due, moreover, to the pervasive turn to austerity of the previous two decades, other countries had become increasingly dependent upon exports to drive growth, while possessing a lower propensity to import than did the US. The rest of the world was therefore capable of helping drive US growth (by pulling up US exports) only after the acceleration of US GDP and import growth had stimulated its own growth … and to a much lesser degree. US exports continued to depend on US imports.

Between 2000 and 2005, the growth of US external deficits thus proved indispensable, once again, in keeping the world economy turning over, just as it had between 1980 and 1985 and again between 1995 and 2000, in which intervals borrowing was also exploding upwards, asset prices were ascending, and manufacturing was plunging into crisis. Between 1997 and 2000, the current account deficit had increased in a way that was entirely unprecedented. But between 2001 and 2005, it rose much further, establishing a historic high every single year and in 2005 arching upward as a percentage of GDP 50 per cent above its then-record level of 2000. As had been the case during the first half of the 1980s and second half of the 1990s, it was the manufacturing trade deficit that did most of the work in propelling the current account deficit upwards, though it was now joined, to a greater extent than earlier, by the rising trade deficit in oil. While manufactured exports in nominal terms increased by 10.6 per cent between 2001 and 2004, manufactured imports soared by 23.7 per cent. The rise of these deficits was rendered all the more alarming because they took place—by contrast to the parallel increases between 1980 and 1985 and 1995 and 2000—despite a significant *decline* in the trade-weighted exchange rate of the dollar, which fell by about 20 per cent between December 2001 and December 2004 (and then came back somewhat in 2005). In fact, between 2000 and 2004, even as the greenback fell by more than 10 per cent, the US share of the world market in manufactures, having remained roughly flat at 11–12 per cent for the long interval between 1987 and 2000, suddenly dropped by a shocking *25 per cent*, from 12.1 per cent to 9 per cent, to its lowest level of the postwar epoch (see p. 326, Figure 15.14). Competitive pressure on the US manufacturing sector was further intensifying.

As between 1980 and 1985 and again between 1995 and 2000, between 2000 and 2005, it was the increase in the trade deficit with the East Asian export-oriented manufacturing economies, including Japan, that accounted for the lion's share of the gargantuan US current account deficit and of its increase. But from around the turn of the century, the Chinese economy took the lead in—and indeed dominated—this movement, as its already spectacular trade-centred developmental process suddenly assumed strikingly greater dynamism. From the early to mid 1990s through 2000, Chinese trade had already been expanding impressively in the wake of the country's turn toward the world market, signalled by the famous southern tour of Deng Xiaoping in spring 1992. In this upward thrust, the turning point came during the first half of the 1990s, when the government opened the way for banks to impose a major tightening of credit and producers to reduce surplus labour in any way they chose, while itself implementing a major devaluation of the renminbi. Over the course of the decade, China's exports grew at the remarkable average annual rate of 15.6 per cent. Even so, by 2000, China's share of world exports was still a bit smaller than that of the Southeast Asian Little Tigers taken together. But from 2000 onwards, the Chinese economy took off as never before, its exports growing at the average annual pace of over 25 per cent over the next four years

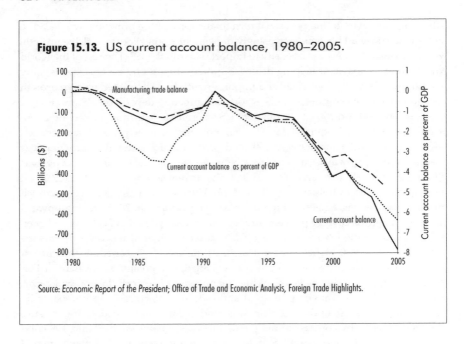

Figure 15.13. US current account balance, 1980–2005.

Source: *Economic Report of the President;* Office of Trade and Economic Analysis, Foreign Trade Highlights.

(despite an increase of only 6 per cent in 2001) and reshaping in the process the commerce of Asia, the US, and indeed the world.

Like that of the Northeast Asian NICs and Southeast Asian Little Tigers, Chinese development derived its extraordinary, and increasing, dynamism from its integration into the multiple triangle trades and production networks that link them to one another, to Japan, and to the US. China's nearly endless supply of low-cost wage labour was, of course, a necessary condition for its spectacular expansion, and particularly its capacity to sustain it. But like its East Asian predecessors, China refused to allow its economy to be shaped by comparative advantage—though it of course made ample use of its cheap wage labour. On the contrary, it achieved extraordinary growth of GDP and GDP per capita by means of rapid technological advance that was itself made possible by its ability to assimilate the technological achievements of its more advanced neighbours. Still, in contrast with the NICs, who like their Japanese predecessors tightly controlled foreign direct investment in statist and mercantilist fashion, China—in this respect more like the Little Tigers of Southeast Asia—enabled its epoch-making growth of trade by welcoming a huge influx of foreign-owned companies, itself facilitated by an enormous flood of foreign investment. Like all its East Asian predecessors, China has thus climbed quickly up the technological ladder by means of the import of ever more sophisticated capital and intermediate goods from elsewhere in East Asia—particularly the NICs and Japan—which has enabled it to export ever more sophisticated consumer goods, above all to the US, and in this way to pay for its imports. But, following in the footsteps of the Little Tigers of Southeast Asia, it has depended in this process of trade-centred growth and—to an extent hitherto unprecedented—upon the relocation of production, no longer just from Japan but now increasingly from the NICs, which have continued to raise their own technological level by themselves sloughing off their lower-end, more labour-using, industries to China. By 2004–05, foreign firms had come to account for no less than one third of Chinese manufacturing output and 55–60 per cent of its exports.

Like its East Asian predecessors, China has, throughout its initial stage of export-oriented growth, focused on the overseas sale of labour-intensive goods like footwear, toys, apparel and sporting goods. But, by relying on foreign-owned firms, especially from Taiwan, China has quickly become a major exporter of high-tech products, consumer electronics and especially what is called information technology hardware —computers and the like. Taiwanese firms led the way in producing for export from China computer peripherals such as power supply units, keyboards, and mice in the early 1990s, moved up to PCs in the mid 1990s, progressed to laptops in the later 1990s, and of late are making liquid crystal displays. Speaking generally, the higher the technological content of the good, the higher the proportion of exports that foreign firms control, and this trend has only intensified. As Chinese exports of industrial machinery were growing twenty-fold in real terms between 1993 and 2003, foreign-owned firms increased their share of the total from 35 per cent to 79 per cent. Over the same period, exports of computer equipment rose from $716 millon to $41 billion, and the share of foreign-owned firms rose from 74 per cent to 92 per cent. All told, by 2002, foreign-owned firms had become responsible for no less than 85 per cent of total exports classified by the Chinese government as high-tech—including pharmaceuticals, aircraft and aerospace, electronics, telecommunications, and medical equipment—up from 74 per cent in 1998. On this basis, by 2002–03 China had passed Japan and the NICs as the largest exporter of high-tech products into the US.[54]

It may be reasonably asked to what extent such a form of expansion of trade, however spectacular, can bring about all-around development in China, given its control by foreign companies. But, there can be no question whatsoever that it has, in a very short time, made China an enormous power in the world market. In the process, following in the footsteps of its East Asian predecessors, China has become a major contributor to the expansion of the US current account deficit and a key perpetuator of over-capacity in international manufacturing. In the brief period 2000–2004, Chinese imports into the US doubled, from $100 billion to $197 billion. In so doing, they increased their share of the US import market in manufactures from 9.6 per cent to 16.3 per cent and accounted for about two-thirds of the increase in the US manufacturing trade deficit during the interval. It is true that the increase in China's share of the US import market also appears to have been largely responsible for the 3 per cent decrease of the share taken by the Northeast Asian NICs and Southeast Asian Little Tigers taken together in this interval, as well as some part of the simultaneous 3 per cent decrease in the share of the Japanese. It is true as well that the trade of China by itself was responsible for virtually all of the *increase* in

54   For this and the previous paragraph I am endebted to, N. R. Lardy, 'The Economic Rise of China: Threat or Opportunity?', in Federal Reserve Bank of Cleveland, *Economic Commentary*, 1 August 2003 (available online); N. R. Lardy, 'The Economic Future of China', in Asia Society, *Resources*, 2005 (available online); N. R. Lardy, 'Trade Liberalization and its Role in Chinese Economic Growth', International Monetary Fund, 14–16 November 2003 (available online); G. J. Gilboy, 'The Myth Behind China's Miracle', *Foreign Affairs*, July–August 2004. Cf. A. Glyn, 'Imbalances of the World Economy,' *New Left Review*, no. 34, July–August 2005.
55   'US Manufactures Imports from Individual Countries' in 'Aggregate Foreign Trade Data, Foreign Trade Highlights', US Office of Trade and Economic Analysis website.

Figure 15.14. Shares of world market in manufactures, 1970–2004.

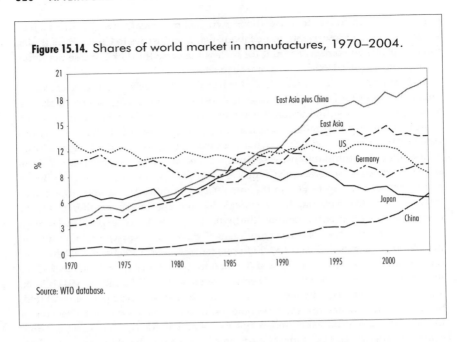

Source: WTO database.

the US manufacturing trade and current account deficits accounted for by the East Asian economies, including Japan, during that period. But it would be quite misleading to interpret these developments as a zero-sum game.[55]

Between 2000 and 2004, Japan reduced the share of its total exports going to the US by 7 per cent. But it simultaneously increased the share of its exports going to China by 6 per cent. The Northeast Asian NICs were doing something similar. Meanwhile, foreign direct investment into China was averaging $53 billion per annum. This sum was greater than that for any other country in the world except the US, and the NICs and Japan were responsible for the greater part of it.[56] What was thus taking place was a still further deepening of East Asian economic integration, with Japan and the NICs stepping up their exports of high-technology capital and intermediate goods to China, there to be processed, often by firms from these places, and sent on to the US. The shrinkage of Japanese and NIC exports to the US thus represents, to a large degree, their reorientation to China so as to better enter, if indirectly, the US market—as well, of course, as the domestic market of China itself. It goes a good way, moreover, toward explaining the remarkable dynamism of China's exports in general and their rapid penetration of the US market in particular. When the US economy gained momentum in 2004, the NICs and Japan, coming back far more slowly from the international recession of 2001 than they did from the international crisis of 1997–98, finally expanded with some vigour. But, they did so far less by raising their exports to the US—which for both Japan and the NICs remained below their levels of 2000—than by stepping up their overseas

56   United Nations Conference on Trade and Development, 'Overview' *World Investment Report 2005*, New York, 2005, p. 2, Table 1.

57   'Asian Demand Lifts Japan's Trade', *BBC News UK Edition*, 26 May 2004 (online).

sales and foreign direct investment in China. It was China's exports to the US, not their own, that took off, but this enabled the NICs' and Japan's commerce and foreign direct investment to grow with them.[57]

Between 2000 and 2004, China, having doubled its share of the world market in manufacturing exports during the previous decade, doubled it again in less than half the time. This was, of course, the same interval in which the US share was suddenly sinking by 25 per cent, and it would be surprising indeed if these developments were unrelated to one another. They manifest the increasing power of a Chinese export machine that has leapt ahead by focusing the energies and capacities of the more advanced East Asian economies upon itself. But that export machine, and the East Asian economies that increasingly both drive it and rely upon it, remains as dependent as ever upon a US market that, for almost a decade, has itself gone forward mainly via borrowing and bubbles and, during the past five years, heavily courtesy of the historic surge of housing prices.[58] (See p. 326, Figure 15.14.)

The prodigious rise of the US current account deficit between 2000 and 2005 depended of course on the willingness of the rest of the world to finance it. During the first half of the 1980s, when real interest rates on US Treasury Bonds soared to historic heights, and during the second half of the 1990s, when the New Economy seemed to offer unprecedented possibilities to prosper both in physical and paper assets, the rest of the world was generally happy to do so. In the latter period, investors from overseas made huge direct investments in the US and bought up enormous quantities of corporate equities and corporate bonds in expectation of endless profits. In so doing, they amplified the equity price bubble and its resulting wealth effect, while keeping the exchange rate of the dollar going up. In that way, without necessarily intending it, they also helped enable their own countries' exports to the US to continue to increase and their own economies to continue to grow. However, following the crash of the stock market and the descent of the US economy into recession in 2000–1, private investors from the rest of the world came to find US assets ever less attractive, especially stocks and direct investments. In the years 1999–2001 inclusive, annual purchases of equities and direct investments in the US by the rest of the world averaged $142 billion and $286 billion dollars respectively. But for 2002–04 inclusive, the analogous figures were just $49.5 billion and $79.5 billion dollars respectively. Indicative of the same trend, in the latter three years, US purchases of the rest of the world's equities and direct investment abroad outran by significant amounts the rest of the world's purchases of US equities and its foreign investment in the US.[59]

As the current account deficit has risen ever higher, downward pressure on the

---

58 The dependence, direct and indirect, of Chinese exports on the US market was apparently confirmed in 2001, when the US recession and the ensuing collapse of imports were accompanied by a star-tling reduction in the growth of Chinese exports, from an annual average of nearly 16 per cent between 1990 and 2000 to just 6 per cent. But noting this is no substitute for an analysis of the deeper sources of Chinese economic growth—as opposed merely to the growth of its exports—which I do not pretend to offer here.

59 FRB, *Flow of Funds*, Table F.107, Rest of the World.

60 Central bank interest rates in the US that have risen higher than in Europe and thus attract invest-ments in dollar-denominated Treasuries are no doubt largely responsible for preventing this. It is also true that US GDP and productivity growth in the past several years has been higher than in Euroland. IMF, *Global Financial Stability Report*, September 2005, pp. 16-18. Still, it is not clear that the latter has actually helped the dollar, since there is little evidence that much European (or other foreign) private money has flowed into

greenback has thus become more intense, leading to a fall in the exchange rate of the US currency against the euro by about one-third between the end of 2001 and the end of 2005 (including a dollar recovery against the euro of more than 10 per cent in 2005). Since the US trade deficit with the Euro-economies rose by more than 70 per cent during that interval despite the euro's revaluation, it is not self-evident how the dollar can avoid falling further.[60] Were the dollar's decline to become more severe, the Federal Reserve could be faced with an excruciating choice: either let the currency drop and invite a wholesale liquidation of US properties by foreign investors that would risk an asset price crash, or raise interest rates to defend the currency and possibly set off a new recession.

In fact, through the end of 2005, the overall decline in the dollar's trade-weighted exchange rate was held to a (still substantial) 12 per cent, because it took place to such a great extent against the euro and to a *relatively* limited extent against the currencies of East Asia. This was the case even though the US trade and current account deficits emerged to such a large degree out of the commerce with East Asia. The dollar held up against East Asian currencies for the straightforward reason that East Asian governments led by Japan and China, but also prominently including the smaller economies of Korea, Taiwan, and Hong Kong, in order to sustain their countries' exports to the US, entered the international currency market, while devoting an overwhelming proportion of their mounting external surpluses to the purchase of dollar-denominated assets, so as to hold down the exchange rate of their currencies against the dollar. Since the demand of overseas *private* investors for US assets could no longer be counted on to finance the US current account deficit and thereby sustain the exchange rate of the dollar, East Asian governments sought to fill the gap in order to make sure that the US market would continue to drive their export-oriented economies. In 2003, East Asian governments increased their dollar reserves by $485 billion and in that way covered no less than 90 per cent of the $530 billion US current account deficit. In 2004, they acquired another $465 billion in dollar reserves and thereby financed roughly 75 per cent of the US's $670 billion dollar current account deficit. By increasing its dollar reserves to the extent it did, the Chinese central bank played a significant part in enabling the US economy to absorb a 57 per cent, $70 billion, increase in exports from China in those two years.[61]

The huge acquisitions of dollar-denominated assets by East Asian central banks not only prevented the US dollar from falling, but kept the US recovery on track by covering the great bulk of the Bush administration's growing federal deficit and in that way keeping the cost of US borrowing artificially low. Between 2000 and

equities or direct investment in the US, especially on a net basis. As a consequence, it is not evident how the marginally greater return on US government bonds can outweigh the apparent risk of dollar devaluation and keep money flowing into the US.

61   These figures for foreign dollar holdings are significantly higher than those to be found in the standard US Treasury reports. The latter understate central banks' buying of Treasuries from the US, because much of this is accounted for by private parties serving as agents for the central banks. The actual increases in central banks' dollar-denominated reserves can be accurately determined, because they are reported annually by the central banks to the Bank for International Settlements. See N. Roubini and B. Setser, 'Will the Bretton Woods 2 Regime Unravel Soon? The Risk of Hard Landing in 2005–2006', New York University, unpublished manuscript, 2005, p. 1, available at Roubini Global Macro website. Compare. M. Higgins and T. Klitgaard, 'Reserve Accumulation: Implications for Global Capital Flows and Financial Markets', *Current Issues in Economics and Finance*, vol. x, no. 10, Federal Reserve Bank of New York, September–October 2004.

2004, as the US federal budget balance fell from 3 per cent of GDP in the black to 3.2 per cent of GDP in the red, overall holdings of US Treasury bonds increased by about $960 billion. Yet private parties in the US not only failed to make *any* net purchases of these Treasuries, but actually slightly *reduced* their Treasury holdings in this period. The Federal Reserve and state and local governments did account for almost one-third of this increase in Treasury holdings. But the rest of the world accounted for slightly more than two-thirds, and East Asian central banks were responsible for the great bulk of the latter. East Asian central banks' enormous subsidy to demand for Treasuries held down US interest rates—by exactly how much is disputed—and thereby enabled the housing market to continue to explode upward and US households to play their assigned part in driving consumption and thereby economic growth.[62] By helping so mightily to close the financing gaps resulting from the US current account and federal budget deficits, East Asian central banks enabled the Fed and the Bush administration to pursue hyper-expansionary policies so as to stoke a recovery that, in the absence of their intervention, would have almost certainly come to grief due to rising costs of borrowing and a declining currency leading to plummeting asset prices.

Nevertheless, the longer East Asian central banks, and in particular that of China, fund the greater part of the US current account deficit, the longer the dollar will stay artificially high and US interest rates artificially low, the larger will be US manufacturing imports from East Asia, and the higher will the US current account deficit climb. In 2005, the latter rose from 5.7 per cent to 6.5 per cent of GDP to set still another record. But given the rising costs it is imposing, it is difficult to see how this syndrome can long be sustained. It requires the East Asian central banks, above all that of China, to count on ever larger future losses by way of the devaluation of their enormous dollar-denominated reserves when the US currency is finally allowed to fall, just as the Japanese had to do between 1985 and 1995. It compels the Chinese to risk the build-up of ever greater internal inflationary pressures as they inject money into the domestic economy in order to buy up the dollars that are derived from both export surpluses and speculative dollar inflows betting on a revaluation of the currency. Perhaps most threatening to stability and growth in the short-to-medium run, as a consequence of the growth of the money supply and the flooding in of funds from overseas, it leads China to sustain ever greater asset price bubbles, the deflation of which could seriously threaten the real economy. At the same time, by virtue of the reduced US interest rates and high dollar that this syndrome perpetuates, it induces the US economy not only to rely for much of the force behind its expansion on debt-based consumption that is dependent in turn on a real estate bubble that can have only a restricted duration, but also to direct its resources toward speculation in financial assets rather than investment in plant, equipment, and software, even as it continues to sustain the erosion of the US manufacturing trade balance and simultaneously its manufacturing productive base. It need hardly be mentioned that a not dissimilar combination of forces brought crash and recession to the world only a few years ago.

At this late date, it is not easy to see how a break from this syndrome can be accomplished without a good deal of pain. The US government, under growing pres-

---

62   Roubini and Setser, 'Will the Bretton Woods 2 Regime Unravel Soon?', pp. 5–10.

sure from an increasingly protectionist Congress, is demanding that China revalue its currency. But the US must be careful what it wishes for. For if China allows the renminbi to rise to any great extent by significantly reducing its purchases of dollar-denominated assets, particularly Treasuries, it is difficult to see how US interest rates can fail to rise and how US asset prices across the board—from government and corporate bonds to corporate equities to residential real estate—can fail to fall, risking a new descent into recession.[63] For its part, the Chinese government is well aware that were it to allow any significant (upward) flexibility in the currency, it would risk, as did much of East Asia from 1995, having to cope with a devastating combination of massive inflows of foreign portfolio capital leading to enormous asset price bubbles and declining manufacturing competitiveness, profitability and exports—in other words a replay of the East Asian financial crisis of 1997–98.[64] In fact, due to what appear to be irreversible political proclivities on the part of both the US and the Chinese, inertia seems likely to prevail everywhere—with China seeking to sustain export-led growth by continuing to finance the US external deficit so as to avoid the wrench of reorienting its dynamic manufacturing economy toward the home market, and with the US seeking to sustain debt-led expansion by leaving the renminbi as it is and continuing to welcome large-scale inflows of Chinese credit so as to avoid the wrench of reducing consumption growth to balance its books. It is therefore difficult to see how one or another form of financial shock can be avoided in the not so distant future … unless the US economy can suddenly find internal sources of radically increased dynamism.

A Weak and Hesitant Expansion

The economic stimulus unleashed by US governmental authorities and buttressed by the East Asian central banks between the start of 2001 and the present—featuring negative real short term interest rates for more than three years and historic federal deficits, supplemented by a significant (if partially limited) devaluation of the dollar—was the greatest in US history. Nevertheless, despite the huge boost to demand, the cyclical recovery remains problematic, its future uncertain. In 2001, 2002, and 2003, the economy struggled, increasing at an average annual rate of just 1.7 per cent, despite an enormous lift in 2003 from the Bush administration's tax rebate and a sharp rise in military spending resulting from the Iraq War. In 2004 and 2005 , GDP growth did jump to 4.2 per cent and 3.5 per cent respectively, and the economy performed well all around. The fact remains that GDP growth during the first five years of this business cycle (2001–2005 inclusive), at 2.56 per cent per annum, was as slow, or slower, than in any other comparable interval going back to 1950.[65]

The weakness of US economic performance between 2000 and 2005 was mirrored, moreover, across the advanced capitalist world. In fact, in the US, Japan, Germany,

---

63   This leaves out of account the damage that would be done by renminbi appreciation to US corporations in China exporting back into the US market.

64   It is true that, in contrast to most of the East Asian economies of the 1990s, China has not opened up its markets in financial capital, so retains a trump card that those economies lacked. Still, it is one thing to have rules restricting foreign financial inflows and outflows; it would be another thing actually to prevent these, under the pressure that would almost certainly emerge if the renminbi were to be allowed to rise and financial assets took off with it.

65   Between 1990 and 1995 US GDP growth was virtually the same as between 2000 and 2005.

and the Euro-15, the average annual growth of GDP, GDP per person employed, the capital stock, and real wages, as well as the level of the unemployment rate, were, in virtually every case, as bad as or worse than during what had hitherto been the worst half-decade of the postwar epoch, 1990–95. Astonishingly, the advanced capitalist economies have continued the very extended process of deceleration, business cycle by business cycle, that has persisted since the 1970s—a process that was interrupted only in the US during the bubble-driven boom of the second half of the 1990s. Even through the first half-decade of the twenty-first century, the long downturn thus remained very much alive and well (see p. 240, Table 13.1).[66]

The objective of the Fed in turning to easy credit and the wealth effect was to pull the US and the world economy from recession and keep them turning over, while allowing time to the corporate sector, especially in manufacturing, to work off its over-capacity, return to health, and resume responsibility for driving the economy. But even through 2005, the contribution of the private business sector was still not much to write home about. Above all, the jobs recovery continued to be by far the least good of the postwar epoch, total employment having risen a paltry 1.1 per cent in the three years of cyclical upturn following the cyclical trough of November 2001, compared to an average of 8.3 per cent for the same interval in previous postwar business cycles.[67] Only in May–June 2005 did private sector employment return to its pre-recession peak of January 2001. Annual jobs growth was in the negative in 2002 and 2003, and much worse than in the 'jobless recovery' of the early 1990s. Even in 2004 and 2005, at 1.3 per cent per annum, the growth of employment was still one-third lower than its average for the whole of the economic expansion between 1990 and 2000, at 2.0 per cent.

To make matters worse, the pattern of job creation offered little evidence that corporations at the heart of the economy had finally embarked on an enduring expansion. As of December 2005, manufacturing employment had sunk to its lowest level in the postwar era, 3.02 million below its amplitude in July 2000 and 78,000 below that of December 2004. In non-manufacturing, employment had still failed to come back to its July 2000 level in information, which includes telecommunications (minus 593,000), transportation and warehousing (minus 44,700), utilities (minus 39,000), and wholesale trade (minus 147,500). For these industries, including manufacturing, taken together, employment was in December 2005 about 3.936 million below its July 2000 level. By contrast, employment had risen above its July 2000 level in retail trade (17,000), construction (45,000), finance, insurance, and real estate (563,000), and leisure (996,000), along with professional and business services (620,000) and other services (25,000), as well as health services and education services (2.411 million). Total jobs growth of 5.285 million in these industries—including a remarkable 1.988 million or 38 per cent of the total in health services alone—insured that total private employment would, by December 2005, rise 1.349 million jobs above its level of July 2000. This amount of employment growth, is without close compar-

---

66   The only exceptions were with respect to GDP per person employed, where US and Japanese performance was better between 2000 and 2005 than they had been between 1990 and 1995.

67   Thanks to Doug Henwood for this calculation.

68   The huge expansion of health services manifested a new takeoff in the cost of medical care in the US, and, while endowing HMOs and insurance companies with outstanding profits, was for the rest of the economy an increasingly difficult burden to bear.

ison, the lowest recorded during the first four years of a cyclical upturn in the postwar epoch. It is, moreover, difficult to see how those industries that have increased employment can play much of role in sustaining the expansion, since jobs growth in the retail trade, construction, FIRE, and leisure industries has been heavily bubble-driven, while that in health services represents the runaway explosion of costs in this sector and will therefore more likely hold down than stimulate growth.[68]

In 2005, largely as a consequence of the historic weakness in employment growth, aggregate real compensation in the private economy (real compensation per employee, multiplied by employment) having increased between 2000 and 2005 at the lowest rate of the postwar epoch—at half the rate recorded between 1980 and 2000—was only 8 per cent higher than in 2000. (See p. 283, Table 15.5.) Meanwhile, even despite its increasing at an average annual rate of 9 per cent in 2004 and 2005, the growth of real non-residential investment in 2005 was only 4 per cent above its level in 2000. As a consequence, the increase of non-residential investment contributed a feeble 0.34 of a percentage point of the total 12.8 percentage point growth of GDP between 2000 and 2005. To complete the picture, in the same interval, annual net exports (that is, the trade deficit) went a further 60 per cent into the red, *reducing* total growth of GDP over the period by 2.4 percentage points or 18.4 per cent. (See p. 318, Table 15.8.)

With the increase in effective demand and thereby GDP growth accounted for by private business so very weak over the course of the recovery, even if significantly better in 2004 and 2005, the economy continued to depend overwhelmingly on the growth of consumption and residential investment, itself dependent upon record household borrowing and dissaving, reliant in turn on rising mortgage equity withdrawals, to keep it going. Over these two years, the growth of private consumption plus residential investment continued to account for 90 per cent of the growth of GDP. Meanwhile, from the third quarter of 2003 through the third quarter of 2005, the personal savings rate tumbled from 2.5 per cent to *minus* 1.8 per cent. This was no doubt made possible by the ascent, during 2004 and the first half of 2005, of mortgage equity withdrawals to almost 9 per cent of personal disposable income. Housing accounted for more than one quarter of the growth of GDP. The salient issue of the day thus continued to be whether private business would generate sufficient investment and jobs growth to keep the economy expanding before the huge economic stimulus petered out, especially as the Fed continued raising short term interest rates and the housing bubble with its wealth effect reached its limit. This appeared all the more pressing in view of the fact that, four full years into the expansion, real long-term interest rates actually fell during 2005, indicating the weakening of aggregate demand and of the economy more generally.

Can Profitability Recover and Revive the Economy?

The necessary, if not sufficient, condition for the sustained growth of US—and global—expenditures on new plant, equipment, and software, as well as productivity, employment, and GDP is a dramatic and sustained increase in the rate of profit, the critical missing factor in the expansion of the 1990s after 1995–97, and of course for the whole period since the end of the 1960s. The average rate of profit in the US non-financial corporate sector during the business cycle of the 1990s did not rise palpably above its level during those of the 1970s and 1980s, remaining about

20 per cent below the average for the postwar boom (1948–69), and proved insufficient to underpin a decisive break from the long downturn. In essence, for the US economy to support a new long upturn, it must resume, and take a good deal higher, the impressive ascent of profitability that began in the mid 1980s but came to grief after the mid 1990s, as the New Economy took off. (See p. 288, Figure 15.3; p. 312, Figure 15.8.)

From the end of the recession in November 2001, the revival of profitability, though at first quite slow, sharply accelerated in 2003 and, especially, 2004 and 2005. Nevertheless, because the profit rate had to come back from such a depressed level, it still had a good distance to go and could well face increasing difficulty in continuing its upward movement. After having declined by about 10 per cent between 1997 and 2000 as the boom reached its apex, the rate of profit in the non-financial corporate sector dived a further 21.3 per cent in the recession of 2001, or a total of 28 per cent between 1997 and 2001, to *its lowest level since 1945* (with the single exception of 1980). By mid 2005, the non-financial corporate profit rate had rebounded impressively, to slightly above its level of 2000. But that still left it at about the average for the whole of the 1990s business cycle.[69] (See p. 282, Table 15.1; p. 334, Figure 15.15.) The failure of the non-financial corporate profit rate to ascend sufficiently to motivate firms to raise to a greater extent than they did their expenditures on new plant, equipment, and software or on increased employment had to have been a major factor in accounting both for the economy's weak response to the government's stimulus programme and for the uncertain character of the recovery right through 2005.

It is a real question, moreover, whether the revival of profitability can be sustained. With output and investment growth muted through much of the cyclical upturn, corporations sought to restore their profit rates primarily by means of raising productivity and holding down wages. In fact, between 2000 and 2004, including the recession year 2001, the growth of real output per hour in the private economy averaged 3.4 per cent, compared to just 2.5 per cent between 1995 and 2000, the years of the 'economic miracle'. As a consequence, some leading economic analysts, not to mention Fed chair Alan Greenspan, have asserted that the miracle of productivity growth that never quite materialized in the 1990s is now upon us, with New Economy technology being implemented more speedily and effectively than hitherto. By implication, a path to longer term profitability revival and economic dynamism has been opened up.[70]

But such a deduction is premature, to say the least. Its Achilles' heel is obvious: so far, increases in output per hour have taken place in the face of a sharp *reduction* in investment growth, that is, the slower introduction of plant, equipment and soft-

---

69 It is evident, moreover, that non-financial corporate profits are over-stated. The underlying corporate profit numbers are gathered not by establishment but by company, which are categorized by the Bureau of Economic Analysis as either non-financial or financial. But since a number of major companies, such as GE, GM, and Ford, categorized by the BEA as non-financial, have made in recent years a huge share of their profits through financial operations, which are nonetheless recorded by the BEA as profits of the non-financial sector, official non-financial profits are misleadingly swelled at the expense of financial profits. In addition, in late 2005, the under-funding of corporate pension plans totalled a staggering $450 billion, formally at least an enormous subtraction from future corporate profits. R. Lowenstein, 'The End of Pensions', *The New York Times*, 30 October 2005.

70 R. Gordon, 'America Wins the Prize with a Supermarket Sweep', *Financial Times*, 20 August 2003.

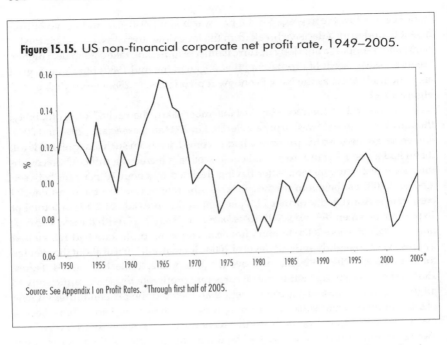

Figure 15.15. US non-financial corporate net profit rate, 1949–2005.

Source: See Appendix I on Profit Rates. *Through first half of 2005.

ware, compared to that of the 1990s expansion. Is it really believable that technological advance speeded up so discontinuously and so rapidly as to yield a rate of private
sector productivity growth between 2000 and 2004 that was 60 per cent higher than
between 1995 and 2000, even though the growth of real capital stock in this interval
was about half as fast as during the second half of the 1990s? The more plausible
explanation is that the recorded gains in productivity largely represent not so much
increased efficiency—meaning more output from the same labour input—as more
output from more labour input per hour, that is, speed-up. It seems telling in this
respect that between 2000 and 2003 the manufacturing sector spearheaded the ascent
of productivity growth by increasing its output per hour at a spectacular rate of 7
per cent per annum, without increasing its capital stock (or output) at all, but *reducing*
hours worked at the stunning average annual pace of 6.2 per cent. It is hard to resist
the conclusion that the manufacturing sector achieved its apparently impressive
increase in productivity during this three-year interval simply by keeping real output
constant, cutting down the labour force by 18.6 per cent, and obliging its reduced
labour force to produce the same amount as before with the same amount of plant
and equipment.

As speed-up was making possible a big jump in recorded productivity growth,
corporations were taking the fruits of the overall increase in GDP to an extent probably unprecedented in US history. During the first three and a half years of the
cyclical upturn, between the last quarter of 2001 and the second quarter of 2005, net
profits (including interest) in the non-financial corporate sector rose a cool 84.1 per
cent, while compensation increased just 15.8. per cent. Put another way, the increase
in profits accounted for an astounding 43.8 per cent of the total increase in net value
added during this interval. On this basis, the net non-financial corporate profit share

(adjusted for indirect business taxes) leaped up by an unheard-of 50 per cent, from 12.6 per cent to 18.7 per cent, in just those three and a half years.

The increase in profitability achieved during the cyclical upturn has thus been made possible, probably to the greatest extent in US history, simply by means of an increase in exploitation—that is, the intensification of labour plus a shift in the distribution of income from labour to capital. Because inflated profits were extracted with relatively little recourse to increases in either labour or capital stock, they were translated more or less directly into increases in the profit *rate*. Yet, one is entitled to ask whether corporations can go much further than they already have in improving their profit rates by extracting still more labour inputs per hour for relatively less pay from their employees, especially if the rate of GDP growth is sustained. The point is that, to the extent that companies must, in future, rely on the more rapid increase of employment, while adding plant, equipment, and software, productivity growth will almost certainly slow and wage growth accelerate, so that the increase of profitability will likely slow. To the degree, on the other hand, they continue to depend on holding down the growth of employment and of wages to sustain earnings, they will continue to place downward pressure on consumer demand. As the cyclical recovery lengthens, the ride toward higher profit rates is likely to become bumpier … yet it will also become more urgent, as the exogenous stimuli that have hitherto driven the expansion rapidly dry up.

Two Scenarios

It is still conceivable that the scenario sought by the Fed will ultimately materialize. For it is possible that the US and world economy have finally sufficiently scrapped high-cost, low-profit manufacturing productive power and have sufficiently reduced unit labour costs—by means of job cutting, intensifying labour, and the holding down of wage growth—to create the prospect of a sustained rise in manufacturing profitability and, in turn, capital accumulation. From the start of the cyclical expansion that began in November 2001, through the end of 2005, manufacturing, and overall industrial productive capacity barely increased. This may indicate that the US manufacturing sector has shed not only a gigantic swathe of labour, but also a significant amount of ineffective, redundant plant, equipment, and software. In 2004, the growth of real manufacturing output leaped to 4 per cent, after stagnating during the previous three years, and manufacturing productivity increase stayed as high as 4.6 per cent, while wage growth remained moderate. Perhaps most indicative that the capacity to supply manufacturing output had fallen back in line with demand, in that year, for the first time since 1994, the price of manufacturing output (the implicit price deflator) actually rose, and by more than 2 per cent, while unit labour costs were prevented from growing at all. Indeed, by 2004, the manufacturing profit rate had increased by 29 per cent over its depressed level of 2001, returning to its level of 2000, still about 15 per cent below its most recent peak of 1995–97. There is some indication, moreover, that, in the first half of 2005, manufacturing investment was surging ahead, while the growth of manufacturing exports (not of course the level) was finally catching up to that of imports.[71]

Were these trends in costs, prices, profitability, capital accumulation, and trade

---

71   A. Aston and M. Arndt, 'A Head of Steam on the Factory Floor', *Business Week*, 8 August 2005.

to continue, it could portend an economy-wide turnaround, for manufacturing was the sector mainly responsible for the fall into recession in 2001 and for holding down the ensuing cyclical upturn … as well as, of course, for the long-term incapacity of the economy to transcend slow growth. Were the profit rate to continue to rise, productivity growth could begin to proceed much more by way of capital accumulation and technological advance relative to speed-up than it has been doing and gain thereby a better chance to sustain itself. It might then be possible to create more jobs and accommodate over the longer run more rapid wage growth and to generate by that means a sustained increase in aggregate demand that could allow the economy to reduce its reliance on consumption growth driven by asset-price bubbles. The same trend could enable, via more rapid exports, at least some stabilization of the current account deficit, and, in particular, a greater willingness of private investors abroad to finance it. Tax returns might accelerate sufficiently to hold down the budget deficit. The underlying point is straightforward: what makes the new century's bubbles and imbalances potentially so lethal is that they have so far covered up and compensated for serious underlying weakness in the real economy. Were the latter to be returned to strength, the threats they pose would not disappear, but would likely be much mitigated. There would be nothing like a healthy economy to dispel financial clouds, and nothing like a manufacturing turnaround to secure a healthy economy.

There is a further consideration. In forging an economic revival, US corporations hold a trump card—a labour force that has, so far, proved not only incomparably more exploitable than, say, those of Western Europe or Japan, but increasingly so over time. Since the end of the New Economy bubble-driven boom, between 2000 and the present, corporations and government have unleashed one of the fiercest assaults on workers in US history. Workers have been unable to prevent huge cuts in employment, especially of higher-paying jobs, a major intensification of work, and a sharp deceleration of real wage growth (excluding benefits), which have made it possible for employers to achieve major gains in productivity and profitability. To this must be added workers' inability, so far, to do anything about employers' increasing tendency to raise their profits by reneging on their enormous, contractually established pension obligations, as well as to negotiate great reductions in what they are obliged to pay for workers' health care, not to mention monumental tax cuts for the very rich, as well as employers. As emphasized earlier, during more than twenty years after 1973, real wages (excluding benefits) in the non-manufacturing sector for production and non-supervisory workers slowly but steadily declined, yet employers in that sector could not take much advantage of this to raise their profit rates, except during the two years between 1995 and 1997, because up through 1995 they were unable to increase productivity at even 1 per cent per annum and because between 1997 and 2000 real wage growth rose impetuously to very much exceed somewhat improved productivity growth. However, between 2000 and 2005, after having averaged 1.6 per cent per annum between 1997 and 2000, the growth of real

72   In the latter part of 2005, Delphi, the country's largest parts producer, as well as Northwest Airlines, appear to have been able to force their workers to accept reductions in hourly wages from the $25–30 range to something like $15, while GM extracted concessions worth several billion dollars per annum in health benefits. Concessions of this magnitude were hitherto unprecedented during the postwar epoch, but they seem likely to prove ever more common for the foreseeable future.

wages (excluding benefits) of production and non-supervisory workers in non-manufacturing averaged less than 0.3 per cent per annum. In fact, in both 2004 and 2005, even as the cyclical expansion lengthened and the growth of GDP and employment gathered steam, real wage growth fell to minus 0.6 per cent per annum.[72] Meanwhile, over the same interval, the rate of non-manufacturing productivity growth did not decelerate, continuing to grow at close to 2 per cent per annum. Were these trends to continue, longer-term prospects for the private economy would brighten, especially if the manufacturing sector could sustain its revival of profitability.

Yet, even today, the weight of evidence appears to point to a different scenario, entailing a still further loss of dynamism by the world economy and the renewal of global turbulence, rather than a break towards sustained growth and increased stability. The titanic, still-continuing destruction of jobs—which was and is the manufacturing sector's main response to the collapse of profitability that it experienced at the turn of the millennium—delivered a shock to demand that for a time threatened deep recession or worse and continues to depress the growth of purchasing power and, in turn, investment. The explosion of household borrowing induced by the Fed to counter it—with indispensable support from East Asian governments—succeeded in temporarily stabilizing the economy by means of jacking up consumption. But, rather than paving the way to the transcendence of the underlying problem it was designed to contain, it may actually have sustained and exacerbated it.

In this scenario, the Fed's interest rate reductions came so quickly and the ensuing housing price bubble so puffed up consumer demand that not only was insufficient productive power scrapped during the brief nine-month recession of 2001, but too much redundant, high-cost means of production was kept in operation during the ensuing cyclical recovery, both in the US and on a world scale. This was all the more the case in view of the fact that, during the epoch-making investment boom of the previous five years, manufacturing production capacity had expanded at a rate hitherto unmatched during the postwar era, growing by close to 40 per cent and very much exacerbating already existing global over-capacity. Meanwhile, East Asia, with China now in the vanguard, continued to expand capacity faster than it could be scrapped system-wide and to rain down torrents of redundant, increasingly high-tech goods upon the world market. It is fundamentally for these reasons that the overall rate of return on capital stock in the US and system-wide has failed to recover sufficiently to motivate a satisfactory new wave of capital investment or job creation. As a consequence, firms across most of the advanced capitalist world have sought to increase profits via two main routes. They have continued to make use of their already paid-for sunk capital, and raised output by way of increasing capacity utilization and confining their productive expenditures to increases in variable capital—raw materials and intermediate goods, as well as wages—rather than expenditures on additional fixed capital. At the same time, they have sought to hold down, if not actually cut back, their employment costs by repressing wage growth, reducing the growth of jobs, and intensifying labour. The result of the implementation of these strategies is that too much capital continues in operation and too little aggregate demand is created. In fact, even though US manufacturing capacity utilization did rise by about 5 percentage points between

2002 and 2005, it remained in 2005 at 78.8 per cent, not only palpably below its level of 2000, but 4–5 percentage points below its 1997 peak and lower than at any previous point since the recession year of 1991. The corporations upon which the world economy ultimately depends thus see the prospective return on new investment in plant, equipment, and software and on the addition of employees as insufficient to justify expanding their productive power, and this because existing productive capacity remains too high and effective demand too low. This is, of course, the same syndrome, marked above all by the weakening of the rate of profit, that has underpinned the long downturn from 1973 through 2005.

It is the fact that realized and prospective returns have been sufficient to warrant only decelerating capital accumulation over such an extended period of time right into the present that explains what has been a slowly ripening crisis of investment on a system-wide scale going back to the 1970s. Even though it increased by a solid 8.5 per cent in 2005, annual real non-residential investment in the US, four full years into the cyclical upturn, barely rose above its level of 2000. Meanwhile between 2000 and 2004, the US private non-residential capital stock grew more slowly than in any comparable period during the entire postwar epoch. This extended still further the slowdown of US capital stock increase that began in the 1970s, continued through the 1980s and into the early 1990s, was briefly interrupted during the remainder of that decade as a consequence of the abortive recovery of the manufacturing profit rate and then the bubble economy, but has resumed after 2000. (See p. 282, Table 15.2.)

The trend towards ever weaker investment has hardly been confined to the US. It has been of even longer standing, more continuous, and recently more pronounced throughout the remainder of the advanced capitalist world. Between 2000 and 2005, in Japan, Germany, and the Euro area, average annual growth of private non-residential investment averaged 2.5 per cent, *minus* 2.1 per cent, and zero per cent, respectively. Moreover, since the 1970s, in Japan, Germany, and Western Europe the growth of the capital stock, as well as the ratio of investment to GDP, has declined decade by decade, business cycle by business cycle, and between 2000 and 2005 both of these indicators of capital accumulation were at their lowest for any comparable period since 1950. (See p. 282, Table 15.2 and p. 341, Figure 15.16.) The Northeast Asian NICs and Southeast Asian Little Tigers, the loci of a three-decade-long investment boom of historic proportions, had long constituted the exception to the rule of secularly slowing investment growth. But, the massive build-up of excess capacity in manufacturing through 1995 and the rise of East Asian currencies between 1995 and 1997 together issued in the great regional-cum-international financial crisis of 1997–98 and the deep recession of 2001. And from these setbacks, the East Asian economies have still been unable to rebound. As a consequence, during the first half-decade of the new millennium, investment in East Asia as a percentage of GDP was about one-third lower than between 1990 and 1995. Whereas private non-residential investment in Korea had grown at an average annual rate of around 11 per cent between 1990 and 1996, and 15 per cent in 1999

---

73   IMF, 'Global Imbalances: A Saving and Investment Perspective', *World Economic Outlook. Building Institutions,* September 2005. See also Bank for International Settlements, *75th Annual Report 1 April 2004–31 March 2005,* Basel, 27 June 2005.

through 2000, it increased at just 5.5 per cent per annum between 2000 and 2005. As the International Monetary Fund observed, 'in the industrial countries ... investment [has] been trending downward since the 1970s', with the result that, over the same period, investment as a percentage of GDP for the world economy as a whole has fallen steadily, declining by about 20 per cent between 1973 and 2004.[73] (See p. 282, Table 15.2 and p. 341, Figure 15.16.)

The accelerating attempt by corporations all across the advanced capitalist world to counter secularly reduced rates of profit that had been forced down further in the post-bubble recession by cutting back sharply on their costs of employment brought the growth of real compensation, like that of capital stock, to unprecedented lows, or near them. Between 2000 and 2005, the increase of wages and benefits per worker in the advanced capitalist economies was at or near the lowest levels of the postwar epoch. In view of the very negative trend in employment growth in the same period, especially in the US, it is therefore unsurprising that, during the same interval in the US, Germany, and Japan, the growth of total private sector real compensation (real compensation per employee times employment) simultaneously dropped to postwar lows, extending a continuous downward trend that, like that of the increase of investment, finds its origins in the 1970s. (See p. 283, Table 15.5.) It is no wonder that the growth of real private consumption expenditures—which also fell without cease in the US, Japan, Germany, and the EU from the 1970s through the present—reached postwar lows in all these places between 2000 and 2005 (see p. 283, Table 15.6) ... or that the world economy has had to rely to such a great extent for the growth of aggregate demand upon the rise of US household purchasing power, itself made possible by rising debt, reliant in turn on the inflation of ever more spectacular financial bubbles.

In the foregoing context, the much-discussed decline of long-term interest rates and of credit spreads so far into the cyclical recovery, seems less paradoxical than it has sometimes appeared to be and requires for its explanation little or no-reference to a so-called 'global savings glut', famously invoked by Ben Bernanke, chair of the Council of Economic Advisers and heir apparent to Alan Greenspan. The supply of savings for the world economy in general and the industrial economies in particular has slowly *declined* during the last couple of decades, and actually dipped more sharply in the last few years. But because demand on the part of non-financial corporations for new plant and equipment has fallen so substantially, their demand for loanable funds has naturally fallen in tandem, and this, by itself, goes a good distance to account for the failure of real long term interest rates to ascend.[74] In the US, over the course of the cyclical expansion between 2001 and 2004, non-financial corporations sharply reduced their average investment as a percentage of GDP to 7 per cent, from 9 per cent at the peak of the boom between 1997 and 2000, with the consequence that they were able to reduce their average demand for borrowed funds as a percentage of GDP in the same interval to a mere 1.7 per cent, from 4 per cent.

With prospective returns on investment less than satisfactory, non-financial cor-

74 See, eg., 'The Great Thrift Shift: A Survey of the World Economy,' *The Economist*, 24 September 2005; For declining rates of saving, see IMF, 'Global Imbalances: A Saving and Investment Perspective, 'p. 92, Figure 2.1. This is in no way to deny, of course, that East Asian, as well as OPEC, *official* purchases of dollar-denominated assets have helped keep down US interest rates.

porations have chosen to use their profits to reward, directly and indirectly, the owners of their shares and stock options, rather than purchase new plant, equipment, and software. Between 2000 and 2004, non-financial corporations paid dividends as a percentage of profits (after interest paid) at the highest level of the postwar period—at an average of 59.9 per cent, compared to 42.5 per cent between 1990 and 2000, 32.6 per cent between 1979 and 1990, and 24.7 per cent between 1969 and 1979. In the first three quarters of 2005, dividends fell back significantly, but rocketing share buybacks by non-financial corporations took their place, leaping to their highest level of the postwar epoch, even above the heights reached during the stock market bubble of 1995–2000. As a consequence, in this same interval, dividends plus share buybacks as a percentage of non-financial corporate profits (before interest paid) also established a postwar record.[75]

The same pattern has been replicated across the globe, notably in such erstwhile manufacturing powerhouses as Germany and Japan, where profit rates at the start of the new millennium were at postwar lows, as well as South Korea. In Japan and South Korea, corporations had already come into possession of far too much plant, equipment, and software at different points during the 1990s. Receiving little encouragement from the world market to add to this, they have since the later 1990s, been not only eschewing investment but devoting enormous sums to paying off the enormous debts that were the legacy of their epoch-making investment booms, the resultant over-capacity, and the ensuing bursting of asset price bubbles.[76] Even the oil giants, whose profits have been driven into the stratosphere by record high prices, have so far nevertheless failed to unleash a new wave of investments, probably mindful of the long stagnation and decline of oil prices that mirrored global economic deceleration from the early 1980s through the later 1990s and apparently not yet convinced that the economic expansion will sustain itself for long enough to enable them to derive adequate returns from capital spending.

The main exception to the rule is to be found in China, where investment-led growth continues at a breathtaking rate, defying and exacerbating world manufacturing over-supply. This is, on the one hand, because the supply of inexpensive Chinese labour that can be combined with ever more advanced technique has till now been essentially unlimited, fuelled by massive disguised unemployment in agriculture and the huge number of layoffs that have stemmed from the rapid contraction of state-owned industry. It is, on the other hand, because the US market has continued to expand, not least as a consequence of ever-larger Chinese purchases of US Treasury bonds, which have facilitated US households' greatest borrowing binge of all time, and in that way, ever-increasing consumer purchases of Chinese (and other) imports. By virtue of the increasingly sophisticated productive techniques that Japanese, Taiwanese, and South Korean exporters to, and foreign direct investors in, mainland China embody in their products, Chinese exports directed toward the US and the rest of the world market rise rapidly up the technological ladder. But, this tends to exacerbate system-wide excess capacity because fast-growing exports from

75   FRB Flow of Funds, Table F.213 Corporate Equities (FRB website); BEA NIPA 1.14 and Fixed Asset Tables 4.7; T. Petruno, 'Buyback Surge is Stoking Debate,' *Los Angeles Times*, 17 August 2005.

76   J. Loeys et al., *Corporates Are Driving the Global Savings Glut*, JP Morgan Research, JP Morgan Securities Ltd, 24 June 2005 (online); R. Miller et al., 'Too Much Money', *Business Week*, 11 July 2005; 'The Great Thrift Shift'.

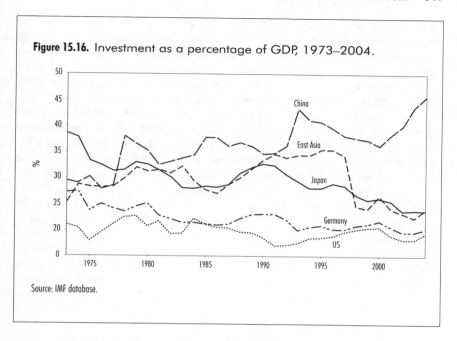

Figure 15.16. Investment as a percentage of GDP, 1973–2004.

Source: IMF database.

China tend increasingly to duplicate goods already being produced elsewhere, only with much lower costs of production and prices. Of course, the fundamental manifestation of this trend is the inexorable rise of the US current account deficit, along with the recent but spectacular rise of the Chinese current account surplus.

The Chinese contribution to the over-supply of manufactures system-wide has, in recent years, been amplified by worsening over-capacity within China itself. In 2005, Chinese fixed investment rose to an estimated 46 per cent of GDP, surpassing the investment shares of Japan and Korea, even at the height of their dynamism. At an annualized pace of almost $1.1 trillion for the first three quarters of 2005, Chinese fixed investment (at market exchange rates) was, remarkably, higher than the annualized totals for the US, at $987 billion, Japan, at $733 billion, and the Euro-zone, at $651 billion.[77] These extraordinary investment numbers are reminiscent of those chalked up by the East Asian economies in the early 1990s, when the pace of their capital accumulation, jacked up like that of the Chinese by an undervalued exchange rate and easy credit on a global scale, also surpassed that of the leading economies ... and soon made for over-capacity and regional cum international economic crisis. Should this trend continue, it implies even stronger downward pressure on prices, and thus on profitability, not only in China, but throughout a world economy that has, four years into the cyclical expansion, shown little inclination to sufficiently revive investment and job creation. Were Chinese capital accumulation and growth henceforth to decelerate—in response to over-invest-

77   S. Roach, 'China Slowdown—Early Not Wrong,' Morgan Stanley Global Economic Forum, 2 December 2005, as well as A. Xie, 'China: The Slowdown Has Begun,' and 'Towards a Deflationary Landing,' Morgan Stanley Global Economic Forum, 2 August and 23 November 2005, available at Morgan Stanley web site.

ment, falling domestic profit rates, and/or tightening domestic credit—the resulting slowdown in Chinese imports would place renewed pressure on Japanese and East Asian producers whose hopes for revitalization depend upon an expanding Chinese market, while forcing up further and faster the US current account deficit with the attendant pressures and risks. The dynamo of the world economy, China is also a looming threat to global economic security.

On the other hand, outside of China and perhaps a few other places like India, because the rate of return on additions to the capital stock remains unsatisfactory and because real long-term interest rates have remained so low, economic surpluses in the hands of both capitalists and workers—the rich and the not-so-rich—tend to be directed toward the purchase of financial assets rather than productive ones. The enabling condition for this trend is, of course, the enormous reduction in short-term interest rates implemented not just by the US Fed, but also by financial authorities across the advanced capitalist world. The European Central Bank was obliged to keep rates down exceptionally long to counter the precipitous rise of the euro between 2001 and 2004. The Bank of Japan engaged in an historic burst of credit creation in 2003–04 to bail the economy out of its most recent recession. These efforts brought the real cost of borrowing systemwide below zero for several years—to their lowest level since the inflationary seventies—and, even today, after a year and a half of tightening by the Fed, the real cost of money has barely risen. As a consequence, according to *The Economist*, the global supply of dollars (the sum of America's monetary base plus global foreign exchange reserves) has been rising at a rate of 25 per cent per annum, close to the fastest pace in the last thirty years.[78]

The outcome of this extended period of ultra-cheap credit and unprecedented borrowing has been to encourage risk and to stoke demand for the on-paper representation of wealth rather than the real thing, which has led, in turn, to the blowing up of innumerable bubbles—in equities, in bonds of all sorts, and, most especially, in residential real estate. Even by the end of 2005, the *cyclically adjusted* price-earnings ratio of the S&P500 index, at 26 or 27 to 1, was higher than at any other time since data became available in 1881, except during the equity price bubbles at the end of the 1920s and the end of the 1990s.[79] In the case of bonds, the search for yield has been pushed so far that the difference between interest rate paid on emerging market debt and that on US Treasury Bonds has plunged from 10 per cent in the latter part of 2002 to just 2.5 per cent in mid 2005, while long-term interest rates in the US have come to just about equal short term ones, especially as the Fed has continued to pursue its campaign to raise the cost of short term borrowing and long term rates have unexpectedly fallen back. Above all, financial speculation has produced a real estate mania that is unprecedentedly global and that has driven up the value of housing in historic fashion. The total value of residential property in developed economies rose by more than $30

78 'Still Gushing Forth: the World Economy,' *The Economist*, 5 February 2005; 'Central Banks Move to Mop Up Excess Cash,' *Reuters*, 1 December 2005.

79 Time series constructed by Robert Shiller and updated by Smithers and Company, London, kindly forwarded to me by Smithers and Company. This is calculation of the price-earnings ratio is far higher than the unadjusted one, because, based on the historical record of previous business cycles, it entails, the expectation that profits growth will decline as the cycle lengthens.

80 'Global Housing Boom'.

trillion over the past five years, to over $70 trillion, an *increase* equivalent to 100 per cent of those countries' combined GDPs. Not only does this dwarf any previous boom in housing prices, it is *25 per cent bigger* than the global stock-market bubble of the late 1990s, which entailed an increase in equity values of 'only' 80 per cent of the countries' combined GDP in five years. 'In other words,' says *The Economist*, 'it looks like the biggest bubble in history'.[80]

There is, in sum, reason to doubt that the downward pressures on the world economy that have long ultimately derived from the persistence of chronic over-capacity in the international manufacturing sector have been sufficiently lifted—and/or that non-manufacturing productivity and profitability have risen sufficiently spectacularly—so that the world economy can generate sufficient dynamism to transcend or integrate its imbalances and cushion the effects of deflating bubbles. This is especially because the result of the US Fed's continuing dependence on cheap credit and asset-price bubbles to provide the subsidy to demand to keep the economy turning over appears to have only delayed, but not really avoided, the economy's obligatory responses to the over-capacity, fall in prof-itability, and asset-price crash of 2000–01. Producers, as expected, moved to restore profits via cutting employment, wages, and capital costs, and this issued, unavoid-ably, in a powerful and extended hit to aggregate demand. But, thanks to the Fed's huge subvention to consumer demand—by way of record household borrowing dependent in turn on runaway home values—they avoided the large-scale bank-ruptcies and scrapping of means of production that tends to be imposed upon business as a result of the fall in aggregate purchasing power that tends to result from its own cost-cutting to restore profitability. They have managed, instead, to maintain already existing plant and equipment in operation and in that way render less necessary stepped-up investment. Instead of purchasing additional capital stock or adding many more jobs, they have tended to turn over their surpluses to shareholders, thereby making additional funds available to the wealthy and in that way for speculation in financial assets. Private business has thus continued to gen-erate little in the way of aggregate demand, but the stimulus provided by easy credit, fiscal deficits, and the declining dollar is evaporating. The odds therefore favour a still further opening up of the already enormous chasm between the income and profits actually produced by the world economy and the paper claims gener-ated by it—the build-up of external surpluses and credit in the hands of East Asia and of external deficits and household debt in the US being one highly sympto-matic manifestation of the broader syndrome. The reversal might come directly through the petering out of demand growth—as a result of a slowdown of invest-ment and/or job creation by corporations dubious about business prospects—or it might come through a fall-off of consumption by households hit by the deflation of the housing bubble, central banks' rising short-term interest rates, and/or a jump in long-term cost of borrowing in response to the increased GDP growth of the last couple of years. Alternatively, it might be set off by way of a run on the dollar or an asset price drop-off, triggered by rising long-term interest rates, themselves the result of a failure to cover the current account deficit. But, whether the reversal takes place with a whimper or a bang, economic slowdown and new turbulence still seem much more likely than a leap into a new long upturn.

Appendix I

PROFIT RATES AND PRODUCTIVITY GROWTH: DEFINITIONS AND SOURCES

I. Profit Rates

The Rate of Profit in the Private Economy and its Component Industries

i). Unless otherwise stated, the rate of profit (r) always refers to the net rate of profit, defined, standardly, as net profits over the net capital stock. Net profits = net value added minus the sum of compensation and indirect business taxes, with net value-added equivalent to gross value-added minus depreciation or capital consumption. Capital stock equals plant and equipment (and also software in the US) and, in this text, is always non-residential unless otherwise stated. So: $r = P/K$.

The profit share (P/Y) is the ratio of profits (P) to output or value added (Y). The output capital ratio (Y/K) is the ratio of output or value added (Y) to the capital stock (K). By decomposing, the profit rate equals the profit share times the output capital ratio. So: $r = P/Y \times Y/K$.

ii). Unless otherwise stated, both compensation and wages mean wages plus benefits. It should be noted that compensation in the context of the calculation of the profit rate includes not only compensation of employees, but also 'compensation of the self-employed'. The self-employed are thus attributed compensation at the same rate per hour or per person as employees in their industry, or the relevant aggregate. Self-employed compensation thus equals employees' compensation per hour or per person times the number of self-employed hours or self-employed persons (full-time equivalents).

iii). Unless otherwise stated, profits are always given with indirect business taxes subtracted, but pre-corporate taxes.

Profit is thus defined as the surplus after depreciation, compensation, and indirect business taxes. This means that it includes net interest paid. The term 'profits' in this text therefore is always meant to include net interest, unless it is explicitly stated otherwise, as in 'profits net of interest', or 'profits minus interest', or 'profits excluding interest'.

iv). The rate of profit is generally given for the 'private economy' or 'private business economy' or a specific major industry. The private economy is, unless otherwise stated, always non-farm and non-residential, meaning that the value-added of farms and that attributed to the residential sector is excluded. The value-added of government enterprises is also excluded. Sometimes profit rates (and other data) are given for the 'business economy,' which refers to the non-farm economy minus the government sector but including government enterprises.

US Profit Rates: The Private Economy and Specific Industries

Below are the sources, unless otherwise stated, for the calculation of profit rates for the US private economy and specific industries, notably manufacturing:

 i). Bureau of Labor Statistics, folders on the business economy and non-farm business economy, available on request;

 ii). Bureau of Economic Analysis, 'Gross Product Originating by Industry', available at the BEA website;

 iii). Bureau of Economic Analysis, Fixed Asset Tables, available at the BEA website.

US Profit Rates: SIC and NAICS

In 2002, US economic statistical agencies switched from the Standard Industrial Classification System (SIC) to the to the North American Industry Classification System (NAICS). Profit rates for the period through 2001 are based on SIC data, unless otherwise stated. Profit rate data for the period from 2001 through the present are based on NAICS data, unless otherwise stated.

US Profit Rates: The Corporate Sector, the Non-Financial Corporate Sector, and the Corporate Manufacturing Sector

 i). Sometimes, the rate of profit is given for the corporate sector, or for the corporate financial sector, or for the non-financial corporate sector (i.e. the corporate sector with the financial sector excluded), or for the corporate manufacturing sector, or the corporate non-financial non-manufacturing sector (i.e. the non-financial corporate sector minus the corporate manufacturing sector). These profit rates are also net profit rates, defined as above. Unless otherwise stated, profits are always after capital consumption adjustment and inventory valuation adjustment. They are always pre-corporate tax, unless otherwise stated.

 ii). The basic source for the calculation of the net profit rate for the corporate sector and the non-financial corporate sector is Bureau of Economic Analysis, NIPA Table 1.14. Net profits here are given after capital consumption adjustment and inventory valuation adjustment. 'Net profits' are here defined as above— i.e. as value-added minus the sum of compensation, capital consumption, and indirect business taxes—but they are net of interest. It is thus necessary to sum 'net profits' and 'net interest' to get a measure of profits as defined above for the private economy and its component industries. The corporate and non-financial corporate profit rates are always 'net profits' plus 'net interest' over net capital stock, unless otherwise stated. Corporate and non-financial corporate taxes, net interest, and dividends are also provided in Table 1.14. Net capital stock for the corporate and non-financial corporate sector can be found in Bureau of Economic Analysis, Fixed Asset Tables, available at the BEA website.

 iii). The switch to the NAICS from SIC introduces a complication, since data in NIPA Table 1.14 are in SIC form through 2000 and in NAICS form from 2001 through the present. In presenting data on profit rates for the non-financial corporate sector, I have chosen to adjust the profit rates calculated on a NAICS basis from 2001 to the SIC profit rates through 2000, rather than simply attach the latter to the former. This makes very little difference, since corporate and non-financial corporate sectors are very similar in the two classification systems.

iv). Calculating profit rates for the corporate manufacturing sector poses certain difficulties, since 'profits' for the manufacturing sector provided by the Bureau of Economic Analysis—on an establishment basis in 'Gross Product Originating By Industry' and on a company basis in NIPA Table 6.16—are without capital consumption adjustment. Since changes in the tax law made over the course of the post-war period affected how much manufacturing corporations declared as their capital consumption allowances, the corporate manufacturing profit figures are not consistent with one another over time; more specifically, the corporate manufacturing profits provided are, over time, increasingly too low. I have therefore calculated the corporate manufacturing profit rate 'from scratch', using the numbers in 'Gross Product Originating by Industry' for the corporate and quasi-corporate sector, i.e. excluding self-employed. This is made viable by the fact that virtually all firms in the manufacturing sector are corporations. This was confirmed by comparing profit rates calculated 'from scratch' with profit rates calculated using corporate manufacturing profits on an establishment basis, from 'Gross Product Originating by Industry' (without capital consumption adjustment), for the early years of the post-war epoch (before significant changes in the tax law) and finding that these were nearly identical. Time series on corporate manufacturing capital stock and capital consumption were kindly provided by the Bureau of Economic Analysis. I wish to thank Shelby Herman for forwarding these to me.

Profit Rates for Japan

The sources for the calculation of profit rates for the private economy are as follows:

i). OECD, *National Accounts*, Volume II, Detailed Tables; OECD, *Flows and Stocks of Fixed Capital*. These have been updated in the new 'STAN' series.

ii). Japanese Economic and Social Research Institute, System of National Accounts. This is available at the Japanese System of National Accounts website: http://www.esri.cao.go.jp/en/sna/menu.html

The profit rate series for the Japanese manufacturing sector depend on the following sources:

iii). Manufacturing net capital stock, current and constant prices, 1955–91. 'Data on Japanese Manufacturing Capital', 28 February 1996: I wish to thank Edward Dean of the BLS for making these series available to me.

iv). Manufacturing net capital stock, current prices (1955–2003), in Japan, Ministry of Finance, Financial Statements Statistics of Corporations by Industry, Historical Data, Assets. This is available at Ministry of Finance website, http://www.mof.go.jp//English/files.htm.

v). 'Underlying Data for Indexes of Output per Hour, Hourly Compensation, and Unit Labor Costs in Manufacturing, Twelve Industrial Countries, 1950–2004,' available on request from BLS, Office of Productivity and Technology. I wish to thank John Rodgers for all his help and collaboration in putting together the Japanese profit rate series.

Profit Rates for Germany

i). OECD, *National Accounts*, Volume II, Detailed Tables; OECD, *Flows and Stocks of Fixed Capital*. These have been updated in the new 'STAN' series.

For the years, 1950–60 and 1990–2000, I rely on time series composed from the German national accounts, and generously made available to me, by Wendy Carlin and Andrew Glyn.

II. Productivity Growth

i). Productivity is always *labour* productivity, unless otherwise specified. It is defined as real value-added per hour or per person.

ii). Unless otherwise stated, the productivity measures given for the US private economy or, equivalently, the private business sector are for the *non-farm non-residential* private economy.

iii). Productivity measures for the US private economy and for individual industries, such as manufacturing, are, unless otherwise stated, based on real value-added indexes provided in 'Gross Product Originating by Industry' and hours provided by the Bureau of Labor Statistics.

iv). Figures on US productivity are often given for the 'business economy', which always means *non-farm business economy*. These are provided by the Bureau of Labor Statistics in its folder on the business economy. Real value-added for the business economy is almost equivalent to that for the private economy as defined above, with the difference that it includes *government enterprises*.

v). Unless otherwise stated, productivity measures for the German and Japanese private economies or private business sector use real value-added figures or indexes and figures for all persons (FTEs), provided in OECD, *National Accounts*, Volume II, Detailed Tables.

vi). Figures for US, German, and Japanese manufacturing productivity are provided directly by the Bureau of Labor Statistics, Program on Foreign Labor Statistics, in 'International Comparisons of Manufacturing Productivity and Unit Labor Cost Trends', news release, available at the BLS website.

vii). The Bureau of Labor statistics publishes data on US real value-added by industry going back only to 1977. For the years 1950–77, I have therefore relied on unpublished, unofficial time series on manufacturing and non-manufacturing real value-added generously made available to me by Bill Gullickson of the BLS Office of Productivity and Technology. I wish to thank Bill Gullickson for forwarding me these series.

viii). The Bureau of Economic Analysis does not publish data on real value-added for the private non-farm sector or the private non-farm non-manufacturing sector. I have therefore relied on an unpublished series for these variables generously made available to me by Brian Moyer and Erich Strassner of the BEA. I wish to thank them for forwarding me these series.

Appendix II

SOURCES FOR MAIN VARIABLES

I. Data on the National Domestic Economies of the United States, Germany, and Japan

United States:
Below are the sources, unless otherwise stated, for the variables listed (there is some overlap):

i). US Department of Commerce, Bureau of Economic Analysis (BEA), 'Gross Product Originating By Industry', current dollars, 1947–present, and chain dollars, 1977–present, BEA website: nominal value-added; nominal compensation of employees; indirect business taxes; proprietors' income; output of government enterprises; corporate profits (plus capital consumption and inventory valuation adjustments); corporate net interest; real value-added; all persons (FTE); employees (FTE).

ii). US Department of Labor, Bureau of Labor Statistics, 'Industry Analytical Ratios' and 'Basic Industry Data': for the Non-farm Business Sector; for Manufacturing; for the Non-Financial Corporate Sector; and for the Total Economy: all persons and employees, 1949–present (numbers and per cent change): nominal value-added; nominal compensation; real value-added; hours at work; hourly compensation; real hourly compensation; value-added per hour (labour productivity); consumer price index; employment. Available on request.

iii). US Department of Commerce, Bureau of Economic Analysis, National Income and Product Accounts, BEA website (numbers plus annual and quarterly per cent change): GDP nominal and real; gross private fixed non-residential investment (structures, equipment, and software) nominal and real; personal consumption expenditures (durable goods, non-durable goods, services) nominal and real. Contributions to per cent change in real gross domestic product by personal consumption expenditures, by gross private non-residential investment, by gross private residential investment, by exports of goods and services, by government expenditures.

iv). US Department of Labor, Bureau of Labor Statistics, manufacturing and non-manufacturing indexes of real value-added, 1950–present. Unpublished series provided by Bill Gullickson. (See above, Appendix 1, on Profit Rates and Productivity Growth.)

v). US Department of Commerce, Bureau of Economic Analysis, Fixed Asset Tables, BEA website: net capital stock current and constant prices, consumption of fixed capital current and constant prices, gross investment current and constant prices.

vi). US Department of Labor, Bureau of Labor Statistics, BLS website: Historical Data for 'B' Tables of the Employment Situation Release, in Employment, Earnings, and Hours from the Current Employment Statistics Survey: earnings of production and non-supervisory workers: total economy, private sector, private non-farm sector, and by industry; employment for total economy, private sector, private non-farm sector, and by industry.

I wish to thank Edwin Dean, John Glaser, Bill Gullickson, Mike Harper, Phyllis Otto, Larry Rosenblum, and Steve Rosenthal of the BLS and Mike Glenn, Shelby Herman, Randal Matsunaga, Brian Moyer, Ken Petrick, George Smith, Erich Strassner, and Bob Yuskavage of the BEA for help with these data.

vii). *Economic Report of the President*, Washington, DC, (annual): unemployment rate, manufacturing capacity utilization; real government consumption expenditures; consumer price indexes; money supply; interest rates; federal, state, and local government current receipts and expenditures.

viii). US Office of Trade and Economic Analysis, Foreign Trade Highlights, Aggregate Foreign Trade Data: goods exports, goods imports, goods trade balance; services exports, services imports, services trade balance; manufactures exports, manufactures imports, manufactures trade balance; exports to individual countries, imports from individual countries, trade balance with individual countries; manufactures exports to individual countries, manufactures imports from individual countries, manufactures trade balance with individual countries.

ix). Federal Reserve, Industrial Production and Capacity Utilization, Table G. 17: historical statistics for production, capacity, and capacity utilization for manufacturing; historical statistics for production, capacity, and capacity utilization for manufacturing industries.

Germany and Japan:

i). OECD, *National Accounts*, Volume II, Detailed Tables, 1960–94: by industry: value added, current and constant prices; compensation of employees; indirect business taxes; all persons at work; employees.

ii). OECD, *Flows and Stocks of Fixed Capital*, various issues back to 1960: for private business economy, manufacturing, and services: gross and net capital stock current and constant prices; consumption of fixed capital current and constant prices; gross investment current and constant prices.

See also above, Appendix 1 on profit rates and productivity growth.

II. Comparative Data on the Domestic Economies of the United States, Germany, and Japan

i). OECD, *Economic Outlook*, Paris (semi-annual): annual per cent change: GDP nominal and real, private; consumption deflators; real gross private non-residential fixed capital formation; unemployment rates; government financial balances; government structural balances;

ii). US Department of Labor, Bureau of Labor, Statistics, 'International Comparisons of Manufacturing Productivity and Unit Labor Cost Trends, 15 countries, 1950–present', at BLS website: manufacturing: total hours, employment, real output per hour, real output per person, real hourly compensation in national currency, nominal hourly compensation, hourly compensation in US dollars, unit labour costs in national currency, unit labour costs in US dollars.

iii). US Department of Labor, Bureau of Labor Statistics, 'International Comparisons of Hourly Compensation Costs for Production Workers in Manufacturing', 29 countries, 1975–present, at BLS website: hourly compensation costs in US dollars for production workers in manufacturing; annual per cent change in hourly compensation costs in US dollars for production workers in manufacturing.

iv). US Department of Labor, Bureau of Labor Statistics, 'Comparative Civilian Labor Force Statistics, Ten Countries, 1959–present', BLS website: civilian labour force employment and unemployment; civilian labour force by economic sector.

III. Data on International Variables

i). Data Archives of the International Monetary Fund: The United States, Germany, Japan, 1950–94: growth of real exports of goods and services; growth of real imports of goods and services; rate of increase of export prices; rate of increase of import prices; per cent share of world exports; nominal exports of goods and services/nominal GDP; exports of goods and services/GDP (price adjusted); growth of exports to and imports from one another in dollars; trade balances with one another.

Korea, Taiwan, Singapore, and Hong Kong, 1950–94: growth of real exports, per cent share of world exports, growth of exports to the US, per cent share of total US imports, growth of exports in US dollars to US, Germany, Japan; growth of imports in US dollars from the US, Germany, and Japan.

(I wish to thank Staffan Gorne and Pete Kledaras of the IMF for forwarding these data to me.)

ii). IMF International Financial Statistics, Washington, DC (monthly and annual): The United States, Germany, Japan, and other countries: nominal effective exchange rates, exchange rates vis-à-vis dollar; goods exports values and volumes; services exports values and volumes; goods and services exports values and volumes; goods imports values and volumes; services imports values and volumes; goods and services imports: values and volumes; goods export prices; goods import prices; goods and services prices.

iii). OECD, *Economic Outlook*, Paris (semi-annual): The United States, Germany, Japan, and other countries: export volumes, import volumes, relative unit labour costs, share in world exports, share in world imports, trade balance, current account balance as a percentage of GDP.

INDEX